Latin American Political History

Latin American Political History

Patterns and Personalities

Ronald M. Schneider

Queens College, CUNY

Westview
PRESS

A Member of the Perseus Books Group

Library of Congress Cataloging-in-Publication Data
Schneider, Ronald M.
    Latin American political history : patterns & personalities / Ronald M. Schneider.—1st ed.
        p. cm.
    Includes bibliographical references and index.
    ISBN-13: 978-0-8133-4341-9 (alk. paper)
    ISBN-10: 0-8133-4341-0 (alk. paper)
1. Latin America--Politics and government. I. Title.

F1410.S377 2006
980—dc22

                                                                        2006003505

07 08 09 / 10 9 8 7 6 5 4 3 2 1

Contents

List of Illustrations

Maps

Photos

Preface

Latin America, embracing the diverse array of countries lying south of the United States in the Western Hemisphere, is both a major part of the world and its richest "laboratory" for understanding the processes of political development and their interaction with economic growth, societal modernization, and cultural influences. Its vast expanse stretches north to south for seven thousand miles from the border between Mexico's Baja California and the most populous state of the United States, California—acquired from Mexico by force over a century and a half ago—to the southernmost tip of Argentina, only a short distance from Antarctica. Since much of the region is farther from the eastern United States than is most of Europe, only a relatively small portion fits the lingering stereotype of being the "backyard" of the US colossus. Moreover, from that same point south of San Diego to the easternmost bulge of Brazil, Latin America extends more than fifty-five hundred miles from east to west—nearly double the width of the hemisphere's hegemonic power and current world paramount.

Latin America's more than eight million square miles of land is divided into thirty-four sovereign political entities plus a handful of vestigial colonial areas (by far the largest and most populous of which is Puerto Rico). The region's differences are so great as to raise the question of whether it has any other than geographical meaning, but the term *Latin America* is firmly rooted in popular usage and embedded in the organization and operations of governments, businesses, and academic institutions. Hence it is much more productive to give it deeper and sharper meaning than to quibble over its appropriateness. When the term is accurately employed, Latin America includes not only all the South American continent, but also Central America and the Caribbean, as well as Mexico.

The diversity among its constituent countries is striking in manifold respects: size, population, ethnic makeup, geography, resources, level of economic development, and societal dynamics, as well as political development. Even with respect to language Latin America is far from homogeneous: Although it is often misleadingly referred to as Hispanic America, nearly a third of its inhabitants speak Portuguese, Haiti is French-speaking, much of the Caribbean is English-speaking, and millions still know only the indigenous languages of their ancestors. And although

Catholicism is by far the predominant religion, there are tens of millions of Protestants and other tens of millions adhering to religions brought over from Africa or practiced in the hemisphere before the arrival of European colonizers. Not surprisingly, but very harmfully, lack of understanding and prevalent misconceptions characterize the fragmented and superficial image of Latin America prevailing in the United States and the rest of the world.

Although the principal focus of this book is comparisons within Latin America, an underlying goal is to bring this region's rich experience into the mainstream of politics and government at the global level. The urgency and timeliness of this task is underscored by the all-too-obvious fact that failures in the realm of political development, particularly of a democratic bent, have been predominant in Africa as well as on most of the Asian continent from the Near East across to Southeast Asia. As a result, the possibility of stable democratic outcomes in such countries has been called into question. In my view as an empirical comparativist with a strongly historical perspective, this pessimism is premature—very possibly by generations rather than just decades—since the democratization of Latin America required over a century and a half.

Many arguments can be made concerning why the several centuries required to achieve stable, representative, constitutional political systems in Western Europe and English-speaking North America should not be necessary for countries whose independence postdates World War II. But propositions concerning rapid political development prove unconvincing when viewed in light of the experience of Latin America, which shares with these fledgling nations much of the same tradition of colonialism with its externally imposed governmental and political structures as well as economic subordination. Although substantial, the time gap between the independence of Latin American countries—typically in the 1820s—and that of the Afro-Asian world, often in the 1950s and 1960s, is significantly less than that between the Afro-Asian world and the emergence of European nation-states in the sixteenth and seventeenth centuries. Hence, a close examination of Latin America's struggles to establish viable participatory political systems provides the most realistic and appropriate yardstick against which to measure the progress (or lack thereof) in this direction by the globe's "new nations." Indeed, what has been accomplished in the real world is the only valid and meaningful standard against which to assess what people are striving to achieve at present. Yet there is a prevalent tendency to substitute for it some empirically groundless concept of what "should" be possible, rooted in little more than the observer's personal impatience to see results during the short span he or she might be around to coach and criticize. Latin America's experience confirms the harsh reality that both political institutions and their requisite congruent political culture are built over generations. Even decades prove time and again to be far too brief for measuring fundamental trends as opposed to mere political fads, fancies, and fashions.

Realistically, a significant permanent expansion of democratic political development in Africa and most of Asia probably remains well in the future. How far in the future is a question social scientists are not yet equipped to answer. Lacking adequate conceptual tools for this task, we must fall back upon the old mainstay of relevant comparative experience. Until we have a deeper understanding of democratization in other regions, concentration upon the criteria and dimensions of relevance is premature—a case of putting the cart before the horse.[1] Since by far the greatest number of recent cases of successful democratization are found in Latin America, this region most urgently requires thoughtful comparative study. Indeed, a major aim of this book is to identify, analyze, and highlight the salient lessons for the current "new nations" of the Afro-Asian world in Latin American experience. In this regard, the 1820–1930 span is more relevant in many respects than recent times, since that is when the countries analyzed here were coping with the array of post-independence problems and challenges of national consolidation that still plague over half the nations of the world.

Will Africa and Asia have to wait as long as it has taken Latin American countries to make lasting progress along the rocky road to political development? Not if leaders in that diverse array of nations pay attention to the lessons painfully learned in Latin America. But before they can possibly do this, it is necessary to decide what these lessons are—something not yet seriously undertaken at the regional level.[2] Since a collective understanding of the experience of many individual Latin American countries has reached a point where appropriate lessons can be drawn, the task of comparison and synthesis is clearly due—indeed overdue. Moreover, at a time when the nations of Eastern Europe, including the former Soviet Union, are still in the early stages of attempting to install viable democratic systems, and those spun off along Russia's Asian borders are even less advanced along this treacherous road, a deeper and more systematic understanding of the analogous processes in Latin America is certainly required. Here the trials and tribulations of the late nineteenth century through the 1920s hold more lessons for them than does recent Latin American experience.

The need for such understanding may be even more acute in the difficult ongoing US–Western European struggles to help establish viable regimes in Afghanistan and Iraq. In both of these cases the cruciality of learning from experience is particularly salient. If we must conclude that hard-learned lessons from bitter failures and painful mistakes were essential to the eventual establishment of democracy in most Latin American venues, then expectations concerning any possible linear scenario for political development in some, if not all, contemporary nation-building endeavors may well need to be tempered and strategies be drastically re-evaluated.

We already know that absorbing the lessons of past traumatic setbacks was crucial in the southern European cases of Spain, Italy, Greece, and Portugal—without going back to earlier democratizations, where the historical context was significantly different. Emergence of stable democracies in Southern Europe is quite recent—dating back only to the mid-1970s for Spain, Portugal, and Greece and back to 1948 in Italy. Hence the widely spread wave of democratizations in Latin America quite soon thereafter and well before the winds of democratic change blew into the former USSR and Eastern Europe would logically seem to have substantial relevance for important parts of the world.

Latin America remains what the distinguished political scientist David Apter recognized it was in the 1970s: the world's most challenging political laboratory, with countries at different levels of development and with varying bottlenecks to be broken through. Moreover, it has a critical centrality to the most sweeping and profound effort to conceptualize the contemporary world's underlying dynamics, Samuel P. Huntington's *The Clash of Civilizations and the Remaking of World Order*, in which the generation's leading political scientist expresses a major uncertainty: Is Latin America a sixth great world civilization–cultural realm, or is it destined to become "one sub-variant of a three-pronged Western civilization"?[3]

Textbooks on Latin American politics, with which I have over fifty years of intimate familiarity, are either so massive as to be prohibitively forbidding to anyone not pursuing advanced coursework on the subject, or so streamlined as to omit any significant historical background or a coherent discussion of individual countries.[4] Adhering to a public policy approach, they opt to focus on present-day governmental structures, political processes, and policy issues, thereby sacrificing analysis of the paths by which countries—and by extension, the region—arrived where they are today. This is precisely the center of my concern: to compare the political development experiences of Latin American nations as well as the region's political panorama during different time periods.

A major challenge to understanding Latin America is its great diversity, underscored by the immense ethnic, historical, and geographic differences among its main components. At first glance, the contrasts between the two nations that together contain over half the region's population overshadow any similarities, an impression only slightly reduced by closer examination and greater familiarity. Brazil is South American, Portuguese-speaking, very heavily African-influenced, and distant from the United States. Mexico is North American, Spanish-speaking, deeply Indian-influenced, and immediately proximate to the United States.

Further complicating the analytical problem, the second most important pair of countries differ strikingly from each other as well as from both of the dominant dyad. Argentina is at the southern tip of South America, whereas Colombia borders the Caribbean and abuts on Central America. The former is largely populated by individuals of relatively recent Italian descent and enjoys close European ties; the latter's population is heavily *mestizo* (mixed Indian-European), with most of its European component having descended from Spaniards who arrived during the colonial era, and it lacks Argentina's close trade and financial links to present-day Europe. Since these four very distinctly different countries contain two-thirds of all Latin Americans, generalizations about the region that fail to apply to them are essentially meaningless, even highly misleading.

Moreover, there is still enormous diversity among the remaining countries. In many ways the Pacific-facing and interior South American nations are heavily Indian, but their proportions of Europeans differ dramatically. A subregion such as Central America contains both Guatemala, which is largely Indian and traditionally dictatorial, and Costa Rica, which is European and intensely democratic, as well as politically volatile Panama, still only one step removed from being a US protectorate. The Caribbean subregion includes French-heritage international basketcase Haiti; the closely US-tied Dominican Republic; US-scorned Cuba; and a slew of former British colonies still in their first generation of independence (with Jamaica and Trinidad and Tobago in the van).

In light of this profound heterogeneity, trying to describe, much less analyze and interpret, Latin America in a single volume is a daunting task. Such a synthesis must navigate the narrow, rock-strewn strait between the Charybdis of homogenization and the Scylla of uniqueness and idiosyncrasies. But having been deeply involved in studying the area for a half century, and acutely dissatisfied with the regionwide works available for teaching about it, I would be remiss—a shirker, if not a coward—if I did not make the attempt. Having developed an approach to explaining Latin America's political life that works in the classroom, I wish to make it available to a far broader audience.

Because I first began to study and observe Latin America in the early 1950s, my views on the past half century are heavily influenced by my often-frustrating, but always enlightening, personal struggle to make sense of what was going on "down there," as I eventually matured from my impatient late teens into my mellower sixties and hopefully wiser seventies. When, for example, I sat in an undergraduate survey course on the region in the early 1950s, the ongoing Peronist experiment in Argentina was the most exciting contemporary event, followed closely by Getúlio Vargas's final, dramatically tragic performance on Brazil's political stage. Then, as I first set foot in the region itself, unwittingly caught up in Cuba's maelstrom of July 26, 1953, which would subsequently prove so momentous, my mind was focused upon Guatemala and its ill-fated effort to break away from the US orbit. With the dramatic events of the Lázaro Cárdenas period in Mexico still close in time as well as space, major concern in the infant field of Latin American politics centered on how much of his legacy might be institutionalized through an exciting new innovation: the hegemonic governing party he had formed, which would cling to control to the beginning of the twenty-first century. As time went on and I traveled more widely in the region, beginning with field research in Guatemala in 1957, then tackling the region's "elephant," Brazil, I developed

Schneider's Law: For the comparative social scientist every apparent contradiction is a call to look more deeply, and each complication should be welcomed as a potential source of enriching the understanding and sharpening the analytical tools. For the real world is the only laboratory we have in political science, so we must make the best possible use of it.

Of all that could, and for the deepest possible understanding probably should, be said about Latin American politics, much more is omitted and excluded than included in this book. Although I seriously take into account the views of country or subregional experts on what is essential to understanding their parts of Latin America, my goal of discerning patterns, as well as my ingrained penchant for comparison, condition and often determine what will be considered in this effort at reasonable synthesis. Personal, rather than arbitrary, my decisions in this respect are rooted in five decades of teaching, an activity in which selectivity is dictated by time restraints even more severely that it is here by limitations of space and readers' patience. This study does not profess to be definitive; opting for geographic inclusiveness by choosing to embrace all of Latin America instead of selected cases, it can aspire to be only systematically suggestive. Such a geographically inclusive and topically selective approach is the most appropriate use to which I can put the perspectives and insights gained over my long span of studying the region. This approach also differs most sharply from those of the books already available.

The outstanding study to date on Latin American politics, Ruth Berins Collier and David Collier's *Shaping the Political Arena: Critical Junctures, the Labor Movement, and Regime Dynamics in Latin America*—written primarily for social scientists—has a very different thrust, including only eight countries and having a sharp analytical focus upon the emergence of labor as a political actor and the ramifications of this emergence.[5] And by now the Collier and Collier patterns with regard to "legalization and institutionalization of a labor movement sanctioned and regulated by the state" in response to political contenders beginning to perceive workers as a constituency, while still relevant, are substantially less useful in explaining present differences. The long-term legacies the Colliers derive have been attenuated by the periods of authoritarian military rule and the transitions to democracy that have followed. Their fundamental approach of focusing on critical transition in the relationship between the state and one particular emerging social actor is, however, still useful for examining the ongoing processes of incorporation of new groups into the political processes. Peter Smith's *Democracy in Latin America: Political Change in Comparative Perspective* provides an impressive marshaling and quantification of data without furnishing continuity on developments in any of the nineteen countries about which it generalizes.[6]

For all its advances since rejection of the intellectually sterile historical, legalistic, institutional approach, inherited from Woodrow Wilson, gained headway in the 1950s, political science still lacks a unified all-embracing theoretical approach.

Simplistic, not necessarily simple, theories about why Latin America lags behind English-speaking North America are inadequate. "Dependency theory," which in the 1960s and 1970s was embraced by the majority of young scholars in the Latin American field, went way too far in putting the blame on external factors and downplaying internal ones. Useful as a corrective to traditional Wilsonian institutionalism as well as deterministic versions of modernization theory, dependence theory threw their babies out with the bathwater. With the demise of the Soviet Union at the end of the 1980s, dependency approaches entered into a steep decline. The vacuum has been partially filled by a mix of "new institutionalism" and the revival of a far less mechanical and more realistic version of modernization theories, tempered with concern for cultural factors. This last approach is close to my slant on analyzing and interpreting Latin American politics, as well as that of a number of other experienced scholars.[7]

Fortunately, the leading political scientists specializing in the region's second most populous country, Mexico, have taken an analytical approach highly congruent with my own, one that is empirical and eclectic in a disciplined and systematic manner. As articulated by Camp:

> Choosing any one approach to explain the nature of political behavior has advantages in describing a political system. In my own experience, however, I have never become convinced that one approach offers an adequate explanation. I believe that an examination of political processes or functions entails the fewest prejudices and that by pursuing how and where these functions occur, one uncovers the contributions of other approaches. An eclectic approach to politics, incorporating culture, history, structures, geography, and external relations, provides the most adequate and accurate vision of contemporary political behavior.[8]

Not only does this approach underlie my writings on Brazil, as well as Camp's impressive scholarly output dealing with Mexico, but it is also incorporated into much of the best historical work on other countries, as well as in the research of a number of other contemporary political scientists specializing on such important countries as Argentina, Colombia, Venezuela, and Chile. These all manifest substantial agreement with Peeler's view that "structures limit possibilities but do not determine outcomes," since purposeful action by political leaders helps shape them.[9]

Although each Latin American country is unique and has its own intrinsic interest and importance, these countries cannot be given equal weight in an analysis of the region's patterns and trends. Equal weighting in the realm of politics would be as fully misleading as it would be with respect to economic factors, where weighting is taken for granted, or demographics, where it is self-evident. Indeed, to so misapply the concept of sovereign equality of nations would be as absurd as considering every component of the former Soviet Union as important as Russia or the Ukraine, or holding that North Dakota or Vermont merits as much consideration as California or New York in the study of US politics.

In keeping with this fundamental logic, Brazil and Mexico receive the greatest stress in this book, justified by the fact that the former constitutes over a third of the region and is not Hispanic, and the latter makes up 30 percent of Hispanic America (having a population almost equal to the next three largest countries combined). In terms of emphasis, Argentina and Colombia follow, then Peru and Venezuela. For these six countries contain more than three-quarters of the region's population, with Brazil and Mexico combining for over half. In the interest of fuller geographic representation, the other four countries of above ten million inhabitants (Chile, Ecuador, Guatemala, and Cuba) will also receive extensive consideration. These ten core countries contain nearly seven-eighths of all Latin Americans and cover 84 percent of the region's area. Moreover, they have exerted and continue to exert very heavy influence upon their smaller neighbors. Hence the smaller countries will appear in less detail and often in terms of variations upon the themes set by the larger countries, but occasionally with emphasis upon their uniqueness.

This selective and weighted approach is justified not only in the present day, but also in the colonial days, when Brazil represented the greater bulk of Portugal's worldwide empire, and present-day Mexico, Peru, Colombia, and Argentina were centers of Spain's viceroyalties in the New World—Chile, Guatemala, Venezuela, and Cuba being seats of their key subordinate entities. This approach also guarantees consideration of the important variations in the critical process of breaking with mother countries and establishing independence. In these regards special attention will also be paid to Haiti, the only country in the Western Hemisphere (including the United States) to win its independence by its own efforts at a time when the colonial power was neither occupied by an enemy nor engaged in mortal combat with a rival.

A region as diverse as Latin America needs to be discussed in terms of tendencies, trends, and common—but not universal—features. To be of significance, these must apply to either the great majority of the region's countries or to the larger ones. In either case, if they do not fit the realities of Brazil and Mexico, generalizations are of limited use, since over half the region and its inhabitants will already have been excluded. Still, conclusions pertaining to a significant range of countries, at times even to a number of smaller countries, may be useful to specific late-developing countries on the other side of the globe.

Latin America is overwhelmingly Christian. It has also been essentially untouched by non-Christian immigration at a time when this has become a significant factor in making both Western Europe and the United States less predominantly Christian. Cultural influences upon the region come chiefly from the United States and Western European countries (especially Spain, Portugal, Italy, and France). Islamic influence is essentially nil, as are Hindu, Confucian, Buddhist, and Shinto influence. Tourist flows are similarly almost exclusively from and to the United States and Western Europe. This orientation is reflected in and reinforced by trade patterns, although not as exclusively. In addition, Latin America continues to increase in potential for economic growth and to expand in population—offsetting the demographic stagnation of Western Europe and the trend in this direction in the United States. The inescapable conclusion is that Latin America's importance as the third leg of the Western Christian world is not only great, but also growing.

The developmental experience of Western Europe and the United States is too remote in time and too heavily rooted in an economic order requiring colonies as sources of raw materials and captive markets to have readily apparent, plausible, and politically acceptable lessons for the late-developing centers of the Afro-Asian world. Since most of these countries have had very limited success in their post-independence development struggles—politically and socially as well as economically—lessons from Latin America may well prove more relevant. If so, these lessons need to be perceived as such. Here the diversity of the region offers a potential advantage, since the experience of the middle and smaller countries may be more appropriate for similar countries in Africa and Asia than that of gigantic and resource-rich Brazil, large next-door neighbor of the United States, Mexico, or quasi-European Argentina and Chile. This book may at least allow scholars in, or at least those interested in, the vast array of countries in Africa and Asia to decide which are the Latin American cases that could be most relevant. Hopefully this interest in turn may spur paired comparative studies focusing not just on present similarities, but on a Latin American country's dealing with specific challenges at a prior point in time and an Afro-Asian country's current problems.

As fundamental change is basically a slow process, and since my primary purpose is to illuminate long-term trends of lasting import, developments over the past century and a third will be dealt with in twenty-five- or thirty-year periods. Thus major challenges can be considered, along with the impact of significant economic changes and societal transformations, rather than fads, fashions, wind shifts, and dramatic events of transitory impact. In analyzing politics there is always a great danger of confusing recent trends with longer-run tendencies, much less permanent changes. Decades have repeatedly proven to be more reliable time units in this regard than are single administrations, and quarter centuries provide a significantly greater discrimination between surface waves, tides, and deeper currents of change. Middle-class democracy lasted sixteen years in Argentina, only to be swept away in 1930; military rule persisted for over twenty years in Brazil before yielding to civilian democracy after 1984; the Sandinista revolution in

Nicaragua was triumphant for thirteen years before its repudiation by the electorate in 1991; and Chile's Augusto Pinochet dictatorship had surpassed fifteen years prior to bowing out in 1989.

The interaction of social, economic, and cultural factors with politics is neither linear nor direct. The impact of profound socioeconomic change upon politics is sometimes gradual and cumulative; in other instances it is delayed, pent up, and hence more explosive. Detailed treatment of all periods and administrations in every country would require a massive multivolume work, its readership inevitably limited to specialists. It is clear that nations, much as individuals, go through critical periods and transforming events as well as long stretches of routine existence. Therefore, in this book country treatment will be sketchy for the latter and fuller for the more dynamic periods. Moreover, only personalities who had a catalytic influence or transforming impact upon their country will be fleshed out and analyzed in depth. The result is a consciously calculated uneven treatment designed to focus on the crucial rather than the routine.

Countries in their development toward stable participatory political processes rooted in a viable economy and functional social structures do not move in a continuous or straight line. Typically there are protracted periods of stagnation or even backsliding as well as times of coasting on ebbing momentum. Fortunately most countries also experience surges of forward movement. Emphasis will be placed on these developmental spurts and the conditions and agents that caused them as well as the conditions that led to their running out of steam. Thoughtful readers will be aware that standards for substantial democracy have changed over time, particularly on the dimensions of effective mass participation and social justice. Hence, at generational intervals, there will be brief reference to the prevailing situation in these respects in the United States and Western Europe.

A major aim of this study is to document the fact that political development in Latin America has rarely been a smooth, steady, and linear process. This effort also involves showing the range of variations and any possible exceptions to this rule. This done, it will be possible to relate such surges to causes in the areas of economic change, societal modernization, political leadership, altered alignments among power contenders and forces, and international factors. Throughout, the analytical spotlight will first be focused upon the four corner pillars (Brazil, Mexico, Colombia, and Argentina), followed by the connecting beams of our interpretive scheme (Peru, Venezuela, and Chile). The middle-sized building blocks (Guatemala, Ecuador, Bolivia, and, from 1898 on, Cuba) will constitute foundations for the walls of the explanatory edifice. Finally, there will be a look at where the smaller countries fit into the designs that have emerged.

Because of a concern with crucial junctures, some countries will receive more attention in one chapter than in others. In the case of the major ones, the fallow period for Brazil is the 1840s through the 1860s; for Mexico, 1875–1910 and

1946–1980; and for Colombia, most of the time from the late 1840s to 1929, with the exception of the turn of the century. Similarly little will be said about Venezuela from the 1850s to 1929 or Chile between the 1840s and World War I. My goal is to explain how countries arrived at where they now are, and this goal does not require close consideration of long stretches when they were marking time, coasting on momentum, treading water, or stuck in a rut. Times of excitement and movement merit attention, for continuity is to a very high degree just the absence of change.

One can, for example, argue that by far the greatest part of political development in France occurred during the eras of Louis XIV, Napoleon Bonaparte, and Charles de Gaulle—essentially the last half of the seventeenth century, a quarter century from 1789 to 1815, and 1945 through 1969—roughly a total of one hundred years during the past four and a half centuries. In Latin America perhaps only Argentina needs to be examined closely in all macrotime periods, as change is a regular feature of its national life, possibly because of its limited colonial heritage and easy achievement of independence, later followed by a tidal wave of immigration.

Like human beings, countries do not get to select their parents or choose when and where they will be born. After widely varying prenatal experiences under colonial rule, they undergo differing degrees of birth trauma before coming into being. They then start life with inherent weaknesses and vulnerabilities, which may crop up at later stages of their lives, and often with inadequate social and economic heritages. Immediately after independence the nation-state system imposes adult responsibilities upon infant political systems. Not surprisingly their performance is usually quite shaky, if not inadequate. They may eventually overcome slow and halting starts, but the very process of having to do so may further handicap them. When it comes to countries, unlike people, "what doesn't kill them" usually does not make them stronger. At least, this is a proposition that needs to be examined carefully in the context of different time periods and situations.

Clearly not all that transpired in Latin America in past centuries has left a clearly discernible imprint upon present institutions and processes. Equally clearly, however, current political-governmental practices, as well as the structures through which they operate, still bear the stamp of developments buried well back in the past. The most salient aspects of this heritage, enshrined in that complex amalgam of attitudes, values, myths, and expectations usually shorthanded as *political culture,* must be explored before the more obviously relevant recent past can be discussed. For with regard to antecedent experiences and historical influences there is no rigid expiration date, much less a statute of limitations, only a rule of relevance—albeit one more stringent the more temporally remote the event. Hence most of the book is concerned with the period since 1930.

Although the book is primarily designed for readers interested in an overview of the entire region, it is possible to follow individual countries from their origins to the present by moving from the section treating them in one chapter to the corresponding one in the next. The consistent aim is to ensure that readers gain a deep understanding of Latin America as the sum of the experiences of its constituent parts.

No one scholar, no matter how long he or she may have labored in this field, has been able to conduct original research on all, or even most, of the countries comprising Latin America. Hence each must rely upon leading scholarship on those places where he or she has not conducted field research. As my direct experience is centered upon Brazil, with previous work on Guatemala, Cuba, and—more remotely in time—Argentina, I lean heavily for understanding of Mexico upon the outstanding scholarship of Roderic Ai Camp, Daniel Levy, Enrique Krauze, and Jorge Castañeda. On Colombia, where I have at least spent a little time, I rely substantially on the writings of Harvey Kline, who, like Dan Levy, published a distinguished book with several revised editions in the series I edited during the 1980s and 1990s on *Nations of Contemporary Latin America/Nations of the Modern World: Latin America*. This authorship of several incarnations of a volume in this series (which followed a common agreement on scope, combined with full freedom of approach) also holds true for Thomas Walker on Nicaragua, Howard Wiarda and Michael Kryzanek on the Dominican Republic, and Juan M. del Aguila on Cuba, where objective scholarship such as his is a very scarce commodity. During this sometimes taxing endeavor, James Morris on Honduras, Daniel Hellinger on Venezuela, Waltrud Queiser Morales on Bolivia, John Booth on Costa Rica, David Schodt on Ecuador, Martin Weinstein on Uruguay, and Patrick Bellegarde-Smith on Haiti, along with Riordan Roett and Richard S. Sacks on Paraguay also earned my respect for their scholarship, as did Peter Calvert on Guatemala and Nigel Boland on Belize. This professional admiration holds true also for Tommie Sue Montgomery, whose work on El Salvador was associated with, although not strictly a part of, that undertaking.

Since several volumes in the series were unfortunately never completed, I drew heavily upon the works of Paul H. Lewis, Robert Potash, William C. Smith, Peter G. Snow, and James W. McGuire on Argentina, Peter F. Klarén and John Gitlitz on Peru, Arturo Valenzuela and Paul Sigmund on Chile, and my long-time colleague George Priestley on Panama. I have also drawn substantially upon Lewis's scholarship on Paraguay as well as on undemocratic regimes throughout the region.[10] The writings of the late John D. Martz have proved very helpful on the countries of northern South America (Colombia, Venezuela, and Ecuador), as has the work of Susan Eva Eckstein on Cuba. With respect to Brazil I have benefited especially by the meticulous historical work of Frank McCann, whose recent book does for that country what Potash's three volumes did for Argentina. As I seek in this book to bring together the insights and understanding found in the country-by-country literature, I owe a collective debt to a host of dedicated laborers in this area of academic endeavor not singled out for individual acknowledgment, as appropriately noted in bibliographic citations. Any flaws in the interpretation of their views are wholly my responsibility, as are the other shortcomings of this work, which has benefited from the thoughtful suggestions of two anonymous, but clearly highly qualified, reviewers.

I must add to my acknowledgment of scholars laboring in this field heart-felt appreciation of the emotional support provided by my wife, Marva Schneider, during the exhausting late stages of an arduous journey that occupied a great deal of my time and energies during recent years. I also benefitted from the joyous distractions from overwork provided by our children Shinelle and John, particularly as they climbed to the top of the martial arts ladder. At Westview, Karl Yambert showed an encouraging enthusiasm for the project and Kay Mariea efficiently guided the book through production, while Margaret Richie performed the onerous task of copy editing with unwavering concern for clarity and insistence upon consistency.

Ronald M. Schneider
Queens College, CUNY
May 2006

Notes

1. The seminal ideas of Dankwart Rustow in these regards are updated and expanded upon in Lisa Anderson, ed., *Transitions to Democracy* (New York: Columbia University Press, 1999).

2. The closest approximation to this discussion is by Howard J. Wiarda, particularly in *Dilemmas of Democracy in Latin America* (Lanham, MD: Rowman & Littlefield, 2005).

3. Samuel P. Huntington, *The Clash of Civilizations and the Remaking of World Order* (New York: Simon & Schuster, 1996).

4. Texts tend to be either topically organized, hence confusingly jumping from country to country, if not between time period to time period, and subject to overreaching generalizations, or organized on a strictly country-by-country basis with little or no explicit comparison and with generalizations of limited scope. (The first type I have inelegantly termed *purees* for their excessive homogenization and lack of texture; the second I have characterized as *stews,* since the countries—no matter how richly portrayed—are readily distinguishable individual chunks floating in a thin broth of bland generalizations. The most satisfactory compromise to this point—one that also bridges dilemma of the single author (with limited country expertise) versus a variety of country experts (each following an idiosyncratic approach) is Howard Wiarda and Harvey Kline, eds., *Latin American Politics and Development,* 5th ed. (Boulder, CO: Westview Press, 2000). A very useful interpretation is the expanded version of this volume's overview chapters, *An Introduction to Latin American Politics and Development* (Boulder, CO: Westview Press, 2001).

5. Ruth Berins Collier and David Collier, *Shaping the Political Arena: Critical Junctures, the Labor Movement, and Regime Dynamics in Latin America* (Princeton, NJ: Princeton University Press, 1991).

6. Peter H. Smith, *Democracy in Latin America: Political Change in Comparative Perspective* (New York: Oxford University Press, 2005).

7. Wiarda, *Dilemmas,* pp. 24–46, presents an excellent critique of theoretical perspectives.

8. Roderic Ai Camp, *Politics in Mexico: The Democratic Transformation*, 4th ed. (New York: Oxford University Press, 2003), p. 9.

9. John A. Peeler, *Building Democracy in Latin America* (Boulder, CO: Lynne Rienner, 1998), pp. xi–xii.

10. Paul H. Lewis, *Authoritarian Regimes in Latin America: Dictators, Despots, and Tyrants* (Lanham, MD: Rowman & Littlefield, 2006).

Acronyms

AAA	Argentine Anticommunist Alliance
ABT	Alliance for the Well-Being of All (Mexico)
AC	A-Combination (Suriname)
AD	Democratic Action (Venezuela)
ADOC	Civil Opposition Democratic Alliance (Panama)
AND	Nationalist Democratic Action (Bolivia)
AL	Liberal Alliance (Brazil)
ALN	Nicaraguan Liberal Alliance
ALP	Antigua Labour Party
ANAPO	National Popular Alliance (Colombia)
ANL	National Liberating Alliance (Brazil)
ANN	New National Alliance (Guatemala)
ANR	National Republican Association (Paraguay)
AP	Popular Action (Brazil)
AP	Popular Action (Peru)
APRA	Popular Revolutionary Alliance of the Americas (Peru)
ARENA	National Renovating Alliance (Brazil)
ARENA	Nationalist Republican Alliance (El Salvador)
ATLU	Antigua Trades and Labour Union
AUC	United Self-Defence Forces of Colombia
BLP	Barbados Labour Party
CAEM	Center for Higher Military Studies (Peru)
CD	Colombia Democrática
CEBRAP	Brazilian Center of Analysis and Planning
CFP	Concentration of Popular Forces (Ecuador)
CGT	General Labor Confederation (Argentina)
CIA	Central Intelligence Agency (US)
CNC	National Campesinos Confederation (Mexico)
CNOP	Confederation of Popular Organizations (Mexico)
COA	Argentine Workers' Confederation
COB	Bolivian Workers Confederation
COMIBOL	Bolivian Mining Corporation
CONADE	National Development Council (Argentina)
CONAIE	Confederation of Indigenous Nations of Ecuador
CONASE	National Security Council (Argentina)
CONDEPA	Conscience of the Fatherland (Bolivia)
COPEI	Independent Electoral Organizing Committee (Venezuela)

CR	Radical Change (Colombia)
CTE	Ecuadorian Workers' Confederation
CTM	Mexican Workers' Confederation
CTV	Confederation of Venezuelan Workers
CUT	Unified Confederation of Workers (Chile)
DAC	Democratic Action Congress (Trinidad and Tobago)
DFP	Dominica Freedom Party
DGM	General Directorate of Military Manufactures (Argentina)
DLP	Democratic Labour Party (Barbados)
DLP	Democratic Labour Party (Trinidad and Tobago)
DLP	Dominica Labour Party
EAP	economically active population
ELN	National Liberation Army (Colombia)
EN	Encuentro National (Ecuador)
EP	Progressive Encounter (Uruguay)
ESG	Superior War College (Argentina and Brazil)
EZLN	Zapatista Army of National Liberation (Mexico)
FALN	Armed Forces of National Liberation (Venezuela)
FAO	Broad Opposition Front (Nicaragua)
FAR	Revolutionary Armed Forces (Cuba)
FARC	Armed Forces of the Colombian Revolution
FDO	National Front for Democracy and Development (Suriname)
FDP	Panamanian Defense Forces
FDP	Popular Democratic Front (Venezuela)
FDR	Revolutionary Democratic Front (El Salvador)
FEB	Brazilian Expeditionary Force
FEDECAMARAS	Venezuela Federation of Chambers and Associations of Commerce and Production
FEI	Independent Electoral Front (Venezuela)
FEP	Evita Perón Foundation
FJ	Justicialist Front (Argentina)
FL	Fanmi Lavalas (Haiti)
FLMN	Farabundo Martí Front for National Liberation (El Salvador)
FN	National Front (Colombia)
FND	National Democratic Front (Venezuela)
FNM	Free National Movement (Bahamas)
FRAP	Popular Action Front (Chile)
FREJULI	Justicialist Liberating Front (Argentina)
FRENAP	National Association of the Private Sector (Chile)
FREPASO	Fatherland Solidarity Front (Argentina)
FRG	Guatemalan Republican Front
FRN	National Reconstruction Front (Ecuador)
FSB	Bolivian Socialist Falange
FSLN	Sandinista Front for National Liberation (Nicaragua)
FUT	United Workers Front (Ecuador)
GATT	General Agreement of Trade and Tariffs
GDP	gross domestic product
GNP	Grenada National Party

GOU	Group of United Officers (Argentina)
GULP	Grenada United Labour Party
IBRD	International Bank for Reconstruction and Development, generally known as the World Bank
ID	Democratic Left (Ecuador)
IMF	International Monetary Fund
INP	National Planning Institute (Peru)
IPC	International Petroleum Company (Peruvian subsidiary of Standard Oil)
IPES	Institute for Social Research and Studies (Brazil)
JLP	Jamaican Labour Party
JUC	Catholic University Youth (Brazil)
LIBOR	London interbank offered rate
LPD	Labour Party of Dominica
M–19	19th of April Movement (Colombia)
MAPU	Movement for Unitary Popular Action (Chile)
MAS	Movement Toward Socialism (Venezuela and Bolivia)
MAS	Solidarity Action Movement (Guatemala)
MDB	Brazilian Democratic Movement
MDP	Pradist Democratic Movement (Peru)
MEP	Peoples' Electoral Movement (Venezuela)
MID	Independent Left Movement (Argentina)
MIR	Leftist Revolutionary Movement (Bolivia)
MIR	Leftist Revolutionary Movement (Chile)
MIR	Leftist Revolutionary Movement (Venezuela)
MNR	National Revolutionary Movement (Bolivia)
MRL	Revolutionary Liberal Movement (Colombia)
MRS	Sandinista Renovation Movement (Nicaragua)
MSC	Social Christian Movement (Ecuador)
MUPP	Pachakutik Plurinational Unity Movement (Ecuador)
MVR	Fifth Republic Movement (Venezuela)
NAFTA	North American Free Trade Agreement
NAR	National Alliance for Reconstruction (Trinidad and Tobago)
NDB	National Democratic Party (Suriname)
NDC	National Democratic Congress (Grenada)
NDP	National Democratic Party (Barbados)
NDP	National Democratic Party (St. Vincent and Grenadines)
NDP	New Democratic Party (Grenada)
NF	New Front (Suriname)
NJM	New Jewel Movement (Grenada)
NNP	New National Party (Grenada)
NPS	National Suriname Party
NRP	Nevis Reformation Party (St. Kitts-Nevis)
OAS	Organization of American States
OPEC	Organization of Petroleum Exporting Countries
OPL	Lavalas Political Organization (Haiti), renamed in 2005 Struggling Peoples' Organization
ORI	Integrated Revolutionary Organizations (Cuba)
ORVE	Venezuelan Revolutionary Organization

PAC	Citizen's Action Party (Costa Rica)
PAC	Political Affairs Committee (Guyana)
PAIS	Open Politics for Social Integrity (Argentina)
PAL	Agrarian Labor Party (Chile)
PAM	People's Action Movement(St. Kitts–Nevis)
PAN	National Action Party (Mexico)
PAN	National Autonomist Party (Argentina)
PAN	Party of National Advancement (Guatemala)
PAP	Peruvian Aprista Party
PARM	Authentic Party of the Mexican Revolution
PC	Conservative Party (Can apply to Argentina, Bolivia, Brazil, Chile, Colombia, Ecuador, Nicaragua, Peru, or Venezuela)
PCB	Brazilian Communist Party
PCC	Cuban Communist Party
PCCh	Chilean Communist Party
PCdoB	Communist Party of Brazil
PCN	National Conciliation Party (El Salvador)
PCV	Venezuelan Communist Party
PD	Democratic Party (Chile)
PD	Dominican Party
PDC	Christian Democratic Party (Argentina)
PDC	Christian Democratic Party (Brazil)
PDC	Christian Democratic Party (Chile)
PDC	Christian Democratic Party (Peru)
P de la U	National Unity Party (Colombia)
PDN	National Democratic Party (Venezuela)
PDP	Peoples' Democratic Party (Chile)
PDS	Social Democracy Party (Brazil)
PDT	Democratic Workers' Party (Brazil)
PFL	Liberal Front Party (Brazil)
PGT	Guatemalan Labor Party
PIR	Party of the Revolutionary Left (Bolivia)
PJ	Justicialist Party (Argentina)
PL	Liberal Party (Can apply to Bolivia, Brazil, Chile, Colombia, Costa Rica, Cuba, Ecuador, Guatamala, Honduras, Mexico, Nicaragua, Paraguay, Peru, or Venezuela)
PLC	Constitutional Liberal Party (Nicaragua)
PLD	Dominican Liberation Party
PLH	Liberal Party of Honduras
PLM	Mexican Labor Party
PLM	Progressive Labor Movement (Antigua and Barbuda)
PLN	National Liberation Party (Costa Rica)
PLP	Progress Labour Party (Bermuda)
PLP	Progressive Liberal Party (Bahamas)
PMDB	Party of the Brazilian Democratic Movement
PN	National Party (Chile)
PNA	National Agrarian Party (Mexico)
PNC	National Christian Party (Chile)

PNC	People's National Congress (Guyana)
PNH	National Party of Honduras
PNM	People's National Movement (Trinidad and Tobago)
PNP	People's National Party (Jamaica)
PNP	Peruvian Nationalist Party
PNR	Nationalist Republican Party (Suriname)
PNR	National Revolutionary Party (Mexico)
POR	Revolutionary Workers' Party (Bolivia)
PP	Popular Party (Brazil)
PPB	Brazilian Popular Party
PPC	Popular Christian Party (Peru)
PPD	Party for Democracy (Chile)
PPP	Progressive People's Party (Guyana)
PPP	purchasing power parity
PPR	Progressive Renewal Party (Brazil)
PPS	Popular Socialist Party (Brazil)
PPS	Popular Socialist Party (Mexico)
PR	Radical Party (Chile)
PR	Revolutionary Party (Guatemala)
PRC	Conservative Republican Party (Brazil)
PRD	Democratic Revolutionary Party (Panama)
PRD	Doctrinaire Radical Party (Chile)
PRD	Dominican Revolutionary Party
PRD	Party of the Democratic Revolution (Mexico)
PRE	Ecuadorian Roldosist Party
PRF	Federal Republican Party (Brazil)
PRI	Institutional Revolutionary Party (Mexico)
PRIAN	Renovating Institutional National Action Party (Ecuador)
PRM	Party of the Mexican Revolution
PRN	National Renovation Party (Brazil)
PRSC	Christian Socialist Reform Party (Dominican Republic)
PRVZL	Venezuelan Project (political party)
PS	Socialist Party (Argentina)
PSCh	Chilean Socialist Party
PSB	Brazilian Socialist Party
PSC	Social Christian Party (Brazil)
PSC	Social Christian Party (Ecuador)
PSC	Social Conservative Party (Colombia)
PSD	Social Democratic Party (Brazil)
PSDB	Brazilian Social Democracy Party
PSOB	Socialist Workers' Party of Bolivia
PSOL	Party of Socialism and Liberty (Brazil)
PSP	Patriotic Society Party (Ecuador)
PSP	Popular Socialist Party (Chile)
PSP	Popular Socialist Party (Cuba)
PSP	Social Progressive Party (Brazil)
PT	Workers' Party (Brazil)
PTB	Brazilian Labor Party

PUN	National Unity Party (Nicaragua)
PUP	People's United Party (Belize)
PUR	Unified Party of the National Revolution (Argentina)
PURS	United Party of the Socialist Revolution (Cuba)
PUSC	United Christian Socialist Party (Costa Rica)
PV	Green Party (Brazil)
RN	National Renewal (Chile)
SENDAS	National Secretariat of Social Assistance (Colombia)
SIN	National Intelligence Service (Peru)
SINAMOS	National System of Social Mobilization (Peru)
SKNLP	St. Kitts-Nevis Labour Party
SLP	St. Lucia Labour Party
SLP	St. Vincent Labour Party
SNI	National Intelligence Service (Brazil)
SRA	Argentine Rural Society
SVLP	St. Vincent's Labour Party
UBP	United Bahamian Party
UBP	United Bermudan Party
UCR	Radical Civic Union (Argentina)
UCRI	Intransigent Radical Civic Union (Argentina)
UCRP	Radical Civic Union of the People (Argentina)
UCS	Civic Solidarity Union
UD	Democratic Union (Argentina)
UDI	Independent Democratic Union (Chile)
UDN	National Democratic Union (Brazil)
UDP	United Democratic Party (Belize)
UFCO	United Fruit Company
ULF	United Labour Front (Trinidad and Tobago)
ULP	Unity Labour Party (St. Vincent and Grenadines)
UN	National Unity (Peru)
UN	United Nations
UNAM	National Autonomous University of Mexico
UNC	United National Congress (Trinidad and Tobago)
UNIR	Revolutionary Left National Union (Colombia)
UNO	National Opposition Union (Nicaragua)
UP	Popular Union (Argentina)
UP	Popular Unity (Chile)
UPD	Democratic Popular Union
UPP	United Progressive Party (Antigua and Barbados)
URD	Democratic Republican Union (Venezuela)
URNG	United National Guatemalan Revolution
US	United States
UWP	United Workers Party (Dominica)
UWP	United Workers Party (St. Lucia)
VHP	United Hindustani Party (Suriname)
VVV	Alliance for Prosperity (Volksallia Voor Vooruitgang) (Suriname)
WTO	World Trade Organization

1

Introduction and Overview

Latin America is a region of contradictions because rapid change in some respects interacts with intractable continuities in others. The effects of economic growth and societal modernization feed the former, whereas the latter are rooted in an authoritarian and corporatist past. Howard Wiarda aptly portrays this area, which he considers predominantly but ambiguously and incompletely Western:

> Democratization takes generations, not years, and often requires complete changes in societies and cultures, not just institutions—all of which require a very long time. In the meantime, during the transitional stages, we should expect a variety of mixed regimes, halfway houses, glasses that are both half full and half empty, and governments that have democratic hope and aspirations, but also exhibit authoritarian tendencies.[1]

Wiarda, a major generalist steeped in knowledge of Latin America, holds that to fundamentally alter institutions may take lifetimes, and the more resistant culture within which they operate even longer. His judgment that this may mean three or four generations is a proposition to be considered carefully throughout examination of the region's political development.

A close-up view of Latin America makes an observer acutely aware of both its bothersome problems and its resistance to change. Yet looking back into its past produces a realization of how much change, some of which constitutes real and substantial political development, has taken place. The differences from a century ago (1905) are more than dramatic, bordering upon profound. Then Brazil had been a republic for only seventeen years and, just a decade before, had traded high-handed despotic military presidents for governments dominated by oligarchic elites perpetuating themselves in power by often manipulated elections involving very restricted participation. Yet a few years ago 120 million men and women over the age of sixteen elected an authentic man of the working class to be president. In the early twentieth century Mexico was still ruled with an iron hand by an entrenched dictator whose nearly thirty years in power would extend yet another five before its violent end ushered in a quarter century of bloody civil strife. But at the beginning of the twenty-first century it managed to transfer power peacefully from a party whose hegemony spanned over seventy years to that party's historical opposition. Over the same time, Argentina went from domination by an agro-producing elite to a mass-based democracy, and Colombia progressed from rule by the victors of a bloody civil war to highly competitive electoral democracy.

Every country's political past influences the present in two ways. First, there is the objective heritage of the governmental structures, political organizations, and policy needs addressed, or ignored, as well as the impinging socioeconomic environment. Equally important is the perceived legacy reflected in the attitudes, values, expectations, and misgivings of the political culture that conditions individuals' actions in the political realm. There is always a significant gap between perception and reality, but excessively distorted perceptions often lead both to believing that the unfeasible is possible and that what might in reality be desirable is unattainable. Hence, paths doomed to failure may be followed while those potentially productive may be eschewed.

What Has Happened: The Course of Events

Although the current situation in the region and the countries it encompasses are discussed in Chapters 13, 14, and 15, an idea of where Latin America has arrived is needed as a starting point for comprehension of the journey, the subject of Chapters 2 through 12. First, a brief overview of the present situation is compared to that prevailing a century ago; it is followed by a snapshot of the political panorama fifty years ago. The reason is that a number of crucial questions are best posed as backward- rather than forward-linked. For example, what aspects of independence gaining can be explained by the preceding colonial experience? Next, what elements of widely varying early postindependence political life had their roots in the particular manner in which independence was achieved? In turn, what differences in the second generation of national life are attributable to first-generation nuances? For in making sense of contemporary Latin America, Wiarda stresses "continuities with the authoritarian and corporatist past," and sage observer Paul Lewis grounds his analysis in an "undemocratic culture" brought from Spain and Portugal that has survived transplantation to this hemisphere for five centuries.[2] To evaluate this fundamental conclusion and its implications, to which I subscribe, a full understanding of the roots of Latin America's struggle for political development is essential.

Hence, although this account moves forward in time, the quest for explanations is essentially retrospective. For great change has come about, but only as a result of the accumulation of lesser changes made over many generations. For example, in just the last hundred years, Brazil, a century ago under a poorly institutionalized republic dominated by narrow elites through manipulated elections, is now a stable democracy with 125 million voters. Mexico, which a hundred years ago was under a dictator for three decades and was heading down the slippery slope to revolution and civil war, is finally a competitive democracy. Argentina, governed a century ago by an elitist regime constructed by a general, has, despite economic problems that at times feed acute social unrest, enjoyed democratic political processes since 1983. Although Colombia is plagued with drug trafficking and protracted insurgency, with twelve constitutionally elected presidents in a row over the past forty-seven years, it is far better off than a century ago, when it was dominated by one party and recovering from a very bloody three-year civil war; it was at the same time absorbing the amputation of its valued province of Panama by the expansionist United States.

A century ago Peru, which still has its full share of problems, was an elite-dominated nation facing decades of conflict between its armed forces and its first popularly based political party. At that time Venezuela, now polarized over an erratic chief executive enjoying the support of the low-income masses, was about to enter a bloodily repressive dictatorship that would last through the mid-1930s. Bolivia and Ecuador were synonymous with rampant instability shading into ungovernability, and Paraguay was for all intents and purposes still mired in the previous century. Cuba was just coming out of US military government to become a de facto protectorate subject to military intervention at Washington's whim, as was Panama, cut in two by Canal Zone, over which the United States enjoyed sovereign rights in perpetuity.

In the early 1900s, conditions in Nicaragua, Haiti, and the Dominican Republic were so bad that US military occupation lasting until the beginning of the 1930s was looming on the horizon. Guatemala, Honduras, and El Salvador were considered laughable "banana republics," leaving only Chile, tiny Costa Rica, and equally minuscule Uruguay as essentially democratic anomalies. Bolivia and Ecuador have now become democracies as have Guatemala, El Salvador, Honduras, and the Dominican Republic. Paraguay has progressed to the point where it is in most ways of the late twentieth century, and Panama is a fully sovereign country enjoying ownership and control of its canal. Cuba, a century ago under US military government like Iraq today, has become a country criticized by many and praised by others, but clearly independent both from the United States and from the sponsor it subsequently chose, the no-longer existent Soviet Union.

A good deal of progress seemed to have been made by the midddle of the twentieth century, but some of this turned out to be illusory and, even more, stood on shifting sands. Hence, the political situation a few years after World War II was both far less participatory and markedly more unstable than it would be near the twentieth century's end. Brazil was about to embark on the last hurrah of populist strongman Getúlio Vargas, and Mexico stood out—at least relatively—as its dominant governing party was preparing for yet another peaceful presidential succession, never mind that there was no real political competition. In Argentina the charismatic General Juan Domingo Perón was readying his forces for an unprecedented reelection bid, with his glamorous wife, Evita, still at his side. Colombia was reeling from the murder of its most popular politician and sinking into a civil war that would claim forty thousand lives in a year.

Venezuela had seen a reformist civilian regime replaced by a military junta, and in Peru an ambitious general who had recently seized power was in the process of legitimizing himself through a sham election. Cuba's military autocrat was waiting for an opportunity to reclaim the presidency from a rapaciously corrupt civilian, so that he and his cronies could profit from partnership with the Mafia. Chile, while remaining a bastion of constitutionality, was experiencing disillusionment with its political parties to such an extent that it would soon elect to the presidency a man who had been a military dictator in the late 1920s. As had been the case fifty years earlier, the smaller countries were, on balance, worse off politically than their larger neighbors.

For most of the region, the 1960s were the disillusioning decade of fragile and shallow-rooted populist experiments collapsing, and the 1970s witnessed a dismaying burgeoning of repressive authoritarian regimes. The sun burst from behind these gray political clouds during the 1980s, with despotism swept away by a wave of democratizing transitions—often building on the lessons of past failure. Finally, the 1990s saw consolidation of these often-imperfect democracies—with the early years of the twenty-first century raising issues of social justice and economic performance.

Changes in Structures and Processes

Of course, a summation of where the countries of Latin America have arrived politically is not an answer to how they got there. What happened (the descriptive, or "what," questions) having been outlined in terms of events, the steps and processes of how it happened need to be examined with an eye to trends and patterns, before attention can shift to causation (the more analytical "why" questions). For although very important variations are depicted in the chapters ahead, a high-above-the-treetops wide-lens survey is necessary to provide perspective on the evolution of politics for individuals down on the ground and often blindly hacking their way through year after year of political underbrush. What is normal, what is backward, and what is exceptional must be tentatively assessed against what is common. Only looking across the region and the periods retrospectively at the end of an examination of cumulative experience (as in Chapter 14) allows judgments about whether a particular country was out of step at any time or with regard to specific challenges. Moreover, at any point, Latin American political development can be compared meaningfully only to the current political development on the European continent, particularly its southern part, rather than to the political development of the exemplary leading cases of Great Britain and the United States—which were very far ahead of their continental contemporaries.

At the time of colonization the only two colonizing powers were Spain and its Iberian neighbor, Portugal, both emerging from feudalism. As depicted by Wiarda:

> Latin America is a product of the Middle Ages, feudalism, and the Counter-Reformation, not of the modern world of the Enlightenment, the Protestant Reformation, the scientific revolution of Galileo and Newton, the capitalist and industrial revolution, or the seventeenth-century movement toward limited, representative government in England and its North American colonies.[3]

So the colonial period witnessed the implantation of political institutions bearing the heavy imprint of medieval corporatism, in which the hierarchically organized church, military, and largely peninsular (Iberian-born) bureaucracy each enjoyed special privileges, and the Creole aristocracy (New World–born Europeans) pursued its interests through interaction with them. Royal authority was maintained through separate lines of authority and, often overlapping if not partially contradictory, instructions to the throne's three sets of representatives (church, military, and administrators). Early on, the bureaucracy became a vehicle for patronage and payoffs to reward and ensure loyalty. With time, the large landlords, particularly those who astutely allied themselves to the corporate pillars, came to be an important political factor. But late in the colonial period, intense rivalry developed between *peninsulares* (born in Europe) and the *criollos* (Spanish for Creoles) over their conflicting commercial interests. And these differences shaped their respective attitudes toward continuation of the colonial relationship. (These themes are fully developed in Chapter 2.)

Independence did not transform the fundamentals of this system, although it did institute a very important change in removing the monarch, who had been both the legitimizer of authority and the arbiter among the rival power factors. With the disappearance of the viceroy as the king's local representative, central governmental institutions were greatly weakened; regions that had been victims of a lopsided center-periphery relationship were often broken off, most frequently by the second level of colonial administration: usually *audiencias,* but in a few cases more executively led captaincy-generals, who had long chafed at subordination to the viceroyalties.

Unconstitutional behavior and rule were almost guaranteed by the decision of the educated urban elites to adopt constitutions copied from that of the only republic of the time, the United States; the presidentialism, the separation of powers, and even the federalism of the US Constitution had no place in countries with nothing to federalize and where legislatures and courts lacked independence. Nevertheless, the urban elites backed the adoption of such constitutions without considering whether these had any connection to their experience and habits, much less their needs. These well-intentioned but naive leaders should have emulated the process of the Founding Fathers in Philadelphia and put together a framework suitable to the local circumstances, backed by broad political support, and legitimized by a fairly rigorous ratification process. Instead, they made no effort to adapt the US constitutional structures, which were as alien to the experience of their compatriots as sudden adoption of Protestantism would have been to these staunch Catholics.

At this time, European political regimes were overwhelmingly still based on divine right monarchy with legislative bodies having extremely restricted roles. The French Revolution led quickly to an imperial regime under Napoleon, a restored monarchy, a Second Republic, and another monarchical government under Louis Napoleon, which lasted until the early 1870s. Prussia and Austria-Hungary would remain near-absolutist through World War I, and Italy came into being after 1868 as a monarchy. Hence, in political development terms, during the nineteenth century Latin America was close to the European norm.

Effective authority in most of Spanish America (but not in Brazil) reverted to audacious regional leaders, who defied the urban elite and used their private armies in a warlord manner to usurp power from those who felt entitled to it, but who generally lacked the skill, determination, and support to resist the *caudillos,* or mobilizers of armed support to seize power. In rare cases members of the Creole elite survived by outcaudilloing their upcountry challengers. Chile, under the leadership of Diego Portales, was the outstanding exception; it shaped governmental institutions to its particular conditions, rather than copy the United States. Brazil avoided this stage by remaining a monarchy under the same Portuguese royal family until 1889. Some countries managed to outgrow caudillism within a generation or less, but in others it would prove a persistent and even adaptable institution lasting into the twentieth century.[4] As Wiarda captures the changes in this period relevant to national politics:

> By the middle of the nineteenth century, most Latin American countries had begun to settle down. They solved earlier border disputes; the church-state issue proved less contentious; the earlier trends toward disintegration ended or slowed. At the same time, population increased, new lands came under cultivation, and foreign investment began to flow in. New economic

institutions (banks, financial houses, and others) opened; armies and bureau-cracies were modernized and professionalized; and governments slowly ac-quired effective control over their own national territories.[5]

Early in some countries and later, even much later, in others, high-status, prop-ertied individuals in the capital used their commercial clout and dominance of for-eign trade to gain control of central governments, even if in the process they ceded a good deal of autonomy to *caudillo* types to act as political bosses in their interior regions. At the same time, powerful landowners built bases of political support through patron-client relationships with their workers, retainers, and other depen-dents. National politics generally became a violent struggle for political leverage, which brought with it decisive economic advantage. As development of national identity and consolidation occurred, in some countries fluid and frequently shifting alliances of urban and rural elites took form, often garbed as conservative versus liberal parties. (The details and variations of the past four paragraphs are analyzed in Chapter 3.)

Beginning in the 1870s, the substantial growth of export trade requiring stable financial arrangements and foreign investment for infrastructure development, particularly of ports and railroads, placed an increasing premium on both stability and control of the national government. As aptly captured by Lewis:

> The heyday of the Latin American Liberal state, from 1870 to 1930, wedded export-led economic growth to elitist politics. Progress in urban services and material improvements in transportation and communications brought enormous benefits to a relatively small portion of the population. Political stability was another mixed blessing. If by the turn of the century the *caudillos* had largely disappeared, they had been replaced by either powerful dicta-tors or exclusive oligarchies.[6]

In Mexico the result was a long developmentalist dictatorship lasting into the early twentieth century; in Brazil the political impact of trade-driven development was accommodated through a shift in dominant elites from the plantocracy of the tropical northeast to the coffee producers of the center-south, within the stabiliz-ing framework of the monarchy. When the rising coffee elites required control of the national executive to benefit the industry that was paying the country's exter-nal bills and serving as the economy's engine, a republican regime was adopted.

In Argentina this quest for stability took the form of a greatly strengthened central government balancing the interests of the interior agro-producers and the Buenos Aires merchant and banking elites; in Colombia it was thwarted by geog-raphy that separated population centers by high cordilleras of the Andes. In most countries both civilian bureaucracies and the armed forces expanded significantly as governmental control structures were strengthened and ambitious individuals were provided with employment opportunities. Since this growth of the state required increased government revenues, many of the smaller countries lagged behind, with *caudillo*-type dictators persisting in areas like Venezuela and Central America. The extent and nature of each country's integration into the world economy were generally the most important differentiating factors.

Political institutions responded to the development of an export-import elite wishing a stronger government, not necessarily one that was more democratic or even more responsive—to others at least—and feeling that they deserved it, since burgeoning foreign trade taxes were paying the bills. In a very broad sense, they wanted a cross between a Bismarckian and a Bonapartist state, certainly not one with the post-1820s Anglo-American emphasis on substantially broadened participation. Elites generally considered military expenditures a necessary investment (from which they might well devise ways of deriving profit), and in some cases, such as Brazil and Argentina, by the 1870s urban bankers and businessmen had joined with agro-export producers to advocate large-scale subsidized European immigration. This immigration drastically transformed already white Argentina and heavily black Brazil while leaving *mestizo* (mixed Spanish-Indian) countries much as they had been. Elites tended to endorse a congress and elections as long as these served their interests, but the several components of the elites agreed that a congress and elections could not be allowed to become vehicles for middle-class demands to gain significant leverage with respect to the allocation of public goods. "Opportunity for us and ours; regulation for you and yours" was the basic public policy rationale of sometimes allied, other times rival elite groups. These developments of course interacted with leadership—forceful in many instances, but farsighted in only a few situations.

The political gap that widened between the modernizing urban sector of society and those practices persisting in traditional interior areas was sometimes dramatic. Where the colonial period had been marked by large landholdings with an essentially captive labor force, or tropical plantation agriculture had been been the burden of African-origin slaves, a patron–client system not only persisted but even set down deeper roots, often becoming the basic sociopolitical institution. Indeed, well into the supposedly modern era, landowners frequently possessed almost absolute power, at times actually reaching as far as life or death, in return for providing dependent clients with physical security in those situations where threats of violence existed, as well as a minimum subsistence plus access to a priest. In situations where agents of the central government were far away, the area's most powerful patron took on quasi-governmental functions, in federal systems often even legally delegated to him, in other situations on his own as the biggest shark in local waters. This phenomenon was particularly widespread and durable in Brazil, where the distances from the central government were immense and communications difficult and attenuated, as well as in Mexico even after amputation of nearly half its area by the United States in the middle of the nineteenth century. Like royal authorities in the colonial period, agents of the national government were generally coopted by the local power holders—money and marriage being the chief inducements. (After all, such officials had to deal with the locals every day, whereas they only had to send reports to a distant bureaucratic superior, reports that he would find difficult—if not politically inconvenient—to question or verify.)

At the same time as the patronal political structure and practices survived, even thrived, in rural areas, political life was becoming more competitive in the cities. In many ways, however, the emergent middle sectors there, composed of government workers, shopkeepers, professionals, and tradesmen, were also significantly dependent on patrons. However, members of the middle class had the advantage of clients' competition for their services since there were multiple political factions seeking their support. Indeed, some of them became middlemen in the exchange of benefits for services or made use of their ability to forge upward links to become the nucleus of a new faction. Aspiring to achieve cadet–candidate status with the elites, some posed as spokesmen and an entering edge for the populace, many times to convince those better situated in the political order that they were worth being coopted rather than left to become increasingly troublesome. A few would remain reformist.

Even in those countries where the traditional system did sustain substantial modification, clientelistic exchanges persisted, with the landowner expecting unconditional loyalty, occasionally to the feudal extreme of bearing arms and at other times blindly voting as the patron wished. For as national politics became more complex, patrons in a local network were often clients in a regional one, where their patron was in turn a client of some bigger fish at the national level. Indeed, even well away from labor-intensive agriculture and ranching, the patron's position rested on his links and contacts at the state or national level. In this regard, by the last quarter of the nineteenth century in the more advanced countries and the first three decades of the twentieth in intermediate ones, a distinction emerged between smaller countries, where the capital city was dominant, and the large or geographically divided ones, where regionalism was a significant factor.

Within the more modern milieu of the cities, this essentially patrimonial style persisted in urban garb. Vertical links and horizontal rivalry morphing into confrontational factional competition might come to involve different kinds of payoffs on the part of patrons—jobs or access to government agencies and social services—but come sundown, the exchange from client to patron involved whatever the latter needed to pay his upward political debts: votes in more democratic systems, bodies in the street in turbulent ones. In towns and small cities the system became one of competing political factions organized around prominent families, establishing patron–client types of relationship with elements whose support was up for grabs. Sometimes this system was incorporated into competing political parties; at other times parties vied for the support of these local machines. By the end of the nineteenth century, Brazil, Argentina, Colombia, Peru, Chile, and Uruguay "had developed arrangements for governing that allowed a modicum of order and material progress while continuing to limit political participation."[7] But until well after the turn of the century there was little or no class or even interest basis to these clientelistically organized building blocks of politics. (The impact on national politics of features discussed in these eight paragraphs is studied in Chapter 4.)

Even in the first part of the twentieth century, changes readily apparent in the urban areas were greatly delayed and diluted in the interior. Indeed, moving from the capital to regional centers, to small towns, and on to the countryside, the trip was politically as much back in time as out in distance. The rural patron found himself ever more in a broker role, intermediating between his clients and influentials in government and the urban private sector, which could help him produce, transport, and market his crops so as to have the where-with-all to pay off his clients. Transactions came to involve credit and subsidies, construction of roads, and, in some areas, irrigation projects. This kind of bargaining rarely took place through political parties, which were usually little more than electoral vehicles and were merely urban clubs of notables during the long stretches between elections.

Before the turn of the century in the more developed countries, but after 1900 in the second echelon, the increased flow of resources from expanding foreign trade greatly accelerated the the government bureaucracy's becoming the source of clientelistic benefits and the president's being viewed as the superpatron. Some countries maintained or even created liberal democratic institutions to determine, or at least ratify, who would be this fortunate individual. In other cases, once in power, the nation's dominant political figure decided to stay, ignoring or eliminating inconvenient legal impediments. In almost all cases this *continuismo* involved support by the military to quell protests or put down attempted coups. In other cases, the erstwhile strongman became just another has-been, if indeed he was able to keep his skin whole.

Conceptualizations of the inception of democratic processes by Dankwart Rustow and by Samuel Huntington on the relationship between social mobilization and political institutionalization and its impact on whether political change might be gradual, pent-up and explosive, or forcibly repressed are useful in analyzing political development up to this point.[8] They are of even greater value from here on—so will be applied in Chapter 14.

The early part of the twentieth century, especially the World War I era, brought an acceleration of industrialization and related "modernization" processes, including the dramatic growth of urban centers, a broadening of economic opportunities, and a partial reordering of society. The result was a continuing increase in the number of people making demands upon national political institutions; hence, in view of the often stringent economic limits on meeting these demands—which needed to be channeled and manipulated, if not controlled—an increase in the system's regulative, responsive, and distributive capabilities was, in turn, required. This broadening of functions and strengthening of implementing structures was accompanied by a broadened scope of issues with which national political institutions had to deal, such as planning, development, and social welfare—leading to increasing specialization and centralization of these institutions. All these factors combined to strain extractive capabilities, with revenues falling behind expenditures, which, in the absence of sustained export growth or high foreign investment, required heavy borrowing.

In those few countries where democratic liberal institutions blossomed, the middle sectors sought entry into the political system—often through parties, but occasionally by way of paramilitary organizations—striving in the process to weaken executive control; their increased political participation was reflected in congress long before they could play a decisive role in electing presidents. Often turned back by fraud and repression, they persisted, their leaders frequently realizing that with the emergence of militant labor elements, elites currently viewing them as rivals might well come to consider them allies against a far greater threat—as many times became the case.

Such an early-twentieth-century flourishing of liberal democracy—notable in Argentina, Chile, and Uruguay, but with fainter reflections in Peru, where it was quickly cut off by a personalist dictator, and Colombia, where its impact was attenuated by the vertical nature of its political parties—was a frustrated goal of the Mexican Revolution, where it was submerged in a protracted civil war. In Brazil, republican government was a full generation newer than elsewhere and elite democracy showed only briefly, then was pushed into *tenentismo*, a movement of reformist young military. Taken together, the very major exceptions of Brazil and Mexico made this democratizing trend a limited one, and the survival of a militarist *caudillo* in Venezuela through the mid-1930s, with counterparts in Central America and the Caribbean, further restricted it. (A country-by-country discussion of the themes of the past five paragraphs is contained in Chapter 5.)

Where it did take place, the dawning of liberal democracy was short-lived, caught between populist pressures for enhanced participation and an abrupt end to the economic growth of the 1920s brought about by the Great Depression, which caused conservative elites to turn to regimes that would protect their particular interests in the face of decreased resources—even at the sacrifice of those democratic gains recently made; landowners had, at best, ambivalent feelings about such democratic trends. The notable, and very major, exception was Brazil, where the 1930 Revolution and the ensuing Getúlio Vargas regime allowed that country to catch up in a number of ways, while the former leaders in political development, such as Argentina and Chile, backslid or at best marked time. Indeed, the Brazilian case—and Mexico once it climbed out of the anguish and destruction of civil war in the 1930s under Lázaro Cárdenas—was in the forefront of a phase in which urban groups, including the new industrialists and labor sectors, bypassed or misused parliamentary and electoral processes to attack executive power. These actions were mediated by political entrepreneurs who, by adapting to changing conditions, became leaders of the emerging popular groups. Rather than revolutionary risings of the masses, the maneuvering of political brokers—displaying varying degrees of personalism—along the border between establishment and emergent populist groups was a hallmark of the period. A significant exception was Peru, where events created an antipathy between its best-organized popular political movement and the armed forces, an antagonism that distorted political life throughout this period. Wiarda eloquently underscores the appeal of essentially corporatist regimes:

> In contrast to the Marxian class-conflict ideologies then also gaining new adherents, corporatism advocated the unity and harmony of capital and labor. It was opposed to liberalism and individualism; instead, corporatism advocated the reorganization of society and politics in terms of "organic," supposedly "natural" functional (or corporate) units: the family, the parish, the neighborhood; groups of entrepreneurs, workers, farmers, fishermen, soldiers, religious orders; and so on. It favored a strong state, an ordered and integrated society, and tripartite cooperation between business, unions, and government.[9]

Politically astute individuals, their varying degrees of skill leading to wide variations in results, sought to use the emerging urban masses to play a quite complex and often sophisticated game of facilitating their rise to power as well as the often more difficult task of holding onto it. Here Vargas (1930–1945 and 1951–1954) overlapped with Juan Domingo Perón (1945–1955 and 1973–1974), starting earlier in a less developed society, leaving office when Perón was entering his own presidency, and his return engagement coinciding with Perón's second term. By this time it had become clear that the majority of Latin American countries had begun to diverge from any general pattern, or more precisely had begun to follow differentiated, but not entirely different, paths. Trends in the interwar period included adoption of often narrow and spottily implemented welfare programs, officially sponsored unionism, and, as already indicated, in the 1930s, corporatist experiments bordering on European fascistic models. Although these programs were often lacking in scope, substance, and depth, they significantly enhanced the regime's cooptative capabilities and affected the nature and operation of political institutions. New political interests were built into the system through essentially bureaucratic means involving channeled, if not controlled, consultation through networks of councils and committees that linked government agencies with the burgeoning agents of sectoral groups; this system was most elaborate in Vargas's "New State" but also readily apparent in Mexico.

Such developments involved serious questioning by many, and rejection by some, of the basic liberal rationale for representative political institutions and policies combined with demands for a more active executive power. Legislative role expansion, until recently viewed as desirable by modernizing factions, lost favor to the degree that it was perceived as decreasing governmental effectiveness by facilitating special interests and fostering stalemates and impasses. Hence, legislative-executive conflicts in the 1930s were generally resolved in favor of the presidents, on the upswing again as they had been around the turn of the century. A major exception to this competition and conflict was Mexico, where congress, glad to be in existence and operating within the straitjacket of a single-party system, had no idea of competing for power with a president of the extreme popularity of Cárdenas. During these years the European continent saw authoritarian to totalitarian regimes installed in all but a few countries, with Benito Mussolini and Adolph Hitler joined by Generalissimo Francisco Franco in Spain (following an extremely bloody civil war) and Antonio de Oliveira Salazar in Portugal. Hence, by comparative standards, politically at least, Latin America was coping reasonably well with very difficult situations.

In a few cases the political role of the military from the 1920s into the 1940s was minimal or brief, and in Mexico Cárdenas curbed it before the end of his term in 1940. As a general rule, however, the armed forces were becoming a major factor in shaping the pattern for incorporation of new groups into the system. This could take the form of the old warlord/*caudillo* style in Mexico before 1934, the cutting-edge role of a relatively modern military in Brazil, or the actions of the more authoritarian faction of officers who paved the way for the rise of Perón in Argentina. Although on balance the military was not a progressive force in this period or even in the immediate postwar years, significant factions within the armed forces—most notably the *tenentes* (lieutenants, a generic term for reform-minded young officers) in Brazil and episodic groups in Chile and Bolivia—occasionally were. In light of the weakness of both parliamentary institutions and revolutionary movements, both leaders on a quest to develop power bases among the masses and the new industrialists often turned to the military, as in the highly illustrative case of Venezuela. There, the military showed both the floor and the ceiling of its progressive tendencies in helping Accíon Democrática come to power in 1945 and then booting this reformist party out in 1948. This seemingly contradictory behavior was closely related to the increasingly middle-class origins of the officer corps, which deeply affected their basic political socialization. Yet, in fact, their role as doorkeepers was essentially consistent—pushing open the door to meaningful participation for the "respectable" middle sectors, but then closing it against the "uncultured" and unruly working class. This was a major dynamic in Brazil even earlier than in Venezuela; the facilitating of the middle class's rise came in 1930, and the blocking of labor's attempt to follow began in 1945. In many instances the Cold War had a major impact—most dramatic in the case of Chile—in dampening military reformism.

The belief that the growth of the middle sectors of Latin American society, rooted in economic development and societal modernization, would lead to greater stability and democracy proved illusory. Much less independent than their counterparts in North America and Western Europe, the Latin American middle classes generally failed to develop a coherent political position. Their ambivalent political role stemmed not only from their heterogeneity, but also from a desire to have both progress and stability, while holding open the opportunity to climb to elite status. To accomplish this, middle-class elements frequently acted as brokers between the dominant forces of the past and those of the future: the existing elites and the emerging masses. Lacking the connections and traditional power capabilities of the oligarchy, on one hand, and the numerical strength and pressure potential of the workers and peasantry, on the other, middle-class groups often turned to the military when a crisis loomed. Hence, in the 1960s, the armed forces, which in the second echelon of modernizing countries, as in the earlier ones sketched above, had recently helped open political doors for the middle sectors, sometimes slammed them shut in the face of working-class elements.

This inconsistency appeared to contemporary observers to be another of the puzzling contradictions of Latin American politics, so it is very helpful to bear in mind Wiarda's refinement and updating of Charles Anderson's conceptualization of Latin America's version of political development:

> Historically in Latin America, new groups could be accommodated to this corporatist system by adding a new corporatist pillar to the old regime. Thus, in the late nineteenth and early twentieth centuries, the rising business-commercial-entrepreneurial class (often foreign born) was accommodated in this way. In the 1920s and 1930s (depending on the country) it became the turn of the middle class—or, since it lacked consciousness as a class, the "middle sectors"—to be absorbed into the system. Argentina, Brazil, Chile, Mexico, and Uruguay, the most developed countries in Latin America, were also the countries with the largest middle class and, thus, led the way in adding new pillars to the historic triumvirate of power.[10]

Having shown a significant power capability, one potentially threatening the existing order—through strikes and demonstrations as well as major electoral potential—leaders of the rising group had to agree that in return for being accepted as legitimate actors on the political stage, they would forgo efforts to supplant, much less destroy, the established power contenders. Hence, this agreement constituted a "fiendishly clever and eminently successful way by which the elites in Latin America maintained power . . ." for:

> while new groups could be added to the system, the old groups remained powerful; the vertical or pillared structure of the corporate system also served to preserve hierarchy, authority, and centralization and to prevent horizontal or revolutionary alliances within and between groups.[11]

By the 1960s, if not earlier, it had become clear to scholars, if not always to practicing politicians, that political development could not precede social structures and processes, which in turn occur in response—often substantially delayed—to economic achievements. The varying experience of major countries also demonstrated that progress in the political sphere might not follow as a matter of course but instead might often lag well behind these socioeconomic factors. When this discontinuity occurred, the potential for a catch-up spurt of political development increased, but whether it occurred or not depended heavily upon the presence of adequate political leadership, which could catalyze and constructively channel the mounting dissatisfaction and effectively spread a realization of the need for significant adjustments in the political-governmental sphere. Such leadership had emerged in Brazil with Vargas, Mexico with Cárdenas, and Chile with Arturo Alessandri. It had come even earlier in Argentina with Hipólito Yrigoyen—renewed by Perón—and in Uruguay with José Batlle y Ordóñez, as well as in an excessively personalistic form with Augusto Leguía in Peru. (This theme is followed throughout the book, with findings pulled together in Chapter 14.)

In the first part of the post–World War II period and into the late 1950s, the incorporation of new groups in a few of the more advanced countries was broadening the base of participation to include a few favored rural groups; the incorporation had already happened in Mexico under Cárdenas and was a harbinger of what would come later in other countries. In most cases it involved continuation of the semicorporatist pattern previously used to incorporate urban labor; mass-based parties of a populist character appeared on the scene in some countries. Peronism rode high in Argentina until late 1955; Vargas's policies were continued after his 1954 demise; and in Mexico the party replaced the personal leader, who at times functioned as its agent as much as its leader. Even in a time when rural countries were becoming urban and agricultural economies were turning into industrial ones, and patron–client relationships persisted as the classic patron, to whom in many cases the factory owner had become a functional equivalent, was supplanted by political brokers bearing different names from one country to another, but all skilled in getting out votes, delivering warm bodies for demonstrations, and distributing low-level favors including local patronage as a service to high-status patrons—who now were often elected officials or upper-echelon bureaucrats. The currency might have changed, but the essential nature of the exchange remained constant. This adaptation to socioeconomic change was also found in nondemocratic political styles. In Lewis's view:

> Whereas the old *caudillo* distributed plunder among his relatives, friends, and clients, the new *caudillo* nurtures his following with the "renewable resources" of the state, buying votes with jobs, contracts, welfare, and graft. Behind this façade of the revolutionary regime or the corporate state, however, lurks the Iberian tradition of personal rule, military-type organization, and crusading intolerance.[12]

Well into the 1950s, there was a pronounced increase in incorporating new groups into political life through mass-based populist parties interacting with government social service agencies of a quasi-corporatist type. In many cases this process operated with substantial continuity; in others it was temporarily derailed and then resumed through popular mobilization. In a few instances the interactions of populist leaders and patron–client relationships developed a unique broad political form such as Peronism in Argentina, but in others, particularly in post–Vargas Brazil, they led to important but more transitory styles that I term *cooptative clientelism* and *patronage populism,* a distinction depending on the particular mix of personal or even charismatic appeal with employment, favors, and services. (The topics of the past nine paragraphs are expanded upon in Chapters 6 and 7.)

In all these cases and many others, a great deal of political bargaining, accommodation, and conflict resolution went on, frequently outside the parties-elections-legislature arena. Much of the deal making took place within the committees, councils, and state enterprises of the administration. But in the late 1950s, presidents proved increasingly unable to successfully orchestrate this type of system. Moreover, the rise of Fidel Castro to power in Cuba, bringing the Cold War closer to Latin America, combined with a new sense of coherence and confidence in the officer corps, led to a new wave of militarism. At a minimum, Castro's rise enhanced the officers' determination to play more actively and decisively the historical role of arbiter, which had declined in the postwar years. Even more, it increased opportunities for arbitration for those military elements that had long harbored such inclinations. As the officer corps perceived civilian chief executives to be ineffective at the same time that the armed forces had become more involved in industrial enterprises and development activities, this activism increased apace.

Thus the late 1950s and early 1960s witnessed an alarming surge in the military playing an increasingly active arbiter role in the political lives of the less effectively institutionalized countries, as well as in cases where the long-dominant leader was gone or had exhausted his political magic. A general had seized power in Colombia in 1953, in Brazil Vargas was gone by late 1954, and in Argentina the military deposed Perón a year later. The tasks facing governments were daunting, and public patience was sorely lacking. This was the trying time at which the "revolution of rising expectations" turned into the "revolt of soaring expectations." A yet-unresolved crisis of legitimacy and authority was intertwined with an insistent demand for broadened and more meaningful political participation; at the same time, economic growth had to be achieved in the midst of often unruly pressures for redistribution and greater equality (the dilemma of "premature" distribution prejudicing saving and investment). The demagogic populism of Jânio Quadros in Brazil in 1961, coinciding with the inability of Argentina's Arturo Frondizi to juggle incompatible Peronist-military demands, brought the "collapse of populism" to the southern part of South America.

Although Mexico's civilianized nonpopulist system survived, whereas Colombia and Venezuela provided a countertrend by moving out of military regimes to democratic civilian governments, and Uruguay and Chile delayed succumbing, the overwhelming majority of the region's countries headed into military rule during the 1960s. Their armed forces were impatient with faltering civilian rule, mistaking uproar for looming revolution and the inevitable messiness and sometimes theatrical confrontation of political bargaining for conflict, so as to perceive a system and society in crisis. Time and time again, the military was ready, usually eager, to "save" the nation from the peril of greatly exaggerated, even imaginary pro-Soviet subversion. From the mid-1960s, through the 1970s, and in some cases into the 1980s, authoritarian and often brutally repressive military regimes dismantled leftist organizations that in many cases existed chiefly on paper and through sporadic street demonstrations. In a few countries, including Argentina and Uruguay, they battled persistent insurgencies. Along the way the military attempted to show that they could run the country better than what they saw as the alternatives: demagogic and irresponsible populist politicians or outdated oligarchs. In places such as Brazil, Peru, and Uruguay, the military themselves learned that they were ill suited to be rulers instead of arbiters. In all cases, plagued by their own failures and shortcomings, with reluctance and reservations they turned power back to civilians, in some instances the very ones they had earlier overthrown. (A discussion of the developments sketched in the preceding four paragraphs and of their causes are found in Chapters 8, 9, and 10.)

Often lost in the glare of the dramatic rebirth of democracy in Latin America in the 1980s and 1990s are the resilience and refurbished rebirth of political

LATIN AMERICA

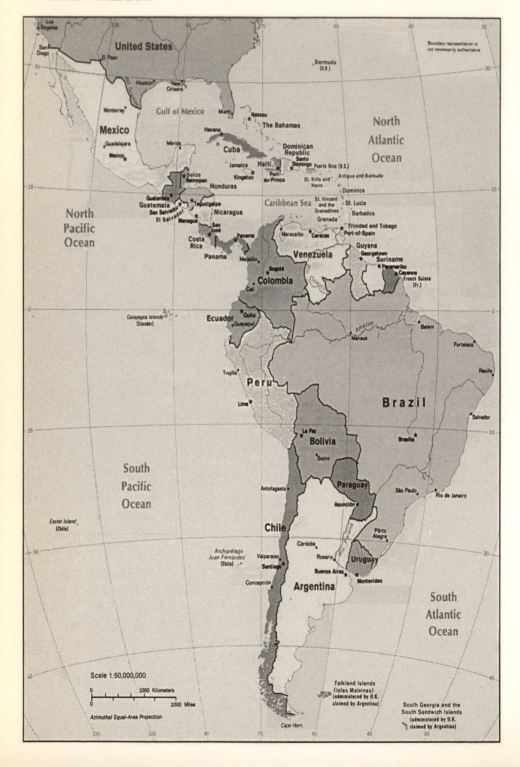

practices with their roots well back in the past. Indeed, this democratic resurgence raises a question of whether traditional Latin American political culture had experienced a resurgence under the military regimes. As Wiarda cautions:

> Latin America has a long history of organic-statism, corporatism, religiosity, elitism, patrimonialism, and authoritarianism that is often pervasive. The political system tends historically to be hierarchical and top-down, its economic system mercantilist and statist, its society strongly class/caste based, its legal system based on civil law and similarly top-down, its religion absolutist, and its educational system deductive. Latin America tends to emphasize group or corporate rights over individual rights, unity and monism over diversity and pluralism, and strong central government over checks and balances.[13]

When military regimes gave way to civilian government, it was generally to groups they had earlier pushed aside in their hurry to seize the reins of power. The return was to what had existed before, not to anything new that had developed during the military suspension of "politics as usual." Argentina went back to the pre-Peronist leading party and its senior surviving leader. Brazil's military relinquished power to elements deeply rooted in the immediate post-Vargas era, electing as president someone who had served in Vargas's cabinet and had been prime minister during a short parliamentary experience in 1962. Peru's bridge away from military rule was the president over whom the military had run roughshod in taking power in 1968. In no case was power turned over to political forces of the left; in most cases it was given to center to center-right establishment political groupings.

No wonder there was no sudden emergence of pluralist political systems; the restored governing elites generally practiced politics essentially as they had learned to in the 1940s and 1950s. As already discussed, in those years the traditional style of national politics had persisted through the transformation of many older clientelistic networks of factional vertical ties into systems that were corporatist in the sense that sectoral interest organizations were built quite directly into the official administrative structure. Instead of autonomous, bottom-up vehicles of interest representation, there were official trade unions, peasant groupings, and business associations legally linked to government agencies such as labor ministries, agrarian reform institutes, and ministries of development or "regional integration." This trend had previously been launched, carried far, and deeply entrenched under Vargas in Brazil and Perón in Argentina, and it was perfected in Mexico after Cárdenas through interest group incorporation into the workings of a hegemonic governing party that monopolized positions in the national executive in a highly fused party-government system. The strength of extraordinary national leaders had allowed these three leading countries to establish a single channel at the top that worked basically like the old royal authority of the colonial period. It didn't eliminate competition for influence among sectoral and regional interests, but it did permit the chief power broker to play off one interest against the other, and in the process to maintain himself at the peak.

When most adept at this political style, as in the cases mentioned above, the maximum leader, bolstered by broad popular appeal as well as effective control structures, held all the strings and operated without significant limitations on his power, except the crucial one: maintaining his ability to make payoffs in the patronage-clientelistic sense up and down the line. He was the ultimate patron ensconced and even institutionalized at the center of all governmental authority. The problems arose when lesser contemporaries and successors found it more difficult to keep the increasingly complex series of personal, patronal, and factional ties together.

Where the president was unable to do this, competition among factions finding support from societal interests percolated up to the top, unleashing the forces of political instability. Unresolved and ineffectively mediated conflicts of interest, sometimes accompanied by violence, gave the most coherent of the existing hierarchical structures, the military, an opportunity to play a praetorian role. But at the end of the 1970s and into the 1980s, the military withdrew or was expelled from ruling, having demonstrated that it was no more adept at governing than the civilians it had replaced. Indeed, meddling and second-guessing by militaries hovering on the verge of stepping in and taking over had been a big part of these governments' perceived failures. Now the chastened armed forces saw their roles reduced in the great majority of countries. At the same time, return to competitive civilian rule proved no panacea, especially in the context of severe economic problems. (The intertwined themes of the past five paragraphs are carefully examined in Chapters 11 and 12, and the several approaches to systematizing these developments are discussed in Chapter 14.)

In the first decade of a new century and a new millennium, the great challenge is deepening democracy and improving its quality. For the first time ever, the four most populous countries of the region—containing 380 million of its 565 million inhabitants—enjoy electoral democracy and constitutional rule at the same time. The next three largest, embracing 70 million citizens, are also governed by popularly elected presidents, even if approval ratings may be on the low side in one of these cases (Peru) and cleavages deep in another (Venezuela). The same democracy also prevails in varying degrees in almost all the remaining countries, a fact obscured because public attention is focused on the grimness of the Haitian exception. The roots of democracy, however, are still rather shallow in most of the region, especially in practice rather than theory. As Wiarda sees it:

On the one hand, democracy as an ideal, as an abstract principle, still enjoys—as it has since the early nineteenth century—widespread support in Latin America. But in the often disorganized and under institutionalized conditions of Latin America, people realize that democracy may not work or work very well in their context. Hence, their preference for strong government, executive leadership, a nationalistic regime, top-down paternalism, and a mercantilist state that also provides abundant opportunities for employment.[14]

Certainly this formulation contains a strong element of truth, yet it may be too sweeping a generalization for such a diverse group of countries. Expert opinions differ as to the severity of the situation. Wiarda has become increasingly pessimistic. His most recent opinion is that

> most Latin American countries have the *formal institutions* of democracy— elections, legislatures, political parties, and so on—but are not very democratic underneath. They are *electoral democracies* but not *liberal democracies*. They have the *institutions* of democracy (relatively easy to change) but not its underlying *practices* or *political culture*.[15]

Peter Smith echoes this concern, saying that "popular support for democratic politics in Latin America is shown to be partial, fragile, and increasingly uncertain. . . . Even without military intervention, democracy could become increasingly 'illiberal' or semi democratic and slide in the direction of autocracy."[16] Hopefully, readers will reach Chapter 15 of this book capable of making an informed decision about the assets and liabilities on Latin America's political balance sheet. (Chapter 13 closely examines contemporary trends and issues.)

It is clear, as the body of this book documents, that political development has been a painfully slow, discouragingly discontinuous, and frustratingly uneven process in Latin America. Yet it has also been faster, less plagued by long-term backsliding, and even more widespread than in other highly diverse, many-nation, far-flung regions of the world. In this respect, comparison with the experience of the southern European countries is both highly informative and essentially encouraging. If their substantially later start along the mine-strewn road to political viability is taken into account, Latin American nations have, in most respects, progressed more rapidly and less traumatically than those on the Mediterranean underbelly of pace-setting Europe.

This is true not only of such mother countries as Spain and Portugal, but also the country of origin of a very sizable proportion of postindependence immigrants, Italy, and the cradle of democracy, Greece. Even the laggards in this march to establish suitable political institutions and a supportive political culture compare reasonably well with the troubled and turbulent lands lying between Italy and Greece. To put Latin America's experience into proper perspective, it must be remembered that any significant degree of stable democracy was attained by Spain, Portugal, and Greece only since the mid-1970s. Moreover, in fundamental ways democratic processes are still incomplete and under stress there. Indeed, their present peril in Italy might be greater than in Brazil, in Spain more than in Mexico. But even to pose this question requires knowledge of the social and economic as well as the political realities of the region.

The Ethnic Mosaic

The racial and ethnic complexity of Latin America is truly impressive, exceeding that of Europe. This dramatically varied complexity, more than any other factor, calls into question the validity and usefulness of the umbrella term *Latin America* for the region. Certainly comparison of developments in one country with those in others cannot ignore the tremendous racial variations, which exceed those of other major world regions. Although some commentators go too far in saying that there are three Latin Americas—white, bronze, and black—the often-underplayed racial differences are all the more crucial because the greatest variations occur in the largest and most important countries; they are not just small exceptions from some sort of regional norm (which doesn't exist).

Brazil, home to nearly one-third of all Latin Americans—185 million of 565 million—has 81 million individuals, 44 percent of its population, with significant African roots, mostly mixed, but significantly black. Yet its 104 million inhabitants of European extraction—roughly as many as in the rest of South America—are quite varied: Those of fairly recent Italian extraction and descendants of early Portuguese settlers are the most numerous, but other Europeans are common and Asian strains are significant in absolute if not relative terms. Although frequently highlighted, Brazil's indigenous population has been reduced to below 0.2 percent (around 350,000 individuals).

Mexicans, who at 110 million comprise nearly a fifth of all Latin Americans, could hardly differ more from Brazilians in their origins and heritage. Persons of mixed Spanish-Indian blood predominate, whereas those of African roots are extremely few. Among Mexico's European population, estimated at only 9 percent, Italians are rare and Portuguese unheard-of. Moreover, Indians at 30 percent still comprise a very sizable proportion of the country's inhabitants, and most of the majority *mestizos* are more Indian than European.

Argentina, with a population of 42 million individuals, is overwhelmingly European, at some 85 percent, having all but eradicated its indigenous population during the nineteenth century. Individuals of Italian extraction are easily the nation's majority, and *mestizos* are fewer than 1 in 7.

Colombia—whose population of 45 million, like Argentina's, makes up about 8 percent of the region's total—is vastly different, bearing a superficial similarity to Mexico in racial and ethnic makeup. Considered a *mestizo* country at nearly 60 percent, it is home to only 700,000 Indians—many with some admixture of African blood. A large proportion of Colombian *mestizos* are markedly more European, hence less Indian, than are most of Mexico's. Blacks and mulattoes are nearly as numerous in Colombia as Europeans—around a fifth of the total population—but are situated at the opposite pole from the Europeans in socioeconomic terms and political influence, perhaps even more than their far more numerous Brazilian counterparts.

These four countries, containing a bit over two-thirds of the region's population, amply demonstrate Latin America's ethnic-racial diversity. But diversity also characterizes the middle stratum of Latin American countries.

Peru, with 5 percent of Latin Americans (nearly 29 million), has Indians and *mestizos*—respectively, 45 and 37 percent—as the very distinct majority, with its 15 percent of European origin, chiefly of Spanish extraction. Peru is distinguished by the fact that Asians are decidedly more numerous than persons of African ancestry.

Nearly as populous (at over 26 million), Venezuela has a racial-ethnic mosaic roughly paralleling that of neighboring Colombia, although with a somewhat higher *mestizo* majority, a lower proportion of African origin, and only 2 percent Indian. Thus, by the time we encounter this first instance in which ethnic-racial similarities between two countries outweigh distinctions, over three-fourths of the region's population has already been accounted for.

Bolivia's population of 9 million fundamentally resembles that of Peru, with 55 percent Indian, 30 percent *mestizo*, and 15 percent white. Ecuador (with 14 million inhabitants) roughly reverses these proportions and adds in a 10 percent African-origin component. Chile, population 16 million, is largely fairly Europeanized *mestizos* and predominantly Spanish-origin Europeans, with only 3 percent Indians, very few Asians, and almost no people of African heritage.

The widely held idea that Central America and the Caribbean are ethnically and racially more homogeneous flies in the face of reality. Guatemala, at 15 million the most populous of Central American countries, bears a fundamental similarity to the Andean countries, with the population 44 percent Indians and most of the rest Ladinos—the local term for *mestizos* and westernized Indians. At 88 percent European and 8 percent *mestizo*, with an African-origin trace, Costa Rica (with only 4 million inhabitants) bears a greater similarity to far-distant Uruguay (a miniversion of Argentina with a population moving toward 4 million) than it does to any of its Central American neighbors. Next door to the south, in

Panama, *mestizos,* at about 70 percent, outnumber people of African origin 5 to 1, and Europeans make up only a tenth of the population of a little over 3 million. To the north in twice as populous Nicaragua, *mestizos* also make up 70 percent; Europeans are a bit more numerous at 1 in 6, and blacks are under 10 percent, with Indians only 1 in 20 (among a population nearing 6 million). For its part Honduras has 7 million inhabitants, 90 percent of whom are *mestizo* with the remaining tenth mostly Indian; both Europeans and those of African ancestry are extremely rare. *Mestizos* predominate even more in El Salvador, where Indians make up only 5 percent of the 7 million population and Europeans just 1 percent. Indeed, the closest parallel to Honduras is faraway Paraguay, where Indians and Europeans total only 5 percent in an ocean of *mestizos* (although most with only a limited proportion of European blood) in a population also of 7 million.

Cuba, the most populous of the Caribbean countries (with 11.5 million inhabitants), contains a majority of African-descended population—51 percent mulatto and 11 percent black—coexisting with a large European component, to the virtual exclusion of *mestizos* and Indians. Haiti and the Dominican Republic, although sharing the same island, differ sharply from each other and also from Cuba. The Dominican Republic is some 70 percent mulatto and 11 percent black, but 1 in 6 of its 9 million inhabitants is European, whereas Haiti, with a population of 8 million, is 95 percent black, the remainder being mostly mulatto, with Europeans in very short supply.

The population of the remaining mini- and microcountries, which comprise only a sliver of the region's inhabitants, are primarily of African descent. Still, even among them, there is racial-ethnic diversity. Guyana's population of 720,000 is 44 percent East Indian compared to 30 percent black and 17 percent mixed African and Amerindian, with a very small number of Europeans. These proportions are not grossly different from those in Trinidad and Tobago, where East Indians and blacks are even, at 40 percent, and 15 percent are mulatto, with trace numbers of other Asians and Europeans among its 1.2 million residents. More populous Jamaica's 2.7 million inhabitants are three-quarters black and 15 percent mulatto, with only 3 percent Europeans, but Belize, an enclave of under 300,000 persons on the Central American coast, is overwhelmingly *mestizo* and Creole, with about one-fifth indigenous elements. Suriname, the 50 percent more populous Dutch foothold in South America, is, like Guyana, just over half East Indian, nearly one-third Creole, and a tenth "bush Negro." Indians and Chinese are traces at 3 percent each.

Given the undeniable facts of such profound diversity, serious consideration needs to be given to whether race and ethnic makeup should not be the chief criteria for subdividing cumbersomely heterogeneous Latin America into meaningful groupings of countries rather than the traditional basis of location and geographic proximity. Certainly ethnic makeup must be a major dimension for classification, since there is abundant evidence that racial and ethnic variation impacts heavily upon politics. It also possesses potential for differentiating the relevance of certain Latin American countries to the several groupings of Afro-Asian nations. In the chapters ahead, significant changes in racial-ethnic composition are discussed, as are shifts in the political relevance of minority elements.

Economics and Geography

In Latin American politics, certain geographic facts cannot be ignored. Brazil, by far the largest of the region's countries (at just over 3.3 million square miles, the fifth largest country in the world), affects much more of Latin America more deeply than does second-largest Mexico. The latter is located at the northern extreme of the region and has its longest and most active boundary with the United States, its massively dominant trading partner. Within Latin America it borders only Guatemala and Belize, one medium-sized by regional standards and the other tiny. In sharp contrast, Brazil, stretching 2,700 miles both north to south and east to west, occupies the heart of the South American continent and borders on the region's third through sixth largest countries (Argentina, Colombia, Peru, and Venezuela), as well as Bolivia, Uruguay, Paraguay, Guyana, Suriname, and French Guiana. Moreover, it has highway connections into Ecuador; Chile is its most distant continental neighbor. Its Atlantic coastline of 4,600 miles equals all coasts of the United States—Atlantic, Pacific, and Gulf. Brazil is distant from the United States, which is an important, but very far from dominant, market; Brazil is closer to Africa and essentially as close to Europe.

For their part, Colombia is situated at the northern tip of South America and Argentina at its southern extreme, positions greatly limiting the number of countries with which they are in direct contact. Of thirty other countries—just a handful having over 9 million inhabitants, and eleven but a fraction of a million—only Peru borders on more than four countries, and most have only two adjoining or adjacent neighbors. Those in the Caribbean have no contiguous neighbors, except for Haiti and the Dominican Republic, which unhappily have just each other.

Because Mexico's international transactions, diplomatic and security-related as well as economic, are all but monopolized by the United States, Brazil's centrality to the region is accentuated. Moreover, its influence is no longer severely limited by Argentina as a hostile rival, since that country's economic well-being requires close cooperation with its huge, overshadowing neighbor, which enjoys a more than 4-to-1 population advantage (at 185 million to 42 million).

There is a prevalent myth that Latin American countries are dominated by their capital cities. Like its cousin, the monoculture myth that most Latin American countries have only a single main product, it bears little resemblance to reality except in the smallest countries—where there is little room for a second metropolis, especially when the first may well not be very impressive. Starting from the top, Brazil contains two of the world's largest cities, neither of them its capital. Metropolitan São Paulo is approaching 20 million inhabitants, and Rio de Janeiro has passed 11 million. Impressive as these figures are, together they comprise only one-sixth of the country's population, which includes eighteen more urban regions of over a million inhabitants, totaling close to 42 million. (Belo Horizonte is over 5 million, Porto Alegre is closing in on 4 million, and Recife, Salvador, Fortaleza, Curitiba, and Brasília all fall in the over-3-million category.)[17]

Mexico City may be the world's largest urban conglomerate, inhabited as it is by at least 23 million souls, but this number falls well short of constituting a quarter of the country's population. Mexico's major cities in the north, led by Monterrey at over 3 million and León, Tijuana, and Ciudad Juárez at well over a million each, along with slightly smaller Torreón and Toluca, are distant from the capital, and even Guadalajara (approaching 4 million) is three hundred miles from Mexico City as the crow flies, but much farther by road or rail over extremely mountainous terrain, as is the somewhat nearer Puebla (well over 2 million). There are also the large port cities of Acapulco on the Pacific and Veracruz on the Gulf coast. Courtesy of its geography, Colombia has a multiplicity of large cities, no single one as populous as Bogotá, with its 7.5 million inhabitants, but together exceeding the capital in numbers. In addition to Medellín, at over 3 million, and Cali, with 2.5 million, there are other important regional centers in this country divided by three cordilleras of the Andes Mountains, including Barranquilla (2 million), Bucaramanga (1 million), and Cúcuta (over 800,000). Lima, nearing 8 million, is Peru's premier city, but again owing to the Andes there is a series of large coastal centers such as Trujillo (700,000) plus the inland metropolis of Arequipa (800,000).

In the fourth, sixth, and seventh largest countries of the region, the capital city is more dominant and has fewer challengers. Argentina is mother to the myth of the huge head with a small body, for the city and province of Buenos Aires do contain nearly half the country's population, while Córdoba (about as far away as Brasília is from Rio de Janeiro or São Paulo) is a very distant second with 1.4 million inhabitants. Rosário (1.2 million) occupies the intermediary spot along the axis that Belo Horizonte does in Brazil, and slightly smaller Tucumán and Mendoza (900,000) are outriders. Caracas and its over 2 million inhabitants leads other Venezuelan cities, with Maracaibo at 1.7 million and Valencia at 1.3 million, but has a relatively small share of the nation's population and is not a port, so its ability to be hegemonic is severely limited, particularly with much of the country's industry located well to the east around Ciudad Bolívar and Cuidad Guyana. Essentially Chile is the Central Valley, with Concepción, Antofagasta, Viña del Mar, and Valparaiso—all between 300,000 and 400,000—playing third or fourth rather than second fiddles to Santiago, but this is a country of only 16 million inhabitants. In Ecuador, Quito may be the capital, containing 1.5 million citizens, but it is not only smaller but also economically less important than Guayaquil, with its 2 million inhabitants, and much of the time "suffers" the indignity of being under a coastal president. In Bolivia, highland La Paz at 1.5 million (with a huge slum city nearby) is rivaled by the economically much richer lowland metropolis Santa Cruz at 1.2 million, trailed by intermediate Cochabamba with a respectable 800,000. Given the small sizes of Uruguay and Paraguay, it is not surprising that Montevideo, with its 1.3 million inhabitants, and Asuncíon, at 1.6 million, are dominant.

Managua is home to a quarter of Nicaraguans; Guatemala City and Tegucigalpa contain a seventh of Guatemalans and Hondurans, respectively; so only relatively small San Salvador, Panama City, and San José, Costa Rica, contain a disproportionate share of their populations. Havana, Santo Domingo, and Port-au-Prince are about the norm for countries with the populations of Cuba, the Dominican Republic, and Haiti.

The combined economic output of Latin America has surpassed an annual $4.0 trillion, raising its per capita gross domestic product (GDP) to nearly $7,400. This amount is in purchasing power parity (PPP), the only meaningful basis for comparison, not the artificial, outdated, and essentially meaningless figures reached by dividing each country's GDP in local currency by the year's average exchange rate with the dollar—a very arbitrary and artificial figure.[18] These regional averages mask extreme variations, including a number of minuscule economies, as well as several of world significance. Latin America includes one of the world's top ten economies, Brazil, at over $1.5 trillion GDP, seeking recognition as being the ninth member of the exclusive trillion-dollar GDP club, behind new inductee China and ahead of Canada and Spain. Latin America also contains the twelfth largest world economy, Mexico, at just over $1 trillion.

Argentina at $450 billion is followed at a distance by Colombia, whose official $270 billion does not fully reflect one of its leading industries, recreational drugs. Thus the four most populous countries account for just over three-fourths of the region's economic output—well above their two-thirds of its population. Peru and Venezuela trail among the major countries with GDPs of $150 million and $130 million, respectively, but since relatively advanced Chile weighs in with an economic output of $160 billion, the seven most populous countries contribute 87 percent of the regional GDP, ahead of their 78 percent of the regional population. Of these larger countries, which contain a high proportion of the region's industry, Argentina has the highest per capita GDP, some $11,000, followed by Chile's $10,000 and Mexico's $9,100. Colombia at $6,100, Peru at $5,300, and Venezuela just above $5,000 are below the regional average in per capita terms, with Brazil is somewhat above it at $8,000.

Variations in per capita GDP are much greater in the smaller countries. Uruguay, with a $43 billion GDP, leads at $12,500 per capita, followed by Trinidad and Tobago's $9,000 per capita on a GDP of $10.6 billion. Costa Rica's GDP of $35 billion comes in at almost $8,000 per capita, well ahead of the Dominican Republic's $6,000 (on a GDP of $54 billion), which is slightly exceeded by Panama's per capita GDP of $6,200 on an economy nearing $20 billion. Haiti's $1,600 per capita (on a GDP of $13 billion) and Nicaragua's $2,100 with a GDP straining to reach $11.5 billion, are at the bottom. In between are found El Salvador and Paraguay at $4,800 with GDPs of $32 billion and $38 billion, respectively. Guatemala follows with $4,100 on a GDP of $58 billion and Jamaica with $3,800 (with GDP of $10.3 billion). The poorest economic performers include Ecuador at $3,500 on a GDP of $47 billion, Cuba at $2,600 from a $33 billion GDP, Honduras at $2,500 and GDP of $18 billion, Bolivia with the same per capita figure on a $22 billion GDP. The very small countries range from $17,000 for the 300,000 Bahamians and $16,400 for the 280,000 inhabitants of Barbados, through $11,000 for Antigua's 70,000 and $8,500 for the 40,000 living in St. Kitts and Nevis, down to slightly over $5,000 in Dominica (population 70,000), St. Lucia with its 167,000 inhabitants, and Grenada (and its 90,000 people). Belize (population 280,000) falls just below that mark. The 720,000 Guyanese at $4,000 and the 440,000 living in Suriname with $3,500 are even worse off, as are the 120,000 people of St. Vincent and the Grenadines, with a per capita GDP of only $2,900.

Leadership, Violence, Democracy, and Religion

Although it has become fashionable to deal with movements rather than personalities, leadership remains a very critical element in the Latin American political equation. Admittedly, as institutionalization advances and organizations comprising the political infrastructure acquire stability and continuity, leadership becomes less crucial as a determinant of political development. Most countries of Latin America, however, are still far from that happy juncture. This should not be surprising, as France needed a charismatic Charles de Gaulle as recently as the 1960s, and Germany required an extraordinary figure such as Willy Brandt into the mid-1970s. Even Britain sorely needed a giant with the stature of Winston Churchill in the 1940s and 1950s and a leader of Margaret Thatcher's unusual talents in the 1980s. Hence, dominant political figures will loom large in this book, though more in the account of how these countries got to where they are than in the saga of the last quarter century. Developmental surges in Latin America have usually involved a major political leader as catalyst, and such episodes have occurred at different times in each country. Unfortunately, the comparative literature on political leadership in this region is quite weak, as, for that matter, is the treatment of Latin American figures in global comparative work.[19] The nature and role of leadership are a major unifying theme of the book. Indeed, a careful reading will put students in a position to critically evaluate the rankings contained in Appendix A.

Leadership is extremely resistant to analytical generalizations. Conditions and situations affect its development and emergence, but they do not determine whether an outstanding leader will come to the fore. Political recruitment processes are an important facilitating or restraining variable, with broadened participation not directly, much less immediately, resulting in wider opportunity to reach the pinnacle of power. Indeed, there is some sobering evidence that democratic electoral processes sometimes reduce the chances of extraordinary individuals coming to hold a country's top office. It is a topic to which attention is given in Chapter 15.

People's fundamental political orientation and basic perceptions of their country are largely formed during their youth. For many, developments in their young adult years, if not before, shape the direction of subsequent political activities. At this stage of their lives, national leaders or even those of recent political myth are often seized upon as role models; for some they may even be mentors. Hence the importance of bearing in mind the context in which political figures grew up. Examples are the late Díaz period around 1900 for Mexico's great reformer Cárdenas; Vargas's final years in the early 1950s and the uneasy period that followed his demise for Fernando Henrique Cardoso, Brazilian president from 1995 to 2002; Argentina's "false dawn" of democracy between 1914 and 1930 for Perón; for Castro, the humiliating spectacle of rampantly corrupt elected governments beholden to the Mafia in Cuba in the mid-1940s; the list goes on. Hence, dates of birth are provided for key political actors to establish in the reader's mind the trail back to the epoch of their socialization, particularly intense from the midteens to the late twenties.

Episodes of large-scale domestic conflict mark the history of those countries that have successfully achieved economic and political development. The US Civil War, Britain's analogous strife 220 years earlier, the French Revolution, Hitler's repressive totalitarian regime and the Holocaust, and the Spanish Civil War come readily to mind as examples of this inability to resolve major political issues by any means other than force of arms. Throughout the Afro-Asian world since the end of World War II, extremely bloody internal conflicts have been, and still are, dishearteningly common. Thus, by comparison, Latin America's political struggles, bloody as some instances have been, are not out of line with global experience. Indeed, the resort to large-scale sustained armed conflict in this region may even be a less common way of resolving intractable differences than in much of the rest of the world. In a balanced assessment, after listing all the tensions existing, Wiarda concludes that "the main process at work in Latin America is still assimilation of the indigenous population into Hispanic life or civilization, though in some countries at some times there will be tension and the potential for breakdown over the degrees and speed of assimilation/autonomy issues." As he sees the current scene:

Latin America has, for the most part, passed the stage where intrastate and identity conflicts are so intense that democracy and human rights issues may, more than sporadically and temporarily, be pushed to the side. But on this issue one needs to distinguish among countries, for Brazil has an increasingly self-conscious Afro-Brazilian movement, and in Bolivia, Brazil, Peru, Ecuador, Colombia, Guatemala, and Mexico, there are sizeable indigenous rights movements that are demanding a say in the political process or even autonomy for their regions. Occasionally, these groups may cause societal disruption, . . . but it seems unlikely that we will see anywhere in Latin America wholesale ethnic conflict, slaughter, and genocide as in Rwanda or large-scale "ethnic cleansing" as in the former Yugoslavia.[20]

Despite the decreased salience of violence, it is still important to look at all major episodes of violence, including those remote in time, and these are covered throughout the book. Besides examining why major organized political violence has occurred at one time or another in almost all Latin American countries, it is important to establish whether and how such traumas have contributed to a quest for ways and means to avoid their recurrence. For if learning does not take place in this field, it is unlikely to do so with respect to less calamitous events. Since there is a persistent myth that violence stems from Hispanic character traits, we will also explore the countercontention that the limited use of violence may be normal in a Latin American political system, or even necessary to its functioning. Given the many types of advantages accruing to those who control the government, emerging groups cannot count upon gaining power merely through the organization of majority support expressed through the ballot box. They may at times have to strike a match, not to burn the system down, but to light a fire under complacent standpatters.

The broadly inclusive acceptance of competitive electoral processes as the means of arbitrating rival political ambitions and policy differences even in tense and polarized situations is still recent in Latin America, so a question arises about how deeply rooted this democratic process may be. As recently as the late 1970s, this sine qua non of stable democracy rested solidly on bedrock only in tiny, highly atypical Costa Rica and, with shallower footing, in Colombia and Venezuela. The wave of democratic transitions that ensued reflected disillusionment with authoritarian military regimes as much as, and very probably more than, abiding faith in the long-term viability of democracy. Despite positive indications in recent years of the growing confidence of key sectors of society in the long-term workability of democratic processes, the question of what kind of democracy merits the careful consideration it receives in the chapters ahead. For as Wiarda cautions, Latin America is "at least in part a particular Hispanic, neoscholastic, counter-reformationary, Thomistic, organicist, semifeudal, corporatist, patrimonialist, precapitalist, pre–Enlightenment, pre–Industrial Revolution, quasimedieval, pre-limited government *version* of the West."[21] This extreme formulation of the persistence of tradition deserves consideration.

With debate raging in the academic community concerning the compatibility of Islam and democracy, it may be informative to bear in mind that a generation ago, and even less time in some quarters, there was a similar intellectual disagreement as to the compatibility of democracy and staunchly Catholic societies. As the experience of Latin America, and southern Europe as well, since the 1970s has resolved this issue in the affirmative, it is vital to document and explore how this salutary trend developed. If future events should prove Islamic societies highly resistant to democratization, there will be a pressing need to compare this impenetrability to that long manifested in Latin America. If democratization hits a wall in the Islamic world, the importance of Latin America to the democratic bloc will be enhanced. For in this region, unlike in others, modernization and westernization did go hand in hand—or at least proved compatible—and ultimately eventuated in democracy for over a half billion individuals. In contrast, current efforts in the Islamic world are for modernization without westernization.

Periodization

Given the size and diversity of Latin America, dates selected for the beginning and end of political eras or generations do not perfectly coincide with significant changes in every country, but they do capture major trends across the area.[22] There is always at least one country in the forefront, playing the role of pathfinder and innovator, while several lag behind the main body of countries—some cases of accumulated retardation. The convenient and conventional "turn of the century" proves useful in 1799–1800 and 1899–1900 as well as in 1999–2000. The choice of 1870 to begin an era is justified by the significant differences from the earmarks of the preceding decades. Even more of a watershed, 1929–1930 serves well for marking a break with the past throughout Latin America, as the impact of the world economic crisis shattered the stability and relative prosperity of World War I and the ensuing decade. This year also heralded the rise of a new generation of political leadership.

The synchronism is weaker for the ensuing break, 1955–1956, as the "crisis of populism" did not erupt in all countries at the same time. Indeed, Brazil began its highest-quality civilian government just as Argentina experienced the fall of Perón, and Colombia and Venezuela were witnessing the decline, to be shortly followed by the demise, of their out-of-phase military regimes. But adopting this juncture rather than the wave of military coups in 1962–1966 allows a focus upon the roots and causes of the ensuing authoritarian regimes, deeply embedded as the coups were in domestic developments rather that a traumatic international crisis (the reverse of the situation in 1929–1930). The 1979–1980 division, although not as all-embracing as that a half century earlier, rather faithfully reflects the 1956–1959 variations in domestic factors. Most important, it catches the early wave of democratic transitions at their onset as well as including the full dynamics of the later ones. Since the heritage of this period is still playing out, adhering to the turn-of-the-century conventional break facilitates the shift from analyzing the past to explaining the present; there is unavoidably much more detail on events and trends that are still unfolding and hence not subject to the winnowing perspective of hindsight.

Against the overview provided in this chapter, the story of how Latin America got to where it is and where it seems to be headed can unfold. Chapter 2, which covers a full three centuries of formative experiences, first describes the region before its "discovery" by Europe, in terms of what Christopher Columbus, Pedro Álvares Cabral, Hernán Cortez, and others found when they reached the Western Hemisphere. It then surveys the period to the end of the 1600s with attention to colonization and territorial claims—that is, how the "New World" was conquered, divided up, and controlled by the European powers. Finally the eighteenth century is briefly examined in terms of the social and economic changes that placed strains upon colonial institutions and practices. The chapter concludes with a sketch of European transformations that facilitated efforts by Latin American elites to achieve greater autonomy—particularly the French Revolution and the onset of the Napoleonic Wars.

Chapter 3 examines decolonization as it made headway and explores the quite varied paths to independence in different parts of the region. It then looks at the ensuing period of unrest and the slow progress toward national consolidation from the 1840s through the 1860s.

Chapter 4 analyzes the differentiation and uneven development that characterized the nineteenth century's final three decades.

Chapter 5 picks up with the emergence of the United States as a major factor and actor, continuing through the collapse of relative prosperity and stability at the end of the 1920s. Chapters 6 and 7 carry the examination of the lives of these countries through the Great Depression and World War II into the first decade of the Cold War.

Chapter 8 explores for the four largest countries the failure of populist democracies and the rise of authoritarian military regimes, down to the decay of those regimes in the late 1970s. Chapter 9 does the same for the rest of the South America and Chapter 10 for Central America and the Caribbean.

Chapters 11 and 12 examine the era of democratization spanning the last two decades of the twentieth century, a period probably more familiar to readers than earlier ones. Once again the four largest countries are covered in one chapter (Chapter 11), and the remaining thirty-one are discussed in another (Chapter 12).

Chapter 13 probes the stresses on the new democratic participatory systems in the early twenty-first century caused by increased demands for sustained growth and reduction of inequalities in the midst of an international environment of globalization and enhanced peril.

Chapters 14 and 15 examine Latin America's future and its lessons for other areas not as far along the road in political development. These chapters address all the issues raised in this chapter's overview of the subject, including (1) the persistence of an authoritarian corporatist political culture; (2) the emergence of patron-client relationships and their adaptation and survival; (3) the role of violence and changing patterns of civil-military relations; (4) leadership and leadership styles from *caudillo* through populist to present-day variants; (5) the relative roles of executives, legislatures, and courts; (6) the nature and extent of political participation; (7) ethnic-racial factors and the delayed incorporation of minorities into national life; (8) ideologies and their political influence; and (9) the emergence of corruption as a political issue, rather than its previous long-term acceptance as a disagreeable fact of life. To the extent reality allows, patterns of political life are discussed and related to paths in political development. An epilogue assesses whether elections during the first half of 2006 have continued the trends laid out in Chapter 13 and bear out the analysis in Chapters 14 and 15. Throughout, the purpose is to guide readers to where, by the time they have finished, they can make three confident statements: (1) "I know what has happened and understand why"; (2) "I believe I understand what is going on now"; and (3) "I have a fairly good idea of where things are headed."

Notes

1. Howard J. Wiarda, *Dilemmas of Democracy in Latin America: Crises and Opportunities* (Lanham, MD: Rowman & Littlefield Publishers, 2005), p. xviii.

2. Wiarda, *Dilemmas,* p. xvi, and Paul H. Lewis, *Authoritarian Regimes in Latin America: Dictators, Despots, and Tyrants* (Lanham, MD: Rowman & Littlefield, 2006), pp. 13–30.

3. Wiarda, *Dilemmas,* p. 3.

4. This is masterfully analyzed in Lewis, *Authoritarian Regimes,* Chapter 1.

5. Wiarda, *Dilemmas,* p. 9.

6. Lewis, *Authoritarian Regimes,* p. 101.

7. Ibid., p. 75.

8. Dankwart A. Rustow, "Transitions to Democracy: Toward a Dynamic Model," *Comparative Politics,* 2:2 (April 1970), pp. 337–363, reprinted in Lisa Anderson, ed., *Transitions to Democracy* (New York: Columbia University Press, 1999), pp. 14–41; and Samuel P. Huntington, *Political Order in Changing Societies* (New Haven: Yale University Press, 1968).

9. Wiarda, *Dilemmas,* p. 10.

10. Ibid., p. 54.

11. Ibid., p. 55.

12. Lewis, *Authoritarian Regimes,* p. 247.

13. Wiarda, *Dilemmas,* p. 37.

14. Ibid., pp. 16–17.

15. Ibid., p. 230.

16. Peter H. Smith, *Democracy in Latin America: Political Change in Comparative Perspective* (New York: Oxford University Press, 2005), p. 335.

17. Figures are from http://citypopulation.de.

18. See *World Development Indicators 2005* (Herndon, VA: World Bank Publications, 2005).

19. The literature on comparative political leadership is sparse and generally weak. Despite a lack of political science conceptualization combined with reliance solely upon English-language sources, Arnold M. Ludwig, *King of the Mountain: The Nature of Political Leadership* (Lexington: The University Press of Kentucky, 2002), is the most comprehensive volume. With the exception of biographical dictionaries, in which entries are individual and usually descriptive, there are a few works of fairly narrow scope, beginning with Robert J. Alexander, *Prophets of the Revolution: Profiles of Latin American Leaders* (New York: Macmillan, 1962), and including Jerome Adams, *Latin American Heroes: Liberators and Patriots from 1500 to the Present* (New York: Random House, 1991); Anton Allahar, ed., *Caribbean Charisma: Reflections on, Leadership, Legitimacy, and Populist Politics* (Boulder, CO: Lynne Rienner, 2001); and Michael Kryzanek, *Leaders, Leadership and U.S. Policy in Latin America* (Boulder, CO: Westview Press, 1992). Useful information on individual figures is available in the compendium *Latin American Lives* (New York: Macmillan Library Reference, 1996).

20. Wiarda, *Dilemmas,* p. 75.

21. Ibid., p. 19.

22. In his very important recent book, Peter Smith opts for a beginning in 1900 and division into three "cycles": 1900–1939, marked by "oligarchic competition"; 1940–1976, embracing the rise and demise of electoral democracy; and 1977–2000, with its transitions to democracy. His own data, however, strongly support my choice of 1929–1930, 1955–1956, and 1979–1980 as divisions between periods. When his three categories of regimes are used, at the first of these dates oligarchies fell by half, just before semidemocracies surged to the forefront. The second marked a clear trough in this latter type of regime, right before democracies showed a sharp upturn. The third coincides with the low point for democracies before they rose to become predominant. This support for my periodization is dramatically displayed in Smith's Figure 1.1. See Peter H. Smith, *Democracy,* p. 27. Smith's quantification gives equal weight to each of the nineteen countries included. When in Figure 12.1, p. 315, he does correlate his cycles with population, the appropriateness of my periods is even more strongly underlined, with the sharp breaks of 1929–1930, the mid-1950s, and the late 1970s leaping off the page to strike the reader squarely between the eyes—the classic "interocular impact test" of significance.

2

The Colonial Background

What the Europeans Brought with Them,
Found, and Ruled

History does not determine the future, but it certainly influences it, often with a heavy hand. Contemporary Latin American politics cannot be understood without some knowledge of preindependence developments. Moreover, the relevance of the region's experience to nations emerging from colonial status in the second half of the twentieth century cannot be evaluated without an understanding of Latin America's prior formative and often deforming colonialism. These dual considerations mandate a selective and focused discussion of the sixteenth through the eighteenth centuries, spanning European intrusion, conquest, exploitation, settlement, domination, and, in some cases at least, development—albeit of a type tailored largely to the needs and convenience of the Old World. The most important and lasting legacies of preindependence times were in the areas of population makeup, religion, cultural heritage, land tenure systems, labor force, role of the state (including administrative bureaucracy and the crown's military arm), and extremely limited experience with self-government. In almost all cases, what went on in the heartland areas would have a far greater lasting impact than occurrences at the periphery. The heartlands would be quite isolated from their hinterlands, and even more so from the other centers of colonization, down to and even beyond independence.

Overview

The vast region "discovered" by the wealth-seeking Europeans, through tentative probing of the Caribbean in the waning years of the fifteenth century and significant explorations of the mainland by the 1520s, proved to be a very heterogeneous New World. The combination of precious metals and a large, territorially stable indigenous population that would attract permanent settlement were found only in the area of today's Mexico and southern Peru—thousands of miles apart. In those two loci the adventurous Spaniards, who would be glorified as *conquistadores* ("conquerors") encountered the Aztec and Incan empires, which had extended their sway over weaker and less advanced peoples and in the process had amassed great wealth.

Successfully decapitating these relatively developed societies (by killing the chiefs and priests and mating with their widows and daughters), the followers of Hernán Cortez in Mexico and the four Pizarro brothers in Peru, after quickly siphoning off their accumulated wealth, would be forced to turn to agriculture, supplemented by mining, using the conquered elites as intermediaries with the essentially enslaved native labor force. Compulsory Christianization had an uneven impact, as many of the indigenous population maintained important aspects of their traditional religious beliefs behind a façade of Catholicism, adopting saints and their statues to stand for the existing gods. In a few places, including present-day Paraguay, the Jesuits, in particular, managed true conversion.

Over the sixteenth century, a basic differentiation emerged in the densely populated core areas of Spanish settlement in what became Mexico and Peru, with viceroyalties established in Mexico City and Lima, at one extreme, and largely ignored peripheral and interior areas at the other. In between, regions of significant economic potential and/or strategic location were settled. In most of these places, slaves from the west coast of Africa soon replaced recalcitrant "Indians," who fled to the interior, starved themselves to death, or refused to reproduce rather than have their children suffer and die in the mines or plantation fields. Moreover, infectious diseases alien to the New World were brought in from Europe, decimating indigenous populations possessing no natural resistance to these scourges. Thus many of the peoples that had inhabited the region before the heavy colonization began were not around to become part of the culture and civilization that developed over the next three centuries, during which the colonial era first thrived, then survived.

Hence, there are very significant variations in both how and how much history impacted upon those parts of Latin America that established independence from their strict Iberian foster parents in the second and third decades of the nineteenth century. These variations are even greater for a country like Cuba, which did not gain its independence until the very end of that century. The states of the "New Caribbean" that continued as European colonies until 1962 or, in a few cases, even longer shared very little of this historical heritage except for the repopulation with slaves from Africa. The recentness of their independence combined with their small size and very small populations prevents them from appearing in this account until far past the period covered in this chapter. For they are "Latin

American" only in a geographical and geopolitical sense, not in the nature of their political culture and governmental processes.

In sharp contrast, what the early settlers encountered is most important to understanding the societies and political systems that subsequently emerged in those few places where pre-Columbian peoples and their cultures substantially survived the conquest and became part of a colonial-era societal amalgam; these are the areas where, as shown in the preceding chapter, their descendents still make up a major component of the population, largely in the areas controlled by the region's two great indigenous empires (the Aztecs in Mexico and the Incas in Andean South America), each of which contained five to seven million of the estimated thirty million inhabitants of the region. Elsewhere indigenous populations were essentially destroyed and their civilizations all but obliterated, the chief exceptions being the Jesuit-protected Guaranis in Paraguay, vestiges of a Mayan heritage in Guatemala (which had at its prime embraced as many people as the Aztecs or Incas), and—in a very limited way—survivors of the millions of Indians who fled into the vast interior of the South American continent, chiefly to what became Brazil, and were both left alone there and isolated from any significant impact on their society.

For these reasons, the discussion here of the sixteenth and seventeenth centuries concentrates heavily upon the Spanish viceroyalties centered in Mexico and Peru, as well as Portugal's rule in Brazil. Moreover, it is focused upon institutions and practices that survived into the postcolonial era. As the aim is to understand the past as it impacted on what followed, the quite different circumstances that gave rise to new viceroyalties in Bogotá early in the eighteenth century and Buenos Aires six decades later are examined less exhaustively, as are the distinctive variations in important outlying regions of the three core colonies. Finally, this discussion leads into consideration of changes in the colonial system that set the stage for the independence movement at the turn into the nineteenth century.

Examination of the three centuries of the colonial period is essential for understanding what followed. As pointed out by Wiarda: "Strikingly, and very much unlike the United States, the colonial legacy of Spanish-Portuguese institutions survived the independence movements of the Latin American territories in the early nineteenth century and the initial stirrings of modernization and lingered on into the early twentieth century."[1]

The Colonizers' Baggage

Overall what the Spanish and Portuguese brought with them from the Old World proved more important in shaping Latin America politically than anything they encountered in the New World. Moreover, changes that occurred on the Iberian

Peninsula from the sixteenth through the nineteenth centuries profoundly affected the colonies. Hence, a brief summary of these developments precedes the account of their incursions into the misleadingly labeled "New World."

The Moorish occupation of over seven hundred years (AD 711–1492) came to an end in Spain just as the discovery of the Western Hemisphere began.[2] This occupation had been imposed in the slow conquest of a mixed population of Euro-Asian origin, including Basques, Indo-German Celts, Greeks, Phoenicians, Carthaginians (for this southwest tip of Europe had been on Hannibal's route to attack Rome), and Romans. Indeed, Romanization of the area long before the arrival of the Moors provides a rough analogue of what descendants of those inhabitants would do much later in and to Latin America. In the Roman imperial tradition, centralized autocratic colonial rule was established by a remote "superior" civilizing power, over a society that would be light-skinned on top and dark at the bottom—whether that was the brown of "Indians" (a name reflecting the ignorance of the "discoverers," who were only partway to India and the East Indies) or the black of the involuntary African immigrants brought over in chains to live and die in slavery.

Much of the material progress of Roman rule in this area had been swept away by Germanic invasions and two centuries of Visigothic domination before the Moorish invasion expanded from its early African footholds and temporarily made what was to become Spain the most advanced part of Europe. The Moors were responsible for a renaissance in Iberia before it appeared in Italy, and they interfered relatively little with Christianity, which during the late-fourteenth- and fifteenth-century reconquest, or *Reconquista,* became militant, absolutist, authoritarian, intolerant, and militaristic—distinguishing features of an aggressively expansionist religion that would carry over into the colonies.[3] Since the peninsula was fragmented into feudalistic kingdoms, the Catholic Church remained strong, and it established close ties with the monarchs of the regions leading the *Reconquista,* particularly Castile and Aragon, where, in Wiarda's words, the Moorish impact had been "less penetrating, less deep-rooted, and less permanent."[4] It became common for the Iberian liberators from Moorish rule to receive not only land for their services to the crown, but also the labor of its inhabitants—practices soon to be enshrined in the New World as the *encomienda* and the *repartimento.* Moreover, the reconquest created a class of warrior adventurers who had discovered that the only way to break through the rigid Iberian social structure was by conquest and plunder.[5]

Portugal had branched off from the rest of the peninsula by the end of the eleventh century and had freed itself of the Moors by the middle of the thirteenth century, attaining full separation from Castile by 1385. During the century remaining before discovery and colonization of the Western Hemisphere, both parts of Iberia experienced consolidation under centralizing royal authority using absolutist techniques. Since significant urbanization took place in this preindustrial era, society was composed of corporate sectors jealously defending their special rights from an expanding state. Although parliaments were born early, they were weak and easily overcome by centralizing monarchs. Corporate units struggled to maintain some autonomy from an expanding, consolidating, absolutist state individually rather than through parliaments. Their generally losing battle was to regain or restore earlier feudal rights of groups, not individual rights or representation. Thomistic and Aristotelian concepts of natural inequalities and hierarchal estates were reinforced by the rediscovery of Roman law. These influences established the political culture and institutions along corporatist rather than pluralist lines, as well as extending the life of divine right monarchy, with its close interrelationship of church and state.[6] But this stream of thought contained a strong Machiavellian undercurrent that diluted and eventually—at least, in the New World—overwhelmed the teachings of St. Thomas Aquinas.

The partial merger of Castile and Aragon through the 1469 marriage of Isabella (b. 1451) and Ferdinand (b. 1452) led to a century of war with France at the same time that colonization of the New World was taking place, further militarizing this process. With a combined population nearing 7 million in 1500 (intermediate between France's 15 million and England's 3 million), Isabella's Castile was by far the senior partner.[7] By 1517, prior to the New World conquests of the Aztecs and Incas, the grandson of these monarchs—born in Belgium in 1500, with roots in Burgundy and already ruling over the Netherlands—became monarch of most of the Iberian Peninsula as King Charles I. He brought with him to Madrid and elevated to power a coterie of Flemish Hapsburgs, who imparted a Germanic tone to Spanish absolutism. Soon the ambitious Charles I bested French and English rivals (Francis I and Henry VIII) to become Holy Roman Emperor Charles V as well as king of Spain. (The Holy Roman Emperor was essentially chairman of the board of directors of postfeudal Europe, chosen by its most important rulers and a few key churchmen. From 1496 to 1519 Maximilian of Austria, patriarch of the Hapsburg dynasty, had held the position.) Still officially king of Castile and Aragon separately, Charles was faced in 1520 with revolts by the elites of "Old Castile," termed *comuneros* (after their desire to organize their cities as communes), that ended only with the fall of Toledo to his armies in late 1521—just when Cortez was capturing Mexico—so the New World was low in the priorities of Charles's government.

Resident in Madrid from 1522 to 1529, Charles married Isabella, sister of Portugal's king, who gave him a son, Philip, in 1527, whose heirs would subsequently lay effective claim to Portugal's throne. But by the late 1530s, Charles's focus of attention was drawn to the Protestant Reformation and his onerous duty as "Defender of the Faith" to lead the Counter-Reformation against the onslaught of Protestant heresy—a task that would keep him out of Spain for as much as fourteen years at a time (1543–1557). Thus, his interest in the New World was exclusively in terms of the revenues it could provide for enormously expensive military campaigns in France, Germany, and North Africa. At the same time, the Society of Jesus, commonly known as the Jesuits, was recognized as a religious order in 1540 and soon assumed an abiding interest in the New World.

Although most of the conquest of the New World occurred under Charles V, much of its consolidation and settlement took place under his successors, the bulk of the emigration to the New World happening in the last decades of the sixteenth century and the first half of the seventeenth. Hence, these emigrants were politically socialized in Spain during the reigns of the next three Spanish Hapsburg monarchs. With the death of Charles, an outstanding example of a divine right monarch (on a par with France's Louis XIV a century later), the mantle of Catholicism's champion passed in 1558 to his son, Philip II, who after the immediately ensuing death of his wife, Queen Mary of England, became preoccupied with the challenge posed by a Protestant England under Mary's younger half sister, Elizabeth I. The vast revenues coming from the Latin American colonies— amounting to 252,000 ducats a year from 1534 to 1543, falling by 50 percent for the rest of the decade, but soaring to over 2 million ducats in 1552–1553—were largely used in this venture, particularly in construction of the great Spanish Armada intended to invade England; after the Armada's destruction in 1588, the Latin American revenues replaced the immense losses.[8]

A union of Spain and Portugal, which temporarily strengthened the former's hand in European affairs, lasted only from 1580—when the House of Aviz died out with the unmarried king, Sebastian, leading Philip to move in to fill the void with twenty thousand veteran troops—to 1640, when Portugal broke away under Dom João, Seventh Duke of Bragança. Cardinal Richelieu—the determined and unscrupulous architect of French policy—backed this fissure in what threatened to become Iberian geopolitical predominance, with the Jesuits helping to rally Brazilian support. By this juncture, conquest of the New World had morphed into permanent colonization. But since Iberians would stubbornly cling to memories of 1492–1588 as the pinnacle of their power and prosperity, this "Hapsburgan model" continued to be the foundation of their colonial system as it had earlier been the bedrock of its implantation. Top-down, authoritarian, hierarchal, rigidly stratified, and church-legitimized were its defining characteristics.[9]

Spain's decline in the seventeenth century would be rapid. To begin with, there were six major mortality crises that caused its population to drop from 8.5 million in the 1590s to 7.5 million in 1717 (before rallying to 10.4 million by 1787). The 1595–1602 bubonic plague outbreak caused 500,000 deaths, equaled in the 1647–1652 epidemic, with 250,000 others perishing in 1682–1687.[10] Moreover, reflecting a serious recession in the New World, its trade with Spain went into a deep depression, falling from 274,000 tons in 1606–1610 to only 121,000 tons for the 1646–1650 period, and royal revenues declined from 11 million pesos in 1596–1600 to less than 4.4 million pesos for 1616–1620, before leveling off. The changing economies of the New World required manufactures not agricultural products—a need Spain was poorly equipped to supply.[11]

Still convinced that they were well in the lead intellectually, Spanish elites turned a cold shoulder to the "heretical"—Protestant-influenced—scientific revolution and even to the great European Enlightenment. Moreover, genetics and inbreeding produced pale shadows of Charles and Philip and led to a line of monarchs who Wiarda judges to have been "weak, ineffective, and ultimately imbecile kings."[12] Indeed, Lynch holds it likely that Philip had his mentally deficient and physically deformed heir, Don Carlos, killed in 1568 and considers Philip III (b. 1577) dull, weak-willed, and overall inadequate; Philip referred so many matters to the various councils—War, the Indies, Castile, Aragon, Italy, Flanders, Portugal, and the Inquisition—that they took an inordinate amount of time to consider and refer their decisions to him for approval.[13] In 1621, this less-than-mediocre monarch was succeeded by Philip IV, a frivolous and irresponsible teenager who never really matured.[14] This deterioration of the royal line only got worse, and Charles II (b. 1661) merited description as "the last, the most degenerate, and the most pathetic victim of Hapsburg inbreeding."[15] Known as El Hechezado ("the Bewitched"), he came to the throne at age four and died at thirty-nine, the last of his line and a cruel parody of his illustrious ancestor Charles I or even the less distinguished Phillip II.

The stream of wealth still being extracted from the colonies was spent by Spain on trying to roll back Protestantism rather than on investing in development. Under these conditions, dissatisfaction with the increasing absolutism of incompetent monarchs, combined with an overgrown local bureaucracy based on sale of offices, created fertile soil for a beginning of speculation by those born overseas as to whether the benefits of Spanish rule outweighed its drawbacks. The rival but mutually reinforcing religious, military, and administrative hierarchies erected early by the crown kept these subversive thoughts from spreading—or at least from having any short-term impact. Meanwhile, the 1600s ended in the mother country with famine and food riots for the masses as a bloated bureaucracy consumed government revenues.[16]

The eighteenth century opened with Iberia in deep crisis; if things couldn't get much worse than they were under infertile as well as feeble-minded Charles II, who finally died in 1700, they would not improve significantly with the ascension of the Bourbons to the Spanish throne. First, the War of the Spanish Succession dragged on until 1713, as other European powers were understandably reluctant to see the Bourbons controlling both France and Spain with their vast colonial empires. In the end Bourbon Philip V, king from 1700 to 1746, was forced to relinquish his claim to the French throne. His heir was the indolent Ferdinand VI, who left the task of implementing the Bourbon reforms to his chief minister, Zenon de Somodeville (b. 1701), marques de la Ensenada.[17]

Spain became a more absolutist state under a streamlined ministerial system in which a single official was directly responsible to the king for each area of policy, a system replacing the old bureaucracy in which responsibility was shared by multi-member councils. Intendants began to take the place of *corregidores* in 1749, and finance, war, justice, and administration were concentrated in a single office.[18] The colonial bureaucracy had by this time become brokers between the Spanish crown and its New World subjects, who liked matters the way they were and perceived greater efficiency imposed by Madrid as impinging on their limited autonomy—especially as the new officials would constitute a new wave of *peninsulares* (those born in the mother country) seeking to please the crown by extracting greater revenues from its colonies. For "the normal instinct of colonial subjects was to question, to evade or modify laws, and only in a last resort obey them."[19]

In 1759, Charles III, half brother of the late king, came to the throne with twenty-five years of valuable ruling experience as Duke of Parma and King of Naples. Seen by Lynch as "a progeny among Bourbon misfits, a marked improvement in the post, and a neglected model for the future," he was determined to tighten the reins and increase efficiency in the empire.[20] Production in the New World from 1747 to 1761 reached the value of nearly 36 million pesos, over 16 million from New Spain (as the viceroyalty centered in Mexico was called) and more than 12 million from Peru (with New Granada trailing at 5.5 million pesos). At the same time private imports were overwhelmingly from the former area, which—favored by much lower transportation costs—enjoyed a three-to-one advantage.[21] Urban riots in Madrid, which the monarch preferred to blame on the Jesuits rather than on those opposed to economic reforms, paved the way for José de Gálvez to assume primacy in colonial affairs by 1775. The first regulations permitting trade between the colonies had been issued by the crown in 1765 and, because of the importance of New Spain as a market for the mother country, pointedly excluded it—as did the extension of freer trade to Peru and Buenos Aires in 1778.[22] Following Gálvez's death in mid-1787 and that of Charles III a year and a half later, trade with other Spanish New World ports was belatedly extended to New Spain. For as the Steins sum up the situation, "One objective of Charles's reign was quietly abandoned: the hope of creating an industrial establishment in the metropole capable of providing manufactures for colonial consumers in populous colonies like New Spain."[23]

With the new intendancy administrative system having proven its worth in Spain, Gálvez (who had been viceroy in New Spain until 1771 and recognized the need for a major overhaul) extended it to the empire. Thus, in the mid-1780s, appointed intendants replaced New World–rooted authorities who had learned to accommodate to the needs of their leading subjects, and the sharp expansion of state functions at the expense of the private sectors reached Spain's Latin American possessions. As Lynch sees it, this reorganization "began the long process of recovering colonial administration from local interests."[24] For "the advance of the Bourbon state, the end of compromise government and Creole participation, and the reduction of links between bureaucrats and local families were regarded by Spanish authorities as necessary steps toward control and revival."[25] In Portugal between 1750 and 1777 the brilliant chief minister Pombal stopped decay and engineered modest improvements, but he could not overcome the twin handicaps of his country's small size and its even smaller population.[26]

As each of the Iberian countries began to modernize, the traditional elements of the Spanish and Portuguese elites still called the shots regarding their overseas possessions. At the same time there was a regression in the quality of governance, as Charles IV was a badly educated forty-year-old with a scandalous wife who would be forced to abdicate in 1808.[27] The already completed rise of Napoleon in France and his subsequent conquest of the Iberian Peninsula were allowing dissatisfaction in the New World to turn into a drive for independence that was too far along to be stopped by the time Spain regained its independence and Napoleon was finally defeated in 1815.

What the Spanish Built in North America

Christopher Columbus's initial voyage in 1492 did not immediately lead to major efforts at Spanish settlement. Its chief landfall was in Hispaniola (now Haiti and the Dominican Republic), not the mainland, and a series of probes followed that were designed to give some idea of the nature of what were still presumed to be islands off the coast of Asia—a misconception that was only slowly dispelled. Caribbean islands, stubbornly labeled the "West Indies," were used as bases for exploration of what turned out to be a landmass far surpassing in size the explorers' wildest imagination. Meanwhile, in light of his failure to match his seamanship in the political and administrative realms, Columbus was stripped of his titles of viceroy and governor general in 1499, and an all-out competition for fame and fortune followed. Cuba was conquered between 1511 and 1515, with Havana founded in 1514 and Santiago a year later, and Puerto Rico had been subjugated by Juan Ponce de León in 1508. Given their relative proximity to Spain they came to overshadow Santo Domingo (on the island of Hispaniola) (established in 1496 and populated in 1502 by twenty-five hundred settlers under Nicolás de Ovando) as jumping-off points for expeditions that reached the mainland.

By far the most important of these incursions was the one that led to the conquest of Mexico—turning it into New Spain and initiating the largest process of integration of the pre-Columbian population with their new European masters. Nearly five centuries later the latter are still very much on top, whereas those whose ancestors lived away from the central region are decidedly at the bottom—in Mariano Azuela's words, "*Los de Abajo*," "the downtrodden Indians," unduly softened in translation as just "underdogs." But in between and making up the majority of Mexico's teeming millions are descendents of those whose blood became mixed during the colonial period—the *mestizos*.

This process began when Hernán Cortez (b. 1485), in defiance of Cuba's governor, Diego Velásquez de Cuellar (b. 1465), who felt he had staked a prior claim by sending his nephew to look things over, led an expedition of 550 men and sixteen horses to the coast of Mexico in 1519, establishing his base at Veracruz, where the Bay of Campeche constitutes the southernmost extension of the Gulf of Mexico. Arriving at a propitious time, he enlisted large numbers of Indians who were resentful of their exploitation by the Aztecs, based well inland at Tenochtilan—today the site of Mexico City. This civilization, advanced in many respects, and operating as an expansionist imperial power, was built on the foundations of the earlier Toltec civilization of the twelfth to fourteenth centuries and had subjugated the descendents of the Mayans, who had populated the Yucatán peninsula centuries before.[28] Hence, these subjects of the Aztecs could view the godlike figures mounted on tall, swift animals and armed with sticks from which a lethal thunder exploded as much as liberators as new conquerors.

Leading his army inland, Cortez, courageous to the point of foolhardiness, refused to be bought off by Aztec ambassadors bearing rich tribute and established control over the center of the Aztec capital while extorting tribute from their emperor, Moctezuma II (b. 1466), who had succeeded his more decisive uncle in 1503. Technological superiority was decisive in the victory of the Spaniards, as the Aztecs, who had copper but no iron, fought on foot with stone-edged wooden clubs and using thick cotton clothing for protection. They proved no match for the Spaniards' horses, artillery, iron armor, crossbows, and firearms (in the form of harquebuses). Yet Cortez was almost done in by his turf war with his nemesis, Velásquez, who in April 1520 sent his agent Panfilo de Narvaez with a sizable force to arrest him and take him back to stand trial for insubordination. In response, Cortez divided his forces, returning to the coast with a major proportion to face the threat from his countrymen. With bribes to the officers and seductive tales of great wealth almost at their fingertips, most of the troops switched their allegiance to Cortez.

Unfortunately, the garrison left in the Aztec capital under Pedro de Alvarado did not behave wisely, and the Aztecs saw the Spanish division offering them an unexpected military advantage. On May 28–29, as the overconfident invaders were surprised and forced to fight for their very survival, Alvarado suffered the devastating loss of half the 120 men Cortez had left behind as well as two-thirds of his horses. The Aztec fear of horses had diminished with familiarity, and they had learned that cavalry was much more effective in battle in open territory than in the narrow confines of city streets.[29] During the revolt Moctezuma was killed by his own people, who perceived him as having erred in seeking to appease the invaders.[30] Cortez decided to abandon the hostile capital and spent almost a year developing plans for a more successful assault.

In May and June 1521, Cortez retook the capital, which had been weakened by a late 1520 smallpox epidemic, with a force of over a thousand Spaniards and large numbers of Indian auxiliaries—plus more horses and thirteen cannon-bearing brigantines that vastly diminished his dependence on the easily defended causeways on which so many of his men had perished in the earlier retreat from the city.[31] At the end of August, the new Aztec ruler, Cuauhtémoc, surrendered, and Cortez—confirmed as governor of New Spain in 1522—found himself master of a country far larger than Spain.

He and his followers immediately consolidated their dominance by killing large numbers of the Aztec nobility—including Cuauhtémoc himself in 1524—and mating with their widows, sisters, and daughters, thus creating a bilingual subelite extremely useful in governing the dense population of the heartland region of the former Aztec empire. Indeed, Cortez had a son with his interpreter, Princess Malintin—granted the distinction of being addressed as Doña Marina—as early as 1522—before fathering children with two of Moctezuma's daughters. Following an expedition to Honduras, Cortez returned to Mexico City to find affairs in disarray, prompting a trip to Spain in 1528 to reestablish his political base. Named the Marques de Valle do Oaxaca, this most fortunate of the *conquistadores* went back to the New World, married a Spanish heiress, discovered California, and retired to the mother country, where he died in 1547. (For not only had Columbus fallen into disfavor and disgrace, but the Pizarro brothers would all meet violent deaths.)

The large amounts of precious metals and jewels sent back to Spain attracted a stream of immigrants, at first mostly would-be *conquistadores* rather than settlers. Between 1506 and the end of the century, Spanish migration to the New World reached 250,000—with another 200,000 arriving between 1600 and 1650. As time went on and opportunities changed, the settlers were mostly artisans and laborers.[32] Meanwhile, the conquest of Central America went forward in 1522–1527, led by Cortez's second-in-command, Pedro de Alvarado, who set up headquarters in the northernmost and most densely populated area, Guatemala.

Finally realizing that it was colonizing the mainland of a New World, not just a string of islands off the Asian coast, the Spanish government—burned by its experience with Columbus and adventurer-type explorers who had followed—established a Council of the Indies in 1524 to supervise the governance of the region. Their greatest concern was, of course, the source of by far the lion's share of wealth and royal revenues—the region opened up by Cortez. For their part, its original *conquistadores,* as it became obvious that the great treasures of the Aztec rulers had been acquired over a considerable period of time and were not all nearby or inexhaustible, settled for large land grants and the services of the Indians living on them. Although these benefits were originally intended to be temporary, given by the crown to reward valiant service, the *encomenderos* (those to whom the native population was entrusted) found ways to hold onto their lands and pass them down from generation to generation. For the *encomienda* was an institution devised to consolidate the Spanish conquest by giving to administrators and loyal soldiers who had received large tracts of land the power to Christianize, protect, use for labor, and tax all adult males in a specific Indian community—usually those already resident on or near the land. Analogous to the *mita* in South America, the *repartimento* provided for compulsory wage labor on roads and public works by Indians not subject to the *encomienda*. The estates resulting from this relationship—highly exploitive unless one overvalued, as much as the Spanish did, the worth of Indians having their souls saved, often against their will—were called *haciendas*.

Those who arrived in the wake of the conquest either had to settle for less or push on to explore and conquer new lands, particularly after affairs were regularized by the arrival in New Spain of its first viceroy, Antonio de Mendoza (b. 1495), in 1535 for a fifteen-year stay. The settlement of this vast addition to the Spanish domains had begun in the densely populated area near the capital, embracing Puebla to the southeast on the way to Veracruz and the sea, then extending northeast toward Tampico and northwest past Guadalajara, established in 1542, then on to Durango by 1561, and finally, by 1596, to Monterrey some five hundred miles north of the capital. The most adventurous and ambitious leaders mounted expeditions up the coast to modern California (Spanish until the middle of the nineteenth century) or down into Central America, which proved early to be essentially devoid of the kind of wealth they were seeking. But during 1540–1560 New Spain enjoyed its first economic and demographic boom, the number of Europeans rising to 63,000 by 1570 (18,000 of them in Mexico City) and to 125,000 by 1646 (48,000 of whom resided in the capital).[33] Small by today's standards, the capital of New Spain compared favorably with European cities of the time.

Since European women remained in extremely short supply for decades, the supply never beginning to close the gap with the burgeoning demand, the mixing of races went on in Mexico, particularly outside the urban centers, for a protracted time. One of the most perceptive students of Mexico, the late Frank Tannebaum, aptly described the resulting society:

> With the mixture of races in Mexico added to by the bringing in of Negroes in sufficient numbers to leave their mark upon the population in certain parts of the country, we have the basis of the social structure that

characterized Mexico throughout the colonial period and in some degree continues to this day. The Spaniard—that is, the born European—was at the top in politics, in the Church, and in prestige. The *criollo,* his American-born child, stood at a lower level. He inherited most of the wealth, but was denied any important role in political administration. The *mestizo* and the dozen different *castas* (racial variants) that resulted from the mixtures of European, Indian, and Negro in their various degrees and kinds were still lower.[34]

Indeed, by 1793 New Spain would have a population of 4.8 million, nearly two-fifths of the 1793 total for Spain's Western Hemisphere colonies. Slightly over half were Indian and a quarter *mestizo*. The 22 percent classified as European, albeit this often was self-declared and not 100 percent so, were deeply divided, as the resentful *criollos* derisively referred to the haughty *peninsulares* as *gachupines,* (sharp-spined creatures rendered as porcupines) a derogatory and scornful term. This ethnic shift was far from entirely the result of miscegenation, as the Indian population of central Mexico declined precipitously from nearly 17 million in 1532 to under 2.7 million in 1558, less than 1.4 million in 1595, and only 1.2 million by 1608. This shocking mortality was largely the result of great epidemics in 1545–1548 and 1576–1581—the second credited with killing at least 40 percent of all Indians in New Spain.[35] To compensate for this labor loss, some 120,000 Negro slaves were brought into New Spain between the conquest and the middle of the seventeenth century.

At the same time as this mixed, highly stratified society was taking shape, administrative structures underwent slow change. With Viceroy Diego Carillo de Mendoza y Pimentel having been forced out in 1624 by riots spurred by Archbishop Juan Pérez de la Serna, it was clear that the triumvirate system (in which the viceroy was head of the government, the captain-general was in command of the army, and the ranking Catholic prelates were expected to work together in the interest of the crown while serving as checks and balances on any one individual's ambitions) was not functioning adequately. The *audiencia,* a chief judicial tribunal headed by a type of judge called *oidores,* was often political in its functioning, and in the instances of Mexico City and Lima (in South America) apt to be controlled by the viceroy—who, after all, legally stood in the king's place. Hence, in 1640, Juan de Palafox y Mendoza (b. 1600) arrived in New Spain as *visitador,* essentially an inspector general, as well as archbishop of Puebla with the task of setting matters right. Two years later this moralistic, even puritanical servant of God and king, accused Viceroy Diego López Pacheco y Bobadilla of harboring Portuguese sympathies—as the joint kingdom had just broken up—and temporarily assumed his office. Subsequently victorious in a power struggle with the new viceroy, García Sarmiento de Sotomayor, in 1647, the archbishop stayed

MEXICO, CENTRAL AMERICA, AND THE CARIBBEAN

on until 1649. (His rival was posted to Lima as viceroy but soon lost favor in Madrid and was replaced in 1649.)

Still, by late in the century, acting as the king's representative could be perilous, for in 1692, hunger-crazed rioters burned the viceregal palace. The fact that by 1710 the Mexican mines at Zacatecas had replaced those at Potosí in Spain's South American viceroyalty as the leading producer of silver had little beneficial effect on New Spain except for the mine owners and merchants, whom it provided with luxury imports.[36] It did, however, reinforce New Spain as the jewel of the Spanish Empire. Its nontreasury exports became more important as its economy diversified (while Peru's exports continued to be almost exclusively silver). As a result New Spain's elites were developing a sense of self-confidence rooted in a strong economic base. Indeed, a growing proportion of its trade was carried on in ships built in the New World, and its merchants began to send representatives to Cádiz and Seville rather than purchase Spanish goods at the Caribbean trade fairs—where prices were sharply inflated. As depicted by Lynch:

> In Mexico the nobility—about fifty families in the eighteenth century— combined a number of roles and offices. One group made its fortunes in overseas trade, invested profits in mines and plantations, and acted primarily in the export sector. Others concentrated on mining and on agriculture producing for the mining industry. They all preferred to co-opt the imperial bureaucracy by marriage and interest rather than confront it in protest and resistance.[37]

Although the role of the military in the colonial period, especially the gradual replacement of Spanish officers by *criollos* and the increasingly important role of militia, had an impact upon independence and the ensuing *caudillo* era, it contributed relatively little to the longer-run colonial legacy except its existence as a powerful interest group and a blurring of lines between the civilian and military aspects of national life. The legacy of the church would be much broader in scope, profound in impact, and lasting as a crucial component of political culture. The intensely Catholic religious heritage left by Spanish colonialism is critical to understanding Mexico even today. As insightfully summed up by Camp:

> Religion played a critical role in the pre-Conquest Mexican indigenous culture and was very much integrated into the native political processes. In both the Aztec and Mayan empires, for example, religion was integral to political leadership. The Spanish were no less religious. Beginning with the Conquest itself, the pope reached some agreements with the Spanish crown. In these agreements, known collectively as the *patronato real* (royal patronate), the Catholic Church gave up certain rights it exercised in Europe for a

privileged role in the Conquest generally and in New Spain specifically. In return for being allowed to send two priests or friars with every land or sea expedition, and being given the sole opportunity to proselytize millions of Indians, the church gave up its control over the building of facilities in the New World, the appointing of higher clergy, the collecting of tithes and other activities.[38]

Once the Inquisition arrived in New Spain in 1571, the church fully assumed the role of ferreting out religious and political dissenters, for "in practice the Inquisition controlled publishing, assembled a book index that censored intellectual ideas from abroad, and fielded special customs inspectors."[39] In New Spain more than elsewhere the church served as a powerful instrument for promoting political as well as religious orthodoxy—for heretics were automatically assumed to be traitors and subversive to the social order.

As royal income from the South American colonies dropped, Mexico became the "last reservoir" for the Spanish crown's financial needs. From only three million pesos a year it yielded nearly five times that amount by the late 1790s.[40] The late colonial period brought changes not entirely to the liking of that part of the elite with historical roots in the country, rather than close ties to Spain. In 1765, José de Gálvez came to New Spain for a six-year inspection, during which he directed the expulsion of the Jesuits in 1767 and laid the foundations for tightening royal control. Upon his return to Madrid in 1771, he was named Minister of the Indies and, beginning in 1776, worked to extend the intendancy system to the rest of Spain's New World colonies. This ultimate implementation of the Bourbon reforms would go quite smoothly in New Spain and its dependencies, on balance the most satisfied region of the Spanish Empire, but would meet with stiffer resistance in South America, particularly in the viceroyalty of Peru.

What the Spanish Built in South America

With the Atlantic Coast of South America denied to the Spanish in 1494 by the Vatican-imposed Treaty of Tordesillas, which acknowledged Portugal's claims to all territories less than 370 leagues west of the Cape Verde Islands, ambitious Spanish explorers seeking to replicate the feats of Cortez and gain equal riches and fame had to turn their attention to its Pacific side. Francisco Pizarro, from Spain's Estremadura region, had been too young to make a mark in the reconquest, so left Spain in 1501 in the fleet of Nicolás de Ovando on that influential man's way to take over as governor of Hispaniola. Always looking for opportunity, at thirty-five Pizarro was a captain in the expedition headed by Vasco Nuñez de Balboa that crossed the Isthmus of Panama in 1513.

Knowing that he would have to venture farther, Pizarro decided to search for fame and fortune down the coast in areas not yet staked out by anyone with better connections and greater resources. His first expedition reached only part of the way down the coast of today's Ecuador. After his second, which made landfall significantly farther south, the by-now-middle-aged adventurer was at the Spanish court in mid-1528 when Cortez returned there from his triumphs—an event that both further whetted Pizarro's appetite and facilitated his quest for royal authorization and sources of financing. Thus, at the beginning of 1530, Pizarro sailed from Spain in command of a substantial fleet. At the end of the year he started his third expedition from Panama at the head of 168 men and thirty horses, accompanied by his half brothers, Hernando, Juan, and Gonzalo. Landing on the northern coast, the expedition moved inland in 1532.

The Incan empire had gradually expanded from its base in southern Peru between 1200 and the early 1400s, with major new conquests from 1438 to 1471 carrying it northward to Cajamarca and Quito and south into Chile. An industrious consolidator, Sapa Inca Huayna Capac, then succeeded Pachacuti Inca Yupanqui, the architect of this empire building. Fortunately for Pizarro's designs, a war of dynastic succession had broken out in 1525—accompanied by a decimating epidemic—as both Huayna Capac and his heir had died.[41] Atahualpa (b. 1502) commanded strong forces based in the north around Quito, and his brother Huascar was entrenched in the southern stronghold of the empire at Cuzco. Capturing Atahualpa through deceit in mid-November, Pizarro, bolstered in mid-April 1533 by 150 reinforcements, extorted a $7-million ransom in gold and silver before killing his hostage at the end of July. Having founded Lima, City of Kings, as a base on the coast, and bolstered by additional reinforcements bringing their armed strength to 600, the Pizarros battled their way to Cuzco, operating in conjunction with a puppet Inca, Manco.

Success bred complications and dangers for the Pizarros as well as fame and riches. In 1534, Pedro de Alvarado, eager to get in on the action, brought an expedition from his Guatemalan base to the northern region, being bought out by the Pizarros although his men remained. Sebastian de Belalcazar left Quito to establish a port at Guayaquil, and Pizarro's old financial partner Diego de Almagro (b. 1475), after having his head filled with stories of supposed riches to the south, was sent off to explore and conquer Chile—a task that would quickly cut short his life, as the Araucanian Indians demonstrated why they had not been conquered by the Incas.

Reinforced in 1535 by troops attracted by the vast wealth of the first shipload of looted riches and extorted tribute that was shipped back to the crown, Francisco Pizarro sought to defeat the Incan general holding the Quito region. But the Spaniards had behaved so brutally that in April 1536 they were surprised by a massive rebellion in which Juan Pizarro was killed. Reinforcements that arrived for the subsequent siege of Cuzco turned on the veteran followers of Pizarro, whom they envied for having enriched themselves by getting to Peru first and felt should now let the newcomers enjoy the manifold benefits of conquest.

By this time Spanish rule had extended inland to the area around Sucre in modern-day Bolivia, then called Upper Peru; a city had been founded there in 1538 named La Plata (Silver), but it was more frequently called Chuquisaca. Gonzalo Pizarro, newly ensconced as governor of Quito, put down the rebellion there, but with greed and ambition running rampant, the three remaining Pizarro brothers did not enjoy the fruits of their conquests for long. In mid-1541 Francisco was murdered by the son of ill-fated ex-partner Diego de Amalgro, who went on to control Lima for a year before himself being killed in September 1542. Gonzalo, named captain-general at the end of 1540, saw Lima become an *audiencia* and seat for a viceroyalty in 1543. Feeling his authority and power infringed upon by the creation of a viceroyalty, he killed Viceroy Blasco Nuñez Vela early in 1546 and was then himself defeated and executed in April 1548 by forces reestablishing the royal authority he had usurped.[42]

Like Cortez and his associates far to the north in New Spain, the Peruvian *conquistadores* were rewarded with *encomiendas,* generally valid for two lifetimes. By Gonzalo Pizarro's death, virtually all of Peru was in the hands of 480 *encomenderos,* but the Indian population, again decimated by an epidemic in 1546 (with another coming along in 1558–1559), had fallen from the estimated 4 to 15 million at the time of the *conquistadores'* arrival to perhaps 1.5 million—on its way down to 1.3 million by 1570. Introduction of the New Laws of 1542 inspired by Father Bartolomé de Las Casas and extension of the sway of the Council of the Indies (in Spain) aroused a strong negative reaction in the *encomenderos,* and their compliance concerning the rights of Indians and the limits on their own powers diminished with their distance from Lima—which unlike Mexico City was not located near the center of their large landholdings. Open defiance by the *encomenderos* was ended by 1554.[43]

In 1568, a fifth viceroy, fifty-three-year-old Don Francisco Toledo, arrived in Lima to resolve the festering question of what residual partial rule the Incas would exercise over the Indian population. Following a rebellion in 1572 under newly installed Inca Tupac Amaru, the viceroy decided upon a colossal project of grouping the natives into new communities, "reductions," where priests could provide for their true conversion to the Catholic faith, and royal administrators would be available to see that they were not forced to pay exorbitant tribute to the Spanish landowners. Although Toledo accomplished a good deal during the twelve years he remained in Lima, he could not curb the voracious appetite of the mines for Indian labor.

A high concentration of the Indian population and mineral wealth, especially the rich silver deposits discovered at Potosí in 1545 and the availability from Huancavelica after 1563 of the mercury needed for silver refining, made the central Andean altiplano and the valleys to its south the natural seat for the Spanish colonial administration of Upper Peru. In the 1570s, the *mita,* the compulsory service of Indians on public works, was extended to a 200-mile radius around Potosí as workforce needs rose to 13,500 per year. Economically the viceroyalty's tail wagged the dog, since Lima functioned largely as a port for Potosí, which peaked at a population of 150,000—at the time smaller only than London, Paris, or Seville.[44] By contrast, Lima would at best reach 25,000 in 1610 on its way to perhaps 80,000 by 1680. Revival of the mines during the last quarter of the sixteenth century had seen silver production increase sixfold, supplying half of all silver from Spanish America and, until late in the seventeenth century, exceeding New Spain's output. As thousands died from overwork and lack of safety precautions in the mines, the eighteenth century saw bloody Indian insurrections requiring ruthless repression. During this time manorial *haciendas* as well as ranchlike *estancias* differentiated themselves from the less successful landholdings of the *encomenderos,* which had lower managerial and entrepreneurial skills. In the cities, artisan industries, small-scale textile manufacturing, and shipbuilding slowly developed.

Mining continued to dominate the viceroyalty's economy, keeping Potosí not only the most populous city in the Western Hemisphere, but also one of the wealthiest. As the mineral riches were sent immediately to Lima for transshipment to Spain, life for the region's indigenous people underwent little change. Spanish overlords just replaced the Incan ruling caste that had previously lorded over the natives' ancestors. The population of Lima underwent significant qualitative change, since the indigenous population was concentrated in the highlands well away from the coast. Hence African slaves rose in number from 3,000 in 1550 to 4,000 in 1586 and on to 15,000, exceeding the number of nonblacks by 1640. At this point *mestizos* made up a significant proportion of the colony's population, as during the first thirty years, when between 5,000 and 10,000 Europeans came to Peru, only one-sixth of them were women, who never reached 30 percent in the next two decades.[45] The original *conquistadores* had taken the widows and daughters of the Incan nobility as wives and mistresses as a matter of policy as well as necessity. Later arrivals taking up residence on their estates continued the practice, their retainers mating with the most desirable Indian females available—including those whose husbands and fathers might be away working in the mines.

As already pointed out with respect to Mexico, by this juncture Spain needed increased revenues from its colonies to finance its expensive aims in Europe. The gathering of Indians into the reductions had spelled the beginning of the end for the *encomienda* system, as it gave control of the labor force back to the state. Now, in 1593, the *corregidores de Indios* began to collect tribute in place of the *encomenderos*. However, these individuals in essence were private entrepreneurs closely linked to merchants and making a living by forcing the Indians to produce in order to buy goods they really didn't need. Like many Indian agents in the United States in the nineteenth century, they generally abused their office to accumulate wealth much as the *encomenderos* had.[46] Their work with the Indian chiefs, municipal officials, rural priests, merchants, and mine owners served to monetarize the tribute system and bring the Indians into the economy.[47]

Sale of public offices as a means of raising government revenues began in 1559 at the level of notaries, being extended to most low-level offices in 1606, reaching the treasury level in 1633, coming to include *corregidores* and *alcaldes mayores* by 1667, and reaching the prestigious *audiencia* positions two decades later.

Selling imperial offices turned out to be a major mistake. In Klarén's view, "Inexperienced, corrupt, and inefficient officials firmly tied to local interests succeeded in gaining control of many important offices, including the central treasury office in Lima."[48] As sales of office moved toward the higher echelons during the seventeenth century, when the crown increased its demands upon the colonial elites, they squeezed the Indians harder. Yet the quality of administration suffered and crown revenues continued to decrease. On the other hand, the church—right on the spot with its devoted servants—steadily accumulated money and property, albeit not quite as much as in New Spain. As Klarén sums up the results:

> Peru in the seventeenth century had, in many ways, drifted away from Spain—its Creole elites becoming more powerful politically and economically, its economy more diverse and autonomous, and its population increasingly mixed. At the same time, silver produced at Potosí had sharply declined, the transatlantic trade had slowed, and tax remittances to Madrid had dropped.[49]

The mother country's response could best be described as an effort at "recolonization" of an area whose importance had been increased by its resurgence as a source of revenue to the crown and the Spanish economy. This recolonization eventually resulted in the implementation of the Bourbon reforms, including the intendancy system. For between 1730 and the 1790s Potosí silver production recuperated and that from Cerro de Pasco in Peru (opened in the 1630s) was on the rise. With overall production increasing from 2.3 million pesos to 40.6 million and population up to a million (from about 600,000 in 1620) plus 200,000 in outlying regions of the viceroyalty, Peru was again a leading part of Spanish America—which had a total of around 12.6 million inhabitants—being second only to New

Spain and producing a significant internal demand for products, both domestic and imported. Its racial mix was approximately 62 percent Indian, 27 percent *mestizo,* and 13 percent European, with blacks numbering only 40,000.[50]

Spain was shocked by the English capture of Havana, the hemisphere's third largest city, in 1762 during the Seven Years' War.[51] It reacted by raising royal forces in Peru to 100,000—creating vastly increased defense costs, which, like the British in their North American colonies, they felt should be shared by the local beneficiaries—who were not willing to bear the costs of what they viewed as essentially European wars.[52] For their part, much like the colonial militias in Britain's North American colonies, Creoles had come to make up a significant proportion of the armed forces already there—estimated by 1740 at a third of officers and two-thirds of troops, reaching three-fifths and four-fifths, respectively, by the end of the century.[53] Following the abrupt ouster of the Jesuits in 1767, the state auctioned their varied enterprises to the private sector. Still, with local Creole elites forming mutual enrichment alliances with crown officials through bribery, intrigue, and sale of offices, imperial interests were being seriously compromised.[54] When by 1778 trade was opened up in many of the Spanish colonies, including Peru, the market was flooded with cheap imported textiles—a boon to consumers, but a bane to local manufactures. Moreover, sales taxes—the hated *alcabala*—were repeatedly raised, and collection was tightened by ending its privatization, instead making it direct.

Recalcitrant colonial elites were not at all happy over shifts in the tax burden—greatly increased when Upper Peru's silver was abruptly funneled down to upstart Buenos Aires, a great loss of revenue to Peru. In a move to strengthen metropolitan controls as already done in New Spain, in 1784 what remained of the viceroyalty after the establishment of new ones in Bogotá and more recently in Buenos Aires (discussed in the next section) was divided into seven intendancies, the *corregimientos* were eliminated, and their *corregidores* were displaced. Further measures banned all Creole appointments to *audiencias* and added more *peninsulares* to enlarged governmental bodies, with some directly appointed as electoral and cooptative procedures were bypassed—a measure leading in practice to royally appointed executives all the way down to the provincial level. As a result, by 1810, the eve of revolution, Creoles made up only a quarter to a third of the membership of *audiencias.* What might have looked like good sense in Madrid was poorly received in the New World—whose elites were aware that Britain's North American colonies had successfully broken free and seemed to be thriving. As Lynch cogently depicts the situation, after 1792 Spain followed a policy of "short-term extortion and structural atrophy." But, courtesy of the Napoleonic Wars, "the fruits were diverted to foreigners, neutrals, or even enemies."[55] At the same time there was a "radical maturing of colonial society whose more self-conscious members felt increasing

ANDEAN SPANISH AMERICA

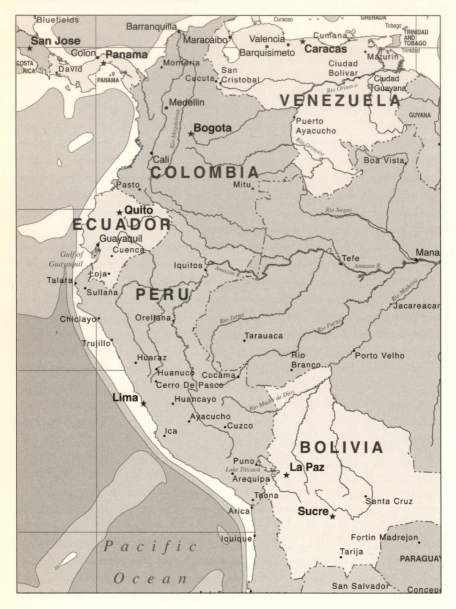

confidence that they could go it alone."[56] In the view of a Mexican scholar, "The growing sense of American identity conflicted with the determination of Spain's eighteenth-century rulers to reduce the New World to the status of a colony."[57]

Moreover, Spanish administrators, particularly after the creation of the intendancies in 1782, of which eight of twelve were in the new viceroyalty of the Rio de la Plata, which picked up the *audiencia* of Charcas—that is, Upper Peru, with all its riches—were frequently changed to prevent them from building an independent base of support. As a consequence, most royal officials were less concerned with local affairs than with accruing financial benefits for themselves during the relatively few years they could count upon being in a position to do so. This ingrained tendency to associate public office with opportunity for personal gain found its way into the political culture of the region's elites and subelites, persisting well into the independence and national periods.

In part because of the rivalry of the *peninsulares* and Creoles, an "us-against-them" mentality developed and fused with the belief that politics was a zero-sum game in which any gains by one group came at the expense of others—if not in direct terms, at least in the form of foreclosed opportunities. Strong personal loyalties and intolerance of opposing views, which would later translate into intransigent partisanship, became prevalent political traits. Moreover, with power in the hands of competing hierarchical groups—the military, the church, bureaucratic authority, merchants, and large landowners—these groups became the arbiters of policy, relying on their power rather than negotiation and compromise. During the colonial era kinship ties were very important because force and intimidation were often applied and the courts were frequently instruments of punishing enemies and rewarding friends and relatives. One could generally rely upon family, not a government that might favor your rivals and, by definition, your ruthless opponents. These views and values all became part of a political culture that demonstrated persistence over the span of generations—for Latin America's long colonial era (lasting three centuries) lasted roughly a century and a quarter more than these countries' independent lives have yet spanned.

Administrative Changes in the 1700s

Although the fundamental elements of the Spanish colonial experience were contained in the two original viceroyalties of New Spain and Peru, adjustments made during the eighteenth century were important in shaping the process of independence and the array of countries that emerged from it. Beginning in the north, by 1522 Pedro Arias de Ávila, better known as Pedrarias, was functioning as captain-general and governor of the strategic nexus Panama. Santa Marta on the Caribbean coast of what would become Colombia served as a Spanish base until overtaken by neighboring Cartegena, established in 1533 by Pedro de Heredia.

Sebastian de Belalcazar moved up from Quito and founded Popayán and Cali in western Colombia in 1536, and Gonzalo Jiménez de Quesada established Santa Fé de Bogotá three years later. The two loose federations of Chibcha Indian "kingdoms" provided little resistance.[58] Indeed, as most of the Indians stayed out of the way of the limited number of Spaniards, scholarly estimates of their ranks vary widely, from 850,000 to over 3 million. By 1549, the northern South American region's development, although limited, did earn it the creation of an *audiencia,* Nueva Granada; an *audiencia* followed in Panama in 1563; and the captain-general in Bogotá was authorized to act independently of the viceroy in Lima. To the east in Venezuela, then more Caribbean than it was South American, Caracas and Maracaibo were founded in 1567.

San Francisco de Quito had been established in 1534 on the ruins of an Incan secondary capital, being attached to the viceroyalty of Peru when it came into existence nine years later. In 1563, it gained some degree of autonomy as an *audiencia,* and in 1720 Ecuador was transferred from Lima's jurisdiction to that of the new viceroyalty centered in Bogotá—although its communications with that city were even more difficult and attenuated than with Lima. (Thus the Peruvian viceroyalty, unlike New Spain's, suffered amputations to the north as well as to the south and west.)

As early as the period 1605–1628, Juan de Boya, as captain-general of New Granada and president of the *audiencia* of Bogotá, fought a series of Indian wars with a very high degree of autonomy from the viceroy in Lima—an autonomy virtually inevitable in light of the geographic barrier imposed by multiple cordilleras of the Andes. In 1675, Medellín was founded as the center of a region isolated by mountains from Bogotá, and 1717 witnessed the establishment of a viceroyalty of Nueva Granada centered on Bogotá and embracing northern South America—spurred by a significant production of gold and gemstones, but triggered by the deposing of the governor/captain-general by the members of the *audiencia.* Abolished in 1723 because of its high costs, the viceroyalty was restored in 1739, still without Venezuela, linked instead to more accessible Santo Domingo.[59] But in 1776, essentially for military purposes, Venezuela (including Trinidad) was made an intendancy, gaining its own captain-general the following year. For mining purposes, between 9,000 and 13,500 black slaves had been brought into New Granada by this time.[60]

In the aftermath of his mediation of the 1778–1782 *comunero* revolt in New Granada (like those in Peru directed against the Bourbon reforms), Archbishop Antonio Caballero y Gongora was named its viceroy.[61] Prudently refusing to install the intendancy system and taking advantage of the relative inaccessibility of Bogotá from Spain, he often consulted with the local Creoles, whom he courted by achieving free trade with Mexico and Venezuela in 1789. In Venezuela, 1795 saw a serious slave uprising in its sugar-producing region, followed two years later by an abortive independence conspiracy.

South of Peru the disastrous 1534–1537 expedition of Diego de Almagro did not go unpunished. In 1540–1541 Pedro de Valdivia carried out a bloody conquest of the *Mapuche* Indians and founded Santiago, but between 1551 and 1664 some twenty thousand lives and a fortune were expended trying to subdue the Araucanians, who launched a major revolt in 1655. By 1598, Spanish influence south of the Bio-Bio River (near the city of Concepción, established in 1550) was nonexistent. Indeed, Valdivia had been beheaded by Indians in 1554, and the same dire fate befell Martín García de Loyola, sent as governor and captain-general in 1592. A proven Indian fighter and brilliant horseman, he was killed in battle by the Araucanians at the end of 1598. In 1609, an *audiencia* was set up in Santiago, which was destroyed by earthquakes in 1647 and 1730 (Concepción met the same fate in 1751).

In the center of the continent, Upper Peru remained closely tied to Lima for most of the colonial period. It increasingly developed trade down into the La Plata region by way of Paraguay, as well as a thriving contraband commerce with Brazil. Far from any center of supervision, early developments in the La Plata region were quite chaotic and lacking in continuity. There was a failed effort to establish a permanent settlement at Buenos Aires in 1536, but the next year Asunción was founded well upriver, much nearer the riches of Upper Peru. Domingo Martín de Irala took advantage of its isolation to seize power there, being rewarded by appointment as Paraguay's governor in 1555. The next year he put down a major Indian revolt, in which over 1,300 Guaranis were killed.[62] By that time Santiago del Estero in the northwestern interior of modern Argentina had been established by an expedition down from Peru, with Mendoza being founded from Chile in 1561 and Tucumán from Peru four years later.

In 1573, the governor of Tucumán founded Córdoba, and in 1582 the southern city of Salta came into existence. By this time Buenos Aires had recently been reestablished, this time from Paraguay—gaining its autonomy from Asunción under a local governor in 1617—as Spain came to value it chiefly as a way to shut off the La Plata route to Upper Peru in order to maintain its close links to Lima.[63] From only a thousand inhabitants in 1615, Buenos Aires grew to seven thousand by the end of the century, thriving largely on contraband from Upper Peru. Upriver, where the Jesuits were very active, in 1724 the governor of Paraguay, with three thousand troops—for that time and place an immense army—wiped out the Jesuit-led Guarani militia. In the first half of the next decade *Comunero* revolts took the lives to two governors before they were crushed by forces from Buenos Aires.

In 1680, the Portuguese had established a fort at Nova Colonia do Sacramento across the estuary from Buenos Aires. Captured by the Spanish in 1702, the colony went back to the Portuguese eleven years later at the end of the War of the Span-ish Succession. Spain was supposed to regain it in 1750 in return for ceding the Jesuit missions in Paraguay to Portugal, which intended to resettle thirty thousand Guarani Indians on Spanish lands. When the terms of the agreement were not ful-filled, Spain took the city of Sacramento by force in 1762, only to have to return it the next year through the Treaty of Paris that ended the Seven Years' War. It finally passed into Spanish hands in 1777 through the Treaty of San Ildefonso—just after Buenos Aires had become the seat of a viceroyalty as Don Pedro de Cevallos ar-rived with 120 ships and twenty thousand men in a major demonstration of Span-ish determination to retain control of the La Plata region.[64] In a basic sense this was a response to the 1763 move of Brazil's capital from Salvador to Rio de Janeiro and continued Spanish-Portuguese strife over the upper shore of the La Plata estuary. Clearly the infant viceroyalty of Buenos Aires could not become nearly as firmly rooted as the original pair of New Spain and Peru, which dated back to the first half of the sixteenth century. Even Bogotá, being a somewhat sen-ior viceroyalty to Buenos Aires, could not do so. In New Spain and Peru, the colo-nial bureaucracy had long become in effect brokers between the Spanish crown and its American subjects, and there were strong nuclei of *peninsular* bureaucrats tied to the mother county.

Back in Central America, where exploration and conquest had been com-pleted by 1527, as well as in the Caribbean, changes were relatively minor. In 1542, the *audiencia* of Panama, established four years earlier, was replaced by an Audiencia de los Confines extending all the way up to Chiapas and the Yucatán. San José was founded in lower Central America in 1736 but remained a town more than a city. The area was accustomed to relative neglect, for it had little to contribute economically and lacked strategic importance. However, 1786 wit-nessed the establishment of an intendancy embracing most of Central America and Chiapas, centered in Guatemala, where the old capital of the preceding *audi-encia* had been destroyed by an earthquake in 1773. Essentially insignificant throughout the colonial period, this subregion would remain so for another cen-tury before gradually attaining greater prominence during the first half of the 1900s and projecting itself more effectively after World War II.

The Portuguese-Brazilian Variant

Half of South America was not subject to Spanish colonization, and it would eventually become Latin America's most important country. Brazil's development as a nation has been essentially evolutionary, with few sharp breaks or drastic dis-continuities. Indeed, in no instance has there been a real rupture because one powerful group has felt dispossessed by another; instead, the group in power has adjusted to sharing control with emergent elements. Such emergent groups have not appeared suddenly but have typically been on the political scene for quite some time before causing what can best be described as changes of regime rather than of the underlying system. Even in the most important of these substitutions of one political regime for another, the old elites have never been plowed under, or even permanently swept aside. Generally old regimes have in the short run been displaced, not replaced. Such apparently "revolutionary" events in the political realm as independence (1822), the shift from monarchy to republic (1889), the overthrow of the oligarchic republic in 1930, the seizure of power by the military in 1964, and the return to civilian rule in 1985 were not in any instance accompanied by sharp social transformations or even dramatic economic innovations. Rather, they were in large part the result of substantial change in these realms of national life that had built up over time, and each landmark change of political regime was, in turn, a watershed contributing to a further round of socioeconomic developments that gradually created pressures for yet another major readjustment of the political system.[65]

Hence, a well-known Brazilian historian writing in the 1960s could say that "traveling through Brazil today we are often surprised by aspects that we thought existed only in history books, and if we ponder them as a whole, we see that they are manifestations of things deeply rooted in the past and not simple anachronistic survivals."[66] A bit later, a North American economist pointed out that Brazilian experience has repeatedly demonstrated economic expansion and structural change accompanied by only minimal alteration in the "fundamental relations of power."[67] Given the lasting impact of the colonial order upon the Brazilian society and economy as well as in the political sphere, it is necessary to trace these patterns from their beginnings.

Continuance of the Brazilian monarchy and its ties to Portugal provided this third of Latin America with a unique nineteenth-century developmental experience that completely bypassed the *caudillo* period and put off its initial experiment with a republican form of government to the 1890s. Hence national consolidation took place in a context free from the double rupture that led to the fragmentation and political instability of Hispanic America following independence. For, in the experience of Brazil, and only in the Brazilian case, separation from the mother country and the quest for a new basis of legitimate authority did not occur simultaneously; instead, the two traumas were separated by sixty-seven years of consolidation of national independence under the rule of the very same monarchs who would have governed Brazil had it remained linked to Portugal.

Since Brazil's preindependence experiences had such a lasting impact upon its national life, they merit close attention. Moreover, given the country's vast expanse, the stamp of the long colonial era differed significantly from one part to another, with developments in Pernambuco, Bahia, Minas Gerais, and Rio de Janeiro having the greatest influence at varying points along the road from discovery in

1500 to the eve of independence at the end of the eighteenth century. One constant is that the six million or more Indians inhabiting this subcontinent when the Portuguese began to settle along its coast, in contrast to those in Mexico and its dependencies and in the Andean region, were destined to have a very limited impact. Over time their influence was increasingly attenuated as African slaves replaced them, coming to constitute a majority of the population before the end of the slave trade in the 1850s. Subsequently a subsequent massive influx of European immigrants reduced Afro-Brazilians to 44 percent of the population. Yet, at over eighty million, this is still more than the total of blacks and mulattoes in all the other countries of the Western Hemisphere and at least 230 times the number of remaining descendents of the native population.

In the late fifteenth century, maritime-oriented Portugal was a leading European nation, engaged in a spirited rivalry with Spain in transoceanic discovery and colonization focused upon the East. Prince Henry the Navigator (b. 1394) had actively encouraged the quest for new maritime trade routes until his death in 1460. In 1488, Bartolomeu Dias rounded the Cape of Good Hope and entered the Indian Ocean, and a decade later Vasco da Gama reached India by this eastward route. He and the Portuguese crown felt a need to follow up what it saw as an unsuccessful Spanish effort to reach Asia by sailing west. Perceiving Columbus's error as lying in having sailed directly across the Atlantic into the unexpected Caribbean barrier, in 1500 Pedro Álvares Cabral (b. 1467), an experienced seafarer, was dispatched on a more southward course. A confidant of the king, this nobleman set out on March 9 with an impressive flotilla of thirteen ships to reach Asia. Along the way he was to explore the New World lands accorded to Portugal by the 1494 Treaty of Tordesillas with Spain.[68] Making good time, he made landfall on what he named the island of Vera Cruz (the True Cross), but which would come to be known as Brazil, from *pau brasil*, a type of red dyewood found there. After a very short stay, the Portuguese fleet sailed on to its primary objective, India (with Cabral returning in semidisgrace the next year because of heavy losses of ships and men).

Portugal, whose limited human resources were already stretched almost to the breaking point across a variety of African and Asian colonies of immediate value and strategic concern, was slow to find major interest in the great hunk of South America that had fallen into its hands. A small fleet piloted by Amerigo Vespucci explored the long coastline, but failure to discover precious metals led the Portuguese, numbering under a million and short on capital, to concentrate on their lucrative Asian trade. Isolated trading posts called *factories* were established at some of the fine natural harbors, but permanent colonization came only after 1531— after the Spanish had consolidated their rich incursions into the Aztec and Incan empires. In the meantime, the French trespassed heavily, and other colony-hungry Europeans tested the waters. King João III, ruling from 1521 to 1557, took greater interest in his huge possession, and the Portuguese crown began to make large land grants to aristocratic entrepreneurs, who assumed responsibility for planting colonies and organizing trade. This system of *capitanias* had worked in the Azores, so its extension to South America as a means of consolidating Portuguese presence seemed logical.

Each captaincy consisted of a strip of land at least seventy-five miles wide and extending inland to the ill-defined and undemarcated Tordesillas line. Each *donatário* (the holder of a capitania), the first of whom set out in 1534, was financially responsible for attracting settlers through subsidiary grants of land called *seismarias* and consisting of forty to more than one hundred square miles, for promoting agriculture and commerce, for caring for the settlers' spiritual welfare, and for protecting them from attack. All this amounted to a heavy burden that few of the *donatários* were able to bear, particularly when most of their unruly colonists were religious dissenters or criminals exiled from the mother country and the French were constantly on the prowl for easy pickings.

By 1549, only two of the fifteen captaincies had proven economically viable: Duarte Coelho Pereira's sugar-producing Pernambuco and Martím Afonso de Souza's São Vicente. The latter had commanded the initial 1531–1533 colonizing expedition that had expelled the French from Pernambuco before sailing far south to establish São Vicente, near the present port of Santos, and a tiny inland colony at Piratininga that would eventually grow into São Paulo, now one of the world's largest cities. (But in the context of the times de Souza considered becoming governor of Goa, the small Portuguese enclave in India, a major promotion.) Indeed, at the middle of the sixteenth century, Brazil was still very much a stepchild to the Portuguese, who were generally disappointed that it appeared to lack not only the spices, silks, and jewels found in the Far East, but also the silver and gold discovered by the Spaniards in both Mexico and at Potosí in today's Bolivia.[69] European immigration to the precarious colonies in Brazil had yet to reach fifteen thousand.

Desperate to salvage this foundering "privatized" Brazil, in 1549 the monarch sent Tomé de Souza (b. 1515), experienced as an administrator in India, to Brazil as governor-general, accompanied by a thousand troops and a small group of Jesuits under Manuel de Nóbrega. Salvador, properly named São Salvador da Bahia dos Todos os Santos, on a magnificent harbor halfway down the coast, was chosen as the unified royal colony's capital, remaining so for 214 years. Before returning to Lisbon to be the king's chief adviser on Brazilian matters, de Souza recommended settlement and fortification of mountain-ringed Guanabara Bay as a strongpoint intermediate between the capital and São Vicente. Meanwhile, French admiral Nicolás Durand de Villegaignon had done so, populating his "Antarctic France" with Huguenots seeking the religious toleration denied them in France.[70] After routing the French and their native allies in 1560, new Portuguese governor-general Mem de Sá founded Rio de Janeiro (formally, São Sebastião do Rio de

Janeiro)—today an urban conglomerate of eleven million inhabitants. The area around Rio de Janeiro was secured in 1575 as an expedition enslaved four thousand hostile Tamoios Indians after killing half that many along with two Frenchmen and an Englishman found among them. For despite laws intended to protect Indians, colonists exploited the loopholes for hostile tribes and those captured in "just wars" to make Indian slaves the backbone of their labor force.

With the institution of the governor-general, equivalent to the Spanish viceroy, and reinforcement of the Catholic Church's position with appointment of a bishop, came the first rudimentary elements of a military establishment and the nucleus of an administrative bureaucracy. In the absence of a significant permanent army, large landowners were obliged to maintain private military forces from among their retainers and dependents. These evolved over time into organized militia units under the control of the most powerful regional figures, who not only were responsible for maintaining law and order in the hinterlands but also, given the lack of regular officials in the rural areas, often performed additional government tasks. So began the phenomenon of *coronelismo,* a system of rural political bosses and their machine politics that was crucial through the first half of the twentieth century and still persists in remote interior areas.[71]

Owing to the demise of the Portuguese royal family, from 1580 to 1640 Portugal was united with Spain and was therefore subjected to attacks by that Hapsburg regime's enemies. Sugar was firmly established as Brazil's chief export, one so profitable that it attracted heavy attention from Portugal's European rivals. England, France, and the Netherlands each sought to seize control of inviting portions of the Portuguese domains—since Portugal had a very small population. In Maranhão, midway between Pernambuco and the mouth of the Amazon, the French established in 1612 a fort named for their king; they were removed by force three years later, when the fort's name was changed to the Portuguese São Luís do Maranhão. Belém was founded in 1616 near the mouth of the Amazon River, and in 1621 the two were combined into the province of Maranhão and Grão Pará, reporting directly to Lisbon. The motivation for this effort at closer control over the northern part of Brazil was that by this time one-half to two-thirds of the Brazilian trade was in the hands of Dutch merchants, and a large proportion of Portuguese commerce with their colony was reexported to the La Plata region or even to Upper Peru.[72]

In 1624, the Dutch, who had recently won independence from Spain, temporarily captured Salvador, which was retaken the next year by a joint Spanish-Portuguese force of 12,500 men and 52 vessels mounting 1,200 cannon.[73] In 1630, using the profits from capturing the New Spain fleet at Matanzas, Cuba, in 1628, the Dutch West Indies Company successfully took all of Pernambuco with a fleet of 67 ships equipped with 1,170 cannon and carrying 7,000 men. This sugar-rich area was modernized between the beginning of 1637 and mid-1644 by the extremely able captain-general Johan Maurits, Count van Nassau-Siegen (b. 1604), who expanded the colony south to the Bahian border in 1635 and northward to São Luís in 1641. The previous year an 86-ship Portuguese flotilla carrying 10,000 troops had been outfought by a Dutch fleet half its size, but the Portuguese counteroffensive eventually triumphed in January 1554, when, blockaded for the better part of a year by a 77-vessel armada, the beleaguered Dutch finally surrendered Recife and Olinda—having incurred crushing land defeats at nearby Guararapes in April 1648 and February 1649, in which they suffered, respectively, 500 and nearly 1,000 fatalities.[74]

Consolidation of the Portuguese presence following separation from Spain under the Duke of Braganca progressed slowly in the second half of the seventeenth century, although in 1646 Brazil was granted the rather hollow distinction of becoming a principality rather than a colony. On the local scene, native females served the Portuguese as sexual partners, and these relationships gave rise to a sizable number of *mamelucos* or *caboclos,* mixed-blood offspring with European fathers and indigenous mothers. Because Indians could easily escape into the vast interior, landowners needed a new source of labor not easily able to survive without the protection and security of the *engenhos* and *fazendas* (plantations and large ranches). The solution was the importation of African slaves, already common in Portugal and far from unknown in tropical Brazil, having been imported at a rate of 8,400 a year by 1600, totaling 250,000 by 1650, and reaching 600,000 by the end of the century.[75] Thus the three main elements of Brazilian society were present and mixing through widespread miscegenation early in the colonial period. Unfortunately, Brazil's indigenous population would be reduced—largely through disease but also by interbreeding, assimilation, and, in some cases, violence—by a million a century until there were only 250,000 left by the 1970s. As they retreated into the vast interior to survive and preserve their ways of life, these predominantly hunting-and-fishing tribes left very little mark upon Brazil's national culture—in stark contrast to the heritage of the Aztecs in Mexico or of the Incas in Peru.

Meanwhile, the Portuguese had begun to move inland beyond the intimidating escarpment. Based increasingly in the city of São Paulo, founded by the Jesuits in 1554 on the plateau inland from São Vicente, expeditions called *bandeiras* brought back large numbers of native slaves from as far away as Paraguay, where the expeditioners, or *bandeirantes,* entered into conflict with the Jesuits, who had converted the Indians and brought them into self-sustaining mission villages named *reducciones* (reductions). Later the *bandeirantes* turned their attention to the quest for mineral riches, roving as far as Peru and even up into Colombia. They were rewarded for their daring and diligence in the 1690s by major discoveries of gold in the region north of São Paulo, an area soon labeled Minas Gerais ("General Mines").[76]

Conflict between *Paulistas* (as people from São Paulo are called), who thought this wealth should be theirs alone, and the wide variety of "tenderfeet" who quickly flowed into this heretofore frontier grazing area erupted into the War of the Emboabas (1707–1709). In its aftermath a captaincy of São Paulo and Minas was created separate from that of Rio de Janeiro. Minas Gerais was emancipated in 1720, when diamonds were discovered there, and its boomtown of Ouro Preto ("Black Gold"), near present-day metropolis Belo Horizonte, swollen to 30,000 inhabitants, temporarily became South America's largest city—as Potosí was in decline. Large portions of the coast were drained of population, and some north-eastern sugar planters sold their slaves, or at least their services, to mining entre-preneurs as the 33,000 African slaves in the mining region in 1717 exploded to nearly 200,000 by 1786—over half the province's total population.

With the value of slaves on the rise, in early 1694 Pernambuco planters, rein-forced by an army of hired São Paulo *bandeirantes,* finally destroyed Brazil's—indeed, the world's—largest and longest-lived community of escaped slaves (called *quilombos*), one that had flourished for several decades at Palmares. Established in 1630, when the Dutch had taken over the region, by the 1690s it contained 20,000 inhabitants under an elected chief bearing the title Ganga Zumba and had repulsed six Pernambucan assaults between 1680 and 1686. This brutal repression was rooted in the Pernambucans' conviction that its continued survival would en-courage insubordination among the rapidly growing and much-in-demand slave population.

Not long after, the Brazilians found themselves on the defensive, as in 1710 a French adventurer, Jean-François Leclerc, captured Rio de Janeiro. Unable to hold it, he was killed after surrendering to Portuguese troops sent from Salvador. This "barbaric" murder provided an excuse for René Duguay-Trouin, at the head of a formidable force of nine warships, seven hundred cannon, and fifty-five hundred men, to sack Rio de Janeiro in September–November 1722. In the face of a relief column from Minas Gerais, Duguay-Trouin withdrew, and the governor of Rio and other officials were subsequently hauled off to Lisbon to stand trial for cow-ardliness and dereliction of duty.[77] Back in Pernambuco, the War of the Mascates ("peddlers"), which dragged on from late 1710 to 1715, had shown how deep hostility could run between descendants of the original settlers and newcomers—the former entrenched in control of Olinda and enjoying church support, while the latter were expanding neighboring Recife.[78]

The eighteenth century was crucial in defining Brazil's borders with sur-rounding Spanish domains—generally by force; on occasion smoothed by diplo-macy. The treaties of Madrid (1750), El Prado (1761), and San Ildefonso (1777) saw the southern border move down, then back up, but the final treaty con-firmed the limits of Portuguese expansion far beyond the Tordesillas line and up through most of the Amazon basin. Indeed, the original 250,000 square miles of the Tordesillas treaty had grown to nearly 3,250,000 square miles—a thirteenfold increase. To be nearer the riches of the mining area and the repeated incursions of the Spanish in the south, the capital was moved from Salvador to Rio de Janeiro in 1763. (Salvador was a city of 50,000 by that time—a figure the new capital would reach by 1800.) Equally important, from the middle of the seventeenth century on, Brazil faced relentless agricultural competition from the British, French, and Dutch—all of whom came to produce sugar more efficiently on their Caribbean possessions.

With sugar revenues cut drastically, Brazil's salvation resided in becoming the world's leading source of gold and, after 1729, diamonds as well. But as gold production dropped off sharply in the 1770s, after having supplied as much as four-fifths of the world's supply, and sugar remained in the doldrums, the Brazilian economy stagnated. To make a bad situation even worse, Portugal had dragged Brazil into its marginal position in the British-dominated mercantilist system through a treaty that made Brazilians purchase British manufactures in return for Portuguese wines and agricultural products. Indeed, after 1750 Brazil produced large amounts of cotton to meet England's Industrial Revolution needs.[79]

During a Portuguese resurgence, financed by Brazilian gold, under the long reign of João V (from 1706 to 1750), emigration to Brazil had risen to six thousand a year until banned by the Portuguese government in 1720 due to alarm caused by the population drain from the mother country. Then, in the third quarter of the eighteenth century, Portugal was run in the name of a weak king by Sebastião José de Carvalho e Mello (b. 1699), Marques de Pombal. Named secretary of state for war and foreign affairs in mid-1750, this exceptionally talented individual, who had represented Portugal in London and Vienna, became virtual dictator, with the authority to rebuild both Lisbon and the government in the aftermath of a devastating earthquake in early 1755. In addition to expelling the Jesuits from Brazil in 1759, forcing over six hundred of them out of that subcontinent (initiating a decade-long break with the Vatican), and abolishing Indian slavery in 1775, this towering figure of Portuguese history remerged Maranhão–Grão Pará with Brazil and attempted to set Portugal's administrative and economic houses in order. Following his resignation with the king's death in 1777, many of his policies were reversed under Queen María I, disconcerting some Brazilians.[80]

The Brazil of this period had changed substantially since the beginning of the century. Not only had many thousands of colonists abandoned their agricultural pursuits and rushed to Minas Gerais in quest of wealth for themselves or their masters, but this El Dorado also served as a magnet for immigration from Portugal as well as from other European countries. Although mulattoes had become a significant social element on the coast, it was in Minas Gerais during the first half of the 1700s that African-European miscegenation made them far more numerous than the Indian-European *mamelucos*. By 1818, the country's 1.9 million blacks and 628,000 mulattoes composed 70 percent of Brazil's total population of 3.6 million.[81]

The latter part of the eighteenth century brought events elsewhere that would have a powerful effect upon Brazil's affairs. Establishment of an independent and republican United States was followed by the French Revolution. Some Brazilians, already resentful of the limitation of trade with Portugal, were further alienated by a 1785 Portuguese decree prohibiting Brazilian manufacturing. Subversive talk was rife in urban centers, and in 1789 an unsuccessful conspiracy known as the Inconfidéncia Mineira and still celebrated as the harbinger of independence was broken up.[82] Its leader, Joaquím José da Silva Xavier (b. 1748), known as Tiradentes for his part-time work as a dentist, was executed as a warning to other discontented elements.

A chain reaction of independence plots in Rio de Janeiro (1794), Bahia (1798), and Pernambuco (1801)—although quickly repressed—reflected a dangerous degree of alienation, which would be augmented in the early years of the nineteenth century by the Spanish American wars of independence. By this time hundreds of Brazilians had returned home with degrees from Coimbra University in Lisbon. Most of these "cosmopolitans" viewed Portugal as too limited a country both intellectually and economically, preferring French Enlightenment philosophy combined with some interest in Adam Smith and nascent British liberalism. As the nineteenth century dawned, these disenchanted intellectuals catalyzed a heady mix of growing pride in Brazil, an increased awareness of US and French republican experiences, and economic dissatisfaction—especially over "oppressive" and "onerous" taxes such as the *dizimo,* or tithe, tax and the royal monopoly on the tobacco trade, which was leased to the highest bidder.[83] Hence, many came to view the champions of independence as heroes even if their efforts proved fruitless. When their adventures turned out disastrously, a growing proportion hailed them as patriots and martyrs rather than traitors.

Seeds of Dissatisfaction and Nationalist Stirrings in Spanish America

Questioning the need for European rule was not limited to Brazil. In the viceroyalty of Peru, the European minority were traumatized in 1780 when José Gabriel Condorcanqui Noguera (b. 1732), a physically imposing, moderately wealthy, and educated landowning *mestizo cacique* ("recognized community leader"), organized a large-scale revolutionary uprising in the Cuzco region. This distant descendant of preconquest royalty took the name Tupac Amaro II, after the Inca leader who had risen against the Spaniards in 1572, and he laid siege to the ancient capital of the Incan empire that took an army of 15,000 to break. Although crushed by late 1781 at a cost of around 100,000 lives (out of the viceroyalty's total population of

1.2 million), this native uprising left a legacy of fear on the part of the elites. In reaction the government undercut the rest of the Inca elite by leveling them down to the status of common "Indios."[84] The Peruvian revolt was accompanied by a series of isolated *comunero* rebellions in scattered parts of New Granada, stemming from resistance to the Bourbon reforms.

On top of these unsettling events came traumatizing word of Haiti's violent revolution. There, a revolt against the French began in 1791 and resulted in total independence by 1804—with the extermination of the country's European population. These were developments that threatened the well-being if not the survival of the elites in other colonies, and distant Spain seemed unresponsive and preoccupied with European affairs. Then, too, the United States had carried on a successful struggle for independence, achieving it in the 1780s—albeit with essential French assistance. While that intervention was addressed against long-term bellicose rival England by a French monarchy, European geopolitics could take strange turns, so keeping a weather eye out for an opportunity was only prudent.

Moreover, and underlying the reservations of many of the economic elite, by the latter part of the eighteenth century Spain was an inadequate industrial supplier and a confining trading partner for its growing New World colonies. Britain, by way of sharp contrast, was well advanced into the Industrial Revolution and experiencing rapid expansion of trade, particularly with Latin America, from where payment for British goods in silver was highly attractive within the prevailing mercantilist system. As the original conquest and settlement of the leading colonies was by now two and a half centuries in the past, the structure of society and relations among groups had altered significantly from the early colonial era. Adjustment to this transformation within the bounds of empire was desirable, but if the mother country was not prepared to go halfway, then other options at least merited consideration. As Voss caught the mood, "Expressing concerns and grievances steadily gave way to envisioning new bases for the reconstruction of relations within regional societies, within the empire—and even outside it."[85] This tendency would broaden and deepen during the early years of the new century. It would gain impetus from the monumental European struggle pitting Britain against Napoleon's quest for dominance.

Notes

1. Howard J. Wiarda, *Dilemmas of Democracy in Latin America: Crises and Opportunities* (Lanham, MD: Rowman & Littlefield, 2005), p. 6.

2. See Bernard F. Reilly, *The Contest of Christian and Muslim Spain, 1031–1175* (Cambridge, MA: Blackwell, 1992), and Roger Collins, *The Arab Conquest of Spain, 710–797* (Oxford: Blackwell, 1989). A sound briefer treatment is in N. P. Macdonald, *The Making of Brazil: Portuguese Roots 1500–1822* (Sussex, UK: Book Guild, 1996), pp. 3–48.

3. Wiarda, *Dilemmas*, p. 5.

4. Howard J. Wiarda, *Politics in Iberia: The Political Systems of Spain and Portugal* (New York: HarperCollins, 1993), p. 23. Very useful are Henry Kamen, *Empire: How Spain Became a World Power, 1492–1763* (New York: HarperCollins, 2003), and Hugh Thomas, *Rivers of Gold: The Rise of the Spanish Empire from Columbus to Magellan* (New York: Random House, 2004).

5. Peter F. Klarén, *Peru: Society and Nationhood in the Andes* (New York: Oxford University Press, 2000), provides a wealth of detail on the conquest and settlement.

6. Howard J. Wiarda, *The Soul of Latin America* (New Haven: Yale University Press, 2001), pp. 87–97, 156–174, provides depth on this topic, as does Wiarda, *Corporatism and National Development in Latin America* (Boulder, CO: Westview Press, 1981).

7. John Edwards, *The Spain of the Catholic Monarchs 1474–1520* (Madden, MA: Blackwell, 2000), p. 142, as well as Kamen, *Empire*, pp. 3–47.

8. John Lynch, *Spain Under the Hapsburgs*, 2nd ed., Vol. 1, *Empire and Absolutism 1516–1598* (Oxford, UK: Blackwell, 1981), p. 61. See also Kamen, *Empire*, pp. 49–93. A good deal of detail is provided in Stafford Poole, *Juan de Ovando: Governing the Spanish Empire in the Reign of Philip II* (Norman: University of Oklahoma Press, 2004).

9. Consult Kamen, *Empire*, pp. 151–195.

10. John Lynch, *Spain Under the Hapsburgs*, 2nd ed., Vol. 2, *Spain and America 1598–1700* (Oxford, UK: Blackwell, 1981), pp. 135–137.

11. Lynch, *Spain*, Vol. 2, pp. 1–11, 38, 200.

12. Wiarda, *Politics*, p. 32.

13. Lynch, *Spain*, Vol. 2, pp. 14–22.

14. Ibid., pp. 66–67.

15. Ibid., p. 249.

16. See Kamen, *Empire*, pp. 331–437.

17. Consult John Lynch, *Bourbon Spain 1700–1808* (Oxford, UK: Blackwell, 1989), as well as Kamen, *Empire*, pp. 437–485.

18. Lynch, *Bourbon Spain*, pp. 169–170.

19. Ibid., p. 329.

20. Ibid., p. 247. A brilliant analysis of policymaking during the ensuing period is found in Stanley J. Stein and Barbara H. Stein, *Apogee of Empire: Spain and New Spain in the Age of Charles III* (Baltimore: Johns Hopkins University Press, 2003).

21. Stein and Stein, *Apogee*, p. 72. See also Kamen, *Empire*, pp. 285–329.

22. Stein and Stein, *Apogee*, pp. 145–185.

23. Ibid., p. 355.

24. Lynch, *Bourbon Spain*, p. 173.

25. Ibid., p. 337.

26. Kenneth Maxwell, *Pombal: Paradox of the Enlightenment* (Cambridge, UK.: Cambridge University Press, 1995).

27. Lynch, *Bourbon Spain*, p. 375.

28. The classic work on this topic is Hugh Thomas, *The Conquest of Mexico* (London: Hutchinson, 1993), amplified in his encyclopedic *Rivers of Gold*. Those conquered are sympathetically treated in George C. Valliant, *Aztecs of Mexico: Origin, Rise, and Fall of the Aztec*

Nation, Rev. by Suzannah B. Valliant (Garden City, NY: Doubleday, 1962). For a wealth of detail about Cortez and his companions, see Hugh Thomas, *Who's Who of the Conquistadores* (London, UK: Cassell, 2000).

29. See Thomas, *Conquest,* pp. 98–398, for events through this setback.

30. John Lynch, *Spain 1516–1598: From Nation to World Empire* (Oxford, UK: Blackwell, 1991), pp. 218–225, and Thomas, *Conquest,* pp. 405–406.

31. Thomas, *Conquest,* pp. 454–530.

32. Lynch, *Spain 1516–1598,* pp. 214–215.

33. Lynch, *Spain,* Vol. 2, pp. 219–222.

34. Frank Tannenbaum, *Mexico: The Struggle for Peace and Bread* (New York: Knopf, 1964), p. 36. This unique Columbia University scholar spent more time in Mexico than other observers of his generation, getting to know individuals in all walks of life.

35. Edwards, *Spain,* p. 172.

36. After a sixfold increase in the last quarter of the sixteenth century, the Potosí mines began a long, slow decline in production that dropped its financial contribution from seven million pesos to only two million. For the Mexican economy in this period, see Richard L. Garner, *Economic Growth and Change in Bourbon Mexico* (Gainesville: University Press of Florida, 1993).

37. Lynch, *Bourbon Spain,* pp. 331–332.

38. Roderic Ai Camp, *Politics in Mexico: The Democratic Transformation,* 4th ed. (New York: Oxford University Press, 2003), p. 25.

39. Ibid., p. 26.

40. Lynch, *Bourbon Spain,* p. 349.

41. John Hemming, *The Conquest of the Incas* (New York: Harcourt Brace Jovanovich, 1970), is the best single source on this part of the Spanish colonial period, at least down through the 1570s.

42. As history has repeatedly demonstrated, the rash bravery, unbridled ambition, and exaggerated ethnocentrism that leads to conquest of other peoples often leads to personalist imperial ventures, very few of which turn out successfully.

43. Hemming, *Conquest,* provides a very lively and detailed account of events through the mid and late 1500s.

44. Ibid., p. 407.

45. Lynch, *Spain,* Vol. 2, p. 233.

46. Lynch, *Bourbon Spain,* pp. 334–335.

47. Klarén, *Peru,* p. 62.

48. Ibid., p. 89.

49. Ibid., p. 98.

50. Lynch and Klarén provide somewhat differing demographic statistics, not unusual in light of the remoteness in time and the nature of sources.

51. Stein and Stein, *Apogee,* pp. 51–53.

52. Stuart F. Voss, *Latin America in the Middle Period, 1750–1929* (Wilmington, DE: Scholarly Resources Books, 2001), p. 37.

53. Lynch, *Bourbon Spain,* p. 343.

54. Klarén, *Peru,* p. 103.

55. Lynch, *Bourbon Spain,* pp. 336–337. Voss, *Latin America,* pp. 19–20, discusses the "decolonization of the colonial bureaucracy."

56. David Bushnell and Neil Macaulay, *The Emergence of Latin America in the Nineteenth Century* (New York: Oxford University Press, 1988), p. 11.

57. Jaime E. Rodríguez O., *The Independence of Spanish America* (Cambridge, UK: Cambridge University Press, 1998), p. 19.

58. Anthony McFarland, *Colombia Before Independence* (Cambridge, UK: Cambridge University Press, 1993), pp. 8–16, covers these early years.

59. These developments are treated in ibid., pp. 187–208.

60. Ibid., pp. 71–79.

61. See ibid., pp. 215–277.

62. Lynch, *Bourbon Spain,* p. 180.

63. Lynch, *Spain,* Vol. 2, pp. 194–195.

64. Macdonald, *Making of Brazil,* p. 337.

65. This section is an adaptation of Ronald M. Schneider, *"Order and Progress": A Political History of Brazil* (Boulder, CO: Westview Press, 1991), pp. 24–32, and Ronald M. Schneider, *Brazil: Culture and Politics in a New Industrial Powerhouse* (Boulder, CO: Westview Press, 1996), pp. 35–37. For greater detail see Macdonald, *Making of Brazil,* pp. 93–445.

66. Caio Prado Júnior, *The Colonial Background of Modern Brazil* (Berkeley and Los Angeles: University of California Press, 1969), pp. 4–5.

67. Nathaniel H. Leff, *Underdevelopment and Development in Brazil,* Vol. 2, *Reassessing the Obstacles to Economic Development* (London: Allen & Unwin, 1982), p. 103.

68. Consult Charles R. Boxer, *The Portuguese Seaborne Empire, 1415–1825* (New York: Knopf, 1969). Macdonald, *Making of Brazil,* pp. 51–89, covers 1500–1549 in detail.

69. The late sixteenth century and early 1600s are treated in Macdonald, *Making of Brazil,* pp. 93–198.

70. See ibid., pp. 105–113.

71. The writings of Victor Nunes Leal, available only in Portuguese, are the best foundation for understanding this phenomenon.

72. Lynch, *Spain,* Vol. 2, pp. 61–63.

73. Ibid., pp. 79–82.

74. Macdonald, *Making of Brazil,* pp. 205–238. See also Charles R. Boxer, *The Dutch in Brazil, 1624–1654* (Oxford, UK: Clarendon Press, 1957).

75. Macdonald, *Making of Brazil,* p. 164.

76. See Clodomir Vianna Moog, *Bandeirantes and Pioneers* (New York: Knopf, 1964).

77. Consult Macdonald, *Making of Brazil,* pp. 294–304.

78. Ibid., pp. 305–312.

79. This "double dependency" resulted from the 1703 Treaty of Methuen. See ibid., pp. 347–358. A classic study still meriting close attention is Charles R. Boxer, *The Golden Age of Brazil: Growing Pains of a Colonial Society, 1695–1750* (Berkeley and Los Angeles: University of California Press, 1962).

80. Macdonald, *Making of Brazil,* pp. 339–346.

81. Ibid., p. 408.

82. Consult Kenneth Maxwell, *Conflicts and Conspiracies: Brazil and Portugal, 1750–1808* (New York: Columbia University Press, 1973). A brief discussion is contained in Macdonald, *Making of Brazil,* pp. 377–379.

83. Macdonald, *Making of Brazil,* pp. 380–381.

84. Hemming, *Conquest,* pp. 118–120.

85. Voss, *Latin America,* p. 37.

3

A Region of New Nations from Colonialism to Consolidation

Independence for Latin America combined the selfish economic concerns and personal political ambitions of many actors with the lofty ideals and unrealistic expectations of others. Only a handful of the educated elite were imbued with ideas of liberty, republicanism, and democracy stemming from the US example and the very brief flame of the French Revolution—before it was put out by Napoleonic imperial floodwaters. For the vast majority these developments were virtually unknown or essentially irrelevant. Most Hispanic Americans were passive observers or swept up in the course of events against their will, and politically active elements were in most instances chiefly influenced by perceptions of where advantage lay for their particular interests and where opportunity existed for their ambitions. Landowner-merchant conflict interacted with the *peninsulares-criollos* rivalries in ways that were sometimes crosscutting, but often reinforcing. As one perceptive scholar catches the mood, "By 1808 for Indians, *castas* (mixed bloods), and Creoles alike the Bourbon crown seemed no longer sufficiently protective of their separate interests as a parent ruler, nor sufficiently impartial in mediating conflict and disputes as an arbiter."[1]

The basic common feature with respect to the quite variegated independence movements was that they were decisively facilitated by the monumental and protracted struggle, which we know as the Napoleonic Wars, for supremacy in Europe between globally dominant Britain and continentally hegemonic France. Had Spain not been occupied and thus temporarily incorporated into Bonaparte's domains, its Western Hemisphere possessions, with the exception of Haiti, would not have become independent at this particular time. Spain might very well have managed to preserve its control for at least another generation. Instead, in most countries, independence was obtained by 1830, although with great variations in the effort involved and the leadership generated. The ensuing decades—functionally equivalent to the 1970s through 2005 for most of Africa and much of Asia—witnessed the frustration of high hopes and a substantial persistence of old patterns behind a facade of rhetoric and cosmetic change. More often than not this process took place within a context of instability mixed with dictatorial experiences, as has been the case in the early years of almost all nations in all parts of the world. The economic conditions prevailing in the early decades of independence complicated the construction of stable constitutional governments. Expecting that the dismantling of colonial restraints on Latin American economies would produce a wave of wealth—which in their eyes had always before been expropriated by greedy *peninsulares* and their exploitive Spanish merchant partners—Creoles found their hopes quickly dashed.

Indeed, in many ways the region's economies were poorer and less integrated in the first decades after independence than they had been in the late colonial period. Political disorder was both a cause and a result of this perverse situation. Unable to rely on the old colonial-era taxes for revenue, new governments found themselves in very tight financial straits. Their resulting weakness contributed to political instability, which in turn impeded the reorganization of economic systems disrupted by the independence struggles. In some areas damage from the wars was extensive, and even where the destruction of human life and economic resources was less widespread, disruptions in financial arrangements and systems of labor relations provoked a decline in important economic sectors. Low economic productivity combined with an inadequate financial infrastructure limited both capital accumulation and inflows from abroad. Moreover, in much of the region, new ways had to be found to coerce labor after the tribute and labor drafts of Indians were eliminated. Hence, overall, fundamental economic and social change trailed independence by three decades—in some cases considerably more. A resurgence of development and liberalism would only occur around midcentury under a new generation of leaders not directly involved in the independence struggles. To differing degrees they would eliminate some of the most extreme restrictions on individual liberties and at least partially dismantle the legal framework of corporate special privileges. Where this progress went farthest, as under Benito Juárez in Mexico, and resulted in stringent anticlerical measures—not just rhetoric—it would provoke a sometimes violent reaction. Only in Mexico, however, would reaction triumph, and there it required European armed intervention.

The way in which independence was obtained may have a greatly attenuated impact upon the political life of Latin American countries today, but timing certainly does influence those few left out of the original wave during the Napoleonic era. It is, however, clear that the independence process heavily conditioned the first generation of national life and also significantly influenced the next one. This postindependence era of trial and error produced a number of fascinating figures and dramatic events but, generally, disappointingly little progress or positive change. Variations among countries were significant, often substantial, and in the 1850s and 1860s set the stage for great differentiation during the final decades of the nineteenth century as some countries began to find their way while others marked time or stumbled into dead ends.[2]

Politically, Latin America was ill prepared for independence, a fact that would have grave and long-lasting consequences. In Wiarda's formulation:

> The Spanish (and Portuguese) colonial system, exploitative and authoritarian, had provided absolutely no training in self-government and certainly none in democracy. There were in the newly independent states of Latin America almost no institutions, little of what we now call "civil society," none of what that early-nineteenth century French observer of North American society Alexis de Tocqueville termed a "web of associability" capable of holding society together and mediating between government and governed.[3]

Moreover, the initial rulers of each country, as well as their opponents, would arise from the particular processes and defining events of the country's emergence from colonial status. This fundamental fact led to a significant division between those countries that would long be plagued with a violent pattern of *caudillo* politics, those that would be able to move beyond this negative heritage within a long generation, and the very few that could avoid this rudimentary level of political life—Brazil being the major example and Chile a Spanish American exception. For most of the region, introduction to independent political life was by way of *caudillos* produced by the wars of independence. As cogently explained by Lewis:

> The breakdown of civilization, the spread of chaos, the inability to conceive of a national interest, the parochial outlook, and the easy recourse to plunder that blurred the distinction between guerrilla warfare and banditry produced the local political buccaneer who acted on his own initiative without permission from his nominal commander. With no central authority to rein him in, he could consolidate his local power and enrich himself by pillaging and eliminating his immediate rivals. The wars legitimatised him, made him a prestigious local figure with an armed band at his command.[4]

The independence movement was catalyzed, facilitated, and in part caused not by any example set by the French Revolution, but by the resulting Napoleonic Wars. This monumental and protracted struggle for supremacy in Europe (in the context of their times, the world) had a greater impact on Latin American people than any other event before or after. Through entering into alliance with France in 1795, Spain had opened up a Pandora's box of unforeseen consequences that created economic and political distance between the Iberian mother countries and their American colonies. England, the dominant sea power, used its naval forces to reduce and eventually cut communications, forcing Spain to suspend its already leaky trade monopoly. The ensuing experience with trading legally with other colonies and neutral countries, especially the United States, stoked Creole desires for greater economic self-determination.

The political divide widened and deepened after Charles IV guaranteed Napoleon passage through Spain to invade Portugal, a staunch British ally. The immediate effect was the Portuguese government's move to Brazil and temporarily transforming it into the empire's administrative center. The impact of Spain's error would soon be felt in Spanish America, as in 1808 Napoleon turned on his erstwhile Spanish allies, placing his brother Joseph on the throne in Madrid. Both Charles and his successor, Ferdinand, became French captives, so the "hub of all political authority" for Spain's colonies was removed.[5] Hence, colonial elites struggled with how to maintain control without even the symbol of a monarch at the head of the governmental hierarchy. This loss was truly traumatizing, as New World Spaniards, only a little over three million in a regional population of seventeen million, feared a racial bloodbath such as the one that had recently occurred in Haiti.

This authority vacuum resulted in the elites of both the *peninsulares* and the *criollos* setting up a variety of provisional governments, ostensibly to rule in the king's name, but in the meantime actively advancing their own interests. For at that point the New World bourgeoisie were interested in equality over independence, home rule over separation, and autonomy over emancipation.[6] In Mexico City and Montevideo these caretaker regimes were controlled by *peninsular* loyalists, whereas in Santiago, Caracas, and Bogotá Creoles dominated the provisional juntas. In 1812, a resistance parliament based in Cádiz (under British protection), claiming to represent Spain's colonies as well as the homeland, produced a liberal constitution proclaiming Spain's American possessions to be part of the kingdom, not colonies. Yet the few Creoles participating in that body found themselves grossly underrepresented and virtually powerless. Although in theory Spanish America was entitled to 149 delegates, only 65 took part, two-thirds of them alternates, not the elected members.[7] Back in the New World the spread of *ayuntamientos* ("governing councils") to all major population centers drastically expanded political participation to less substantial businessmen and property owners.[8]

After a careful study of four major cases, a political scientist who set out to test all the generally accepted explanations for revolt against the Spanish throne concludes that "by the beginning of the nineteenth century the Creole elite in all four colonies wanted to nationalize decision-making, appropriating authority for themselves. The critical factor was the political bargaining relationship between local elites and the government of the empire and of each colony."[9] The result of the interruption of royal authority had been that

> conflicts over the allocation of status, power, and wealth in the colonies of the empire remained unresolved when the international crisis struck.
>
> When legitimacy was in question, many groups, both elite Spaniards and Creoles, moved simultaneously to appropriate political legitimacy. . . . Coups and counter coups undermined the legitimacy of each of three colonial governments at the time that the legitimacy of the entire imperial system was in question.[10]

The restoration of Ferdinand to the throne in 1814 pushed Spanish America further toward independence. In Spain twelve thousand liberals were jailed or exiled in a campaign to restore monarchical power, and in the colonies royal use of military force, including substantial reinforcements from the mother country, to repress independence movements hardened Creole resolve. Then, when in 1820 other troops in Cádiz, who were awaiting transportation to reinforce the royalists in Spanish America, mutinied, Ferdinand agreed to liberal reforms. These concessions divided and weakened loyalist support by undermining confidence in the monarchy. Hence, independence struggles, already under way in many parts of the region, forged ahead, proving triumphant during the 1820s. The result was instability and de facto regimes based on the force, not the functioning republican regimes promised during the independence struggles.

Creoles who had expected that freedom from colonial restraints on their commerce would produce a wave of new wealth found their hopes dashed. Political disorder was both a cause and a result of economic malaise. Political instability impeded reorganization of economic systems and stagnant economies added to political dissatisfaction. In varying degrees the independence wars had contributed to this disappointing postindependence economic picture. Where fighting had been intense and prolonged, as in Venezuela, damage from the war was extensive. Even where the destruction of human life and economic resources had been less widespread, disruptions in systems of labor relations and financial arrangements provoked decline in important economic sectors—particularly mining, which in Mexico required half a century to regain preindependence levels of production.[11]

One of the most pressing and, as it proved, enduring problems Latin American nations faced in their first decades of independence was how to establish the legitimacy of their new governments. Impelled by a deeply felt need to break with the colonial era and not follow the path being taken by their ex-rulers, they generally turned to the US republican model without seriously questioning its appropriateness. The lone, but highly important, exception on the mainland was Brazil, but this country was under the same Portuguese royal family, a continuity that the other countries could not duplicate. The other example was Haiti's black empire, a thought that made Hispanic Americans recoil in horror.

Elites were aware that Great Britain, with its parliamentary form of government, was the most advanced country in the world, but to retain monarchy would undermine the Latin Americans' justification for having separated from Spain. Mistakenly, as it proved, there was a upper class-tendency to see Anglo-American political institutions as responsible for the economic progress of England and the United States. Enlightenment ideas of politics were even farther from Latin American reality than from that of France, where the hopefully egalitarian revolution had spawned violent civil strife, followed by popular enchantment with imperial rule by a social upstart. (By the crucial period of the Spanish American wars of independence, the French had a restored the traditional monarchy, imposed upon them essentially by British force of arms.) The real political situation prevailing in Spanish America was one in which

> long term social, political and economic change had differentiated the Spanish American empire internally and had led to the formation of consciously competing groups. When imperial legitimacy broke down, these preexisting groups turned from competition over status and wealth to competition for power. Their unrestrained conflict in the political arena led to a collapse of colonial legitimacy.[12]

Overview

In many ways Brazil experienced an exceptionally easy separation from its mother country, involving a period in which Portugal's government was transferred to Rio de Janeiro, and once this transitional period was over, the heir to the Portuguese throne remained as prince regent. He subsequently became Brazil's monarch, and his son would occupy the throne until 1889. Thus Brazil avoided the double rupture of breaking both with the mother country and with the world's established source of legitimizing political authority, that is, divine right monarchy. At the time, the United States was the only republic in the world—still unproven in a myriad of ways.

Mexico's path to independence was also rather drawn out, but dramatically more violent as popular movements were bloodily repressed before an upstart adventurer proclaimed himself emperor and was soon ousted by force. This train of events opened the way for a long era of *caudillo* politics, in sharp contrast to Brazil's stable monarchy. López de Santa Ana of Mexico and Pedro II of Brazil were antithetical figures, dominating the political stage for their country's first generation of independence, the former into the 1850s, and the latter nearly twice as long.

Argentina's independence came early and with little bloodshed, largely because royalist forces were very limited in this sparsely populated area of—at that time— little economic value. Its liberator would then be off across the Andes to help Chile win its independence and subsequently to fight against Spanish forces in Peru. As a result, there would be a protracted period of instability before a dictatorial *caudillo* imposed order in Argentina. The ensuing Rosas era, lasting just past midcentury, would be followed by efforts, stretching through the 1860s, to unite the coastal metropolitan area to the interior.

Northern South America experienced a long and bloody armed struggle to free itself from the Spanish yoke, resulting by the late 1820s in Simón Bolívar's short-lived Gran Colombia. With Venezuela and Ecuador splitting off in 1830, what remained struggled along without a dominant leader until the slow evolution of an elitist two-party system in the 1850s and 1860s. Venezuela, largely a ranching society, spawned a durable *caudillo* pattern of politics that would continue into the twentieth century, and Ecuador would be racked by conflict between the sierra area around Quito (the regional capital from colonial days) and the coastal region led by merchants of the port city of Guayaquil—a conflict persisting for well over a century. Peru, center of Spanish rule and settlement on the continent, resisted independence currents and had it imposed militarily by Bolívar's armies in the latter half of the 1820s. Hence, the legitimacy vacuum had the most serious effects there, where efforts to construct a viable political system proved extremely difficult, but *caudillo* rule and its legacy were avoided. Upper Peru, renaming itself Bolivia, would seek confederation with its much larger neighbor. When this proved impossible, owing to intransigent opposition by Chile, it wallowed in instability for the next generation.

Chile, having won its independence early with considerable aid from Argentina, enjoyed the best initial leadership of any Latin American country and built the foundations of a stable representative political system in the 1830s. Paraguay, where Spanish presence had been all but absent during the colonial period, would be home to sultanistic dictators, and Uruguay, created at the end of the 1820s, largely at Britain's insistence, as a buffer between Brazil and Argentina, would be subject to heavy interference by its neighbors.

Central America's independence was largely a by-product of Mexico's, but Cuba would remain under Spanish rule for the rest of the century (along with Puerto Rico)—as many parts of the Caribbean and several small enclaves on the South American coast would remain until the 1960s. Thus, the only real battle for independence in the Caribbean took place in Haiti, where the long bloody struggle was won by 1804. The Dominican Republic would split off from Haiti only at mid-century.

Brazil: Peaceful Separation and
Preservation of Monarchy

Both in gaining independence and in filling the legitimacy vacuum that ensued, Brazil's experience differed markedly from that of all parts of Spanish America. Its remaining a monarchy for another full generation resulted in unique facets that would last throughout the nineteenth century. (This uniqueness would be diminished, in a relative sense, only by the autocratic kinglike behavior of a few post-1871 Hispanic American rulers, including Porfirio Díaz in Mexico or Antonio Guzmán Blanco in Venezuela, who would act in quasi-monarchical ways.)[13] The most important permanent result was Brazil's holding together its vast area, in contrast to the amputation of half of Mexico by the United States and the fragmentation of Spanish South America.

The early nineteenth century found Portugal in another of its dynastic binds. Queen María I, an eccentric on her way to outright madness, had married her uncle Pedro, who held the anomalous title of king-consort.[14] With her certification as insane in 1792, their son João ran the government, assuming the title of prince regent five years later. In September 1807, Napoléon issued an ultimatum that Portugal must declare war against Britain, its longtime protector, or face the consequences of French occupation. Hence, in late November, the Portuguese royal family, accompanied by the civil and military bureaucracies, set sail for Rio de Janeiro under British naval escort. During a brief stopover at Salvador in January 1808, the prince regent (the future King João VI) opened Brazil's ports to trade with Britain and other countries—as much a price for British support as a sop to the colonists. Subsequently, manufacturing was permitted, institutions of higher education were founded, and naval and military academies were established. Most important in the long run, a new army composed of a mixture of Portuguese troops and local recruits was created. To coopt the local elites, in 1815 Brazil was accorded the status of a kingdom, formally coequal with Portugal—for João had declined to return to Lisbon.

By the end of the Napoleonic Wars, the colony was outgrowing its mother country, which at that time had a population just over 3 million, not intimidating to Brazilians, who by now numbered 4.5 million and were well aware of Portugal's weakness and relative poverty. Portuguese liberals convoked a legislature in which they enjoyed a safe majority. Not surprisingly, its measures to reestablish most of Portugal's previous domination catalyzed separatist sentiment in Brazil. Thus, when João, who had become king in 1816, was summoned home in 1821 by a parliament that had taken power following a revolt, he advised his twenty-two-year-old son, Pedro, who was staying behind as prince regent, to lead the independence movement should it appear to be getting out of control.[15] Pedro soon had cause to heed his father's advice. In the midst of clashes between Brazilian-born elements and Portuguese troops, he rejected an October 1821 order of the Portuguese parliament to return to Lisbon. Pedro's "Fico" ("I'm staying") of January 9, 1822, was followed by the appointment of a cabinet headed by native Brazilian José Bonifácio de Andrada e Silva (b. 1763). Efforts by Lisbon to tighten its hold over Brazil resulted in Pedro's dramatic cry of "Independence or death!" on September 7, 1822—commemorated as Brazil's Independence Day. Within ninety days of this challenge, he was crowned (on his twenty-fourth birthday) "Constitutional Emperor and Perpetual Defender of Brazil."[16]

Commencing national life under the rule of the individual who had been governing in the name of the mother country enabled Brazil to avoid the vacuum of legitimate authority that plagued most of its neighbors, whose path to independence combined rupture with Spain and adoption of a radically different and untried political regime. Brazil's emancipation was quick, although not totally peaceful. Repeated skirmishes and prolonged confrontations with provincial authorities and Portuguese troops loyal to João VI and the Lisbon government were handled by Brazilian troops under the command of Francisco Alves de Lima e Silva, giving a first taste of battle to the country's leading military hero—and important political stabilizer—his son Luíz (b. 1803). While these conflicts were still continuing in the north, Brazil's first constituent assembly began to function on May 3, 1823, but after six months of executive-legislative conflict, Pedro used the army to shut the assembly down (exiling José Bonifácio until 1829). The emperor's version of a basic governmental charter was promulgated by decree on March 25, 1824. He appointed provincial presidents and senators (for life, from lists submitted by provincial legislatures); the lower house was indirectly elected by a very restricted suffrage.

Despite violent reaction to the establishment of a centralized regime, Brazil's territorial integrity was preserved. As if a spate of regional uprisings were not problems enough for the new nation, the emperor engaged in an expensive and unsuccessful war with today's Argentina over what would eventually become Uruguay. Indeed, by the end of the decade, the stiff-necked, impulsive, and short-tempered monarch found himself in an untenable position.[17] The ouster of French king Charles X in July 1830 had a sharp impact upon those political figures who feared Pedro's actions were influenced by the fact that he was still heir to the Portuguese throne. In the intensifying legislative-executive conflict, the military leaned in the opposite direction from 1823, leading the emperor to abdicate in favor of his five-year-old son, Pedro. In the tripartite regency that ensued, General Lima e Silva saw his initial dominance undercut by establishment of the National Guard as a counterweight to the army. Liberal Diogo Antônio Feijó (b. 1784), who as minister of justice supervised this new armed body, came out on top. The Additional Act of August 1834, which modified the governmental system in the direction of decentralization, eliminated the Council of State and instituted a single regent—a post to which Feijó was elected in April 1835 by a national vote of 2,826 to 2,251. Faced with a resurgence of the Conservative's strength, he gave way in September 1837, being replaced in April 1838 by Pedro de Araújo Lima, the future Marques de Olinda.

Back in power, the Conservatives curbed provincial autonomy through the Interpretive Law of 1839, a blow that led the Liberal Party to engineer a parliamentary coup that brought Pedro II to the throne in July 1840 at the ripe age of fourteen.[18] The man who would be the young emperor's chief adviser and military bulwark, Luíz Alves de Lima e Silva, followed up a successful 1841 campaign in Maranhão with defeat of a Feijó-led São Paulo revolt the next year (gaining each time a military promotion and a higher patent of nobility). He could then turn to the revolt in Rio Grande do Sul that had been festering since 1835, restoring order by 1845. Elevated to the Dukedom of Caxias (commoners John Churchill, First Duke of Marlborough, and Arthur Wellesley, First Duke of Wellington, had received dukedoms in Britain in analogous situations) Latin America's most accomplished military commander was named commander of the Brazilian troops sent in 1852 to help overthrow Argentine dictator Juan Manuel de Rosas, subsequently becoming war minister, a post he would hold much of the time into the 1870s—along with being president of the council of ministers (prime minister) in 1856, 1861–1862, 1866, and 1875–1878.

Meanwhile, by 1850 the elements were in place that would allow Brazil to enjoy political stability accompanied by modest economic development and limited social progress down well into the 1880s. Its population had risen to near 7.5 million from just over 5.3 million in 1830, and Rio de Janeiro had grown to a city of 250,000. With British pressure bringing the slave trade to an end after 1852, more than 2.5 million slaves made up one-third of the country's inhabitants. Nevertheless, as Brazil attacked the slavery problem gradually, by 1872 over 85 percent of Brazilians were free (8.6 million out of 10.1 million). Although the main flood of immigration was still ahead, recent European arrivals were already a key component of the population in the southernmost states. The increase in economic development had averaged 1.6 percent annually between 1822 and midcentury, but industrialization remained in low gear.

Although its great expansion was still to come, coffee already provided half the country's export—twice that accounted for by sugar, which it had surpassed in the 1830s. From Rio de Janeiro state, coffee was moving into the interior of São Paulo state, with a consequent fundamental shift in the locus of economic power—first reflected in the emergence of the coffee nobility as a social force, but having more profound political ramifications by the 1870s. In the 1830s, Brazil supplied 30 percent of the world's coffee, rising to 40 percent in the next decade and to 50 percent from the 1850s through the 1870s. As the center-south became the repository of the nation's wealth, railroad construction picked up steam, tying

BRAZIL

coffee-producing areas to booming ports, although, given Brazil's great size, not only transportation but even communications were essentially inadequate.

During the monarchy's heyday, a fairly homogeneous political class oriented to national unity bolstered stability. The large landowners and export producers enjoyed considerable political power, but there remained significant scope for autonomous action by middle-sector political-bureaucratic elements occupying the higher echelons of the centralized state administrative apparatus. The elite's ability to coopt emerging urban elements rested upon a *cartorial* state, in which appointments were exchanged for electoral support and public employment was used to provide positions in response to the clientelistic political needs of the elite. Away from the capital, decentralized but politically potent power was exercised by the provincial landed class. Given the great distances and poor communications, the Brazilian state—even at the apogee of the monarchy—had to recognize the existence of powerful local interests. These could constrain policy choices of the national government, although not force it to follow their preferred course of action.[19] In the final analysis, the emperor remained the respected and legitimate balance wheel of the system—something sorely lacking in other Latin American countries.

As the fourth branch of the Brazilian constitutional system, the moderating power *(poder moderador),* the emperor could change the party in office when in his judgment such a change would reduce legislative-executive friction. Elections were indirect, with increasingly stringent income requirements moving up the ladder from local voters to provincial electors and on to those eligible to be elected. The Conservative Party, backed up by the National Guard and often manipulated by the emperor, and the Liberal Party were the linchpins in a system in which controlled elections for the national legislature were a means of legitimizing a ministry that had already been chosen by the emperor. During his long reign (1840–1889) Pedro II alternated the parties in office eleven times, always taking into account an intricate political game of intraelite interests and ambitions, which he understood as well as he did the maneuverings of notables at the provincial level to build patronage structures and establish ties with influential figures in the capital. Of course, the price for this stability was the loss of any capacity for parties to serve as instruments of modernization and change, which, by the way, political parties did very little of at this time in other Latin American countries.

When the Liberals returned to power in 1862, they had to turn their energies to a major international war that strained the nation's resources to the limit and allowed the Conservatives to regain control of the central government in time to garner the credit for the war's eventual success. Uruguay's independence had brought little stability to the River Plate region, and during the early 1860s, Brazil intervened to aid the Colorado Party (liberals) in its struggle with the Blanco Party (conservatives), who turned to Paraguayan dictator Francisco Solano López for help. Small, but highly militarized, Paraguay at the end of 1864 sent forces across Argentine and Brazilian soil to reach Uruguay. With a population in excess of nine million and the beginnings of an industrial plant, Brazil, like the North in the contemporary US Civil War, had significant material advantages over its warlike foe. At the outbreak of hostilities, Paraguay had 64,000 men under arms to only 18,000 for Brazil. When the Triple Alliance (Brazil, Argentina, and Uruguay) saw their 65,000 troops—57,000 of them Brazilian—bog down in front of Humaitá, Caxias agreed to take command, but only if the emperor brought the Conservatives back to office.[20] Caxias captured Humaitá in August 1868 and occupied the Paraguayan capital at the beginning of 1869.

The war had a profound impact upon Brazil, as during the more than five years it lasted, nearly 200,000 men were mobilized, some 139,000 sent to the war zone, and at least 30,000 killed or wounded. The burdensome financial cost fed inflation and forced the Brazilian government to increase its foreign debt substantially. When the National Guard, which had provided a power base to regional political dynasties, was absorbed into the army, the political system never fully recovered from the dislocations and strains intensified by the war. Upset at having been ousted abruptly from power, the Liberals initiated a decade in opposition by issuing a manifesto in 1869 calling for electoral reform, elimination of the moderating power, and even the abolition of slavery. In 1870 alienated Liberals formed the Republican Party to work for an end to the monarchy, which nonetheless would survive another two decades. So Brazil successfully navigated the treacherous voyage from colony to nation (at a time when Germany and Italy had not yet fully achieved unification). But this accomplishment contrasted sharply to the Spanish American experiences.

Mexico: *Caudillo* Dominance and Foreign Intervention

Events in New Spain, that giant-sized viceroyalty stretching from California across to Texas and down through Central America, were critically important to Spain. The source of two-thirds of Spain's colonial revenues, especially silver production, the region, governed out of Mexico City, had a population of over 6.5 million (half of all Spanish subjects in the Western Hemisphere—overwhelmingly Indians and *mestizos*)—governed by only 15,000 Europeans. Having routed in late 1808 the Creole autonomists who argued that Mexico should be a constitutional kingdom under the Spanish crown, the *peninsulares,* who were absolutists, were determined to preserve the colonial status quo.[21] They deposed the viceroy and persecuted Creoles before welcoming weaker viceroys, whom they were confident they could dominate.

Contesting the legitimacy of this Mexico City regime and other juntas set up in the wake of the French occupation of Spain, popular uprisings began in 1810, led by radical priest Miguel Hidalgo y Costilla (b. 1753), himself an educated *criollo* (whose family had been pushed to the brink of bankruptcy by royal tax collectors) but able to inspire the Indian masses to revolt through his stirring "Grito de Dolores" (Cry of Pain).[22] As Indians made up 60 percent of the population, and *mestizos* another 22 percent, this unprecedented development panicked the dominant European minority—ever mindful of what had recently occurred in Haiti.

By late in the year, Hidalgo's revolutionary army of 80,000 was at the doors of Mexico City, which, with a population of 170,000, was the hemisphere's largest city. During this campaign the movement for independence began to take on characteristics of a race and class war as the revolutionaries attacked the persons and property of not only *peninsulares*, but also Creole elites.

Repulsed outside the capital by better-armed and disciplined government forces, the popular horde executed hundreds of Europeans once back in their own strongholds. By the time of the final defeat of Hidalgo's forces in early 1811 and the execution of their leaders, some two thousand of New Spain's fifteen thousand *peninsulares* had lost their lives. With Hidalgo's death, Father José María Morales y Pavón (b. 1765), of poor *mestizo* origins, assumed his mantle, mobilizing increased Creole as well as *mestizo* support. Militarily unsuccessful, this second great martyr of Mexican independence was captured and executed in late 1815.[23] Restored to power in Spain in May 1814, King Ferdinand had annulled the liberal reforms of the Cádiz provisional *Cortes* (national legislature) that had so upset New World conservatives. In late 1816, a conciliatory new viceroy arrived in Mexico, but 1820 witnessed a revolt in Spain against royal absolutism. The ensuing elections of representatives to a new Cortes in Madrid resulted in victory for Mexican auton-omists, who viewed the prime concerns of the Spanish legislature as largely irrele-vant to their needs, hence to their vision of Mexico's interests. Mexican military officers and merchants and its Catholic Church were anxious over the Spanish lib-erals' threat to the special privileges of the armed forces and religion. Wanting to keep these pillars of the established social order strong, and confident in their abil-ity to keep popular forces in check, they felt a break with Spain provided their best option. Hence, in this very important part of Latin America, independence was a conservative maneuver to preserve stability and order. Against this backdrop, insurgents, led by uneducated *mestizo* Vicente Guerrero (b. 1783), were suffi-ciently troublesome for the viceroy to send Colonel Agustín de Iturbide (b. 1783) against them.[24] This ambitious young officer, feeling inadequately rewarded for his service to the crown, allied his thousand men with the eight hundred of his erst-while foe behind the February 1821 Plan of Iguala. Inspired by Napoléon's ex-ample and events in Haiti, by September of that year this son of a Basque merchant and a Mexican mother had, on his thirty-eighth birthday, crowned him-self "regent of the Mexican Empire," and by May of the following year he would be saluted as Emperor Agustín I. On his maps, his short-lived realm may have run from Oregon to Panama, but he exercised effective control over only a small part of this far-flung domain.

General Guadalupe Victoria (b. 1785 as Miguel Fernández) had risen in revolt against Iturbide in October 1821 and was subsequently supported by the coun-try's future strongman, Antonio López de Santa Ana (b. 1794), son of recent Span-ish immigrants and himself a former royalist officer. After being forced to abdicate in March 1823, Iturbide attempted a comeback sixteen months later and was promptly executed. By the time a federal republic was launched in 1824, with Victoria at its helm, perhaps 600,000 deaths had occurred in the struggles begun in 1810—a tenth of the total population of slightly over 6.2 million. Thus, although Mexico was the first major part of the Spanish Empire to become independent, viable political processes would remain a distant dream as force remained the arbiter of power. In addition, damage to the economy was severe: not only a disturbing drop in silver production, but also the disintegration of large estates and increases in transportation costs, as 90 percent of foreign trade was funneled through the narrow Valley of Mexico to Veracruz corridor.

Establishment of the republic failed to bring a significant measure of stability, much less a taste of democracy. In the absence of political parties, politics within the restricted elites often involved the rival Masonic lodges, the York Rite and the Scottish Rite secret societies being bitterly opposed. Indeed, stability would have to wait until the 1870s, and democracy would flourish only briefly at widely separated intervals until well into the twentieth century. Even the road to consolidation proved more than bumpy; it was traumatic and nearly fatal. The blatant and brutal interference of the United States in midcentury, culminating in US annexation by force of half of Mexico's territory, would obscure the significant leadership talents of its first dominant political figure, Santa Ana. Then the very great promise of the hemisphere's most authentic representative of the indigenous masses to reach power, Benito Juárez, would be undercut by military intervention by France, which diverted him from reform to survival.

By 1828, the York Rite faction of the Mexico City elite won out, engineering the election of General Manuel Gómez Pedraza (b. 1789), negated through a December 1828 coup by Guerrero, Victoria, and Santa Ana. Installed as president, Guerrero abolished slavery in 1829 and forced Spanish citizens to leave the country. Santa Ana, demonstrating unusual bravery in repelling a French invasion, earned promotion to major general and became known as the "Hero of Tampico" on his way to becoming Mexico's "Man of Destiny."[25] Overthrown at the end of 1830 by his centralist vice president, Guerrero attempted a countercoup and was promptly executed. This conflict-ridden scene set the stage for a federalist coup in 1831 that brought Santa Ana to the presidency the following year—for the first of his eleven stints in office. In 1835, this oft-absent-from-the-capital *caudillo*—since he abhorred the routine of governing and having to deal with the demands of whining politicians and clamoring businessmen—suspended the 1824 Constitution and repressed a resulting federalist revolt in the north. He turned power over to his reliable vice president, Valentín Gómez Farias, in 1833 and again in 1835—as he would in 1839, 1842, and 1843, withdrawing to his extensive holdings near Veracruz. By this time the Mexican army was made up of elements that had until recently been fighting against each

BENITO PABLO
JUÁREZ GARCÍA

other—a phenomenon that would be repeated with severely negative effects in the aftermath of the 1910 Revolution.

Captured by Sam Houston's forces when trying to quash the Texas secessionist movement in 1836 (in large part motivated by the Texans' desire to maintain slavery), Santa Ana was coerced into recognizing that region's independence. He soon redeemed himself by repelling a French invasion force at Veracruz in 1838, losing an arm in the process. This resilient *caudillo,* who opportunistically aligned with liberals or conservatives as the occasion dictated, returned to the presidency in 1843, only to be ousted the next year. Then in 1845 the United States annexed Texas (in clear violation of its treaty obligations with Mexico) and shortly thereafter provoked a war. This crisis provided Santa Ana with an opportunity to return from exile. After fighting General Zachary Taylor to a draw in the north at Buena Vista in February 1847, he forced-marched to Veracruz, where he was trounced by General Winfield Scott's vastly superior forces. Santa Ana's failed defense of the capital seven months later brought about his resignation and led to exile in Colombia. Thus the shrewd politician avoided having to sign the humiliating 1848 peace treaty with the United States. As Krause captures the essence of this great *caudillo,* "In Santa Anna there was a semblance—an often grotesque mixture—of royal and popular legitimacy combined."[26] In retrospect, Santa Ana's view that it would be a century before the Mexican people would be fit for democracy turned out to be not far off the mark. In his eyes, in the meantime, there was no reason despotism could not embody wisdom and virtue.

Although midcentury witnessed Mexico's first fully constitutional transfer of power, a Conservative-backed coup in early 1853 furnished Santa Ana a final turn in the presidency, this time supposedly as a bridge to a future European monarch.

To this end he abolished the 1824 Constitution. His final, abrupt departure from power in mid-1855 was precipitated by the Liberals' Revolution of Ayutla, which brought to center stage a compelling political figure starkly different in almost every dimension from the durable *caudillo*. For after November 1855 uncompromising centralist Liberals were in power in a country whose population was around 7.7 million. Benito Pablo Juárez García (b. 1806), a Zatpotec Indian descended from the region's historical indigenous nobility and married to an essentially Spanish woman, had been governor of Oaxaca, and now became justice minister in the Juan N. Álvarez (b. 1790)–Ignacio Comonfort (b. 1812) government. Under the law bearing Juárez's name, the *fueros* (special legal rights) of the church and the military were abolished. Following Álvarez's resignation in favor of Comonfort, the Lerdo law (named after Miguel Lerdo de Tejada) in mid-1856 drastically changed the land tenure system, and the landmark 1857 Constitution disestablished the Catholic Church.[27]

These drastic measures led by 1858 to civil war, with the Conservatives behind militarily adept General Miguel Miramon (b. 1831) controlling Mexico City, and with Acting President Juárez, ably seconded in the military field by General Santos Degollado and in the political realm by Melchior Ocampo, resisting out of Veracruz. Victorious at the beginning of 1861, the Liberals indulged in violent anticlerical actions and expelled the country's bishops—the result being the kidnapping and murder of Ocampo in May of that year. Juárez was elected president for the term ending in December 1865, at which time he was scheduled to turn the presidency over to the chief justice, General Jesús González Oretayo. But events would drastically alter that timetable.

Unable to best the Liberals internally and firmly believing that they were the country's only bulwark protecting order and decency against Godless anarchy, the Conservatives and the church looked for help from abroad. They found a willing partner in French emperor Louis Napoléon, in power for over a decade and looking for a means to escape from the image of being just the great Bonaparte's nephew. Juárez's suspension of foreign debt payments in 1862 gave the ambitious French ruler the pretext for which he was looking, and after taking Mexico City in 1863, his invading army maintained Austrian archduke Ferdinand Maximilian von Hapsburg (b. 1832, two years after his much more fortunate brother, Franz Josef) on a Mexican throne hastily created in 1864 with the wholehearted collaboration of the Conservatives and the Catholic Church.[28] Juárez's legitimate Liberal government was forced to wage guerrilla warfare from the mountains. But after Prussia's shocking defeat of Austria in the 1866 Seven Weeks' War, Napoléon III withdrew his troops in anticipation of the Prussian-led invasion of France, which eventually came in 1870. Thus, militarily orphaned, Maximilian was captured and executed in mid-1867. These events brought Juárez and the Liberals back to power older, if not entirely wiser, than before, with ambitious General Porfirio Díaz chafing at the bit for his chance to show how the country should be run.

Argentina: *Caudillo* Rule to Elite Democracy

Compared to most of the rest of Spanish America's and in stark contrast to Mexico's, Argentina's independence would come easily—albeit followed by much more turbulence than in Brazil. On the other hand, Argentina's becoming a nation would be even more difficult, eluding the efforts of the founding fathers and being accomplished only by a subsequent generation. For the Creole merchants of Buenos Aires, finally free of colonial restraints on commerce, sought with considerable success to maintain their economic dominance over the interior, while it strove mightily to maintain autonomy.

In the area around Buenos Aires, the British strove to take advantage of the opportunities created by the Napoleonic Wars by attempting invasions in 1806 and 1807. These were repulsed by local militia under the command of a French-born officer, Santiago Linares—who was repaid by being overthrown by Baltasar Hidalgo de Cisneros in mid–1810 and promptly executed. Since this still-provincial city had become the center of a viceroyalty only in 1776 and before that had been governed from distant Peru by extremely tenuous communications across the Andes and down through the Gran Chaco, the Spanish military presence was very weak and the *Porteños*, as Buenos Aires residents were known, had to shoulder the burden of repulsing the British largely on their own. This experience gave these Creoles, who had already deposed an incompetent viceroy, a sense of identity and capability.[29] As a consequence Spanish rule was effectively ended at the earliest date in Latin America: May 1810. This perhaps premature independence for a vast region with fewer than 600,000 inhabitants only ushered in a chaotic succession of juntas and "directors," generally with a fragile hold on the city and ephemeral control over any significant part of he interior. Although the best-remembered figure of these early years was José de San Martín (b. 1778), who had been serving as an officer in Spain, he did not govern, moving on instead with a fifty-five-hundred-man army across the Andes to Chile in early 1817; he would never return, dying in France in 1850. By this point, following a pair of short-lived triumvirates and a supreme director, Juan Martín de Pueyrredon had been elevated to that post as head of the United Provinces of the Rio de la Plata. He moved this entity's congress from an interior city to Buenos Aires before being forced to resign in mid-1819, his resignation inaugurating a period of near anarchy.

As governments came and went in a revolving door in 1820, the issue of federalism versus a unitary regime came to the fore, with Bernardino Rivadavia (b. 1780) leading advocates of the latter, and some interior strongmen (provincial *caudillos*) allying themselves with like-minded José Gervasio Artigas (b. 1764) across the La Plata estuary in Montevideo. Artigas defeated the Spanish, only to be defeated in turn by the Brazilians, who moved quickly after their independence to lay claim to all of the area that Portugal had long claimed. By 1825, Rivadavia had forged a provisional national government, but Buenos Aires landowners opposed to his economic liberalism and modernizing policies brought about this government's dissolution in mid-1827 in the context of war with Brazil over the area that would soon become Uruguay.

Order came, but at an extreme price, as in 1829 Juan Manuel de Rosas (b. 1793), a very wealthy and extremely well-connected landowner who had played no part in the independence struggles, was named Buenos Aires governor with extraordinary powers. A shrewd and ruthless *caudillo* who quickly became renowned for his courage and strength and feared for his cruelty toward enemies, he ruled Buenos Aires with an iron hand and extended his sway over much of the interior through alliances with provincial strongmen formalized as the Federal Pact. Cloaking himself as a federalist against Rivadavia's *Unitários* (advocates of a unitary system), Rosas, riding the crest of successful desert and Indian campaigns, gained absolute power in Buenos Aires through an 1835 plebiscite. Reminiscent of some of Napoléon's votes, the announced results were an implausible 9,315 to 5.[30]

The self-styled "restorer of the laws," known to his opponents as Bloody Rosas, used a terrorist secret police, the Mazorca, to supplement his wily intelligence. Behind a slogan of "Death to the Vile, Filthy, Savage Unitários," he engineered an Argentine Confederation in which his Buenos Aires government represented the other provinces in the fields of defense and foreign affairs. Between 1843 and 1851 Rosas kept his enemies penned up under siege in Montevideo. A rancher himself, he demonstrated considerable skill in maintaining alliances with provincial *caudillos* to prevent their ganging up against him until after midcentury.

Finally, in 1851, *caudillo* governor Justo José de Urquiza (b. 1801) of Entre Rios turned against Rosas and forged an uneasy alliance with the *Unitários,* Brazil, and Uruguay, decisively defeating Rosas at Monte Caseros the following year. Thus Argentina had a durable *caudillo* autocrat deposed at about the same time as Santa Ana finally lost out at the other end of the region in Mexico. But instead of Juárez and the liberals aligned against European intervention as in Mexico, Argentina would see a series of elite leaders eventually bringing the metropolis and the interior—totaling close to 1.4 million inhabitants—together before heading toward a less authoritarian analogue to the Díaz regime. Argentina's Constitution of 1853, with amendments to meet changing times, is still in effect today (after being temporarily replaced between 1949 and 1956).

The struggle to unite the Buenos Aires region with the interior, this time under some form of democratic order, occupied the next decade and a half. Buenos Aires stayed out of the confederation formed in 1853, since the rather haughty

ARGENTINA AND CHILE

Porteños did not want to share the revenues from control of foreign trade, much less run the risk of being governed by people they considered inferior in both education and breeding. Under the leadership of General Bartolomé Mitre (b. 1821), they battled Urquiza. Exiled by Rosas in 1837, Mitre fought for the Uruguayan Colorados and spent time in Chile. His victory at the battle of Pavón in September 1861 ended the interior confederation and left Mitre, compared to his foes a veritable Renaissance man, in the driver's seat, so Buenos Aires gradually entered the nation, with Mitre becoming Argentina's president in 1862.[31] Entrenched in power, he frequently used force against troublesome provincial *caudillos*. His effort to dominate the country's political life for a prolonged period failed, as the population considered the war with Paraguay "his," not theirs, and he had to swallow the bitter pill of the 1868 election of his archrival, cosmopolitan intellectual Domingo Faustino Sarmiento (b. 1811).

Born in the northwest, Sarmiento, whose motto was "to govern is to educate," was an acute critic of the provincial "barbarism" he witnessed there. His most famous book, *Facundo: Life in the Argentine Republic in the Days of the Tyrants: Civilization and Barbarism*, published in 1845, made famous Facundo Quiroga, a provincial *caudillo* of La Rioja province (until his death in 1834), while perpetuating the *Porteños'* sense of superiority, and provided a rationale for his stress on modernization and Europeanization.[32] When Sarmiento came to office, Argentina had a population of 1.8 million, 500,000 living in Buenos Aires province and almost 180,000 in the city itself. British investment was flowing in to build railroads across the fertile pampas, and—with government encouragement—immigrants from Italy and Spain were beginning to arrive in significant numbers. A golden era for Argentina was on the horizon.[33]

Uruguay: Independent in Name, Not Fact

Following the establishment of Uruguay as an independent buffer state between Brazil and the Argentines in 1828, these larger neighbors continued to intervene actively in its affairs—an easy task, since its population continued to grow slowly from 1820's mere 70,000. Indeed, Argentina recognized its independence only after Rosas's fall in 1852.

Uruguay's first president, Fructuoso Rivera (b. 1784), chosen by the legislature (and serving a second time beginning in 1839), was the personification of the urban Colorado faction of this city-state's small elite. General Manuel Oribe (b. 1792), his successor, serving from 1835 until forced by Rivera to resign in 1838, led the interior-based conservative Blancos. With the liberal Colorados controlling the capital, Oribe allied with Rosas to control the hinterland and lay siege to Montevideo from 1843 to 1852—capitulating to Argentina's Urquiza and Brazilian forces when the beleaguered Rosas could no longer provide significant assistance.[34] Venáncio Flores (b. 1808) held power in the immediate aftermath and, after revolting against Blanco governments of Bernardo P. Berro (1860–1864) and Antonio C. Aguirre (1864–1865), returned to office from 1865 to 1868 with the support of Argentina's Mitre as well as the help of Brazilian troops. This development led to Paraguayan dictator López's ill-advised attempt to aid the Blancos in their 1870 uprising against the government of Lorenzo Batlle (1868–1872), an action that provoked Brazil and Argentina to declare war against Paraguay. For Uruguay's Colorados this event ushered in a very long era of hegemony—in its first stages under the baton of military figures.

Paraguay: Isolation That Breeds Delusions

In extremely isolated Paraguay, populated by about 100,000 Guarani Indians and perhaps an equal number of *mestizo* descendents of traders and Jesuit priests, who had been the dominant European influence from 1607 until their expulsion in 1767, an absolute dictator, José Gaspar Rodríguez de Francia (b. 1766 of Brazilian parents) arose. Insisting on being addressed as El Supremo ("the Supreme One"), he was in control from helping to defeat an Argentine force in 1811—which sealed independence from the former viceroyalty as well as from Spain—until his death in 1840 and sought order and tranquility through isolation from the rest of the world. Educated at the University of Córdoba, he felt held back by enemies' allusions to possible mulatto blood. Starting as the junior member of a three-man junta, he had achieved absolute power by 1814. This ironfisted nationalist gained favor with the masses by confiscating church- and European-owned lands and leasing them to the poor while setting up a system of state farms, with surpluses being parceled out to the poor. Ironworks and factories for armaments and even shipbuilding (for river traffic) were established. His regime has been aptly labeled a "socialist Barracks state" and described as "premature to early" in terms of developments in other parts of the region.[35]

A less dictatorial and more paternalistic autocrat, Carlos Antonio López (b. 1792), a lawyer and rancher, ruled as first consul from 1841 until 1862, reducing Paraguay's paranoid isolation. He built schools and enlarged the army while strengthening relations with the outside world. His son, Francisco Solano López (b. 1826), corrupted by his absolute life-and-death sway over his subjects and influenced by the pretensions of his French-born mistress, embarked on a disastrous venture to intervene militarily in Uruguayan affairs. By the mid-1860s this rash act had involved the country in a hopeless war with Brazil and Argentina, so the last years of the 1860s found him and his few surviving followers fighting a doomed, rearguard action in the interior, ended by the increasingly paranoid dictator's death in action in 1870 and Brazilian occupation until 1876. Between 60 and 65 percent of all Paraguayans died in the war, and the country's population declined from 550,000 to not much more than 230,000—less than one-eighth adult males.[36] Brazil took 160,000 square kilometers along its border, while Argentina helped itself to a somewhat smaller slice from the western side of the country. As a result of this trauma, Paraguay's political development, as well as its economic growth and societal modernization, would be long delayed.

Northern and Western South America:
Gran Colombia plus Peru Divided into Six Nations

As in Mexico, reverses and frustration marked the early stages of the independence struggle in upper South America. Francisco Miranda, who had been radicalized during a stint of army service in Spain in the 1770s, launched an 1806 revolutionary invasion of Venezuela at the head of a small group of foreign volunteers. This Quixotic venture failed to find support, although the local Creoles wanted an expansion of free trade to benefit their plantation economy; with the very recent events in Haiti much in mind, they feared the threat to their power that might result from the removal of Spanish control. Hence, Miranda's initial venture to break Spain's hold was easily crushed.

In New Granada a strong loyalist faction in Bogotá, seat of the viceroyalty, did not prevent a junta in Cartagena from declaring independence in 1809. A clique of patrician Creoles who did not want full independence ousted the viceroy and proclaimed social and economic reforms in 1810. Having become radicalized (as had analogous figures in the American colonies thirty-five years earlier) in March 1811 this group of notables proclaimed the Republic of Cundinamarca in Bogotá, but unaided could not withstand royalist/loyalist forces. This Pátria Boba ("Foolish Fatherland"), inspired by Antonio Nariño, was reconquered by 1815.

Miranda's second attempt to mount a revolution by way of Venezuela at the end of 1810 had resulted in his capture in mid-1812 and subsequent death in a Spanish prison. Assuming his mantle (like Morelos vis-à-vis Hidalgo in Mexico), Simón Bolívar (b. 1783)—son of a wealthy cacao-growing family—briefly established himself in power in Venezuela in 1813 and captured Bogotá at the end of 1814. A few months later a royalist army of ten thousand men landed in Venezuela and in little over a year had retaken Bogotá.[37] The struggle heated up with Bolívar's return to Venezuela from his Jamaican exile at the end of 1816. In a little more than a year the man who went down in history as the "Liberator" had forged an alliance with José Antonio Paéz (b. 1790) and his *llanero* ("cowboy") cavalry. Aware of the need to strike Spanish royalist authority at its heart, Bolívar marched toward the seat of the viceroyalty in Bogotá, declaring the entire region independent in December 1819 at a congress he had convened at Angostura. There he was named president of Gran Colombia, embracing today's Colombia, Venezuela, Ecuador, and Panama. The trick, as had been the case in the United States after the Declaration of Independence in July 1776, was to make this assertion into a permanent fact through force of arms.

Having won a major victory at Boyacá in August 1817 on the way to the capital (where the forces numbered only three thousand on each side), Bolívar consolidated his grip by triumphing again back at Carabobo in Venezuela in mid-1821. Leaving his vice president, Francisco de Paula Santander (b. 1792) in Bogotá, he moved west into Ecuador, where he had previously sent Antonio José de Sucre Al-calá (b. 1795) to support Guayaquil-based independence forces. Victory at Pichin-cha, near Quito, on May 24, 1822, sealed the independence of the northern portion of the viceroyalty of Peru and paved the way for a final offensive against the remaining loyalist stronghold. Bolívar's forces triumphed at Junin in August 1824 and at Ayachucho in December. Troops under Sucre moved on to Upper Peru, which would constitute itself as Bolivia in August 1825, and in late 1826 Bolívar would leave Lima to return to Bogotá to face problems with Santander as well as with Paéz in Venezuela (suspending many of Bolívar's liberal reforms).[38]

Colombia

In 1830, Bolívar's dream of unity for the northern tier of South America came tumbling down, burying this great historical figure in the process.[39] In addition to personal ambitions and regional rivalries, which all but doomed the dream from the start, Gran Colombia was plagued by very poor transportation and communi-cations, which played into the hands of those on whom Bolívar—sitting isolated in high-altitude Bogotá—counted to do his bidding in the peripheral areas. Even in the capital, many of the local elite who remembered their former privileged ac-cess to viceroyal authorities viewed the Liberator as a Venezuelan outsider. Re-signing in despair, Bolívar died on the arduous journey to the coast on his way out of the country that had proven so ungrateful.

Freed from Bolívar's shadow, Santander, a lawyer from near the Venezuelan bor-der, emerged as the dominant figure, holding the presidency of Nueva Granada as a constitution was drafted in 1832; he was granted a new four-year term the fol-lowing year. In a bloody 1837 civil war a civilian, Dr. José Ignacio de Marques, won out over Santander's choice, General José María Obando. Surviving a revolt by elements seeking greater regional autonomy, de Marques was succeeded in 1841 by General Pedro Alcántara Herrán. Following adoption in 1843 of a consti-tution strengthening the executive, Herrán gave way in 1845 to yet another Boli-varian general—in this case, his own father-in-law, Tomás Cipriano de Mosquera (b. 1798), an aristocrat from Popayán.[40] A split in Conservative ranks then let the Liberals slip back in as the congress chose General José Hilario López in 1849, ushering in a period of reform legislation in a country nearing a population of 2.4 million—double that at the time of the independence struggle.

Colombia's two-party system was solidly in place, but this did not mean that they would confine their intense rivalry to the ballot box. Indeed, both the Liber-als and Conservatives were loose coalitions of factions and caudillos. As insightfully portrayed by Lewis:

The party leaders were those *caudillos* with the broadest networks of relatives, friends, and clients. Minor *caudillos* attached themselves to those leaders in the expectation of sharing the rewards of victory. Defeat or disappointment might cause them to change sides, however, so the inner logic of *caudillo* politics demanded that the chief *caudillo* "must continuously find new resources of wealth which can be distributed to his following, or he must attach resources which replenish themselves."[41]

Early in other areas as well as in Colombia, the chief spoils were crown possessions and the property of royalists; then came the communal lands of Indians and church holdings; finally, it was *caudillos* taking from rival *caudillos*. In some cases, a particularly ambitious and able *caudillo* would grab power at the national level and use the spoils "to modernize his army, overwhelm his rivals, and impose the 'blessings' of orderly despotism."[42]

Because unity was nearly impossible to achieve in mountainous Colombia, the beginning of the distinguishing feature of Colombian politics down to the present emerged: two vertically organized, elite-led parties retaining a monopoly on organized political life, generation after generation. For over a century and a half, the Liberals and Conservatives have retained the support of the vast majority of politically active Colombians, dooming all efforts to create new parties—efforts successful in almost every other Latin American country—to failure. This phenomenon has also spared the country *caudillo* rule and has limited militarism (in terms of the political involvement of professional career officers) to only one four-year outbreak (1953–1957).

With General José María Obando (b. 1795) in office in 1853, the deeply divided Liberals fell victim to an 1854 coup by General José María Melo, whose effort to change the constitution to extend his term as well as to increase executive powers paved the way for the selection of Conservative civilian Mariano Ospina Rodríguez in 1857. By mid-1861 the Liberals had won out in an armed struggle, returning General Tomás Mosquera to power, enacting anticlerical measures, and adopting an extreme form of federalism that made the country essentially a confederation—as each province had its own army. After being reelected once again in 1866, Mosquera fell victim to a coup in May 1867 that was followed by thirteen more years of Liberal rule. By this time the 1863 Rionegro Constitution had established a system closer to that found wanting by the United States in its early days—federal in name, but confederal in substance. Sovereignty resided in the federated states, and each had its own army, with the central government handling foreign relations and having some powers in the case of foreign wars.[43]

Venezuela

After declaring Venezuela's independence from Gran Colombia in 1830, José Antonio Paéz, a light-skinned *mestizo* lacking any formal education, but an able cavalry commander, launched a tradition of *caudillo* rule in this country of fewer than 800,000 inhabitants that would persist there for over a century—longer than in almost any other place in Latin America. For seventeen years his Conservatives kept their Liberal rivals in check as production of cacao, coffee, and hides recovered from the disruption occasioned by the armed struggles for independence. President from 1831 to 1835 and again from 1839 to 1843, Paéz hung like a shadow over the presidencies of José María Vargas (1835–1837) and Carlos Soublette (1837–1839 and 1843–1847). More similar to Mexico's Santa Ana than Argentina's Rosas, albeit from far humbler beginnings, Paéz came back from his large estate in 1846 to head the army in a civil war, rebelling again in 1848. By this time Antonio Leocádio Guzmán (b. 1801) had established the Liberal Party as a counterweight to the dominant landowners.[44]

Following Paéz's next-to-last ouster, stability proved an elusive goal and the politically dominant Monagas brothers, Generals José Tadeo (b. 1784), president 1847–1851 and 1855–1858, and José Gregorio (b.1795), president 1851–1855, were faced with a protracted and extremely bloody armed conflict known as the Federal War between 1858 and 1863—during which 300,000 persons died in this sparsely populated country, which had managed to reach a population of 1.3 million from its preindependence 760,000. The Liberals won the struggle only after they brought Paéz back from his New York City exile in 1861 and granted the old *caudillo* near-dictatorial powers, which he exercised only briefly. Of great importance for the future was the development of Guzmán's son, Antonio Guzmán Blanco (b. 1829), into a military leader of the Liberal-federalist forces, resulting in a political career that would dominate the rest of the century.

Juan Cristosomo Falcón (b. 1820), a leader of the Liberal-federalist side in the civil war, became president in 1863; his vice president, wealthy financial expert Antonio Guzmán Blanco, ran the country day to day. In 1868, José Tadeo Monagas, reincarnated as a Conservative, returned via a coup for a last brief hold on the presidency before the new era dawned—as the younger Guzmán captured Caracas, seized power in mid-1870, and set out to crush the Conservatives (and all other opposition). He would be the prototype of a new breed of Liberal *caudillos* in the region.

Ecuador

In its first generation of independence this medium-sized country wedged between Colombia and Peru experienced a series of strongmen, each of whom encountered great difficulty in bridging the deep gap between Quito, with its mountainous hinterland, and the distant coastal region. Freed of Spanish rule by Bolívar's forces in May 1822, Ecuadorians then fought against the loyalist forces in Peru. Given the conditions of its independence, the dominant figure in Ecuador's national life from 1830 to 1845 was dark-skinned and nearly illiterate Venezuelan General Juan José Flores (b. 1801). Following Ecuador's September 1830 separation from Nueva Granada (Colombia), which had been preceded by a border dispute between Gran Colombia and Peru, in which Guayaquil was nearly destroyed, Flores merely switched his title from governor of the Southern District (of Gran Colombia) to president of the Republic of Ecuador—which gave him rule over perhaps 550,000 persons.

Chiefly concerned about survival in power and surrounded by Quito area personages, Flores faced a rebellion in 1834 by forces desiring to replace him with Vicente Rocafuerte y Rodríguez de Bejarano (b. 1783) of the Guayaquil-based Liberals. Pragmatically, Flores sponsored Rocafuerte for the presidency in 1835 but stayed on as army head. He was returned to the presidency by Congress in 1839 (with Rocafuerte going back to be governor of Guayaquil) and held power until a Guayaquil-centered revolt in reaction to election rigging and alleged plans to turn the country into a monarchy under Spanish sponsorship with himself as king forced him out of both the presidency and the country in 1845. By this time, less than 20 percent of Ecuador's roughly 650,000 inhabitants were of European stock, so that elitist electoral politics had a very narrow base.[45]

The turbulent post-Flores period pitted coastal Liberals led by General José María Urbina, president via a coup 1851–1856, against Quito-based Conservative Party behind the dynamic figure of Gabriel García Moreno y Gómez (b. 1821)— born in Guayaquil and another example of an ambitious individual from a humble background marrying into an elite family. The latter graduated from the university at twenty-three and subsequently represented Quito in the congress—where he opposed the Flores, Rocafuerte, and Urbina governments. Peruvian-sponsored efforts in 1859 by local *caudillos* to break away from the central government led García Moreno to team up with General Flores to successfully put down these local rebellions. Installed in power as a result, this highly educated part tyrant, part nation builder went beyond making Catholicism the country's official religion, which he did in a modern 1869 Constitution, by formally dedicating the nation to the Sacred Heart of Jesus in 1873. Priests having the temerity to criticize him were replaced by foreign ones.[46] Repelling, again with the aid of Flores (who lost his life in the process), an attempt by Liberals to seize power in 1864, García Moreno remained in office through manipulated elections—in which only 5 percent of the population had the right to vote—until cut down on the steps of the government palace by a machete-wielding assassin in 1875. The Liberal Party had despaired of getting him out of power in any other manner.

Peru

The area that had been the core of Spain's Spanish American empire was most
deeply affected by the postindependence power vacuum. Benefiting from colonial
monopolies, and fearful of the type of social violence the late-eighteenth-century
indigenous revolts had threatened, many Peruvian Creoles had not been anxious
to break with Spain. Having been a royalist stronghold, and with most of its elites
tarnished as loyalists, Peru began its life without a national hero or a patriotic
force—and with its population reduced to not much more than 1.2 million. After
Argentine San Martín's 1821 stint as "protector" had been cut short by royalist
resurgence, Bolivian-born upper-class General Andrés Santa Cruz (b. 1792),
headed the government left behind in Lima by Bolívar in 1826–1827, being followed in power by Ecuadorian general José de la Mar from 1827 to 1829—
arranged by the congress without resort to elections. Aristocratic aspirant General
Agustín Gamarra, a former royal officer who had switched sides and become
leader of the Lima–north coast based Conservatives, held the presidency in
1829–1833 and 1839–1841; the Arequipa–southern Andes centered Liberals, who
had backed de la Mar, returned to power in 1833–1834 behind Luis de Orbegoso.
Santa Cruz's case was only the most prominent of repeated instances in which
mestizos who had gained distinction in the independence wars would be pushed
aside by the white elites. The first part of this period would see no government in
full control of the country, as civil strife prevailed in many areas.[47]

In 1836, through military force, Santa Cruz, who after losing out in Lima had
entrenched himself in control of Bolivia, forged a Peruvian-Bolivian Confederation, which was broken up in 1839 as a result of defeat by Chile in the First War of
the Pacific. Instability became accentuated as Peruvian president Agustín Gamarra
(b. 1785) was killed in battle attempting to reannex Bolivia. His death left General
Manuel Ignácio Vivanco as dictator, with a mild penchant toward education and
the untangling of government finances, until he was ousted in 1844 by the new
king of the political hill, General Ramón Castilla (b. 1797). At last Peru had a
long-term strongman, as Castilla, benefiting from rising export earnings from
guano, held the presidency from 1845 to 1851 and, after the ouster of his successor, José Rufino Echenique—architect of a controversial and corruption-tainted
debt consolidation—by an Arequipa-based revolt, again from 1854 to 1862.
Emancipation of 25,500 slaves brought the number of free blacks to over 40,000.
Castilla astutely maintained a position midway between the liberals and the conservatives. (He had fought in the Spanish army against San Martín and later under
the Chilean flag against the Peruvian-Bolivian Confederation.) By midcentury
the Peruvian state was dominated by the merchant elite and their planter allies.[48]

By Castilla's time Peru had almost doubled its population from an independence day 1.2 million to near 2.3 million and had experienced a guano export

boom of sufficient proportions to attract foreign investment, so this middle-class *mestizo* could carry out limited modernization and a partial professionalization of the military. Unfortunately, his constructive work was followed by a decade of chaotic fraternal strife, leaving the country in disarray.

Bolivia

Isolated from the center of peninsular power in Lima, Upper Peru had experienced independence movements as early as July 15, 1808, with a revolt led by Pedro Domingo Murillo, followed by installation of a governing junta in La Paz the following year, which had the temerity to proclaim independence, in practice a declaration of self-rule with respect to Lima. The revolt was crushed at the end of January 1810 by five thousand troops sent up by the viceroy of Peru, and its leaders were executed. Soon thereafter an uprising occurred in support of the independence of Buenos Aires. The protracted Fifteen Years' War ensued, really a series of clashes with royalist forces that hazarded the long trek to restore the Spanish yoke. Once San Martín and Bolívar closed the noose on Peru, General Antonio José de Sucre (b. 1795) defeated the ten-thousand-man army of Viceroy de la Serna at Ayacucho on December 9, 1824. Royalist forces in Upper Peru were routed at the beginning of April the following year.

In this isolated area with a population of one million, which named itself after Bolívar to escape remaining Upper Peru, Venezuelan Sucre, a mild reformist, became president in 1826 but was forced out in August 1828 by Peruvian general Gamarra, an old comrade in arms. (Sucre's subsequent assasination in 1830 then opened the door for Santa Cruz to move in from Peru). In May 1829, the two warhorses' conflict over power was resolved when Gamarra became president of Peru and former Peruvian chief executive Andrés Santa Cruz took over in Bolivia with dictatorial powers. After balancing the budget and launching a public works program, as noted above the ambitious Santa Cruz united Bolivia and Peru by force, proclaiming the Peruvian–Bolivian Confederation in October 1836. For the short time he presided over the confederation, General José Miguel Velasco governed its Bolivian component. Defeated by Chilean general Manuel Bulnes in 1839, Santa Cruz was forced into European exile. By this time the practices and traditions that would make Bolivia synonymous with extreme political instability had become established. (Some compilations list 190 governments in its first 165 years.)[49]

In 1840, Velasco won a power struggle for the vacant presidency. Until midcentury he occupied it four times, his longest stay being a bit over two years—a distant and minor league parallel to Santa Ana in Mexico. General José Balleván (b. 1805), a self-educated *mestizo*, held office in 1843–1847, increasing exports of guano and quinine. Then Velasco's final presidency in 1848 was extremely brief, as he was promptly ousted by General Manuel Isadoro Belzú (b. 1808)—the country's first populist *caudillo* president—whose policies favored the Indians and other underdog groups. Author of a nationalist mining code and a new constitution (Bolivia's fifth in sixteen years) in 1854, he had the country's first census taken; it revealed the population to be 2.3 million—sizable by the standards of the time. Upon leaving office in 1855, Belzú became the first Bolivian president to finish his constitutional term, but his son-in-law, who was his successor, lasted only two years.

Although 1857–1861 saw Bolivia's first civilian president, José María Linares, he was overthrown by his own cabinet and succeeded by tyrannical General José María de Archa. At the end of 1864 Archa was in turn ousted by a rival *caudillo*, Mariano Melgarejo (b. 1820)—but not until he had slaughtered seventy of his political rivals.[50] The period from 1864 to 1871 was marked by the bloody dictatorship of this uneducated upstart sergeant and self-proclaimed general, who personally killed Belzú when he attempted to regain power. Melgarejo was overthrown only after having ordered his army to march to the relief of Napoleon III in Paris—a feat impossible even with the aid of chewing coca leaves and a testimony to Melgarejo's poor grasp of geography. In his insatiable appetite for wealth, this drunken brute of a *mestizo* sacked the national treasury, then corruptly sold a piece of the country to Brazil and signed extremely disadvantageous treaties with Chile.[51] After alienating his peasant base with a law allowing communal Indian lands to be seized and sold, the degenerate autocrat was overthrown in January 1871 (and subsequently slain by the brother of his favorite mistress, an appropriate end to the worst of Latin American tyrants).

Chile

The independence of the southernmost Andean country was inextricably tied up with the leadership of Bernardo O'Higgins. Born well south of the Central Valley in 1778 as the illegitimate son of Ambrosio O'Higgins, an Irish colonel serving in the Spanish army, his birth coincided with Chile's becoming a captaincy-general—bringing increased autonomy from Peru. Nine years later, his father became head of Chile's colonial administration, and in 1796, he was promoted to viceroy of Peru, dying there in 1801. (His successor was Gabriel de Áviles, who had followed him as governor of Chile and, after a stint as viceroy in Buenos Aires, was promoted to king's representative in Peru.) Raised by friends of his distant father, in 1794 Bernardo was sent to Spain to further his education, but he quickly moved on to England, where he came in contact with Francisco Miranda and his revolutionary ideas concerning Latin American independence.[52]

With Chilean elites divided over who should govern in King Ferdinand's name during the French occupation of Spain, O'Higgins became a lieutenant colonel of cavalry and was elected to the Chilean congress at the beginning of 1811. Defeated by Spanish forces at Rancaugua in late 1814, he fled to Argentina, returning with San Martín two years later. In early 1817, they won the decisive Battle of Chacabuco. A few months later O'Higgins triumphed at Maipó and began a six-year stint as newly independent Chile's "supreme director." After resigning in 1823 in the face of mounting opposition to his reform measures from large landowners and the church, he assumed a field command under Bolívar for the final stages of the war in Peru, dying in Lima in 1842.

Following O'Higgins's departure from office in 1823, Liberal general Ramón Freire, champion of the *pipolos* ("novices") was in and out of power until the *pelucones* ("bigwigs") won the 1829–1832 civil war and inaugurated three decades of Conservative rule. By this time the country of one million inhabitants had produced a leader strikingly different from the era's typical *caudillo* ruler. After April 1830, Diego Portales Palazuelos (b. 1793), a brilliant and energetic businessman from Valparaiso serving as minister of war, navy, interior, foreign affairs, and finance—first under president Francisco Ruiz Tagle and then, after engineering that president's ouster, under General Joaquín Prieto—dominated government policy. Viewing the Catholic Church and the landowning aristocracy of the Central Valley as bulwarks of order, he created a Civil Guard to maintain order and act as a political counterweight to the army.

During the short time before his tragic early death this exceptionally able statesman engineered a settlement between the Conservative-centralist and Liberal-federalist factions that brought political peace. His views on a centralized presidency were in large part incorporated into Chile's long-lived 1833 Constitution, under which an indirectly elected president, eligible for a second five-year term, appointed the intendants who headed the provincial governments and were held in line by his extensive emergency powers.[53] A bicameral congress was chosen indirectly by an electorate restricted by literacy and property qualifications. Although presidents often fixed elections, this system was advanced for the times. (Britain only began to expand its very limited electorate in 1832, and the United States was still adapting to Jacksonian democracy.)

In addition to creating conditions for economic progress, Don Diego, as he was respectfully called, placed heavy emphasis on education. He worked assiduously for Chilean victory in the war against the Peruvian-Bolivian Confederation, instituting conscription and acting as de facto quartermaster general. His life was abruptly ended when he was bayoneted in 1837 by rebellious troops being sent to the First War of the Pacific, and he became an iconic heroic model. Prieto, who had been reelected in 1836, presided over the final military victory at the battle of Yungay in early 1839. Hence, in 1841, General Manuel Bulnes, nephew of Prieto and popular hero of Indian and antibandit campaigns even before earning battlefield laurels, was elected president and presided over a postwar economic boom. Facilitated by his close relationship to the outgoing chief executive and his engagement to the daughter of the 1827–1829 president, Bulnes's accession provided for a peaceful transition of power. (His favorable reputation would carry his son Aníbal to the presidency in 1876, a John Adams–John Quincy Adams–like father-son phenomenon that would be repeated on several other occasions, and as late as the 1990s.)[54] Liberal Manuel Montt Torres (b. 1809), Bulnes's interior minister, became president in 1851 after his predecessor defeated Conservatives rebelling against the loss of their preferred position. Chilean elections were still heavily manipulated by the executive, albeit no more so than elsewhere in the region.

Chile continued on its remarkable stable constitutional road in 1861, after Montt's second term, in which he stressed communications, transportation, and education. Although the outgoing chief executive strongly preferred Antonio Varas, his former interior minister, the victor was conciliation candidate José Joaquín Pérez Masayano (b. 1801), who included all significant factions in his cabinet and permitted a modestly larger role for the congress. Hence, in 1866, Pérez was unopposed for a second term. Tensions were greatly eased by the emergence of Chile as the world's leading copper exporter, so the outlook for the ensuing period was bright—in sharp contrast with that of its Andean neighbors.

Central America:
Easy Independence, Disunity, and Diversity

Central America had been attached to Mexico during the colonial period as an *audiencia* under a captain-general based in Guatemala. Divided into four intendancies after 1786 (including Chiapas, which would be annexed by Mexico), this region of about 1.3 million inhabitants, chiefly Indians and nearly half living in today's Guatemala, found itself in a vacuum when Mexico became independent. Geographically dispersed elites declared it independent from Mexico in mid-1823, adopting a constitution the next year as the United Provinces of Central America and uneasily holding together until 1839.[55] Following a three-year civil war, in 1829 the Liberals, under Honduran Francisco Morazán (b. 1792), son of an unsuccessful West Indian businessman, forcefully ejected the Conservatives from power and moved the capital to San Salvador.

In 1838, Conservatives rallied behind Guatemalan José Rafael Carrera (b. 1814), a young proclerical, mixed-blood *caudillo* who, on the basis of talent and determination, had risen from his humble origins as a swine herder, attaining power through a peasant revolt. Carrera's control of the federation led Honduras, Nicaragua, and Costa Rica to secede. Although he decisively defeated Morazán near Guatemala City in March (Morazán was executed in Costa Rica in 1842),

Carrera was unable to reunite the region. Exiled from his Guatemalan base in 1847–1848, he promptly staged a comeback and, after militarily defeating his foes, became president for life in 1854, dying in power (from alcoholism) in 1865.[56] The legacy he left behind enabled his Conservative successors to hold onto power in the northernmost and largest country of the subregion until 1871.

Meanwhile, El Salvador—its population moving toward 400,000—was governed by Carrera ally Francisco Dueñas, in power from 1851 to 1856 and reinstalled in 1863. His governance was ended by a coup in 1871. Similarly, in Honduras, home to fewer than 200,000 individuals, a Carrera ally, Francisco Ferrera, occupied the presidency from 1839 to 1845, subsequently running the country through his control of the army.[57] In the aftermath of near anarchy and foreign meddling in Nicaragua, the regional strongmen in 1863 also put into power in Nicaragua a dictatorial general who lasted through 1871. In isolated and very sparsely populated Costa Rica—still well under 100,000 in population—Juan Mora Fernández held sway quite peacefully from 1824 through 1833 within the framework of the regional federation. From 1835 to 1842, he was followed by Braulio Carrillo Colona (b. 1800), who, having led the country out of the decomposing federation, was ousted by Morazán-led forces (before Morazán's violent death). In the next few years, coffee production expanded substantially. The decade 1849–1859 saw Juan Rafael Mora run the country until ousted by a coup when seeking a third successive term. Attempting to seize power the following year, he was executed. Subsequently the country's political life became increasingly militarized and subjected to control by wealthy coffee producers.[58] In 1870, Colonel Tomás Guardia Gutiérrez overthrew President Jesús Jiménez and proceeded to break the power of the conservative landowners.

Nicaragua, whose population did not reach 200,000 until 1830, underwent the most colorful political course in the region during these formative decades. Much of its Caribbean coast was part of a puppet Kingdom of Mosquito, controlled by the British out of an enclave carved into Guatemala and southern Mexico and confusingly called British Honduras. For the main part of the country, politics centered chiefly on the bitter rivalry between the population centers of León in the north and Granada in the south. As midcentury neared, Cornelius Vanderbilt was operating a profitable steamboat-coach-wagon line across the country under a concession obtained from a Conservative government. Rival US financial interests contemplating a railroad backed the Liberals by bringing in a small group of mercenaries under William Walker in 1855. This feisty diminutive adventurer assumed the presidency before being defeated in 1857 by a Central American army supported by Vanderbilt.[59] Walker (b. 1824) made another bid for power in 1860 before being summarily executed. This whole demoralizing episode helped discredit

Liberals in Central America for a decade and a half. In Nicaragua specifically, it led to a long period of Conservative rule.

The Caribbean: Haiti's War for Independence and the Dominican Republic

Haiti's uniqueness is only in part a result of having been a French colony, stemming instead essentially from being the only country in the Western Hemisphere to have gained its independence exclusively through its own unaided efforts. By 1500, overwork and disease had decimated the indigenous population—which had originally stood at nearly a million—so by 1570 the backbone of the labor force across the island of Hispaniola was African slaves. By this time Cuba had become a more important center, and the mainland had eclipsed these early settlements.

By the end of the first quarter of the eighteenth century, administration by trading companies had failed in the western third of the island, which since 1697 had become French-controlled Saint Domingue, so direct administration was implanted there. As the eighteenth century wore on, Saint Domingue became responsible for some two-fifths of France's foreign trade, producing large amounts of sugar, coffee, cotton, and cocoa on some eighty-five hundred plantations. By the late 1700s, society had become quite complex, having at its apex a "plantocracy" composed of about five thousand of the thirty thousand Europeans, only a fifth of whom had been born on the island. Some freed mulattoes *(affranchis),* many of whom had fought in the US Revolution under French general Jean-Baptiste de Rochambeau, were smaller landowners. Some of them were soon-to-be insurgent leaders, including Henri Christophe, a future Haitian king. Still over a half million slaves constituted the overwhelming mass of a population that would number only 650,000 in 1820.[60]

The bloody process that in less than a decade and a half would lead to independence began with an abortive *affranchi* revolt in 1791, in which 50,000 insurgents killed 1,000 whites, at a cost of 10,000 rebel fatalities. As a result 10,000 whites fled to the United States, and Spain in 1792 and England the next year sent in military expeditions to restore order. When the original leader of the insurgents was killed, François Dominique Toussaint (b. 1743) assumed command, defeating the Spanish in 1795 and the British two years later, and capturing the city of Santo Domingo in the eastern part of the island in 1801. After crushing a mulatto uprising against his control, he assumed power for life under the name Toussaint L'Ouverture. His Saint Dominigue was only nominally a French colony, so in 1802 Napoléon, recently ensconced in power in postrevolutionary France, sent a force of twenty-two thousand veteran troops under his brother-in-law to attempt to reestablish control. Unfortunately, Haiti's first great figure died the following year in a French prison.

The independence struggle continued under General Jean Jacques Dessalines (b. 1758) with 100,000 Haitians and half as many French combatants dying before the liberator's final victory at the end of 1803. The killing of 2,000 to 3,000 of the reduced number of remaining white civilians at this point effectively ended European presence in Haiti, whose independence was reluctantly recognized by major powers in 1804. Sadly, early independence brought Haiti no advantage in the realm of political development. Dessalines proclaimed himself Emperor Jean Jacques I, but fearing that he was siding with the ex-slave masses, the new elite of *affranchis* had him executed in 1806. His death led to a division of the country, with educated, freeborn, relatively light-skinned General Alexandre Sabes Petion (b. 1770), son of a Frenchman and a free mulatto woman, as president in the south and Henri Christophe (b. 1763), a black originally from St. Kitts, ruling as a tyrannical king in the north. This division continued until their respective deaths in 1818 and 1820. By this time the roots of competition between brown and black elites had been established in a country whose total population was only 650,000.[61]

Much larger Santo Domingo—sparsely inhabited by 50,000 whites, an equal number of mulattoes, and only 25,000 blacks—was brought under Haitian occupation in 1822 by Jean-Pierre Boyer (b. 1776), a free mulatto who succeeded Petion as president of Haiti, and this situation was uncomfortably maintained for twenty-two years. Santo Domingo's successful bid for independence in 1844 coincided with a period of extreme instability in Port au Prince, where four presidents followed on each other's heels in 1844–1846 after the ouster of "President for Life" Boyer. The pendulum soon swung in the opposite direction as Faustín Soulouque (b. 1788), an illiterate and superstitious black who turned on the mulatto elite, followed the example of Louis Napoleon in France and became Emperor Faustín I in 1849, holding power for a decade, but failing to recapture Santo Domingo. He was overthrown in 1858 by Fabre Nicholás Geffrard, who, although ruling dictatorially did negotiate a concordat with the Vatican and establish diplomatic relations with the United States before being overthrown in 1867.

The eastern two-thirds of Hispaniola, which had been neglected by the Spanish after 1550, got off to a late and troubled start as an independent country. Fought over by Haitians, French, British, and Spanish between 1804 and 1809, it reverted to Spanish control until 1821, when it was occupied by Haiti. With Venezuelan backing, Juan Pablo Duarte established the Dominican Republic's independence in 1844, but continued attacks by Haiti had the effect of "preventing renewed economic development, discouraging immigration and investments, keeping the country from stabilizing politically or developing functioning institutions of its own, and renewing the now often-desperate calls for a foreign protector."[62] Duarte was quickly pushed into exile by Pedro Santana (b. 1801) and Buenaventura Baéz (b. 1810). This dictatorial duo alternated in the presidency: Baéz had five terms (1849–1853, 1856–1857, 1865–1866, 1868–1873, and 1876–1878) to Santana's three terms (1844–1848, 1853–1856, and 1859–1861). Following a brief negotiated return to Spanish rule in 1861–1865 and Santana's death, quasi-perpetual president Baéz's plan for annexation by the United States failed to win approval of the US Senate by a single vote.[63]

Latin America in 1870

Clearly most Latin American countries experienced very halting progress toward political development during the first half century of independence. The long period of colonial rule, some three centuries, had left them poorly prepared for self-government. As an aggravating factor, they generally rushed into adopting, often with little adaptation to their real needs, a governmental blueprint and institutions badly suited to prevailing conditions. Some of the educated elites, particularly in Chile, did insert realistic modifications into their constitutions. In other cases such tailoring of the US model of federalism, separation of powers, and separation of church and state occurred in practice without formal incorporation into the basic charters. As characterized by Wiarda:

> . . . Recognizing the need for strong leadership in these often disorganized, chaotic societies, the Latin American founding fathers entrusted the executive with broad powers, while weakening the influence of the congress and courts. The president was also given vast emergency powers frequently needed in these fractured, disorganized polities to declare a state of emergency, suspend the constitution, and rule by decree. . . . The Catholic Church was often established as the official church and Catholicism as the official religion.[64]

By the end of the 1860s, Latin American countries were in many basic political and politically relevant ways significantly more different than they had been on the eve of independence. A greater number of colonial differences had been accentuated by the wide variations in the processes of gaining independence than had been softened or blurred, and the gaps were then widened by distinctive initial experiences in their lives as separate nations. The second generation of independent existence was so heavily shaped by the experiences of the 1830s and 1840s that differentiation in some cases accelerated and in others hardened. Only in the 1850s and 1860s did countries sharing certain racial and economic features begin to follow somewhat parallel developmental paths. It would be in the last three decades of the nineteenth century that these paths began to produce common patterns.[65] Yet the years since independence heavily shaped and conditioned developments in each country, roughly analogous to the political socialization of individuals. As formulated by the most systematic student of this phenomenon, "Earlier events in a 'premodern' period, established the institutional design that was consolidated in the latter part of the nineteenth century, molded state expansion, and helped to explain the so-called 'oligarchic states' of the early twentieth century and their radical transformation after the 1930s."[66]

Notes

1. Stuart F. Voss, *Latin America in the Middle Period, 1750–1929* (Wilmington, DE: Scholarly Resources, 2001), pp. 44–45. Solid sources on the region's independence and its aftermath include Richard Graham, *Independence in Latin America: A Comparative Approach* (New York: McGraw-Hill, 1994); Leslie Bethell, ed., *Spanish America After Independence c. 1820–c. 1870* (Cambridge, UK: Cambridge University Press, 1987); Jamie E. Rodríguez O., *The Independence of Spanish America* (Cambridge, UK: Cambridge University Press, 1998); David Bushnell and Neil Macaulay, *The Emergence of Latin America in the Nineteenth Century* (New York: Oxford University Press, 1988); Jay Kinsbruner, *Independence in Latin America: Civil Wars, Revolutions, and Underdevelopment* (Albuquerque: University of New Mexico Press, 1994). John Lynch, ed., *Latin American Revolutions 1808–1826: Old and New World Origins* (Norman: University of Oklahoma Press, 1994), is a useful collection of readings.

2. See Jorge I. Dominguez, *Insurrection and Loyalty: The Breakdown of the Spanish-American Empire* (Cambridge: Harvard University Press, 1980).

3. Howard J. Wiarda, *Dilemmas of Democracy in Latin America: Crises and Opportunities* (Lanham, MD: Rowman & Littlefield, 2005), p. 7.

4. Paul H. Lewis, *Authoritarian Regimes in Latin America: Dictators, Despots, and Tyrants* (Lanham, MD: Roman & Littlefield, 2006), p. 14.

5. Lynch, *Latin American Revolutions,* p. 88.

6. Rodríguez O., *Independence,* p. 2.

7. Ibid., p. 103.

8. Ibid., p. 89.

9. Dominguez, *Insurrection,* p. 249.

10. Ibid., p. 250.

11. On the economic situation on the eve of independence, see Richard L. Garner, *Economic Growth and Change in Bourbon Mexico* (Gainesville: University Press of Florida, 1993).

12. Dominguez, *Insurrection,* p. 253.

13. This section draws heavily upon Ronald M. Schneider, *"Order and Progress": A Political History of Brazil* (Boulder, CO: Westview Press, 1991), pp. 32–52, abridged in Ronald M. Schneider, *Brazil: Culture and Politics in a New Industrial Powerhouse* (Boulder, CO: Westview Press, 1996), pp. 37–43. Excellent on the period is Roderick J. Barman, *Brazil: The Forging of a Nation, 1798–1852* (Stanford, CA: Stanford University Press, 1988), with events leading up to independence covered in pp. 42–96 and the intricate maneuverings of the initial period of independence detailed in pp. 97–129.

14. See N. P. Macdonald, *The Making of Brazil: Portuguese Roots 1500–1822* (Sussex, UK: Book Guild, 1996), pp. 440–445.

15. Ibid., pp. 465–487, treats these developments.

16. Neil Macaulay, *Dom Pedro: The Struggle for Liberty in Brazil and Portugal, 1798–1834* (Durham, NC: Duke University Press, 1986), provides a nuanced treatment of this controversial figure.

17. Macaulay portrays Pedro as less absolutist than his Brazilian biographers generally do and depicts his enemies as far from truly liberal, whereas Barman, *Brazil,* stresses the continuing desire of Brazilians to cut the Portuguese-born down to size. Concerned with his brother Miguel's seizure of the Portuguese throne in 1828 to the detriment of Pedro's nine-year-old daughter (Miguel's child wife), Pedro may well have viewed his abdication as exchanging a new and somewhat uncomfortable crown for a time-honored throne near the European center of world affairs.

18. Pedro's extremely long reign is ably analyzed in Roderick J. Barman, *Citizen Emperor, Pedro II and the Making of Brazil, 1825–91* (Stanford, CA: Stanford University Press, 1999).

19. See Richard Graham, *Patronage and Politics in Nineteenth-Century Brazil* (Stanford, CA: Stanford University Press, 1990).

20. Most of the useful sources on this war are in Portuguese or Spanish, the most comprehensive being Augusto Tasso Fragoso, *História da Guerra entre a Triplice Aliança e o Paraguay,* 5 vols. (Rio de Janeiro: Imprensa do Estado Maior de Exército, 1934).

21. First-rate histories of Mexico include Michael C. Meyer and William H. Beezley, eds., *The Oxford History of Mexico* (New York: Oxford University Press, 2000), and Colin M. MacLachan, *Spain's Empire in the New World* (Berkeley and Los Angeles: University of California Press, 1991). Rodrígues O., *Independence,* pp. 159–168, analyzes the process of Mexico's separation from Spain.

22. Enrique Krauze, *Mexico, Biography of Power: A History of Modern Mexico, 1810–1996* (New York: HarperCollins, 1997), pp. 91–102, treats the period of Hidalgo's preeminence.

23. Krauze, *Mexico,* pp. 103–111, covers Morelos's revolutionary enterprise.

24. Ibid., pp. 121–129, treats this monarchical interlude.

25. Ibid., pp. 135–158, recounts the ins and outs of the Santa Ana era. Lewis, *Authoritarian Regimes,* pp. 19–21, captures the essence of his political style. A detailed, highly negative biography is Robert L. Scheina, *Santa Anna: A Curse upon Mexico* (Washington, DC: Brassey's, 2002).

26. Krauze, *Mexico,* p. 142.

27. Ibid., pp. 159–172, 192–204, deals with Juárez's presidencies.

28. Ibid., pp. 173–191, covers Maximilian's ill-fated rule.

29. The standard historical survey is James Scobie, *Argentina: A City and a Nation*, 2nd ed. (New York: Oxford University Press, 1971). On the independence process, consult Rodríguez O., *Independence,* pp. 123–130.

30. See John Lynch, *Argentine Caudillo: Juan Manuel de Rosas* (Wilmington, DE: Scholarly Resources, 2001). Lewis, *Authoritarian Regimes,* pp. 18–19, presents a vivid sketch of the man and his regime.

31. Lewis, *Authoritarian Regimes,* pp. 88–89, provides an insightful sketch of Mitre.

32. Consult Ariel de la Fuente, *Children of Facundo: Caudillo and Gaucho Insurgency During the Argentine State-Formation Process (La Rioja, 1853–70)* (Durham, NC: Duke University Press, 2000).

33. Very useful is Fernando López Alves, *State Formation and Democracy in Latin America, 1810–1900* (Durham, NC: Duke University Press, 2000). For the intellectual flavor of this period, consult William H. Katra, *The Argentine Generation of 1837: Echeverria, Alberdi, Sarmiento, Mitre* (Madison, NJ: Fairleigh Dickinson University Press, 1996).

34. See López Alves, *State Formation,* as well as Martin Weinstein, *Uruguay: Democracy at the Crossroads* (Boulder, CO: Westview Press, 1988).

35. Consult Lewis, *Authoritarian Regimes,* pp. 31–37. On his long-term legacy, see Riordan Roett and Richard S. Sacks, *Paraguay: The Personalist Legacy* (Boulder, CO: Westview Press, 1990).

36. See Chris Leuchars, *To the Bitter End: Paraguay and the War of the Triple Alliance* (Westport, CT: Greenwood Press, 2002).

37. Consult Anthony McFarland, *Colombia Before Independence* (Cambridge, UK: Cambridge University Press, 1993), pp. 332–346, and David Bushnell, *The Making of Modern Colombia: A Nation in Spite of Itself* (Berkeley and Los Angeles: University of California Press, 1993), pp. 32–41. Specifics on the independence struggle are covered in Rodríguez O., *Independence,* pp. 150–157.

38. See Bushnell, *Making of Modern Colombia,* pp. 55–60. Another reliable history is Frank Safford and Marco Palacios, *Colombia: Fragmented Land, Divided Society* (New York: Oxford University Press, 2002).

39. Bushnell, *Making of Modern Colombia,* pp. 67–73, evaluates his exercise of power from 1826 to 1830.

40. Ibid., pp. 83–99, deals with 1832–1848. See also López Alves, *State Formation,* in which Colombia is compared with Argentina and Uruguay.

41. Lewis, *Authoritarian Regimes,* . . . , p. 29, quoting Scheina, *Santa Ana,* p. 175.

42. Lewis, *Authoritarian Regimes,* p. 27.

43. Bushnell, *Making of Modern Colombia,* pp. 122–125.

44. Lewis, *Authoritarian Regimes,* p. 23. On the legacy of this type of beginning, see Daniel C. Hellinger, *Venezuela: Tarnished Democracy* (Boulder, CO: Westview Press, 1991). On the independence struggle, consult Rodríguez O., *Independence,* pp. 109–122. Also useful is Robert L. Gilmore, *Caudillism and Militarism in Venezuela, 1810–1910* (Athens: Ohio University Press, 1964).

45. For background see David Schodt, *Ecuador: An Andean Enigma* (Boulder, CO: Westview Press, 1987).

46. Highly favorable assessments are Father Jean du Saveur, *García Moreno: The Intrepid President of Ecuador, 1821–1875* (St. Jovite, Quebec: Editions Magnificat, 1989), and John C. Moran, *In Memoriam: Gabriel García Moreno, 1875–1975* (St. Paul, MN: Dawn Heron Press, 1976).

47. See Lewis, *Authoritarian Regimes,* pp. 25–26. Peter F. Klarén, *Peru: Society and Nationhood in the Andes* (New York: Oxford University Press, 2000), provides a sound historical treatment of the period.

48. An unpublished manuscript by John Gitlitz was very helpful on the interaction of economics, social change, and politics in Peru's development.

49. See Herbert S. Klein, *Bolivia: The Evolution of a Multi-Ethnic Society*, 2nd ed. (New York: Oxford University Press, 1992). Rodríguez O., *Independence,* pp. 130–136, treats the independence of Bolivia along with that of Paraguay and Uruguay.

50. On this period, consult Waltrud Queiser Morales, *Bolivia: Land of Struggle* (Boulder, CO: Westview Press, 1991).

51. See Lewis, *Authoritarian Regimes,* pp. 26–27.

52. A useful source is Simon Collier and William E. Slater, *A History of Chile, 1808–1994* (Cambridge, UK: Cambridge University Press, 1996), which provides details on O'Higgins and his role. See also Rodriguez O., *Independence,* pp. 136–144.

53. Consult Lewis, *Authoritarian Regimes,* pp. 38–42. There is considerable dispute among Chilean political scientists on the contribution of this governmental framework to the country's relative stability. For a measured view on this issue, see Federico G. Gil, *The Political System of Chile* (Boston: Houghton Mifflin, 1966).

54. For perspective on this juncture see Collier and Slater, *History.*

55. Consult Ralph Lee Woodward, Jr., *Central America: A Nation Divided*, 3rd ed. (New York: Oxford University Press, 1999).

56. Lewis, *Authoritarian Regimes,* pp. 21–22.

57. See James Morris, *Honduras: Caudillo Politics and Military Rulers* (Boulder, CO: Westview Press, 1984).

58. See John A. Booth, *Costa Rica: Quest for Democracy* (Boulder, CO: Westview Press, 1998).

59. Consult Thomas W. Walker, *Nicaragua: The Land of Sandino* (Boulder, CO: Westview Press, 1981).

60. See Patrick Bellegarde-Smith, *Haiti: The Breached Citadel* (Boulder, CO: Westview Press, 1989). For a broader perspective of the area, consult Franklin W. Knight, *The Caribbean: The Genesis of a Fragmented Nationalism* (New York: Oxford University Press, 1990).

61. Alex Dupuy, *Haiti and the World Economy: Class, Race, and Underdevelopment Since 1700* (Boulder, CO: Westview Press, 1989), is perceptive on this generally misunderstood country.

62. Wiarda, *Dilemmas,* p. 93.

63. Consult Howard J. Wiarda and Michael Kryzanek, *The Dominican Republic: A Caribbean Crucible* (Boulder, CO: Westview Press, 1982).

64. Wiarda, *Dilemmas,* p. 7.

65. Voss, *Latin America,* up to p. 162, provides an overall conceptualization of trends but does not treat variations and differentiation.

66. López Alves, *State Formation,* p. 8.

4

Consolidation and Development

Latin America, 1871–1899

A number of unifying themes with roots in the colonial period ran through the first half century of independence down into this new period. Violence, although not at the levels attained during the independence struggle, ran high as force continued to decide who would hold power in many countries. Even where there were no *caudillo*-type power struggles or foreign invaders to be expelled, as had just occurred in Mexico, large-scale bloodshed broke out. The 1870s began with an extremely bloody war between Brazil and Paraguay, and subsequently Brazilian authorities ruthlessly exterminated a large community of poor rural dwellers on the implausible justification that they were subversives seeking to restore the monarchy (abolished in 1889).

In Argentina violence took the form of virtual genocide against the country's indigenous population. Colombia ended the nineteenth century with an intense three-year civil war between Conservatives and Liberals—on both sides staunch Catholics. Chile, Peru, and Bolivia became involved in a Second War of the Pacific, one with even more sweeping consequences than those of the 1830s. Central America saw continued efforts to reunite the subregion by force, and tens of thousands of Cubans perished in attempts to gain independence from Spain. In almost every instance labor seeking to organize was met head-on by repression involving the army, not just police forces.

Authoritarian mind-sets stymied most efforts at establishing republican processes with a significant democratic component, and very little headway was made in broadening political participation. In most places executive authority dominated national legislatures, a trend most pronounced in Mexico's autocratic Díaz regime (which continued in power a decade into the next century). Yet, in one notable case, Chile, an attempt at presidential role expansion was stopped dead in its tracks in a violent confrontation resulting in the president's ouster and suicide. As is spotlighted in this chapter, leadership styles became more varied, as did opportunities for corruption.

Although there were major continuities, in several important ways Latin America underwent very significant changes during the last three decades of the nineteenth century. In the first place, Brazil made the watershed transition from an enlightened monarchy to an aristocratic, if not oligarchic, republic, and Mexico slipped into the unique developmentalist tyranny of the thirty-five year Díaz era. Argentina moved to institutionalize a viable elitist republican regime while consolidating recentralization. On the negative side, Colombia's efforts at an elitist democracy deteriorated into bloody civil war in a still deeply regionalized country. The elites involved in each of these major countries were heavily influenced by positivism, an ideology stemming from the writings of French philosopher Auguste Comte. A symbiotic fit with the goal of development, it called for controlled, evolutionary modernization. As Wiarda explains its appeal to the elites and emerging middle sectors in Latin America:

> It advocated change and progress but not through revolutions. It was change led by the educated elites, devolving little power upon the masses. It stood for development but not genuine democratization or popular participation. It was not divisively individualistic in the U.S. sense but was centralized, organic, top-down, and corporatist in accord with long-standing Latin American traditions.[1]

Peru, Chile, and Bolivia coped, each in its own way, with the Second War of the Pacific and its heritage while seeking ways to reconnect with the world economy—Chile having the most notable success, Bolivia the least. Venezuela continued its *caudillo* pattern; in many of the other countries, a significant degree of stability emerged, under "respectable" conservatives, from the often chaotic postindependence epoch, whether it had been *caudillo*-dominated or not. The Caribbean, other than Haiti and the Dominican Republic, remained under foreign rule, although Cuba experienced a protracted armed struggle for independence from Spain. National integration attenuated but did not eliminate caudillism, an often much misunderstood, but important, feature of Latin America's political heritage. It was a unique form of personalist rule widely prevalent during the first generation of independence, and even more, it helped to explain political life in those many places where, with some modifications, it persisted into the twentieth century. This persistence required caudillism, first, to survive the latter part of the nineteenth century, as it spectacularly did in nearly pristine form in Venezuela and Guatemala, and with modification, but not transformation, in the Dominican Republic, Honduras, Nicaragua, Paraguay, and, in a far less pure form, Mexico and

Peru. Moreover, in many instances national consolidation was brought about by one *caudillo's* dominating his rivals, the result being a dictatorship or a group of *caudillos* forming a national political machine of a warlord nature, in which they preserved local control and shared in the profits of national revenues and patronage—all this while reducing the risk of elimination by central authorities.

As demonstrated in the preceding chapter, caudillism in all its variations involved use of personal appeal and leadership qualities, often bordering on the charismatic, as well as bravery and audacity, to promote allegiance to an individual in a situation where the traditional basis of monarchical authority had disappeared and no new base for institutionalizing legitimacy had yet emerged. It was particularly frequent in countries with a deep cleavage between capital city and peripheral rural regions, in which a would-be *caudillo* could build his clients, dependents, and retainers into a private army, then descend on the urban center and, conquering it, rule the country.[2]

Caudillo rule had the effect of retarding the emergence of constitutional legitimacy, even as structured political authority did emerge. The true *caudillo* had a degree of personalist allegiance that ordinary dictators lacked, although in the real world there were certainly dictatorial *caudillos* and, particularly after the emergence of organized armed forces, caudillistic dictators. The ideal type of postindependence caudillism could not, finally, survive the establishment of a professional military, but it could coexist symbiotically with the jerry-built nonprofessionalized armed forces that many countries had. In some places, including Venezuela and Guatemala, caudillism and militarism would eventually merge, Venezuela's Juan Vicente Gómez being the outstanding example of a leader beginning as a *caudillo* in the first decade of the twentieth century and ending up as a militarist dictator by the 1930s.

The persistence and transformation of caudillism in some countries, contrasted sharply with the emergence of dominant elites, in some cases true oligarchies, stands out as the most important differentiating factor in Latin America during the latter third of the nineteenth century. In most cases the original generation of leadership was gone by the early 1850s. A second coming to power between the mid-1840s and the mid-1850s, had a different destiny in some countries than in others. The outstanding exception was Brazil, where the monarchy provided for extraordinary institutional continuity, with one monarch on the throne from 1830 to 1889. As already shown, national unity in combination with viable economic development had gotten under way in a number of countries during the 1860s, but in more cases it was be delayed to the 1870s and 1880s, and in a few instances even longer. Most countries experienced some type of developmental surge, either under oligarchical formal democracies or behind *caudillo*-type dictators. Conservatives relied on indirect political participation and limited regional and local self-government, and Liberals advocated an enlarged and invigorated state and testing the limits of participation in representative republican politics.

Greatly augmented demand in Europe and the United States for the region's raw materials and foodstuffs provided a favorable economic environment. Moreover, foreign capital flowed into mining, export agriculture, and the infrastructure required by a quantum leap in the movement of goods. Small local industries burgeoned along with commercial enterprises; banking and financial institutions flourished. Foreign perceptions of order and stability were essential to a continued stream of investment and access to loans. Of course, some countries were left out of this progress, such as Paraguay, and to a lesser extent Bolivia, as well as Caribbean laggard Haiti. Then, too, the general trends appeared in diminished scale and more clouded form in Central America.

In examining political change in the late 1800s, not only is it necessary to establish a basis for comparing which countries would be farther along the road to political development at the period's end, but attention must also be given to the extent of progress made by countries entering this period already trailing far behind the exemplary leaders. Indeed, some countries made more progress than others but were still behind them in political development at the period's end. Assessment is complicated because headway was often made on one dimension while absent in other areas. Voss captures the prevailing situation as one in which "the cumulative effect of the notables' response to the expanding opportunities of a market economy and of modern republican politics had reached a critical turning point by the 1870s. Their large and well-structured families enabled them steadily to broaden and deepen their involvement in the economy and public affairs."[3] He sees the behavioral transition as one in which the family retained its paramount role, whereas the parish and the community lost theirs as a new generation of institutions became the foundations of an industrial capitalist economy featuring greater commercialization of production and an unprecedented influx of foreign capital that "augmented the horizons of Latin America's prominent families. As a result the notables distanced themselves from those below and tightened relations with an activist national state."[4]

Overview

By 1871, several of the region's countries had fared better since independence than others, and a few had relatively, if not absolutely, stood still. Brazil entered the period with its monarchy functioning full throttle and coming off its crushing defeat of Paraguay. The shift of its economic center of gravity from the northeast and its tropical plantation products to the center-south, where coffee had become king, was well under way, bringing with it the broad stream of European, particularly Italian, immigration. Mexico had just thrown off the alien monarchy imposed upon it by Louis Napoleon and returned to the Liberal reforms of the Juárez era the monarchy had interrupted. Argentina had finally been unified and was being governed by leaders who were among the most intelligent and educated in the region. With peace and unity it was able to attract the torrent of Italian immigration that rapidly transformed its society. Compared to these three, Colombia was little changed from the preceding period, entering into its coffee era without the immigration from which Brazil and Argentina were benefiting or political leadership comparable to that of any of them.

Peru, which had experienced a conflict-ridden decade in the 1860s, saw its first civilian president and first peaceful transition from one elected civilian to another soon after the period opened. Subsequently the rule of its first outstanding president was interrupted by a second disastrous war with Chile. During this time Peru would undergo substantial economic diversification, leading to intense intraelite rivalries. Venezuela entered the period just out of its bloody civil strife and had a long period of stability and economic growth and modernization under a relatively benevolent Liberal *caudillo*—the first time it was catching up to its neighbors instead of falling farther behind, and doing this under the least undemocratic government it would have until the late 1930s.

Chile began the period as the most democratic country in Latin America and in many ways rested on its laurels, bolstered by high nitrate exports. Ecuador's Conservative strongman was assassinated in 1875, and the country was plagued by violent conflict for all but the last few years of the period. Bolivia was farther behind in terms of political development, entering the 1870s racked by violence, which would continue through the period's end. Already in poor political straits, Uruguay and Paraguay essentially marked time—as did the five countries of Central America, along with Haiti and the Dominican Republic.

More often than not, the prevailing situation at the end of the century was stability that benefited the upper classes, sometimes reflected in strongman rule. This varied from a sophisticated and, for the times, not undemocratic regime of channeling and balancing forces in Argentina under General Julio Roca to a harshly authoritarian regime with the most threadbare veil of republican structures and processes in Mexico under General Porfirio Díaz, this latter model lasting a decade into the twentieth century. In Brazil, where a republic replaced monarchy only at the end of the 1880s, elite figures started a rotation in office at the century's end, to be continued and perfected in the early twentieth century. Colombia, unfortunately, was caught up in a bloody civil war, but Peru managed to get under stable elite civilian during the late 1890s, while Venezuela regressed politically after the death of durable Liberal *caudillo* Guzmán Blanco. How these conditions came about requires close examination.

Brazil: From Monarchy to Republic

Latin America's largest country worked its way into and through a major systems change. Although a Republican Party was founded in 1870 and the number of recent European immigrants was rising just as the ranks of slaves were thinning, the monarchy that made Brazil unique in Latin America—indeed the Western Hemisphere—was still functioning smoothly.[5] Despite three decades in power, Pedro II, just turning forty-five, was in his prime. Although the costs had been great, Brazil was enjoying the final victorious phase of the Paraguayan war, including military occupation of its troublesome neighbor. Swelling of the officer corps from roughly fifteen hundred to nearly ten thousand created a major demobilization problem, and the country had too many military heroes who aspired to influential governmental positions—seeing themselves as worthy successors to the country's great aging icon, the newly elevated Duke of Caxias. Hence the seeds of the post-1880 decay of the monarchical system may well have been sown during the Paraguayan war, needing only sufficient irrigation during the superficially calm 1870s to ensure subsequent germination.

The war had brought with it a significant spurt of industrialization, but with a built-in lag factor before it would affect society sufficiently to have a heavy impact upon politics. Meanwhile the Liberals, smarting from their abrupt ouster from power during the war, had initiated a decade in opposition—the longest such stint in their history—calling for electoral reform, elimination of the Emperor's moderating power, the disbanding of the National Guard, and even the abolition of slavery. The new generation of Conservative Party politicians was loyal to the monarchy, but unlike their distinguished predecessors, they had not experienced the "chaos, anarchy, and threatened disintegration" that had marked the 1830s.[6]

The passage of the Rio Branco Law (the law of free birth) in September 1871 assuaged antislavery forces by declaring that children henceforth born to slave mothers would be free—but only when they came of age. As a result, by 1884 the number of slaves declined to 1.24 million, and a new law then freed all over sixty years of age. By 1887, some 723,000 slaves (plus 500,000 of their children) constituted only 5 percent of Brazil's growing population—which by the early 1880s had reached 12 million (finally surpassing that of Mexico).[7] Yet this reduction in the scope of the slavery problem heartened abolitionists to press for a full end to what they viewed as a retrograde abomination.

As in the societal realm, change in the economy was significant yet circumscribed, making its impact upon politics slow and sure rather than sudden and destabilizing. Under the forward-looking emperor the government subsidized a wide variety of economic activities, including coastal steamboats, railroad construction, modernization of the sugar industry, and European immigration. From 20 percent of central government expenditures in 1879, economic development rose to 33 percent by the monarchy's end in 1889—still well behind the cost of the military and civil bureaucracies. Foreign trade remained the major source of government revenue, and failure of agriculture to generate sufficient income was the major restraint on industrialization. Unlike the more favorable situation of rival Argentina, Brazil's problem of a small domestic market for manufactured goods was aggravated by high internal transportation costs stemming from the long distances involved.[8] Economic growth had recovered during the Paraguayan war but, after undergoing a downturn in 1876–1877, rallied strongly for the rest of the decade. Meanwhile, the land law of 1850, benefiting the coffee producers and facilitating the continuation of large plantations and *fazendas* ("latifundia") in older areas, remained the basis of a land tenure system that would prove resistant to change into the twenty-first century.

As Brazil moved through the 1870s and into the 1880s, the abolitionists and republicans provided the monarchy with an increasingly divisive political agenda. Yet these vociferous civilian groups by themselves were no threat to the system. The armed forces were a very different matter. A series of reform measures passed in 1873 and 1874 temporarily satisfied much of the officer corps but, as is the wont of reforms, whetted the appetites of more radical figures. For replacement of the old system of forced recruitment—the so-called manhunt (essentially kidnapping by press gangs)—by a semblance of a conscription system was long overdue.[9] Moreover, the implementing legislation gutted this reform, reducing it to a moribund, if not completely dead, letter.

Those younger officers whose wartime experience had led them to want vigorous reform of their service were discontented over indifference, if not opposition, to their proposals for modernization. The civilian elite, lulled into complacency by the absence of political adventures by the army during the long span of its dominance by the Duke of Caxias (who presided over the council of ministers for the final time in 1875–1878), blindly perceived no risk in taking the military for granted (this at a time when under Díaz the military was in the driver's seat in Mexico, and when Roca was rising to dominance in Argentina on the basis of his military exploits). Thus the horizon was already clouded when economic depression was aggravated by a coffee crisis after 1880—the year in which Caxias died.

The landmark 1881 Saraiva law made parliamentary elections direct by a single class of electors, which included, for the first time, non-Catholics, freedmen, and naturalized citizens. Yet, at the same time that it took this forward step, this "reform" reduced the number of eligible voters from over 1.1 million to just above 145,000 (by eliminating the preliminary steps of the old multilevel process). The subsequent October elections dealt the first electoral reverse to the party in power in the nation's history, as the emperor maintained an unaccustomed posture of impartiality. But the establishment adapted rapidly to this modification of the rules of the political game, and clientelism at least partially replaced coercion in maintaining the essence of the old electoral politics: manageability. The Liberals' leading military figure, Marshal Manuel Luíz Osório, had passed away just before Caxias, leaving the army without prestigious old-school figures to help contain discontent. Indeed, Caxias's and Osório's heirs in the military hierarchy would ride this wave to power instead of seeking to stem it.

The growing divorce between the political elite and the military contributed to acceptance by the great majority of the officer corps of a coup engineered by a small, radicalized faction drawn chiefly from the post–Paraguayan war generation. The government, including an aging emperor deprived of his trusted judge of the military's mood, failed to realize that military leaders could provide a very different type of opposition from that the churchmen had mounted in the 1870s on the "religious question" when the state clashed with the upper clergy over prerogatives. When civilian governments, both Liberal and Conservative, provided members of the military with issues that united rather than divided them, they could subordinate partisan inclinations and personal rivalries to a prickly sense of corporate pride and strong institutional interests. While the Conservatives and Liberals fell over each other cultivating the generals and admirals, the small Republican Party began to work on the younger officers—particularly those who had manifested signs of dissatisfaction with the status quo. Moreover, as proved the case in many other countries, making politics a major factor in promotions and appointments proved to be a sure way to politicize the armed forces.[10]

The impact of the abolitionist cause was most strongly felt through its overlap with republicanism, as sympathy for the former led to support for the latter. By 1884, Lieutenant Colonel Antônio de Sena Madureira had twice become the center of a controversy between the military and the government over officers' rights to speak out on political issues. Meanwhile, Marshal Manoel Deodoro da Fonseca (b. 1827), although a confirmed monarchist, was becoming increasingly alienated from the government. Having experienced combat in the civil strife of the 1840s, he— along with his five military brothers—found an opportunity to distinguish himself in the Paraguayan war. A colonel by the conflict's end, the able, ambitious, and egoistic Deodoro was promoted to brigadier general in 1874. Advanced to field marshal, the equivalent of major general, in 1884 and named quartermaster general the next year, in 1886 he was assigned to command all military forces in Rio Grande do Sul—where the government also appointed him first vice president of that key border province. This career success fed his belief that he was the logical heir to the great influence previously exercised by Caxias. His subsequent involvement in the political dispute over the miserable state into which the army had been allowed to deteriorate was not only logical but would be far from the last time an apparently nonpolitical general with a long career marked by professionalism and adherence to authority would abruptly become highly politicized and play a key role in a regime change bordering on system transformation (as in 1955 and 1964).[11]

When Sena Madureira was censured for violation of a gag order, Deodoro aligned with the opposition Liberal Party. The prime minister's decision to relieve Sena Madureira of his command proved as fatal to the government as would the Spanish Republican regime's decision in the early 1930s to do the same to General Francisco Franco. Well aware of the emperor's advancing age and declining health, Deodoro led younger officers in establishing the Clube Militar ("Military Club"), which was to play a significant role in the impending crisis as well as subsequent ones.[12] Although a fairly sharp cleavage on political issues had existed between the Paraguayan war generation and the junior and midgrade officers imbued with the positivist ideas of the leading military intellectual, Benjamin Constant Botelho de Magalhães (b. 1836), common corporate interests now crystallized in the no-holds-barred debates within the Military Club—with Deodoro as its president and Constant as vice president. Indeed, this forum for a continuing exchange of views outside the rigid hierarchy of the command structure greatly facilitated discussion moving toward action.

Moreover, the War College, created in March 1889 as an extension of the Military Academy for advanced and specialized training—and commanded by Constant—had a faculty loaded with military reformers who would be part of the coming coup's leadership. Located next to cavalry and artillery barracks, the War College "infected" these line troops, rather than being contained by them. Hence, although the economic effects of abolition and their political ramifications had some impact upon the termination of the monarchy, the antislavery campaign had brought officers together with civilian advocates of a republic within the framework of a common social reform cause. Intelligently the Republican Party members forged an alliance by temporarily downplaying their major goal in favor of concentrating on issues of greater immediate concern to the military—including federalism, which did not require open opposition to the constituted authorities of the empire but at the same time carried the young officers a step down the road in the direction of such a break. By early 1888, "the officers had absorbed so much republican propaganda in their studies at the military school and the Superior War School that they were ready to substitute abolitionist sentiments with republican ones as necessary to make Brazil a free Pátria."[13]

On May 13, 1888, while acting as regent, Pedro's daughter and heir decreed the end of slavery—a move directly affecting only 650,000 blacks (who became unemployed freedmen instead of employed slaves). The modicum of popular support gained was offset by the bitter alienation of provincial landowners, who were still important in the Conservative Party, which in June was brought back into power. Republican leaders, their party having been credited with less than one-seventh of the vote in the August 1889 elections (as blatantly manipulated as the vote that would bring down the "Old Republic" in 1930) realized their need for a prestigious military leader at the head of their movement. Heavily influenced by Constant, thirty-four-year-old Major Hermes Rodrigues da Fonseca helped convince his uncle, the malcontented Marshal Deodoro, to head the revolutionary government. When adjutant general Floriano Peixoto (b. 1839), who, on disability leave in out-of-the-way Alagoas, had avoided involvement in the events leading up to the revolt, on November 15 added his two thousand troops to the six-hundred-man rebel column in Rio de Janeiro, the empire was at its end. The graying emperor was still respected, but the emerging elites could not accept the prospect of an empress dominated by an arrogant French husband—the Conde d'Eu—detested by much of the officer corps. So the royal family was sent off to Europe, where Pedro died in Paris two years into his forced retirement.[14] As McCann eloquently captures the essence of this development:

> The overthrow of the empire was a coup d'etat rather than a popular revolution; the republic was the product of an officer corps defending its particular interests and allying itself to a political minority. In fact, only a portion of the corps was directly involved; some officers were motivated by fears for their institution and for their own welfare, some by republican ideology or the desire to be up-to-date with international trends, but no officer displayed his willingness to die for the empire.[15]

As in 1930, and even more in 1964, the coup's rapid success benefited from the government's having grossly overestimated its military strength *(dispositivo militar)*, seriously misjudged the probable actions of key military figures (including the emergence of a critical "swingman"), and relied on popular support, which did not arise to defend the regime at the time and place where the crucial events were taking place (Rio do Janeiro in the first half of November). In comparative and analytic terms the decay of Brazil's imperial regime corresponded closely to Huntington's generalization concerning the fate of centralized traditional monarchies: "Such political systems ordinarily have a high degree of legitimacy and effectiveness so long as political participation is limited. Their political institutions, however, remain rigid and fragile in the face of social change. They are unable to adapt to the emergence of middle-class groups into politics."[16]

In basic outline subsequent events followed Huntington's scenario:

> The pattern of politics in the displacement of the traditional or oligarchic rule by military coup d'etat resembles in a more restrained and limited fashion the familiar Crane Brinton model of revolution (beginning with "treason of the intellectuals," fall of the old regime, revolutionary honeymoon,

PEDRO II

and reign of terror through the "thermidor"). In the construction of the coalition of military and civilian elements to carry out the coup, it is usually necessary to stress those objectives which have the broadest appeal and to place at the head of the coup a moderate, conciliatory military leader who is able to acquire the confidence of all the groups participating in the coup and also has more ties than other members of those groups with the old regime.[17]

Over its sixty-seven-year life the monarchy had served its purpose. For by the time Brazil discarded it and embarked on the republican road—which had proven so perilous and fraught with traumatic episodes for the other countries of the region—many of the most serious challenges to national integrity and identity had been overcome. Not only had the vast territory been held together, when Spanish America had fragmented, but significant gains had also been made in the process of securing borders, across which there were now eight separate Hispanic American countries plus surviving British, French, and Dutch colonies. Moreover, national political institutions and processes had been consolidated, the establishment of professionalized armed forces and the alternation of parties in power being the most significant accomplishments. On the other hand, little had been lost in political development by the lateness of this adoption of a presidential republic. Mexico's republican experience had led only to loss of half its original territory and the Díaz dictatorship. In Argentina the double break with Spain and monarchy had ushered in the dictatorship of Rosas and the political separation of Buenos Aires from the rest of the country, which was finally ended in 1861 by the military victory of the metropolis over the provinces. Even the long parliamentary experience of Chile had deteriorated by the end of the 1880s into a civil war between forces backing the supremacy of the congress and those supporting a president bent on augmenting his powers.

Now, with the monarchy's end, for the first time in Brazil's history a dictatorship was in control, legitimized only by its monopoly of force and significant, but far from overwhelming, popular support for a republic. The crucial factor in the future course of Brazil's political development was that the Republicans had turned to the armed forces as the one institution that could put an end to the monarchy without precipitating drastic change in the distribution of power among contending social groups. For the Republican Party wanted only an alteration in the framework of government to accommodate the economic and social changes that had already occurred. With coffee's almost 5.6 million 132-pound sacks in 1889 providing two-thirds of the country's exports, the coffee producers and their mercantilist associates sought greater say in national policy than the monarchy, with its ties to ossifying parties, provided. Hence, this regime change did not usher in any sharp break in economic policy or new departures in the social realm. Serving in the last parliament of the empire were two Republican Party deputies, elected in 1884 from São Paulo, who soon would become the nation's first civilian presidents: Prudente José de Morais Barros (1894–1898) and Manuel Ferraz de Campos Salles (1898–1902). But first Brazil would have to weather a stormy period of rule by a pair of autocratic militarists.

The provisional government that found itself suddenly in office on November 15, 1889, was not agreed upon what kind of a republic should be installed (much as was to be the case again after the 1930 revolution). Historical republicans, Jacobin army officers, and traditional notables seeking to salvage what they could from the sinking of the empire all vied for office and influence. Headed by a conservative militarist who had never believed in republicanism, the new government, after a short period of turmoil and strife, saw the old local and regional elites reassert their control over all but the most urban and industrializing parts of the increasingly dualistic country. Ruy Barbosa (b. 1849), the epitome of the well-meaning and excessively optimistic republican civilianist cadre, as the republic's first finance minister implemented a moderate degree of protectionism, considering it to be politically crucial in consolidating the new regime. With no constitution in effect, banks emitted so much currency that the money supply almost doubled in 1890 and expanded by over 50 percent the next year. As economic interests scrambled to take advantage of the prevailing preoccupation with the nature of the emerging governmental institutions and political processes, the republican regime consumed nine finance ministers during its first seven years.

For all the government's initial uncertainty and hesitation, Brazil continued to change. Its racial composition underwent transformation as European immigrants, with Italians as the backbone, flowed in even faster than had African slaves in earlier periods. From 10,000 a year in the 1850s and 1860s, these new arrivals doubled to nearly 20,000 annually during the 1870s before exploding to over 450,000 in the 1880s—on their way to a record 215,000 in 1891. Indeed, of the 10 million that would come to Latin America between 1870 and 1930, nearly two-fifths would settle in Brazil—and their numerous progeny would profoundly alter its society.[18] By filling the workforce needs of the developing coffee areas, this immigration kept the former slave population at the bottom of the socioeconomic pyramid. (Over the longer run, these immigrants' impact would be felt in the political socialization they had brought from the Old World—where Italy achieved political unity only in 1868, followed by Germany in 1871.)

At this point Brazil's literacy rates, 19 percent for males and 10 percent for females, reflected the absence of educational opportunity for the vast majority of the population. As Europeanization went forward, the Afro-Brazilian proportion of the population decreased, and the indigenous population nearly disappeared. Having declined precipitously (to under 1.5 million by 1750, only 800,000 by 1819, and a mere 0.5 million by 1867), its numbers were far less than those of immigrants arriving in any two-year period. Overall, Brazil's population had risen to 14.3 million in 1889 from 11.8 million in 1880, with over two-fifths still living in the economically declining northeast region. The economic heart of the country had shifted southward into São Paulo, whose 1890 population of 1.4 million was on its way to 4.6 million by 1920, largely as a result of immigration. Still, just 11 percent lived in cities of over 10,000 inhabitants, and industry accounted for only 10 percent of GDP.[19]

Shadows of these changes could be discerned in the political realm. Although some planters had supported the Republican Party, from November 1889 to 1894, control of the government was largely in the hands of predominantly urban-oriented individuals, chiefly military, who took some steps inimical to the planters' interests. The nation's center of gravity had moved to the center-south, with Minas Gerais, the country's most populous state at 3.1 million in 1890, occupying a pivotal position as link between the former heartland and the soon-to-be-dominant region. Having dissolved the Chamber of Deputies and eliminated the life tenure of Senate members, Deodoro assumed the title Chief of the Provisional Government, and military men took power in a majority of states. In the view of leading political sociologist Fernando H. Cardoso (son of a general and destined to be Brazil's president from 1995 through 2002), "At the level of real political organization the dismantling of the imperial institutions left a vacuum that, in the short run, could only be filled, as it was, by the great bureaucratic structure that came unglued from the Imperial State: the armed forces."[20] Yet they would do a poor job of providing stability, much less good government. As McCann aptly sums up the situation:

Military intervention in politics and society is a sign of weakness of both the state and society. But to apply the statement to Brazil is to say the obvious. During the nineteenth century the monarchy and the army were the sole national institutions in a remarkably weak state and society. The coup of 1889 left the army as the republic's core institution but without the ideology, structure, experience, personnel, political mandate, or will to embrace fully such a role.[21]

Even before becoming war minister at the end of April 1890, Floriano Peixoto wielded great power, replacing Ruy Barbosa as first deputy chief a few months later. At least four major groups had collaborated in the republican revolution and were represented in the provisional government: the historical republicans, particularly strong in São Paulo; the young civilian revolutionaries; the positivist-oriented junior officers who followed Benjamin Constant (and would be orphaned by his death in early 1891); and the senior military, who had joined or accepted the movement because of Deodoro's and Floriano's lead. At the extremes of polarization were the authoritarian-oriented Jacobins and an alliance of promonarchy naval officers and São Paulo coffee-producing elites. As would be the case again in 1930 and 1964, differences over policy as well as personal rivalries soon emerged. When the constituent assembly that was elected on September 15, 1890, met in November, the administration presented it with a draft constitution, which after some grumbling it promulgated on February 24, 1891. The following day Deodoro was chosen president over Prudente by a vote of 129 to 97, and Floriano was elected vice president by a larger majority of 153 to 57. Ominously for the future, opposition to Deodoro was engineered by Admiral José Custódio de Melo, politically ambitious president of the Military Club— with the backing of Floriano.[22]

Unable to adapt to the restrictions of governing within the limitations of a constitution, Deodoro had difficulty in dealing with an often hostile congress. Reacting to what he viewed as unjustified obstruction, the thin-skinned president dissolved the legislature in November 1891 and imposed a state of siege. A revolt broke out in Rio Grande do Sul, and promonarchy admiral Custódio de Melo incited most of the fleet to revolt on November 23. Recognizing his position as untenable, Deodoro angrily resigned. Those who had overthrown him fared little better at governing the infant republic, narrowly avoiding institutionalizing a resort to force as means for deciding the control of political power. In the absence of channels for resolving elite differences, the military remained an uncertain arbiter. Devious where Deodoro had been direct, impassive rather than emotional, distrustful rather than open, and cautiously calculating rather than impulsive, Floriano aroused extremes of feeling. Caught between monarchical sentiment in the navy and the support of some army officers for the deposed president, and also impelled by his own authoritarian nature, Floriano was almost as far from a democratic executive as Deodoro had been.[23]

He immediately fomented a series of local military movements *(derrubadas)* to oust all provincial presidents who had backed Deodoro in the recent crisis, thus beginning a pattern of using federal military forces to influence local power struggles that would be more the rule than the exception into the 1930s. To avoid the necessity of a direct presidential election, Floriano maintained the fiction of being the "vice-president in exercise of the presidency" In February 1892, he forced dissenting flag officers into involuntary retirement. Admiral Custódio de Melo, who considered himself the author of Deodoro's ouster, interfered in government affairs beyond the normal scope of a navy minister who was also president of the Military Club. In April 1893, this ambitious officer openly broke with Floriano, and when in September federalists invaded Rio Grande do Sul from neighboring Uruguay, he led a major revolt of the fleet. After the United States thwarted his ill-conceived plan to force Floriano out of office by bombarding Rio de Janeiro, he sailed south to continue the civil war, leaving the more politically adept Admiral Saldanha da Gama and Military Club president Admiral Eduardo Wandenkolk to lead opposition to "iron marshal" Floriano in the capital until faced in March 1894 with the arrival of a new progovernment squadron of ships hurriedly purchased in Europe. All this disorder facilitated the spread of constitutionalist sentiments for civilian rule to elements of the armed forces who lamented the negative effects on professionalism, the loss of unity, and the sacrifice of their ability to act as the moderating power (a responsibility they felt the military had assumed by eliminating the emperor).[24]

In this trying situation, Floriano, caught up in the inexorable logic of the calculus of survival and plagued by declining health that would lead to his death within a year, had to give up any intention of staying in office in order to be able to put an end to the civil war. Agreeing to the election of a representative of the São Paulo coffee elite brought him the state troops needed to keep the rebels bottled up in the south as well as support in congress for the requisite financing. Moreover, there was an increasing tendency in many areas of the country to question the armed forces' assumption of the right to interfere in all spheres of political life and their highhanded infringement of civil liberties in the name of national security or military honor. This dissatisfaction was fueled by the government's tendency to overuse the specter of a monarchist threat (much as the communist issue would be used in the 1960s).

Elections on March 1, 1894 (which Floriano had postponed from the preceding October), made Federal Republican Party (PRF) nominee Prudente de Morais Brazil's first civilian president by a margin of 277,000 votes to only 38,000 for young Afonso Augusto Moreira Pena (whose day would come a dozen years later). Beginning with this experienced politician's inauguration, representatives of the São Paulo elites occupied the presidency for twelve consecutive years. Cautious, persistent, and tenacious, new chief executive Prudente was aided by the cessation of hostilities in the south by mid-1895. Yet, to many of Floriano's supporters, found almost exclusively among the military, this taciturn representative of the São Paulo aristocracy seemed soft on reactionary interests. The relative freedom accorded to monarchist groups, contrasted to their repression under the preceding military presidents, made Prudente suspect in the eyes of exalted republicans and militant military Jacobins. For as McCann perceptively points out:

> The Prudente de Morais administration sought to quiet passions by bringing the war in the south to a negotiated end, with amnesty for the rebels. Even the general officers, who Floriano had expelled, were allowed to return to active duty. Moreover, Prudente weakened the army's archrepublican faction by furthering the careers of anti-Florianistas.[25]

The tragic affair of Canudos soon presented these critics with an opportunity to exploit the weaknesses of Prudente's position. Only in an atmosphere of extreme political passions could the existence of a small colony of impoverished religious fanatics in the backland be seen as a monarchist plot and threat to the existence of the republic. Yet cynical manipulation of this situation created a politicomilitary crisis.[26] For Bahian officials and embarrassed military spokesmen found this conspiracy theory a convenient explanation for the inability of three successive military expeditions to defeat the small, out-of-the-way community founded by Antônio Conselheiro, a primitive mystic. National uproar exploded in March 1897 after a federal force of 1,300 trained troops, accompanied by artillery, was all but wiped out. Aware that the various military factions, whose differences and rivalries had thus far allowed him to govern, might unite now that the army's reputation was on the line, Prudente sent a new war minister into the field with 10,000 men. On October 5 the fortified shantytown was completely demolished and its defenders were annihilated. Thus, with a total loss of some 5,000 lives on the government side and the lives of at least 15,000 humble, uneducated peasants, the traumatizing affair was ended—just in time for the choice of Prudente's successor. Paradoxically, a badly managed and perhaps unnecessary use of military force redounded to Prudente's advantage when an abortive Jacobin coup in early November left him appearing courageous, if not heroic. As McCann reminds us:

> The empire may have been overturned in a bloodless coup, but the bloodshed of the succeeding decade more than made up for it. If some hoped that Canudos would launch a military-dominated republic, the result was the opposite. The disaster strengthened the control of officers who wanted to lessen military influence on the government.[27]

Election of fifty-seven-year-old São Paulo chief executive Campos Salles as Brazil's second civilian president in March 1898 took place in an atmosphere of comparative calm, the winner receiving 420,000 votes to 39,000 for his out-gunned opponent. The new president was a moderately conservative successful agriculturalist.[28] Often considered the restorer of Brazil's shattered finances and credit, he inherited a chaotic financial situation rooted in a decline in coffee revenues. Under his predecessor a wide range of banks had, until 1897, been authorized to issue currency. As coffee prices continued to drop, in good part in response to an unbridled increase in production, devaluation of the exchange rate had been stepped up, causing a fall in imports and a consequent reduction in customs receipts—an important component of government revenues. This deterioration led, by mid-1898, to the necessity of a negotiated debt moratorium. All payments on existing foreign debt were suspended for thirteen years, the creditors insisting in return upon both elimination of the budget deficit and the withdrawal from circulation of currency equal to their funding loan. In a foretaste of debt problems that would be aggravated much later by the 1988 constitution, that of 1891 had permitted provinces and even municipalities to contract foreign debt—a privilege they promptly abused. Much of the money borrowed was used to cover operating deficits, and by 1898 foreign debt had risen 53 percent since the establishment of the republic—requiring over half of all federal government expenditures for its service. Putting the country's finances in order required unpopular deflationary and recessive policies. The elites were chiefly interested in keeping labor plentiful and cheap through European immigration, which had the secondary effect of helping their desire to "whiten" the country's population.[29]

Campos Salles's most lasting legacy was in the political field. Reversing the policy of his predecessors, he ceased to be preoccupied with maintaining supporters in power at the provincial level, preferring instead to accept whoever won the power struggle in each state as long as their representatives in congress lent him their support. Under the "politics of the governors," electoral fraud and coercion by state machines were tolerated, and victories by their opponents were not recognized by the Chamber of Deputies. In turn, the governors extended to local elites a similar deal of patronage and services for votes. This arrangement strengthened the municipalities as a basic political unit, but in such a way as to reinforce the hold of the regional oligarchies and local clientelistic machines.

Thus, in the context of insufficient institutionalization and the persistence of the traditional sociopolitical order in the rural areas making up most of the country, the introduction of formal democracy through extension of the franchise worked not so much to make change as to bolster entrenched elites. There was a reestablishment of duality between centralized power over national matters in the hands of the federal executive and local autonomy, often bordering on license, in "lesser" matters—although these were often of life-or-death import to the bulk of the population. Under these circumstances politically active military elements disenchanted with the course of events concentrated on holding eroding positions at the provincial level, meeting with greatest success on the periphery. Undercut by the political tactics of Campos Salles, which were followed in the 1920s by a successor (Artur Bernardes) they viewed even less favorably, the military "modernizers" began thinking about how to regain control of the national government.[30]

The political patterns of the Old Republic, as the 1889–1930 regime was called, were not what the young positivist disciples of Benjamin Constant had had in mind when they had toppled the monarchy as outdated, if not retrograde. Now, a decade into the republic, their child had been perverted at the hands of an unholy alliance of the new São Paulo elites and the ex-monarchical bosses in the traditional boondocks. The civilians' handiwork was, in the positivists' view, almost as distant from parliamentary democracy as was the military interregnum, since in the end much of the patriarchal society was preserved. The real abomination was that local and regional oligarchies not only survived but also actually found their hand strengthened—at least on their home ground—against the new political forces that had begun to challenge their domination. The survival of what was known during the monarchy as *coronelismo* ("rule by the rural 'colonels'") was rooted in the fact that going from empire to republic at the national level did not alter basic conditions in the traditional rural areas, especially in the northeast and the north. Rural society continued to reproduce an authoritarian paternalism that provided a continuing basis for patrimonial politics.[31] There was still a long way to go before change in political processes would catch up with the switch in governmental institutions.

Mexico: Authoritarian Modernization

Mexico, whose population had reached 9.1 million by 1872, was a model of stability and economic development in the late nineteenth century, a sharp contrast with its preceding troubles (as well as with what would soon ensue). This sharp departure from the course it had hitherto followed was of an essentially authoritarian nature under an extraordinarily effective strongman whose rule would last a decade into the twentieth century and earn itself a one-word title—the Porfiriato (after Díaz's commonly used name, Porfirio)—that became a shorthand term much like *Bonapartist* or *Bismarckian* in Europe.[32] The mid-1872 death of the great Liberal statesman Benito Juárez, only months after his reelection as president, opened the way for the rise to power of an individual who would mark the transition to a kind of institutionalized autocratic rule that made a mockery of his liberal origins.

General José de la Cruz Porfirio Díaz (b. 1830) was an acutely intelligent *mestizo* from southern Mexico who abandoned education for the priesthood in favor

JOSÉ DE LA CRUZ PORFIRIO DÍAZ

of a military career. When Juárez became governor of Díaz's native state, the ambitious young man hitched himself to this rising star. After Juárez and many other Liberal leaders went into exile when Santa Ana again seized power in 1853, the bellicose Díaz mounted guerrilla warfare. With the French intervention, this experienced military leader was promoted to brigadier general in 1862. In an audacious move he ran for the presidency against the elderly Juárez in 1871 on the slogan of "Effective Suffrage, No Reelection," which would be turned against him four decades later. Left out in the cold by a postelection Juárez–Sebastian Lerdo de Tejada alliance that gave the latter the vice presidency, Díaz essayed a failed uprising. When Lerdo (b. 1827), who succeeded to the presidency following Juárez's death, sought reelection in 1876, Díaz rebelled again, as did the head of the Mexican supreme court. Defeating Lerdo's federal forces, Díaz began his thirty-five-year domination of Mexico's political life—an era that would serve as a goal, if not a model, for subsequent Latin American strongmen.[33]

This battle-tested veteran of the struggle against the French stepped aside for a close ally, General Manuel González, in 1880, resuming the presidency in 1884 with ritual reelections at the end of each subsequent term. His rule was marked by economic development and modernization from above based on a blueprint devised by a group of positivist technocrats known as Los Científicos ("the Scientific Ones"). Bearing a basic similarity to the young officers who ended the Brazilian monarchy, as well as to many Argentine intellectuals of the Sarmiento-Roca era, when push came to shove they often ended up stressing the first part of their slogan of "Order and Progress." In Camp's judgment, "Positivism became a vehicle for reintroducing conservative ideas among Mexico's liberal leadership." As aptly expressed by this leading student of Mexican politics:

> After years of political instability, violence, and civil war, these men saw peace as a critical necessity for progress. Their explanation for the disruptive preceding decades centered on the notion that too much of Mexico's political thinking had been based on irrational or "unscientific" ideas influenced by the spiritual teaching of the church and that alternative political ideas were counterproductive.[34]

In their view, this new moderate liberalism could best be inculcated in the next generation of leaders of the country through carefully supervised public education. The National Preparatory School in Mexico City was the keystone institution in their effort to create a homogeneous elite political culture. There the heirs of the upper and aspirant upper-middle classes from all over Mexico would study under the same dedicated and highly qualified teachers. Influenced by Herbert Spencer's version of social Darwinism, they used a strategy for forging a modern Mexico that was based on the idea that

> now it was time to enter the scientific stage and propel Mexico along the path toward Industrial society. But, as Comte and Spencer also taught, progress can come about only through order. Someday Mexico might become a free society, but in the meantime an enlightened, scientific elite would have to modernize the country by force.[35]

Convinced that foreign investment was the key to Mexico's future, Díaz created an environment of stability and financial responsibility conducive to such investments, particularly in the areas of revitalizing mining and vastly improving transportation through construction of roads and railroads. He also, as were many other governments of the time down through South America, was generous in making attractive concessions to maintain a steady, heavy flow of foreign investment. Between 1884 and 1910 foreign investment increased more than thirtyfold. Railroads grew from a mere 700 miles of track to over 12,000—and exports went up 600 percent during the Díaz era.

Viewing Mexico's Indian masses with disdain, and, indeed, envying Argentina for not being cursed with such a drag on development, Díaz and his associates imported European capital and technicians instead of workers (whereas Brazil and Argentina imported workers). For although the government did try to attract immigration, Mexico ended up with small numbers of large landowners who bought public lands at bargain prices. The privileged groups that allied with them as they diversified their investments into mining and manufacturing shared in the country's sustained economic growth; all others benefited little. It has aptly been said by many figures that under Díaz Mexico became the "mother of foreigners and stepmother of Mexicans." Although this attitude was politically feasible for a generation, it resulted by the end of the century in a frustrated group of upwardly mobile *mestizos* whose progress appeared blocked for lack of the right connections. Yet for decades Díaz staved this reaction off by coopting many in the emergent middle class through expansion of the federal bureaucracy—much as had been done by viceroys in the colonial era. For the Mexican state grew immensely under Díaz's Porfiriato.

Successfully negotiating consolidation of Mexico's foreign debt and starting a steel industry, Díaz presided into the new century over sustained economic development fed by foreign investment. By the end of the 1890s, manufacturing employed 500,000 workers and mining another 100,000, as lead, zinc, and copper supplemented gold and silver. Precious metals dropped from 80 percent of exports to 60 percent, and other raw materials doubled from 15 to 30 percent. Urbanization helped transform the country, as Mexico City doubled its population and Monterrey and Veracruz each grew by over 450 percent. In the two-tiered society providing benefits for those of European descent and a fortunate few educated *mestizos,* while ignoring the masses, Catholic schools were permitted to serve the needs of a dependent middle stratum—as long as the church stayed clear of political affairs; Díaz's Mexico needed obedient masses as much as it did enlightened and thinking elite sectors.

Nationally Díaz placed fellow military men in many key positions, but as in the later case of Francisco Franco in Spain, after a quarter century in power these old comrades were increasingly replaced by young, technically better-qualified civilians. Order was maintained in the countryside not by the regular army, but through a brutal militarized police force, the Rural Guard—commonly known as the Rurales, some sixteen hundred gunmen, many former bandits. Peons who fled the system of wage slavery or permanently inherited indentured servitude were hunted down and ruthlessly made examples of to discourage others from attempting to escape to the growing towns and cities. Political patronage went to those who loyally served the authoritarian system and its autocratic helmsman. As Lewis describes politics under this durable despot:

On returning to power in 1884, Díaz began tightening his grip on Mexico. He divided Mexico into eleven military zones that often were large enough to encompass two or three states. These zones were then divided into smaller military regions, and those were subdivided into even smaller subregions. Díaz personally chose the commanders of these divisions, battalions, and regiments, being careful to make sure that they were loyal. Those officers were well paid, given opportunities for graft, and frequently shifted. Thus the twenty-seven states were crisscrossed by military commands whose top leaders were capable of keeping the governors under control.[36]

By the midpoint of his rule, Díaz had put together a reliable set of governors who were reelected in noncompetitive elections as regularly as he was. It was a huge patronage machine in which "relatives and in-laws as well as old friends and military comrades" were taken care of first. Key regime figures included his father-in-law, Manuel Romero Rubio, as interior minister, the clever José Limantour as treasury minister, and Justo Sierra in charge of education. Crucially for the future, Díaz rejected advice to establish a political party to help institutionalize the system, preferring a style of unfettered personal leadership. Thus, when his time eventually came to an end, there could be no question of a smooth transition.

As the century drew to a close, the entrenched dictator could and did feel superior to the bumbling erstwhile military masters of Brazil and the São Paulo oligarch Prudente who had succeeded them in office for one puny term. Neither Díaz nor the yes-men collected around him had any inkling that down in Argentina a much greater degree of institution building was going on under General Julio Roca, whose heritage would live on when Díaz's work had been swept away by revolution and his name had become a curse. For as cogently captured by Camp:

> Because Díaz held the presidency for some thirty years, a personality cult developed around his leadership. His collaborators conveyed the message that progress, as they defined it, was guaranteed by his presence. His indispensability enhanced his political maneuverability. On the other hand, Díaz put in place a political system that was underdeveloped institutionally. In concentrating on his personality, political institutions failed to acquire legitimacy. Even the stability of the political system itself was at stake because continuity was not guaranteed by the acceptability of its institutions, but by an individual person, Díaz.[37]

The very significant degree of economic development brought about by a quarter century of Díaz's policies had led to changes in the urban sector of society that were undermining the foundations of the regime's political control. But as the century came to its close, decay of the Porfiriato was not yet in sight. Indeed, its demise was still a decade away. No one imagined that in the ensuing period the country would experience protracted civil war and stretches of near chaos. But this was the ultimate result of a repressive regime mortgaged to the strength of a single individual.

Argentina: National Consolidation and Elite "Democracy"

Argentina entered this period in a situation of uneasy semistability, being governed by Domingo Sarmiento, with his predecessor, Bartholomé Mitre, as his archrival. Successful in having Nicolás Avellaneda, his education minister, elected to succeed him in 1874, Sarmiento had to join the new chief executive in defeating a revolt led by Mitre, who had fervently aspired to return to the presidency. This campaign elevated young General Julio Argentino Roca to national prominence. Then in 1880 Argentina, at this point a country with a population of about 1.8 to 2.4 million (the problem of estimating the number of Indians and keeping up with the influx of immigrants preventing precision), gained a new dominant figure in the person of Roca. Well aware of how Rosas had risen to power a generation before, he had worked his way up through the army to become a very young war minister and in the late 1870s had defeated both the Indians and the Buenos Aires province militia. His election inaugurated the epoch known as the *Unicato*, the centralization and concentration of power by strengthening the federal government relative to the provinces and the president vis-à-vis congress.[38] Now the rapidly growing capital became a federal district, the province being given a new capital thirty miles eastward at La Plata.

Roca's career was characterized by the kind of rapid advancement through military success that had marked the Duke of Caxias in Brazil or Díaz in Mexico. (Indeed, it bore a striking parallel to Napoléon's earlier meteoric rise in France.) Julio was born in 1843 as the middle of seven children of a relatively poor interior family. As a youth his *Unitário* father had fought under San Martín in Chile and Peru. By age sixteen Julio was already an artillery officer under Justo José de Urquiza in his unsuccessful battles against Mitre's forces. The outbreak of the war of the Triple Alliance in 1864 found him a captain; the courageous young officer rose to the rank of colonel by age twenty-eight. Helping Avellaneda defeat Mitre's rebellion in 1874 made him a general at thirty-one.

Having married into a rich Córdoba family, Roca became war and navy minister in 1877 and a national hero through his desert campaign against the Indians in 1878–1879. Glorified as the Conquest of the Wilderness, this campaign allowed ranching to move south and west, leaving the rich soil of the pampas for grain, particularly wheat. Roca skillfully used this springboard to overcome *Porteño* opposition as the presidential candidate of a so-called League of Governors. When taking office in October 1880 he was only three months past his thirty-seventh birthday. At this point a crucial bargain was made between the pampean landowners and their unruly interior counterparts, who for a share of the Buenos Aires customs revenues agreed to end their provincial *caudillo* pattern of disruptive uprisings.[39]

Roca saw the cohesive pampean elite, organized into the Argentine Rural Society (SRA) in 1866, become the backbone of the National Autonomist Party (PAN) after its formation in 1874. Controlling a productive and profitable agro-export economy, this elite—based upon a concentration of landowning dating back to the Rosas Era, and further stimulated under Sarmiento—accumulated capital in local and foreign currency. As viewed by a modern scholar, this was "a landowning elite that was sufficiently homogeneous in economic activity and geographical concentration to allow it to constitute a national state as opposed to a set of regional fiefdoms."[40] Hence, the underlying situation was very different in Argentina than in either Brazil or Mexico, since the former, given its vast area and varied regions, could not form a centralized dominant political party, and the latter was under an entrenched dictator with a network of ties to regional bosses who needed no modern electoral machine. Hence, in the closing years of the nineteenth century Argentina was run by:

> a fluid, loosely organized clique of notables that chose its candidates through informal negotiation and settled disputes over credit and railway access through backroom deals called *acuerdos*. Having settled these internal conflicts, the PAN leaders doctored voting lists, bought votes, and used intimidation (taking advantage of the absence of a secret ballot) to undermine candidates running under ephemeral opposition labels.[41]

Governing firmly and with authority during his six-year term, Roca then democratically gave way to Miguel Juárez Celman, his brother-in-law, who encountered a serious economic crisis and was faced with an attempted rebellion in the face of his institutionalization of electoral fraud before leaving office in 1890. Serving out the end of Juárez Celman's term, Vice President Carlos Pellegrini managed to straighten out the problems of the Bank of the Argentine Nation and get the country on the road to economic recovery. Luis Saénz Peña then occupied the presidency from 1892 until 1895, when he was replaced by Vice President José E. Uriburu. By this time heavy Italian immigration—half the region's total—and substantial British infrastructure investment, the underpinnings of a sustained economic growth of over 5 percent a year, was converting Argentina into Latin America's most economically developed country. Elected for a second time to the presidency in 1898, nearly two decades after his original rise to power, Roca was still in his prime when passing the presidency to his friend Manuel Quintana in 1904.

By 1890, urban modernizing elements led by Leandro Além (b. 1842) had founded the Radical Civic Union (UCR) to pursue reforms through the electoral process. Originating as a student movement in 1889, it was temporarily joined the following year by dissident elements of the pampean elite behind Mitre, a man who had never been satisfied by any presidency other than his own back in 1862–1868. Faced with the barrier of electoral manipulation and fraud under the conservative civilian presidents, the Radicals attempted coups in 1890 and 1893. Although failing at both the ballot box and the barricades for more than two decades, they would triumph in the long run. The Argentine Socialist Party (PSA), founded under another name by Juan B. Justo in 1894 but dropping the limiting words *international* and *workers* the next year, encountered far less success. Competing with the anarchists for influence over the immigrant urban workers already politically socialized in Europe, they would be the losers until well after the turn of the century and then face new competition from the communists. Headway for the Radicals and illusions of progress for the Socialists would have to wait until after Roca's death in 1914 left both the nation and the military without a strong hand at the helm.[42] In sharp contrast to Díaz, Roca had worked through parties and elections to increase the capabilities of the political system (the true measure of political development), rather than functioning as the irreplaceable autocratic executive.

Colombia: An Elite "Democracy" Degenerating into Civil War

Following the unstable caudillism of 1830–1866, the Liberals were in power from 1867 to 1880, moving against the Catholic Church—at that point, by far the country's leading landowner. For the Liberals held that the church was a retrograde force obstructing progress, not the glue holding the social order together as maintained by the Conservatives. Colombia's extreme federalism, with the central government (installed in 1863) handling little more than foreign affairs, continued into the 1870s. During that time civil wars and violence were rampant, with over fifty insurrections—many directed at the state administrations, which carried on most governmental activities.

In 1879, dissident Liberal Dr. Rafael Nuñez Moledo (b. 1825)—a positivist moving toward the right, whose 1877 coup attempt had been defeated—allied with Conservatives in a coalition known as the National Party, promising "regeneration."[43] President in 1880–1882 and reelected in 1884, Nuñez ran the country, which was nearing three million inhabitants, until his death a decade later. His lasting contributions were shaping the 1886 unitary constitution that remained in force for over a century, establishing a strong position for the Catholic Church through a concordat with the Vatican in 1887, founding a national bank (as part of an active government role in the economy), and instituting a protective tariff. Elected to a third term in 1892, he died in office two years later. Economically the country still lacked a consistent foreign exchange earner, a vacuum increasingly filled after the barren 1870s by coffee as Colombia became a major competitor with dominant Brazil in this field.

As time went on, power within the coalition shifted into Conservative hands, and the near-hegemonic Conservatives absorbed the National Party. From the mid- to late 1890s Miguel Antonio Caro, author of much of the 1886 constitution, held the presidency. Elections were rigged not only to deny Liberals a chance at the presidency, but also to keep them out of the congress, until by 1896 General Rafael Uribe Uribe was the sole Liberal in either house of the congress. Under such circumstances a Liberal resort to violence was a logical outcome. So in the last years of the century the situation deteriorated into one of the bloodiest civil wars in Latin American experience—a vicious struggle that lasted until 1902. Undoubtedly Colombia was the period's greatest backslider, a case of political decay rather than even stagnation, much less development.

The Second Tier: Divergent Paths and Uneven Modernization

Certainly Brazil, Mexico, Argentina, and Colombia followed very different paths in the 1870s, 1880s, and 1890s. Peru, Venezuela, and Chile also each took a road distinct both from one another's and from those of the four larger countries. There might be important common elements, but in significantly varying combinations. Uruguay established a working arrangement between two historically antagonistic parties, and Bolivia remained dominated by mining interests. Isolated Paraguay went through a disastrous war, from which it would take the rest of the period to recover.

Peru: The Road to the "Aristocratic Republic"

Peru continued a complex political development path replete with contradictions and partial disruptions stopping short of clear ruptures—in part because of the lack of a single center dominating all regions. Hence, it would continue to traverse a course with almost as many ups and downs as the Andes themselves. It emerged from an unstable decade of crises in 1872 with enlightened coastal aristocrat Manuel Pardo y Lavalle (b. 1834) as its first full-term civilian president, but only after War Minister Tomás Gutiérrez ousted President José Balta. Soon Balta, Gutiérrez, and two of his brothers were dead, the last three at the hands of an incensed Lima mob. Pardo, who survived a series of revolts fomented by Nicolás de Piérola, Balta's ambitious finance minister, was followed in 1876 by Manuel

Prado—who found that with a population reaching 2.7 million the country was more complex than it had seemed before he had assumed the helm. His assassination in 1878 opened the door for the wily and ambitious Piérola (b. 1839) to seize power. By this time the guano boom had ended, leaving the sugar-growing *hacendados* (hacienda owners) in the driver's seat. But railroad building, done chiefly for the mining sector, made possible livestock *haciendas*. Wool in the south became important (as would oil subsequently in the north). Intraelite conflict in the 1870s was intense.

Piérola's first stay in office was turned into a nightmare by another military defeat at the hands of Chile in the 1879–1883 Second War of the Pacific, a crushing setback that resulted in the humiliation of Lima's occupation as well as Piérola's ouster from office in late 1881, when Lima fell to the Chileans. The war also devastated much of commercial agriculture and seriously impaired mining output. In its aftermath Peru developed an array of export axes resulting in a more complicated structure of regional elites and mass strata. Sugar was produced in the sunnier and better irrigated valleys of the north central coast, cotton dominating in the less watered valleys of the far north and the central coast. Wool in the south and rubber extraction in the east also increased in the 1890s. The large-scale sugar barons, often of immigrant origins and economically in the ascendant, became the backbone of the so-called oligarchy, with prewar "plutocrats" surviving on cotton as a declining second line of the elite.

Resistance hero General Andrés Caceres (b. 1833), who had carried on the struggle against Chile after the fall of Lima, emerged by 1886 as the dominant postwar political figure, leaving the presidential office in 1890 to a friend, but retaking it in 1894. The next year the "civilianists," who had cooperated with his first administration, allied with Piérola and his newly founded Democratic Party to overthrow the personalist chief executive in a bloody civil war. President until 1899, this fiery but fundamentally conservative *caudillo* of a populist and provincial cast guided the country into the inception of the twenty-five-year period known as the Aristocratic Republic, which would last well into the new century.[44] His most notable move was bringing in a French mission to modernize Peru's decrepit military. Little did he dream what a political monster he was creating.

Venezuela: Modernizing Caudillism

Coming to power by coup in mid-1870 as the country neared a population of two million, Antonio Guzmán Blanco was in many ways a Díaz-type developmentalist, building roads, railroads, aqueducts, port facilities, and telegraph lines. As a Liberal in the mold of his father, one of the Liberal Party's founders, he undercut the Catholic Church at every opportunity. Arising from the national elite, he had been a participant in the Federal War and then served as President

Falcón's successful finance minister (a post in which he amassed a personal fortune). Having been raised in Caracas, he had no regional base from which to combat local *caudillos,* but he convinced many of them to support his efforts to provide a stable environment for foreign investment in return for a share of the increased government revenues.

Putting an associate in temporarily in 1877, Guzmán Blanco returned to the presidency in early 1879, a scenario he repeated in 1884–1886 with Joaquín Crespo (b. 1845) as the beneficiary.[45] During his eighteen years of dominating the country he modernized the capital and upgraded the educational system. Infatuated to the point of near obsession with France and all things French, he spent his long 1877–1879 and 1884–1886 sabbaticals there. After two final years in power, he turned the presidency over to General Juan Pablo Rojas Paul, going into retirement when Rojas forcefully asserted his independence. Crespo seized power in 1892, regaining election two years later and serving until 1898. His handpicked successor could not withstand the onslaughts of the country's next *caudillo*, Cipriano Castro from Táchira, who seized power in late 1899.

Chile: Role Expansion for Parties and Congress

In this essentially democratic country, the region's most politically advanced in this period, new political alignments had emerged by the end of the 1860s, and the Catholic Church was reemerging as a powerful political factor. The Liberal-Conservative Fusion Party and the National (Monttvarista) Party, which had been effective vehicles for coopting newly wealthy elements, were soon faced with a challenge from the more urban and middle-class Radical Party. The changing of the guard was reflected in the fact that the chamber elected in 1870 contained no less than five future presidents. A ban on reelection enacted in 1870 put an end to the almost automatic decade-long two-term presidencies. Subsequent Chilean presidents, some of them sons of pre-1850s chief executives, served single five-year terms. Fusionist Liberal Federico Errázuriz Zanartu (b. 1825) held office in 1871–1876 before his power base fell apart over anticlerical legislation, and a Liberal-Radical coalition subsequently enacted a series of reforms, including restrictions on the use of emergency powers, reduction of senate terms from nine to six years, and dropping of property requirements for voting. As parties became better structured in a country whose population had reached two million by 1880, restrictions on freedom of speech and assembly weakened.[46]

The smashing 1879–1883 military victory over Peru and Bolivia in the Second War of the Pacific was enough to make most Chileans all but forget the demoralizing bank collapse of 1877–1878, and the acquisition of nitrate-rich regions in the peace settlement would pay dividends down through the 1920s. In 1881, following the capture of Lima, Conservatives attempted to regain power behind the candidacy of war hero General Manuel Baquedano, but he was defeated in a violent and bribery-ridden election by Domingo Santa María, a member of the incumbent cabinet. Santa María fought a rearguard action against demands of congressional leaders for a greater say in cabinet appointments and free elections and sought to reduce the influence of the Catholic Church. José Manuel Balmaceda Fernández (b. 1840), Santa María's loyal interior minister, was elected in 1886, subsequently denouncing "congressional dictatorship" resulting in what he decried as a "bastardized parliamentary system," and advocating a more active state and greater regulation of the foreign-owned nitrate companies. Hence, in January 1891 a strong majority of national legislators voted to depose the potential tyrant, who clearly aspired to be a strong chief executive in the mold of Roca or Díaz. This confrontation unleashed a civil war that was won, after eight months of fighting, by procongress forces only when troops commanded by German general Emil Körner Henze switched sides. Balmaceda reacted to the collapse of his dream of dominance by committing suicide.[47]

Thus late 1891 witnessed the election of Admiral Jorge Montt Álvarez (b. 1845) as president in what was now a system of a very strong congress and active political party competition—a far cry from Brazil's dominance by military presidents, Díaz's stranglehold on Mexico, Roca's centralization and concentration of authority in Argentina, and Colombia's resort to a bloody civil war to establish one-party hegemony. Elected in 1896, Federico Errázuriz Echaurren (b. 1850) died in mid-1901, but the pattern of the "parliamentary republic," in which presidents were less important than in any other Latin American country, would last to 1924. Indeed, as the century came to its end, Chilean democracy was rooted in the economic prosperity resulting from the country's favored position as a nitrate producer, just as this mineral was in demand not only for fertilizer, but even more for explosives in the age of European arms races featuring battleships utilizing ever larger cannon and hence needing increased amounts of explosive. What would prove extremely destructive for Europe was a boon to Chile.

Ecuador: From Conservative Rule to a Liberal Dynasty

Following Conservative *caudillo* Gabriel García Moreno's violent death in 1875, Ecuador experienced political volatility punctuated by military dictatorship. The following year provisional president Antonio Borero y Cortazar was forced out by a coup, and successor Ignácio de Vientemilla's March 1882 unconstitutional bid to extend his hold on the presidency in the midst of a web of scandals led to his ouster through a 1883 "war of restoration." Two Conservative civilian presidents then governed this country of just over 1.1 million inhabitants before 1888, when the new Progressive Party, under Antonio Flores Jijon, son of Ecuador's original president, sought to bridge the intense Conservative-Liberal chasm. For with the emergence of cacao as a major export crop, the old and essentially declining sierra economic elite faced an increasing challenge from a new agro-export stratum including merchants and bankers and centered on the fast-growing port of Guayaquil.[48]

In 1895, Liberal general José Eloy Alfaro Delgado (b. 1842), a persistent plotter with a bit of both Díaz and Roca in his makeup, seized power in his native Guayaquil and in a year of bloody struggle ousted President Luis Cordero and subjugated the sierra as well as the coast. Alfaro's sway lasted well into the twentieth century, his Liberals being in the driver's seat for three decades. This flamboyant personality, a *mestizo* married to a wealthy woman from Panama, would partially serve as a role model for Ecuador's key figure of the 1930s through the 1970s, José María Velasco Ibarra.

Bolivia: The Challenge of Tin to Silver

In the aftermath of the assassination of the tyrannical Mariano Melgarejo, Bolivia had five presidents in as many years. Authoritarian general Agustín Morales assumed the presidency by way of a coup at the beginning of 1871. His assassination after a brief sample of the perks of power was yet another indication that up on that high Andean altiplano, occupying the presidency could be extremely dangerous to one's health. Indeed, President Adolfo Ballevián died suddenly in 1874, and his own war minister ousted his replacement in 1876. Thus Hillerión Daza, once an officer under Melgarejo, was at the helm when Bolivia (along with Peru) was maneuvered into the disastrous Second War of the Pacific with Chile. Indeed, it was largely brought on by his greedy attempt to alter trade contracts with Bolivia's southern neighbor. By December 1879, Bolivia no longer had a coastline, and Daza was on his way out, proving that in politics nothing fails like traumatic failure. His congressionally selected successor to govern this land of 1.5 million persons was undistinguished general Narciso Campero.

In the 1880s, political parties finally replaced military strongmen, serving as vehicles to protect the economic interests of a new ruling class composed of the old landed aristocracy and the mining elites. The Conservative Party, led by Mariano Baptista, supported a national policy of peace, traditionalism, respect for the Catholic Church and preservation of its rights, and—perhaps above all—order and the sanctity of property. The party's spokesmen in the presidency, chosen by the congress and starting with Gregorio Pacheco in 1884, representing the interests of the Sucre-based silver mining oligarchy, dominated the Bolivian political scene down to the end of the century, putting government revenues into building the railroads needed to lower production costs. The power of the Conservative Party's "oligarchy" lasted to 1899.[49]

The ascendant Liberal Party supported the rise of the new tin-mining elite (which would dominate the first quarter of the twentieth century). This party was for secularism and federalism. With the presidency essentially a conservative fiefdom, the Liberals often used the congress as a base for challenging conservative policies. Like their rivals, they firmly believed that economic development required upper-class civilian governments. Hence, "as long as the political parties represented the establishment interests of the silver and tin barons, a certain degree of political infighting and instability was permitted, and indeed harmless."[50]

The so-called Federal Revolution erupted in 1898 over keeping the out-of-the-way city of Sucre as the country's capital or legally recognizing that La Paz had become the center of government. Based in the southern cities of Sucre and Potosí, the silver barons and landed elite of the Conservative Party were opposed to the rising tin-mining and commercial elites who were based in the northern cities of Oruro and La Paz and who were the backbone of the Liberal Party. Unable to gain control of the presidency through elections, the Liberals did so by force, ousting Severo Fernández Alonso in early 1899. They replaced him with General José Manuel Pando, whose administration carried over to the early years of the twentieth century, when Bolivia experienced more instability.

Uruguay: Still Far from a Stable Democracy

The continent's smallest country (with a population nearing 230,000) had a series of military presidents from the mid-1870s to 1890 who strengthened the central government relative to the interior *caudillos*. Civilian José Ellauri was ousted in 1875, Lorenzo Latorre governing for the rest of the decade. The 1880s saw Máximo Santos and Maximo Tajes (1886–1890) in the presidency, followed by fellow Colorado Julio Herrera y Obes. During this time urbanization continued apace, with Montevideo in the van. There was a significant influx of both immigrants and foreign capital. Light manufacturing, small commercial establishments, and service enterprises were largely in immigrant hands. Wool had become the country's chief export.

The return to civilian rule witnessed high-handed actions by chief executives and was seriously marred by the assassination in 1897 of Colorado president Juan Idiarte Borda in the midst of a revolt against his government led by part-Brazilian Blanco leader Aparicio Saravia (b. 1855). In 1872, the Colorados had agreed to cede control of four of the country's thirteen departments. Now, to buy peace they agreed to Blanco control of six of the country's nineteen provinces as well as one-third of the legislative seats if they received a quarter of the vote. Uruguay's better days were still around the corner of a new century's dawn.[51]

Paraguay: The Difficult Task of Rebuilding

The end of the Brazilian occupation in 1876 brought little relief to this devastated inland country. Its massive war reparations were not paid off until mid-1880. By that time the Liberals, who called for representative democracy, free elections, and minimal state intervention in the economy, were challenging the Colorados, political heirs of the old regime. The former, favored by Brazil, allowed a growing foreign presence and sold off state-owned lands while dominating political life until 1904. For following a coup that resulted in the death of the incumbent civilian president, the coup's leader, General Bernardino Caballero, was selected by the congress and presided over an administration featuring education, immigration, and massive sale of public lands (some sixteen million acres, mostly to foreigners) as a major source of revenue. Since Caballero remained the country's strongman as boss of the National Republican Association (ANR), generally referred to as the Colorados, his successor in the presidential office, Patricio Escobar, guided the country toward belated economic recovery in the 1890s. Not the absolute authority figure that Francia and the two Lópezes had been, virtual gods as they were to the Indian masses, Caballero still reigned for twenty-seven years more supreme over this still prostrate country than did chief executives in more developed countries—which at that point included every other country in Latin America.[52]

Central America: Different Paths, but Not to Political Development

On balance Central America was a backwater area lying between Mexico and Colombia. The countries were small, their populations were smaller, and their contribution to the US-European economy was insignificant. Hence it is not surprising that they were at the periphery of what was going on in the larger region and that the patterns of the earlier period would not be seriously modified.

Guatemala: A Modernizing Caudillo Dictator

In good part as a heritage of the late quasi-charismatic Rafael Carrera, Guatemala in the last three decades of the nineteenth century experienced the type of *caudillo* dictator that had gone out of fashion in many countries but would prevail in Guatemala through World War II. A Darwinian process of survival of the fittest following the 1865 death of Carrera brought his antithesis, Justo Rufino Barrios (b. 1835), a white lawyer, to the presidency from 1873 to 1885, when he died in battle in El Salvador pursuing his dream of reuniting Central America by force. Governing a country that by 1880 had a population of over 1.2 million at a time when coffee had replaced cotton as the country's chief export, he followed policies basically similar to those of fellow Liberals Díaz in Mexico and Guzmán Blanco in Venezuela—building railroads and port facilities as well as reforming the bureaucracy and professionalizing the military. Indeed, in exile in Mexico in 1869–1871, he had close contact with Juárez and the Lerdo de Tejada brothers. In power he mounted a campaign against the Catholic Church and sold land to foreign investors for commercial agriculture. Not surprisingly, exports of cattle, coffee, and bananas expanded significantly. Even more than Guzmán Blanco, his Venezuelan counterpart, he stressed education while enacting a "vagrancy law" to force Indians to become at least part-time plantation laborers. Barrios proved a tough act to follow, and his nephew was assassinated in 1898 when he tried to stay on as president after the congress had refused to reelect him.[53] Soon, however, Guatemala would produce another *caudillo* dictator.

Costa Rica: Starting on the Road to Democracy

Costa Rica got its only prototypical *caudillo* president in 1870, when Colonel Tomás Guardia Gutiérrez (b. 1831) came to office and, after relinquishing the presidency in 1876, oversaw this country of only 170,000 inhabitants as head of its army until his death in 1882. Leader of the Liberal Party, he was in some respects as much a Costa Rican Guzmán Blanco as he was a clone of Barrios (his Venezuelan and Guatemalan contemporaries). Like them and Mexico's Díaz, he was an authoritarian modernizer. Guardia began his stewardship with a new constitution enhancing presidential authority while providing for a unicameral legislature. He went on to strengthen the state and rationalize the national bureaucracy. Investing heavily in education and public health, he also began railroad construction. These expenditures required substantial tax increases, some of which went for his pet project of modernizing the armed forces. Like Díaz in Mexico, he was interested in results and had little concern about constitutional niceties and no qualms about repressing those who got in the way.

By the time of Guardia's death, the power of the coffee planters had been seriously undermined, if not broken. Yet, given the lack of effective competitors, they moved to refill the vacuum. Wrapped in the banner of the Liberal Party, Guardia's successors, beginning with Prospero Fernández Oreamundo (b. 1831), in office from 1882 to his death in 1885 and mentor to multiterm future presidents Ricardo Jiménez Oreamundo and Cleto González Víquez, enacted anticlerical policies aimed at limiting the growing influence of the once-weak Catholic Church, which reacted by mobilizing its supporters to participate more actively in politics. This development became yet another reason that the elites could not return to the old ways of competition among personalist factions and agreed on agroexport liberalism as the appropriate economic policy.[54] Education had increased the politically participant citizenry, and growth of the state was spurring a slow

growth of the still small middle class. The railroad had given rise to the banana industry and diversification of the economy.

Thus, although elections were still indirect, the political parties made unprecedented appeals for popular support in the 1889 presidential race to succeed
Liberal Bernardo Soto. The newly formed Catholic Union Party outpolled the
startled Liberal Party by four to one. When the military attempted to bar the
winner from taking office, militant popular protests made them back down.
Hence, José Joaquín Rodríguez became president in mid-1890 in the country's
first constitutional transfer of power from one party to its opponents—a mile-
stone in the development of democracy. Pulling themselves together, the Liberals
returned to power in 1893, subsequently banning the Catholic Union Party, and
thus inaugurating a period of fraudulent elections and authoritarian governments
lasting until 1905.

Nicaragua, El Salvador, and Honduras

Nicaragua, with its 400,000 inhabitants, experienced Conservative Party rule from
1857 to 1893 through regular succession each four years. This time of peace was
marked by the rise of Managua as the country's center and coffee as its chief product. In 1893, conservative dominance ended as the Liberal Party's José Santos Zelaya (b. 1853) began a sixteen-year autocratic, development-oriented regime with
nearly equal components of Díaz and Guzmán Blanco.[55]

In El Salvador, the period began with Santiago González wresting the presidency by force from Francisco Dueñas, thus inaugurating a protracted period of
Liberal Party dominance that would extend to 1944—while ending an epoch of
violence that had seen twenty-five major armed conflicts since the end of Spanish
rule. Abolition of communal landholding in 1881–1882 forced much of the indigenous population off their ancestral lands, a problem in a small country whose
population had swelled to 600,000. The resulting concentration of land left power
firmly in the hands of a small elite of major coffee growers, some also holding
army rank, from whom the succession of virtually indistinguishable presidents
came. The Rural Police, created in 1884, became the National Police and would
be supplanted in 1912 by a National Guard.[56]

In Honduras, with a population reaching 300,000 by 1880, it was the liberals
on top with the modernizing administration of Barrios-backed developmentalist Marco Antonio Soto (b. 1846) from 1876 to 1883—when he resigned following a quarrel with regional leader Barrios—marking a political high point
not to be reached again until the late 1950s. As the end of the century neared,
banana production grew dramatically, briefly elevating the country to the position of world leader. In the process US companies became critical actors in
Honduran political life, with United Fruit and Standard Fruit vying for influ-

ence. Local elites and the gradually emerging middle class largely fell into their orbits as clients and dependents.[57]

The Caribbean: Better Days for Haiti, but Instability in the Dominican Republic

After some instability during the 1860s, Haiti underwent a period of relatively high foreign investment and development during the years paralleling the Díaz regime in Mexico, Roca's dominance of Argentine political life, and Nuñez in Colombia. In retrospect, Haiti's true golden age started under Etienne Felicité Lysius Salomon (b. 1815), who, after eleven years of turmoil, became president in 1879 via a legislative vote of 74 to 13. Having been Emperor Faustin's long-term finance minister and married to a French woman, he was the leader of the nationalist faction of the elite. In addition to increasing French influence, he put down mulatto rebellions and decreed a new constitution in 1886 before resigning under extreme pressure two years later. Florvil Hypólite, president in 1889–1896, continued this political progress, which proved to be a false dawn, as 1908–1915 would see seven presidents and be followed by two decades of US occupation.[58]

The last three decades of the nineteenth century witnessed little basic change in the late-blooming Dominican Republic. Frequent-president Buenaventura Baéz, who, in a last-hurrah ending in March 1878, left the country bankrupt, overthrew a reformist administration in office during 1874–1876. Despite this long period of treading water, the Dominican Republic did participate in the region's widespread trend toward autocratic modernizers. General Ulises Heureaux (b. 1845), a black from Haiti, held effective power for most of the period from 1882 to 1899, building an economic infrastructure, modernizing the army, and encouraging the production of sugar, coffee, and cacao at the cost of crippling international borrowing. This determined autocrat was also the most brutal of his contemporary strongmen, certainly more so than Mexico's prototype, Díaz. His 1899 assassination by an opposition leader opened the door to a protracted struggle for power between ambitious and opportunistic Juan Isidro Jiménez and Horácio Vásquez (b. 1860), one that would characterize the opening decade and a half of the next century.[59]

Latin America in 1899

The turn of the century found most Latin American countries at some point along the continuum of changes begun from five to twenty-five years before. In only a few instances it marked a sharp watershed. Brazil was adjusting to civilian republican government, but not otherwise making significant progress along the road to political development. Mexico was at the peak of the Porfiriato, moving ahead economically while stagnating in the political realm. Argentina was in the middle of the productive Roca Era, which would pave the way to its finest days, in the early twentieth century. While Colombia was entering a bloody civil war, Peru was half a decade into its reasonably productive Aristocratic Republic—productive compared, at least, to what had gone on before. Venezuela was witnessing the emergence of a lesser *caudillo* dictator, looking back at a great one, and on its way to another autocratic giant. Chile was nearing the finish of the first decade of its Parliamentary Republic, with its civil war scars barely noticeable, and Cuba was in the process of exchanging Spanish rule for US domination.

For the area's relatively more advanced countries, politics had come to revolve around the question of whether the notables could still control the state to which they had mortgaged their future. As Voss poses the problem, "The scale and scope of national institutions were reaching levels outpacing the ability of notable family networks to master them."[60] Government functions had greatly expanded; there was a growth in increasingly specialized bureaucracies that went beyond security and tax collection to work on public education and health, with regulation of workers and unions just around the corner.

Among the lesser countries, in Bolivia the Conservative Party and the rising tin-mining and commercial elites of the Liberal Party squared off in a 1898–1900 civil war won by the latter. Ecuador was under one of its most efficient and memorable strongmen, who had recently triumphed in a violent civil war. Uruguay had resolved a Blanco revolt in 1897 by guaranteeing this minority party "coparticipation" in governing, and Paraguay had been enjoying a brief period of relative peace and economic recovery that ended in 1898.

In Central America, Guatemala saw a president maintain himself in power illegally in 1897, only to be assassinated the following year; Nicaragua was at the midpoint of a sixteen-year dictatorship, but one less repressive than what had come before or would come after; and Honduras enjoyed relative stability under Liberal Party elites as the banana industry and mining investment boomed modestly. The Dominican Republic was poised on the edge of a violent internal power struggle, and matters in Haiti were better than they would be for at least another century.

In many countries the changes since 1870 might not have been earthshaking, but in retrospect political developments everywhere after 1900 were intelligible only against the backdrop of this preceding period. This was especially true of three of the four major countries—Brazil, Mexico, and Argentina—where transformations were under way. At the other end of the spectrum, a number of countries' failure to make significant political progress paved the way for some of the next period's most dramatic, and in many ways traumatic, events: US intervention and occupation.

Notes

1. Howard J. Wiarda, *Dilemmas of Democracy in Latin America: Crises and Opportunities* (Lanham, MD: Rowman & Littlefield, 2005), p. 9.

2. See Paul H. Lewis, *Authoritarian Regimes in Latin America: Dictators, Despots, and Tyrants* (Lanham, MD: Rowman & Littlefield, 2006). The best sources on this phenomenon are brought together in Hugh M. Hamill, ed., *Caudillos: Dictators in Spanish America* (Norman: University of Oklahoma Press, 1992).

3. Stuart F. Voss, *Latin America in the Middle Period, 1750–1929* (Wilmington, DE: Scholarly Resources, 2001), p. 163.

4. Ibid., pp. 189–190, 206–207.

5. This section draws substantially on Ronald M. Schneider, *"Order and Progress": A Political History of Brazil* (Boulder, CO: Westview Press, 1991), pp. 52–87, covered in less detail in Ronald M. Schneider, *Brazil: Culture and Politics in a New Industrial Powerhouse* (Boulder, CO: Westview Press, 1996), pp. 43–50.

6. E. Bradford Burns, *A History of Brazil*, 2nd ed. (New York: Columbia University Press, 1980), p. 156.

7. See June E. Hahner, *Poverty and Politics: The Urban Poor in Brazil, 1870–1920* (Albuquerque: University of New Mexico Press, 1986), p. 40.

8. Ibid., pp. 84–89 and 107.

9. Consult Frank D. McCann, *Soldiers of the Pátria: A History of the Brazilian Army, 1889–1937* (Stanford, CA: Stanford University Press, 2004), p. 3.

10. For a meticulously reconstructed account of these developments see ibid., pp. 3–10.

11. The individuals referred to here are Marshals Henrique Duffles Teixeira Lott (war minister, 1955–1960) and Humberto de Alencar Castelo Branco (president, 1964–1967). Their early careers are discussed in McCann, *Soldiers,* pp. 156, 253, 348.

12. Ibid., pp. 6, 62, 91, 218, 263–264.

13. Ibid., p. 4.

14. Useful for this period is Frank Colson, "On Expectations—Perspectives on the Crisis of 1889 in Brazil," *Journal of Latin American Studies,* 13:2 (November 1981), pp. 265–292. On how much the lack of a male heir may have weighed in the monarchy's demise, consult Roderick Barman, *Princess Isabel of Brazil: Gender and Power in the Nineteenth Century* (Wilmington, DE: Scholarly Resources, 2002).

15. McCann, *Soldiers,* p. 15.

16. Samuel P. Huntington, *Political Order in Changing Societies* (New Haven: Yale University Press, 1968), p. 199.

17. Huntington, *Political Order,* pp. 204–205.

18. See Samuel L. Baily and Eduardo José Miguez, eds., *Mass Migration to Modern Latin America* (Wilmington, DE: Scholarly Resources, 2003).

19. Hahner, *Poverty,* p. 7. Also see Richard Graham, *Britain and the Onset of Modernization in Brazil, 1850–1914* (Cambridge, UK: Cambridge University Press, 1968), pp. 51–72.

20. Fernando H. Cardoso, "Dos Governos Militares a Prudente-Campos Salles," in *História Geral da Civilização Brasileira,* Tomo 3, Vol. 1, *Estrutura de Poder e Económia, 1889–1930* (São Paulo: Difusão Européia do Livro, 1975), p. 38.

21. McCann, *Soldiers,* p. xvii.

22. Ibid., pp. 17–20.

23. Consult June E. Hahner, *Civilian-Military Relations in Brazil, 1889–1898* (Columbia: University of South Carolina Press, 1969), pp. 51–72, and McCann, S*oldiers,* pp. 20–23.

24. McCann, *Soldiers,* pp. 24–28, and Hahner, *Civilian-Military Relations,* pp. 125–182, provide detail on these events.

25. McCann, *Soldiers,* p. 30.

26. See ibid., pp. 31–61, as well as Robert M. Levine, *Vale of Tears: Revisiting the Canudos Massacre in Northeastern Brazil, 1893–1897* (Berkeley and Los Angeles: University of California Press, 1992).

27. See McCann. *Soldiers,* p. 63.

28. Francisco de Assis Barbosa writing in in Afonso Arinos and Jânio Quadros, *História do Povo Brasiliero,* Vol. 5, *A República, as Oligarquias Estaduais* (São Paulo: J. Quadros Editôres Culturais, 1967), p. 121.

29. McCann, *Soldiers,* p. 65.

30. See ibid., pp. 66–80.

31. Consult Victor Nunes Leal, *Coronelismo, Enxada e Voto: O Município e o Regime Representativo no Brasil* (Rio de Janeiro: Revista Forense, 1948).

32. For overviews of the Díaz period, see Michael C. Meyer, William L. Sherman, and Susan M. Deeds, *The Course of Mexican History* (New York: Oxford University Press, 2002), Chapters 26–30, as well as Colin MacLachlan and William H. Beezley, *El Gran Pueblo: A History of Greater Mexico* (Englewood Cliffs, NJ: Prentice Hall, 1994), and Charles A. Hale, *The Transformation of Liberalism in Late Nineteenth Century Mexico* (Princeton: Princeton University Press, 1989).

33. Enrique Krauze, *Mexico, Biography of Power: A History of Modern Mexico, 1810–1996* (New York: HarperCollins, 1997), pp. 205–237, covers the Díaz era.

34. Roderic Ai Camp, *Politics in Mexico: The Democratic Transformation*, 4th ed. (New York: Oxford University Press, 2003), p. 35.

35. Lewis, *Authoritarian Regimes,* p. 55.

36. Ibid., p. 57.

37. Camp, *Politics,* p. 39.

38. A reliable political history is James Scobie, *Argentina: A City and a Nation*, 2nd ed. (New York: Oxford University Press, 1971).

39. See James W. McGuire, *Peronism Without Perón: Unions, Parties, and Democracy in Argentina* (Stanford, CA: Stanford University Press, 1997), p. 30. Also very useful is Fernando López Alves, *State Formation and Democracy in Latin America, 1810–1900* (Durham, NC: Duke University Press, 2000), which covers Colombia and Uruguay as well as Argentina.

40. McGuire, *Peronism,* p. 32.

41. Ibid., p. 32. McGuire goes on to argue persuasively that because of this flawed foundation, Argentina went on to a series of incumbent-party hegemonies, including that of the PAN, until its fragmentation in 1909, that of the Radicales from 1916 to 1930, and that of Peronism after 1946.

42. Consult David Rock, *Politics in Argentina, 1890–1930: The Rise and Fall of Radicals* (New York: Columbia University Press, 1975); Peter G. Snow, *Argentine Radicalism: The*

History and Doctrine of the Radical Civic Union (Iowa City: University of Iowa Press, 1963); and Karen L. Remmer, *Party Competition in Argentina and Chile: Political Recruitment and Public Policy, 1890–1930* (Lincoln: University of Nebraska Press, 1984).

43. Consult David Bushnell, *The Making of Modern Colombia: A Nation in Spite of Itself* (Berkeley and Los Angeles: University of California Press, 1993), pp. 130–146. Another excellent history is Frank Safford and Marco Palacios, *Colombia: Fragmented Land, Divided Society* (New York: Oxford University Press, 2002). Also see the parts on Colombia in López Alves, *State Formation*.

44. Very thorough is Peter F. Klarén, *Peru: Society and Nationhood in the Andes* (New York: Oxford University Press, 2000).

45. See George S. Wise, *Caudillo: A Portrait of Antonio Guzmán Blanco* (New York: Columbia University Press, 1951). Also of use is Robert L. Gilmore, *Caudillism and Militarism in Venezuela, 1810–1910* (Athens: Ohio University Press, 1964).

46. A solid work is Simon Collier and William F. Slater, *A History of Chile, 1808–1994* (Cambridge, UK: Cambridge University Press, 1996).

47. Useful is Brian Loveman, *Chile: The Legacy of Hispanic Capitalism* (New York: Oxford University Press, 1979).

48. See David Schodt, *Ecuador: An Andean Enigma* (Boulder, CO: Westview Press, 1987).

49. An excellent and perceptive history is Herbert S. Klein, *Bolivia: The Evolution of a Multi-Ethnic Society*, 2nd ed. (New York: Oxford University Press, 1992).

50. Waltrud Queiser Morales, *Bolivia: Land of Struggle* (Boulder, CO: Westview Press, 1991), pp. 60–61. Also consult Herbert S. Klein, *Parties and Political Change in Bolivia, 1880–1952* (London: Cambridge University Press, 1969).

51. Consult López Alves, *State Formation*, as well as Martin Weinstein, *Uruguay: Democracy at the Crossroads* (Boulder, CO: Westview Press, 1988).

52. See Harris G. Warren, *Paraguay and the Triple Alliance: The Postwar Decade*, 1869–1878 (Pittsburgh: University of Pittsburgh Press, 1979), and *Rebirth of the Paraguayan Republic: The First Colorado Era, 1878–1904* (Pittsburgh: University of Pittsburgh Press, 1985), as well as Paul H. Lewis, *Political Parties and Generations in Paraguay's Liberal Era, 1869–1940* (Chapel Hill: University of North Carolina Press, 1993).

53. Convenient on the region is Ralph Lee Woodward, Jr., *Central America: A Nation Divided,* 3rd ed. (New York: Oxford University Press, 1999). Chester Lloyd Jones, *Guatemala: Past and Present* (Minneapolis: University of Minnesota Press, 1940), is still sound on the last half of the 1800s and the early twentieth century.

54. John A. Booth, *Costa Rica: Quest for Democracy* (Boulder, CO: Westview Press, 1998), pp. 40–41. Also see Deborah J. Yashar, *Demanding Democracy: Reform and Reaction in Costa Rica and Guatemala 1870s–1950s* (Stanford, CA: Stanford University Press, 1997).

55. See Thomas W. Walker, *Nicaragua: Living in the Shadow of the Eagle*, 4th ed. (Boulder, CO: Westview Press, 2003), as well as Richard Millett, *Guardians of the Dynasty: A History of the U.S.-Created Guardia Nacional de Nicaragua and the Somoza Family* (Maryknoll, NY: Orbis Books, 1977).

56. Consult Tommie Sue Montgomery, *Revolution in El Salvador: Origins and Evolution* (Boulder, CO: Westview Press, 1982).

57. See James Morris, *Honduras: Caudillo Politics and Military Rulers* (Boulder, CO: Westview Press, 1984).

58. Consult Patrick Bellegarde-Smith, *Haiti: The Breached Citadel* (Boulder, CO: Westview Press, 1989), as well as Alex Dupuy, *Haiti and the World Economy: Class, Race, and Underdevelopment Since 1700* (Boulder, CO: Westview Press, 1989).

59. See Howard J. Wiarda and Michael Kryzanek, *The Dominican Republic: A Caribbean Crucible* (Boulder, CO: Westview Press, 1982).

60. Voss, *Latin America,* p. 255.

5

The New Century Dawns

Great Promise to Sobering Reality, 1900–1929

Just as there had been continuities from the first half century of Latin American independence into and even through 1871–1899, there would be from that time into the first decades of the new century. As already discussed, caudillism would take less local and more national forms, morphing, as will be shown, into dictators bolstered by national armies. In Venezuela, Guzmán Blanco as a financial expert exercised a very different leadership style from that of the uneducated Paéz early in the country's history. Now Juan Vicente Gómez would use the national army he had largely forged against the traditional *caudillo* types, but his tactics regarding how to treat opponents still followed pages out of the playbook of Guzmán Blanco, or even from that of Paéz.

In Brazil the turn of the century brought no significant changes, certainly not like the shift from monarchy to republic that had been the crux of the antecedent period. In Mexico profound changes would wait a decade (not three as in Brazil), and in Argentina major changes would break through after more than a decade of undermining of the established order. Mexico's road toward political development would pass through the greatest wave of violence the hemisphere has ever witnessed—protracted civil war from 1910 deeply into the 1920s; Argentina's functional equivalent would be bloodless. Why such a difference can be understood only by contrasting the final decade of the Porfiriato with the gradual decompression of Roca's Unicato in Argentina. Colombia was binding up its festering wounds from its "thousand days" of intense civil war, and Chile was a model of stability and—by the global standards of the time—democracy. Peru's path involved an autocratic populist's breaking the hold of the oligarchical elites.

Through a flood of heavy, sustained European immigration beginning in the 1870s, Brazil, Argentina, and Uruguay experienced profound change in their ethnic composition: The first became slightly more white than black and mulatto, and the other two became predominantly white. Such an ethnic shift was unique to the period 1870–1930, and its effects would heavily condition, although not determine, subsequent political life. Hence, the truly great transformational leaders of Brazil, Mexico, and Argentina would be working their political magic on very different audiences in an era when racial thinking heavily impacted political life in Europe as well as the Americas.

For Central America and the Caribbean, the salient factor of the new period would be an aggressively expansionist United States (long before experienced by Mexico) attempting to shape politics through military intervention, including long-term occupations of Haiti and the Dominican Republic, as well as protectorate powers written into treaties with Cuba and Panama.

But without the benefit of such informed scholarly observations rooted in 20-20 hindsight, the twentieth century opened for most of Latin America on an auspicious note that gave rise to hopes that gains made in the preceding period were a foretaste of what lay ahead. The dawn of the century found Brazil having completed a decade of turbulent republican life, Mexico twenty-five years into Porfirio Díaz's development-oriented authoritarian regime, Argentina enjoying almost as much stability as Mexico and even more development along with considerably greater freedom under Roca, but Colombia caught up in a bloody three-year civil war. This was from the high hopes and dreams of the engineers of independence, and conditions in many other countries were less promising.

Latin American nations would undergo substantial changes from the end of the nineteenth century to the eve of the world's Great Depression of the 1930s. In an encouraging number of cases something approaching that era's less demanding standards for democracy would be approximated, but only in a few of these experiences would such gains become sufficiently rooted to survive the lack of fundamental consensus and the persistence of high-stakes, often winner-take-all, competition. Yet in a majority of countries some rough and imperfect adaptation of politics to the fundamental economic and social transformations that were taking place did occur. Even if fragile and narrowly based democratic walls subsequently could not resist the enormous strains occasioned by the Great Depression and tumbled down, foundations often survived upon which sturdier and more enduring political structures could subsequently be built.

The period around World War I witnessed a new wave of essentially middle-class-led aspirations for democracy as narrowly understood by the middle sectors of the time. This development was frequently complicated by the efforts of urban labor in the more industrially advanced countries to be included in the broadening of participation—a trend viewed with considerable misgivings, if not downright hostility, by many middle-class elements. Hence, not only was progress in this direction very uneven, but what was accomplished almost always lacked firm enough underpinnings to withstand the traumatically adverse impact of the global economic crisis that brought this period to an end. Yet the incorporation of labor into the political process did begin in a number of countries, especially where the middle sectors had begun to be incorporated in the preceding period.

Overview

At the turn of the century Brazil was an agricultural country only a decade removed from monarchical rule and striving to establish viable civilian government after an authoritarian military regime and a regional civil war. It would experience a brief and rather half-hearted military reformism between 1910 and 1914 before going back to a series of undistinguished representatives of the traditional elite. This return to old-style politics would spark abortive young officer revolts in 1922 and 1924–1926, and as the structures and processes of the oligarchic republic proved outdated and inadequately representative by the end of that decade, the stage was set for revolution.

In Mexico the entrenched Díaz regime would last a decade into the twentieth century before a middle-class-led revolution would be required to try to achieve what would soon be peacefully accomplished in Argentina, or at least to catch up with Brazil in terms of extent of political competitiveness. Instead, the revolution in Mexico would usher in two decades of bloody civil war among the elements that had quickly forced the old dictator to cut and run, but then could not agree on who or what would take his place. This process consumed the lives of three presidents, a potentially great peasant leader, and millions of common citizens before a new strongman imposed some degree of order upon warlord-style politics in 1928.

In Argentina Roca returned to the presidency in 1898 and provided a significant degree of stability that lasted through his death at the beginning of World War I. Bereft of the leadership he had furnished since 1880, conservatives acquiesced in electoral reforms that averted the threat of revolution and that, by 1916, had ushered in a period of democracy under Radical Party presidents lasting down to an essentially counterrevolutionary outcome in 1930. During the intervening fourteen years Argentina would shine, not just within Latin America, but also on the world scene, as a democratic beacon.

Colombia started the new century coming out of a bloody three-year civil war, to that point (and until overtaken by Mexico) the largest scale of such fraternal strife in the Western Hemisphere outside the United States. Colombia would then show a surface stability under the victorious Conservatives while slowly moving toward a split in their ranks that by the period's end would raise the prospect of elections in which the Liberals, losers of the civil war, might replace the victors in power.

In Peru at the turn of the century advocates of civilian and military rule were still debating the blame for Peru's defeat in the Second War of the Pacific. The country would then briefly stand out as getting on a modernizing path in 1912–1914, only to return to more traditional politics before ending the period under an eleven-year reign of the same contradictory individual who had held the presidency in 1908–1912.

Starting this period in something of a vacuum after the end of the Guzmán Blanco era, Venezuela, economically and socially the laggard of the region's larger countries, in 1908 entered the rule of its rough equivalent of Mexico's Díaz, a general who would remain firmly in control of the country into the 1930s, along the way getting it launched as a major oil producer.

Chile began the twentieth century recovered from the trauma of its civil war and with a quasi-parliamentary system in place. It would then experience a roller-coaster ride featuring a reformist president whose 1920–1925 term would be interrupted by an ambitious military figure who would rule from 1927 to 1931.

Bolivia witnessed a gradual disintegration of relatively stable two-party oligarchic rule as the liberals split by 1920, and a bloody uprising in 1930 set the stage for a repressive and foolhardy government. Ecuador experienced instability that bordered on ungovernability aggravated by the intense hostility between the sierra and coastal regions. Uruguay flourished during the early part of this period under the one truly outstanding leader it has produced, and Paraguay remained mired in the nineteenth century as South America's most backward nation.

Guatemala would spend the first two decades under a *caudillo* dictator, followed by protracted maneuvering to see who would be the next long-term strongman. The status quo essentially held in El Salvador and Honduras, so Costa Rica was the only semidemocratic country in Central America and the Caribbean.

Cuba began the period under US military rule. Once it was accorded nominal independence, the United States continued to intervene, using force in 1906–1907, 1912, and 1917. Cuba then saw a popularly elected president decide that he was the indispensable man and stay in power as a dictator until ousted by force in 1933. Haiti and the Dominican Republic spent much of the period under US military occupation, as did Nicaragua, and Panama became a firmly held US protectorate, all the more so once the Panama Canal opened in 1914.

Brazil: The Long Process of Escaping São Paulo Domination

The twentieth century opened with São Paulo agriculturist Manuel Ferraz de Campos Salles, described as "moderate, opportunist, and vigilant against the excesses of the multitude," halfway through his term as Brazil's fourth president, but only the second civilian one.[1] Generally considered the restorer of the country's shattered finances and eroded credit, he consolidated Brazil's foreign debt. Reacting against the unrest and turmoil of his predecessor's term, he ceased to be preoccupied with maintaining his supporters in power at the provincial level, preferring instead to accept whoever won the power struggle in each state as long as their representatives in the congress lent him their support. This "politics of the governors," as continued by his successors, served as a means for presidents to stay above the disputes of shifting factions with little programmatic content by ceding a high degree of provincial autonomy, hence buying temporary equilibrium at the price of future crises. Electoral fraud and coercion by state political machines was tolerated as long as they played ball in national politics. By virtually eliminating any possibility of peaceful alternation in power at the state level, this concentration on the country's heartland to the neglect of other regions set up tensions that would come to a boil and burst through after 1910.

Thus, in a context of inadequate political institutionalization and the persistence of a patrimonial sociopolitical order in the rural areas that made up most of the country, formal electoral democracy with a severely limited franchise facilitated a political comeback by conservative elites entrenched at the state level— once they accepted a republic. There was a pronounced duality between centralized power over national matters in the hands of the federal executive and a wide scope for local autonomy.[2] As McCann painstakingly reconstructs the sentiment of the times:

> The Brazilian middle class saw the country controlled by rural landowners, or *coroneis*, who with their armed hangers-on constituted irregular military forces that limited the central government's ability to enforce national law. And worse, from the middle-class point of view the *coroneis*, through an elaborate alliance system, actually controlled the central government. A strong military under middle-class control might be able to impose their vision of Brazil.[3]

Grounded in the absence of real national political parties, the president's manipulative policy had the effect of further weakening those feeble party structures that did exist. A chaotic scene of shifting factional alliances predominated, based on the interplay of center-state, interstate, and intrastate maneuvering in a highly federal governmental system. Under these circumstances, the military elements, which had been set back by the virtual counterrevolution implicit in the *Paulista* consolidation of power, concentrated on attempts to hold their eroding positions at the provincial level. They met with greatest success on the country's periphery, where they could still use army influence over federal machinery to enhance their power in what traditionally had been local rivalries. Only when undercut in this enterprise by a president they viewed less favorably than Campos Salles would military reformists concentrate on regaining control of the central government.

In an environment of domestic peace—despite economic troubles—combined with manipulable political competition, Campos Salles chose as his successor the incumbent president of the province of São Paulo, aristocratic fifty-four-year-old Francisco de Paula Rodrigues Alves. Having served as finance minister under both Marshal Floriano Peixoto and his civilian successor, Prudente de Morais, he was admirably prepared for the presidency as shaped by his predecessor. His election in 1902 by a vote of 316,000 to 25,000 demonstrated that the system of succession via agreement among the heads of key states was working smoothly. Continuing movement toward making the federal government a condominium of conservative oligarchies, he was faced at the midpoint of his term with a revolt as proponents of a positivist military dictatorship sought to escalate into a coup the popular dissatisfaction with compulsory smallpox vaccinations. The November 1904 uprising, in which cadets from the military academy took an active role, was firmly put down.[4] In a move that would have deep unforeseen ramifications, the academy was temporarily transferred to Porto Alegre, where the future army officers came into close contact with the Rio Grande do Sul student politicians just down the block at the law school—in some cases marrying into their families. Together, led by Getúlio Vargas, João Neves da Fontoura, and Pedro Aurélio de Góes Monteiro, they would subsequently organize and make the 1930 Revolution.

Economically, and to some extent socially as well, Brazil had moved ahead during the dozen years of relative peace and stability under representatives of the São Paulo coffee growers and exporters. The population at the turn of the century had passed 17 million, as immigration during the 1890s had risen sharply, despite civil war and economic ups and downs, to over 1.2 million, some 690,000 of whom came from Italy. The economy, which had grown only 16 percent from 1889 through 1899, expanded 4.2 percent a year from 1900 to 1909. From 1898 through 1910, coffee accounted for 53 percent of exports, and rubber rose to 26 percent. Indeed, coffee production exploded from 5.6 million sacks (of 132 pounds each) in 1891 to 16.3 million in 1902—as Brazil's share of global coffee production soared to 75 percent. Highly concerned about finances, Rodrigues Alves began the economic *reerguimento* (resurgence) characterized by tight monetary policies having recessive effects offset by amplified public works programs stressing rail and port facilities, with sewer and water systems for the capital city, which now boasted a population exceeding 800,000.[5]

In March 1906, a new chief executive—Afonso Augusto Moreira Pena (b. 1847) of Minas Gerais—was chosen, ending the hold of São Paulo on the presidency. But since Minas had replaced Rio de Janeiro as the second leading coffee state, this did not signify any major change in the distribution of power away from the highly influential, though not fully hegemonic, coffee elite. For Pena was an old classmate of Rodriguez Alves and had also served as his vice president. Yet a *Mineiro* presidency did reflect the emergence of a new balance wheel in the politics of the governors, coopting and channeling, as well as accommodating, the interests of states other than São Paulo and Minas Gerais. In August 1905, Senator José Gomes Pinheiro Machado of Rio Grande do Sul launched a brief king-making career by articulating Pena's candidacy with sufficient skill to convince São Paulo to get on board. As Minas Gerais was still number one in population, size of the electorate, and number of congressional seats, elevation of its former chief executive to the presidency was logical. Essentially unopposed, Pena received over 288,000 votes to fewer that 5,000 for his token electoral sparring partner. Since the Federal Republican Party (PRF) was little more than a rather loose "club of oligarchs," the military, even with its internal divisions, was Brazil's closest approximation to a national political institution. For as McCann views the situation:

> The formation of Brazil, as a political entity, required that the central government weaken the independence of the Pátrias. The process of state formation had not been completed under the empire and continued on into the republic. Indeed, the republic expanded the power of the Pátrias, the former provinces now called states, and at the same time searched for a formula that would hold the country together.[6]

Aware of restlessness among junior and midgrade army officers, Pena, as a wary *Mineiro* (a person from Minas Gerais), prudently chose as his war minister Marshal Hermes da Fonseca (b. 1855), articulator of the 1889 coup against the monarchy and legalist hero of the 1904 crisis. Disunity and intransigence among the civilian elites soon created a vacuum he could readily be convinced to fill, for to important elements of the armed forces he seemed to combine the best qualities of his uncle, ex-president Deodoro, with Floriano's "overlooked" virtues.[7] Hence, civilian and military founders of the republic faced off in the 1910 election. Determined to combat any resurgence of Florianism, leading intellectual Ruy Barbosa (b. 1849), the epitome of civilian Brazil's finest flower, launched his own antimilitarist candidacy with the backing of his home state of Bahia, São Paulo, and Rio de Janeiro, his adoptive home. Although the champion of the "civilist" (civilian) cause carried the cities of the south, the combination of state machines and military support was decisive in the interior. Official figures registered a win for Hermes by 404,000 to 223,000—both a record turnout and a record low margin of victory, as well as the first time the candidate supported by São Paulo had failed to win.

Inaugurated on November 15, 1910, the twenty-first anniversary of the republic, Hermes followed the precedent of his two military precursors rather than the live-and-let-live stance of the four intervening civilian presidents. Influenced by a new alliance of middle-class military with like-minded civilian reformers, he launched a series of "salvations," aimed at freeing oligarchic machines of local political chiefs and powerful landowning families allied with Pinheiro Machado and his embryonic Conservative Republican Party (PRC). Influenced by Roca's policies in Argentina and aware of what Díaz had done in Mexico, Hermes felt a need to undercut the nearly complete control of political life in their states that governors maintained through clientelistic deals, nepotism, and use of patronage; electoral corruption bordering on the obscene; and violence pure and simple. Such a system of well-mounted political machines consolidated leadership of the regional chief in the states and of the *coronel* in the municipalities in such a way that the peasantry was practically feudalized. The survival of this traditional system made emergence of coherent national political parties capable of disciplining legislative politics all but impossible.[8]

But all Hermes, hamstrung by the single four-year term, which left presidents semi-lame-ducks by the end of their third year in office, could accomplish was a partial rotation of oligarchic elites and effective undermining of Pinheiro Machado's efforts to make the PRC into a real national party. Late in his administration Hermes was plagued by a Canudos-type situation with major political implications in a remote area disputed by the southern states of Paraná and Santa Catarina. In a period rife with corruption, unemployment, and speculation, the Contestado insurgency (named after the disputed area) survived the death of its leader in October 1912, being finally crushed by a field army of over 7,000 men in 1915 at a cost of over 300 government troops and perhaps twenty times that number of rebels killed—almost all of them humble people participating in an essentially spontaneous protest by those marginalized by the existing social order and political process.[9]

In the March 1914 elections forty-six-year-old Wenceslau Bráz Pereira Gomes, vice president under Hermes, polled 92 percent of the roughly 550,000 votes, giving Minas Gerais its second president. In September 1915, Pinheiro Machado was murdered, and the PRC collapsed, leaving a situation in which the army's adoption of conscription raising the socioeconomic level of the enlisted men was viewed as a step toward making the army more representative of the Brazilian people. As McCann's careful examination of the period reveals:

> The war in Europe rather than that in the Contestado provided the backdrop against which the reform and reorganization plans that had been developed during the previous years were put into practice. Obligatory military service became a reality, and some officers hungered to have their expanded army join the fighting in Europe. That desire was frustrated, but the physical expansion resulting from obligatory service further extended the army's reach throughout Brazil and thereby increased the central government's ability to intervene in the states.[10]

With World War I in progress, the 1918 election of São Paulo's Rodrigues Alves for a second stint as president aroused little opposition, and in keeping with the new scheme of "coffee with milk" politics (São Paulo and Minas Gerais), he had Minas Gerais chief executive Delfim Moreira da Costa Ribeiro as his running mate. As the official slate polled 99 percent of a 400,000-vote turnout, stability appeared assured. But Rodrigues Alves died in January 1919, and the vice president was too ill to take over the presidency. The compromise choice in the resulting special election was Epitácio Lindolfo da Silva Pessôa (b. 1865)—who had headed Brazil's delegation at the Versailles peace conference but would normally have been ruled out of consideration because he came from the small northeastern state of Paraíba. On April 19 he received 71 percent of the fewer than half million votes cast, as Ruy Barbosa, the William Jennings Bryan of Brazil, in his last hurrah, was credited with 119,000 votes to the victor's 341,000.

This first civilian president from outside the center-south was called upon to govern a Brazil that had changed significantly since the early 1900s. Its population had passed 22 million in 1910 on the way to 30.6 million by 1920. Rio de Janeiro was a city of nearly 1.2 million, and São Paulo, with 580,000 inhabitants, had started on the expansion that would make it the continent's premier city, but the economy, which had expanded by 77 percent from 1900 to 1913, an expansion leading to a per capita GDP rise of 35 percent, had slowed to a modest 2.4 percent annual growth rate between 1914 and 1918. Although coffee still accounted for over 47 percent of the nation's exports in the 1914–1918 period, this percentage was down from its nearly 62 percent during the Hermes years. Rubber, source of 20 percent of Brazil's foreign exchange earnings during that period, declined to 12 percent by 1922. Although immigration had fallen off during the first decade of the century, the total of 650,000 was substantial, and between 1910 and 1919 the flow rose once more, to 820,000. Although still low, literacy rates had risen by 10 percent to 29 percent for males and 20 percent for females.[11]

World War I clearly focused the attention of both elites and government on the need to diversify industrial production so as not to be caught short in any future international crisis. Consequently, during the 1920s the government provided incentives and extended subsidies to certain priority industries. The issue of price supports for coffee became more divisive after a 27 percent fall in coffee revenues in 1920 led to further expansion of the money supply on top of the troublesome inflation of the wartime years. Political passions ran high through Pessôa's truncated tenure. The officer corps took umbrage at this cosmopolitan international jurist's appointment of civilians as service ministers and the employment of six thousand troops in an intervention in Bahia in favor of a political ally. Although nomination of Minas Gerais chief executive Artur da Silva Bernardes (b. 1875) for the 1922–1926 term was agreed upon by the nation's leaders in early 1921, the fact that it earmarked the presidency in 1926 for São Paulo's governor caused Rio Grande do Sul to join with Rio de Janeiro, Bahia, and Pernambuco in the "republican reaction" alliance.[12] Hermes da Fonseca, returning from six years in Europe, threw his very considerable support to this opposition slate, which already enjoyed the backing of young military reformists and even the venerable Ruy Barbosa.

The March 1922 balloting saw the government candidate win as always. But with intellectual sectors sensitized by the centennial of independence, the republican reaction refused to accept the announced results as valid, and Hermes, presiding over the Military Club, called for a "tribunal of honor" to verify the electoral results. When Bernardes was proclaimed president-elect on June 7 with the smallest margin yet (56 percent of the vote, or 467,000 to 318,000), Hermes reacted with a provocative declaration that led to his arrest. The reaction of his supporters was a revolt designed to bring the armed forces back to power. Romantic young officers organized the uprising on very short notice, and Hermes's failure to turn it into more than a gallant but futile gesture spelled the epitaph for Florianism. But out of the heroic behavior of the junior officers who faced almost certain death a more potent force—*tenentismo* (a reform movement of young officers)—was born as a modern movement freed from the shackles of seeking to emulate successes of an earlier era. Indeed, over a span of decades it would be unique in the annals of Latin America and in some ways of the world.[13] McCann defines its context:

> As in the 1880s a "military question" beset Brazil's political system at a time when multifaceted frustrations gripped the army officer corps. In both periods a progressive wave had raised the level of debate about professionalism. Slow promotions discouraged junior officers who found senior officers, who had accommodated themselves to the reigning system, blocking their upward mobility.[14]

In the perspective of 1922, however, the young military rebels looked like anything but the wave of the future. Fort Copacabana under Captain Euclides Hermes da Fonseca, son of the marshal, rebelled in the early morning hours of July 5, but these gallant rebels soon found themselves in isolated resistance against the full force of the government. Under heavy fire the most militant young officers embarked upon a suicidal sally against the ground troops besieging them; only the seriously wounded Antônio de Siqueira Campos and Eduardo Gomes—twice a presidential candidate after World War II—survived to become national heroes. Bernardes was inaugurated on November 15 under the cloud of this bloodbath, and during his four years in office he enjoyed little respite from crises. Civil war broke out in Rio Grande do Sul over the outcome of the November 25 gubernatorial voting, and old scores from earlier armed struggles were settled by acts of violence crossing the line into barbarism. Moreover, Bernardes ineptly handled a dispute in Rio de Janeiro involving conflicting claims to be the legitimate state government. Long before the Rio Grande do Sul strife came to a close at the end of 1923, plans for a new revolt against the increasingly repressive Bernardes government were going forward in the nation's center under leaders with greater skill and coherence. Striking on the second anniversary of the 1922 revolt, the insurgents controlled São Paulo city before withdrawing to the interior on November 27 in the face of air attacks.

This was only the beginning of what would develop into the overture to Brazil's 1930 Revolution. Captain Luís Carlos Prestes managed to ignite the chronic powder keg of Rio Grande do Sul and after two months of holding off government forces, marched northward to join with the São Paulo rebels, a feat achieved in April 1925. With Prestes as chief of staff and Juarez do Nascimento Fernandes Távora, destined to be presidential runner-up in 1955, as commander of one of its columns, the rebel movement fought fifty battles in a 15,000-mile campaign through the country's vast interior before going into exile in Bolivia in February 1927. This saga, which outlasted the term of the target of their animosity, caught the country's imagination. Catalyzed by this dramatic insurgency, a new civilian–military coalition was emerging—one that within a short time was capable of pushing aside the decaying structures of the past four decades much as the military Jacobins, Deodoro and Floriano, and the Republican Party had done away with the empire.[15]

In the lull before the storm, the presidential succession of 1926 was one of the smoothest the republic had yet experienced. The government candidate was São Paulo chief executive Washington Luís Pereira de Souza (b. 1869), with his Minas Gerais counterpart as running mate. The official results of 688,000 to 1,116 gave a grossly misleading impression of national consensus. Large coffee planters, São Paulo professionals, and the newer generation of the traditional middle class formed the Democratic Party in February 1926 to challenge the long-entrenched Paulista Republican Party. At the same time, Antônio Carlos Ribeiro da Andrada reached the presidency of Minas Gerais, from whence he contemplated becoming Brazil's next president. In Rio Grande do Sul the Liberator Party (PL) was established in March 1928. Tory reformism, which had carried the day in Argentina on the eve of World War I, was finally under way, but the situation was fast slipping past the point at which its equivalent might be enough. Indeed, by 1928 the oligarchic republican regime had reached a point of deterioration similar to the decay of the empire in the mid-1880s. Those in power, however, certainly did not see the situation in such gloomy terms. Indeed, they felt that they had already weathered the worst.

The spread of insurrectionist sentiment among the military coincided with an increasing alienation of urban progressive groups from a political establishment unresponsive to the desire by middle sectors for a significant say in policymaking and indisposed to yield to demands for any type of electoral reform. (Their Argentine counterparts had taken the high road in this respect and had been shut out of power since 1916.) Dissension within the political elite over presidential succession combined with the impact of the world economic crisis to make the regime vulnerable and to catalyze the formation of a revolutionary coalition capable of overthrowing the established political order. This time, in contrast to the termination of the monarchy four decades earlier, nationwide mobilization and substantial fighting were required to bring about a revolution.

As the 1920s drew to a close, Brazil's population had passed 35 million, with Rio de Janeiro a city of 1.5 million and São Paulo nearing 900,000. After stagnating in 1924 and 1925, economic expansion recovered to a robust 11 percent a year for 1927 and 1928—but on a fragile basis. This relative prosperity was highly mortgaged to coffee, responsible for over 72 percent of export earnings from 1924 through 1929, a year in which GDP growth plummeted to a mere 1.2 percent—well below the population increase. For between September and December, coffee prices fell by one-third, and by the second half of 1930 they were down an additional 70 percent because of a massive harvest and disastrously declining international demand. Under these conditions the president felt compelled to keep the government under control of reliable *Paulista* coffee interests; reneging on the understanding with Minas Gerais, he anointed São Paulo chief executive Júlio Prestes de Albuquerque as his successor. The president was soon to find that in politics, hell hath no fury like a proud and determined presidential candidate scorned.[16]

Indeed, by the late 1920s the Brazilian political system was clearly in a state of debilitating disarray and heading for outright decay—just as had been the case with the monarchy a third of a century earlier. This deterioration was a function of the lack of flexibility and capacity to modernize shown by the political structures and processes, on the one hand, and of the accelerating pace of economic change and resultant societal tensions, on the other. This time bringing about a major regime change would require a serious economic crisis and the grave errors in political judgment this crisis engendered on the part of the administration. Events over the past twenty years underscored the resilience of the oligarchic structures and demonstrated that—in contrast to circumstances in Argentina—the middle class could not hope to break through to power without the military serving as its cutting edge. For Brazil was not yet a country where the urban industrialized region could determine the course of national affairs. As Hahner aptly summarizes the situation, "Quarrels within this strong, unified elite, with its regional alliances cemented by control of a rural-based elite, never degenerated into bloody fights which might have encouraged some politicians to seek worker support to counterbalance rivals."[17]

Institutions and processes that were at least marginally suitable for the first years of republican government had failed over four decades to evolve beyond the amalgam with traditional practices that had been carried over from the monarchy. The electoral process was highly fraudulent, national parties simply did not exist, and protests against the inequities of the established order were increasingly met with repression rather than compromise and evolutionary reform. In Argentina, by the middle of World War I, middle-class reformers had come to power through honest elections, and half a decade earlier Mexicans had risen up to overthrow an entrenched autocrat. But in Brazil arbitrary executive authority lacked the compensatory merits of strength and effectiveness, and the spokesmen of the often patriarchal and essentially patrimonial regime could not point with pride to outstanding accomplishments to justify their continuing stewardship of the nation.

Mexico: Dictatorship, Revolution, and Civil War

The new century opened with Mexico firmly under the control of the most powerful ruler in its history. The Porfiriato was in its prime, and Mexico City had swollen under Díaz's development-oriented policies to 345,000 souls, on its way to 470,000 by 1910—in a land that had reached 15.2 million inhabitants. The countryside was another matter, as entire villages were having their meager holdings expropriated in order to be handed over to already large landowners or foreign land development companies. By 1910, over half of Mexico's farmland was owned by a few thousand *hacendados,* many of them foreigners, and US timber companies had forced Indians off their ancestral lands. Small farmers were being reduced to the lowly status of peons for lack of documentation of ownership and money to fight eviction through the courts. Then, in 1906, recession struck the country—all the more shocking because of the sustained growth of the Díaz era during its first thirty years.

Díaz's developmental programs had given rise to significant changes in Mexican society. As vividly captured by Lewis:

A middle class of urban professionals, government officeholders, shopkeepers, and—perhaps most significantly—industrialists had emerged. These latter were mainly small entrepreneurs running family businesses: iron- and steelworks in Monterrey, textile factories in Puebla, food and beverage plants in various parts of the country. These entrepreneurs increased in number, thanks to the government's desire to promote national industry through protective tariffs. Still, they had little access to bank credit, for their factories were labor rather than capital intensive and could compete only if they kept down wages.[18]

These new forces were acutely aware that Díaz, who was nearing eighty years of age, was not the indispensable man he had been in his prime. As an astute student of Mexican politics encapsulated the Díaz legacy:

> As Mexico emerged from the first decade of the twentieth century, it acquired a political model that drew on Spanish authoritarianism and paternal heritages. Like the viceroys before him, but without reporting to any other authority, Díaz exercised extraordinary power. He built up a larger state apparatus as a means of retaining power, and although he strengthened the role of the state in society, he did not legitimize its institutions. While he did succeed in building some economic infrastructure in Mexico, he failed to meet social needs and maltreated certain groups, thereby continuing and intensifying the social inequalities existing under his colonial predecessors.[19]

Juárez-style liberals had been marginalized, not destroyed, during the Porfiriato's long run, and new ideas and the germ of a spirit of revolt were emerging, fed by the writings of progressive journalists such as Ricardo Flores Magon, whose paper *La Regeneracíon*, founded in 1900, quickly picked up an intelligent and critical readership. Although the government closed it and arrested Flores the next year, a seed had been planted, as liberal clubs had been founded throughout the country. A loosely organized circle of state governors and their supporters, mostly landowners and businessmen like themselves, were increasingly taking issue with the *Científicos*, looking down the pike to the old dictator's eventual retirement or death. As the yet inchoate dissatisfaction took form,

> business as usual might have continued if there had not existed widespread discontent among . . . commercial farmers, medium-size domestic businessmen and merchants, and the significantly enlarged professional and intellectual classes—as well as among more marginal elements such as shopkeepers, retail merchants, and the group generally called the petite bourgeoisie.[20]

As the time for his ritual reelection in 1910 neared, Díaz played his habitual reluctant dragon act, complaining of the sacrifices he had made for the nation and the Mexican people—complaints that had been repeatedly followed by agreement to serve one more term. This time he gave an interview to this effect to a journalist, who published it as if the dictator was serious about having competitive elections. At this point three opposition currents came together: Francisco Ignácio Madero (b. 1873), from a wealthy landowning family in the north, and his political reform movement, embodied in the Anti-Reelectionist Party; protest movements of peasants who had been pushed off the land by concentrations of ownership; and elements of the urban working class who perceived themselves as being left out of Mexico City's booming times—particularly when economic growth rates were not what they had been until 1897.

A group of educated middle-class businessmen and liberal professionals rose to the occasion behind Madero's candidacy. Arrested by Díaz, he was released after the dictator's reelection had been announced in September 1910. Fleeing to Texas, this rather bookish individual—with graduate education in Paris and at the University of California—who had suddenly become a popular hero, launched a revolt in November 1910 behind the slogan "Effective Suffrage, No Reelection."[21] Following Madero's February 1911 invasion from Texas, which triggered uprisings in the north led by Francisco "Pancho" Villa and in the south led by Emiliano Zapata, Díaz found that his vaunted army existed more on paper than in reality (for commanders had long overstated their troop strength in order to pocket the surplus salaries). After three months of the defeat of his dispirited forces, Díaz decided the game was no longer worth the risk, resigned, and went into European exile in May 1911. (This pattern is strikingly similar to that of the downfall of Fulgéncio Batista in Cuba four decades later.) The tyrant had been overthrown, but hopes for democracy would soon be dashed. Indeed, Mexico would enter the bloodiest and most chaotic period in its life as a nation, one that would entail by far the greatest death toll anywhere in the Western Hemisphere, with the exception of the US Civil War.

A cautious man with a strong idealistic streak, Madero moved slowly, concentrating on electoral reforms that he believed would permit a truly representative government, which could then address the country's problems in an orderly and moderate manner. Meanwhile, as president—legitimized in November by the freest elections in Mexican history—he followed Díaz-like economic policies while leaving social policy to the governors. But labor organizers and particularly the leader of southern peasants, Emiliano Zapata (b. 1879), had a more revolutionary outcome in mind, one that stressed a serious social agenda for the nation.[22] The moderate Madero had left many individuals from the Porfiriato undisturbed in government positions and had disbanded the revolutionary army. These were fatal mistakes, as they enabled General Victoriano Huerta (b.1845), a top-ranking officer of Madero's army and an Indian, to carry out a conspiracy against him. Francisco León de la Barra (b. 1863), as interim president after Díaz's resignation, had backed Huerta's campaign against Zapata in August 1911. Under Huerta's command the federal army repressed a revolt by Bernardo Reyes in mid-December 1911 and crushed a 1912 rebellion in Chihuahua headed by General Pascual Orozco—for which Madero promoted the ambitious militarist to major general. Félix Díaz, nephew of the deposed dictator, rose up at Veracruz in October 1912 but was captured and imprisoned. Then, in February 1913, a senior general freed Díaz and Reyes, a development that led the overly trusting president to place Huerta in command of the riotous capital city, where more than five hundred died in two days of fighting. The opportunistic Huerta would soon repay Madero by betraying him.

With a change of administrations looming in Washington, Republican Ambassador Henry Lane Wilson—a Díaz admirer who lamented the strongman's ouster, detested Madero, and knew that Democrat Woodrow Wilson would soon replace him—sped up his secret plotting. On February 18, Huerta arrested Madero, as Ambassador Wilson brokered a pact that gave Huerta the presidency and made young Díaz his successor. With this implicit blessing, Huerta had Madero cowardly murdered on February 22. This power grab by a would-be Díaz emulator ushered in the longest and most destructive civil war Latin America has seen, with a death toll well in excess of one million. The immediate reaction of three northern reformist governors was to take to the battlefield as the constitutionalists (portraying Huertz as an illegitimate usurper), with Cuahuila's Venustiano Carranza (b. 1859), Madero's war minister, as Primer Jefe ("First Chief"), backed up by the duo of Villa (b. 1878) of Chihuahua and Sonora's Álvaro Obregón (b. 1880).

Huerta the usurper was a victim of fate in that the 1912 election in the United States had involved a split in Republican ranks between President William H. Taft and ex-President Theodore Roosevelt that let Wilson in as a minority president. Republicans of the time felt reassured to have a guarantor of stability and property rights in office in Mexico—as had been the case for nearly thirty-five years with Díaz—but a Democrat of Wilson's strong views on democracy considered Huerta a murderer. Not only did Wilson deny Huerta's de facto regime diplomatic recognition, but he also sent troops to seize the port of Veracruz to cut off supplies of weapons to Huerta's forces. Hence, defeated in June 1914 at Zacatecas by Villa's forces, and with constitutionalist armies closing in on the capital from several directions, Huerta was forced out of the presidency in July 1914. Once again, however, those who felt that the worst was over and that stability was in sight were destined for disappointment.

In October 1914, some 150 revolutionary generals met in the Convention of Aguascalientes, joined by a slew of Zapata's anarchist intellectual advisers (as the uneducated Zapata's personal skills centered on exceptional horsemanship and his image as a lover), with the constitutionalists' First Chief exercising presidential-type powers and keeping this unwanted gathering at arm's length. Convincing the United States to withdraw its troops from Veracruz in November 1914, Carranza used it as his base to wage war against the so-called conventionists. By the next August he was militarily successful. An imposing individual at six feet four inches, with a flowing white beard, this son of a comfortably fixed *hacendado* had served as governor of Coahuila in the early stages of the revolution. A moralist reformer, he was very image-conscious, wanting to be "another Juárez, to command like Don Porfirio, and to avoid the errors of Madero."[23] "Rectification" (correction) of liberalism

MEXICO

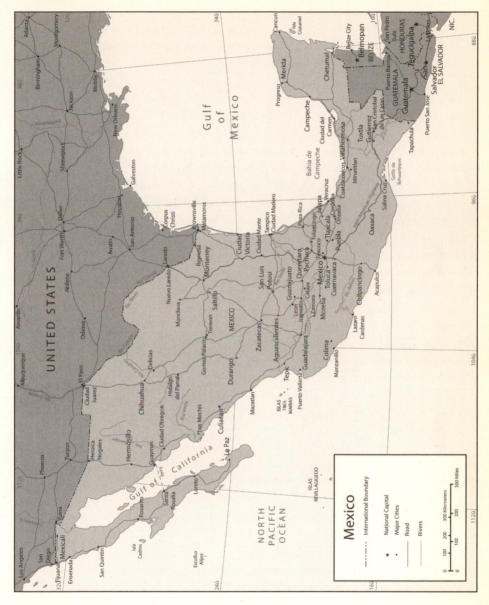

Mexico

- – – – International Boundary
- ★ National Capital
- • Major Cities
- —— Road
- —— Rivers

0   100   200   300 Kilometers
0   100   200   300 Miles

and the revolution was his leitmotif. To younger revolutionaries he was the "old man," a somewhat antiquated carryover from a past era.

The irrepressible Villa continued to provide a challenge to the chief executive.[24] This son of a sharecropper who had developed a reputation as a *bandido* (bandit) in his youth had convinced much of the populace of his northern region that, like the James brothers in the United States, he had just been reacting to oppression and injustice. His army of intensely loyal followers had reached sixteen thousand men by the time he defeated Huerta, giving him significant weight in what was to a high degree a warlord type of political situation. Miffed by Carranza's preference for disciplined soldier Obregón over himself—darling of the international media (with a laudatory film being made for the US public), at the end of 1915 Villa attacked Sonora, Obregón's fiefdom. The latter would lose an arm—shades of Santa Ana—in defeating Villa, being ably seconded in this feat by Plutarco Elías Calles (eventually to eclipse Obregón politically). Villa, now a hunted guerrilla, crossed the border into New Mexico and sacked the small town of Columbus. The punitive expedition under General John "Black Jack" Pershing never managed to catch up with Villa in the deserts of northern Mexico, but the headlines would carry Pershing to command of the US Expeditionary Forces in World War I.

When Carranza's government turned a cold shoulder to their demands for "land, bread, and a roof over their heads," Zapata and his followers caused as much trouble in southern Mexico as Villa had in the north. Rebelling behind a platform, the Plan de Ayala, calling for immediate transfer of land to those who tilled it and direct election of a new government, Zapata only temporarily gained the beleaguered Villa as an ally. While liberal Carranza still had the support of the more "Jacobin" Obregón against these agrarian radicals, the elimination of Huerta had only further divided the revolutionary forces, as the sterner would-be democrat Carranza stressed the need to establish political reforms, rather than split the middle-class leadership of the revolution over the radical social measures being pushed by Zapata and Villa and their substantial armies. In 1916, Zapata was attacked by a thirty-thousand-man federal army and pushed deep into his rural base. After putting up a good guerrilla struggle, he was lured into an ambush and shot in April 1919.

With a temporary lull in the fighting, in late 1916 Carranza convoked a constitutional convention at Querétaro (north of the capital) to draft a legal framework for the revolution. In this assembly, largely comprising lawyers and intellectuals, the radicals defeated Carranza's supporters on all major issues. Hence, the convention produced a document whose beauty was only exceeded by its impracticality. The constitution's very idealism condemned it to remain a revered statement of aims and aspirations for several decades, not a blueprint for Mexico's governments to follow. In a country whose rich mineral deposits were largely controlled by foreign investment, this constitution declared all subsoil resources to belong to the people. With an economy still dominated by large landowners who felt entitled to act as the ultimate authority over their peons, it called for agrarian reform. In a society where factory owners were accustomed to lord it over their workers, it gave the latter the rights to organize and strike. In a highly Catholic country, it stripped the church of authority and rights that had withstood Juárez's Liberal reforms a generation before. In short, it was a "wouldn't it be loverly" type of constitution, raising many hopes and expectations that, under the circumstances, could not be fulfilled—but would be of great importance farther down the road.[25] But this constitution did serve to weaken Zapata's support by projecting the image of a reform-minded government.

Gifted by the constituent assembly in May 1917 with a term as constitutional president, which he would soon find did not guarantee peace or even long life, Carranza soon faced revolt from Obregón, Plutarco Elías Calles (b. 1877), and Adolfo de la Huerta (b. 1881)—all, like him, generals by grace of their military exploits since 1911. Having drifted in a conservative direction and entered into an accommodative alliance with elements of the old dominant class, Carranza attempted to block Obregón—whom he correctly viewed as a potential threat to the principle of a single presidential term—from winning the 1920 elections. Behind the Plan of Agua Prieta, the Sonoran trio took up arms against him, and when the dust settled, Carranza, having again retreated to Veracruz, was killed in May 1920. The way was now open for the presidency to fall into the hands of Obregón after a short rest in the interim grasp of de la Huerta.[26] Purging Carranza supporters, the much younger Obregón soon cut the size of the army sharply from 100,000 to 50,000 men. At the same time he increased the number of officers, buying off generals and colonels by putting them on the government payroll.

Obregón, who got off on the right foot by naming progressive José Vasconcellos as education minister and lauding the great revolutionary muralists—Diego Rivera, José Clemente Orozco, and David Alfaro Siqueiros—had not hesitated to enrich himself during the civil war. Now, as his term progressed, having taken care to distribute land to former Zapata followers, he moved to the right in order to conciliate businessmen and military elements opposed to agrarian reform as well as to avoid becoming dependent on labor. Hence, the Sonorans grew apart, with treasury minister de la Huerta exiting in 1923 (the year of Pancho Villa's assassination) to run for a full presidential term in the next year's balloting against Calles, who was on the ticket of the Mexican Labor Party (PLM). When, after being declared the loser, de la Huerta revolted, in what had become a habit in Mexican politics, nearly half the federal army sided with him. Obregón, who enjoyed US endorsement, crushed them as he had Villa, killing seven thousand, including many of his erstwhile comrades in arms.

Calles's victory was assured by his PLM's putting a workers' militia in the field allied to Obregón's National Agrarian Party (PNA) and its peasant army. Son of an alcoholic who had neglected his family's property holdings, Calles had been a Lieutenant colonel in Obregón's Sonoran army in 1913, subsequently "moralizing" (attacking ingrained corruption) that state as governor.[27] After working for Obregón's election, he served in the key post of interior secretary. Having traveled in Europe following his election, Calles had many ideas about what his administration needed to do. The Bank of Mexico was founded in 1925, and new petroleum and land laws were enacted—the furor they aroused in the United States being dampened by Ambassador Dwight Morrow after 1927. The National Bank of Agricultural Credit was established in 1926, and railroad rebuilding, highway construction, school building, and irrigation projects went ahead as the state's role in the economy was substantially expanded. Meanwhile, as Obregón was off crushing the Yaqui Indians and bloodily smashing Sonoran opponents, Calles guided a constitutional amendment allowing nonimmediate presidential reelection. The strong-minded president also created a diplomatic issue with the United States by sending armed expeditions to Nicaragua in support of the Liberal Party's Juan Sacasa against the US-preferred Conservative, Adolfo Díaz.

Calles's partiality to the PLN pushed the PNA into opposition, but this development was lost in the uproar around his decision that, unlike Obregón, he would implement the strong antichurch provisions of the 1917 Constitution. Restrictive 1926 decrees set off in rural areas a bloody revolt of Catholic peasants protesting "atheistic, socialist" excesses. In what was known as the Cristero Rebellion for its rallying cry of "Viva Cristo Rey" ("Long live Christ the King"), Catholic peasants burned schools that had been turned over to public secular education, often killing the "socialist" teachers, and blew up troop trains. For its part, the government closed down convents, and even in the capital, nuns and priests were subject to arrest for wearing clerical garb in public. Although the government could handle the National League for Defense of Religion, the devoutly Catholic peasants and their guerrilla tactics were another matter. The death toll reached at least 25,000 Cristeros—with government troop losses and those unfortunates caught in between bringing the total to 70,000.[28] At least 200,000 persons fled to the cities, and 450,000 left the country for California.

With almost every surviving revolutionary general aspiring to the presidency, Calles, looking to his own future, saw Obregón safely through a second election in 1928, immediately benefiting from the president-elect's assassination by a fanatic Catholic in July before he could take office. This event, rather than any law or court ruling, established that the revolution's motto of "no reelection" meant never, not just immediately. Under Calles's leadership and in line with his pledge to transform Mexico from "a country of men to a country of laws," this ban was incorporated into the constitution, the presidential term was extended to six years, and the National Revolutionary Party (PNR) was created in 1928. Starting as a holding company with the surviving warlord *caudillos* and regional political bosses at its center, the PNR would take on a greater and more institutionalized role in regularizing presidential succession, in the process bringing sorely needed peace and stability. Calles was the senior survivor of the 1910 Revolution and the country's sole living ex-president as well as head of its instantly dominant political party. Thus he saw the Cristero revolt to its end and in December 1928 appointed Emílio Portes Gil (b. 1891) as provisional president. For the time being, Mexico would be run by Calles as First Chief, one in no hurry to give way to a president chosen by the people.

Argentina: The False Dawn of Democracy

Returning to the presidency of Argentina in 1898 from his position as highly respected ex-president, Julio Roca governed with the provincial elites that had banded together in the 1870s in the National Autonomist Party (PAN). Turning the presidency over to his friend Manuel Quintana in 1904, he retired to the status of the country's most revered personage. Roca's 1914 demise left the nation and the military without a strong hand at the helm, but he left behind a positive heritage of economic development possessing sufficient momentum to carry on under lesser successors. Courtesy of the Roca Era, by the end of the first decade of the twentieth century Argentina was the world's ninth leading nation with respect to foreign trade, but with three-fourths of its businesses owned by foreigners—overwhelmingly British. Its population of 3.9 million in 1895 doubled by 1913, almost half at that point being immigrants or their children—predominantly from Italy—and enjoyed a level of living higher than that of the Swedes or the Swiss. A country that had only 1.8 million inhabitants in 1869 experienced an immigration of over 2.8 million between 1880 and 1905, and the flood continued. Buenos Aires grew five times over between 1880 and 1914, to become a world-scale metropolitan center of 1.5 million. The railroad network fanning out from it across the rich soils of the pampas had burgeoned from only 2,400 miles in 1880 to 22,000 miles by the outbreak of World War I.[29]

The *estanciero* (large ranchers and farm owners) ruling class had responded positively to the opportunities provided by international markets from 1910 through World War I. Commercial agriculture adopted the latest methods and technology, diversified, and grew rapidly. By 1913, grain and meat made up 90 percent of exports, 85 percent going to western Europe, chiefly Great Britain. During this sustained economic development society became more complex, as new interests emerged to challenge the hegemonic leadership that the pampean producers had consolidated over the regional bourgeoisies and society in general. These *estancieros* and their merchant and banking allies had developed a flexible network of oligarchic state institutions that afforded the means for coopting opposition elements through incorporation into the system.[30]

JULIO ARGENTINO ROCA
(Credit: Witcomb. Archivo General de la Nación)

In the political processes of the post-Roca era socioeconomic conflicts were funneled into the political arena by carefully channeled participation and representation within the oligarchic state. Those in power consciously decided to keep politics in a struggle within a bureaucratic political class, as preferable to the alternative of a pattern of revolt and repression, which would leave an increasingly unreliable military, whose officer ranks were rapidly filling with the offspring of recent Italian immigrants, in the position of arbiter of the national destiny. For although the Radicals' 1890 revolt had failed to overturn the system, it did combine with a severe financial crisis to bring about the resignation of President Juárez Celman. The second resort of the Radicals to force, in 1893, encountered more sympathy from junior officers, and the third UCR (Radical Civic Union) revolt, in 1905, appeared to generate significantly broader support.[31]

In this context Argentina's first democratization began in 1910 with the elevation of Roque Sáenz Peña (b. 1851) to the presidency. This "tory reformer" came to power as the result of a split within conservative ranks involving supporters of ex-presidents Roca and Carlos Pellegrini that saw the PAN disintegrate in 1909—a year marked by a week of class conflict in Buenos Aires that left a dozen dead and 80 injured—into a multitude of conservative provincial parties. Moderate conservatives turned reformist in fear that accelerated social mobilization could not be contained within the existing political institutions. Thus, in a strong legislative position since the Radicals had boycotted the elections, in 1912 Saénz Peña pushed through the congress a law providing for a secret ballot and expanding the electorate to all males over eighteen, including immigrants who had completed military service obligations. The law also guaranteed the second-place party in each province one-third of its legislative seats. For glancing over their shoulders at Mexico and Brazil and looking ahead to the challenge to the socioeconomic order posed by the emerging urban working class, Sáenz Peña and his followers saw the middle-class Radicals as a potential ally against the masses and the emergent Socialist Party.

Federal supervision of the 1914 congressional elections provided a trial run for fair voting and honest ballot counting. Although Sáenz Peña (as well as Roca) died that year, Victorino de la Plaza carried through on his project. Most UCR leaders being dissident oligarchs, moderate conservatives could contemplate a Radical victory much as British Conservatives had proved able to live with Liberal wins in 1911. Moreover, when the dust settled after the 1916 balloting, the Conservatives still controlled the senate and eleven of fourteen provinces—even though the Radicals had received 46 percent of the national vote and the Socialist Party 9 percent. Still, by making it much harder for conservative parties to win elections, the 1912 reforms made them less attractive vehicles for the landowners' political activities and fed their aspirations for almost any kind of return to the good old days of "dependable" electoral outcomes.[32]

New president Hipólito Yrigoyen (full name Juan Hipólito del Sagrado Corazón de Jesús Yrigoyen Além) was a far different kind of leader from Roca. Born in 1853, only a few months after the Battle of Caseros had toppled Rosas from power, he was the son of an impoverished French Basque immigrant. As a young lawyer in the early years of the Roca Era, he was a police supervisor before opting for a career as a teachers' college professor. Although several of his romances produced children, Yrigoyen never married, becoming something of a political Jesuit, devoting his very considerable talents and energies to politics—where he excelled in intrigue and behind-the-scenes wheeling and dealing. The suicide of his uncle and rival, Leandro Além, in 1896 opened the way for Yrigoyen to emerge as uncontested leader of the UCR, and he carefully honed his leadership skills in the two decades before being elected president. A compulsive micromanager, he couldn't delegate authority and hesitated to give the congress any significant autonomy. This taciturn and at times enigmatic individual presented radicalism as a cause, if not a crusade, and considering his opponents evil and enemies of the nation. Initially Yrigoyen was more amenable to labor's demands than previous presidents, often taking an evenhanded approach to worker-employer conflicts and settling strikes with significant concessions.[33]

Although Yrigoyen used his constitutional authority to intervene in the provinces frequently and with apparent gusto, it was only under heavy military pressure that he reluctantly agreed to repress the violent January 1919 metal

HIPÓLITO YRIGOYEN

workers' strike in Buenos Aires, an event stimulated in part by the recent Bolshe-vik revolution in Russia. The legacy of this "tragic week," in which at least 750 died, would hang heavy over Argentina's political life and greatly reduce working-class support for the radicals. (In this respect, it created the opportunity for Perón's rise to political domination of Argentine labor.) Among the accomplishments of Yrigoyen's administration were the establishment of an agency to develop sub-stantial oil deposits discovered in 1907, a land reform program involving nearly twenty million acres (mostly on the frontier), and a landmark university reform. Unfortunately, Yrigoyen—like his contemporaries in Brazil and Mexico—was too traditional to perceive the potential of political parties as vehicles for incorporat-ing new elements into politics. Hence, the stage was set for a situation by the 1940s in which "Argentina's least cohesive and least-organized social class became the one most fully incorporated into party politics, whereas its most cohesive and best-organized social classes were the least fully incorporated into party politics."[34]

Constitutionally limited to one term at a time, Yrigoyen reluctantly gave way in 1922 to fellow Radical Party stalwart Marcelo Torcuato de Alvear (b. 1868), a member of the Argentine Rural Society (bailiwick of the country's agricultural interests). Not wanting a pro-Yrigoyen general or a civilian to fill the critical post of war minister, he tapped Colonel Augustín Justo for the job.[35] Selection of this anti-Yrigoyen officer, the son of an ally of ex-chief executive Bartolomé Mitre, positioned Justo for a political rise reminiscent of, but less spectacular, than that of

Roca in the 1880s. (At this juncture the *tenentes* had just staged their protest revolt in Brazil, and Mexico's professional military had been displaced by the generation of revolutionary generals that would produce the country's presidents through World War II.) By midterm Alvear's supporters were shifting to the right, often voting in the congress with the conservatives and ending efforts to incorporate workers into party politics through the UCR. Indeed, in 1926 the powerful railroad workers' union joined municipal workers to form the Argentine Workers' Confederation (COA) as an independent political force. By this time Yrigoyen's supporters were actively hamstringing the government.

During Alvear's competent, but uninspiring, administration, Yrigoyen deeply split the party by insisting at age seventy-six upon returning to the presidency. The aging, egoistic Radical leader, austere and mysterious rather than a spellbinder, whose support now included a larger lower-middle-class component and even some moderate elements of skilled labor, was successful in this bid. On April 1, 1928, he received 839,000 votes to 414,000 for his chief rival, selected by Alvear and tacitly backed by the Conservatives. In accomplishing this personal electoral triumph, Yrigoyen created a fatal division of the party between his followers and partisans of Alvear, who wore the term *antipersonalists* as a badge of honor and would not reconcile with their rivals for over a half century (finally accomplished at the 1983 elections, only after decades of political turmoil and national trauma). At first, affairs progressed normally, but when the international economic crisis, the Great Depression, began to swamp the country, this representative of a fading generation had no rabbits to pull out of his top hat to salvage Argentina's hypersensitive economy. He intervened actively in interior states prior to the March 1930 congressional elections, but still he and the government UCR was easily overthrown by a virtually bloodless coup on September 6, 1930. By this time UCR leadership had become heavily middle-class instead of dissident aristocrats, and as the party consolidated its electoral majority, it came to be viewed as a major threat by the country's conservative forces and their military allies. Indeed, the armed forces were so alienated that archrivals Uriburu and Justo cooperated in Yrigoyen's peaceful ouster.[36] (Clearly his nonviolent expulsion from power contrasted sharply with contemporary events in Brazil, bearing a much greater similarity to the overthrow of Pedro II in Brazil a generation earlier.)

Outstanding in many ways as a leader, but flawed by a sense of destiny that convinced him he was irreplaceable, Yrigoyen was favored by having no major political figure with whom to share the Latin American spotlight. José Batlle in Uruguay had far too small a stage, and many of Chilean Arturo Alessandri's best years were after 1930. Vargas burst on the scene just as Yrigoyen exited it, and Mexico's Lázaro Cárdenas emerged from obscurity only during the 1930s. Yrigoyen's bad luck was being in his late seventies during his second term in office and having to face the onset of the Great Depression.

This first, perhaps in a basic structural sense premature, democratization of Argentina was extremely significant not only for that country, but for Latin America more generally. At that time Brazil was still encapsulated in an oligarchic republic rooted in elite accommodations and electoral fraud. It would break out of this pattern only through revolution and a populist authoritarian regime headed by a personalist, although paternalistic, strongman. For its part, Mexico took the revolutionary road in 1910 and found itself mired in civil war through the 1920s. In Colombia the Conservatives were entrenched in power, enjoying the fruits of victory in the bloody struggle that had ended the past century. Chile, like Argentina, would attempt the reformist road a few years later but would fall into military dictatorship by 1927, and Peru was to experience continued instability and Venezuela suffocating stability under a *caudillo* dictator. Hence, Argentina's peaceful installation of a middle-class democracy at the time of World War I justifiably merited close attention, as did this noble experiment's abrupt collapse in the face of global economic crisis in 1930.

Colombia: Reconstruction and Maintenance of Control

No country in Latin America, perhaps none in the world, entered the new century under as unfavorable circumstances as did Colombia. The bloody civil war begun in mid–1899 ran well into 1902 and left the country prostrate. Commerce was in ruins and the currency almost worthless. The one positive note on the political side was that extremist factions in both the victorious Conservatives and the defeated Liberals bore the onus for having caused the disastrous conflict. Hence, the moderates of each "political religion" realized that some degree of cooperation would be necessary to rebuild the devastated economy. But before reconstruction was under way, the country received another staggering body blow—the 1903 amputation of the strategic and economically vital province of Panama by the expansionist United States.[37]

Beginning the new century in the middle of warfare, the faction of the Conservative Party, hoping for peace talks, overthrew aged president Manuel A. Sanclemente in 1900, but, elevated from vice president, José Manuel Marroquín continued all-out warfare. Four years later, with the civil war over and Panama lost, the moderate Conservative Party leadership realized that the country required a strong leader, and in 1904 they nominated General Rafael Reyes Prieto (b. 1850) for the presidency, which he easily won. An upper-class man from the provinces who admired Díaz and had more than a little of Argentina's Roca in his makeup, Reyes acted decisively and with self-assurance. In the name of reconciliation he forced the Conservatives to accept minority Liberal representation in the cabinet as well as the national legislature. Indeed, he replaced the existing bicameral congress with a national assembly made up of three representatives from each department (as Colombia's provinces are called), indirectly chosen by department officials whom he had appointed to office.

Following a protectionist trade policy to encourage growth of domestic industries, and building a railroad from Bogotá to the sea, Reyes realized that obtaining foreign investment and expanding trade—especially the sale of Colombia's coffee—required normalized relations with the United States. Hence, he negotiated a treaty that of necessity included recognizing the independence of the breakaway republic, Panama. Of course, this provision met heavy public resistance, since Colombians quite naturally felt that they had been victimized by a shameless land grab by a rapacious pretender to regional hegemony. Indeed, the issue of ratifying the Thompson-Urrutia Treaty invigorated the until-then quiescent opposition, and Reyes suspended the congress.[38]

Thus, in June 1909 an alliance of historical Conservatives and Liberals came together in the Republican Union and won a majority in the elections for a reestablished congress. Stunned by this setback, Reyes resigned and left the country. Under the presidency of Carlos E. Restrepo from 1910 to 1914, the Republican Union held together as conservative landowners and liberal merchants found common ground in advancing the export of coffee, which had become the country's leading agricultural product. As Paul Oquist explains with regard to this country, which by 1912 contained 5.1 million inhabitants, "The state was strengthened to accommodate Colombian society to capitalist socioeconomic structures, to accelerate integration into the world capitalist system, and to compensate for the decline of traditional mechanisms of social control."[39] Conservative José Vincente Concha (1914–1918) initiated the trend for governments to become more partisanly Conservative, the principle of some Liberal Party participation survived.

When men socialized under this regime reached maturity, memories of this experience would lead them to adopt coalition government as the way out of the horrendous experience of 1948–1956 (see Chapter 6). As Marco Fidel Suárez, the illegitimate son of a peasant girl, piloted the country through the immediate post–World War I period, a group of young upper-class emerging leaders formed a group known as Los Nuevos ("The New Ones") to consider what changes were called for in light of the loss of Panama (and the opening of the canal there under US control), with no special consideration for neighboring Colombia, and the growing importance of foreign capital. Advocating a more active role for the state in guiding Colombia's development, Los Nuevos would furnish important political leadership from the 1930s on.

The 1920s were known as the "dance of the millions" for unprecedented public spending as $173 million was borrowed abroad and $25 million was belatedly paid by the United States as an indemnity for the kidnapping of the Panama Canal project (being the amount offered Colombia in the nonratified treaty prior to Panama's secession).[40] The decade got off to a bad start politically as President Suárez resigned in 1921 in the face of substantiated charges of financial improprieties. Following an interim chief executive, Pedro Nel Ospina (b. 1858 during the presidency of his father, Mariano Ospina Rodríguez) became president in August 1922 and, like Reyes, emphasized transportation. He was followed in 1926 by Miguel Abadía Méndez.

Change began to come in the late 1920s as oil and bananas became significant new exports and gold dropped to less than 5 percent of export earnings. Coffee, however, remained supreme—accounting for 80 percent of export earnings—as, from one million sacks in 1913, production had doubled by 1921 and would reach three million sacks by 1930. A protracted and violent strike of workers on the United Fruit Company banana plantation at Santa Marta on the Caribbean coast in 1928 provoked two opposite reactions. Most Conservatives approved of the repressive action taken by the Méndez government, whereas progressive Liberals saw it as a sign that the time had come to consider the needs and demands of the working class. Debate mounted as the next presidential elections drew near.[41]

The Second Tier: Each in Its Own Path

As in the preceding period, the four largest countries had followed strikingly different paths: Brazil's consolidation of a republican system under an elite-dominated regime; Mexico's overthrowing the old order and battling for the spoils; Argentina's perhaps too rapid progress toward middle-class democracy; and Colombia's hegemonic rule by the Conservative Party. The roads followed by the remaining South American nations would also be distinct. Peru's efforts at political development, focusing on finding an effective leader, would pass through a highly personalist regime that, unlike Mexico or Argentina, would leave the country halfway along the way to modernity. Venezuela's unique experience would center on an autocratic *caudillo*-type dictator presiding over the inception of an oil-based economy. Chile, somewhat like Argentina, would see its stability threatened at the end of the period. Ecuador saw domination by the Liberal Party, in contrast to Conservative paramountcy in Colombia. While Uruguay experienced its golden age of progressive democracy under an extraordinary reformist leader, Paraguay was still mired in the nineteenth century. Bolivia continued its record of ineffective presidents shuffling into and out of power through coups and rigged elections.

Peru: Finally Strong Leadership and Its Rejection

The 1895–1919 period for Peru, generally called the aristocratic republic, saw suffrage severely restricted to literate adult males, a category that would include nearly 15 percent of Peruvian men by the end of World War I. (Voting turnout in 1894 was a mere 4,500; a decade later it was 147,000 of a population nearing 5 million.) With party agreements and partisan control of the electoral machinery largely predetermining the outcome of elections, as in most of the rest of the region, the cooperating elites grouped in the Civilist and Democratic Parties decided presidential succession in all but one instance during this quarter century. The first significant event after the turn of the century was Augusto B. Legúia's 1908–1912 presidential term. This shrewd practitioner of the political arts was succeeded by a brief and in some ways artificial equivalent of Argentina's middle-class democratic flourishing, led by the well-intentioned Guillermo E. Billinghurst. In 1914, Colonel Oscar R. Benevides headed a coup that threw this idealist out, but Benevides found himself too junior in the army hierarchy to hold onto power.

Legúia's long return engagement as conductor of Peru's political life after World War I took place in a society significantly changed from that existing at the beginning of the century. The economic transformations were more complex than those in Brazil, Mexico, Argentina, and Colombia—if only because Peru lacked a single dominant economic focus or sector. Coffee provided this dominance for Colombia, and to a lesser extent for Brazil, and for Argentina it was beef and wheat, the agro-pastoral dyad of the pampas. In Mexico the deciding political factor after 1910 was brute force on the battlefield, which temporarily relegating socioeconomic factors to the political sidelines; besides, the economy was devastated by the near-continuous warfare and the pre-1910 elites' having been displaced without yet being replaced.[42]

These political developments occurred in a context of economic and social change. In the early decades of the twentieth century under the "aristocratic republic," Peru's economy was undergoing significant changes, leading to shifts in the power of elite sectors that would have a cumulative and in the long run profound impact upon national politics. Sugar production, which had expanded rapidly in the mid-1890s, was overtaken by cotton as the country's leading export crop after 1910. Increased cotton production also fueled a growing textile industry in the Lima region. Copper replaced silver as the major mining export, the US-owned Cerro de Pasco Company becoming dominant by the 1920s. Wool was still significant in the south, rubber had dropped sharply, and oil was just beginning to be a factor. These economic trends were reflected in the social realm as sugar "barons," chiefly of immigrant origin, slowly became the core of the elite, bolstered by largely native-born cotton planters and commercial and financial interests tied to British investment. For sugar production was both large-scale and rather highly mechanized, requiring access to foreign credit for viability. Mining as well as the plantation crops relied heavily on seasonal migrant labor, including former black slaves and Chinese coolies, as well as sierra Indians.

During this period export of Peruvian products and import of foreign capital and consumer goods became increasingly funneled through Lima and its adjacent port of Callao. Linked to British commercial capital, financial and commercial sectors of the Peruvian "oligarchy," really a group of connected elites, were by early in the period concentrated in Lima, where they paid close attention to government activities. The capital was also home to the handful of Peruvian families that still owned small mines. Under protection afforded a depreciating silver-based currency and tariffs imposed by a financially strapped government in the late 1890s, some agro-exporters, foreign firms, and immigrants began to invest in import-substitution manufacturing located in Lima. With this expansion of commerce and industry, Lima began the growth that would elevate it to hegemony among Peru's urban centers, experiencing a population surge of nearly 30 percent between 1908 and 1920, from a modest 175,000 inhabitants to 225,000. After 1910 industrial growth slowed, and as inflation outpaced increases in import prices, tariff protection eroded, while the extremely successful performance of export sectors during World War I drew capital away from manufacturing. Although well-financed foreign factories survived, small immigrant entrepreneurs did not fare as well.

Not all socioeconomic developments leading to political changes were located in the capital region; others took place in the south. By the opening of the twentieth century, descendants of local, English, Basque, and Catalonian wool merchants had become the core of a closely knit Arequipan elite. Extension of the southern railroad inland to Cuzco in 1907 opened new areas to the wool trade. *Haciendas* owned by interior landlords or acquired by the elite expanded at the expense of peasant communities, provoking a wave of localized rebellions. This usurpation of community land largely stopped by the end of World War I, as the increasingly powerful urban middle sectors pressured the central government to show sensitivity to peasant protests. This shift in public policy gave rise to a realization that future profitability was possible only through technological improvements like land enclosure, selective breeding, and improved pasturage. Such modernization was opposed by both types of rural labor—*colonos* (peons), who by tradition enjoyed the right to graze their own animals on *hacienda* land, and *comuneros* (residents of Indian communities), who continued to graze surreptitiously on land they considered theirs by right. Efforts to modernize wool production had bogged down by the 1920s, and for the moment, alpaca exports remained more important than sheep's wool.

These changes in composition of the elite and relations among its components underlay politics for much of the period, although the emergence of middle-class sectors enriched and complicated political life, especially as Peru moved through the 1920s. The electoral law of 1896 had replaced local caucuses with a centralized electoral system, shifting competition for control of the electoral machinery to the national level. Since suffrage was still limited to literate male citizens, the coast and the cities carried the heaviest weight in presidential elections. With regard to congressional elections, however, the rural regions were heavily overrepresented in both houses owing to quirks in the criteria for apportionment. Unlike Brazil, Mexico, Argentina, and Colombia, Peru was not a federal system, and provincial political elites were linked to competing factions at the center by a system of political brokers, rather than acting through governors.[43]

In the first decade of the aristocratic republic and essentially down close to World War I, the basic modus vivendi among the dominant elite blocs was not seriously challenged. A liberal political economy benefited both the agro-exporters and the commercial interests of the coast, and the sierra landlords retained effective local autonomy. Middle- and working-class voters were either clientelistically tied to the Civilists, a party dominated by agro-exporters, commercial interests, and the upper crust of the professions, or attracted to Nicolás de Piérola's Democrats, a hodgepodge coalition led by a fiery but fundamentally conservative *caudillo* with a populist and provincial bent. Traditional landowners could be found in either of these major parties or in the ranks of the lesser Constitutionalists and Constitutional Federalists. Both this high degree of elite consensus and the low level of central government revenues, still just half those attained during the previous period's guano boom, kept a larger role for the state at the margin of political discourse.

After 1904, during the first presidency of José Pardo y Barreda (b. 1864), son of earlier president Manuel Pardo, the alliance of the Civilists and the Constitutionalists upon which the aristocratic republic rested began to lose control of the electoral machinery recently centralized to retain power. At the same time the emerging urban middle sectors started pressing for a more active government sensitive to their concerns and for change in the system of congressional representation, which inordinately favored rural landowners. These issues were center stage in Argentina, about to become so in Mexico, and arousing concern in Brazil, but unique to Peru, a number of intellectuals were beginning to question openly the quasi-feudal subjugation of the Indians. Although these pressures led to a splintering of the major parties and the emergence of new political movements, they did not cause a clear-cut realignment of the party system carried down from the preceding period.

Two governments undermined, but did not destroy, the aristocratic republic. Dissident Civilist president Augusto B. Leguía (b. 1863), taking power in 1908, tilted toward the urban middle sectors and undercut his party's hegemony by decentralizing the electoral machinery. In 1912, he threw his support to protopopulist Guillermo E. Billinghurst (b. 1851), who rode to victory on a massive mobilization of the Lima-area working class. Implementing policies favoring the urban middle and working sectors, such as electoral reform and labor legislation, and using mob violence as a political resource, Billinghurst provoked the elites to instigate a coup, which cut short both his presidency and his life in 1914. His intentions had been laudable, but his tactics imprudent. Peru was far from being Argentina at that point, where Conservatives acquiesced in facilitating the Radical Party's rise to power and the watershed British political events of 1911 (when the Conservatives reluctantly but peacefully agreed to the Liberals' demand to curb severely the role of the House of Lords) had no relevance to this underdeveloped, Indian-majority country, a fact lost on some intellectuals.

Provisional president Colonel Oscar Benevides (b. 1876) cobbled together elite support for a unity candidate for election in 1915, former president José Pardo, who coasted through wartime on the illusionary prosperity of inflation while mollifying the capital region constituency that had supported Billinghurst by continuing progressive labor legislation there, although not in the rest of the country. It was in this partially transformed and still changing socioeconomic context that in 1919 the astute Legúia assembled a broad reformist coalition of urban middle sectors, artisans, and workers to confront the die-hard elements of the elite coalition that constituted the backbone of the aristocratic republic. Refusing to be deprived of victory by electoral fraud, Legúia seized power. Acting in some ways parallel to Yrigoyen and the Radical Party in Argentina, and foreshadowing to a limited extent what Getúlio Vargas would do in Brazil after 1930, Legúia, during his eleven-year presidential tenure, destroyed the Civilist Party. In place of this underpinning of the old order, he cultivated new political brokers in the provinces.[44]

Legúia's long rule, carrying through the relatively favorable decade of the 1920s, was a lost opportunity for political development. Corruption, nepotism, and cronyism undermined the development of effective class and interest organizations, and he did not construct a new political party to replace those he had relegated to irrelevance. His Democratic Reform Party would not continue to be a significant factor, leaving a vacuum once Legúia was himself off the political stage. Starting in a promising manner with an eight-hour day for factory workers, price controls on food and housing, legislation designed to protect indigenous communities, and a broadening of workmen's compensation, Legúia moved toward the center right when export prices fell in 1923. The backbone of his constituency became the expanding government bureaucracy, the incipient industrial bourgeoisie, and the more commercially oriented landowners—white-collar workers being coopted with limited health and pension benefits not extended to the proletariat. Cognizant of the calculus of survival, Legúia split the navy from the purview of the war ministry and established a civil guard and a militarized republican guard, as well as an aviation corps under the navy minister.

Peru's autocrat was a Yankeephile who had started out as an agent for a US insurance company. Foreign experts were brought in not only as advisers, but also to head new agencies requiring technical training and experience. In some ways

AUGUSTO B. LEGUÍA

reminiscent of Díaz in the 1890s, he favored US over British capital, which had long ties to the Civilists, now his opponents. Seeking to resolve the lingering dispute with Standard Oil subsidiary International Petroleum Company (IPC)—a contentious issue that would have extremely deleterious effects in the 1960s—he granted it control of Peru's major oil field, low taxes, and exemption from royalties in return for a cash payment of $1 million and assistance in placing bonds in US capital markets. Leading to a short-term rise in oil production, this agreement was a time bomb.[45]

The stability Legúia provided attracted foreign investment, reflected in an eruption of foreign debt from $12.4 million when he returned to power to $88.4 million by 1929—the year of his third consecutive election. In addition to expanding the government, the influx of financing allowed for the first major public works program since the guano boom. This program stimulated all industries related to construction, as well as extension of the railroad system and overdue modernization of Callao's port facilities. Five major coastal irrigation projects initiated the creation of a new group of middle-class farmers, and over 10,000 miles of roads and hundreds of bridges stimulated internal commerce. Tightened tax collection helped treble government revenues to nearly $100 million a year by the late 1920s, with expenditures pushing $80 million. The expanded role of the state under Legúia had been written into a new constitution in 1920—which borrowed heavily from that idealistic document framed by Mexico three years earlier. As in Mexico, many of its advanced social provisions would wait another generation for implementation.

Not surprisingly, Lima grew by two-thirds during the Legúia Era, beginning in the 1930s at 375,000, including a sizable middle class. Whereas large factories were chiefly foreign-owned, individuals of recent immigrant origin predominated among the owners of smaller industrial establishments. Japanese Peruvians, descended from indentured servants, migrated to the cities and opened small commercial establishments or workshops, and Italians arriving in the 1920s moved into food processing and leather working. Legúia's policies made enemies of the agro-exporters, and his extension of governmental authority and his own political machine into the provinces alienated many traditional landlords. Concentration of urban improvement projects in the Lima area also aroused resentment in the interior. Hence, as unemployment and consequent unrest rose in the wake of the late 1929 financial crash, an effort to overthrow the autocrat was inevitable. It would come in August 1930.

Venezuela: Caudillism Transformed to Militarism

In Venezuela, where two *caudillos* dominated the first seventy years of national life, a third, General Cipriano Castro (b. 1858), took power in 1899 at the cost of some three thousand lives. Brutal, self-indulgent, and corrupt compared to the gentlemanly Guzmán Blanco, he frequently faced foreign interventions to collect debt and saw Great Britain claim a sizable swath of land in the eastern part of the country. The forerunner of a series of dictatorial leaders from the Andean province of Táchira, Castro opted to consolidate power through development of a centrally controlled national army. Strong-arming the capital's bankers to obtain the requisite credits and raising commercial taxes, he entrusted construction of the army to his right-hand man and vice president, Juan Vicente Gómez (b. 1857), a self-made successful rancher and businessman. In a series of campaigns entailing some twelve thousand deaths, Gómez crushed all would-be *caudillos*.

The high-living Castro lost control of the government to Gómez in 1908 when going to Europe for medical care (for kidney problems related to his high living). Gómez would never relinquish power, although entrusting the presidential office to close collaborators in 1915–1922 and 1929–1931. He established a firm control that would last until his death in 1935, twenty-seven years later. Holding all the reins of power in his own hands, this centralizing personalist ran the country from his stronghold a few hours outside Caracas.[46] His government was staffed with relatives, cronies, and retainers to an extent that put even Díaz to shame.[47] The political instability of the nineteenth century had prevented the emergence of an oligarchy based upon large landholdings, and Gómez maintained his power base, as had previous *caudillo* rulers, by distributing land to his cronies. Still, he would become the country's largest landowner—a feat that would be imitated by Rafael Trujillo in the Dominican Republic and Nicaragua's Anastasio Somoza.

During the middle years of Gómez's autocratic rule, oil began to become a major factor in Venezuela's still rudimentary economy. Marginal compared to coffee or even cacao as late as 1921, oil exports earned well more than three times the total of these traditional products by the middle of the decade—a ratio that would reach seventeen to one by the end of Gómez's rule. Showing a degree of foresight, the strongman limited the duration of all oil concessions to fifty years. Bringing the first significant European immigration since colonial days, the oil boom also helped shift the locus of power away from the Andean region. With everything going his way, Gómez found a student uprising in 1928 little more than a minor annoyance. He was mellowed from his most brutal days and enjoyed being depicted as the model of "democratic caesarism." Hence, he permitted the uprising's leaders to go into exile instead of eliminating them—a decision that would have profound positive implications for the country, as these students would become the backbone of the forces working effectively to build a democratic Venezuela after Gómez's demise. (Indeed, their most prominent leader, Rómulo Betancourt, would twice occupy the presidency.) Many of the less illustrious, however, were imprisoned and put to forced labor. As the period ended, Gómez was still in complete control of the country, although enjoying a sabbatical from the presidency.

Chile: Democracy Faces Militarism

The new century brought no sharp change to Chile, as the "parliamentary republic," with its emphasis on parties and legislative politics (along with British investment in nitrate production), continued, under a series of highly respectable, if undistinguished, presidents beginning with Germán Riesco Errazuriz in 1901, followed by yet another Montt, this time Pedro (b. 1846), in 1906, and ending with José Luis Sanfuentes in 1915–1920.[48] As nitrates, source of half the country's foreign exchange earnings throughout this period, were again in high demand (after a slump caused by synthetic alternatives), stability ruled through World War I—although five men occupied the presidency in the decade following Montt's 1910 resignation brought on by ill health. Socioeconomic normality had changed drastically by 1920 with a precipitous fall in demand for this vital component of explosives, and copper had not yet come to fill the gap. Politics was taking on an increasingly urban cast, as Santiago had reached 500,000 inhabitants on its way to 713,00 by 1930. The Central Valley agricultural elite managed to maintain the entrenched clientelistic system by absorbing commercial and incipient industrial eléments. Yet dissident regional oligarchies in the north and south combined with new urban middle sectors and dissident middle groups to press for the political and social reforms their Radical counterparts were achieving in Argentina.[49]

Intransigence of the Conservatives and Liberal Parties, in sharp contrast to the flexibility recently shown by their Argentine equivalents, led in 1920 to the centrist wing of the latter joining the Radicals and Democrats in the Liberal Alliance behind Arturo Alessandri Palma (b. 1869), who had been first elected to the Chamber of Deputies in 1897 and to the Senate in 1915. Lacking a majority in the congress, Alessandri resigned in September 1924 when right-wing obstructionism led to military interference in governmental affairs. In March 1925, Alessandri was back under a new, more presidential constitution providing for direct election of the president for a six-year term, separation of church and state, elimination of congressional votes to censure ministers, and a requirement that the legislature act promptly on proposals deemed urgent by the president. Proportional representation applied to twenty-nine chamber constituencies and ten senate constituencies. Governing by decree at the sufferance of war minister Colonel Carlos Ibañez del Campo (b. 1877), Alessandri resigned for a second time in October, almost at the end of his term. Running in a context of economic recovery, Ibañez gained election as president in March 1927. Like so many other Latin American chief executives, he fell afoul of the economic crash. With prices in a free fall, vital foreign exchange earnings from nitrates began a fall in 1930 that would reach 70 percent by 1933. Not surprisingly, Ibañez's dictatorial regime ended in chaotic 1931.[50]

Ecuador: Uneasy Liberal Dominance

Ecuador, the small country wedged in between Colombia and Peru, began the new century as it had ended the preceding one—enjoying the cacao boom. Liberal Eloy Alfaro, in power since 1895 and godfather of the regime that had established control of the state by the coastal agro-exporting bourgeoisie instrumental in making Ecuador the world's ranking cocoa producer, yielded the presidency to ex-protégé General Leonidas Plaza Gutiérrez (b. 1865) in 1901, and Plaza passed it on to a civilian in 1905. Alfaro regained office by ouster in 1906, adopting an even more anticlerical stance, pushing public education, presiding over the completion of the vital Guayaquil-Quito railroad, and witnessing development of the banking system as the major link between the agricultural elites and the government. Following a brief civil war with Plaza's followers in 1911, this controversial leader met a violent end at the hands of an enraged mob the next January (thus ending tragically, as had his earlier Conservative counterpart, García Moreno).

This bloody outcome let Plaza return to power in 1912 amidst a civil war dragging on to 1916.[51] A railroad builder with close ties to the cacao-growing sector of the economic elite, he had to cope with the residual strength of traditional sierra elites whose *haciendas* still controlled a large proportion of the rural labor force. (Attempting to return to power in 1925, he was executed.) Presidents of the 1916–1925 period—Alfredo de Baqueriza, José Luís Tamayo, and Gonzalo Cordova—were front men for coastal banking and agricultural interests known as *la argolla* (those stuffed to the gills, more colloquially, "fat cats") for their close ties to the Commercial and Agricultural Bank of Guayaquil—a major source of loans for political purposes. With collapse of the cacao boom in 1925, corruption of the political process became less tolerable, so a period of strikes, unrest, and mounting violence was followed by a coup by young officers from the highland region. Called the Transformacíon Juliana (for the month in which it came to power), this mildly reformist military regime, which made hesitant efforts to pick up the pieces from the estrangement between government and business elites resulting from collapsing commodity prices, lasted until 1931.[52] One of its legacies was the 1929 extension of the vote to women.

Bolivia: Elite Democracy and the Rise of Tin

With the dominance of the conservatives broken in 1898–1899, General José Manuel Pando (b. 1849), president until 1904, and assassinated in 1917, and General Ismael Montes (b. 1861), in power from 1904–1909 and again from 1913–1917, inaugurated an era of Liberal Party rule marked by overextension of public works. A spilt in the party occasioned by Montes's second election, and involving both ex-president Pando and future presidents Bautista Saavedra and Daniel Salamanca, gave birth to the Republican Party in 1914. In the face of electoral fraud in 1917, three years later the Republicans staged a bloodless coup—heartened by the developments in Argentina that had brought the Radical Party to office. Once in power, the Republicans split in two (as the Argentine Radicals were in the process of doing), each headed by a highly personalist political boss. In place of the oligarchic two-party system that had served for a generation, Bolivia now had a "less stable and more populist multiparty system."[53] Salamanca led the Genuine Republican Party and Saavedra the Socialist Republican Party. The former represented the urban upper class, frightened by the prospect of the rising middle class as well as the traditional rural patricians. The latter's constituency was middle-class liberals, who had resented the mother party's close ties to the tin-mining interests. Politics now began to reflect underlying class conflict, partially overshadowed by the personal animosities of party leaders.

As president from 1921 to 1925, Saavedra (b. 1860) enacted progressive social and labor codes while doubling taxes on the mining sector. He vigorously repressed the first general workers' strike in 1922 as well as a miners' strike and an Indian uprising the following year. While the economy yo-yoed with the price of tin, he negotiated private international loans on disadvantageous terms and encouraged foreign investment, particularly Standard Oil of New Jersey drilling for oil in the southwestern lowlands. Hernando Siles Reyes (b. 1881), an intraparty rival of the president, was the Socialist Republicans' successful presidential candidate in 1925. However, at midterm he formed the Nationalist Party and joined in with the Genuinos of Salamanca in attacking the previous administration for political repression, economic mismanagement, and a sellout to foreign interests. Yet in 1927 he invited Princeton University economics professor Edwin Kemmerer to shift his advising mission from Peru to Bolivia. Having built roads, railroads, and telegraph lines, but burdened with responsibility for obtaining foreign loans on increasingly unfavorable terms, Siles rashly attempted to amend the constitution to extend his term. This bald power grab boomeranged and resulted in his ouster by a bloody coup on June 25, 1930.[54] But with the world economic crash under way, his ouster would not mean better days ahead for Bolivia.

Uruguay: Flowering of Democracy

This period would prove to be Uruguay's golden age, in which it established a well-deserved reputation for progressive democracy upon which it would later coast. In 1903, the election by the congress of José Batlle y Ordóñez (b. 1856), son of former president Lorenzo Batlle, remembered for a lackluster administration when his son was an infant, set off an eighteen-month civil war, which did not stop him from launching a program of social, economic, and political change that was clearly ahead of the times in the Latin American context. Indeed, this greatest of Uruguayan leaders, a cosmopolitan who blended in when in Paris and other European haunts, would exit the political scene just as Yrigoyen and the Radicals opened their stand in Argentina.[55] His policies would not, however, be reversed, as happened after 1930 in Uruguay's across-the-river neighbor.

Batlle was almost immediately faced with a serious armed challenge to his authority. The election losers, the National Party under Aparicio Saravia, challenged him for having broken the 1897 agreement on coparticipation, for he strongly favored fully competitive elections based on proportional representation. The full-fledged civil war that ensued ended only with Saravia's death in battle in 1904. To implement effectively his option for party (partisan) government, Batlle first had to consolidate his hold over a divided Colorado Party, accomplished through the 1905 Chamber of Deputies elections and the senate balloting the next year. Subsequently he was more successful than Yrigoyen would be in Argentina fifteen years later in finding a loyal successor who would carry on his policies and facilitate his return to office.

Elected in 1907, Claudio Williman maintained, but did not advance, Batlle's reforms, as the country experienced greater prosperity than during the last half of Batlle's term. Upon his reelection in 1911, Batlle moved to unify and modern-

JOSÉ BATLLE Y ORDÓÑEZ

ize his party so as to put an end to the unstable, personalistic, and at times autocratic politics of the preceding period. His goal was to establish a "model country" with "an educated, secular, economically secure working class linked
politically to the Colorado Party; and a fully democratic political system, ruled by
a non-presidential, nine-person council, the *colegiado*."[56] An economy dependent
on the export of livestock and hides was to be industrialized at the same time as
dependence on foreign investment was greatly reduced. To this end, the government encouraged immigrant capitalists to come to Uruguay and shifted toward
bonds rather than investment as the main source of foreign capital. Government
companies were founded to replace foreign ones. A prosperous and satisfied society would be created through free primary and secondary education, an eight-
hour workday, and an old-age pension system. To minimize class conflict, labor
would be given the right to organize and strike, plus maternity leave and curbs
on child labor and an opportunity to participate freely in the electoral process.
This sweeping reform program, strongly opposed by the country's business elites,
and including full separation of church and state, finally passed the congress in
the last year of his administration.

His Colorado successor, Feliciano Viera, known, for his appearance, as El Indio,
found himself in a political dilemma. Although the Colorados had won the July

1916 elections by 52 percent to 48 percent, 9 percent of their share had gone to a faction opposed to Batlle's project to scrap the presidential system. Needing their support to govern, Viera broke with his predecessor. The dissident leader founded a new party and allied with the Nationals (Blancos) in the February 1917 chamber elections. Although Batlle's supporters won this balloting, they could not push the *colegiado* through the constituent assembly until 1917–1918, when bipartisan approval was achieved on a system of a president who supervised defense, foreign affairs, and internal security and a nine-man National Council of Administration handling all other matters.

Impasse prevailed over the first decade of the new governmental system. Already strained, Colorado unity came to an end with the deaths of ex-presidents Viera and Batlle; Batlle had been serving as head of the National Council of Administration since 1926. One candidate determined to fill the Colorado leadership vacuum was Gabriel Terra, an opponent of both Batlle's social reforms and the council, but a more effective politician than any of Batlle's disciples. He would have an essentially negative impact in the 1930s.

Paraguay: Still a Century Behind

The Liberal Party ended the generation-long Colorado dominance of Paraguay's rudimentary political life through an Argentine-backed coup in 1904 that removed Colorado Juan A. Escurra, a supporter of longtime dominant political leader General Bernardino Caballero, from office and replaced him with Benigno Ferreira. This marked a shift from strong rule by military men to weak rule by civilians as petty factionalism led to fifteen presidents in the next eighteen years. In an excessive demonstration of equal opportunity, eight Liberals occupied the presidency during the first eight years. With the absence of significant foreign trade, they all continued to raise revenues by selling large tracts of land to foreigners. Then *caudillo* Eduardo Schaerer tried to impose stability through his version of radical statism, financed by foreign loans, but he saw his successor, Manuel Franco, die three years into his term, once again setting off the presidential carrousel.[57]

Civil war came in late 1921 as Colorados unsuccessfully backed Schaerer's bid to return to power. Eligio Ayala, backed by two-time president Manuel Gondra (1910–1911 and 1920–1921), held office until mid-1924. For the next dozen years there was relative stability under the Liberals—as the Colorados boycotted the elections. By Paraguayan standards this began as a progressive period, including the 1926 land reform. But once Gondrista Liberal José Patricio Guggiare took office in August 1928, the border incidents began with Bolivia, which would lead to the calamitous Chaco War.

Central America: More of the Same, Except for One

The opening three decades of the twentieth century saw dramatic change in only one of the Central American countries: Costa Rica. Elsewhere, patterns from the 1890s persisted as these countries encountered great difficulty in moving beyond *caudillo* politics and foreign domination.

Guatemala: Banana Republic Dictatorship

The largest of the region's countries opened the century in the firm grasp of Manuel Estrada Cabrera (b. 1857), an admirer of Justo Rufino Barrios and the model for Nobel Prize–winner Miguel Angel Asturias's memorable novel *El Señor Presidente*.[58] Having succeeded to power when José María Reyna Barrios was murdered in 1898, Estrada Cabrera, a lawyer by profession, turned more repressive after surviving an assassination attempt during his second term in office. He was decidedly more conservative than Barrios, and his policies became increasingly bizarre and repressive, evoking scorn by the educated strata of society. The viability of Estrada Cabrera's long rule was assured by the heavy investments of the Boston-based United Fruit Company in the country's transportation and communications infrastructures and the resulting burgeoning banana exports. Indeed, this reliance on foreign investment had started under Barrios with port and railroad facilities.

Reelected without opposition in 1910 and 1916, Estrada Cabrera became a morbid recluse, finally being declared mentally unfit by the congress in 1920. Within a few months his civilian successor was overthrown by General José M. Orellano, who passed away in 1926, and in turn the delicate health of his successor, Lázaro Chacón, gave out in 1930—by which time the military was clearly the real power. A new dictator was waiting in the wings.

El Salvador: Consolidation of an Oligarchy

The agro-exporting elites held this little country in the palms of their hands throughout the period, one usually described as moderate modernization in a context of the rise of coffee as the country's chief cash crop. In 1913, rich agriculturist Carlos Meléndez reached the presidency. After a second term from 1915 to 1919, his brother Jorge occupied the presidency to 1923, so the family's hold on the office lasted to 1927. Although power did not always reside so blatantly in the hands of a single family, the country's renowned "fourteen families" did constitute a tightly knit oligarchy.[59]

Honduras: The "Banana Republic"

More than any other country, Honduras was the prototypical "banana republic." By the turn of the century, conditions there were deteriorating. Manuel Bonilla became president in 1903 but in 1907 was ousted and replaced by Miguel Dávila in a revolt that involved invasion by Nicaragua (whose president saw this as a step toward reuniting Central America). Bonilla and US banana entrepreneur Samuel Zemurray launched an uprising in 1912 that, with forceful US mediation, resulted in Bonilla's reinstatement in office before dying early the next year.[60] The country's future strongman, Tibúrcio Carías Andino, was elected in 1923, but the Liberal Party controlling the congress erected obstacles to his taking office. The resulting US mediation led to the inauguration of his running mate, Miguel Paz Baraona, at the beginning of 1925. The Liberals regained the presidency in 1929 behind Vicente Colindras, who would govern to 1932.

Costa Rica: Consolidation of Democracy

Adoption of the secret ballot and universal male suffrage in 1902 was followed by the election in mid-1902 of Ascensíon Esquivel. A gradually broadening and differentiating electorate elevated the National Union Party's moderately conservative Cleto González Víquez (b. 1858) to power in 1906. His permitting free elections (in advance of both the Mexican Revolution and the Sáenz Peña reforms in Argentina) brought the more reformist Ricardo Jiménez Oreamundo (b. 1859) to office in 1910. Legislation in 1913 during González's second term made elections more direct and open well in advance of those of any other country in the Mexican–Central American–Caribbean region. For in Costa Rica the coffee-producing elites preferred classical liberal-representative devices to the uncertainties of military dictatorship, and the gradual spread of banana cultivation did not give foreign companies a dominant position from which to interfere in political life, as they had interfered and did interfere in the politics of Costa Rica's northern neighbors. Dissatisfied elements of the coffee aristocracy backed a coup led by Federico Tinoco that overthrew Alfredo González in 1917, but failure to obtain US recognition caused the would-be strongman to throw in the towel in mid-1918. In December the Liberal Party's Julio Acosta was elected to serve until 1924, and Jiménez was brought back to office for the 1924–1928 term, being followed by fellow ex-president Cleto González (whom he would succeed in 1932).[61]

Nicaragua: US Intervention

In Nicaragua the new century dawned with José Santos Zelaya having already been seven years in power. A "relatively benevolent, modernizing, authoritarian nationalist," this Liberal dictator presided over a Díaz-like spurt of development.[62] His patriotic but unrealistic refusal to grant the United States effective control of part of Nicaragua's territory for an interoceanic canal turned Theodore Roosevelt's attention to Panama as an alternative. Then negotiations with the British and Japanese over a canal, as well as his efforts to reunite Central America, put Santos Zelaya on Washington's hit list. Thus, the United States supported a Conservative Party-backed uprising that ousted Zelaya in 1909. José Madrez, José D. Estrada, and Juan J. Estrada each briefly kept the presidential chair warm until Washington found its man, installing Adolfo Díaz in office in May 1911. When he and his backers could not establish control over the country, US marines were sent in to bolster them in 1912. Díaz was propped up until 1916, when, following the signing of the Bryan-Chamorro Treaty giving the United States exclusive canal rights and making Nicaragua a de facto protectorate, Emiliano Chamorro became president through an election in which the Liberal Party was kept from campaigning. He was succeeded by a relative in 1921, and Carlos Solórzano was elected in 1925. When Chamorro ousted him the next year the United States dictated a compromise in which the usurper would stay in office only until new elections in 1928.

Overconfident about the popular base for their client Conservative Party president, US officials had withdrawn the troops in August 1925. The 1926 revolt brought a return of US forces the next year and subsequent engineering of a peaceful election in 1928 that put the Liberal army commander, General José María Moncada, in the presidency of a country whose independence was only nominal and whose sovereignty was essentially a legal fiction—as was also the case at that time in the Dominican Republic, Haiti, and Panama, as well as, less openly, Cuba. With unforeseen consequences for the future, one of the new president's lieutenants, Augusto César Sandino, had become alienated and radicalized, turning to armed insurgency. Another, Anastasio Somoza García (the country's future durable dictator) obtained a commission in the US-organized National Guard.

The Caribbean: US Intervention for All

This subregion emerged as a problem area early in this period, strategic and economic considerations making it even more the "backyard" of the United States than was adjoining Central America. Its largest country, Cuba, was a new nation just coming out from under Spanish colonial rule.

Cuba was born as a nation only as the nineteenth century came to its close. The island was not only settled early by the Spanish but was also closest to Spain in terms of transportation and communications. Tobacco and coffee gave way to sugar, which brought with it a greatly increased use of slave labor. As Juan de Aguila aptly summarizes, the political results were that "lacking either clear separatist objectives, a commitment to social revolution, or an effective political/military strategy, Cuba's creole class accepted Spain's periodic concessions, preserved slavery, and accumulated wealth, exchanging political quiescence for economic and social privileges."[63]

Having lost most of its American empire, Spain after the 1820s clung even harder to what remained, especially Cuba. Hence, the first bid for Cuban independence was delayed until less prosperous planters in the eastern region, far from Havana, rose up in October 1868 behind Carlos Manuel de Céspedes (b. 1819), with Máximo Gómez (b. 1836) and Antonio Maceo y Grajales (b. 1845)—a poor free Negro—as military leaders in an ill-fated decade-long armed struggle. Loss of perhaps 200,000 Spanish and 50,000 Cuban lives guaranteed there would be a lengthy lull before the effort to win independence by force resumed. As US interests in Cuba burgeoned to a point where Cuba was economically tied more closely to the United States than to distant and capital-poor Spain, both Spanish concessions and an autonomist movement failed to stem the spread of sentiment for independence. Fighting resumed on a large-scale in 1895, with José J. Martí (b. 1853) as intellectual mentor and stateside advocate, becoming a national idol with his death.[64] Just as armed French intervention had been crucial to US independence in the 1780s, direct US involvement was necessary to shift the military balance against a determined Spain. Seizing upon the wave of enraged public reaction to the "dastardly" sinking of the US battleship *Maine* in Havana harbor, the Republican McKinley administration joined the war in mid-1898, bringing it to a quick conclusion.

The immediate result was not independence for Cuba, but US military occupation. Once protectorate status was guaranteed by incorporation into the Cuban Constitution of the Platt Amendment's menu of justifications for future US interventions, Cuba became nominally independent. But its subsequent history is both illustrative and critical. For poor as were the self-government experiences of Haiti, the Dominican Republic, and Nicaragua, at least they did exist. In Cuba elder statesman Tomás Estrada Palma (b. 1835) of the Partido Moderado had been installed as president in May 1902 under a US-shaped 1901 constitution (much as during recent experiments in nation building and force-fed political development in Afghanistan and Iraq). A corrupt reelection in 1905, which the Liberal Party boycotted, led to a coup the following year. This in turn resulted in the second US military occupation from 1906 to 1909, which ended with the highly US-tutored election of Liberal general José Miguel Gómez, known as the Shark (El Tuberón) for his limitless greed in using the national treasury as his personal bank account. He was followed in 1912 by Mário García Menocal (b. 1866), who was given a second term by a small electorate in 1916.

In the face of accusations of ballot rigging, the United States intervened heavily (with twenty thousand troops, compared to only three thousand the first time) to prop up García Menocal, an action that graphically demonstrated where ultimate authority rested. Thus Alfredo Zayas (b. 1861), elected in 1920 with García Menocal's endorsement, had General Enoch Crowder constantly looking over his shoulder. US investment in sugar soared, but with the profitable refining operations transferred abroad, only raw sugar was exported until Hershey set up a refinery in 1925, with others following. Total US investment had grown to $160 million plus $37 million in bonds by 1906, then leaped to just over $1 billion direct and $100 million in bonds by 1927. In 1924, General Gerardo Machado y Morales (b. 1871) was elected president, subsequently gaining substantial support through an ambitious public works program. This nominal liberal clung to office by force when his constitutional term ended in 1928, ushering in a period of escalating repression and violence. His blatant *continuismo* led to an increasingly critical political role for the Cuban army, whose senior ranks were lavishly courted by the beleaguered president.[65] This would be a heavy legacy for the next three decades.

The Dominican Republic would come under increased US control during this period, which opened with Juan Isidro Jiménez tenuously clinging to the presidency—before being overthrown by his vice president, Horácio Vásquez. An interim president in 1907 agreed under pressure to a US customs receivership that had the United States apply 55 percent of Dominican export revenues against the country's mountain of foreign debts. Ramón Caceres, ex-dictator Hereaux's assassin, subsequently provided five years of modestly responsible government before his own violent death in 1912. With Caceres's demise, the political situation deteriorated just as World War I began. President Juan Isidro Jiménez's impeachment in 1916 (after a year and a half back in power) triggered a US occupation (as had already occurred in Haiti) that lasted eight years. Since guerrilla resistance was quite limited, the occupation was less oppressive than at the other end of the island and was terminated in 1924 with the election of the old political warhorse General Horácio Vásquez.[66] After extending his term in 1928, Vásquez was forced out in 1930.

By the turn of the century, conditions were deteriorating in Haiti. Northern peasant revolts had been occurring for a generation. Presidents Nord Alexis (1903–1908) and Antoine Simon (overthrown and killed in 1911), as well as the five individuals passing through the presidency in the next four years, could not keep politics in the urban centers from deteriorating to a point where, in mid-1915, President Jean Vilbrun Guillaume Sam had 173 of his political enemies executed before his own assassination triggered a US takeover. This proved to be the least successful of Woodrow Wilson's experiments with installing democracy at the point of a bayonet. Behind the puppet presidents Sudre Dartiguenave—who in 1917 suspended the national legislature for twelve years—and Louis Borno, US control of the economy was consolidated, and a war of extermination was carried out against resistance in the countryside. Labeled as bandits by the United States, some 50,000 opponents of the occupation were killed both before and after their leaders, Charlemagne Peralte and Benoit Batraville, were hunted down and shot in 1919–1920. By the time the repression was completed in 1929, perhaps a tenth of the country's two million inhabitants had fled to Cuba or the Dominican Republic.[67] (The occupation would continue until 1934.)

Latin America in 1929

In many ways Latin America appeared to have made significant progress during the first three decades of the twentieth century. Although a considerable degree of violence had been involved, it had been largely confined to Mexico and its epic civil strife. Unfortunately the shallowness of the roots of development and modernization would be exposed by the traumatizing impact of the Great Depression—triggered just as the relatively progressive and prosperous 1920s drew to their close. Argentina had enjoyed the greatest forward movement, briefly ranking as one of the world's leading democracies. Mexico had gained the biggest headlines for its revolution and was showing signs of emerging from the violent power struggle that had ensued. Brazil was viewed as having its early-1900s progress running out of steam, and Colombia was held up as a model of stability combined with elite democracy.

Chile was recognized as going through difficult days but was credited for having performed well for all but the most recent years. Cuba was perceived through a very relativistic lens as having moved along reasonably well in light of the recentness of its independence. Peru under Leguía seemed to be lurching toward modernity, and Venezuela was praised for stability under a dictator given a pass on his arbitrariness because of the country's rising oil exports. Uruguay was seen as a "quaint" little democracy and Paraguay as an insignificant unknown, whereas Bolivia and Ecuador were saddled with the image of being virtually ungovernable. It was understood that the two parts of Hispaniola, along with Nicaragua, were the domain of the US occupying forces busy constructing democracy by building roads, schools, and hospitals as well as "reliable" security forces—while vigorously repressing "bandits" standing in the way of such "Wilsonian" nation building carried on by his Republican successors. The Central American countries were lumped together as banana republics from which little could be expected, and Panama was seen, not inaccurately (except in a formal juridical sense), as a US protectorate. But the real test was about to begin with the hurricane-like impact of a world economic crash.

Notes

1. See Francisco de Assis Barbosa in Afonso Arinos and Jânio Quadros, *História do Povo Brasileira,* Vol. 5, *A República, as Oligarquias Estaduais* (São Paulo: J. Quadros Editôres Cultur-

ais, 1967), p. 121. This treatment of Brazil draws heavily upon Ronald M. Schneider, *"Order and Progress": A Political History of Brazil* (Boulder, CO: Westview Press, 1991), pp. 84–114, and the less detailed version in Ronald M. Schneider, *Brazil: Culture and Politics in a New Industrial Powerhouse* (Boulder, CO: Westview Press, 1996), pp. 50–58.

2. This thesis is explored in Joseph L. Love, "Political Participation in Brazil, 1881–1969," *Luso-Brazilian Review,* 7:2 (December 1970), pp. 3–24.

3. Frank D. McCann, *Soldiers of the Pátria: A History of the Brazilian Army, 1889–1937* (Stanford, CA: Stanford University Press, 2004), p. 88.

4. See ibid., pp. 89–92.

5. The modernization of Rio de Janeiro is ably treated in Jeffrey D. Needell, *A Tropical Belle Epoque: Elite Culture and Society in Turn-of-the-Century Rio de Janeiro* (New York: Cambridge University Press, 1988). For a perspective from the hotbed of Brazil's southern politics, see Joseph L. Love, *Rio Grande do Sul and Brazilian Regionalism: 1882–1930* (Palo Alto, CA: Stanford University Press, 1971).

6. McCann, *Soldiers,* p. xxi.

7. Hermes is analyzed in ibid., pp. 94–95.

8. The first part of Hermes's presidency is discussed in ibid., pp. 107–121.

9. See ibid., pp. 121–157, as well as Todd A. Diacon, *Millenarian Vision, Capitalist Reality: Brazil's Contestado Rebellion, 1912–1916* (Durham, NC: Duke University Press, 1991).

10. McCann, *Soldiers,* pp. 158–159; an exhaustive treatment of the army's modernization extends to p. 186.

11. Consult June Hahner, *Poverty and Politics: The Urban Poor in Brazil, 1870–1920* (Albuquerque: University of New Mexico Press, 1986), p. 88.

12. See Love, *Rio Grande do Sul,* pp. 199–215.

13. Consult McCann, *Soldiers,* pp. 210ff.

14. Ibid., pp. 218–219.

15. Neil Macaulay, *The Prestes Column: Revolution in Brazil* (New York: Franklin Watts, 1974), provides a detailed account of these events. McCann, *Soldiers,* pp. 259–279, makes use of a much wider array of sources.

16. Useful for understanding politics at this juncture is Mauricio Font, *Coffee, Contention, and Change: In the Politics of Brazil* (London: Blackwell, 1990). For the socioeconomic situation at the end of the 1920s, see Michael L. Conniff, *Rio de Janeiro in the Depression Era, 1920–1937* (Stanford, CA: Stanford University Press, 1975).

17. Hahner, *Poverty,* p. 291.

18. Paul H. Lewis, *Authoritarian Regimes in Latin America: Dictators, Despots, and Tyrants* (Lanham, MD: Rowman & Littlefield, 2006), p. 59.

19. Roderic Ai Camp, *Politics in Mexico: The Democratic Transformation,* 4th ed. (New York: Oxford University Press, 2003), pp. 39–40.

20. Rodney D. Anderson, *Outcasts in Their Own Land: Mexican Industrial Workers, 1906–1911* (DeKalb: Northern Illinois University Press, 1976), p. 243.

21. Enrique Krauze, *Mexico, Biography of Power: A History, of Modern Mexico, 1810–1996* (New York: HarperCollins, 1997), pp. 245–273, deals with Madero and the revolution, as does Michael C. Meyer, William L. Sherman, and Susan M. Deeds, *The Course of Mexican History,* 7th ed. (New York: Oxford University Press, 2002), Chapters 31, 32. See also

Charles C. Cumberland, *The Mexican Revolution: Genesis Under Madero* (New York: Greenwood Press, 1952). On US involvement, consult Robert E. Quirk, *An Affair of Honor: Woodrow Wilson and the Occupation of Veracruz* (Lexington: University of Kentucky Press, 1962).

22. Robert E. Quirk, *The Mexican Revolution: 1914–1915* (New York: Norton, 1970), provides perceptive analysis. The most detailed treatment of this period is Alan Knight, *The Mexican Revolution*, 2 vols. (Lincoln: University of Nebraska Press, 1990). Also very useful is Peter H. Smith, *Labyrinths of Power: Political Recruitment in Twentieth Century Mexico* (Princeton: Princeton University Press, 1979). Zapata is discussed in Krauze, *Mexico,* pp. 274–304, as well as in John Womack, Jr., *Zapata and the Mexican Revolution* (New York: Knopf, 1969), and Samuel Brunk, *Emiliano Zapata: Revolution and Betrayal in Mexico* (Albuquerque: University of New Mexico Press, 1995).

23. Krauze, *Mexico,* p. 344. The Carranza period is covered in pp. 334–373; these years are also discussed in Meyer, Sherman, and Deeds, *Course of Mexican History,* Chapters 33–35.

24. Krauze, *Mexico,* pp. 305–333, deals with events involving Villa.

25. See Charles C. Cumberland, *The Mexican Revolution: The Constitutional Years* (Austin: University of Texas Press, 1972).

26. Krauze, *Mexico,* pp. 374–403, covers the Obregón era, as does Meyer, Sherman, and Deeds, *Course of Mexican History*, Chapter 36.

27. Krauze, *Mexico,* pp. 404–437, deals with events during the period of Calles domination.

28. On the religious conflict, see David C. Baily, *Viva Cristo Rey! The Cristero Revolt and the Church-State Conflict in Mexico* (Austin: University of Texas Press, 1974), and Robert E. Quirk, *The Mexican Revolution and the Catholic Church, 1910–1929* (Bloomington: Indiana University Press, 1973).

29. Consult David Rock, *Politics in Argentina, 1890–1930: The Rise and Fall of Radicalism* (London: Cambridge University Press, 1975), as well as David Rock, *Argentina, 1516–1987: From Spanish Colonization to Alfonsin* (Berkeley: University of California Press, 1987). Other sound political histories include Luis Alberto Romero, *A History of Argentina in the Twentieth Century* (University Station: Pennsylvania State University Press, 2002), and James Scobie, *Argentina: A City and a Nation*, 2nd ed. (New York: Oxford University Press, 1971).

30. See Paul H. Lewis, *The Crisis of Argentine Capitalism* (Chapel Hill: University of North Carolina Press, 1990), and William C. Smith, *Authoritarianism and the Crisis of the Argentine Political Economy* (Stanford, CA: Stanford University Press, 1989).

31. Peter G. Snow, *Argentine Radicalism: The History and Doctrine of the Radical Civic Union* (Iowa City: University of Iowa Press, 1965), and Rock, *Politics,* are valuable sources.

32. See Douglas Madsen and Peter G. Snow, *The Charismatic Bond: Political Behavior in Time of Crisis* (Cambridge: Harvard University Press, 1991), p. 41.

33. Consult James W. McGuire, *Peronism Without Perón: Unions, Parties, and Democracy in Argentina* (Stanford, CA: Stanford University Press, 1997), pp. 37–43.

34. See ibid., p. 44.

35. Consult Robert A. Potash, *The Army and Politics in Argentina*, Vol. 1, *1928–1945: Yrigoyen to Perón* (Stanford, CA: Stanford University Press, 1969), pp. 18–22.

36. Ibid., pp. 42–57.

37. David Bushnell, *The Making of Modern Colombia: A Nation in Spite of Itself* (Berkeley and Los Angeles: University of California Press, 1993), pp. 148–154. Also reliable and perceptive is Frank Safford and Marco Palacios, *Colombia: Fragmented Land, Divided Society* (New York: Oxford University Press, 2002).

38. Bushnell, *Making of Modern Colombia,* pp. 155–160, treats the Reyes era.

39. Paul Oquist, *Violence, Conflict, and Politics in Colombia* (New York: Academic Press), p. 154.

40. Vernon Lee Fluharty, *Dance of the Millions* (Pittsburgh: University of Pittsburgh Press, 1957), is the classic work on this period.

41. Bushnell, *Making of Modern Colombia,* pp. 164–180, covers the post-Reyes years.

42. An excellent history is Peter F. Klarén, *Peru: Society and Nationhood in the Andes* (New York: Oxford University Press, 2000).

43. Consult Peter F. Klarén, *Modernization, Dislocation, and Aprismo* (Austin: University of Texas Press, 1973), as well as his more recent *Peru: Society and Nationhood in the Andes* (see note 42).

44. See Howard L. Karno, *Augusto B. Legúia and the Modernization of Peru,* Ph.D. dissertation, University of California at Los Angeles, 1971.

Author not available, *The Downfall of the Constitutional Government of Peru: Historical Analysis of the Military Revolution of July 4, 1919 That Established the Dictatorship of D. Augusto Bernardino Legúia in Peru* (New York: DeLaisne & Rossboro, 1927), provides a sense of the times.

45. *El Convénio Greene-De la Flor y el Pago a la IPC* (Lima, Peru: El Populista, 1979).

46. See Lewis, *Authoritarian Regimes,* p. 64. The atmosphere of this period is caught in Thomas Rourke (pseudonym of D. J. Clinton), *Gómez: Tyrant of the Andes* (New York: William Morrow, 1936).

47. Lewis, *Authoritarian Regimes,* pp. 63–68, provides an excellent vignette on Gómez.

48. For perspective, see Brian Loveman, *Chile: The Legacy of Hispanic Capitalism* (New York: Oxford University Press, 1979), as well as Simon Collier and William F. Slater, *A History of Chile, 1808–1994* (Cambridge, UK: Cambridge University Press, 1996).

49. See Karen L. Remmer, *Party Competition in Argentina and Chile: Political Recruitment and Public Policy, 1890–1930* (Lincoln: University of Nebraska Press, 1984).

50. For details on the latter part of the period, see Frederick M. Nunn, *Chilean Politics, 1920–1931: The Honorable Mission of the Armed Forces* (Albuquerque: University of New Mexico Press, 1970).

51. Consult David Schodt, *Ecuador: An Andean Enigma* (Boulder, CO: Westview Press, 1987), as well as the early part of Anita Isaacs, *Military Rule and Transition in Ecuador, 1972–92* (Pittsburgh: University of Pittsburgh Press, 1993).

52. See John D. Martz, *Ecuador: Conflicting Political Culture and the Quest for Progress* (Boston: Allyn & Bacon, 1972).

53. Indispensable is Herbert S. Klein, *Parties and Political Change in Bolivia 1880–1952* (London: Cambridge University Press, 1969).

54. Consult Waltrud Queiser Morales, *Bolivia: Land of Struggle* (Boulder, CO: Westview Press, 1991).

55. See Milton Vanger, *José Batlle y Ordóñez of Uruguay: The Creator of His Times, 1902–1907* (Cambridge: Harvard University Press, 1963), as well as Martin Weinstein, *Uruguay: Democracy at the Crossroads* (Boulder, CO: Westview Press, 1988).

56. Consult Milton Vanger, *The Model Country: José Batlle y Ordóñez of Uruguay 1907–1915* (Waltham, MA: Brandeis University Press, 1980).

57. See Paul H. Lewis, *Political Parties and Generations in Paraguay's Liberal Era, 1869–1940* (Chapel Hill: University of North Carolina Press, 1993), and Harris G. Warren, *Paraguay: An Informal History* (Westport, CT: Greenwood Press, 1982)—a reprint of Warren's 1949 gem—as well as Riordan Roett and Richard S. Sacks, *Paraguay: The Personalist Legacy* (Boulder, CO: Westview Press, 1990).

58. Miguel Angel Asturias, *El Señor Presidente*, trans. by Francis Partridge (New York: Atheneum, 1964), is a masterful fictionalization of the Estrada Cabrera regime. Lewis, *Authoritarian Regimes,* pp. 70–71, sizes up this despot. Very useful on the broader context is Deborah J. Yashar, *Demanding Democracy: Reform and Reaction in Costa Rica and Guatemala 1870s–1950s* (Stanford, CA: Stanford University Press, 1997).

59. Consult Ralph Lee Woodward, Jr., *Central America: A Nation Divided*, 3rd ed. (New York: Oxford University Press, 1999). For the social unrest that would soon inundate the country in blood, see Thomas P. Anderson, *Matanza: El Salvador's Communist Revolution of 1932* (Lincoln: University of Nebraska Press, 1971).

60. See James Morris, *Honduras: Caudillo Politics and Military Rule* (Boulder, CO: Westview Press, 1984).

61. Consult John A. Booth, *Costa Rica: Quest for Democracy* (Boulder, CO: Westview Press, 1998).

62. See Thomas W. Walker, *Nicaragua: The Land of Sandino* (Boulder, CO: Westview Press, 1981).

63. Juan M. de Aguila, *Cuba: Dilemmas of a Revolution* (Boulder, CO: Westview Press, 1984), p. 11. A basic historical source is Hugh Thomas, *Cuba: Or the Pursuit of Freedom*, updated ed. (New York: Da Capo Press, 1998). A wealth of detail is in Jorge I. Dominguez, *Cuba: Order and Revolution* (Cambridge, MA: Belknap Press of Harvard University Press, 1978). A useful perspective is provided in Jorge Ibarra, *Prologue to Revolution: Cuba, 1898–1958* (Boulder, CO: Lynne Rienner, 1998).

64. On this figure raised to a mythical hero by Castro, consult John M. Kirk, *José Martí: Mentor of the Cuban Nation* (Tampa: University Presses of Florida, 1983).

65. See Louis Perez's three studies: *Cuba Between Empires, 1879–1902* (Pittsburgh: University of Pittsburgh Press, 1983); *Army Politics in Cuba, 1898–1958* (Pittsburgh: University of Pittsburgh Press, 1976); and *Intervention, Revolution, and Politics in Cuba, 1913–1921* (Pittsburgh: University of Pittsburgh Press, 1978).

66. Consult Howard J. Wiarda and Michael Kryzanek, *The Dominican Republic: A Caribbean Crucible* (Boulder, CO: Westview Press, 1982).

67. Start with Patrick Bellegarde-Smith, *Haiti: The Breached Citadel* (Boulder, CO: Westview Press, 1989); Alex Dupuy, *Haiti and the World Economy: Class, Race, and Underdevelopment Since 1700* (Boulder, CO: Lynne Rienner, 1989); and David Nicholls, *From Dessalines to Duvalier: Race, Colour, and National Independence in Haiti* (Cambridge, UK: Cambridge University Press, 1979).

6

From the Great Depression into the Cold War

Brazil, Mexico, and Argentina, 1930–1955

The abrupt end of the essentially prosperous post–World War I decade followed by its antithesis, the Great Depression, had a profound effect throughout the Western world. Not only would this catastrophe reinvigorate the interest in Marxism-Leninism, which had ebbed during the 1920s good times, but it would fuel a rise in the fascist regimes that would dominate most of western Europe even before the Axis powers resorted to war in late 1939 to seek domination. Fascism came to power in Italy behind Benito Mussolini in the mid-1920s, with Adolf Hitler and his Nazis gaining control of Germany in 1933. Holding sway over much of Spain after its civil war broke out in the mid-1930s, Generalissimo Francisco Franco's Falange organization, a crossbreed of Spain's traditional authoritarian Catholic corporatism with modern fascism's rejection of individualism and many aspects of modernization, was in full control of that country by the 1940s (and would prevail until the mid-1970s). A similar regime was already entrenched in Portugal under Antonio de Oliveira Salazar.

Given the close historical links and blood ties between most Latin Americans and Spain, Italy, and Portugal, interest in the competing ideologies of communism and fascism rose sharply during the first half of this period. The former, a hard sell in deeply Catholic societies, created a great deal of concern while failing to develop into a mass political movement. In Brazil, Vargas would play these two forces off against each other, not only neutralizing them, but also essentially neutering them by 1938. In postrevolution Mexico, with no significant Italian population, fascism never got beyond the curiosity stage, and Cárdenas defanged communism. In Argentina, where the potential was much greater, the Peróns coopted communism's labor base and absorbed fascism within their populist version of authoritarian corporatism. Staunchly Catholic Colombia, which did not receive a significant influx of European immigration in the decades before or during this period, was barren land for both these modern ideologies. In different ways this would be the case in the medium-sized and smaller countries as well.

In this international context for Latin America the years from 1930 through 1955 were a maelstrom in which countervailing and contradictory trends were at work as each country strove to cope with its particular form of often-traumatic impact resulting from the global economic crisis, World War II, and the US-Soviet confrontation escalating into the Cold War—giving this period the character of a three-act play with no comedy, some tragedy, and a great deal of drama. Through it all, the pace of socioeconomic change varied greatly across the region, accompanied by major differences in its political effects. Still, as in the preceding period, violence and destruction had been minor compared to that in Europe or Asia, hosts to the two world wars.

Although the timing and the directions might be nearly unique to the country, few of the region's countries avoided dramatic swings of the political pendulum. To add a good deal of excitement to events, in keeping with a world trend that produced Winston Churchill, Franklin D. Roosevelt, Adolf Hitler, Joseph Stalin, Benito Mussolini, Francisco Franco, and Mao Tse-tung, a number of truly remarkable political leaders came to the forefront across Latin America. Indeed, these exceptional individuals outnumbered the region's total of such salient figures up to that time and have not come close to being matched in subsequent periods. Their heritages are still strongly felt today. In large part because of these great leaders, for three of the four major countries this was the most significant and transforming period in their national life. It spanned the entire Vargas era for Brazil; included the developments preparing the way for Perón's rise in Argentina, as well as his stay in power; and covered the establishment, institutionalization, and flourishing of the hegemonic governing-party system in Mexico. As will be seen in the next chapter, it was also the period in which Venezuela, Bolivia, and Guatemala broke free from nineteenth-century-type situations and ceased to fall farther behind the leading Latin American countries, while Colombia surged forward before a traumatic regression.

Overview

All these considerations and the accompanying drama were highly apparent in Brazil, where Getúlio Vargas came to power in 1930, survived a civil war and both communist and fascist armed revolts during the 1930s, was ousted in 1945, and, after triumphantly returning to the presidency through popular election, died by his own hand in 1954. His political legacy, especially as applied to industrialization and the incorporation of the urban working class, would stretch on as a determining factor well beyond the end of this period, so that understanding this legacy is imperative for comprehending the political development path Brazil has since followed.

In Mexico Lázaro Cárdenas, a dedicated and effective populist reformer, as close to a reincarnation of Benito Juárez as might ever be seen, threw off the tutelage of his erstwhile patron, Elías Plutarco Calles, and transformed politics and society more in six short years, from 1934 through 1940, than in the quarter century since the 1910 Revolution—or would be over the next six decades. Largely on the momentum he built up, the dominant party would cruise through not only the rest of this period but also the following one, and on into the 1980s.

Argentina went through a failed effort to return to the oligarchic past, followed by an attempt to limit the damage and get back on a democratic track. Impossible as this was with World War II breaking out, especially in light of the tensions between a British-controlled economy and an essentially Italian population, this balancing act gave way in the mid-1940s to the rise of populist-nationalist-authoritarian Peronism under Juan Domingo and Evita Perón—clearly both among the region's all-time most charismatic leaders. By the end of this period Evita Perón was dead, and Juan Perón was on his way into exile. But Peronism would remain a potent factor in Argentine life, not just through the ensuing decades but also into the next century.

Brazil: The Vargas Era

For Brazil this was a momentous period, one dominated from beginning to end by one man, Getúlio Dorneles Vargas (b. 1883).[1] Taking place in an atmosphere of economic crisis, the 1930 elections were the traditional system's last chance to show whether it could adapt to the country's changing circumstances, and the governing elites of the Old Republic (1889–1930) failed the test. Never in the four-decade life of the republic had the government's candidate lost, and these arrogant movers and shakers saw no reason to change what seemed to them to be natural, if not ordained by God. Hence, many people inherently averse to revolution ended up throwing themselves into one behind a moderate leader who personally sought compromise and conciliation until the last moment—indeed, one who would have been pleased to become president in partnership with the established elites, if they had only let him attain office through the electoral process.[2]

Urban middle classes—including the military—took a leading part in the 1930 Revolution but lacked the independence to formulate a political program or establish autonomy from dissident elements of the oligarchy, who also participated in the revolution or quickly aligned themselves with the new regime once it was established. These eventually conservative groups realized that electoral democracy under the existing socioeconomic system would result in a return to power of the class of landowners and export merchants whose political dependents and hangers-on greatly outnumbered the urban middle-class vote. Thus, finding in Vargas a leader in whom they could place their trust, the emerging middle-class groups submerged their reformist ideas and accepted a paternalistic regime without parties or elections, but one in which they could play a major role in a rapidly expanding bureaucracy.

As in 1889 the army was the vehicle for dissident elites and the middle class to overturn old governmental institutions. When the military returned to the barracks, civilian middle sectors could not hold onto political power in a still essentially patrimonial society, yet they could reap individual benefits from the clientelistic-*cartorial* system by again agreeing to be coopted. Hence, instead of a pluralist democracy, a populist authoritarian regime emerged under Vargas and built up the urban working class as a potential power factor in a corporative institutional structure (one based upon societal groupings, not individual pluralism). The middle class gained control of the *cartorial* state apparatus but did not come to control the political system as a whole. Government continued to serve the interests of the class that controlled the economy, while it looked out for the immediate needs of a middle class that asked for little more than guaranteed employment by the state.[3] As the industrial bourgeoisie developed as a potentially significant political factor basically sympathetic to modernization, the astute Vargas began to move toward also using the industrial, essentially urban, working class as a political base for his increasingly developmentalist and nationalist policies.

During the Vargas period the state employed, with substantial success, the powerful instrument of patronage to coopt effectively much of organized labor into a "system of State tutelage and control" that would persist beyond the 1960s.[4] Most critical to the failure of the 1930 Revolution to develop into a sharp rupture with the past was the fact that the *tenentes* (lieutenants), rebellious young officers who constituted the cutting edge of the movement for political reform, had no one view of an appropriate role for the working class. Indeed, the civilian middle class, for all their espousal of political democracy, were not strongly inclined toward social reforms. This being the case, the armed forces became the key factor in events of the Vargas period, exercising "the function of arbiter that the body politic destined for them."[5]

Yet, even without rupture, Brazil was transformed under Vargas: During the fifteen years of his initial stint at the nation's helm, the hegemony of the traditional agricultural elites was broken, new industrial elements came to exert significant influence on national policy, and the middle class developed political muscle and savvy. Under stop-and-go government sponsorship, determined by Vargas's reading of the political winds and tides, the working class gradually assumed a position on the political stage, although no more central than upstage left.[6] Vargas's long stay in power accelerated economic development; created a structured, if coopted, la-

GETÚLIO DORNELES VARGAS

bor movement; strengthened the central government immensely; and greatly expanded the scope of the government's activities—in the process, raising and broadening aspirations for political participation. In most ways the transformation exceeded that achieved after 1945 by Perón in Argentina, since Vargas needed to cover ground already traversed by Argentina under the Radical Party in 1916–1930.

The original core of the revolutionary movement that eventually triumphed in October 1930 was the *tenentes*, who had gained conspiratorial experience as well as a significant degree of popular renown during the four years of their armed struggle against the Bernardes government. The revolutionary movement's success, however, required alliance with a broad coalition of political forces with power bases in a number of key states, a feat for which an experienced leader would have to be found outside the *tenentes'* ranks—a role tailored to Vargas's multifaceted talents. Born in the late years of the monarchy on a ranch in the interior of Rio Grande do Sul (Brazil's most southern and rebellious state), and raised the son of a leader of state militia forces involved in that frontier area's bloody civil strife of the 1890s, he joined the army at sixteen but resigned from the military preparatory school as result of a disciplinary incident, an action that left him something of a hero to his classmates and greatly facilitated his dealings with his generation of military leaders. Returned to the ranks as a sergeant, this feisty cowboy type (gaucho) saw brief combat service during a 1902 border dispute with Bolivia.

Entering state politics in 1908, shortly after graduation from law school in Porto Alegre, where he established a reputation in student politics, Vargas was immediately recognized as possessing unusual leadership talents. Elected to the state legislature in 1909, he rose to majority leader within a decade. In 1922, Vargas was elected to the national congress, where he functioned as leader of his state's delegation. In 1926, he achieved the rare distinction of being appointed Brazil's finance minister despite not coming from the São Paulo–Minas Gerais coffee elite. In November 1927, Vargas was elected governor of his home state, where he cemented his close relationship with rising young officers who had attended the military academy in Porto Alegre while he and his closest associates were studying down the street at the law school.

As it took form during 1930, the revolutionary movement was a heterogeneous amalgam of groups desiring sweeping political changes, if not a new social order, with elements violently opposed to the incumbent administration's control of presidential succession but devoid of any wish for more than moderate political and administrative reforms. Both the civilian and the military components of the movement were essentially bourgeois. Presidential succession served as the concrete issue around which fragmented opposition forces could join in a movement cohesive at least insofar as its immediate objective—attainment of power—was concerned. Indeed, the Liberal Alliance (AL) went forward on the national level after its birth in Rio Grande do Sul because some of its leaders saw it as a means of pressuring the president to make either Vargas or his Minas Gerais counterpart, the aristocratic Antonio Carlos Ribeiro de Andrada (who deeply resented having been passed over), the official candidate instead of São Paulo governor Júlio Prestes de Albuquerque.

If government leaders thought that the 1930 election might defuse the growing crisis, they were sorely mistaken. Although Minas Gerais and Rio Grande de Sul jointly gave Vargas nearly 600,000 votes, he was credited with only 200,000 in all the rest of the country, whereas the official candidate was given a national total of 1.1 million. Credibility was the issue in a country with a long tradition of creative vote counting, as the government felt obliged to admit that Vargas had run much more strongly than any opposition candidate before, an admission leading his backers to believe fervently that this was tantamount to admitting that he had been the real winner. This certainty of fraud grew as the Liberal Alliance totaled up their estimates of actual voting in the rest of the country—beginning with Rio de Janeiro, where the electoral books did not come close to balancing. Yet, despite more than a year of contingency planning, the civilians and military who would soon mobilize the most extensive revolutionary movement in Latin America's history were still wary and distrustful of each other.[7]

Catalyzing the decision to raise the banner of revolt was the assassination of Vargas's running mate on July 26. Forty-year old Lieutenant Colonel Pedro Aurélio de Góes Monteiro, a native of the northeastern state of Alagoas, although his military education as well as his in-laws were based in Rio Grande do Sul, rapidly emerged as the movement's effective chief of staff. Launched on October 3 in Rio

Grande do Sul, the revolt immediately drew into its wake the powerful 14,000-man federal force there, as well as the state militia. Marching northward and picking up reinforcements in Santa Catarina and Paraná, by week's end the rebel column was preparing for battle with legalist forces loyal to the government massed in southern São Paulo. Meanwhile rebel units had scored a series of successes in the distant northeast, and by October 23 rebel forces from Minas Gerais were on the verge of invading Rio de Janeiro. Aided by the intervention of the archbishop, senior generals convinced the president to resign on October 24, taking power temporarily as a "pacifying junta." Ten days later Vargas assumed office, promising a program of "national reconstruction," an amalgam of the Liberal Alliance program and a laundry list of demands of the diverse groups that had supported the revolt. The army was left deeply divided since, as shown by McCann, it had been split into six groupings: the *tenentes;* Góes Monteiro's moderates; opportunistic adherents; resisters; pacifiers; and fence sitters.[8]

Through moves more heavy-handed than those adopted in 1889 by Deodoro da Fonseca after overthrowing the monarchy, the provisional government established itself as a dictatorship with vast discretionary powers. Representative bodies were dissolved, and interventors appointed by Vargas to replace elected governors had nearly total powers in the states. Large numbers of politicians associated with the ousted government were arrested. Senior military officers who had viewed Vargas only as a lesser evil than an extensive civil war were alarmed by the influence of the *tenentes,* whom they viewed as undisciplined, politically ambitious upstarts. Historical revolutionaries (those who supported the 1920s rebellion) distrusted senior officers and midgrade legalists (officers who had remained loyal to the elected government) as opportunists lacking loyalty to revolutionary goals. Moreover, the *tenentes* and the dissident oligarchs had become belated allies only as events moved from the electoral arena to armed revolt. Key to the situation as 1930 ended was that

> 1930 was a reformist movement rather than a truly revolutionary one. It did not intend to eliminate poverty or even redistribute national wealth or income; it did not propose to cut up the huge fazendas that dominated agriculture and restructure landholding more equitably; it did not set out to eliminate illiteracy. The revolutionaries wanted an honest government that would promote modernization that included industrialization and economic development but with little re-stitching of the social fabric.[9]

Far from homogeneous in their political orientation, the *tenentes* generally shared several attitudes setting them apart from the civilian liberal constitutionalists. The latter were preoccupied with democratic forms, and the former were more concerned about the substance of often vaguely articulated social and economic reforms. They also generally manifested an elitist approach to "national regeneration" from the top that frequently shaded into authoritarian nationalism, a tendency also found among rising Argentine officers of the same generation. Although the communists and other radical movements were quite weak, their noisiness led both old elites and the emerging middle sectors to a near obsession with the proletarian threat. Many failed to grasp the wisdom of Vargas's creation of a labor ministry so as to better control the workers and his subtle use of manipulative paternalism.

The elements considering themselves legitimate owners of the revolution were so varied as to defy classification, much less orchestration. Hence, Vargas's ability to work with them all and keep them from each other's throats was more phenomenal than merely exceptional. Its roots went back into his youth, when he undertook a military education that, even if not completed, gave him deep insight into the thought process of the contemporary military generation as well as close personal ties with many of them. Well aware that the Liberal Alliance's common denominator was opposition to the Washington Luís government rather than hostility toward the established order, Vargas also understood all the feuding civilian components of the movement that had brought him to power just as well as he understood the military. Moderately conservative to liberal, the dissident elites of advanced states such as Minas Gerais and São Paulo wanted a system of formal representative democracy in which the power of the rural oligarchic machines had been curbed by elimination of their ability to manipulate electoral results. This degree of political development had been accomplished in Argentina at the time of World War I, so the Brazilians thought it could be done in their country in fairly short order. Groups opposed to the old government in many of the smaller states were even less interested in reform. They only wanted to receive from the new government what their rivals had gotten from the old regime. Progressive elements saw electoral reforms as an opening to empowerment of the middle sectors to carry through an agenda of economic and social reforms.[10]

Before Vargas could do more than allot power at the state level to trustworthy elements and establish a minimally effective federal executive, he was faced with a counter-revolutionary threat. The São Paulo uprising, which threatened disaggregation of the revolutionary forces, erupted in part because Vargas's interventor was an outsider, rather than a *Paulista*, underscoring how much the former holders of power had lost—for instead of governing the country, as they were accustomed to do, they were not even allowed to govern their own state. Essentially the revolt occurred because São Paulo had not been militarily defeated during the revolution: Its congressional representatives in the capital had given up in the face of the federal army's withdrawal of support for the government at the same time as people back home in São Paulo were preparing for a battle they were confident they could win. Hence, Vargas's conciliatory convocation of May 1933 elections for a constituent assembly had no effect, and the proud *Paulistas'* resort to force to reverse a course of affairs desired by most Brazilians cost them dearly in the long run by confirming suspicions that the São Paulo Democratic Party believed in democracy only as long as it served the party's hegemonic designs.[11] (Thus, even today São Paulo's congressional representation is capped at 70, when population would entitle the premier state to at least 113.)

Rio Grande do Sul remained loyal to Vargas, and Minas Gerais sent state militia against its old partner, dooming the May 1932 revolt to failure—as 80,000 federal troops took five months to crush the valiant struggle against more professional forces by 70,000 *Paulistas* hoodwinked by their leaders into believing that help would come from other states. These oligarchs failed to enlist the support of the state's growing working class, for whom they harbored disdain and distrust. Following a policy of conciliation with the people of São Paulo, if not with the revolt's instigators, Vargas held elections on May 3, 1933, for a National Constituent Assembly. These elections were marked by a confusingly large number of new parties, often existing only at the state level as fronts for established interests and old leaders. The 214 winners were joined by 40 hand-picked representatives of social groupings. With senior officers replaced by individuals who had proved their loyalty and ability on the battlefield, and with the prospect of a united *Paulista* opposition eliminated through appointment of a favorite son to govern there, Vargas was in a strengthened position. Moreover, *tenentismo* was nearly eliminated as a political force, and the army "came closer than at any previous time to enjoying a monopoly of force within Brazil."[12]

Chosen president in July 1933 for the 1934–1938 term by the National Constituent Assembly by a vote of 175 to 59 over his Rio Grande do Sul civilian rival, Vargas would govern under a constitution reflecting the divisions within Brazil's body politic. The core of the 1891 charter and its classic presidential institutions were preserved, with the addition of political reforms dear to the liberal constitutionalists and socioeconomic guarantees demanded by the *tenentes* and their reformist civilian counterparts. Transition from dictator to constitutional chief executive led Vargas to pay more attention to the claims of organized political groups. Ineligible to succeed himself, he had to deal with presidential ambitions and their impact on the 1934 congressional elections and the subsequent indirect selection of governors. With his skillful support, forces supporting Vargas's interventors came out on top in all major states, in many cases confirming the intervention as elected governor. Yet political polarization soon disrupted the atmosphere of harmony accompanying Brazil's successful recovery from the Great Depression, which had played a major role in the 1930 Revolution, for strong ideological movements of the left and right took center stage away from the intramural squabbles of the government's supporters.

By 1935, Luíz Carlos Prestes for the Communist Party and Plínio Salgado for the incipient fascistic movement calling itself the Integralists were attracting the attention of the urban populace. In March 1935, the National Liberating Alliance (ANL) was launched as a united front for the illegal Brazilian Communist Party (PCB) and other radical leftist forces, including some alienated *tenentes*. Poorly planned, the November 1935 Communist-led revolt was a total fiasco that left an anticommunist legacy in the military that was still operative a generation later. Allying the Catholic Church and propertied interests with the military to combat most progressive forces, it enabled Vargas to lay the groundwork for his own coup and establishment of a long-term dictatorship.[13]

The year 1937 was the most momentous for Brazil since 1930. While the public's attention was focused on the contest for Vargas's successor, scheduled for election in January 1938, crucial developments were taking place behind the scenes, where the president skillfully undermined political rivals and created a favorable situation among the military. At the end of 1936 he installed General Eurico Gaspar Dutra (b. 1883) as war minister, and soon after, his amicable rival Aurélio de Góes Monteiro (b. 1889) became armed-forces chief of staff. (The relationship between these two able and ambitious generals was similar to that in New York between Governor George Pataki and Rudolph Giuliani, Mayor of New York City.) By mid-1937, both the presidential campaign and Vargas's conspiracy to derail it were in high gear. One candidate—Armando de Salles Oliveira—was depicted as a *Paulista* oligarch dedicated to restoring that state's hegemony; the other—José Américo de Almeida—was pictured as naive and dangerously demagogic. Both portrayals were quite close to the truth. Hence, much of the political elite and a growing number of the middle class were susceptible to the idea that the elections should be postponed if a suitable unity candidate could not be found. Astutely riding on a controlled escalation of the crisis, Vargas fostered polarization by, on the one hand, encouraging the Integralists to act openly and aggressively and, on the other, reactivating the specter of communist subversion through the hoax of a sensational communist plan that created an atmosphere of near hysteria.[14] Yet the most important element in establishing an authoritarian regime was the army, and its support for Vargas's initiatives required agreement on a mutually beneficial plan for the years ahead. As reconstructed by McCann:

Central to the relationship between Vargas and the generals was a pledge, or *compromiso,* that he had made to equip and arm the army and navy in return for social and political peace in which his government would develop Brazil's economy and infrastructure. The Patria was to be made safe. Generals Pedro de Góes Monteiro and Eurico Dutra believed that they were saving Brazil from catastrophe and insuring its future security.[15]

With full military support and a sigh of relief from many sectors of society, on November 10 the congress elected in 1934 was closed, and a new constitution was declared to be in effect. The eight-year run of the Estado Novo ("New State," named after the corporatist regime of Antônio de Oliveira Salazar in Portugal) had begun. Its early weeks were filled with initiatives reminiscent of the first moves of the provisional government seven years earlier. Vargas was able to assume the stance of a unifying symbol in a situation where polarization provided salience to both communism and fascism, while the majority rejecting either extreme were divided between the traditional socially sterile constitutionalism of one presidential candidate and the fundamental, often incoherent populism of the other. As the 1937 constitution's articles concerning representation and legislation never went into effect, Vargas continued to enjoy the power to legislate by presidential decrees. Long-term stability rested upon the fact that

> he and the generals shared a dream, perhaps not with the same details, but they dreamed of a great prosperous nation spread over a gloriously beautiful portion of the earth, living and producing in security and happiness. Vargas was dedicated to the improvement of Brazil and was confident in his ability to make the right decisions for his country. However, he was careful to seek advice and not to get too far ahead of elite opinion.[16]

The communists having eliminated themselves from contention through their 1935 fiasco, the only challenge to Vargas's new order came in May 1938, when the Integralists joined with some liberal constitutionalist conspirators in a poorly executed coup attempt. Suspicious that political parties might prove a vehicle for the rise of rivals, Vargas also viewed them as electoral trappings irrelevant to his needs and objectives. His basic pattern of manipulative paternalism, shifting gradually toward personalistic populism, required no intermediary structures. In this area Vargas was not innovative, preferring to turn existing forces to his use and to destroy those he could not utilize. He also preferred to exploit personal rivalries among leading figures, often turning yesterday's opponents into today's allies rather than having to deal with institutionalized power contenders. He did not drastically change his political style or the institutional structure of the Estado Novo during the seven years of its existence, but he did adapt pragmatically to altered conditions as the processes of industrialization and urbanization gradually modified the societal foundations of the polity.

National integration continued to progress, and the federal executive developed capabilities far beyond those of the pre-Vargas era. An array of administrative agencies was established to deal with matters previously outside the scope of public policy, but now of concern to the centralized, increasingly interventionist state.

Moreover, a wide variety of government corporations and mixed capital enterprises came into being to play ever more important roles in development—along with a network of organizations designed to tie urban workers to the government through both a dependent union movement and a rudimentary social welfare system. In contrast to the simplicity of the central government during the federalist Old Republic, a proliferation of institutes, autonomous agencies, and consultative councils were formed in the Estado Novo. There was a lack of mechanisms for effective coordination below the president, but this administrative tangle fulfilled its principle political purpose of "transferring the conflict among the different dominant groups to within the state bureaucracy itself through self-representation of interests in these technical organs."[17]

There were multiple interests seeking to influence public policy, but after 1937 there was no legislative arena and no opportunity to mobilize electoral support and bring it to bear upon the executive. Vargas was an exceptionally astute political balancer, conciliator, and manipulator, but he was overextended, requiring development of structures for linking state and society. With parties ruled out, the answer was an informal, but effective, network tying together the Vargas-appointed interventors, the growing array of governmental agencies, and sectoral organizations fostered by the basically corporatist design of the regime. Masterfully orchestrated by Vargas, this arrangement provided a means for accommodating emerging interests while easing the decline of traditional elites by continuing to provide opportunity to influence the decisions most vital to their economic interests. The resulting system of cooptative clientelism enhanced the viability of the Vargas-designed system by channeling the concerns of politically relevant elements into narrow struggles over policy in particular areas—hence away from questions of the regime's basic orientation and underlying priorities. On balance it worked better than the system uneasily in place in Argentina, that being forged in Mexico, or even the electoral democracy in Colombia.

The Brazil of the 1940s had evolved considerably since the 1930 Revolution. Population had grown to over 41 million (on its way to 52 million by 1950), with the state of São Paulo surpassing Minas Gerais (as California would do to New York State a bit later in the United States). By 1940, urbanization had lifted Rio de Janeiro to 1.9 million inhabitants, followed by São Paulo with 1.3 million. A sustained surge of import-substitution industrialization was narrowing the gap between agriculture and industry as proportions of GDP, although the former still provided two-thirds of employment. Internal economic activity was overtaking external demand as the principal determinant of the accumulation of capital. The hegemony of the traditional coffee bourgeoisie had ended because coffee had fallen as a proportion of agricultural production from nearly 50 percent in the 1920s to 30 percent by the mid-1930s, and only 16 percent after 1939. Urban, modernizing sectors of society were increasingly penetrated by the governmental capabilities of the executive, and as the central government came to affect the lives of a larger proportion of the population directly, more frequently, and in a wider variety of ways, the regime built a multiclass base, even if it was not yet reflected in the sphere of political organization. The foundation for significant political mobilization had been laid.

World War II had a profound impact upon the Brazilian armed forces, especially officers of the *tenente* generation. Initially this was all to Vargas's advantage as he channeled military energies into the war effort while rallying popular support in the name of national defense. Politically active officers were sent to the United States for training, then on to Italy to fight, and in general the armed forces were pleased with the new equipment they received and the favorable position relative to Argentina that Brazil came to enjoy. Both Dutra and Góes Monteiro—whose rival ambitions Vargas played off against each other as skillfully as Napoléon had done with Charles Maurice de Talleyrand and Joseph Fouché—underwent a shift from sympathy for Hitler's Germany to support of hemispheric solidarity. But this transformation carried the generals on to becoming champions of liberal democracy, and they would eventually join the movement to oust the dictator from power—if only to avoid the danger of being dragged down with him in the face of growing sentiment for a return to representative government. The Brazilian Expeditionary Force (FEB) would return from Italy covered with glory just in time to take part in the intense political maneuvering that characterized the second half of 1945.[18]

Aware that the Estado Novo could not carry over into the postwar era without major modifications, in 1943 Vargas had begun preparations for an eventual return to competitive politics by forging a political organization capable of mobilizing public support for a contest at the polls. Building upon the foundation of amplified social programs for urban workers and the government's close control over their unions, he began to organize a machine that could rapidly be transformed into a party. Industrialization became the touchstone of a program designed to appeal not only to workers, but to urban commercial and entrepreneurial interests, government employees, and the military as well. The sage politician realized that he was faced with a challenge far different from those of 1932 and 1937, as presidential aspirant Dutra could not be expected to support his continuation in power, and the opposition's Brigadier Eduardo Gomes was the leading paladin of the *tenentes*—now pushing into senior office ranks. Determined that if he could not hold onto power directly, it must pass to his allies and supporters rather than to his critics, Vargas played out what seemed to be a losing hand in such a way as to maximize the possibilities of a future comeback.

On April 7, 1945, representatives of all political currents opposed to Vargas founded the National Democratic Union (UDN); Vargas immediately countered with the Social Democratic Party (PSD), essentially a holding company of state political establishments, under the direction of the interventors. Elections were convoked for December 2, and on July 17 Dutra was nominated by the PSD, being succeeded as war minister by army chief of staff Góes Monteiro. Vargas shifted his attention to launching the Brazilian Labor Party (PTB), a vehicle for channeling electoral support from the government-controlled labor unions. By yielding to the irresistible, Vargas was able to depart from office with honor and dignity and, more important, without having opened an irreparable breach with the armed forces. As Vargas was suspected by the United States, burned by Perón's successful maneuvering in Argentina at this time, Dutra's military supporters allied with those of the UDN's Brigadier Gomes to thwart any continuist designs the president might harbor, and Góes Monteiro proclaimed himself "commander in chief of the army." In the face of suspicions that this military leader of the 1930 Revolution was positioning himself for a possible seizure of power, the head of the Brazilian supreme court temporarily assumed the presidency on October 30. The Estado Novo was over, but Vargas was still politically potent and the institutional structure he had devised remained untouched.

Elected to the Senate from both São Paulo and Rio Grande do Sul, as well as to the lower house of the congress in six states, this short, middle-aged man would continue to cast a long shadow over Brazilian politics. His ouster was largely a reaction by the old landowning and mercantile elite, in alliance with much of the middle class, against the processes of change that threatened to undermine the continued conservative dominance of politics and their use of the state to further the interests of the dominant groups rather than those of an emerging urban working class. In this the elite and the middle class were rowing against the current, much as their Argentine counterparts had done in the 1930s, and the ambivalences of the middle sectors would in the longer run lead them back to Vargas. For at this juncture the Brazilian middle class was undergoing a transformation catalyzed by the entrance of a new generation of technical and administratively oriented personnel and a "new intelligentsia" concerned about development problems. In the immediate postwar period these still insecure elements feared losing their recent gains through the rise of the working class and the extension of expensive social benefits to them.

The growing middle class, more concerned about its patronage positions than about radical changes in the system, permitted consolidation of democratic forms without correlative social policies. Hence, in the view of a young scholar who would become the country's culture minister at the turn of the century, "All the important organizations functioning as mediators between the State and the individual are really entities annexed to the State itself rather than effectively autonomous organizations."[19] (This was true of the Mexican political system through the 1980s.) In a framework of contact between the state and the urban masses through the intermediary of populist leaders, personalities took precedence over programs, and even more, over ideologies. In sharp contrast with Mexico or even Peronist Argentina, Brazil's political parties, suffering from a lack of coherence and organization, as well as from their essentially conservative orientation, were inadequate vehicles for the socialization of the new urban masses entering the electorate.

Thus, as would be repeated in the 1980s, whereas vociferous nationalists proclaimed the advent of the era of ideological politics and were followed by the relatively highly politicized leadership of unions and "popular" organizations, the masses turned instead to a direct link between their votes and a political leader with a significant degree of charisma. Clientelism continued to serve as the basis for holding much of the middle class to the established political leadership and the existing parties in terms of an exchange of votes for employment or a specific favor. But this arrangement could not work for the urban masses as a whole when the electorate expanded far beyond the patronage potential of even the *cartorial* state. From roughly a million in 1908 and 2.7 million for the 1934 balloting, the electorate had already grown to over 7.4 million by 1945 (before exploding to eleven times that figure by 1989).

Even Dutra's December 2, 1945, election depended far more upon the durability of the forces solidly in control of a majority of the states plus the urban masses' response to Vargas's populist appeals than on the lackluster candidate. For its part, Gomes's campaign had difficulty in avoiding an essentially negative image of being against everything Vargas stood for. With almost 6.2 million individuals voting, the vast majority for the first time, Dutra defeated the opposition's Gomes by a margin of better than three to two (3.25 million to 2.04 million); the Communist Party standard bearer trailed with nearly 570,000. Well over 60 percent of the victor's margin came from São Paulo and Rio Grande do Sul, with much of the rest run up in Minas Gerais—as the Vargas-founded PSD and PTB delivered massive pluralities. In congressional voting PSD candidates received nearly 43 percent, and the PTB, limited to urban centers, added another 10 percent, while the UDN—which had actually expected victory—came away disappointed with less than 27 percent.

The Dutra government turned out to be a temporary interruption of Vargas's work, not its derailment, much less its end. The sixty-year-old career army officer, who took office on January 31, 1946, was experienced only in the intraregime politics of the Vargas era. Owing to his cautious nature, Brazil failed to receive strong or imaginative presidential leadership during this crucial period of transition from a relatively closed discretionary regime to an open, competitive, and representative system. Without guidance from Dutra, the new congress produced in September 1946 a constitution designed to curb executive power and guarantee the preservation of federalism. State elections in January 1947 resulted in former interventor Adhemar de Barros's creating the Social Progressive Party (PSP) and becoming São Paulo governor. This creation of a party dominant in the leading state would have the effect of preventing the development of true national parties, as the PSD, UDN, and PTB would be relegated to secondary importance in the country's most populous and important state.[20]

Indeed, the most negative heritage of the ballyhooed "restoration of democracy" was failure to lay a foundation for a functional party system, a detrimental shortcoming that handicaps Brazilian political development down to the present. Vargas's continuation as the potentially dominant figure for two of the three major parties, combined with the fact that opposition to him was the unifying factor and guiding principle of the other, drastically inhibited the development of parties along modern programmatic lines or into institutionalized vehicles for political mobilization. The PSD, preeminently the party of the political "ins," supplied the majority in the 1946–1950 congress, occupied most executive positions under Dutra, and controlled the greater proportion of state administrations. Essentially nonideological, it combined dominant rural machines of the post-1930 period with businessmen and industrialists who had benefited from Vargas's increasing orientation toward economic development. It had the support of a high proportion of the new bureaucratic stratum, and its ranks were swelled by patronage-seeking opportunists (an element adhering to all subsequent governing parties).

In its early years the UDN was an alliance of political "outs," and the PSD was a coalition of holders of power. It originally brought together the political chiefs of rural cliques not favored by the interventors, including some of the most reactionary landowners, with urban commercial-industrial interests containing a high proportion of bankers, administrators of large companies, and offspring of prestigious families, as well as independent professionals and white-collar employees from the private sector. Despite a classically liberal tendency in the larger cities, because of malapportionment of congressional seats it came increasingly under the sway of its conservative rural wing. At this point its antithesis, the PTB, was important only in the major industrial centers.

Governing with little opposition from the UDN, Dutra strove to establish the basis for long-term stability, but his antilabor as well as anticommunist orientation made his term largely one of drift and accommodation of retrograde forces. Many of the vices of the Estado Novo were eliminated, but most of its virtues were also lost, and some of the least desirable features of the pre-Vargas system reemerged. Indeed, return to regular elections and a functioning congress enabled the old agricultural interests, through their controlled voters, to regain much of the power they had held before 1937—if not before 1930. Large agriculturalists and associated mercantile interests strove to preserve an economic order based on agro-exports and unhindered access to imported manufactured goods. This resurgence of rural interests conflicted with the demands of business, banking, and an emerging industrial sector for fiscal policies promoting industri-

alization and tariff protection for their products. Despite unimaginative governmental policies, annual real GDP growth under Dutra averaged 6 percent, fully
double the rate of population increase.

By 1950, there was a generalized nostalgia for the dynamic Vargas years. On
April 19, his sixty-seventh birthday, Vargas accepted the PTB nomination, having
already reached an agreement with Adhemar de Barros for PSP support—critical
in São Paulo. He used his still-heavy influence within the PSD to assure the selection of a weak candidate with appeal limited to the same sectors as that of the
UDN standard bearer. Vargas also made deals with PSD gubernatorial and legislative candidates who wanted PTB votes in return for supporting him in the presidential balloting. Thus, although PSD candidates were victorious in most of the
country, Vargas carried seventeen states plus the federal district (Rio de Janeirio
city) with 3.9 million votes (nearly 49 percent) to 2.3 million (almost 30 percent)
for the UDN's Eduardo Gomes (b. 1896) and fewer than 1.7 million (better than
21 percent) for the demoralized PSD nominee. The marriage of the predominantly rural-based traditionalist PSD and the largely urban, development-oriented
PTB that Vargas forged in 1950 would survive, although with mutual infidelity
and bickering, until 1964. Vargas's blend of clientelistic and populist policies
shaped the PTB, deeply affected the PSD, and thwarted repeated efforts to infuse
programmatic or ideological content into these parties. The proportions of the
mix were to vary, as the PTB grew in strength relative to the PSD and developmentalists and reformers increased within their ranks.[21]

Accustomed to governing relatively free from restraints, Vargas was not comfortable operating within an institutional structure designed in 1946 to minimize
his freedom of action. Moreover, Dutra's narrow interpretation of presidential
powers and hands-off attitude with respect to party politics created a situation in
which each move by Vargas to provide strong presidential leadership was criticized
by the opposition as an indication of dictatorial proclivities. In turn the president
was impatient with the short-sighted obstruction of policies designed to modernize the nation and attacks upon his evolutionary approach to social welfare for the
urban working class—whom, as Cárdenas had done in Mexico and Perón was doing in Argentina, he wished, in a neo-Bismarckian manner, to bring in to politics
within the system under the auspices of a government-linked party. Vargas wanted
to function as before as manipulator of existing political interests as well as mediator between these and the interests of emergent groups, being at his best as the re-
sourceful conciliator of policy alternatives put forth by contending political forces.

Beginning in a favorable economic context resulting from the demand for
Brazilian products spurred by the Korean War, Vargas strove to make industrialization and diversification common denominators for an economic policy involving
an active role for the state and a significant degree of government planning. As
long as the US administration of Harry S Truman was willing to provide technical

assistance for basic planning studies, Vargas turned a deaf ear to radical nationalists while maintaining his populist stance by advocating measures of economic nationalism. Near the end of 1951 he submitted to the congress a bill creating a mixed-capital corporation to explore and exploit Brazil's oil resources—which US experts had declared were extremely limited. Conservative military elements not reconciled to Vargas's victory over *tenente* hero Gomes lent a ready ear to Washington's laments over Vargas's unwillingness to join in the Korean War, embracing the perverse logic that participation in World War II created a moral obligation to align with the United States in subsequent conflicts. (Wrongheaded Washingtonians persisted in viewing Brazil as a willfully wayward adolescent.)

Hence, radicalization of political life took place during the latter half of 1953, a period in which the end of the Korean conflict eroded demand for Brazilian exports, and a hostile Republican government replaced a sympathetic Democratic administration in the United States. With Vargas's term having reached midpoint, elements of the armed forces not only once again suspected Vargas of harboring designs to continue in office, but this time felt he had backing from Argentine strongman Perón. As would be the case again in the early 1960s, inflation served as the catalyst of social tensions and raised dilemmas of financial policy that the administration had sought to avoid. Wage restraints and credit restrictions, essential for economic purposes (as a former finance minister, Vargas was unique among Brazilian presidents—and most other Latin American chief executives—in recognizing the importance of sound fiscal and financial policies), undercut his efforts to build up support among labor and the new industrialists. The cost of living had risen 21 percent in 1952, double that for the preceding year, and inflationary pressures were growing. The US administration of Dwight D. Eisenhower, with its policy largely shaped by Secretary of State John Foster Dulles, refused to consider any moral obligation to continue Truman's commitment for developmental assistance. Instead, Brazil was told that it should make conditions more attractive for US private investment. As a gesture of good faith, Vargas should withdraw support for Petrobrás, the state petroleum company recently approved by the congress.[22]

The backbone of the anti-Vargas movement polarizing politics and pushing confrontation in place of conciliation was an alliance of the UDN with the strongly anticommunist wing of the armed forces. Defeated at the ballot box in 1945 and 1950, the commitment of this alliance to democratic processes had worn thin. An abortive attack on the life of strident Vargas critic Carlos Lacerda on August 5, 1954, gave the bitterly frustrated outs an opportunity to destabilize the president. As a military-run investigation uncovered involvement of Vargas cronies and advisers in unsavory dealings, and as leading generals refused his offer to take a leave of absence, the seventy-one-year-old Vargas shot himself on August 24. His suicide note swung public opinion against his enemies, whom he depicted as greedy reactionaries and unpatriotic instruments of rapacious foreign interests.

With Vargas abruptly gone from the stage he had dominated for so long, tension between pro- and anti-Vargas forces dominated the political scene. In the midst of advanced stages of campaigning for the October 3, 1954, legislative and gubernatorial elections, and with presidential balloting only a little over a year away, Vice President João Café Filho (b. 1899) assumed a caretaker role, supported by a mixture of non-Vargist political forces, including the pro-Dutra wing of the PSD. The outcome of elections held only forty days after Vargas's death was surprisingly normal, resulting in a standoff between Vargas's heirs and his foes. As usual, the chief concern of politicians was to win, so national issues took a back seat to local questions and alliances of convenience. When the dust settled, the PSD held onto its leading position with 114 Chamber of Deputies (lower house) seats, the PTB edged up to 56, and the UDN slipped to 74.[23] Thus, Café Filho and his successors would have to govern all the way to February 1959 with the congress little changed from that elected with Vargas in 1950.

With a president to be chosen, Brazil had no respite from campaigning, as the PTB and PSD allied behind Minas Gerais governor Juscelino Kubitschek de Oliveira (b. 1902) on the basis of Vargas protégé João Belquior Marques Goulart (b. 1918) for vice president. Ranking *tenente* Juarez do Nascimento Fernandes Távora (b. 1898) ran for the UDN-PDC coalition, with Adhemar de Barros (b. 1901) making a determined São Paulo–based bid. Largely on the strength of a home state margin of 430,000 votes, Kubitschek, with nearly 3.1 million votes, beat Juarez Távora by a 470,000-vote margin—while receiving only 34 percent of the record 9.1 million ballots cast. Anti-Vargas forces tried in vain to block inauguration of the personable medical doctor, managing to install the presiding officer of the Chamber of Deputies acting president in November, but the PSD-PTB coalition thwarted this ploy by substituting the Senate's president, who, backed by the war minister, held office until Kubitschek took over in early 1956.

Although Vargas was gone, this rotund grandfatherly figure would continue to cast a long shadow, and the political patterns he had fostered would persist. Although his legacy was not embodied in a party as Cárdenas's was in Mexico or Perón's was in Argentina, it would be every bit as profound and lasting. Up through the military takeover in 1964, Brazilian governments would be based on a loose coalition of industrialists, commercial sectors linked to the internal market, technical elements of the middle class, and the organized component of the working class. But when the process of development threatened to bring significant socioeconomic changes, the military with support of conservative interests and the traditional sector of the middle class would intervene. Progressive forces failed to create a new party, resting instead on the inadequate basis of an eroding alliance between the PSD, strong in the congress, and the PTB, with popular support in urban areas. Vargas's heirs would run up against a hard wall of obstruction thrown up by political elements closely linked to the old agrarian interests and entrenched in the government machinery.

Mexico: Institutionalizing the Revolution

Within the National Revolutionary Party (PNR), the holding company of regional political bosses and near warlords created by recent ex-president Plutarco Elías Calles in 1929, this Godfather-like inveterate political schemer and manipulator managed to be kingmaker and power behind the throne in a system called the Maximato in honor of his title as Jefe Maximo ("Maximum Chief") of the revolution.[24] Pascual Ortiz Rubio (b. 1877) of Michoacán was the candidate imposed by the boss-of-bosses for November 1929's less-than-honest presidential election. Revolutionary intellectual José Vasconcellos's campaign against the official candidate faced an impossible uphill battle, including intimidation, as in March Calles's paramilitary "Gold Shirts" fired on a mass rally in Mexico City. The almost automatic uprising in Sonora was repressed at the cost of a thousand dead and twice as many wounded—which, in a country inured to counting fatalities in the tens of thousands, was taken as good news and a favorable portent.

The decisive factor in Mexican elections at this point was not casting votes but their creative counting, in which the PNR excelled as much as Argentina's conservatives—or as much as the Brazilian oligarchic regime would for the last time in 1930. When Ortiz Rubio vacated the presidency in September 1932, having found out that being president did not provide the freedom of initiative and action it had before the straitjacket of a Calles-run government party, Calles replaced him with Abelardo Rodríguez (b. 1889), who had become wealthy as a rumrunner during the US prohibition era and who seemed happy to have the job.

During the Maximato, Lázaro Cárdenas del Rio (b. 1895), a *mestizo* who was the former governor of Michoacán, led an ascending reform faction within the Party seeking to revive the Sonorans' strategy of an alliance with popular sectors. Seen by Calles as the most solid of the competing revolutionary generals, he had been a captain during the intramural bloodletting of 1913–1914 and became a colonel before the end of 1915 and a brigadier general in 1920. While excelling as a staff officer, he had fought against Zapata, Villa, the Yaqui Indians, Carranza, and de la Huerta—becoming a major general in 1928 at age thirty-two. November 1930 had found this rising politician presiding over the PNR, a post he held—and used to good advantage—until August 1931. Moving over to govern Michoacán, with radical Francisco Mugica as a mentor, he embarked on a dramatic acceleration of land reform.

At the 1933 party convention Cárdenas secured the presidential nomination, saw his campaign program adopted as the PNR's "six-year plan," and changed the basis for membership in the party to individual instead of affiliation of entire or-

LÁZARO CÁRDENAS DEL RIO

ganizations, the better to use it as a mobilization vehicle. At the center of his political strategy was what scholars call state building, particularly the need to strengthen still fragile political institutions. In this respect Calles's PNR, within which he rose to power, was not the kind of party Cárdenas felt Mexico needed. He would give it one good renovation and then guide his successor toward another thorough overhaul. The result would be a party that could get the job done for another fifty-five years with ordinary drivers at the wheel.

Easily elected after a vigorous campaign in which he sought as much to get to know the Mexican people as to become a friendly paternalistic personality to them, exuding simplicity and sincerity, the thirty-nine-year-old Cárdenas reinvigorated agrarian reform, distributing vast amounts of land to individual *campesinos* (loosely translated as "peasants") and even more to Indian villages in the traditional communal landholding form of the *ejido*. By the end of six years he had distributed 18 million hectares (over 43 million acres) to 800,000 peasants and rural laborers. Cárdenas also implemented the provision of the 1917 constitution for seventh-day pay, giving workers the equivalent of a 16 percent pay raise, and greatly increased investment in education, particularly at the primary level and in small towns and rural areas long overlooked by the federal government. Proponent of a mixed economy, Cárdenas worked to make the state sector stronger and more autonomous. In June 1935, Cárdenas made his coalition with labor both stronger and more open. This action brought his conflict with Calles, who had long chafed at his independent ways, to a head and resulted in an intense power struggle that Cárdenas won, ending Calles' ability to be more than a stone in his shoe by shipping him off to California in April 1936. Remaining members of Calles's faction could prove an annoyance in the 1938 congressional elections, but most of the grief then came from elements on the right longing for some of the coziness they had enjoyed with governments during the Maximato.

Establishing civilian control over the praetorian military was one of Cárdenas's priority tasks in pursuit of his goal of strengthening and fortifying a viable political system that could be entrusted to civilian rule without military interference. This was no small task as the army had come to play an important, or at least favored, role under Díaz, was a crucial factor in the 1911 to 1919 outright civil war, and was featured in the sporadic resort to force during the 1920s. Although as a stopgap the government built up worker and peasant militias, the longer-run institutional solution was to establish an academy to educate lower-class young men to become highly professionalized, apolitical officers. In the years before they could have a cumulative effect on the ethos of the Mexican military, largely composed of self-made officers who had earned commissions and promotion on the battlefield and become retainers of the regional warlord class that had emerged from the decades of conflict, other steps would have to be taken. Cárdenas's war minister put into effect, with Cárdenas's firm backing and his prestige as having been a revolutionary general, such fundamental measures as transferring officers without reassigning their men with them and directly paying soldiers instead of having this done by "their" officers. A decree limiting military service to a maximum of thirty years meant that all who began their careers with the revolution would be out at the beginning of his successor's term.[25]

The government's close ties to both labor and the peasantry were institutionalized in 1936 through the Mexican Workers Confederation (CTM), an umbrella union organization, and the National Campesinos Confederation (CNC), a massive outreach to peasants and rural workers in 1938. Then in March 1938 Cárdenas reorganized the PNR as the Party of the Mexican Revolution (PRM), composed of four functional sectors: the workers, organized in the CTM; the peasants, embodied in the CNC; the military; and the "popular sector" embracing the middle class, particularly organized public employees along with some liberal professionals.

The last two years of Cárdenas's presidency began with the bold nationalization of the country's petroleum resources and turning them over to development and production by a state entity, Pemex (Petroleos Mexicanos). With war clouds darkening over Europe, Cárdenas with great skill took advantage of an international window of opportunity. Using a provision of the 1917 constitution reaffirming the Spanish royal principal that all subsoil resources belong to the nation, he took physical possession of the oil fields, agreeing to subsequent payment within strict limits. Given the perilous situation they found themselves in, Britain and the Netherlands had more urgent matters on their plate than jumping to the defense of Royal Dutch Shell, which Cárdenas would then put forward as a model for resolution of the compensation issue with US companies.

With many US investors already up in arms over the land expropriations, media uproar and congressional lobbying were raucous—full of accusations of communism and demands for military intervention. The situation was defused by the fact that Franklin D. Roosevelt, rather than a Republican, was in the White House and that, with war on the horizon, he did not want a disgruntled neighbor on the long, exposed land border. Hence, he sent Josephus Daniels as a special envoy. A respected southern gentleman newspaper publisher from South Carolina (and FDR's boss as secretary of the navy in World War I), his endorsement of Cárdenas as a nationalist reformer, not a communist, averted an official crisis. As Cárdenas and his advisers must have expected, adverse economic fallout from the oil expropriation was heavy and damaging, leaving the economic situation for 1939 and 1940 alarmingly bleak.[26]

Cárdenas pulled back from populism near the end of his administration with a sharp reduction in land distribution and choice of his long-term associate, the moderate Manuel Ávila Camacho (b. 1897), as his successor.[27] Most likely he decided, quite wisely, that after the hubbub and turmoil of his term, and the major long-term programs he had launched, a period of consolidation was in order. Aware of the mounting opposition that his sharp turn to the left had aroused, he could best preserve political order by agreeing to a more centrist successor and wrapping the publicly little-known candidate in his legitimizing cloak. Besides, Ávila Camacho had just enough of a revolutionary background not to be a red flag to military elements, who still had most of their teeth and claws and were being recruited by an opposition candidate. In making his decision on such sound political considerations, Cárdenas taught an important lesson to the PRI presidents ahead about taking the needs of the next six years into account as much as continuity of their policies or personal preferences in making a wise choice of successor. In any case, the great man's decision not to try to keep a hand on the tiller or a foot on the accelerator once he had passed the sash on to his successor was a salutary example—particularly in light of Calles's penchant and precedent in the opposite direction. Indeed, it was appropriate not just for Mexico, but for other countries as well.

The election of this rancher, who had served as Cárdenas's chief of staff in 1919 and was his defense minister in 1940, found an old revolutionary general, Juan Andreu Almazán, running against him with support of the large industrialists centered in Monterrey, aggrieved foreign investors, diehard praetorian elements of the military, and middle-class sectors feeling threatened by the rise of labor. In the face of electoral defeat, merited or fraudulent, Almazán rebelled, but the uprising found less support than similar reactions had in the past, and it would be the last serious effort to contest Mexico's presidency by force of arms. If Cárdenas's had been a transformational government, Ávila's Camacho's presidency was in many ways a transitional one. It began a shift away from social reform toward industrial modernization that quickly coopted much of Almazán's support, converting some into enthusiasts (since many political participants as well as observers had assumed that Cárdenas, still in his prime of life, would attempt to control his successor à la Calles). As the war in Europe and the subsequent direct involvement of United States lifted Mexico out of the economic slump of 1939–1940, the new administration's investments in infrastructure and public works rose sharply. A treaty of the farm workers *(braceros)* with the United States eased unemployment.

Accepting counsel from ex-caretaker president Rodríguez rather than the rival Calles or Cárdenas factions in the party, and spurning its far left fringe, Ávila Camacho forced Soviet sympathizer Vicente Lombardo Toledano out of the leadership of the CTM, bringing in Fidel Velásquez, who would serve to keep labor in line with the party and government through the 1980s. There was no sharp break in the government-labor domestic relationship; it just ceased to be monogamous on the government's side. This shift was gradual and sweetened by establishment of a social security system in 1941 and its gradual implementation over the next few years. Ávila Camacho also consolidated civilian control over the military.[28]

Ávila Camacho's aim of increasingly subordinating the party to the government required a preliminary move and new legislation before a drastic restructuring of the party at the end of his term. In the 1943 congressional elections active involvement in the nominating process resulted in a significant increase in the political weight of the popular sector, reorganized into the national Confederation of Popular Organizations (CNOP), which came away with 75 of the PNR's 144 seats in the lower house, to 46 for the *campesino* sector and only 23 for labor. The 1946 election law strengthened electoral machinery while centralizing control, done of course in the name of reducing fraud at the local level. It also eliminated regional and ad hoc parties by requiring a membership of at least thirty thousand with a minimum of one thousand members in each of two-thirds of Mexico's states. Ideological parties were restricted by a ban on those of the extreme left or right, acceptable in a context of the war against fascism just ending and the threat of international communism just rising, as well as proscription of religious parties—a preemptive strike against the possibility of the conservative Catholic National Action Party (PAN), founded in 1939 by Manuel Gómez Marín, seeking to recast itself as a Christian democratic party, as was happening in Italy and Germany. The PAN had been allowed in 1943 to participate in the congressional balloting, giving the political camel a chance to stick its nose into the electoral tent. Indeed, beginning with 4 of its 110 Chamber of Deputies (lower house) candidates recognized as winners in 1946, this little acorn would by the end of the century have grown into a sturdy tree.

After declaring in December 1945 that he was personally a "believer" (code word for Catholic), thus reducing tensions carrying over since the 1920s, Ávila Camacho—who had appointed the 1929 victim of electoral fraud to head a splendid new national library (Biblioteca Mexico)—continued his pursuit of national unity by amending the constitution to remove its most onerous anti-Catholic restrictions in the field of education. Then, at a national convention in January 1946, he unveiled ideological and structural changes packaged as being in keeping with the brave new postwar world of which Mexico was an increasingly important part. With "Democracy and Social Justice" unveiled as the new slogan (replacing "For a Workers' Democracy"), and the Institutional Revolutionary Party (PRI) as the government party's new name, membership was henceforth individual and direct, not collective and intermediated by the sectors. In recognition of the progress made in professionalization of the armed forces, the military was folded into the popular sector, and this was made more accessible to private-sector white-collar workers, professionals, and small businessmen. The net result was a more centralized and hierarchical party in which sharply reduced debate within the no-longer-autonomous sectors would soon be reflected in lessened debate in the congress and a decisive strengthening of the government's position vis-à-vis the party. Calles had built a party, Cárdenas had made it his kind of party, and now Ávila Camacho had transformed it into "the" party, if not for all times, for the next half century—requiring only periodic tune-ups.

The presidency of Miguel Alemán Valdés (b. 1902), Ávila Camacho's interior minister, marked a turning point in Mexican politics in several ways. With his 1946 election the torch was passed to a new generation of civilian politicians not only without personal participation in the revolution, but having had little involvement in the ensuing period of civil war.[29] As Alemán was the son of a revolutionary officer, the age of the generals was over, and the military accustomed itself to a low profile within an increasingly civilian-dominated PRI. Alemán's term represented consolidation in the power of a PRI faction far more probusiness and hence dramatically less nationalistic and reform-minded than the waning Cárdenas wing. This trend would reach the point where pursuit of political stability through economic growth would become the basic premise of the political system, seen as an operational imperative by subsequent administrations. Increasingly the quest to sustain economic growth would lead first to opening the doors wider to foreign investment, then to massive international borrowing and a burgeoning foreign debt. It would, unfortunately, also mark the emergence of large-scale corruption as a distinguishing characteristic of Mexican politics.

In order to promote growth without generating high inflation, a priority in a country that by 1950 had reached a population of 27.8 million, Alemán's government acted through PRI-affiliated unions to suppress labor's wage demands. A new strategy of stable development was instituted, based on promotion of industrialization through subsidizing domestic industries and a massive infrastructure improvement program featuring expansion of generation and transmission of cheap hydroelectric energy. A balance-of-payments problem and rising inflation led to an unpopular devaluation of the peso in 1948, followed by another in 1952. The lessons seem to have been learned, and there would not again be an economic crisis until 1976. But at the end of his term Alemán, much later to die as one of Mexico's richest businessmen, faced opposition not only to his policies, but also to his divisive, rather than consensual, style. Running roughshod over party factions and refusing to enter into traditional negotiating over selection of governors, he was determined to impose a conservative candidate over party leaders who felt it was time for the pendulum to swing in the other direction before reformist elements might begin to feel the party had deserted them.

Further undermining the autocratically inclined president, since the government's heavy involvement in the economy provided ample opportunities for large-scale corruption, its tolerance by the administration eventually sparked public outcry and even protests from within the PRI. As captured by a close student of Mexican politics, the Alemán administration became noted for "the corruption accompanying all of these [grandiose economic] projects, and for the very profitable economic strangleholds reputedly held" by some of its insiders and their favorites.[30] Indeed, corruption became an integral part of the Mexican political system—a problem that would only worsen by the 1980s, when billions of dollars from drug trafficking would lead to rampant graft and fraud not related to productive economic growth.

Hoping to restore faith in the ruling party, Alemán compromised on Adolfo Ruiz Cortines (b. 1890), his interior minister and a former governor of Veracruz, who enjoyed a reputation for probity.[31] General Miguel Henríquez Guzmán insisted on running as a dissident in the 1952 election, getting 16 percent of the vote. This would prove to be the last time in three and a half decades that the PRI would come up against an unwanted electoral challenge as it completed its transformation into a hegemonic, near-monopolistic official party allowing only marginal and essentially symbolic opposition. Waving the banner of "consolidation and moral reform," Ruiz Cortines moderated his predecessor's policies without abandoning their basic thrust. The economy continued to grow, and as the construction boom ebbed, money was channeled into public health programs and improvement of benefits to those workers already eligible rather than reformers' demands for extension of coverage to other groups. Concentration of new jobs in urban areas in and around Mexico City gave rise to the proliferation of shantytowns and a growing urban underclass.

Continuation of Alemán's sharp cutback in land distribution to the rural populace nourished a reappearance of the Cárdenas faction of the party as champions of the agrarian and labor constituencies, which were as heavily emphasized in the party's formal facade as they were marginalized in its policymaking functions. This progressive sector was opposed by a hard-right Alemanist faction, which allowed the president to assume the role of evenhanded mediator and spokesman for the party's center. Thus,

> The very existence of [contradictory] interpretations of the Revolution made it both necessary and possible for President Ruiz Cortines to exercise judgment independent of both and fully responsible to neither. He took a moderate stand in the center of the broad political spectrum embraced by the PRI.[32]

In exercising this leadership style, Ruiz Cortines relied on the power of his office and the machinery of government, not personally being or seeking to seem a particularly strong or dominating leader. In an important sense this stance simplified the succession dilemma, to which Ruiz Cortines turned his attention after the 1955 midterm congressional elections, in which women could vote for the first time, a right they had acquired in the first year of his term.

Argentina: From Democracy's "False Dawn" to Perón

The Argentine 1930 Revolution had very little in common with the simultaneous events in Brazil, much less what had taken place in Mexico in 1910, except for a misleadingly similar name. It was in reality a great leap backward, as conservative forces in alliance with right-wing members of the military sought to reestablish an updated approximation of the pre-1912 system. The fascistic "integral nationalists" led by General José Félix Uriburu moved quickly to fill the vacuum left by Hipólito Yrigoyen's quite peaceful ouster on September 6. Heavily influenced by a German military adviser when serving as army inspector general during the 1922–1928 Marcelo Alvear government, this ambitious officer was close to a secret "lodge" of disaffected officers and retired early in Yrigoyen's 1928–1930 encore administration. Far more extreme politically than the mainstream of the officer corps, Uriburu's provisional government included Lieutenant Colonel Álvaro Alsogaray, who would much later be an inveterate plotter, as head of the military side of the presidential staff. Thwarting Uriburu's ambitions as well as those of the fascistic Argentine Civic Legion, General Agustín P. Justo (b. 1878), the leader of the constitutionalist wing of the army, assumed the presidency through elections in November 1931. When Alvear's candidacy was vetoed by the government, the antipersonalist Radicals decided to boycott the election.[33] Since Yrigoyen and his followers contested the revolution's legitimacy, maintaining that he was still the legal president and would be into 1934, they were banned from taking part in the election.

Justo, an Alvear-era (1922–1928) war minister who had led the opposition to Yrigoyen's return to power, represented the Concordáncia, an alliance of Conservatives and antipersonalist radicals. His six-year administration (beginning in

February 1932), although not the second coming of Roca, compared favorably with the administrations of most of his contemporaries, although not with those of Vargas and Cárdenas. In 1933, Justo's government signed the much-criticized Roca-Runciman Pact, which granted the British preferential economic treatment in return for pledging to keep their beef purchases at the 1931 level. Given Argentina's heavy dependence on meat exports, chiefly to Britain, this pact was as essential to Argentina as Vargas's moves to prevent a collapse of coffee sales were to Brazil. (Mexico's agriculture was still recovering from the devastation of two decades of internal warfare, so foreign markets were not a major concern for Cárdenas.) Surviving the impact of the world depression better than less-developed neighbors, but with foreign exchange reserves drained, Argentina left the gold standard the same year, 1933 (which also saw Yrigoyen's death). Import-substitution industrialization provided gradual recovery from the depression. In the process pampean landowners learned to compromise with industrial entrepreneurs and foreign financial interests.[34]

This so-called infamous decade of the 1930s, in which both the November 1935 gubernatorial elections and the March 1936 congressional balloting were rigged, witnessed a changing of the guard when antipersonalist Radical Roberto M. Ortíz (b. 1886) became president through a late 1937 election, the second in succession in which extensive fraud was used to frustrate the Radical Civic Union (UCR), which believed that Alvear was the true winner despite the 57 percent of the vote officially credited to Ortíz. This well-intentioned centrist, who had been Alvear's public works minister and Justo's finance minister, upon taking office in February 1938 enjoyed the full backing of Justo, still the respected role model for much of the officer corps. Indeed, Justo and other constitutionalist officers blocked a coup attempt that had Ortíz on the ropes in August 1938. Subsequently the president stepped up efforts to cultivate support among the officer corps.[35]

The economic policies of the Ortíz government were essentially inward-looking with growing state involvement, but the political atmosphere was increasingly marked by cynicism, corruption, disillusionment, and resignation. The traditional agricultural elites were determined to regain control of the presidency in order to use the government to defend their interests in the face of the lingering depression. (This situation contrasted with Brazil, where analogous groups were already in control of the government and other interests needed to break their hold.) Real wages had doubled during the 1920s, so workers were far from happy when they only held level through the 1930s.

With the radicals controlling the lower house, but the conservatives holding a majority in the senate, Ortíz followed a reasonably moderate course until blindness resulting from diabetes forced him to hand over power in mid-1940 to sixty-seven-year-old conservative vice president Ramón S. Castillo. With war already raging in Europe, its impact on Argentine politics was heavy. In World War I, when both Britain and Italy were on the same side, Argentine sympathy had been solidly for the Allies. Now business sectors were again on the side of Britain and the Allies, but much of the military, given their overwhelming Italian origins, sided with the Axis. Working to block Justo's interest in returning to the presidency à la Roca four decades earlier, Castillo had been able to name his own cabinet after Ortíz's formal resignation in August 1940. As the 1943 elections grew nearer, Castillo threw his support to the extremely right-wing presiding officer of the Senate, Robustiano Patrón Costas. A wealthy sugar planter from the interior, this political boss of Salta had a bad reputation with respect to treatment of his workers and was viewed as imperious and inflexible.

Higher field-grade army officers, majors to colonels, despite division into semisecret groupings known as *logias*, increasingly agreed on one thing: The elections could not take place under Castillo's direction, since under his government's concept of "patriotic fraud," in the counting of ballots, if not in their casting, Patrón Costas would be the certain winner. Wide as their ideological differences were on traditional left-right continuum, they shared a nationalist orientation with an inclination toward national power and independence that led them to support industrialization. None of these views were compatible with those of the British-capital-linked agro-export producers hoping to see Patrón Costas lead the country into the postwar era. Moreover, the senior officers were very upset over the heavy US military aid to archrival Brazil after it joined the Allies in August 1942. But with the war shifting against the Axis powers, a particularly acute shift with respect to Italy, Castillo was wed to the Patrón Costas option in the presidential balloting scheduled for September 1943. Many officers were increasingly reluctant to be associated with yet another fraudulent election.[36]

One of the most important of activist officers by 1943 was Colonel Juan Domingo Perón. Perón was decidedly the most important individual in twentieth-century Argentina, very probably the outstanding leader in the country's history, and a strong contender for that distinction with regard to all Latin America. A far more complex figure than the rather cardboard caricature in the musical *Evita,* he was in many ways a typical Argentine, although on a larger-than-life scale.[37] This exceptional man came from family roots similar to those of much of Argentina's population. His paternal great-grandfather, a Perrone, had migrated from Sardinia in 1827, had married an English girl, and had become a moderately successful merchant specializing in imported footwear. Hence, Juan Domingo's grandfather could become a doctor and man of letters of considerable material worth and substantial social standing. He further broadened the family's gene pool by marrying a Uruguayan of southern French ancestry. This distinguished Buenos Aires man-about-town's early death at age fifty had a decidedly adverse impact upon Perón family fortunes.

JUAN DOMINGO PERÓN

Juan Domingo's father had been born in 1867, and his mother was a Spanish-Indian woman not formally married to Don Marío Tomás Perón. The future Argentine strongman came into the world on October 8, 1895, in a small town on the pampas, moving as a little boy to a sheep ranch in Patagonia, which his downwardly mobile father managed. Sent to the capital for schooling in 1904, the embryonic charismatic *caudillo*, lacking money for the private schools required for pursuing a medical career, entered the National Military School in 1911. Thus his socialization spanned the late Roca era and overlapped the ferment that preceded the rise of the radicals to power.

Making his mark more in sports than in the classroom, having early in life become an expert horseman and excelling at boxing and fencing, Perón, the youngest in his class, graduated 43rd of 110 in December 1913. After several routine assignments, the twenty-four-year-old first lieutenant began teaching at the Noncommissioned Officers' School in the capital, a post he would hold until March 1926. By then a captain, he undertook studies at the Superior War College (ESG), graduating near the top of his class in January 1929 and marrying at that point. Having demonstrated intellectual capacity, as well as leadership potential, he continued to teach military history while assigned to the general staff. Playing a cautious and discrete role in the 1930 Revolution, which included a brief flirtation with the Uriburu faction, Perón became a supporter of General Justo and was promoted to major at the end of 1931. During Justo's presidency, Perón wrote intensively, manifesting an affinity for the ideas of Oswald Spengler and admiration for Alexander the Great, Julius Caesar, Frederick the Great, and Napoléon as well as expressing strong views on the state's need to avoid internal conflict by regulating all aspects of national life. After two years as military attaché in democratic Chile, Lieutenant Colonel Perón returned to his beloved Buenos Aires in 1938. In the aftermath of his twenty-nine-year-old wife's tragic death from uterine cancer, he was sent in February 1939 to observe Mussolini's crack Alpine troops. While in northern Italy he assiduously read the basic documents of the fascist regime, took advantage of his proximity to Milan to take courses in organizational theory, and toured wartime Europe, visiting Nazi Germany and returning by way of Franco's Spain. Once home in early 1941, Perón, tall and handsome with widely recognized leadership abilities, rapidly emerged as a key figure within the not-so-secret military "lodge" founded in March 1943 and known as the GOU (Group of United Officers), with its slogan of "Government, Order, and Unity" and General Edelmiro J. Farrell as its patron. With Justo's early 1943 death (following those of Alvear and Ortíz) having removed a constitutionalist restraining influence over the still largely apolitical mass of the army, a broad-based conspiracy ousted Castillo on June 4, 1943, eliminating the prospect of elections through which the *concordáncia* would remain in power. As ten thousand troops marched on the presidential palace and fatalities were held to seventy, few observers had any idea that this would be the end of civilian rule until 1958.[38]

The initial president of the de facto regime, pro-Ally Arturo Rawson (twelfth in seniority among active-duty generals), who considered breaking diplomatic relations with the Axis powers, was swept aside in two days and replaced by the war minister, General Pedro P. Ramírez, the chief organizer of Castillo's ouster (and sixth in seniority), whose views were closer to those of the GOU, with General Farrell becoming war minister. (At this point Juan Carlos Onganía, who would govern Argentina in 1966–1971, was just a first lieutenant.) Perón became Farrell's undersecretary, maneuvering skillfully through the politically dangerous shoals. In what was by late 1943 a "Francoist" regime—that is, one bearing basic similarities to Spain under Francisco Franco—Perón became head of the national labor department in October and was upgraded two months later to a cabinet post as secretary of labor and social security. When the vain and somewhat lazy Farrell replaced Ramírez as president in late February 1944, a month after his sudden severing of relations with Germany and Japan, fast-rising Perón became minister of war in June and vice president in July before adding the title of president of the National Council for the Postwar Era the next month. While heading the war ministry he astutely built support by greatly expanding the upper levels of the officer corps. The army's general officers were increased from 25 to 37, with full colonels upped by 25 percent and lieutenant colonels from 233 to 420. Needless to say, Perón had a great deal of say in the ensuing orgy of promotions and an even louder voice in reshuffling assignments.[39]

The strategy Perón had evolved for ensuring his country's advancement without undue disorder in a conflictual world called for a systematic effort by the state to organize workers and channel social conflict in order to prevent revolution. This effort would require someone with an enlightened mind coupled with unwavering determination to be at the helm for a lengthy time. Such an individual would need to combine the strong points of Franco and Mussolini with an updated version of Roca's political sagacity and understanding of the Argentine people. Looking around, but not long or far, Perón found no one fitting the bill for Argentina's providential man nearly as well as he himself did. (History has amply confirmed his judgment, as much as it has the certainty of Churchill, Charles de Gaulle, and FDR that they were what their country sorely needed in its particular time of crisis.)

With his eye on the need for a power base outside the armed forces, Perón worked assiduously to gain influence and followers within the labor movement, which to that point had embraced only a small fraction of the working class, a situation government sponsorship could quickly change. In 1943, a minimum wage was instituted, a system of labor courts was set up to adjudicate employee-employer disputes, and an end-of-year "thirteenth month" bonus was required. In 1944, Perón reached out to the rural underclass with a "Statute of the Peons" extending to them some of the rights and benefits previously accorded to urban labor. Between 1943 and 1946 the number of people covered by social security trebled. Meanwhile Perón forged a single national labor central, the General Labor Confederation (CGT), and issued a corporatist labor code similar to that already proclaimed by Vargas in Brazil. Hence, in October 1945, on the eve of his fiftieth birthday, Perón was in a position to bid openly for the presidency.[40]

Possessed with astute political acumen and adroit skills at manipulation, coupled with a magnetic personality and flair for showmanship, Perón polished the latter with enthusiastic and extremely close coaching from twenty-six-year-old Eva María Duarte. A kindred spirit, Evita, also born without the church's formal blessing, had made it in from the boondocks and up from the street the hard—or easy—way, depending upon one's perspective, and was an extremely ambitious and strikingly attractive actress cum radio personality who knew a winner when she saw one. Soon she moved in with the tall, handsome widower Perón, launching a symbiotic partnership that would end only with her greatly premature death in mid-1952.[41] Conservative forces were panicked at the possibility of Perón's rising even higher and in mid-September 1945 organized a mass march—perhaps nearing 250,000 persons—for "the constitution and Liberty," but a coup attempt by disaffected army units a few days later in Córdoba fizzled out. Still, encouraged by this demonstration of anti-Perón sentiment, his enemies and rivals within the regime, jealous of his popularity and wary of being eclipsed by his meteoric rise, convinced insecure President Farrell to dismiss him on October 9, 1945, for having used his government position to further his electoral ambitions. Trying to put the best face possible on this potentially crippling setback, Perón claimed to have voluntarily resigned in order to pursue his presidential candidacy without conflict of interest. He asked for, and received, a chance to bid the Argentine people farewell, using it to announce a major wage increase that he "hoped" the government would honor. Alarmed by his audacity and the favorable public response it had elicited, on October 12 his enemies arrested Perón and had him confined on an island in the La Plata estuary (where he would be sent again by military opponents in September 1955).[42]

Throwing caution to the wind, Evita infused backbone into hesitant labor leaders and effectively stirred up Buenos Aires's urban masses—the *descamisados* ("shirtless" in the sense of not wearing collars). A highly vocal demonstration in the city's center on October 17, involving a march sponsored by the CGT, the largest demonstration Buenos Aires had ever seen, involving 300,000 persons, convinced the vacillating Farrell to reverse course. Moreover, Perón's intramural foes were unwilling to shed blood over the issue, with General Eduardo J. Ávalos—remembering the "tragic week" a quarter century earlier—opening the gates by refusing to repress the demonstrating masses. Thus Perón returned in triumph, making a devastatingly dramatic appearance in front of a hysterical mass of *Porteños* from the balcony of the presidential palace at the centrally located Plaza del Mayo.[43] He then resumed the whirlwind campaign leading to a decisive victory in Argentina's first fully free and competitive election since 1928. To this end, on October 24 he announced formation of the Partido Laborista ("Labor Party"). In December the cowed government, reconciled to his election, issued a wage and bonus decree clearly bearing his stamp.

In recognition of her crucial role when Perón's fate hung in the balance and of her immense popularity with the lower classes, Evita became Señora Perón at a private ceremony on October 23 and would soon be Argentina's youngest and most glamorous first lady, indeed very likely the hemisphere and even global leader in these respects. Still, many senior army officers considered her unfit for that lofty position, and further elevation would be a bone of contention between Perón and the other generals. The campaign was an intense and spirited one, with the radicals allying with socialists and communists behind a unity slate composed of somewhat antiquated José Tamborini for president and Ricardo Balbín, leader of the Radical Civic Union, for vice president. To counter, Perón selected J. Horténsio Quijano, a dissident radical, as his running mate. The US government, viewing the opposition Democratic Union (UD) with favor, was bitterly opposed to Perón and less than two weeks before election day released a "blue book" denouncing his supposed fascist ties. This blatant attempt to influence the election had a boomerang effect, giving credence to Perón's attacks upon the opposition slate as an unholy "capitalist/communist alliance." On February 24, 1946, Perón received 52.4 percent of the record vote, ten percentage points ahead of the UD coalition standard bearer. His 2.84 million votes was far-and-away the most any president had ever received, coming from an electorate of males eighteen and over, some 700,000 larger than that in 1937—of whom all those under twenty-six had never before voted for a president. He had 304 of 376 votes in the electoral college, a two-thirds majority in the lower house, 28 of the 30 senate seats being contested, and all provincial governors. With his gala inauguration on June 4, the Perón Era, Argentina's most defining period, was fully under way.[44] In a sign of his authoritarian side, all supreme court judges were summarily replaced.

The country over which General Perón (promoted on the eve of his taking office) would govern for nearly a decade was far more complicated than it had been at the time of his political socialization. Fed by immigration, mostly from Italy, its population had passed 15 million, with almost 3 million in the capital and another 1.5 million in its suburbs. Although industry had surpassed agriculture as a proportion of GDP, most of it was small and low-tech. The country's industrial plant and infrastructure were rundown after a long lack of renovation stemming from the depression and wartime. Although the country had been neutral during the war and had faced only an imagined threat from Brazil, the armed forces absorbed 43 percent of federal government outlays, 6 percent of GDP, with most of it going to the 138,000-man army. The General Directorate of Military Manufactures (DGM), established in 1941, was expanding into a wide variety of ancillary activities. Since all but two of the army's forty-four generals were senior to Perón, they had some difficulty in accepting the sudden role reversal—subordination to their former subordinate. Unlike the president, two-fifths of them had been born in Buenos Aires and half were sons of immigrants.[45]

For Perón, becoming president was more like a return to power than a transition. His determination to do things his way was exemplified by his choice of an inexperienced thirty-three-year-old as finance minister. So that until 1949 the real economic czar would be Miguel Miranda, operating out of the Central Bank presidency. It was clear that import-substitution industrialization was bottlenecked, requiring either a broadening of the internal market or expansion of exports, optimally both. October saw the proclamation of a five-year plan featuring an ambitious program of industrialization, the implementation of which was marred by a good deal of inexperience, substantial mismanagement, and more than a hint of corruption. Yet, between 1943 and 1948, GDP rose over 25 percent, hitting 8.3 percent in 1946 and a very impressive 13.8 percent in 1947.

In January 1947, some 150 million British pounds ($750 million) from the blocked (nonconvertible) sterling accounts run up by Britain during the war were used to purchase the country's railroads—psychologically satisfying, but creating a drain on already-strained government finances for badly needed repairs and reequipment as well as operating costs. Similar expenditures buying out British-owned public utilities imposed the double burden of a high purchase price and the need to make heavy investments in maintenance and expansion. At that juncture, a young Radical politician, Arturo Frondizi (destined to be elected Argentina's president in 1958), denounced a proposed oil exploration deal in Patagonia with Standard Oil of New Jersey as a betrayal of nationalist principles. It would be a long time before Perón could again be criticized for insufficient nationalistic zeal, but when it did happen during his second term, it would inflict a serious political wound. (At this point, Alejandro Lanusse, the future military president who would find himself compelled to hand the presidency back to Perón in 1973, was a cavalry first lieutenant.)

Heavily conditioned by political considerations, Perón's development policies contained fundamental contradictions. His encouragement of light industry required increasing capital goods imports, but with investment in agriculture down, failure to generate sufficient export earnings created a severe bottleneck. Perón's nationalism discouraged foreign investment, and its prolabor and anticapitalist rhetoric put off domestic entrepreneurs—especially with regard to long-term investments. Yet there is no question that the first years of Perón's government were better for Argentina's workers than even the preceding Farrell-Perón regime had been. Between 1946 and 1949 real wages went up 60 percent, even more for unskilled workers than for skilled ones. Consumption was stimulated and pressure was put on prices as purchasing power rose. To come up with the vast increase in revenues required by his social programs, Perón elevated protective tariffs and heavily taxed rural exporting elites. In 1946, he established the state-controlled Argentine Institute for Trade Promotion, deeply infringing on a sphere that had been the private sector's.[46]

Perón made no secret of his distaste for parties, considering them anachronistic and stressing that Peronism was a movement, not just a party. As soon as the Labor Party had served its electoral purpose, he dissolved it, forming in June 1946 the Unified Party of the National Revolution (PUR) in its stead. By 1949, this would become the Peronist Party, but he wanted it to remain an electoral vehicle and not gain autonomy or play a major role in government. To this end he kept the Women's Peronist Party under Evita's leadership separate and used the Evita Perón Foundation (FEP) along with the CGT to dispense patronage. Indeed, throughout his career Perón took pains to see that potential rivals would not find an organizational base in a structured, hierarchical party.[47] As part of his preference for establishing direct links to the populace, Perón gave Evita wide leeway to expand the activities of her foundation. Already in charge of the labor secretariat, she gathered funds for the FEP from unions and "voluntary" contributions from businesses (even less voluntary than are campaign contributions for unions and businesses in the United States). The vast sums collected were used to build apartment complexes, orphanages, homes for the elderly, clinics, and even schools. They also funded programs for distributing food, clothing, and medicine to the needy. As intended, this wide array of social welfare functions blurred the line between Peronism and the government, leaving grateful beneficiaries feeling indebted to the Peróns.

In the March 1948 congressional elections, the Peronists received 60 percent of the vote and a two-thirds majority in the lower house (the Senate being chosen indirectly by the provinces). Needing to amend the constitution to permit reelection, Perón held elections in December for a constituent assembly to revise the 1853 constitution, winning 66 percent of the vote and two-thirds of the assembly's seats. After only two months' work the assembly produced a new constitution, which was promulgated on March 11, 1949—strengthening presidential powers, permitting reelection, and confirming Perón's 1947 extension of the vote to women. But a major economic crisis in 1949 was kicked off with a January stock market crash triggered by Perón's dismissal of economic czar Miguel Miranda, who had held his position since the administration's inception. The dropping of the economic pilot was triggered by a precipitous drop in economic growth—from 1947's almost 14 percent GDP to a scant 1.2 percent in 1948 on the way to a negative 4.6 percent for 1949. Moreover, inflation shot up from 13.1 percent in 1948 to 31.1 percent for 1949. The exhaustion of the game plan, if not the basic model, resulted in large part from the fact that the drive for industrialization had created a great jump in imports just as export earnings dropped in response to sagging prices and a loss in world market share.

Perón's reelection would not be nearly as much of a civic festival as his initial elevation to power had been. The campaign was marked by harassment of opposition candidates and use of government machinery on behalf of the Peronists. A long-simmering feud between Perón and Alberto Gainza Paz, the internationally renowned publisher of the country's most prestigious newspaper, *La Prensa,* came to a head in January 1951 with its closing, aggravated by its expropriation in April. Perón's intention to make Evita even more of a coleader by elevating her to the vice presidency stirred up opposition from those elite sectors still considering her that immature, upstart *puta* ("whore"), a reference to her bed-hopping rise from obscurity.[48]

Significant elements within the military felt that Perón had to be stopped before achieving a second term. By early 195,1 Major General Eduardo Lonardi (who would be Perón's bête noire in 1955) was the center of one group of plotters, and retired brigadier general Benjamin Menéndez was the hub of a rival conspiracy. With the elections moved up three months to November 11, time was running short. An abortive coup by Menéndez on September 28 weakened the anti-Perón movement's base by triggering a wave of purges and forced retirements, but these left deep scars that would come back to haunt the nation's strongman. A State of Internal Warfare was decreed, remaining in effect for the rest of Perón's presidency. An honorable man, Lonardi requested retirement so that he could continue plotting in good conscience.

The conspirators had been undercut by Evita's announcement at the end of August that she was resigning the vice-presidential nomination that had been bestowed upon her. By this time it was a very poorly kept secret that she had been suffering from uterine cancer for some time, refusing to undergo a hysterectomy until November 5. The balloting six days later saw an enthusiastic turnout of 7.6 million, including, for the first time in a presidential election, women, who had been extended the vote in late 1947. Perón finished well ahead with 61 percent of male votes and 64 percent of women's; 32 percent of voters, some 2.4 million, cast their ballots for the radicals' Ricardo Balbín (who would try again for the presidency in 1958). Peronism came away with all governors and 135 of 149 lower-house seats.[49] Vice President Quijano died just before the April 1952 reinauguration, which was also marred by the beloved (by the many) and hated (by the few) Evita's excruciating illness. Her tragically premature death on July 26, 1952, led to a massive outpouring of grief and sympathy, with 2 million mourners for her state funeral, but down the road it would create very serious problems for the charismatic, but already overextended, leader of the Argentine nation.

In February 1952, facing high inflation, 36.7 percent in 1951 and 2 percent higher in 1952, along with the prospect of a foreign exchange crisis, the government announced the most ambitious economic stabilization program in Argentine history. It included a two-year wage freeze and, perhaps even more jolting to Argentines, deep cuts in domestic beef consumption to allow increased exports. Growth, which had recovered to 4 percent in 1951, plummeted to an unprecedented negative 6.3 percent for 1952. To emphasize that these sacrifices were temporary, Perón unveiled a second five-year plan at year's end. The situation was not helped by persistent rumors propagated by the opposition that as much as $700 million had been diverted through the Evita Perón Foundation into overseas bank accounts. Then, too, central government payrolls had soared as federal public employees rose from a little over 200,000 in 1945 to nearly 400,000 by 1955.[50]

Perón was never one to stay on the defensive for long. In an act of major symbolic import, the Jockey Club, shrine of the country's propertied elites, was burned to the ground on April 15, a fate shared by the headquarters of the Socialist Party. Then, in July 1953, in a surprise turnaround, Dr. Milton Eisenhower, brother of the incumbent US president, arrived on a special mission. This highly publicized rapprochement with the United States was followed by a much-relaxed investments law, which made possible foreign investments in the exploration and development of Argentine oil fields and signaled a new era in Perón's hitherto quasi-neutralist foreign policy. Economic growth recovered sharply to 7 percent in 1953, remaining at a satisfactory 3.8 percent in 1954.

Under these at least temporarily favorable conditions, Perón called elections for the congress and a new vice president for late April 1954, with Peronists getting 69 percent of the vote and filling the vacant vice presidency with Admiral Alberto

Tessaire. Perón also moved ahead with organization of a Peronist Movement, having the Peronist Party, the Women's Peronist Party, and the CGT as its three pillars. Hence, as late as October 1954, Perón appeared solidly in power. Indeed, Arthur P. Whitaker, a distinguished Ivy League historian and leading scholar of Argentine affairs, ended his *The United States and Argentina* with a seemingly well-founded prediction that there was no reason he might well not remain in power for another decade. Within little more than a year, however, Professor Whitaker would be industriously at work on a volume entitled *The Argentine Upheaval,* explaining why Perón had fallen out of power almost before his previous book was on the shelves of bookstores.[51] (Many of the factors cited by Professor Whitaker for a long future for the Perón regime were, however, borne out by Perón's subsequent return to power and the longevity of Peronism.)

The crisis that would topple Perón by September 1955 began to take form a year earlier. Worn down from riding the two horses of keeping the military in line while partially filling the void left by Evita's death by dealing with labor and the masses, the fifty-eight-year-old president filled the void in his personal life with fourteen-year-old Nelly Rivas. But this lapse in morality would be more a pretext for the church's turning against him than its actual cause. In point of fact, the church had long felt deeply threatened by the state's moving into the social welfare field, which it considered its private preserve, even if it was indirectly through Evita and her foundation's multifarious activities. A divorce law passed in December 1954 was a further serious provocation.[52]

Having the pretext for a break with Perón, the church needed opportunity. Negative popular and military reaction to his April 1955 contract with Standard Oil of California to explore for oil in Patagonia left Perón looking vulnerable. Thus, when the next month the government removed religious instruction from public schools, replacing it with what the church considered political indoctrination under the guise of citizenship, the church, almost certainly in consultation with the Vatican through the papal nuncio, girded for war. Unwisely, as it proved, Perón was ready, even eager, to meet this remaining institutional bastion of independence on the political battlefield. The congress immediately passed a law calling for elections to a convention to revise the constitution on all aspects relating to the church. With backing from disgruntled sectors of the armed forces, the church defied Perón by organizing a 100,000-person Corpus Christi procession in the center of Buenos Aires in early June.

When Perón retaliated by expelling two non-Argentinean members of the church hierarchy, he was publicly excommunicated on June 16. The church rallied support by publishing an "Episcopal Declaration Denouncing Religious Persecution in Argentina." It continued to defy Perón by going ahead with organization of the Christian Democratic Party (PDC) along the lines of the dominant political force in Italy, in whose formation the Vatican had played a key role in the immediate postwar years. It was no coincidence that on the same day marine corps rear admiral Samuel Toranzo Calderón led a revolt, which was bloodily repressed. The church, now further upset by the regime's organization of youth branches and re-scinding of long-established subsidies to Catholic schools, added its encourage-ment to that of the restive conservative elites, now out of power for a dozen long years, both encouraging the military conspirators.

The original leader of the second coup was Major General Pedro Eugenio Aramburu, recently appointed to head the Superior War College (ESG). When he backed off, retired General Eduardo Lonardi took over, launching the revolt in Córdoba on September 16, three months after its ill-fated precursor. Rear Admiral Isaac Rojas threw his weight behind Lonardi in a self-styled "revolutionary coun-cil" and its pretentious claim to be the "liberating revolution." Perón sought to ride out the storm, but hundreds of civilians were killed when navy pilots strafed the Plaza de Mayo in front of the presidential palace (Casa Rosada) in an effort to kill Perón. Although his most fanatical followers retaliated by attacking priests and burning churches, he threw in the towel in the face of air force threats to destroy valuable oil refineries and demolish port facilities. Following Perón's resignation on the night of September 19, two days later the interim military junta gave up negotiating, and on September 23 Lonardi was duly sworn in.[53] Military purges occurred rapidly, with all admirals except Rojas as well as 45 captains forced into retirement from the navy, a fate in store for 63 of 86 generals and about 1,000 of-ficers of less elevated rank. Lonardi's most serious mistake may have been an act of omission: failure to name Aramburu war minister. For this well-connected active-duty general pushed Lonardi out on November 13, not quite as quickly as Ramírez had pushed Rawson out in 1943. Aramburu found himself originally hemmed in by a "revolutionary military council," soon downgraded and more prosaically renamed the Military Advisory Board. So the momentous period that had opened in 1930 with Yrigoyan still living in a fool's paradise ended with Perón on his way to exile and Aramburu believing that the tasks facing him were manageable and would mark an end to Peronism—indulging in a pipe dream, for Perón would return to power in the 1970s and Peronists would be governing the country through the 1990s and in the early years of the next century.

The Situation in 1955

The three-fifths of Latin Americans living in Brazil, Mexico, and Argentina enjoyed political development along with substantial economic growth—the fruits of which were still heavily skewed toward the elites and more favored elements of the middle sectors. Organized elements of the working class were recipients of social welfare benefits, although more in Argentina than in Mexico, with Brazil still lagging in this field—but closing the gap. Mexico's gains were the most institutionalized and so would survive the next period. A reversal was under way in Argentina but would be delayed nearly a decade before occurring in Brazil. Only Mexico, where the military were no longer a major political factor, would escape the wave of authoritarian military regimes that marked the next period.

Notes

1. The place to begin on this enormously important figure is J.W.F. Dulles, *Vargas of Brazil* (Austin: University of Texas Press, 1967). See also Robert M. Levine, *Father of the Poor: Vargas and His Era* (New York: Cambridge University Press, 1998), as well as Levine's *The Vargas Regime: The Critical Years, 1934–1938* (New York: Columbia University Press, 1970).

2. This treatment draws heavily on Ronald M. Schneider, *"Order and Progress": A Political History of Brazil* (Boulder, CO: Westview Press, 1991), pp. 106–186, as well as the less detailed version in Ronald M. Schneider, *Brazil: Culture and Politics in a New Industrial Powerhouse* (Boulder, CO: Westview Press, 1996), pp. 58–75.

3. Helio Jaguaribe, "Brazilian Nationalism and the Dynamics of Its Political Development," *Studies in Comparative International Development,* 2:4 (1966), p. 59.

4. June E. Hahner, *Poverty and Politics:, The Urban Poor in Brazil, 1870–1920* (Albuquerque: University of New Mexico Press, 1986), p. 292.

5. See María do Carmo Campello de Souza, "O Processo Político-Partidário na Primeira República," in Carlos Guilherme Mota, ed., *Brasil em Perspectiva*, 3rd ed. (São Paulo: Difusão Européia do Livro, 1971), p. 225. Frank D. McCann, *Soldiers of the Pátria: A History of the Brazilian Army, 1889–1937* (Stanford, CA: Stanford University Press, 2004), pp. 259ff, delineates with care the divisions within the army as well as its ambivalences and hesitations.

6. On labor see Kenneth P. Erickson, *The Brazilian Corporative State and Working Class Politics* (Berkeley and Los Angeles: University of California Press, 1977).

7. João Neves da Fontoura, *Memorias,* Vol. 2, *A Aliança Liberal e a Revolução de 1930* (Porto Alegre, Brazil: Editora Globo, 1963), pp. 307–329 details these events. See also their reconstruction in McCann, *Soldiers* pp. 280–300.

8. McCann, *Soldiers,* p. 299.

9. Ibid., p. 308.

10. See Carlos E. Cortes, *Gaucho Politics in Brazil: The Politics of Rio Grande do Sul, 1930–1964* (Albuquerque: University of New Mexico Press, 1974), pp. 24–67.

11. Consult McCann, *Soldiers,* pp. 310–334.

12. Ibid., p. 331.

13. On the Communists and their uprising Levine, *Vargas Regime,* pp. 100–124, can be supplemented by J.F.W. Dulles, *Brazilian Communism, 1935–1945: Repression During World Upheaval* (Austin: University of Texas Press, 1983), as well as John W.F. Dulles, *Anarchists and Communists in Brazil, 1900–1935* (Austin: University of Texas Press, 1973), pp. 233–306. Newer sources are reflected in McCann, *Soldiers,* pp. 372–388.

14. Roots of the Estado Novo are ably analyzed in McCann, *Soldiers,* pp. 406–439.

15. Ibid., p. 405.

16. Ibid., p. 434.

17. Consult Eli Diniz, "O Estado Novo: Estrutura de Poder. Relações de Classes," in *História Geral da Civilização Brasileira,* Tomo 3, Vol. 3, p. 114.

18. See Frank D. McCann, *The Brazilian-American Alliance, 1937–1945* (Princeton: Princeton University Press, 1973). Later years are covered in Sonny B. Davis, *A Brotherhood of Arms: Brazil–United States Military Relations, 1945–1977* (Niwot: University Press of Colorado, 1996).

19. Consult Francisco Weffort, "Politica de Masses," in Octavio Ianni, ed., *Política e Revolucao Social no Brasil* (Rio de Janeiro: Editóra Civilização Brasileira, 1965), pp. 163–175.

20. Michael L. Conniff, *Urban Politics in Brazil: The Rise of Populism* (Pittsburgh: University of Pittsburgh Press, 1981), provides useful analysis. On the opposition see Maria Victoria de Mesquita Benevides, *A UDN e o Udeniismo: Ambiguidades de Liberalismo Brasileiro, 1945–1965* (Rio de Janeiro: Editora Paz e Terra, 1981), pp. 62–76. Ademar de Barros and his PSP are discussed in John D. French, "Workers and the Rise of Adhemarista Populism in São Paulo Brazil, 1945–1947," *Hispanic American Historical Review,* 68:1 (February 1988), pp. 1–43.

21. Detail on this period can be found in J.W.F. Dulles, *Vargas of Brazil,* as well as J.W.F. Dulles, *Unrest in Brazil: Political Military Crises, 1955–1964* (Austin: University of Texas Press, 1970).

22. See Peter S. Smith, *Oil and Politics in Modern Brazil* (Toronto: Macmillan of Canada, 1976).

23. For comparison with the previous presidential balloting see Ronald M. Schneider, *Brazil Election Factbook* (Washington, DC: Institute for the Comparative Study of Political Systems, 1965), pp. 53–61. The campaign is detailed in Edward Anthony Riedinger, *Como Se Faz um Presidente: A Campanha de JK* (Rio de Janeiro: Editora Nova Fronteira, 1988).

24. Krauze, *Mexico,* pp. 438–480, treats the Cárdenas era, as does Meyer, Sherman, and Deeds, *Course,* Chapter 38.

25. See Joe C. Ashby, *Organized Labor and the Mexican Revolution Under Lázaro Cárdenas* (Chapel Hill: University of North Carolina Press, 1967), and Roderic Ai Camp, *Generals in the Palacio, the Military in Modern Mexico* (New York: Oxford University Press, 1992).

26. See Edmund D. Cronon, *Josephus Daniels in Mexico* (Madison: University of Wisconsin Press, 1960).

27. Krauze, *Mexico,* pp. 491–525, deals with Ávila Camacho's term, as does Meyer, Sherman, and Deeds, *Course,* Chapter 50. Useful on this generation is Howard F. Cline, *Mexico: Revolution to Evolution, 1940–1960* (New York: Oxford University Press, 1963).

28. See Krauze, *Mexico,* pp. 508–510. Ávila Camacho's appointment by Cárdenas as war minister in 1940 had given him control over the army in the run up to the election.

29. Krauze, *Mexico,* pp. 526–600, analyzes the Alemán government.

30. Robert C. Scott, *Mexican Government in Transition* (Urbana: University of Illinois Press, 1964), p. 250.

31. Krauze, *Mexico,* pp. 601–624, surveys the Ruiz Cortines administration.

32. Scott, *Mexican Government,* p. 207.

33. A meticulously researched account of political-military developments up to Perón's coming to power is found in Robert Potash, *The Army and Politics in Argentina,* Vol. 1,

1928–1945: Yrigoyen to Perón (Palo Alto, CA: Stanford University Press, 1969). The 1931–1935 period is covered in detail on pp. 57–90.

34. Solid histories include Luis Alberto Romero, *A History of Argentina in the Twentieth Century* (University Station: Pennsylvania University Press, 2002); David Rock, *Argentina, 1516–1982: From the Spanish Colonization to the Falklands War* (Berkeley and Los Angeles: University of California Press, 1985); and James Scobie, *Argentina: A City and a Nation*, 2nd ed. (New York: Oxford University Press, 1971). Economic factors are treated in Laura Randall, *An Economic History of Argentina in the Twentieth Century* (New York: Columbia University Press, 1978); Carlos Diaz Alejandro, *Essays on the Economic History of Argentina* (New Haven: Yale University Press, 1970); and Tomas Roberto Fillol, *Social Factors in Economic Development: The Argentine Case* (Cambridge: Massachusetts Institute of Technology Press, 1961).

35. The 1936–1939 period is treated in Potash, *Army,* Vol. 1, pp. 91–140. Of interest is Mark Falcoff and Ronald H. Dolkart, eds., *Prologue to Perón: Argentina in Depression and War, 1930–1943* (Berkeley and Los Angeles: University of California Press, 1975).

36. Potash, *Army,* Vol. 1, p. 183. The 1937–1943 period is examined on pp. 141–199. Valuable insights into the ensuing years are contained in Frederick C. Turner and José Enrique Miguens, eds., *Juan Perón and the Reshaping of Argentina* (Pittsburgh: University of Pittsburgh Press, 1983).

37. Biographical studies include Joseph Page, *Perón: A Biography* (New York: Random House, 1983); Robert J. Alexander, *Juan Domingo Perón: A History* (Boulder, CO: Westview Press, 1979); and Robert D. Crassweller, *Perón and the Enigmas of Argentina* (New York: Norton, 1987).

38. Events from the coup to consolidation of Perón's presidential bid (in October 1945) are discussed in Potash, *Army,* Vol. 1, pp. 200–282.

39. Perón's cultivation of army support is detailed in ibid., pp. 249–252. Also useful is Donald C. Hodges, *Argentina 1943–1987: The National Revolution and Resistance,* expanded ed. (Albuquerque: University of New Mexico Press, 1988). Economic policies in their political context are discussed in Paul H. Lewis, *The Crisis of Argentine Capitalism* (Chapel Hill: University of North Carolina Press, 1990), and William C. Smith, *Authoritarianism and the Crisis of the Argentine Political System* (Stanford, CA: Stanford University Press, 1989).

40. Invaluable from late 1945 on is Robert Potash, *The Army and Politics in Argentina,* Vol. 2, *1945–1962: Peron to Frondizi* (Palo Alto, CA: Stanford University Press, 1980).

41. On Evita Perón consult Alicia Ortiz, *Eva Perón* (New York: St. Martin's Press, 1993), and Nicolas Frazer and Marysa Navarro, *Eva Perón* (New York: Norton, 1985), as well as Eva Perón, *My Mission in Life* (New York: Vantage Press, 1953).

42. The best account is found in Potash, *Army,* Vol. 1, pp. 269–282.

43. This pivotal "bonding" event is discussed in Douglas Madsen and Peter G. Snow, *The Charismatic Bond: Political Behavior in Time of Crisis* (Cambridge: Harvard University Press, 1991), pp. 46–51. See also Jean Kirkpatrick, *Leader and Vanguard in Mass Society: A Study of Peronist Argentina* (Cambridge: Massachusetts Institute of Technology Press, 1971).

44. Potash, *Army,* Vol. 2, p. 44, discusses the election, with the socioeconomic situation on pp. 6–8. Also see Peter H. Smith, "The Social Base of Peronism," *Hispanic American His-*

torical Review, 52:1 (February 1972), pp. 55–73, reworked in his *Argentina and the Failure of Democracy* (Madison: University of Wisconsin Press, 1974).

45. José Luis de Imaz, *Los que Mandan (Those Who Rule)* (Albany: State University of New York Press, 1970), provides a wealth of information on the social composition of the Argentine army.

46. The early chapters of Smith, *Authoritarianism*, and Lewis, *Crisis,* treat the economic situation, and Potash, *Army,* Vol. 2, pp. 92ff., provides detail on the 1949 crisis.

47. James W. McGuire, *Peronism Without Perón: Unions, Parties, and Democracy in Argentina* (Stanford, CA: Stanford University Press, 1997), pp. 59–66, discusses Perón's negativism toward parties, an attitude shared by Vargas during his first fifteen-year stay in office.

48. Perón was probably aware of Evita's illness and wished to reward her with the vice presidency, as she could not wait for the next time. He could not let military leaders in on her impending death, so he had to absorb the serious political costs of offending senior officers and then backing down.

49. The election is covered in Potash, *Army,* Vol. 2, pp. 135ff.

50. See the discussion of the Evita Perón Foundation in McGuire, *Peronism,* pp. 64–73. Lewis, *Crisis,* p. 202, estimates that as much as $700 million were diverted to overseas accounts (which stood Perón in good stead after his ouster in 1955).

51. Arthur P. Whitaker, *The Argentine Upheaval: Perón's Fall and the New Regime* (New York: Praeger, 1956).

52. Potash, *Army,* Vol. 2, pp. 171ff., covers the Perón-church split. A more Peronist perspective is in McGuire, *Peronism,* pp. 66–75.

53. Potash, *Army,* Vol. 2, p. 197, treats the Lonardi-Aramburu relationship.

7

Depression, the Cold War, and Weak Leadership

The Fate of All but the Big Three

The rest of Latin America did not undergo the great corporatist-populist experiences of Vargas's Brazil, Cárdenas's Mexico, or Perón's Argentina. Instead, the countries followed diverse paths in surviving the external buffeting forces without the buffering resources and capabilities of their three larger siblings. So, unlike them, most did not come out of the period with their middle class fully integrated into national political life and the incorporation of the working class well under way.

Overview

Colombia was the most tragic victim of the inability to participate in the forging of great and essentially positive legacies à la Brazil, Mexico, and Argentina. After starting out well, in the late 1940s it descended into the depths of bloody civil war and repressive dictatorship after its candidate for transformational leadership was brutally murdered on the eve of attaining power. By the end of the period democratic forces were rallying for a successful comeback.

Peru's tortuous political trajectory began with the vacuum left by Augusto Legúia's overthrow and ended with the eight-year rule of a military strongman. Its constant dominant theme was the emergence of the Popular Revolutionary Alliance of the Americas as the country's most deeply rooted political movement and the intransigent refusal of the armed forced to allow this nemesis access to power. This impasse would persist through the ensuing period as well.

For Venezuela, this quarter century opened with one dictator and closed with another, but in between, momentous developments took place that would soon after usher in an era of stable democracy. Juan Vicente Gómez finally passed away in 1935, initiating a transition that eventuated in reformist civilian rule in 1945–1948. Although a military authoritarian then emerged, civilian democratic forces dramatically reasserted themselves by 1958.

Chile saw the fall of its military strongman in 1931, leading to a string of responsible civilian governments including even the return of General Carlos Ibáñez as elected constitutional president for the 1952–1958 term.

Ecuador experienced the rise of José María Velasco Ibarra, whose series of trips to the presidency embraced not only each decade of this period, but also the 1960s and on into the 1970s.

Bolivia in 1932 began a disastrous war with Paraguay that had as its aftermath a 1936 military coup and a short-lived reformist military government leading to its watershed 1952 Revolution.

Paraguay, isolated from the rest of the world, experienced little change. Although it was the nominal winner, it was long traumatized by the mid-1930s war with Bolivia. The rest of the period saw the rise to power of General Alfredo Stroessner, who exercised heavy-handed control of political life up through most of the 1980s. Paraguay remained South America's most backward country.

Uruguay came out of the doldrums to reassert its claim to being the Switzerland of Latin America, although obviously a sociopolitical, not a geographic, conceit.

In Central America, Guatemala began the 1930s with yet another transition from one *caudillo* dictator to another but underwent a revolution in 1944 that ushered in a turbulent decade culminating in a US-backed counter-revolution in 1954. After starting well under a reformist civilian, El Salvador went downhill, with a long dictatorship marked by a bloody repression of an attempted revolution leading to a military monopoly on the presidency. A *caudillo* dictator dominated Honduras until 1949; then a liberal government was soon ousted by a coup. For Nicaragua the period became the Somoza era, as dictator Anastasio Somoza not only held sway almost the whole time, but also established a durable nation-strangling regime passed on to his sons after his assassination in 1956. In sharp contrast Costa Rican democracy overcame its greatest challenge in 1948 and was squarely back on the track before period's end, and at that point Panama's depressing status as a de facto US protectorate began to improve—slowly.

In the Caribbean, the path of Cuba during this time was both dramatic and traumatic as US intervention aborted the 1933 revolution and led to the emergence of the army as the proxy arbiter of politics, with its leader, Fulgéncio Batista, the country's dominant figure. Although Batista permitted elections in 1944 and 1948, the resulting governments were so corrupt as to discredit democracy in the eyes of many Cubans. Hence, Batista returned to power, becoming increasingly dictatorial as opposition mounted in the mid-1950s. The stage was set for drastic and lasting upheaval—which would not be long in coming. In the

Dominican Republic the protracted personalist authoritarian regime of Rafael Trujillo began at the inception of this period, duplicating Nicaragua in terms of a country run for the benefit of a single family. (This dictatorial regim would end only with his death in 1961 and would leave a heritage continued into the mid-1990s by a close disciple.) Haiti also experienced the end of US occupation but failed to develop either stability or democracy the stage was set for a bloody tyrant to emerge at the beginning of the next period.

Colombia: From a Promising Start to Rampant Violence

The quarter century opening in 1930 was to be a very turbulent one. Beginning with a return to civilized, if intense, competition between the two historical parties, Colombia would move through roughneck competition with virtually no-holds-barred until the rivalry literally became cutthroat—involving tens of thousands of throats cut along with hundreds of thousands of victims of other very personal means of slaughtering one's political enemies. Relative peace would be restored through military dictatorship before the parties would agree to bury the hatchet, or rather the machete, in order to launch a unique experience in co-government.[1] During this time, as the power of the state increased, so did the benefits of its control not only as a vehicle of patronage, but also of economic success, as the "increasing 'state-orientation' of the economy and the social order led to a point where it became impossible to conceive of any large-scale enterprise in any sector of activity without the protection and goodwill of the state."[2]

Colombia's 1930 elections were heavily impacted by the onset of the world depression. Not having run a candidate in 1926, the Liberal Party took advantage of divisions in Conservative Party ranks to come back with a "national concentration coalition." This was engineered by Enrique Olaya Herrera (b. 1881), who made use of his good relations with US bankers to win support of those conservative businessmen most concerned with continuing a flow of foreign investment. The mainstream Conservatives were split over the administration's draconian anti-subversive laws passed in the wake of 1928 labor unrest. Divisions in the Liberal's ranks were chiefly between a reformist wing led by future president Alfonso López Pumarejo (b. 1886) and a center-right faction headed by Bogotá newspaper publisher Eduardo Santos, another future president, which at this juncture supported Olaya. Even after being elected Olaya felt he needed to cooperate with the Conservatives in the interest of his number one goal, reactivating the economy. He included prominent Conservatives in his cabinet as a means of gaining bipartisan support for his priority legislation. Olaya's main ally in this political venture was influential Antioquía Conservative Party leader Carlos Restrepo, willing to collaborate with moderate Liberals in the interest of Colombia's stability, a prerequisite

ALFONSO LÓPEZ PUMAREJO

for foreign financing and investment. These moderate Conservatives were primarily concerned about maintaining the status quo, which was, after all, chiefly of
their making. Olaya never did figure out how to get reforms started without precipitating a break between moderate and reformist Liberals or how to satisfy the
partisan appetites of Liberals in the countryside while governing in partnership
with Conservatives. For Colombia's political culture viewed political domination
as the supreme objective of both the parties, since this ensured a monopoly of patronage and the spoils of the political war, whereas failure to control the government meant at best the short and dirty end of the stick.[3] In 1931, the moderate,
even behind-the-times, Law 83 recognized the right to form unions (subject to a
slew of conditions), and economic policies combined protectionism with a rather
timid taste of state intervention. But by 1934 exports were back to their prede-
pression value, and industry was growing at the same modest rate as before 1929.
Partisan confrontations in rural areas and growing class cleavages in the cities were
toned down by a 1933 Peruvian invasion of Leticia, a small southeastern protru-
sion, resulting in a war that led to an increased sense of national unity.

In 1934, López gained election as president but did not initially have control of
the congress. Unlike his predecessor, he believed in party government, not bipartis-
san coalition. Gaining a congressional majority in 1935, he managed to enact important parts of his Revolucíon en Marcha, a very rough functional equivalent of
Roosevelt's New Deal, although a relatively pale shadow of Cárdenas's program in
Mexico. Overhaul of the regressive tax system to include levies on income and
wealth, expansion of education, an import-substitution program of industrialization bolstered by protective tariffs, and a beginning of agrarian reform were
among his major accomplishments, along with a 1936 election law that ended lit-

eracy and property requirements for voting. However, even this was too much for much of the moderate wing of what was after all an elite-led Liberal Party. Critics thought it differed too little from the preaching of "wild radical" dissident Jorge Eliécer Gaitán Ayala (b. 1898) and his Revolutionary Left National Union (UNIR, Spanish for "to unite"). Those who had any inkling that López wanted to bring Gaitán and his followers back into the Liberal Party fold and use them to move it leftward were irate toward the president.[4]

In 1937, López lost control of both the congress and his party, in part a victim of the single four-year term, which had the effect of prematurely clipping his political wings. Liberal rural bosses were unhappy with his emphasis on urban labor and concerned over his lack of cooperation with their efforts to regain ground at the local level lost during the long era of Conservative domination, a venture that required both patronage and use of government agencies to disadvantage, if not harass, political enemies. For if Conservatives might be considered rivals in the cities, in the countryside, where politics was a bare-knuckle game—make no bones about it—they were your enemies, often backed up by blood feuds going back at least as far as the turn of the century Thousand Days' War. This intraparty dissatisfaction led to a shift away from reformist López toward the moderate wing, in which Eduardo Santos (b. 1888) was the rising star. By late 1937, Santos defeated Dário Echandia, López's choice, for the Liberal Party nomination. The still-divided Conservative Party decided not to run a candidate against Santos, backing him as a great improvement over the "radical" López. So in 1938 Santos became president in a walkover. Santos's four years in office were marked by a reorientation of policies toward capitalist industrial and agricultural development. His most significant reform was to remove education from control by the Catholic Church, and he reached agreement with the Vatican requiring that henceforth bishops and higher prelates be Colombian citizens.

López staged a comeback in 1942, since the moderates lacked any eligible candidate of his national stature, and Gaitán's radical wing was only in the process of reintegration into the party. Defeating a dissident moderate Liberal backed by Santos, who received an impressive 41 percent of the vote in an election lacking a Conservative Party contender, López pledged to complete the unfinished work of his "Revolution on the March." Unfortunately, wartime economic conditions were not conducive to costly social programs. The moderate factions of the Liberals and Conservatives voted together to control the congress and thwart López. Aided greatly by Santos's *El Tiempo*, the country's most influential newspaper, López's intraparty rivals and interparty foes capitalized on a series of improprieties by members of the president's family, although none by the president himself, to keep him on the defensive and wear him down. After the embarrassment of being held prisoner by army officers in the southern city of Pasto, López decreed a state of siege, using the exceptional powers it gave him to greatly accelerate organization of unions. This strengthening of a labor power base sparked intensified personal attacks from ex-president Santos and his followers.[5]

López, who had already experienced the uncomfortable feeling of impending lame-duck impotence in 1937, resigned in 1945. The uneventful remaining year of his term was served by young Alberto Lleras Camargo, who considerably later would be enshrined in the pantheon of outstanding Colombian presidents alongside López, but certainly not for anything he did in this caretaker stint—during which he avoided being politically sandwiched between Santos and Gaitán by forming a National Union government with the moderate Conservative faction of Mariano Ospina Pérez.

By 1946, the Liberal Party was so deeply split that, like US Republicans in 1912, they had two candidates competing on election day. Gabriel Turbay was a moderate with long mainstream service to the party. Jorge Eliécer Gaitán, a unique figure in the annals of Latin America, not just Colombia, was a charismatic spellbinder and as much an outsider, more for his dark color than for lower-class origins per se, as Benjamin Disraeli had originally been to the British political establishment in the mid-nineteenth century. Turbay was running for an office he had had his eye set upon since youth, and Gaitán, a spoiler at this point, was running to take the party away from him and move it to the left. The last-minute candidacy of Ospina Pérez (b. 1891), scion of a highly respected traditional conservative family, ended sixteen years during which that party had not put up a presidential candidate. Ospina Pérez received only 566,000 votes (42 percent) to Turbay's 437,000 votes Gaitán had obtained 364,000 votes and clearly cost Turbay a probable victory.[6]

For his first two years, Ospina maintained the National Union coalition from the Lleras Camargo interregnum, not feasible over the long haul once the radical and bellicose Gaitán took over the Liberal Party leadership in 1947, and strikes and civil unrest in urban areas supplemented the usual rural violence accompanying a shift of power from one party to its enemies (as the antagonism went well beyond the bounds of rivalry). By that time Ospina was losing strength within the Conservative Party to one of the most destructive leaders to master the art of turning a political drama into a tragedy: Laureano Eleutério Gómez Castro (b. 1889), leader of the reactionary faction of the Conservatives, who favored restructuring the state and society along corporatist lines. For him, this required reestablishing Conservative Party hegemony as it had been at the beginning of the century, no matter if this necessitated approximating genocide. Like inquisitioners of the sixteenth and seventeenth centuries, he was doing God's will, an end justifying any means.[7]

Gaitán's faction won 55 percent of the Liberal votes in the 1947 congressional elections, in which the Liberal total of 806,000 significantly exceeded the conservatives' 654,000. So the Liberal Party decided by late 1947 that it would march into the late 1950 elections united behind Gaitán. Given the decided demographic edge they held over Conservatives Party voters, this decision made Gaitán's election a near certainty, and he would not stop short of a Cárdenas–type revolutionary administration, as López had, but would go beyond it. The radical transformation of Colombia he had in mind would leave the Conservative Party with no political future as surely as Perón's regime was doing in Argentina. The task of stopping this political "anti–Christ," as Gómez viewed Gaitán, could not be left to the ballot box; a bullet would be much surer. On April 9, 1948, in the heart of Bogotá, the deed was done.

In the short run Gaitán's murder triggered the *Bogotazo* (rampant rioting in the capital), in which at least 2,000 perished in an orgy of rioting, and much of downtown Bogotá was destroyed. In the medium run it opened the way for Gómez to become president. In the slightly longer run it unleashed *La Violencia* ("The Violence"), the closest approximation to genocide Latin America has experienced, ravaging the country through 1953 and leaving nearly 300,000 bodies in its wake.[8] A virtual lame duck, and with liberals and conservatives rapidly approaching a state of civil war in the countryside, Ospina banned all public meetings in March 1949 and then removed liberal governors from office, putting an end to even a pretense of national union. In November Gómez refused to consider any accord with the liberals (to him "damned heretic Protestants"), the liberals proposed impeachment of Ospina Pérez, and the president reacted by declaring a state of siege entailing closing of legislative bodies and suspension of civil liberties. With elections moved up a year to November 27, 1949, Gómez was chosen president by a vote of 1.14 million to 14 as the Liberal Party boycotted what it considered fraudulent elections. Gómez had long wanted to be president in the worst possible way. Now he was.

Gómez was a reactionary's reactionary, classifiable as an ultraright, near-fascist, fanatical Catholic. Often expressing a desire to return Colombia to the days of Ferdinand and Isabella, he officially called for a "Hispanic counterrevolution." An end to separation of church and state was an early priority goal, and fiscal austerity and attraction of foreign capital were cornerstones of his rather primitive economic policy, centering on dismantling almost everything done under Liberal presidents. Still, favorable exports and increasing foreign investment provided a reasonable degree of prosperity. But with deaths from politically motivated violence passing 200,000 with no end in sight, Gómez went too far when he tried to push through a constitution involving a concentration of powers that would make the president a near autocrat, reduce the congress to a rubber stamp, and centralize authority in Bogotá. He had been on leave from the presidency since November 1951 because of health problems, leaving the conduct of governmental affairs in the hands of presidential designate Roberto Urdaneta. Attempting to reassume office in June 1953, Gómez was blocked by a coalition of all political factions except Laureanista conservatives, and Colombia's first successful military coup in over a century installed General Gustavo Rojas Pinilla (b. 1900) in power.[9]

Starting with broad support, this general, whose political ties had been to the Conservatives, alienated supporters. For he was an ardent of right-wing Dominican dictator Rafael Trujillo, who blatantly attempted to entrench himself in power garbed in the much more elegant political robes of a Peronist. Originally Rojas staffed his government with Ospinista Conservatives, but early on he offered an amnesty to Liberal insurgents. Assuming a more populist stance, he made late 1953 and 1954 tax reforms that angered coffee growers and industrialists, who were hardest hit. Heavy public works expenditures led to balance-of-payments problems, accompanied by inflation and capital flight. The final straw was setting up a National Secretariat of Social Assistance (SENDAS) along the lines of the Evita Perón Foundation and putting his daughter in charge. When she was booed at the Bogotá bull ring, Rojas Pinilla turned his security goon squads loose on the offending spectators.

As the period ended, leaders of the Liberals and Conservatives were beginning to consult on a plan for Gómez's removal. The dictator's efforts to fuse urban workers and the peasantry together in a political base to counter the elite's traditional domination of Colombia's politics posed a threat to both parties, and his reduction of the death toll of *La Violencia* by half through repression did not win him the allegiance of the middle sectors—not with this improvement still translating into at least fifteen thousand deaths a year.

Peru: The Army Versus APRA, Doom for Democracy

The depression-influenced overthrow of Leguía in 1930, given his modernizing and populist, if not deeply reformist, orientation, like Yrigoyen's ouster in Argentina, allowed the return to power of backward-looking advocates of the old order. It was in opposition to this retrograde tendency that Victor Raúl Haya de la Torre would build the Popular Revolutionary Alliance of the Americas (APRA) into a mass movement. But the military would not permit the *Apristas* to come to power, even outlawing the party from 1934 to 1945. In that year conservative Manuel Prado—in power since 1939—allowed APRA limited legality, soon erased by a military coup leading to the decade-long semidictatorial regime of General Manuel Odría.[10]

By 1930, Leguía's policies had earned him the animosity of important groups: Agro-exporters were alienated by his economic policies, traditional landowners resented his expansion of political organization into "their" fiefdoms, and the provinces in general looked askance at his lavishing public works upon Lima while turning a cold shoulder to their wants. Economic decline, which was reflected in unemployment and popular dissatisfaction, left the autocratic chief executive vulnerable in much the same basic way as were his counterparts in Brazil, Argentina, and Colombia when the full weight of the depression was felt. Hence, the man who was probably the most outstanding political leader Peru had yet seen fell in August 1930 before a coup headed by Colonel Luis Sánchez Cerro (b. 1890), commander of the Arequipa garrison.

Initial consensus dissipated rapidly as it became clear that the new administration, like that of General Uriburu in Argentina, was heading back toward the pre-Legúia days, perhaps even toward conditions that had prevailed before Legúia had first come to power in 1908. Challenged by rival governments controlled by middle-sector elements in regional centers, Sánchez Cerro agreed to new elections in October 1931. He used his anti-Legúia role, Indian appearance, lower-class background, and personal appeal to build an ad hoc movement of an updated *caudillo* nature. He was opposed by the programatically based APRA, a mass movement that would mobilize plurality support up through the 1980s. Founded in Mexico in 1924 by Victor Raúl Haya de la Torre (b. 1895), the unchallenged leader well into his, and the party's, old age, APRA preached a complex populist ideology with a near-religious fervor, operating out of a network of "houses of the people." Born into a downwardly mobile family, Haya de la Torre had been imprisoned and exiled to Mexico following the failure of a violent protest against Legúia in 1923. Thus he bore firsthand witness to the Calles period of trying to bring order out of Mexico's revolutionary chaos.

Mixing Andean indigenist and Marxist ideas, *Aprismo* (as the movement, its program, and the ideology originally expounded by Haya de la Torre's mentor, José Carlos Mariátegui [1895–1930] were all called) advocated an anti-imperialist and antioligarchic alliance of middle sectors, workers, and peasants, placing the latter in the central role Marx had reserved for the proletariat. APRA's 1931 program featured a state-led mixed economy complete with central planning, government development banks, and nationalization of strategic economic sectors, with foreign investment on terms set by the state. Tariff protection, progressive direct taxation of export sectors, agrarian reform, and universal adult suffrage for a corporatist-structured government were other key proposals. In short, from the viewpoint of the conservative groups that had overthrown Legúia, *Aprismo* was much more threatening than programs they had already found clearly unacceptable.[11]

A hierarchical structure, with Haya even more its maximum chief than was Calles in Mexico, APRA expected to come to power through the 1931 election. As the electorate embraced 25 percent of all adult males compared to only 15 percent in 1919 (and only 15 percent of them registered as white), APRA's confidence seemed justified. But when the vote tabulating was finished, the official results gave Sánchez Cerro 51 percent to Haya's 35 percent. The "outdated, reactionary personalist" had managed to combine victory in the landlord-controlled interior provinces with support from Lima's *lumpen* proletariat to thwart political progress. In *Aprista* eyes—and not unreasonably, given both the past history of Peruvian elections and the situation in other Latin American countries at the time—the elections had been fraud-ridden and hence were invalid. Had not this been the outcome in Brazil a short year before? Violence and near civil war followed the outlawing of the party. Having witnessed many of their comrades massacred by the army, *Aprista* rebels near the northern city of Trujillo seized control of their leader's hometown in July 1932 and killed imprisoned army officers before laying down their arms. Rather than being forgotten over time, a sense of outrage would be kept alive in the mythology and lore of the Peruvian military and used as a justification for barring from power the "cowardly murderers," a category extended to embrace all *Apristas*, even if they had not been born at the time. This veto would have a paralyzing and distorting effect upon Peruvian national life until the mid-1980s. Still, on occasion APRA would find some sympathy in the form of junior officer support for its revolts—like the sympathy the Radical Party had encountered in Argentina in the 1890s.

In April 1933, *Apristas* retaliated for the slaughter of their supporters after the Trujillo incident by assassinating Sánchez Cerro, giving General Oscar Benevides a chance to come back to power; he was selected by the constituent assembly to serve out Sánchez Cerro's term. When *Apristas* rebelled again in 1934, the party was again outlawed, being subjected to severe repression until 1945. Benevides came into office with the depression having shrunk government revenues to only $19 million and his predecessor having defaulted on Peru's foreign debt. In 1933, petroleum provided three-fifths of the government's meager income. As other sectors of the economy stabilized, a rise in revenues to $50 million reduced dependence on petroleum to one-fourth. Establishing a social security system for industrial workers and building low-cost housing in Lima as well as highways everywhere, Benevides rode out the depression, along the way canceling the 1936 electoral outcome and extending his term, even adopting some of the reforms proposed by the *Apristas*, if only to appease and coopt part of their potential electoral base.

Taking over in 1939 as the official candidate in a controlled election, civilian aristocrat Manuel Prado Ugarteche (b. 1889) allowed unions to organize, doubled the number of government jobs for the middle class, and reduced the cost of basic foodstuffs in the cities. A much more able politician than his military predecessor, Prado relaxed persecution of the *Apristas* without endangering internal order. In so doing he made skillful use of a successful border war with Ecuador in 1941 as well as improved wartime economic conditions. The political situation, already improved under Prado, looked even better after World War II. Peru took part in the region's general swing toward democracy in the immediate postwar period.

In 1945, a broad center-left coalition carried a distinguished jurist from the Arequipan middle class into office. José Luis Bustamante y Rivera (b. 1894) received two-thirds of the vote—a significant part of it from *Apristas* integrated into his National Democratic Front. At 28 percent of the adult male population, voting was up modestly from the last competitive balloting in 1931. Continuing the trend of the Benevides and Prado governments, Bustamente's policies favored industrialization and the urban middle and popular groups. Export sectors were hit hard by tax increases, and tariff and credit policies benefited industry. Housing and school construction programs were continued. Still, the coalition fell apart as APRA sought to dominate the administration from its dominant position in the congress. As APRA bested the communists within the labor movement and sought advantages for rural workers and tenants opposed by landlords, the political situation wavered between polarization and impasse. In July 1947, Bustamonte's conservative opponents used an obscure legal provision to close the congress, allowing the president to rule by decree.

Following an attempted coup by APRA, on October 27, 1948, the military seized power behind General Manuel Odría (b. 1897), who would hold office into 1956 by way of an election in 1950 legitimizing his occupation of the presidency. Odría's chief backers were the agro-exporters, anxious to be back on top, where they were certain God intended them to be. Odría's personalistic authoritarian regime, under which APRA was heavily repressed, attracted foreign investment and stimulated industrialization, although much of it was by multinationals. US direct investment grew rapidly, heavily concentrated during the 1950s in mining before subsequently diversifying into manufacturing and banking. Large increases in exports followed on the heels of these investments, and the US strategic stockpiling of minerals in the early 1950s stimulated exports of lead and zinc as well as copper and iron ore. New irrigation projects on the coast led to rapid increases in production and export of sugar and cotton, but existing oil fields neared exhaustion.[12]

Proclaiming himself "anti-union, but pro-worker," the paternalistic authoritarian provided substantial material benefits to the most organized mass strata. Creating a labor ministry, he extended social security coverage and lavished special attention upon the housing field. Straddling the old and the new in a simpler version of what Vargas had done in Brazil, he built a network of political support among conservative landowners through rather traditional political brokerage and massive irrigation projects for the sugar and cotton producers, at the same time cultivating a new personal power base among the teeming population of the squatter settlements ringing Lima (the *callampas,* or "mushroom slums"). With an eye on both Perón's Argentina and the Peronist-type governments in Bolivia and Chile after 1952, he used his wife's charitable activities to cultivate slum dwellers' community organizations.

Odría calculatingly harked back to Legúia as architect of the good old days, launching a trebling of construction expenditures during the Korean War export boom. But that ended, and by 1955 he faced increasing political opposition, beginning with the agro-exporters, who felt he had abandoned them, his original backers, for the populist road. Again, as at the end of the preceding period with earlier strongman Legúia, the provinces resented the concentration of public works and expenditures in the capital region. By late 1955, Odría was encountering formidable political opposition for the first time. The next year he would give in to it and hold elections—the first in which women voted—and see his candidate trounced.

Venezuela: Dictatorship, Democracy, and Dictatorship Again

The 1930s in Venezuela found Juan Vicente Gómez and his cronies still firmly entrenched in power as they had been for two decades. Hence, nothing changed until after his death from natural causes at the end of 1935. Even then he cast a long shadow, as General Eleazer López Contreras (b. 1883), the dictator's defense minister, presided over a controlled transition—confirmed as president by the congress—until 1941. Tolerant of change at first, he tightened up under criticism from his peers and expressions of concern by foreign investors—before relaxing restrictions again after a general strike. In that initial liberalizing phase, Rómulo Betancourt (b. 1908) and fellow young Marxist associates formed the Venezuelan Revolutionary Organization (ORVE), which then joined in the "April bloc" with other progressive parties that had sprung up. The congress, a carryover from the Gómez Era, reacted harshly to all this unwonted, and to them unwanted, leftist activity, which also involved a flurry of union organization.[13]

The July 1936 constitution was a major disappointment to liberals and radicals, since it did not contain major reforms and they had been hoping for something at least along the lines of the 1917 Mexican revolutionary constitution. In October the umbrella National Democratic Party (PDN) was denied legalization. A hastily enacted labor law, to be the carrot in a carrot-and-stick approach by the government toward the working class, fell short of both the 1931 Brazilian law and the 1924 Chilean one. Then in 1940, López Contreras, now cozied up to the conservatives, withdrew legal recognition from a third of the existing unions. Shortly thereafter he turned the presidency over to his defense minister, General Isaias Medina Angarita (b. 1897)—ratified by an election in which under 5 percent of the population voted.

In the favorable political climate of the World War II period, party activity finally flourished, led by Democratic Action (AD), successor to the ill fated PDN; the Independent Electoral Organizing Committee (COPEI); and the Democratic Republican Union (URD). Medina agreed with Betancourt and AD on a mutually acceptable presidential candidate for 1945, but health problems undercut this effort at unity, and AD joined young officers in an October 1945 coup. Thus began the *trienio,* three years of boisterous, dramatic, and—in the short run—unsuc-cessful radical political reform. The initial seven-man junta contained four repre-sentatives of AD and two from the army, with Betancourt soon presiding over a "Revolutionary Governing Council." He quickly changed the 1946 petroleum law to provide for an unprecedented 50-50 split of revenues between the oil com-panies and the government. Moreover, foreign companies in Venezuela were re-quired to invest in nonextractive productive activities, and a new constitution with a social welfare orientation was promulgated. Elections at all levels were made di-rect, with all citizens over eighteen entitled to vote.

Although abruptly ended by a military coup in late 1948, this learning period would result in the successful implantation of democracy a decade later. In this process Betancourt, who had spent his second exile in 1939–1941 observing Chile's democratic practices, gained experience that would prove invaluable as he guided the country's destinies in the 1958–1963 period. For under his youthful leadership AD polled nearly 1.1 million votes (71 percent of the total) in the late 1946 elections for a constituent assembly, giving them 137 of 160 seats, and with support from 70 percent of the electorate, it won control of the congress and placed respected novelist Rómulo Gallegos (b. 1884) in the presidency in Decem-ber 1947—as the electorate exploded to over 35 percent of the population (as women voted for the first time).[14] With a high degree of fusion between party and state, Betancourt remained the country's chief political operator, and another future president from the generation of 1928, Raúl Leoni, served as the extremely active labor minister. Land reform and organization of the peasants received prior-ity attention, enrollment in primary education nearly quadrupled, and govern-ment oil revenues doubled. Yet this "damn the torpedoes, full speed ahead" strategy, by going too far, too fast, on too many fronts, catalyzed a classic backlash mobilization, one aggravated by US Cold War desire for stable anticommunist regimes—particularly one in a major supplier of oil located in close proximity to the Panama Canal. Other parties were alienated by the "arrogant, monopolistic" stance of AD, which denied them an opportunity to build a popular base, and concerned by Betancourt's oil policy, the military listened to US interests.[15]

Opposition coalesced around López Contreras; then conspirators who found that ex-president too right-wing gravitated to Medina Angarita. Awareness of this plotting pushed AD into a more antimilitary mood, leading to consideration of arming organized workers and setting up a peasant militia as had been done in early 1930s Mexico. The sense of impending crisis spurred AD to further speed up the already hectic pace of organizing both urban and rural masses. In October 1948, a radical agrarian reform law was enacted. The AD government's relations with COPEI, a Christian Democratic Party, and the Catholic Church deteriorated from uneasy to openly hostile. Hence, COPEI founder Rafael Caldera Rodríguez (b. 1916), a leading spokesman for the "generation of 1935" (activist university students at the end of the Gómez era), and rising leader Luis Herrera Campíns (b. 1925)—both future presidents—shed no tears when on November 24, 1948, many of the same officers who had helped AD come to power in 1945 staged a coup to oust it. Although conservative economic interests and the international oil companies were jubilant over this turn of events, Venezuela's communists were also far from unhappy, since AD had been squeezing them out of an erstwhile dominant role in the urban labor movement.

Developments in the political sphere disappointed the parties that had opposed the Gallegos government. Colonel Carlos Delgado Chalbaud (b. 1909), minister of defense during the *trienio,* originally headed the military junta, which set out to dismantle the state-labor alliance and demobilize AD's organized popular base. The party was banned, as was its labor arm, the Venezuelan Workers Confederation, and AD leaders went to jail or exile, or they hid. In November 1950, before he could try to become constitutional president, as his contemporary Odría had just done in Peru, Delgado Chalbaud was murdered by security agents linked to one of his junta mates, the extremely ambitious Colonel Marcos Pérez Jiménez (b. 1914). PJ, as he came to be known, controlled the government from his post as minister of defense until seizing the presidency at the beginning of December 1952. He went beyond his ill-fated predecessor in reversing the economic and social policies of the AD *trienio*, particularly in rural areas.[16]

Close to Dominican Republican dictator Rafael Trujillo and attuned to developments in Peru as well as Argentina, Pérez Jiménez established an Independent Electoral Front (FEI) to carry him through an election in which COPEI and the URD could safely be allowed to participate as legitimizers, with the stronger AD banned and repressed. This scenario was knocked into a cocked hat when voters overwhelmingly cast their ballots for the URD's Jovito Villalba. Alleging widespread power failures, the dictator interrupted the vote counting; a week later he was announced as the winner. Since the URD was understandably reluctant to accept perhaps the greatest electoral fraud ever perpetrated in a region that was accustomed to the manipulation of election returns, it, too, was outlawed. By the beginning of 1953, the country was free of any organized opposition activity.

Once again Venezuela was under the heel of a *Tachirense* (a native of the Andean province of Táchira) *caudillo* dictator—one at least as ruthless as his professed role model, Gómez, had been, but nowhere near as able. Still, conditions were favorable for Pérez Jiménez, as industry grew rapidly for a tremendous expansion of oil production because the dictator abandoned the AD program of husbanding this precious nonrenewable resource. More effective at repression than construction, this authoritarian regime would survive only into 1958 (shortly after its counterpart in Colombia under Rojas Pinilla had met its end).

ARTURO ALESSANDRI

Chile: Redemocratization and the Old Dictator as a Populist

The period from 1930 through 1955 would see a good deal of political change in Chile. Oddly, it began with Colonel Carlos Ibáñez del Campo's losing his hold on dictatorial power and closed with retired General Ibáñez halfway through a term as a freely elected president governing Chile as a semi-Peronist. In between, the country had a brief experience with revolving-door presidents, an encore performance by 1920s democratic chief executive Arturo Alessandri, a popular front government, and a Cold War–era president elected with communist votes but shifting to the right. Meanwhile, copper would assume the importance previously held by nitrates.[17]

When Ibáñez formed the congress in 1930, the seats were allocated among the political parties according to previous negotiations, with Ibáñez's infant new organization getting a junior partner's share. The 1931 elections produced a victory for Juan Esteban Montero Rodríguez, the military strongman's minister of interior, supported by the Conservative, Liberal, Democratic, and Radical Parties. Unable to develop an effective program, as these parties supported different policies and had different ideas about Chile's political future, Montero drifted to the right until overthrown in June 1932. After extreme instability a self-declared "socialist republic" headed by Colonel Marmaduke Grove lasted only twelve days in September 1932 before being replaced by the moderate Carlos Dávila Espinoza, who shifted back toward Ibáñez-like policies during his brief passage through the presidency.

Two additional provisional presidents later and Alessandri was back in office, courtesy of an October 30, 1932, election in which he received 54.7 percent of the vote to 17.7 percent for Grove, running from exile. Candidate of the Democrats and Radicals, he was supported by many Liberals tired of the political turmoil and, in retrospect, reacting positively to his earlier presidency. (As pointed out in Chapter 1, nothing makes a president look better than less successful successors.) As in Yrigoyen's encore performance in Argentina after 1928, and as it would be with Alfonso López in Colombia a decade later, those who expected a renewed wave of reform measures were quickly disappointed as Liberals and even Conservatives played major roles in policymaking. Conservative Gustavo Ross as treasury minister followed orthodox recovery-from-depression policies designed to get business on its feet. In a development that would have its major impact substantially later, the Chilean Socialist Party was founded in 1933. For the upper and middle classes the uneventful Alessandri administration was even more comforting than the Justo administration was to their counterparts in Argentina.[18]

The 1938 elections found politically conscious Chileans concerned about the sad turn of events in Spain, where the Civil War had turned in favor of Franco's fascistic Nationalists. The Comintern's policy of popular fronts of democratic and antifascist forces made the Chilean Communist Party (PCCh) available for alliances, so right-wing Radical Pedro Aguirre Cerda (b. 1878) had both Socialist and Communist backing, along with that of the fading Democrats, and also received considerable support from admirers of Ibáñez and elements of the right unhappy with the Liberal-Conservative coalition's candidate. These two parties of the right came away from the polls with 48 percent of the seats in the lower house, compared to 40 percent for the popular front parties, led by the Radicals at 20 percent and the Socialists with 13 percent. In this politically uncomfortable situation, centrist Aguirre Cerda found himself reassuring the right because of his unwillingness to rely on the left. In fact, this was the dilemma of the Radical Party, with a wing leaning in each direction. By the premature end of Aguirre Cerda's government in 1941, immobilism was its hallmark—although there had been some industrialization, expansion of the state's role, and respect for workers' rights.

On February 1, 1942, Juan Antonio Ríos Morales (b. 1888), another right-leaning Radical, was elected president over ever-available Ibáñez, the candidate of the right—in part owing to ex-president Alessandri's pushing the Liberals into the Ríos camp. With a cabinet extending over into Liberal and business ranks, and under the slogan "To govern is to produce," Ríos promoted social stability. Suspected of profascist sympathies, he reluctantly joined the Allies at the beginning of 1943. One by-product of his administration was the ouster of Marmaduke Grove as head of the Socialist Party (for being too collaborationist) and his replacement by young Salvador Allende Gossens (b. 1908), who would be a key protagonist in the political drama and tragedy after 1955. Allende produced no miracles as the party's presidential candidate in 1946, receiving a very anemic 2.5 percent of the vote. The Socialist Party had become discredited for collaborating with a government that had produced no significant reforms and whose economic policies had allowed deterioration of working-class income relative to the income of other social sectors that were supporting opposition parties. Meanwhile, both president Ríos's possible accomplishments and potential failures were cut off when ill health forced him out of office near the end of January 1946.

On September 4 Gabriel González Videla (b. 1898), a leader of the left wing of the Radical Party, was elected president in an extremely close election over a near-reactionary candidate, with Fernando Alessandri Rodríguez as the third contender. The margin of González Videla's victory was provided by the Communist Party, which received three seats in his cabinet—which also included as finance minister future president Jorge Alessandri Rodríguez, another son of "Don Arturo." However, under heavy US pressure in 1948 González Videla enacted a "Law for the Defense of Democracy," which proscribed the PCCh, replacing it in his coalition with Liberals who had opposed his election. This was one of the most dramatic impingements of the Cold War upon politics in any Latin American country.

Foreign observers, but not individuals closely following Chilean politics, were surprised when Ibáñez, who had been serving as a senator, won the September 4, 1952, presidential election as candidate of an array of newly formed electoral vehicles (ad hoc political organizations brought into being only for one-time electoral purposes) and older splinter parties: the Agrarian Labor Party (PAL), the Popular Socialist Party (PSP), the Peoples' Democratic Party (PDP), the Doctrinaire Radical Party (PRD), and the National Christian Party (PNC), among others. In a general rejection of the traditional parties, a near majority of the electorate (46.8 percent) decided to gamble on Ibáñez's recent rebirth as a Peronist—in the first balloting that included women. The candidate of the right received less than 28 percent, and the candidate of the left, Socialist senator Salvador Allende, trailed badly with a mere 5.5 percent. (Eighteen years and three tries later, he would come out on top—a victory that had fatal consequences.) Electoral reform and legalization of the Communist Party led the list of Ibáñez's political accomplishments, although there was little positive on the economic side of the ledger. As the period ended, Ibáñez was pondering the implications for him and his government of Perón's recent fall from power.[19]

Bolivia: National Trauma and Revolution

This would be a crucial period for Bolivia, probably the most decisive of its life. As the 1930s opened, the new president, Daniel Salamanca Urey (b. 1868), a leader of the 1920 and 1930 coups, found that he had finally come to power—at the wrong time. He quickly lost patience with social and political unrest stemming from his inability to get a handle on the country's escalating economic crisis (as if anyone could under the circumstances), ruthlessly repressing all opposition, including that of those who had been his allies in ousting Bautista Saavedra from office shortly before. Aggressively supporting Bolivian colonization of the Gran Chaco, a large disputed border area, he led the country into a debilitating war with Paraguay. In this venture Salamanca was influenced by a false belief that the area in dispute was rich in oil, an opinion propagated by foreign advisers.

The Chaco War lasted from 1931 to 1935, the final peace treaty coming in 1938. Bolivian soldiers, chiefly highland Indians, fell prey to the lowland diseases of the war zone, and Argentina began to furnish aid to Paraguay. Hence, the campaign was an unrelenting series of Bolivian defeats. Of a national population totaling around 2 million, at least 50,000 troops perished, and the mobilization of 200,000 men—largely Indians—undermined the established social order. By 1952, the political fallout would have unleashed a zigzag and extremely messy run-up to a transforming revolution. As aptly described by a scholar with close ties to the country:

> The Chaco War was the catalyst that started the process of undermining the traditional economic and social system of Bolivia. Arousing the spirit of nationalism and the social consciousness of the youth of the upper and middle classes of the cities, it also had disintegrating effects on the life of the Indians, who were the great majority of the population. The war, by shattering the social and economic equilibrium of the old order, led to widespread political mobilization and intellectual ferment.[20]

A half year before the war's inglorious end, Salamanca was ousted from the presidency, with his vice president taking over as a caretaker. Elections scheduled for the end of May 1936, in the midst of continued depression resulting from the low world demand for tin, were aborted when Colonels Davíd Toro and Germán Busch (b. 1904) led a coup installing a reformist government pledged to protecting the rights and interests of veterans and labor. Under Toro's baton, its plans to build a mass party upset the established political parties, and the government sought to gain support from new political elements through nationalizing Standard Oil of Bolivia in March 1937 (more than a year before Cárdenas nationalized oil in Mexico) and creating the Bolivian National Petroleum Company. Then, in July 1937, Busch ousted his erstwhile companion in arms, his coup leading the next year to an attempt to institutionalize the postwar reforms in a radical and nationalist constitution. Falling victim to political polarization, the constituent assembly was abruptly closed down in October 1938. Beset with virulent opposition from the extreme left as well as the intransigent right, Busch committed suicide or was murdered in August 1939. During his two years in power he had established ministries of labor as well as of mines and petroleum, legalized the Confederation of Bolivian Workers, and decreed a labor code. These accomplishments would serve as a foundation upon which the progressive forces coming to power through the 1952 Revolution could build.

This noble, albeit in the short run, failed experiment to bring Bolivia up to the times led to new political alignments, which once more faced off in disloyal competition, roiling the waters of national life for a dozen years. A Socialist Party had been formed in 1936 and espoused nationalist and corporatist ideas. Composed chiefly of intellectuals and students, it quickly split, with the Independent Socialist Party giving birth to the National Revolutionary Movement (MNR) at the beginning of 1941 behind two men who, from the 1950s into the 1980s, would together accumulate five full and one fractional presidential terms. Victor Paz Estenssoro (b. 1907), an economics professor with experience working for the Patiño tin mining company, was destined to become the most influential political leader in the country's history, and Hernán Siles Zuazo (b. 1913) would rank within the next four or five.

The MNR's chief middle-run opposition came from the Bolivian Socialist Falange (FSB), founded in August 1937 by individuals familiar with Chile and its loud, but insignificant, Nazi Party and attracted to the Spanish fascistic movement of 1920s strongman Miguel Primo de Rivera. It found initial support among Catholic high school students in Bolivia's second city, Cochabamba. Among an array of small Marxist parties the Party of the Revolutionary Left (PIR), founded in 1940, temporarily stood out. With roots among the teachers' and railroad workers' unions, it advocated a nationalist bourgeois revolution in alliance with a multiclass movement, but it became politically irrelevant by 1950. The PIR faced competition from the Revolutionary Workers' Party (POR), founded in exile at the end of 1934 and containing a strong Trotskyite current. In the early 1940s, it was absorbed into the Socialist Workers' Party of Bolivia (PSOB). This confusion of names and ideologies on the far left proved to be of little consequence, since the MNR would steal the wind from its sails much as Peronism emasculated the Marxist and Marxist-Leninist parties in Argentina. (The fractionalized extreme-left would first fascinate, then quickly alienate, young Ernesto "Che" Guevara when he arrived in Bolivia from Argentina, in what proved to be a long journey winding up fatally back where it started.)

The oligarchy's return to power after Busch's convenient demise was both uneasy and short-lived. Strongly pro-Allies conservative General Enrique Peñaranda was put in through a rigged election in 1940, only to preside over the massacre of Catavi tin miners at the end of 1942, in which three hundred strikers were killed, an event that would eventually lead to his ouster by a field-grade officers' coup a year later. Lieutenant Colonel Gualberto Villaroel (b. 1908), leader of a secret military lodge roughly equivalent to Argentina's GOU, followed an orientation basically similar to that of the martyred Busch. Overthrown by an "antifascist democratic front" and lynched by an enraged mob in mid-1946, Villaroel was succeeded by agents of the absentee "tin barons." This effort to bring back the past would end with a bang in 1952 as a real revolution would bring to power the young middle-class radicals who had imparted a reformist tone to Villaroel's ill-fated government. For beginning in 1940 the middle class and part of the upper class shifted their support from the traditional parties, providing the MNR with a multiclass constituency.

Although he was forced to campaign from exile in Argentina, Paz Estenssoro emerged the victor in May 1951 presidential balloting, with 43 percent of the still extremely restricted electorate of well under 200,000 in a country with a population of 3 million. In the absence of a candidate with a majority of the vote, the final electoral decision rested with the congress. At this point President Mamerto Urrolagoitia evaded responsibility by turning power over to the ranking officer of the armed forces. Annulling the elections, he in turn installed General Hugo Ballián as interim president. This was one effort too many by the beneficiaries of the old order to "hold the lid on the garbage can." On April 8, 1952, the minister of internal security opened up the La Paz armories to the MNR and its aroused supporters, and on April 11 the top military officers fled into exile. On April 16 Paz Estenssoro arrived from Buenos Aires and was sworn in as president. As had been the case in Brazil in 1930, he was considered the constitutional president as the presumed winner of the 1951 elections.[21] Intelligent and politically astute, Paz realized that long-run success depended on defining a new model of political economy within which society could develop and also constructing stable links between state and society through construction of new political institutions.

Events moved far and fast during Paz's first administration, when the practical dilemma was accumulating capital while at least partially meeting demands for social justice. Economically Bolivia was light-years behind Perón's Argentina. Electoral reform gave the vote to women, did away with literacy restrictions, and reduced the voting age to eighteen for married citizens (it remained at twenty-one for singles). Hence, the 1960 electorate would jump to a million, with 26 percent of the population voting instead of only 5 percent. The tin mines of the Patiño, Aramayo, and Hochchild family enterprises were nationalized and merged as the state-owned Bolivian Mining Corporation (COMIBOL). This action alone transferred from the private to the public sector the control over 85 percent of Bolivia's tin production and 95 percent of its foreign exchange receipts, and the generation of 50 percent of central government fiscal revenues.[22]

Acutely sensitive to the fact that the army had blocked them from attaining power in the 1947–1951 period, the MNR government began to politicize and proselytize it, favoring MNR sympathizers in promotions and assignments and establishing party cells within its ranks. Efforts to establish control over unions, particularly the miners' union, ran into difficulty owing to the influence already embedded in them by extreme left-wing parties and movements. The way was more open in the rural field, where direct action by organized *campesinos* pushed the government's hand, bringing about an agrarian reform that was in good part an effort to legalize and channel what was already taking place semispontaneously. Bolivia's rural working population had previously been familiar only with the short and dirty end of the stick. At the time of the Chaco War, only twenty years back, most of them had been landless peasants *(colonos),* performing laborious services for their landowner patrons in return for a roof over their heads. Indeed, their conditions of life were very similar to those of Mexican peons before the 1910 Revolution. Despite limited improvement during the few periods of reformist governments, including that of the MNR after 1952, these *campesinos* were very much an exploited underclass. By the mid-1950s, they were increasingly unwilling to tolerate this injustice, as the ensuing periods would demonstrate.

Ecuador: Velasco Ibarra Versus the Field

The 1930s were an especially turbulent decade for Ecuador, with fourteen individuals occupying the presidency, most in very brief provisional or interim capacities. In August 1931, President Isidro Ayora resigned and fled the country, and the campaign for the end-of-1933 elections involved considerable bloodshed. On the political scene in the 1920s and running unsuccessfully for the presidency in 1928, but gaining a national following as presiding officer of the Chamber of Deputies, José María Velasco Ibarra (b. 1893) was swept into power by the voters in 1934. This charismatic demagogue would occupy center stage in Ecuador's national life as the providential man not only of the 1930s, but also of every decade into the 1970s. Within a year of first coming to office, he was ousted after attempting to dissolve the congress and jail his leading opponents. Following an interim military junta until constituent assembly elections in mid-1938, in 1940 "the Great Absentee" (a title stemming from his repeated exiles) returned to mount a dynamic campaign.[23]

Robbed of victory by fraud perpetrated in a limited-participation election by supporters of Liberal Carlos Alberto Arroyo del Rio (b. 1893), Velasco Ibarra was able to make a comeback in the aftermath of a disastrous 1941–1942 war with Peru that cost the country 200,000 square kilometers of land containing access to the headwaters of the Amazon River. Running in 1944 as the candidate of a heterogeneous coalition called the Ecuadorian Democratic Alliance and including both the Communist and Conservative Parties, he stormed to victory in the June elections—even though he had to campaign from exile—as enraged followers forced Arroyo del Rio to resign on May 29. Shifting to the right in the nascent

Cold War context of 1946, the stormy petrel of Ecuadorian politics was expelled by a military coup the following year.

Velasco Ibarra's second expulsion from office ushered in Ecuador's first sustained experience with constitutional civilian electoral rule. In September 1948, Galo Plaza Lasso (b. 1906), a decendent of 1860s–1870s president Leonidas Plaza Guitiérrez, narrowly defeated the Conservative Party's candidate and reaped the benefits of a banana boom that by 1950 had made this tropical fruit the mainstay of the economy and made Ecuador the leading banana-producing country in the world. In this economically favorable context Velasco Ibarra not only was elected in 1952 but actually served out his full term. The "national personification," as he relished being called, came to power this time with the support of the Guayaquil-based Concentration of Popular Forces, but he would still govern with his intensely personalistic style. Velasquismo was the movement that introduced mass politics to the country and under which a large proportion of individuals playing leading political roles to the end of the century experienced their political socialization.[24] It would dominate most of the ensuing period.

Uruguay: Hard Days for Democracy

This was an extremely trying time for Uruguayan democrats. Colorado Gabriel Terra (b. 1873) was duly elected in 1930 but made himself dictator in 1933 through a coup abetted by the Blancos under their longtime leader Luis Alberto de Herrera (b. 1875). A new fully presidential constitution gave Terra a term lasting to 1938, when he saw his brother-in-law and war minister, General Alfredo Baldomir (b. 1884), elected to the presidency in the first election that included women. In 1942, Baldomir attempted to end the coalition agreement with the Blancos, adding fuel to the country's political fires. He was replaced in 1943 by Juan José Amezaga. Luis Batlle Berres (b. 1897), nephew of the great Batlle y Or-dóñez, came to the presidency in 1947 after Amezaga died, and he engaged in a power struggle with his cousins until the end of his term in 1951. Then the constitutional amendment instituting a plural executive with the titular presidency rotating yearly among its majority members went into effect.[25]

Paraguay: Another War Before
Recovery from the Last Catastrophe

Not yet fully recovered from the devastating war of the 1860s, Paraguay went to war with Bolivia in 1932 over the remote and desolate Chaco region. Holding off the German-trained Bolivian troops, Paraguay achieved an honorable truce in 1935, and in the 1938 treaty it gained title to almost all of the 20,000-square-mile contested area—at the cost of thirty-five thousand troops killed. War hero Rafael

Franco (b. 1897) seized the presidency in early 1936, ousting Eusebio Ayala and ending thirty-two years of Liberal Party rule. This founder of the *Febreristas* (a name taken from the month of their successful revolt) began a program of agrarian reform but was ousted in mid-August 1937 by a Liberal coup that put Marshal José Félix Estigaribia (b. 1888), another hero of the war, in office as a cloak for their partisan orientation. Siding with the "new Liberals" committed to reform, he dissolved the congress and ruled as a dictator, leaving behind a brandnew constitution providing for an all-powerful state when he died in a plane crash in 1940.[26]

Pro-Nazi Higínio Morínigo (b. 1897), benefiting from wartime prosperity, held office for eight years, outlawing the "old Liberals." Trimming his sails in keeping with international winds, Morínigo revoked his ban on party activity and formed a coalition cabinet including the wary *Febreristas*. Federico Cháves (b. 1882), unable to best the rabble-rousing and less aristocratic Juan Natalicio González, built up goon squads to seize power for his branch of the Colorados. Declaring a state of siege in mid-January 1947, Morínigo defeated a revolt with help from Perón and support from Colonel Alfredo Stroessner, soon to become the country's long-lived dictator. Since the vast majority of the army had been involved in the insurrection, the Colorados were in a position to rebuild the officer corps. In the aftermath of the rigged election of González, Morínigo was ousted by a bloodless palace coup in mid-1948. Early the next year, when the interim president wanted to escape his tutelage, Cháves seized power, aided by Stroessner. Legitimized by election in mid-1950 and reelected in 1952, he managed to hold on until becoming a coup victim in May 1954. Cháves was briefly replaced by a coalition provisional president until elections in which Stroessner was the only candidate brought this, in his own eyes at least, Franco-like figure to power in mid-August—ushering in one of the longest-lived dictatorial regimes in South America's experience, one that would more than span the ensuing period.

Central America: Falling Less Far Behind

The beginning of the 1930s to the middle of the 1950s saw the countries of Central America follow increasingly differentiated paths, events in Guatemala being the most dramatic in their ups and downs, those in Costa Rica the most promising, and those in El Salvador the bloodiest.[27]

Guatemala: Revolution to Counterrevolution

In the subregion's largest country, General Jorge Ubico y Castañeda (b. 1878) came to office in 1930 and proved to be the last of Guatemala's old-style political strongmen. Having been war minister as early as 1921 and an unsuccessful presidential contender in both 1922 and 1926, he was essentially a restorer of the Estrada Cabrera model of dictatorial rule. Governing in harmony with the United Fruit Company and showing his devotion to the cause of democracy by expropriating German-owned coffee plantations, which he used for the benefit of his family and friends, Ubico tightened restrictions on the underclasses, requiring men to work far from home during the banana harvest and on public works programs. Destabilized by democratizing influences permeating rising groups in a slowly developing society in the context of World War II, he stepped down in the face of a well-orchestrated campaign of civil disobedience in April 1944.[28]

Within a few months the interim military regime was ousted by an armed movement enjoying the support of midgrade officers, and the 1944 Revolution was truly under way. The resulting junta presided over the country's first fully free direct popular election of a chief executive in March 1945. Dr. Juan José Arévalo Bermejo (b. 1904), returning from fourteen years as a professor in the interior of Argentina, hardly a relevant experience in light of the day-and-night differences between these countries, was the landslide victor in elections that for the first time included women. A self-styled "humanistic socialist," he had to govern a country with no meaningful experience in competitive politics and a severely backlogged agenda of pressing public policy issues. Moreover, Arévalo had within his government the two military members of the preceding junta, both of whom were eager to succeed him in the presidency.

The determining event of Arévalo's administration occurred in July 1947, when Chief of the Armed Forces Francisco Arana, the candidate favored by the established interests—including landowners, the United Fruit Company, and the US government—was killed by henchmen of War Minister Jacobo Arbenz Guzmán (b. 1913). The latter was supported for the presidency by the progressive and radical forces enjoying influence for the first time under the highly democratic Arévalo. The ensuing uprising by Arana's enraged supporters was repressed through arming the railroad workers and teachers, who constituted the backbone of Guatemala's fledgling labor movement. With his chief rival eliminated, Arbenz handily won the 1950 elections, becoming president in March 1951.[29]

Arévalo basically brought Guatemala belatedly into the twentieth century with his emphasis on education, establishment of a social security system, enactment of a labor code, and founding of an institute to support industrial growth—an agenda less radical than the one that would be followed in Bolivia after 1952. It remained for Arbenz to grapple with the thorny issue of agrarian reform, an issue arousing intransigent opposition from the United Fruit Company (UFCO), which controlled the country's railroads, telecommunications system, and port facilities, as well as much of its most productive land and was therefore viewed as the "Octopus," its tentacles being in all strategic sectors of national life.

The mid-1952 agrarian reform law, although largely based upon Cárdenas's 1930s program in Mexico, was partially couched in language used by eastern European communist regimes. Moreover, its implementation was largely entrusted to the Guatemalan Labor Party (PGT), the local communists. In any eventuality, United Fruit was determined to use its very considerable influence in the Eisenhower administration in the United States to protect its vested interests. Since UFCO's agents and allies possessed very close ties to US Secretary of State John Foster Dulles and CIA Director Alan Dulles, as well as a number of influential Republican senators, its intense lobbying efforts would result in a policy of isolating Guatemala internationally while preparing a covert operation to oust Arbenz from power. Supporters of the late Colonel Arana, led by Colonel Carlos Castillo Armas, were clandestinely trained in Honduras, and John Peurifoy, fresh from overseeing the final stages of the defeat of the communists in the Greek civil war, was brought in as US ambassador to Guatemala.

The drama played out rapidly in a polarizing situation. Arbenz, heavily influenced by his wife (an alienated and highly radicalized member of a Salvadorian elite family), moved closer to the local communists, while the opposition, ably abetted by the United States, drove a wedge between him and perplexed armed-forces leaders. Within nine days of a June 1954 invasion by US-backed exiles, Arbenz was himself on his way to exile, and shortly thereafter Castillo Armas was installed as president. The 1944 Revolution was ended but could not be entirely buried, although a series of would-be political undertakers would try their best to bury it.[30]

El Salvador: The Rise of Militarism

The region's only single-coast country finally enjoyed essentially honest and open elections in early 1931 under the aegis of liberalizing president Pio Romero Bosque. A moderately reformist large landowner, Arturo Araújo, was chosen by the limited electorate as his successor, only to be ousted in December after only nine months in office. This development brought to power his vice president, General Maximiliano Hernández Martínez (b. 1882). A communist-led uprising quickly followed, inspired by Augustín Farabundo Martí (b. 1893). This rebellion was soon suppressed, with over thirty thousand deaths, a very large proportion of those killed being suspected sympathizers who had taken no active part in the revolt.[31] This bloody affair, enshrined in history as La Matanza ("The Slaughter"), rather than bringing progressive change, vastly strengthened the position of the military as protectors of the established social order.

When Hernández Martínez was ousted in May 1944—in much the same manner as Ubico had been a month earlier in Guatemala—General Salvador Castañeda Castro was elected to replace him, and the leader of the 1944 revolt was exiled. (Although the franchise had been extended to women in 1939, this was their first opportunity to exercise it.) When Castañeda attempted to engineer his continuance in office, he was booted out in December 1948 by a group of midgrade officers. The strongman of the ensuing junta, Major Oscar Osório (b. 1910), was legitimized in March 1950 with three-fifths of the votes cast. Following a developmentalist orientation, roughly similar to that of Odría in Peru at that time, Osório was able to effectuate election of Lieutenant Colonel José María Lemos as his successor in March 1955. By this time the presidency had become the top rung on the army's promotion ladder.

Honduras: The Army as Ruler

In October 1932, General Tibúrcio Carias Andino (b. 1876), a National Party of Honduras (PNH) politico closely allied with the United Fruit Company, was elected to the presidency. Having narrowly failed to grab the brass ring in 1923 and 1928, when he had been blocked by the United States, he was not disposed to relinquish power so belatedly attained. The most nearly charismatic of Central American dictators of the era, "standing over 6 feet, barrel-chested, with penetrating eyes and flowing white mustache,"[32] he would eventually pass the presidential sash to his war minister, Juan Manuel Gálvez Durán (b. 1887), through elections in 1949. A split occasioned by Carias's desire to return to power led to an election in 1954 that enabled the Liberal Party's (PLH) Ramón Villeda Morales (b. 1908) to creep in as a minority president. This idealist was soon expelled from office by his vice president, who in turn was ousted by a military coup that made Julio Lozano Díaz dictator and ushered in an era of military rule that essentially vitiated the right to vote that women had gained.

Nicaragua: The Somoza Dynasty

The years 1930–1955 would quickly become the Somoza era in Nicaragua, extending through the subsequent period. The long-entrenched US occupation authorities had accepted a Liberal Party victory in the 1928 elections, and another Liberal, Juan B. Sacasa, was elected in 1932. But trouble was brewing, as in 1927 Augusto César Sandino (b. 1895) had launched guerrilla opposition to the government and the US occupying forces he rightly believed were the country's real rulers. When the US troops withdrew in January 1933, Sandino agreed to a truce. By this time Anastasio Somoza García (b. 1896) had been installed as commander of the US-organized National Guard. Having a business degree from a US college and married into one of Nicaragua's elite families, this ambitious and engaging young man of impressive stature and bearing approved the capture and execution of Sandino in February 1934.[33] The country then had both a new strongman (So-moza) and an eventually symbolically powerful martyr (Sandino).

In 1936, Somoza, who had participated in a failed coup back in 1926, pushed aside President Sacasa, staging his own election as replacement five months later. Adopting a populist style of professing concern for the victims of the depression, he relied on close relations with the United States to stay in power. Occasionally placing a puppet in the presidential office, as did his Dominican contemporary Trujillo, he based his ironclad control of the country upon his domination of the military. Bolstered by wartime prosperity, he kept the population satisfied while gaining control of very large landholdings and lucrative businesses. Owing to his careful foundations for a dynasty, his assassination in September 1956 at the peak of his power would leave no vacuum, as one son assumed the presidency, backed up by another as head of the National Guard. In a cosmetic gesture, women were granted the essentially meaningless—at that time at least—right to vote.

Costa Rica: Birth of a Stable Democracy

The 1930s opened very differently for Costa Rica than for the rest of Central America, or for that matter for Latin America in general. Ex-president Ricardo Jiménez was the popular choice again in 1931, but the Republican Party elected León Cortes Castro (b. 1882) in mid-1936 as a reaction to three decades of Liberal Party rule. Although organized labor and the Communist Party gained strength during World War II, coffee aristocrat Dr. Rafael Angel Calderón Guardia (b. 1900)—who had broken with his predecessor over Cortes Castro's pro–German proclivities—came to dominate the Republican Party and became president in 1940. Assuming a populist stance, he adopted social Christian reformism as es-poused by the country's Catholic archbishop, enacting a social security law in 1941 and a labor code in 1943. As his handpicked successor, Teodoro Picado, fol-lowed a similar orientation, the conservative opposition rebelled behind the new National Unity Party of newspaper publisher Otilio Ulate Blanco (b. 1892), whereas middle-sector elements led by José Figueres Ferrer (b. 1906) put forth a moderate social democratic alternative.[34]

The 1948 elections led to a serious crisis, the outcome of which has shaped Costa Rican politics to the present. Calderón Guardia's effort to perpetuate him-self in office through electoral fraud ignited a brief but bloody civil war in which the diminutive, but dauntless, Figueres's National Liberation forces defeated the army and its communist labor allies. The ensuing junta revised the 1871 constitu-tion to eliminate the army and extended the vote to women and blacks. In 1949, it turned power over to Ulate, the previous year's electoral victor. At the end of his term in 1953 the National Liberation Party swept into office behind the highly popular Figueres, who garnered 65 percent of the record vote. The result was the consolidation of Costa Rica's democracy.

The Caribbean: Strongmen and the Legacy of US Occupation

This period in the Caribbean was marked by countries going from US military control to rule by personalist authoritarian figures installed in power under the auspices of the United States.[35] By the mid-1950s, like the Somozas in Nicaragua, these individuals were still in the driver's seat, most firmly in the Dominican Republic and shakily—for lack of sponsors in Washington—in Haiti. In Cuba the Batista regime seemed entrenched, but its end was drawing near.

The Dominican Republic: The Rise of Trujillo

The inertial stability provided by Horácio Vásquez in the aftermath of the US occupation of the Dominican Republic came to an abrupt end in 1930. When the aging *caudillo* sought to hold onto the presidency in 1930, riding the wave of economic panic resulting from the beginning of the Great Depression, rebels easily toppled him—with the US-organized and US-trained National Guard first facilitating their task and then, after the president had been ousted, neutralizing them by following the orders of Trujillo, the National Guard's chief of staff. Thus, Trujillo, a onetime sugar plantation guard and telegraph operator, was elected president in May 1930 with an announced 99 percent of the votes cast. The authoritarian regime, which would last into the 1960s, had begun. Rafael Leonidas Trujillo Molina (b. 1891) was essentially a product of the US occupation, having entered the National Guard in 1918 and risen to colonel in a short seven years and brigadier general at age twenty-seven. Son of a rather unscrupulous and not very successful small-town businessman, Trujillo ruled the country with a steel grip until his assassination in 1961. One of his protégés, Dr. Joaquín Balaguer, would be the country's leader for most of the ensuing period and up through 1996.[36]

Just eighteen days after Trujillo took office, a hurricane leveled Santo Domingo. Armed with sweeping emergency powers granted by the congress, he rebuilt the city and renamed this second oldest of the region's cities Ciudad Trujillo. Successfully managing the country's economic recovery, Trujillo constructed a system in which his family controlled three-fifths of the GDP—beginning with monopolies of salt, milk, beef, insurance, and newspapers. Consolidating his power during his first four-year term, Trujillo established the Dominican Party (PD) as his vehicle of political control, along with the armed forces, which he favored with nearly half government expenditures as well as ample extralegal opportunities for enrichment. When it came to terror and repression, Trujillo was at least the equal of Venezuela's Gómez and much tougher than Nicaragua's Somoza, not sharing the latter's desire to be popular. Carefully cultivating close ties to the United States, Trujillo appeased nationalist sentiment by having more than ten thousand "illegal" Haitian harvest workers slaughtered in 1937. As Lewis captures the essence of this dictator's dictator:

> He had a forceful and dominating personality, a good memory, and a command of details. He thoroughly controlled the people under him through a combination of methods that included economic pressure, exile, murder, and the ubiquitous presence of spies and informers. Even his closest associates were afraid of him, for their wealth and power depended entirely on his whim. Outside of his immediate family Trujillo had no permanent loyalties. He was suspicious of everyone and would frequently turn on those around him, humiliating them publicly and even sending them to prison and ruin. He was a shrewd judge of men, and an excellent organizer and administrator.[37]

Trujillo's sultanistic style involved requiring undated resignation letters from all appointees, including the Dominican supreme court judges, and using them without any advance notice. Anyone who had a profitable business soon had Trujillo as a not-so-silent partner. The war increased the Trujillo clan fortune and also provided funds for costly public works. Trujillo's pose as the region's leading anticommunist provided cover for draconian repression of domestic opposition, and Trujillo played this role to the hilt once the Cold War opened. Meanwhile, he entrenched his family in key military and political posts while currying favor in 1942 by granting women the hollow right of voting.

Haiti: Failure to Find Political Viabiliity

As part of a sweeping end to overt military occupations, in 1934 the US Roosevelt government withdrew US troops from Haiti, but not before pressuring President Louis Borno out of office in April 1930, with the legislature then choosing conservative mulatto elitist Sténio Vincent (b. 1874) to finish out his term. Vincent was followed in office in 1941 by Elie Lescot (b. 1883), a corrupt tyrant who continued to favor lighter-skinned elements of the small Haitian elite and operated under the influence of Trujillo. When Lescot tried to hang onto power in late 1946, he was ousted by a coup that briefly brought to power Colonel Paul Eugene Magloire (b. 1907), who was determined to help the black majority seize power from the mulatto elite. This effort ushered in a stormy period of attempted change and reform—in keeping with broader currents in the region during the immediate postwar years. Dumarsais Estimé (b. 1900), a black congressman from the interior installed as president by the national assembly in mid-1946, oversaw a brief experience with progressive middle-class government that left the foreign-dominated economic situation essentially intact. With corruption running rampant (as it was in Cuba at the time), Estimé was overthrown in 1950 by Magloire, the same military leader who had toppled Lescot in 1946. Hence the newly won right to vote had little meaning for Haitian women. The ensuing regime of General Magloire, a member of the most elite black stratum, followed reasonably centrist policies, ending with a coup at the end of 1956, when Magloire resorted to the old ploy of illegally extending his presidential term.[38] As it turned out, he was only paving the way for a dictator who would make even Trujillo seem civilized, if not soft: François Duvalier.

Cuba: Still Only Half Independent

The young country of Cuba began the 1930s headed into a major crisis, as the autocratic Gerardo Machado was highly dependent on the goodwill of the United States, which would shift with Franklin Roosevelt's accession to power. As internal opposition mounted, Washington "mediated" a compromise in which the dictator agreed to take a leave of absence in mid-1933. In a development that would leave an important legacy for the future, the Popular Socialist Party, as Cuba's communists were called, opportunistically withdrew their support of a general strike in return for legalization by the about-to-be-ousted strongman.

Trading on very little but his name, Carlos Manuel de Céspedes Júnior became president, lasting only a month before being overthrown by a watershed noncommissioned officers' coup headed by the ambitious mulatto Fulgéncio Batista y Zaldivár (b. 1901), a figure fundamentally similar to Somoza in Nicaragua or Trujillo in the Dominican Republic. By September, university professor Ramón Grau San Martín (b. 1887) had become head of a "revolutionary" government that established an eight-hour workday and limited foreigners' land purchases. This government's failure to gain acceptance from the United States or to develop an effective political organization (a task hardly feasible in a few short months) led to the abrupt end of this experiment in mid-January 1934.[39]

With the politically astute Batista acting as king-maker and running the show from behind the scenes, the essentially figurehead presidency had a confusing array of incumbents during the next few years. Carlos Hevia was president for two days in January 1934, followed by Manuel Marquéz Sterling for a day and Carlos Mendieta for all of twenty-two months. By this time no longer needing the Platt Amendment, which had granted sweeping powers to intervene, the United States had abrogated it, confident that the Batista-led military would act as its proxy—as Somoza and Trujillo were doing. Strikes forcing Mendieta out, his vice president lasted five months before being succeeded by Miguel Mariano Gómez (b. 1890), who would survive for four months between a Batista-engineered election and removal by a Batista-ordered impeachment. Vice President Federico Laredo Brú (b. 1875) then held office for four years by realizing who actually held the power. Finally, his puppet master, Batista, decided to come out from the wings to center stage and triumphed in a 1940 election, becoming Cuba's wartime president. Since the Soviet Union was US ally for all but the beginning of his term, Batista made peace with the local communists. Indeed, three of them participated in his cabinet—including Carlos Rafael Rodríguez, who would later be Castro's vice president.

As Batista, anticipating Washington's desire for maintenance of democratic forms, returned to his arbiter role as unquestioned boss of the military, 1944 witnessed the election of Grau San Martín of the Auténticos with 55 percent of the vote, compared to the 42 percent with which he had been credited in 1940 in losing to Batista. Having had to wait a full decade to return to the presidency after the United States had frozen him out, he and his cohorts were older, but greedier rather than wiser, carrying graft to a new high. Eduardo "Eddy" Chibas (b. 1907), Grau's public works minister in 1934, broke with his erstwhile mentor and founded the Party of the Cuban People, popularly known as the Orthodoxos, in 1947, but the next year Carlos Prio Soccarás (b. 1903) of the Auténticos was elected with 900,000 votes, compared to Chibas's 325,000—gained through his slogan "Honesty over money." As soon as inaugurated, Prio proceeded to pillage the public even more than had his predecessor, and politically connected gangsterism continued to thrive in a context in which the US Mafia was consolidating its position as the dynamic force in a three-way partnership with the government and army commander Batista.

During the next campaign, mercurial demagogue Chibas dramatically committed suicide in August 1951 on his popular radio program, having realized that in his quest for the presidency he was bucking not only the US government but also US investors, particularly the newly entrenched organized-crime associates of Meyer Lansky. As a preface to his self-destruction, Chibas informed his followers that even if elected, he wouldn't have been able to carry out his reforms against such formidable guardians of the status quo.[40] The trauma occasioned by the death of this paladin of democracy and civic probity radicalized many of his young followers, most importantly Fidel Castro Ruz (b. 1926). The electoral vacuum allowed a March 1952 Batista coup, which in turn led to Castro's quixotic July 26, 1953, attack on the Moncada barracks in Santiago. Arrested after most of his followers had been killed, Castro used his trial to make a stirring "history will absolve me" speech, which put the regime on trial in front of public opinion. As Batista followed advice not to make Fidel a martyr, sentencing him to prison instead of death, Castro soon benefited from an amnesty designed to improve the climate for Batista's election of a puppet president, going into exile in Mexico and leaving Batista, to all appearances, firmly in the driver's seat. For Cuba, and to a significant degree for the rest of Latin America, this would prove to be the lull before the storm.

Latin America in 1955

At the midpoint of the 1950s the region was in a state of flux, with few strong clues to what the next quarter century would bring. Brazil was still absorbing the demise of Vargas, and Argentina was reeling from the ouster of Perón. Mexico's stability stood out and led many analysts to apologize for the nondemocratic aspects of PRI rule. Colombia was under a military regime, something it had not previously experienced in the century. Peru was seven years into another of the many military regimes it had seen, and Venezuela was growing increasingly dissatisfied with its subjection to the whims of a personalist military man. Chile had brought a failed militarist of the late 1920s back in as a neo-Peronist, but his mentor had been ousted next door. Bolivia was in the early years of its revolutionary experience, and Ecuador was in one of its frequent presidencies of Velasco Ibarra. Uruguay was experimenting with a plural executive, and Paraguayans didn't yet realize that Stroessner was not just another military strongman, but an autocrat who would eclipse Díaz's Western Hemisphere record for longevity in office.

Away from South America, Guatemala was attempting to turn back the clock and dismantle the programs and institutions of its 1944 Revolution, as Nicaragua was making a smooth transition from the elder Somoza to rule by his sons. Honduras's brief flirtation with progressive democratic government was about to end, just as Costa Rica was institutionalizing its return to democratic ways and El Salvador's military were awkwardly striving to turn their regime into a miniature version of Mexico's—ignoring the salient, and inconvenient, fact that the PRI was a civilian structure, not a front for military rule. The Dominican Republic witnessed Trujillo's dictatorship at its acme, and Haiti was on the eve of attaining stability at the price of terroristic authoritarianism. Cuba was the poster child for a country with no idea of what the near future was to bring, as Batista—with his military and Mafia partners—seemed firmly in control, having banished the advocates of revolution to Mexican exile. All this ensured that Latin America's next period would be not only turbulent, but even truly momentous.

In terms of the basic themes laid out in Chapter 1, the authoritarian corporatist political culture, still dominant in the 1930s, had been seriously eroded in three of the major countries but still had a firm hold in Colombia and most of the smaller nations except Chile, Uruguay, and Costa Rica. Even in Brazil, Mexico, and Argentina, patron-client relationships were still the bedrock of politics, although less visible in the rapidly growing urban centers. With peace having come to Mexico, violence was down from the preceding periods in most of the area, although it was raging across the Colombian countryside. Leadership had changed greatly in both its nature and its style, most of the remaining *caudillo*-type dictators still looking strong, but actually on their last legs (much as Díaz had been at the beginning of the antecedent period in 1900). Of the giants who had graced the political scene for much of this period, Vargas was recently in his grave, Cárdenas long in retirement, and Perón just overthrown—although he still had a whopping comeback left in him. The leading figure of the next period, Castro, had yet to begin his rise (from prison after his failed 1953 revolt, followed by exile). Most of the populist figures that had emerged after World War II would soon be swept aside by the wave of military seizures of power that characterized the 1960s. Under some of them, national legislatures were in many cases less ineffective than they had been, but they were still clearly junior partners of the executive. Chile, Costa Rica, Venezuela, Uruguay, Colombia, and Brazil (in descending order) had the most politically significant congresses in the region. But these legislatures were soon to be plowed under by authoritarian military regimes—with Costa Rica the sole exception. A few countries had managed to establish civilian control over their armed forces. Mexico, by creating a hegemonic party, and Costa Rica, by abolishing its military altogether, were the major exceptions. At the time, it appeared that Brazil, Chile, and Uruguay also belonged in this category, but events were soon to prove the contrary. In almost all cases the armed forces were the arbiter of executive-legislative conflicts, not the courts, and this "moderator" role could lead to deep political involvement.

Political participation had greatly expanded in recent years, but it, too, would be largely negated by the surge of authoritarian military regimes. Substantial progress having been made in incorporating the middle classes into politics, the focus had shifted to the urban working class. In most places racial minorities remained politically marginalized—but remember the civil rights movement in the United States had yet to get going, so they were not greatly behind the times. Indeed, blacks were prominent on top Latin American soccer teams well before Jackie Robinson finally broke the color barrier in US major league baseball. Revolutionary ideologies flourished essentially as slogans of leftist intellectuals who made far greater gains in the media than they did in building a popular base. As to corruption, it remained more an accepted fact of life than a cause for indignation, much less a political issue—except in Cuba.

Notes

1. Sound histories include David Bushnell, *The Making of Modern Colombia: A Nation in Spite of Itself* (Berkeley: University of California Press, 1993), and Frank Stafford and Marco Palacios, *Colombia: Fragmented Land, Divided Society* (New York: Oxford University Press, 2002).

2. Paul Oquist, *Violence, Conflict, and Politics in Colombia* (New York: Academic Press, 1980), p. 152.

3. Ibid., p. 14.

4. See Richard E. Sharpless, *Gaitán of Colombia: A Political Biography* (Pittsburgh: University of Pittsburgh Press, 1978); Herbert Braun, *The Assassination of Gaitán: Public Life and Urban Violence in Colombia* (Madison: University of Wisconsin Press, 1985); and W. John Green, *Gaitanismo, Left Liberalism, and Popular Mobilization in Colombia* (Gainesville: University Press of Florida, 2003).

5. This period is well covered in Harvey Kline, *Colombia: Democracy Under Assault*, rev. ed. (Boulder, CO: Westview Press, 1994).

6. For an interpretation of politics up through Gómez, consult John D. Martz, *The Politics of Clientelism: Democracy and the State in Colombia* (New Brunswick, NJ: Transaction, 1997), pp. 53–62.

7. Consult James F. Henderson, *Colombia: The Laureano Gómez Years, 1889–1965* (Gainesville: University Press of Florida, 2001).

8. On La Violencia, see Orlando Fals Borda, *Subversion and Social Change in Colombia*, trans. by Jacqueline Skiles (New York: Columbia University Press, 1969), and Mary Roldon, *Blood and Fire: La Violencia in Antioquía, Colombia, 1946–1953* (Durham, NC: Duke University Press, 2002).

9. The Rojas Pinilla period is covered with the freshness of recent occurrence in Vernon Lee Fluharty, *Dance of the Millions* (Pittsburgh: University of Pittsburgh Press, 1957), and John D. Martz, *Colombia: A Contemporary Political Survey* (Chapel Hill, NC: University of North Carolina Press, 1962).

10. A sound history is Peter F. Klarén, *Peru: Society and Nationhood in the Andes* (New York: Oxford University Press, 2000). Paul H. Lewis, *Authoritarian Regimes in Latin America: Dictators, Despots, and Tyrants* (Lanham, MD: Rowman & Littlefield, 2006), pp. 110–112, provides an insightful sketch of developments from 1930 to 1955.

11. The literature on APRA includes Grant Hilliker, *The Politics of Reform in Peru: The Aprista and Other Mass Parties of Latin America* (Baltimore: Johns Hopkins University Press, 1971), and Peter F. Klarén, *Modernization, Dislocation, and Aprismo* (Austin: University of Texas Press, 1973). See also Robert J. Alexander, *Aprismo: The Ideas and Doctrines of Victor Raul Haya de la Torre* (Kent, OH: Kent State University Press, 1973), an edited selection of his writings.

12. Odría's years are treated in Klarén, *Peru,* and Hilliker, *The Politics of Reform in Peru*. He looks better in retrospect than he did to contemporary observers, since most later chief executives performed worse than he did in providing eight years of stability with moderate economic growth. Although no Perón, he was more politically astute than near contemporaries Rojas Pinilla and Pérez Jiménez, a significant cut above Bolivian military presidents of the time (more equivalent to Banzer from the 1970s), and at least the peer of Chile's Ibáñez.

13. See Daniel C. Hellinger, *Venezuela: Tarnished Democracy* (Boulder, CO: Westview Press, 1991), and David E. Blank, *Politics in Venezuela* (Boston: Little, Brown, 1973).

14. Robert J. Alexander, *Rómulo Betancourt and the Transformation of Venezuela* (New Brunswick, NJ: Transaction Books, 1982), covers the *trienio.*

15. John D. Martz, *Acción Democrática: Evolution of a Modern Political Party in Venezuela* (Princeton: Princeton University Press, 1966), is the standard work on the AD.

16. Consult Phillip B. Taylor, Jr., *The Venezuelan Golpe de Estado de 1958: The Fall of Marcos Pérez Jiménez* (Washington, DC: Institute for the Comparative Study of Political Systems, 1968).

17. Informative histories include Brian Loveman, *Chile: The Legacy of Hispanic Capitalism*, 3rd ed. (New York: Oxford University Press, 2001), and Simon Collier and William F. Slater, *A History of Chile, 1808–1994* (Cambridge, UK: Cambridge University Press, 1993).

18. A solid political analysis is Federico G. Gil, *The Political System of Chile* (Boston: Houghton Mifflin, 1966).

19. Consult Donald W. Bray, *Chilean Politics During the Second Ibáñez Government*, microfilm/microform (Palo Alto, CA: Stanford University, 1961).

20. Waltrud Queiser Morales, *Bolivia: Land of Struggle* (Boulder, CO: Westview Press, 1991), pp. 74–75.

21. Essential is Herbert Klein, *Bolivia: The Evolution of a Multi-Ethnic Society*, 2nd ed. (New York: Oxford University Press, 1992). An optimistic assessment of the revolution is Robert J. Alexander, *The Bolivian National Revolution* (New Brunswick, NJ: Rutgers University Press, 1958).

22. See James M. Malloy, *Bolivia: The Uncompleted Revolution* (Pittsburgh: University of Pittsburgh Press, 1970), and James M. Malloy and Richard S. Thorne, eds., *Bolivia Since 1952* (Pittsburgh: University of Pittsburgh Press, 1971).

23. On this case of enchanting the electorate and maintaining support without fulfilling promises, see Carlos de la Torre, *Velasco Ibarra, Populist Seduction in Latin America: The Ecuadorean Experience* (Athens: Ohio University Center for International Studies, 2000). The other side of the coin, Ecuador's armed forces, are the central focus of John Samuel Fitch, *The Military Coup de Etat as a Political Process, 1948–66* (Baltimore: Johns Hopkins University Press, 1977).

24. David Schodt, *Ecuador: An Andean Enigma* (Boulder, CO: Westview Press, 1987), and John D. Martz, *Ecuador: Conflicting Political Culture and the Quest for Progress* (Boston: Allyn & Bacon, 1972), provide perspective on the country's situation at this juncture.

25. A sound work on Uruguay is Martin Weinstein, *Uruguay: Democracy at the Crossroads* (Boulder, CO: Westview Press, 1988).

26. For perspective, see Riordan Roett and Richard S. Sacks, *Paraguay: The Personalist Legacy* (Boulder, CO: Westview Press, 1990). Very thoughtful are Paul H. Lewis, *Political Parties and Generations in Paraguay's Liberal Era, 1869–1940* (Chapel Hill: University of North Carolina Press, 1993), and Paul H. Lewis, *The Politics of Exile: Paraguay's Febrerista Party* (Chapel Hill: University of North Carolina Press, 1968), as well as Paul H. Lewis, *Socialism, Liberalism, and Dictatorship in Paraguay* (New York: Praeger, 1982).

27. For a comparative overview, consult Ralph Lee Woodward, Jr., *Central America: A Nation Divided*, 3rd rev. ed. (New York: Oxford University Press, 1999).

28. See Kenneth J. Grieb, *Guatemalan Caudillo: The Regime of Jorge Ubico: Guatemala, 1931–1944* (Athens: Ohio University Press, 1979).

29. Consult Ronald M. Schneider, *Communism in Guatemala 1944–1954* (New York: Praeger, 1958), as well as Deborah J. Yashar, *Demanding Democracy: Reform and Reaction in*

Costa Rica and Guatemala, 1870s–1950s (Stanford, CA: Stanford University Press, 1997), and Robert H. Holder, *Armies Without Nations: Public Violence and State Formation in Central America, 1821–1960* (New York: Oxford University Press, 2004).

30. On the regime's demise, consult Piero Gleijeses, *Shattered Hope: The Guatemalan Revolution and the United States, 1944–1954* (Princeton: Princeton University Press, 1991), and Ronald M. Schneider, *Communism,* pp. 301–322.

31. See Thomas P. Anderson, *Matanza: El Salvador's Communist Revolution of 1932* (Lincoln: University of Nebraska Press, 1971), and Tommie Sue Montgomery, *Revolution in El Salvador: Origins and Evolution* (Boulder, CO: Westview Press, 1982).

32. James Morris, *Honduras: Caudillo Politics and Military Rulers* (Boulder, CO: Westview Press, 1984), p. 9. Also useful is Thomas J. Dodd, *Tiburcio Carias: Portrait of a Honduran Political Leader* (Baton Rouge: Louisiana State University Press, 2005).

33. See Thomas Walker, *Nicaragua: The Land of Sandino* (Boulder, CO: Westview Press, 1981), as well as Richard Millett, *Guardians of the Dynasty: A History of the U.S.-Created Guardia Nacional de Nicaragua and the Somoza Family* (Maryknoll, NY: Orbis Books, 1977), and Richard Millett, *The Regime of Anastasio Somoza, 1936–1956* (Chapel Hill: University of North Carolina Press, 1993).

34. Consult John A. Booth, *Costa Rica: Quest for Democracy* (Boulder, CO: Westview Press, 1998); Charles D. Ameringer, *Don Pépe: A Political Biography of Jose Figueres of Costa Rica* (Albuquerque: University of New Mexico Press, 1978); and Yashar, *Demanding Democracy.*

35. For perspective on the region, see Franklin W. Knight, *The Caribbean: The Genesis of a Fragmented Nationalism,* 2nd ed. (New York: Oxford University Press, 1990).

36. See Howard J. Wiarda and Michael Kryzanek, *The Dominican Republic: A Caribbean Crucible* (Boulder, CO: Westview Press, 1982). Useful biographies include Robert D. Crassweller, *Trujillo: The Life and Times of a Caribbean Dictator* (New York: Macmillan, 1966) and Bernard Diederich, *Trujillo: The Death of the Goat* (Boston: Little, Brown, 1978).

37. Lewis, *Authoritarian Regimes,* pp. 155–156.

38. On Haiti, consult Patrick Bellegarde-Smith, *Haiti: The Breached Citadel* (Boulder: CO: Westview Press, 1989), and Alex Dupuy, *Haiti and the World Economy: Class, Race, and Underdevelopment Since 1700* (Boulder, CO: Westview Press, 1989), as well as Robert Rotberg, *Haiti: The Politics of Squalor* (Boston: Houghton-Mifflin, 1971).

39. Excellent sources include Juan M. del Aguila, *Cuba: Dilemmas of a Revolution,* rev. ed. (Boulder, CO: Westview Press, 1994); Jorge I. Dominguez, *Cuba: Order and Revolution* (Cambridge: Belknap Press of Harvard University Press, 1978); Louis A. Pérez, Jr., *Cuba: Between Reform and Revolution,* 3rd ed., (New York: Oxford University Press, 2005); and Hugh Thomas, *Cuba: On the Pursuit of Freedom,* updated ed. (New York: Da Capo Press, 1998).

40. Useful is Jorge Ibarra, *Prologue to Revolution: Cuba, 1898–1958* (Boulder, CO: Lynne Rienner, 1998). The extent of US-organized crime's partnership with the Batista regime and its contribution to anti-Yankee sentiment in Cuba have often been underestimated. New York's fabled Meyer Lansky, relocated to Miami, was the architect of entrenching the Mafia in the unimaginably profitable triad of gambling, drugs, and prostitution— euphemistically termed "tourism"—that brought Cuba the roisterous teamsters on a howl/Las Vegas blow-off-steam type of visitors. Through accidentally being in Havana on

the occasion of Castro's July 26, 1953, attack on the Moncada barracks, I had an unwonted firsthand opportunity to observe the symbiotic relationship between the pillars of the dictatorial regime and their North American *compadres*. Understandably, many Havana residents resented the assumption by hordes of drunken "gringos" that if they were female, their favors were for sale. Although still in college, I was not naive concerning political machine relationships, as for four years I was ensconced near Chicago while the senior Richard Daley was being groomed as heir to "Colonel" Jake Arvey as Cook County's organized-crime-connected unquestioned boss. On Lansky, consult Robert Lacey, *Little Man: Meyer Lansky and the Gangster Life* (Boston: Little, Brown, 1991), as well as Dennis Eisenberg, Uri Dan, and Eli Landau, *Meyer Lansky: Mogul of the Mob* (New York: Paddington Books, 1979). The extensive literature on Daley and Chicago's mob-ridden politics begins with Mike Royco, *Boss: Richard J. Daley of Chicago* (New York: Dutton, 1971), and William F. Gleason, *Daley of Chicago: The Man, the Mayor, and the Limits of Conventional Politics* (New York: Simon & Schuster, 1970).

8

Inferno and the Hard Road Back

Brazil, Mexico, Argentina, and Colombia, 1956–1979

By the mid-1950s, Latin American politics had become essentially nonideological. The PRI's dominance over Mexico had reached the point where it had in effect become the *Institutional* Revolutionary Party, a vast patronage-dispensing machine that might well have caused Cárdenas to roll over (and over and over) in his grave. In Brazil a doctrine of "developmentalism" was taking hold under the guidance of the new president, Juscelino Kubitschek. At just that point the Argentine armed forces ousted Perón from power but found little resonance for their negative message of antipopulist anticommunism. Relieved by a decrease in the horrendous violence of 1948–1953, Colombia was torn between the reactionary brand of authoritarian corporatism preached by Laureano Gómez, clearly in decline, and the business-oriented liberalism gaining favor among sectors of the entrepreneurial stratum. *Aprismo* was losing meaning if not necessarily supporters in Peru, having become a political party more than a movement, much less an ideology.

But among the armed forces, catalyzed by the Cuban 1959 Revolution, a national security doctrine developed and took on an ideological nature. It would be used not only to justify the sweeping wave of military coups that characterized the 1960s, but also to rationalize the armed forces' actions. In some cases, most traumatically following overthrow of the Allende government in Chile and the "Dirty War" in Argentina a few years later, these authoritarian military regimes would carry ruthless repression to the extreme of institutionalized terrorism. In other countries, such as Brazil and Peru, insurgencies would be mercilessly crushed without a societywide reign of terror.

Thus, the quarter century from the middle of the 1950s to the end of the 1970s, saw most Latin American countries falter in their efforts to make representative systems work and fall instead, many for protracted periods, under the ironfisted control of authoritarian military regimes. Indeed, competitive, constitutional, democratic governments and political processes were so eclipsed as to appear to be a scattered few exceptions to the rule of the collapse of populism and rise of a new militarism—often institutionalized in the "national security state." By the mid-1970s, such repressive regimes were overwhelmingly predominant in the region, much more than elected civilian governments had been at the beginning of the 1960s. Just as these promising civilian governments had been inundated by the flood tide of rampant militarism beginning in 1962, the late 1970s witnessed a resurgence of effective demands for political liberalization and democratization, unleashing forces that would blossom within a few years into a tidal wave of transitions to democracy.

In retrospect, leadership was not as lacking in the downhill first half of this period as often perceived by observers and students of the area. Indeed, a strong case can be made that presidents in a quite wide range of countries grappled responsibly and tenaciously with problems that were beyond resolution, given the unfavorable conditions prevailing at the time. Juscelino Kubitschek in Brazil and Rómulo Betancourt in Venezuela were the outstanding success stories, although at the time overshadowed by the dramatic appeal of Fidel Castro in Cuba, but Colombia's Alberto Lleras Camargo, Arturo Frondizi of Argentina, Peru's Fernando Belaúnde Terry, Eduardo Frei Montalva in Chile, and Bolivian multiterm president Victor Paz Estenssoro represented effective democratic leadership under very trying circumstances, as did—within a strikingly different institutional framework—Adolfo López Mateos in Mexico.

In something of a paradox, outstanding political leadership was not a major factor in the climb out of the depths of the political inferno that got under way in important parts of the region during the late 1970s, although its absence among the military did contribute to erosion of support for the authoritarian option. Failure of authoritarian regimes to deliver on promises of greatly improved economic performance and the waning of fears of possible leftist revolutions that had led elites and panic-stricken middle sectors to turn to the military in the 1960s played much more important roles in this democratic recovery. This chapter puts the region's four largest countries under the microscope as the most important cases; the rich experiences of the other South American countries are examined in Chapter 9, where an effort is made to discern a pattern. Then, in Chapter 10, this analysis is extended to Central America and the Caribbean. For behind the apparent commonality of establishment of military regimes, a good deal of difference was rooted in distinct previous national experiences.

Overview

Brazil entered this quarter century on the upswing from the jolting crisis that had brought about Vargas's demise. Juscelino Kubitschek de Oliveira, elected in late 1955 and taking office early the next year, would prove to be one of the most effective chief executives in the history of the republic—ranking very high even in the wider regional experience. After broadening and deepening the foundations for sustained development that Vargas had begun, he presided over an election in 1960 that brought a more-than-somewhat-quixotic populist to power—only to crash under the weight of his own grand schemes and manipulations less than a year later. Very ordinary João Goulart, the vice president who succeeded Jânio Quadros, was no match for a polarizing situation, being ousted at the end of the first quarter of 1964 by a conservative military movement enjoying wide support from civilian elites and middle sectors. By the end of the 1970s, a series of military presidents would have led the country down into a repressive, although economically successful, authoritarian regime and then turned the corner to put it on a path of liberalization morphing into political opening.

By contrast, Mexico would leave the period as firmly under the control of its long-hegemonic party as at the beginning, although with pressure for change mounting. Thus it would be the only country (except for small virtual city-state Costa Rica) to avoid government by the armed forces.

These twenty-five years would be both turbulent and violent for Argentina. Beginning with military rule in the aftermath of Perón's ouster, the country would undergo a protracted period in which neither military nor civilian governments could provide long-term stability. Perón returned to power triumphantly in 1973, only to die the next year, when he was the key factor in averting a slide into undeclared civil war. Back in power by 1976, the military would still be searching in vain for a blueprint for political viability when the 1970s came to an inglorious close.

Colombia would emerge early from an essentially hideous ten years to find not only political viability, but also democracy under a series of coalition governments operating within the innovative framework of the National Front. By period's end it would be plagued by insurgency and massive illegal drug-trafficking enterprises threatening to become a state within a state.

Brazil: The Road into and Back from Military Takeover

Even after the substantial modernization of government and politics during the quarter century of the Vargas era, personalities continued to take precedence over programs. Alongside still relatively effective clientelistic politics, new types of populist leaders emerged, some owing more and some less to Vargas's example. The basically conservative orientation of major parties and the heavy, if not predominant, rural influence in their leadership prevented close identification of urban voters with them. Hence, the masses turned instead to a direct link between their votes and a political leader with some degree of charisma. Clientelism continued as the basis for holding the middle class to established political leadership and existing parties in terms of exchange of votes for employment or favors. But it could not work for the urban masses, as the electorate ballooned beyond the patronage potential of the *cartorial* state.[1] From 1 million in 1908 and 2.7 million for the 1934 balloting, the electorate had passed 7.4 million by 1945 and grew exponentially thereafter.

As Vargas left no true heir, the peculiar Brazilian form of populism he had embodied, combining features of urban machine politics with personalism, emotional appeals, and effective performance in the material realm, assumed several distinct forms as aspiring leaders adapted it to the peculiar characteristics of the constituents they were wooing in their state. João Goulart (b. 1918) on the left, rooted in Rio Grande do Sul, attempted rather ineptly to carry on the labor-oriented nationalism of Vargas, only to be outdone by his own brother-in-law, Leonel Brizola (b. 1922), who modernized the appeal to workers with a more stridently ideological brand of nationalism. Like his nemesis, Carlos Lacerda (b. 1914), he effectively exploited the new medium of television to transcend the limitations of public appearances to communicate with the masses. For on the right in Rio de Janeiro it was the crusading anticommunist zeal of Lacerda and his mystique of intransigent opposition, in a system where opportunism and accommodation predominated, that gained a fanatic following. Centered in São Paulo was the conservative brand of Adhemar de Barros (b. 1901), blending massive public works expenditures with demagogic campaigning and skillful exploitation of graft and patronage to electoral ends. The antithesis to this patronage approach was the moralistic messianism of Jânio da Silva Quadros (b. 1917), the ascetic giant-killer capitalizing on the popular desires for an end to the corruption and controversy of Adhemarism and Goulart's perversion of Vargism. These strains of populism shared an appeal to the swelling mass urban population, which had been poorly assimilated and was plagued by the insecurities of city life as have-nots. Restless, but largely nonradical, the middle sectors also gave substantial support to populist politicians.

First up was the transitional Juscelino Kubitschek de Oliveira, the quintessential Brazilian "cordial" man, impossible to dislike and folksy in a natural-seeming manner. Elected with a plurality in November 1955 in a close three-way race, this grandson of a Czech immigrant earned a unique place in the annals of Brazilian politics by being more popular at the end of his term than at its beginning. Indeed, he is often considered Brazil's best single-term president. Born in Minas Gerais in 1902, after being orphaned he worked his way through medical school,

JUSCELINO KUBITSCHEK DE OLIVEIRA
(CREDIT: ALEJANDRA KUBITSCHEK)

graduating in 1927 and doing surgical internships in Paris, Vienna, and Berlin. Serving in the congress during Vargas's first democratic period (1934–1937), he returned there in 1946 after having been mayor of Belo Horizonte, Brazil's third largest city. Elected governor at the time of Vargas's triumphal 1950 return, this leader of the moderate and modern wing of the Social Democratic Party (PSD) earned a reputation as a builder and an effective developmentalist that propelled him to the presidency.[2]

Kubitschek brought to that office all the legendary facility for political maneuvering and compromise of an experienced *Mineiro* politician. His Program of Goals ("Programa de Metas") promised "fifty years' progress in five" and emphasized transportation, energy, steel, manufacturing, and construction of a new capital in the sparsely populated interior. Offering something to nearly every relevant group, his program's long-run effect was consolidation of Brazil's industrialization by building up the requisite infrastructure while implanting heavy industry—especially automotive—and fostering a capital goods sector. A dynamic and pragmatic centrist, "JK" gave economic development marked priority over social welfare measures, which he postponed for an expected second term in 1961–1965. He carefully avoided the kind of confrontation that had cost Vargas his office and life, leaving the economic and political interests of the landowning forces so powerful in his party untouched in exchange for their support in promoting industry and some steps toward modernization of urban society—in a rapidly urbanizing country. The significant and painless economic growth of his term, averaging over 8 percent, could not be duplicated by his immediate successors owing to the limits of import-substitution industrialization and the high level of inflation that was the legacy of his single-minded determination to attain goals his critics had scorned as impossibly ambitious.

Marshal Henrique Duffles Teixeira Lott (b. 1894) as war minister was both a strong bulwark against plotting and conspiracies and a restraint upon the president's freedom of action. Kubitschek's amiability and moderate nationalism dispelled lingering suspicions among the officer corps concerning his Vargista origins, and his infectious enthusiasm for Brazil's future disarmed all but the most hardened of his opponents, moving the country closer to a national consensus on many basic issues than had existed since before the 1920s. Thus, his term was the apex of reasonably functioning representative politics, and the October 1958 congressional and partial gubernatorial elections were largely free from polarization. The 326-member Chamber of Deputies chosen to serve for the last two years of his term and the first years of his successor's was little changed from that elected four years earlier. Since Kubitschek could not stand for immediate reelection, the outcome of governorship races had important implications for the future, particularly Brizola's win in Rio Grande do Sul and the defeat of Adhemar de Barros by Quadros's candidate in São Paulo.[3]

A stiffening of attitudes by the US government and international financial institutions, frustrated in efforts to force the determined Kubitschek to cut sharply back on his development program in order to curb inflation, had unfortunate effects. The structuralist-monetarist controversy, previewed under Vargas, but sidestepped by the Café Filho government in 1954–1955, was joined full force as Kubitschek would not risk the stagnation that austerity programs had brought, and was bringing, to other countries in the region. In mid-1959, this chilling of relations was aggravated by a negative US response to a Kubitschek proposal for a joint crusade against underdevelopment in the hemisphere (this Operation Pan-American would be the inspiration for the John F. Kennedy administration's 1961 Alliance for Progress). Kubitschek's failure to give in to US wishes infuriated top policymakers, especially Secretary of State Dulles.[4] Inside Brazil the consensus on developmental nationalism that Kubitschek had skillfully forged began to disintegrate in the face of polemical exchanges between economic liberals' advocacy of orthodox fiscal measures and radical nationalists' attacks on foreign capital and external influences.

Viewed by many Brazilians as a fearless patriot standing up to the forces that had laid Vargas low, Kubitschek preserved his prestige and personal popularity by staying above the partisan squabbling engendered by the proximity of presidential succession. Brazil's population was up to 70 million, with over 31 million classified as urban dwellers. Life expectancy was nearing fifty-three, compared to under forty-three in 1940, and infant mortality was dropping dramatically. The doubling of industrial production during Kubitschek's term was reflected in the presence of

2.9 million employees of industry in the labor force of 22.7 million—a significant rise from 1.6 million in 1940. Indeed, by 1960 industry accounted for 25 percent of GDP compared to 23 percent for agriculture. Exceeding most of his goals, Kubitschek had built an automotive industry from scratch to 321,000 vehicles in 1960. He had laid the foundation for Brazil's post-1967 economic takeoff, but the first three years of his successor's poor management in the midst of renewed political instability led to the overturning of the political system Kubitschek's adroitness and economic successes had bolstered.

By 1960, the balance in the PSD–Brazilian Labor Party (PTB) alliance had shifted to a point where the latter could demand a greater say in picking the presidential candidate, with nationalist credentials of key importance. Kubitschek acquiesced in the choice of Marshal Lott, despite his lack of popular appeal, since an opposition victory served his longer-run objective of not facing a formidable candidate in a 1965 comeback bid. Hence, the electorate's hopes came to rest upon Quadros, a new and exciting type of populist politician promising to reform or dismantle the system rather than manipulate it. Viewed by many as a political messiah, as well as São Paulo's first real chance to regain the presidency it had lost in 1930, Quadros pledged to sweep out the accumulated corruption and inefficiency of three decades of the Vargas succession while setting Brazil's administrative house in order, maintaining the momentum of development, and remembering the common people, whose interests had been largely neglected by Kubitschek's emphasis upon infrastructure growth over social development.[5]

Quadros appeared to much of the electorate to be the best bet for a sound administration, if not the nation's savior. To the National Democratic Union (UDN), having lost three times in a row with distinguished *tenentes* as candidates, he was the sole hope of finally attaining power. For in contrast to Kubitschek's step-by-step rise through the PSD machine, "Jânio," as he was popularly known, relied upon a charismatic appeal and highly unorthodox campaign techniques, in which he frequently changed party label in order to build an image and a following that transcended the lines of Brazil's fragmented political organizations. But in a bid for national office he needed the electoral machinery of a major party, hence accepted UDN endorsement. Having been catapulted to national prominence by his dramatic 1954 defeat of Adhemar de Barros for the São Paulo governorship, he was elected to the congress in 1958 and on October 3, 1960, sailed into the presidency with nearly 5.6 million votes to Lott's fewer than 3.8 million and de Barros's distant 2.2 million. In amassing a record plurality, he carried all of Brazil's major states, something not even Vargas had accomplished. The PTB's Goulart's narrowly achieving reelection as vice president seemed to be of secondary import at the time.

Quadros began the lamentable process of dissipating the positive heritage left by Kubischek, a development that would pave the way for the most dismal decade in Brazil's life as a nation, 1963–1973. Betrayal of the people's hopes through erratic Bonapartist behavior (updated via Charles de Gaulle and Fidel Castro) left a pall of disillusionment when the providential man irresponsibly fled after eight short months, contributing to a perilous radicalization as some sought in doctrinaire programs or radical ideology to remake institutions and practices that the demagogic populist leader had so completely failed to deliver. Lending depth to the crises of 1962–1964 was a growing tension between modernizing sectors of Brazilian society and those opposed to fundamental change in the patrimonial order—rooted in clientelism, cooptation, and the *cartorial* state—that had successfully withstood the 1930 Revolution and the postwar "reestablishment of democracy." As the progressives were concentrated in the center-south and traditional forces were still dominant in the northeast and north, efforts to bridge this cleavage through accommodation and conciliation fell flat. Direct popular election of the president combined with gross underweighting of the modernized regions and excessive overrepresentation of the most backward states guaranteed a congress far more conservative than the executive.

By the early 1960s, economic development had so transformed urban Brazilian society that the old rules of the patrimonial political game no longer applied. But these changes had not yet reached the hinterlands, still the locus of power between presidential elections because of the grotesque legislative underrepresentation of the most populous states. This duality would prove a debilitating dilemma for civilian governments and be a thorny problem for the military ones that took over after 1964. The classic urban-rural gap had its most negative impact in sprawling, federal Brazil. At the local and state levels of the northeast, north, and center-west, patrimonial political structures proved highly resistant to the limited reflections of the ongoing economic and social transformation of the area below the eighteenth parallel. Moreover, cooptation rather that true representation was rooted in the fact that strong governmental structures had been established before the mobilization of social groups. From this tenacity of traditional politics in the interior stemmed repeated electoral victories at the state level that enabled these rural-based conservative elites to exert heavy influence, if not always control, within the decentralized national structures of the UDN and the PSD.[6]

Through this pernicious phenomenon, patronage politics and clientelism persisted at the national level even in the face of sustained economic growth and strong modernizing influences in society. In a system in which sectoral organizations rather than parties were the vehicles for urban interest groups, the inadequately organized middle classes would, under perceived threat to their level of living, come to view the army as the defender of their basic interests, a shift in viewpoint that led to breakdown of the developmentalist coalition of forces that had originally been shaped by Vargas, and that had functioned effectively during the all-too-short Kubitschek era. (It is tantalizing, as well as frustrating, to ponder how events might have played out if presidential reelection had been permitted in 1960, rather than not being adopted until the 1990s.)

Quadros, saddled with the congress elected in 1958, before the modernizing impact of Kubitschek's policies had been felt, realized that in dealing with grave financial problems and the woeful state of administrative machinery he would encounter strong opposition from entrenched interests and alienate much of his UDN backing. Unable to communicate his face-to-face persuasiveness to the nation as a whole from the isolation of the still-raw, new capital Brasília, far distant from major population centers, Quadros opted for risky measures to impact an inherently slow-moving congress. In August 1961, he found to his dismay that Brazil was not 1958 France, and he was not de Gaulle, as a plan to mobilize popular pressure on the congress to grant him extraordinary powers backfired and the all-out gamble of a resignation ploy ended his presidency. The best he could do was a resignation letter on August 25 along the lines of Vargas's suicide note.

While Goulart meandered home from a state visit to China that had focused attention upon his leftist inclinations, congressional leaders and the military ministers, anxious to avoid a clear rupture of constitutionality, but unwilling to trust Goulart with full presidential powers, worked on a compromise solution. On September 2 the congress approved a parliamentary form of government, and five days later Goulart became president with a Council of Ministers headed by Tancredo de Almeida Neves (b. 1910), an experienced Minas Gerais politician who had held the justice portfolio at the end of Vargas's last term). The disaster of civil war had been avoided, but it was a stay of execution, not a permanent reprieve. During the two and a half years of Goulart's presidency, crucial events occurred that carried Brazil down the slippery road to a crisis of the system, not just of the regime, resulting in two decades of authoritarian military rule. Political issues, particularly those with deep social and economic roots, went quickly from highly divisive to positively indigestible.

Traditional agrarian interests at first continued to find allies in the congress to thwart executive initiatives. Then, when the 1962 elections resulted in a weakening of conservative numbers and resolve, the agrarians responded by allying with urban elites, who were being dislodged from the levers of political power, to do away with electoral and legislative processes that no longer served their purposes. To accomplish this, they exploited the government's mistakes to convince centrist elements of the dire threat posed by "demagogic" radicalism. Even more important, their allies inside the armed forces did the same vis-à-vis moderates within that ultimately decisive institution. For there was a well-defined military nucleus frustrated by the fact that each time the military had pushed Vargas and his heirs out of power (1945, 1954, and 1960), the "misguided" electorate quickly opened the door for their return (1950 by again electing Vargas, 1955 by choosing Kubitschek, and, through Quadros's resignation, 1961). A tragic case of political mobilization for structural reforms leading instead to a preemptive counterrevolution gave the right its chance to take power by force. (There are strong parallels in this respect between 1961–1964 in Brazil and what had taken place in Venezuela in the years immediately preceding 1948, as well as what would occur in Chile just before 1973. In addition, it happened at virtually the same time as the military was ousting the civilian president in Argentina.)

The polarization leading to the breakdown of Brazilian democracy was fed by both shortsighted opposition to change by intransigent conservative elements and detachment from reality on the part of the extreme left, which let wishful thinking run wild during 1963 and early 1964—eventually turning into suicidal self-delusion reminiscent of that of the National Liberating Alliance militants in 1935. Goulart's manifold shortcomings aggravated the crisis and hastened its unfortunate denouement, but the very real dilemmas in the situation of the early 1960s would have severely tested the mettle of Kubitschek or even Vargas. Goulart, spooked by the prospect of being outflanked on the left by brother-in-law Brizola and convinced of the need to recover full presidential powers, responded to the October 7, 1962, congressional election campaign by shifting to a stridently radical nationalist stance. On that day 15 million Brazilians, of the 18.5 million eligible, chose a congress scheduled to hold power until February 1967, as well as governors in half the states. Money poured into conservative campaigns by the United States served to neutralize patronage favors and massive expenditures for left-wing candidates made by the Goulart administration—and also served to further inflame passions. Brizola launched himself onto the national scene by receiving a record vote for congress from Rio de Janeiro even though his entire political career had been in Rio Grande do Sul.[7]

The resulting Chamber of Deputies saw the PSD, PTB, and UDN at relatively equal strength with 119, 104, and 97 seats, respectively, leaving just 89 to the ten minor parties. Only if Goulart would walk a tightrope between insistent demands for basic reforms coming from the majority component of his PTB and the conservative rural-based core of the PSD could the Vargas-designed alliance be maintained and the administration retain a viable congressional base. Unfortunately the event marking the high point of Goulart's abbreviated term also distorted his political perspective. On January 6, 1963, a plebiscite favored a return to presidentialism by 9.5 million to only 2 million opposed. By interpreting this five-to-one preference for a presidential system as a vote of confidence and a personal mandate, Goulart grievously miscalculated his position. Pushing for policies injurious to the interests of the established power structure, he catalyzed a backlash mobilization capable of swamping the left's noisy campaigns and demonstrations when push really came to shove.

Under pressure from the extreme left, Goulart abandoned the three-year plan worked out by finance minister Celso Furtado. Wage increases spurred inflation to over 80 percent for the year as per capita GDP growth turned negative. Since even in politically troubled 1961 the economy had grown by 7.9 percent, Goulart was vulnerable to charges of economic mismanagement. As presidential succession was scheduled for 1965, the semi-lame-duck president had to cope with rival political ambitions within as well as between parties. The situation was greatly complicated by the fact that marriage to the sister of Goulart's wife made the highly ambitious Brizola ineligible, driving him toward increasingly extreme positions involving, at the minimum, militant demands for constitutional change and at the maximum, threats of political pyromania. Goulart's brand of patronage-oriented, paternalistic populism, largely devoid of ideological content, proved inadequate in the rapidly polarizing political situation, and he became increasingly open to rash and ill-considered advice. His most egregious error was an October request to the congress for a state of siege, which cost him the support of a very large proportion of the legalist-democratic majority in the officer corps, upon whose constitutionalist scruples his tenure in office effectively rested.

For by this time the broad-based conspiracy that soon brought down Goulart and his government was already well advanced. Retired General Golbery do Couto e Silva (b. 1911), later to be the chief idea man of the moderate wing of the military rulers, used the Institute for Social Research and Studies (IPES) as a nexus for antiregime planning, taking an active role in the search for a prestigious senior general in the Rio de Janeiro area to assume a leadership position. General Humberto de Alencar Castelo Branco (b. 1897) filled the bill admirably. A hero of the Italian campaign who enjoyed a reputation for scrupulously avoiding involvement in civilian political affairs, he had developed a large following among those who were by now middle-grade officers during a long tenure with the Command and General Staff School, and among more senior officers through his service as commandant of the Superior War College (ESG). By late 1963, he had conditionally agreed to assume military leadership of the movement, as long as plans to move against Goulart rested upon his violation of accepted rules of the political game.[8]

At the end of February 1964, Goulart took a number of measures bordering on demagoguery that indicated that he had stopped listening to Kubitschek and was falling more under the influence of Brizola. Deciding to go all out for mobilization of mass pressures for basic structural reforms, he imposed agrarian reform by executive decree on March 13, also nationalizing private oil refineries. Yet these measures, announced at a popular rally, were overshadowed by Brizola's denunciation of the congress and call for a popular revolution. As the Easter holidays neared, governors of five of the country's six most important states undertook close cooperation and distanced themselves from the federal executive. When two thousand discontented servicemen gathered at a communist-controlled union on the night of March 25, Goulart stepped over the line by agreeing to demands, including appointment of a new navy minister. Within a few days, essentially conservative Minas Gerais was in open revolt. As troops descended on Rio de Janeiro on the night of March 31, Goulart fled to his home state, leaving the incendiary Brizola the impossible task of mounting armed resistance.

The forces that overthrew the Goulart government with surprising ease were united chiefly by agreement that the radicalization and lack of discipline of the preceding weeks was intolerable. Beyond a shared determination to end "subversion," the various components of the March 31 movement possessed no consensus as to what should come next. As had been the case in 1930, the wide scope of participation brought with it a high degree of heterogeneity. Historical conspirators within the military who advocated a prolonged period of purges stood alongside conservative UDN elements who wanted the lengthy period of political dominance they had expected to have after the 1960 election. These two groups coexisted uneasily with moderates for whom Goulart had been acceptable as long as they could expect a return of Kubitschek to power by 1966. Relations were equally shaky with legalists who had reluctantly acted only when they were convinced of Goulart-Brizola efforts to subvert military discipline and "illegitimately" change the constitution.

Having gone farther than ever before in exercising the moderating power, the armed forces decided to establish a semiconstitutional regime to replace the provisional Revolutionary Supreme Command immediately set up by General Arthur da Costa e Silva (b. 1899). Castelo Branco was the near-consensus pick of the military conspirators to serve out at least the remainder of Goulart's term, and the congress duly ratified this choice on April 11. By this time the Revolutionary Supreme Command had issued an "institutional act" barring the "corrupt" and "subversive" elements linked to the overthrown regime, including elected officeholders, from political life for ten years.[9] Under heavy pressure from Costa e Silva, who stayed on as war minister, Castelo agreed to deprive Kubitschek of his political rights on June 8, a move designed to forestall pressures for an early election. Against the wishes of the hard-liners *(linha dura),* the president let his major discretionary powers under the first Institutional Act expire, bolstering the reservations of these younger officers of a radical rightist position that the Castelo government was overly concerned about moderation and rationality. Indeed, there was a general feeling among the military that power could not be allowed to fall back into the hands of the Vargas lineage as in 1951, 1956, and 1961. How long the military should itself hold power was another matter. Forces advocating the traditional arbiter function with a quick turnover of power to reliable civilians carried the day in April 1964 and remained in control of the situation until October 1965. Only with the 1967 presidential succession did it become apparent that a long authoritarian night under elements determined to be the nation's ruler was inevitable.

Castelo and his close advisers, including generals Golbery do Couto e Silva and Ernesto Geisel, believed that basic flaws in the country's political structures needed to be remedied and that the punitive phase of the revolution had to be put behind them so that the government could come to grips with underlying structural problems. Meanwhile, economic recovery was essential, so Planning Minister Roberto de Oliveira Campos was free from the considerations of political feasibility and electoral repercussions that had constrained previous stabilization efforts. GDP growth of 3.4 percent in 1964, 2.4 percent in 1965, 6.7 percent in 1966, and 4.2 percent the following year were remarkable for a period of adjustment and austerity, leaving cosmopolitan diplomat Campos with an enviable international reputation.

Despite dire forecasts by those opposed to rapidly reopening political competition, Castelo insisted on going ahead with direct election of governors in October 1965 in the eleven states where they had been chosen in 1960. This test of public reaction to his brand of tutelary democracy saw candidates associated with the revolution carry most states, but the public perception was one of repudiation of the administration in major population centers. In the resulting behind-the-scenes military crisis, a sweeping Second Institutional Act was issued, and Costa e Silva consolidated his position as the leading contender to succeed Castelo, with existing political parties dissolved and choice of the new president resting with the congress. Soon a two-party system was imposed, consisting of the government-sponsored National Renovating Alliance (ARENA) and nominally opposition elements banded together in the Brazilian Democratic Movement (MDB). Although the latter had only 21 senators and 150 deputies, they came from such a wide range of interests and ideological positions that the party would never achieve a significant degree of unity or even coherence.

In February 1966, the Third Institutional Act decreed indirect selection of governors, convoked congressional elections for November 15, and made mayors of state capitals appointive. In these conditions the MDB decided not to contest the presidential race, so on October 3 Costa e Silva became president-elect under circumstances closely paralleling those of Floriano's selection to succeed Deodoro nearly three quarters of a century before. (This move to a more authoritarian regime occurred at almost the same time as Argentina was taking steps in the same direction.) While the regime shaped a new constitution, congressional balloting strengthened the government's hand, with ARENA winning over two-thirds of the Chamber of Deputies seats and electing eighteen of twenty-two senators on well over 8.7 million votes to not quite 4.9 million for the MDB. Yet in a harbinger of things to come, the opposition won by large margins in Rio de Janeiro and Rio Grande do Sul and came close in São Paulo.[10]

The inauguration of the amiable, rather ordinary Costa e Silva to succeed austere military intellectual Castelo ushered in a protracted period during which the presidency was occupied by someone committed to the idea of the armed forces as the country's proper and semipermanent ruler. Well-intentioned in a number of ways, but also ill-prepared in many areas of public policy, Costa e Silva found himself facing a "broad front" of opposition linked to ex- and would-be presidents (Kubitschek, Quadros, Goulart, and Lacerda). More troublesome was criticism from the Catholic Church and student organizations. Many hard-liners around the president confused the church's newly found social conscience with giving aid and comfort to subversive agitators, a category in which they lumped all politically activist students—a large proportion of whom had their roots in church-sponsored youth organizations such as Popular Action (AP) and Catholic University Youth (JUC). Caught up in Cold War conceptions, the conservative military were dismayed by the church's lack of appreciation for their self-perceived saving of Brazil's Catholic values from destruction by Marxist-Leninist forces.

Lack of presidential leadership by the later part of 1968 combined with an insubordinate mood in the congress and terrorist acts from both political extremes to create a crisis. When on December 12 the Chamber of Deputies refused to strip an aggressively hostile young congressman of his parliamentary immunity, the government reacted with unexpected vigor. The truly draconian Fifth Institutional Act (AI-5) granted broad discretionary powers to the president and began a new round of cancellations of legislative mandates and suspensions of political rights. Brazil moved to the brink of unrestricted military dictatorship. At least 1400 individuals were punished under AI-5, and all elections scheduled before November 1970 were canceled.[11] Then, as August 1969 ended, the nation awoke to the news that Costa e Silva, who had been considering moves to ease political restrictions, had suffered an incapacitating cardiovascular problem. The service ministers vetoed assumption of the presidency by the civilian vice president, forming a junta instead. For the fourth time since 1964, progress toward political normality was bulldozed into oblivion by military imposition of a more arbitrary regime than had previously existed. A military equivalent of the College of Cardinals both chose General Emilío Garrastazú Médici (b. 1905) as president and decreed an extensive set of constitutional amendments further increasing centralization of power in the hands of the federal government and augmenting the already heavy concentration of authority in the executive. After ten months of forced recess, and minus the large number of its most independent members who had fallen afoul of the Institutional Act, a chastened congress was summoned back to ratify the military's decision.

"Project Brazil: Great Power" was the leitmotif of Médici's administration, one in which high rates of economic growth coexisted with ruthlessly effective repression. Energized by the death of the most prominent guerrilla leader, Médici made it clear that in his "revolutionary state" the president retained emergency powers as leader of the revolutionary movement as well as chief executive. Economic growth had held at 9.5 percent in 1969, after an astounding jump to 9.8 percent in 1968, and was accelerating. As Brazil won its third soccer World Cup champi-onship in the past four tries in mid-1970, making up for 1966's failure, the regime had relative ease in diverting public attention from politics. After state legislatures confirmed presidential choices for governors, on November 15 congressional elections afforded the registered electorate of 29 million (in a population ap-proaching 95 million) a chance to chose between ARENA loyalists and surviving MDB candidates. Not surprisingly the government party garnered 220 of 310 lower-house seats and victories in 40 of 46 Senate races, on the strength of 10.9 million valid votes to the MDB's 4.8 million. Yet the opposition retained a solid base of support in the most advanced regions of the country.

The Médici government combined improved intelligence, systematic use of torture, and more sophisticated counterinsurgency tactics to destroy the violent left. Brutally efficient, and focused, repression was not on nearly the same scale or marked with as great a disregard for human life as in Argentina. Much of the pub-lic remained mesmerized by economic growth, which, fueled by heavy industrial investment, steamed ahead at 10.4 percent for 1970, 11.3 percent in 1971, 12.1 percent during 1972, and 14.0 percent for 1973. Hailed as the "economic mira-cle," this growth involved low rates of inflation (under 20 percent a year), a tenfold increase in foreign exchange reserves, and sharply rising exports at $4 billion in 1972 and $6.2 billion the following year. The flies in the ointment were extremely inequitable income distribution, failure of growth to improve levels of living for the underprivileged masses, and neglect of pressing social problems, such as health, housing, and education. Still the government scored resounding victories in the November 1972 municipal elections. Moreover, Médici did not lose control of the succession process as had his predecessors.[12]

Highly respected army minister General Orlando Geisel, to whom Médici delegated authority in the matter of the succession, decided that his younger and more intellectual brother, Ernesto (b. 1908), was best qualified for the job. An-nounced as the government candidate in June 1973, Ernesto Geisel was named to the presidency on January 15, 1974, by an electoral college composed almost exclusively of the incumbent congress. This choice of a close disciple of late ex-president Castelo Branco had momentous implications for Brazil, as it restored control to moderates rather than right-wing ruler types. The next five years would be a reversal of the past half decade, as champions of the military as arbiter outwitted and outfought the entrenched hard-line advocates of indefinite mili-tary rule. The new president and his team of Castelo Branco heirs—in the face of heavy resistance within the armed forces and only limited understanding and sporadic cooperation from a distrustful civilian opposition—steered the country through a phase of decompression of the repressive authoritarian regime and set it firmly on the path to political "opening" *(abertura)* before selecting a successor to carry this process on to democratization. To this final end, Geisel installed General João Baptista de Oliveira Figueiredo (b. 1918) as head of the National Intelligence Service (SNI).

Although coming to power in the midst of a continuing economic boom, the austere German Lutheran was clearly not going to outperform his predecessor in the growth realm. The global energy crisis had already begun during the last quarter of 1973, so the boom was due to moderate, although not end. To repeat the economic rationality of the Castelo period, Geisel appointed João Paulo dos Reis Velloso (b. 1931) as planning minister, with brilliant young economist Mário Henrique Simonsen (b. 1935) as finance minister. Closely advised by Golbery do Couto e Silva, Geisel operated with a flexible timetable for dismantling the repressive apparatus that had burgeoned under Médici and for subsequently turning the country out of the cul de sac of authoritarianism. His first task was to become effective leader of the military institution as well as head of government.

At the center of Geisel's decision to begin decompression *(distensão),* as blueprinted by Golbery largely on the basis of the ideas of Samuel P. Huntington, was his perception that under Médici the security apparatus had gained a dangerous degree of autonomy.[13] Being held responsible by the public for human rights violations had widened the gap between the military and the centrist-to-moderately-reformist elements of Brazilian civil society. With the guerrilla threat having been eliminated, repression was dysfunctional, and its practitioners needed to be reined in. If Geisel had to act autocratically at times to remove obstacles to *distensão* or if he even had to resort to authoritarian measures to avoid losing essential military support, so be it, as he was concerned about the end result, not popularity along the way.

The first step was handpicking governors, all duly confirmed by state legislatures in October 1974. Then he insisted on holding essentially free congressional elections on November 15. With an electorate of 35.8 million in a population nearing 105 million, the turnout of 29 million matched 1970's total of voter registration. The balloting resulted in a strong MDB comeback, scoring a 16 to 6 victory in senate races and electing 45 percent of the lower house. The government was sobered more than shaken by the poor showing of its party's senatorial candidates, since ARENA retained a decisive 204 to 160 edge in the lower house—compared to its previous 220 to 90 advantage—and an even more comfortable margin in the upper house, where holdovers gave it 46 seats to the MDB's 20. Indeed, in the view of its strategists, opposition gains were healthy in that they reflected the return to normal channels of electoral politics by alienated elements that had abstained or nullified their ballots in 1970.

March 1975 saw resumption of full functioning of the congress, but in May the president invoked the extraordinary powers of AI-5 after years of disuse. By the last quarter of the year, hard-line elements, particularly in São Paulo, were heating up the issue of subversion in answer to opposition efforts to focus attention upon torture and violations of civil liberties. When a crusading journalist and then a worker accused of distributing communist propaganda died while in the authorities' hands, the president immediately relieved a personal friend of army command there. Approved by many officers tired of hard-line excesses, this step caused a rift between Geisel and his army minister. Since General Sylvio Frota (b. 1910) was a hard-liner who harbored presidential aspirations, a confrontation was inevitable. Geisel skillfully engineered it to occur when and where he was ready to do battle. Meanwhile, in the local elections of November 1976, some 18 million votes were cast for ARENA candidates compared to 13 million for the MDB's. Yet the opposition elected mayors or a majority of councilmen in 63 percent of cities of over 250,000. Still the most important result was confirmation of the government's belief that it could retain sufficient control of the system at the national and state levels in 1978 with ARENA as its vehicle, although this feat might require some judicious tinkering with electoral rules.

Relaunching *distensão* in 1977 was complicated by mediocre performance in the economic realm. The government's ambitious Second National Development Plan for 1975–1979 had been undermined by the soaring price of crude oil and the heavy investments required by consequent efforts to reduce dependence upon petroleum imports. During 1974, problems were most evident in trade, as doubling imports resulted in a $4.7 billion deficit. Foreign exchange reserves dropped, and foreign debt rose. GDP growth, largely a carryover from the Médici years, was 9 percent, but inflation edged up to nearly 35 percent. This economic downturn was more evident in 1975 as GDP growth declined to 6.1 percent and inflation leveled off. Although in 1976 expansion of GDP improved to 10.1 percent, inflation jumped to 46 percent. But the last years of the Geisel government took place in a deteriorating economic environment as growth fell to 5.4 percent for 1977 and 4.8 percent in 1978. With a rapid rise in foreign debt, balanced trade in 1977 and 1978 wasn't enough, since surging debt service required a large sustained inflow of capital.

Structurally, the Brazilian economy of the late 1970s was substantially changed since the military's seizure of power. By 1978, agriculture was down to 14 percent of GDP and industry up to 33 percent. Annual steel production exceeded nine million tons by 1979, triple that of 1964, with the auto industry producing nearly a million vehicles. Electrical generating capacity had doubled between 1964 and 1971 and again by 1978. This transformation was reflected in the workforce, where by 1978, 20 percent of the economically active population (EAP) was employed in industry and 40 percent in the service sector, with agriculture down to 36 percent—compared to 14, 26, and 60 percent, respectively, in 1950. Indeed, during the 1970s, industrial employment grew by well over 500,000 a year and jobs in the service area by nearly 900,000 annually.

In 1977, Geisel and his advisers were faced with finding a way to guarantee an ARENA victory in the next year's national elections while heading off Frota's unwanted presidential candidacy. Placing the congress in temporary recess, Geisel decreed changes in the rules of the electoral game, including extending his successor's term to six years. With one senator from each state chosen indirectly, the government was assured of retaining control of the upper house, thus reinforcing its majority in the electoral college. By reaffirming Geisel's determination to keep decompression within limits and control its pace, these decisive moves contributed to the military support necessary for dealing with the succession question. Frota was astutely maneuvered into overplaying his hand and was dismissed in October. His dismissal was followed in April 1978 by Figueiredo's nomination by ARENA, preceded by elimination of the sweeping powers of AI-5. So on October 15 the electoral college ratified Figueiredo, and the selection of governors went smoothly with the exception of São Paulo, where upstart Paulo Salim Maluf (b. 1931) defeated Geisel's choice at the ARENA convention.

With Brazil's electorate up to 46 million in a population of 114 million, nearly 38 million of whom went to the polls on November 15, the government party elected 231 federal deputies to 189 for the opposition. Yet even more than had been the case in 1974, the gross underrepresentation of populous urban states was crucial to ARENA's comfortable margin of seats; in terms of popular vote, the difference was only 250,000 votes—at a bit over 15 million to 14.8 million. The government also won fifteen of the twenty-three Senate seats at stake (despite the popular vote being 57 to 43 percent in favor of the MDB).[14] State electoral colleges chose twenty-two other seats, with ARENA gaining all but one. These mixed results were advantageous for the process of political decompression and its transformation into *abertura*, since the electoral vitality of the MDB convinced wavering elements associated with the regime of the need for continuing political reforms, and ARENA's firm control of congress and state legislatures forestalled any reaction by hard-line elements in the armed forces. A moral victory for the opposition drew it further into the game of liberalization through elections—the slow and conflict-free road. Indeed, the extreme left, especially its violence-oriented and minimalist components, was essentially irrelevant from this point on, and its irrelevance helped the new government to contain attempts by the radical right to derail *abertura*.[15]

Following Geisel's end-of-year revocation of banishment orders against a number of exiles, Figueiredo was inaugurated as constitutional chief executive on March 15, 1979. For the first time since 1926, one Brazilian administration was followed by another committed to continuing its policies. Not only did Golbery do Couto e Silva continue as presidential chief of staff, but Simonsen also stayed on, though shifting over to the planning ministry. Thus, this was a government reflecting all major currents within both the military establishment and the technocratic stratum—as Costa e Silva–Médici–era economic czar Antônio Delfim Netto (b. 1928) took over the agriculture ministry. The economic legacy was mixed, as GDP growth reached 7.9 percent for 1979, but inflation doubled to 77 percent. Defeated on the question of making adjustments to the harsher economic realities imposed by the global energy crisis, Simonsen gave way in September to Delfim Netto and his idea of a quick fix by way of a 30 percent currency devaluation.

In any case, attention was focused on that month's sweeping amnesty law and the November reformulation of the party system. The Social Democracy Party (PDS) replaced ARENA as the government's electoral and legislative bulwark, and the MDB became the Party of the Brazilian Democratic Movement (PMDB); the Popular Party (PP), the Brazilian Labor Party (PTB), and the Democratic Workers' Party (PDT) were also legally recognized. As all had roots from before the military took power, the only really new factor on the party scene was the Workers' Party (PT), headed by São Paulo metalworkers leader Luis Inácio Lula da Silva (b. 1946). Far from having the immediate impact many observers predicted for a socialist party, or being a transitory phenomenon, it would gain the presidency—but not until early in the next century.[16]

Mexico: Institutionalized Stability and Economic Viability

For Mexico this quarter century, in comparison to both the preceding one and the one to follow, would be remarkably unremarkable and, in contrast to the rest of the region, free of crises. The hegemony of the PRI continued essentially unchallenged under a series of competent, but noninnovative chief executives, with only Adolfo López Mateos (1958–1964) doing much to instill some traces of new life into the graying party still coasting on the conquests and accomplishments of Cárdenas in the late 1930s. Weathering a few significant ripples of discontent stemming in part from the example of the Cuban Revolution, the well-institutionalized system demonstrated residual momentum combined with occasional dashes of resilience.

The period opened with Adolfo Ruiz Cortines well past the midpoint of his uneventful administration, and with the economy on the upturn. The 1958 elections brought his choice, former labor minister López Mateos (b. 1910), to the presidency with just over 90 percent of the votes cast.[17] The conservative National Action Party (PAN) put up a sacrificial opposition candidate, Luis H. Álvarez, a textile manufacturer from Chihuahua, and the two other legal parties, existing primarily to give an appearance of democracy and legitimacy to the process, entered congressional candidates but voted for López Mateos. The Popular Socialist Party (PPS) had been founded by the aging Vicente Lombardo Toledano after his

Marxism had found no welcome in the PRI. The Authentic Party of the Mexican Revolution (PARM) was a club of retired army generals serving as window dressing on the right of the PRI as the PPS did on its left. For an improved public image of the regime, the PAN was credited with six chamber seats—one more than in 1952 and the same as in the 1955 midterm balloting.

In a term that overlapped the Cuban Revolution, for which many Mexicans felt a visceral sympathy, López Mateos made a swing back to the center from his predecessor's more probusiness policies—packaging it as a move to the left and a return to Cárdenas-like policies. Benefiting from substantial prosperity, he cultivated an image of being "widely loved and a great compromiser."[18] Yet his power base was rooted firmly in the party, and he carefully avoided offending any significant faction. Hence, in a context of a booming economy, López Mateos kept unions relatively satisfied and moderately extended social services. Progress in these respects in the urban sector, as well as public works, particularly low-cost public housing, partially masked the continuing poverty of the rural masses, which the president sought to appease by stepping up distribution of land. At the end of his term López Mateos boasted that he had turned over more land to the *campesinos* than even Cárdenas had. He failed to note, however, that, compared to the prime lands given out by Cárdenas, much of this land was semiarid and unproductive, located in some degree of proximity to hydroelectric complexes, but often lacking developed irrigation systems. But he demonstrated some concern about distribution of the wealth built up under his predecessors.

In 1964, election of Gustavo Díaz Ordaz (b. 1911), López Mateos's minister of *gobernacíon* (like Britain's Home Secretary, with control over public safety and justice) went smoothly: The PRI candidate received 89 percent of the ballots cast. Congressional and gubernatorial elections confirmed the PRI's political stranglehold. Díaz Ordaz's *sexénio,* as Mexico's nonrenewable six-year presidential term is known, did not go as smoothly as that of his predecessor. Provisions had been made in 1963 for a small number of congressional seats to go to parties obtaining at least 2.5 percent of the vote, even if they failed to carry any of the 178 districts. This reform resulted in a lower house in which the PRI had 175 seats for its 86.3 percent of the vote, compared to 20 for the PAN on 11.5 percent of the vote, balanced by 10 for the tame PPS and 5 for the even tamer PARM even though their slivers of the electoral pie had been only 1.4 percent and .7 percent, respectively.[19] Taking office near the end of 1964, Díaz Ordaz came to exemplify the strength and power of the presidential office independent of leadership shortcomings on the part of its incumbent. Unlike López Mateos, he lacked the will and ability to conciliate rather than alienate important interests within the broad inclusive type of hegemonic party the PRI had become. Power contenders around him were frustrated by his failure even to communicate the idea that compromise was viable. (In this sense he was a throwback to Alemán.)

Luck was certainly not on Díaz Ordaz's side. He would have to cope with the severe political unrest of 1968 on the occasion of Mexico's hosting the Olympic Games—only two years before it was scheduled do the same in an election year for the soccer World Cup on the fiftieth anniversary of the 1910 Revolution. On October 2 thousands of students took to the streets to protest the lack of political liberty, the economic decline, and the failure to meet the social needs of a rapidly expanding population. They were fired upon by the police and army, leaving 325 killed and many more wounded, with large numbers roughly rounded up and jailed.

The 1970 succession was heavily influenced by this violent student unrest of the second half of 1968. Government figures preferring negotiation to repression were discredited in the president's eyes, as were professors in general. The elimination from consideration of the presidential chief of staff and Mexico City's mayor, both early-line betting favorites, opened the way for the hard-line interior minister, Luis Echeverría Álvarez (b. 1922). Indeed, a number of well-placed insiders have claimed that the rather Machiavellian Echeverría stoked, if not lit, the fires that consumed the presidential ambitions of his two main rivals, who, after the bloody massacre of student demonstrators, saw their prospects in steady decline. Echeverría's chances were aided in early 1969 by Díaz Ordaz's serious eye operation, his wife's nearing insanity, and his son's drug problems. By June 1969, Echeverría knew that he was the president's choice, and in late October, he was formally endorsed by the party.

Although Echeverría's election was not quite as easy as that of 1964 (he was credited with "only" 86 percent of the votes), neither was it a real contest in the sense of any possibility that he might lose. On the congressional side, the PRI came away with all 178 district seats (on 80.1 percent of the vote), and the PAN received 20 of the national bonus for its 13.9 percent of electoral preferences (with the PPS and PARM holding the same insignificant share of the vote they had in 1964). Echeverría had the distinct benefit of presiding over an oil-exporting country during the good years of high crude prices, so he could maintain the image of a populist without having to really upset those economic fat cats with whom the PRI had developed a close, sometimes almost incestuous, relationship. His policy of "shared development" called for the workers and peasants to receive a more equitable share of a growing economic pie, but without that share's coming at the direct expense of the middle class or the entrepreneurial stratum. His goals of doubling production of petroleum, electricity, and steel required heavy foreign borrowing, and this would lead to an economic crisis toward the end of his term analogous to that in the final stage of Alemán's stewardship. (Yet, by comparative standards, particularly within Latin America, a quarter-century spread between economic crises was a noteworthy accomplishment—credit for which belonged to Ruiz Cortines, López Mateos, and even Díaz Ordaz, not the man under whom the streak came to its end.)

If Díaz Ordaz had demonstrated, by Mexican standards, inept, sometimes hesitant, and sometimes arbitrary leadership, Echeverría went to the other extreme, showing "a style of rule [that] was neither institutionalized nor bureaucratized. It was extremely, urgently and intensely personal."[20] In the eyes of another perceptive student of Mexican politics, he "exemplified the degree to which the authoritarianism inherent in his office could be used to fit the personal style of the incumbent, in this case the style of an insatiable power seeker."[21] Most damaging to the party was his virtual Kulturkampf with the business community, at least those large-scale elements aligned with the PAN. Showing how far Echeverría had come from the Alemanista model, he massively increased public intervention in the economy, requiring, in the eyes of many, an alarming degree of deficit financing. As depicted by Camp:

> During the early 1970s the government bought or gained control of hundreds of businesses and industries, placing more economic and human resources in the hands of government managers than at any time before. At the end of his administration, Echeverría further alienated the private sector by attempting to expropriate valuable lands in the northwest.[22]

With increasing petroleum exports, large international loans were obtained for development projects.

By the end of Echeverría's term, the country faced an economic crisis requiring a measure that PRI governments had avoided since 1954, a substantial devaluation of the peso. This would, of course, be left until the 1976 election had been safely won, not difficult since the PAN was too internally divided to field a candidate, making the election a walkover. A three-year stabilization agreement was signed early with the International Monetary Fund (IMF), with the requisite austerity measures in terms of limits on the deficit, cuts in expenditures, more careful husbanding of revenues, and wage restraints left on his successor's doorstep as an unwanted housewarming present. Yet in Mexico, and certainly most other countries, as long as one's predecessor bequeaths the presidency to one, and not to a bitter rival, complaining about the legacy would be in bad political taste.

Echeverría had begun his term giving the impression that his interior minister was close to being heir apparent. But this young contender, still in his thirties, became a stalking horse, if not a decoy, as the president shifted his support to an individual of much more limited political assets, hence more likely to realize that he owed his rise to El Presidente.[23] Echeverría realized all too well that in choosing him, Díaz Ordaz had not found a successor who had any strong sense of loyalty. Indeed, by the end of his first year as president, the split between Echeverría and his predecessor was complete. The transition had taken place in a context of economic growth, but this would deteriorate, and with it the natural heir apparent,

Mário Moya Palencia. At thirty-seven the youngest interior minister in Mexico's history, he fell victim to the tradition of each age cohort's getting two bites at the presidency. Echeverría turned increasingly to the more mature José López Portillo.

Brash and overconfident, the perils of youth, Moya built too much of an independent political following, a no-no in a system in which presidents sought to have a successor who would feel indebted to them for such a great honor and opportunity. Brought into the government in late 1971, López Portillo (b. 1920) was appointed finance minister in 1973. Although foreign debt quadrupled from $5 billion to $20 billion between 1970 and 1976, López Portillo received high grades in management of the economy from a president harboring some quite particular ideas concerning finance and fiscal policy. In selecting López Portillo to be his successor, Echeverría was seeking to minimize the chance that he would be reduced to a limping duck as political interest in general and interests as actors turned their attention to the man who would be the country's boss for the next six years. In an attempt to salvage his place in history, Echeverría lowered the voting age to eighteen and embarked on a last-minute campaign of distributing land to peasants.

Elected easily at the end of 1976, with 94 percent of the vote, López Portillo enjoyed support of an enlarged Chamber of Deputies, in which the PRI had all 195 district seats on the strength of 80.1 percent of voter preferences, and the PAN retained its 20 allotted national pool seats despite a drop in its share of the vote to 8.5 percent. The PPS saw these "good behavior" seats rise to 12 and the PARM to 9—as they raised their vote to 3.0 percent and 2.5 percent, respectively.[24] The new president had considerable success in reducing the harm and alarm his predecessor had left behind, working assiduously to heal the rift between the government and the private sector. Like Ruiz Cortines and López Mateos, he radiated confidence and political stability, adopting an economic discourse stressing an "alliance for profits" soothing to business sectors offended by Echeverría's populist stance. A combination of the Arab oil embargo and the growing Mexican petroleum reserves allowed for a trebling of production and a twelvefold increase in earnings by 1980—making Mexico, or at least its government, wealthy. López Portillo invested billions in a highly touted rural development effort with highly disappointing results, and corruption and graft reached new highs.[25]

López Portillo played as fast and loose with prudent financial policies as he had facilitated Echeverría in doing. After chafing under restraints of the IMF agreement, interpreted by him more as guidelines than as rigid limits, by the end of his term he turned developmentalist. Unrealistically expecting continuing high crude prices to produce growing revenues, López Portillo followed unwise policies similar to those of John V. Lindsay as mayor of New York City in the early 1970s—essentially spending next year's projected higher revenues this year. Foreign debt, both public and private, continued to soar in the face of profligate spending—on the way to $60 billion by the end of López Portillo's term in 1982, a tripling in only six years. Although the first half of the next period would see more of the same, the 1990s would witness a democratic transformation of Mexican politics.

Argentina: Peronism Versus Military Rule

The complexity of Argentine politics during the 1956–1979 period all but defies explanation. Starting and ending with authoritarian military figures in power, in between it saw presidencies by each wing of the Radicals as well as a dramatic return to power by Perón. During this time a variety of economic game plans would be introduced, then generally abandoned in midstream as a new chief executive abruptly took power. Several grandiose strategies were devised by heads of government and their brain trusts, failing because of either faulty premises or excessive rationality detached from any deep understanding of persisting, although perverse, political realities.[26]

Although he was out of power and in exile in Spain, Perón's long shadow would loom over Argentina not only until his death in 1974, when he was back in the presidency, but through the rest of the century and into the next. No matter what strategy the forces that ousted him might adopt, they could not break his hold over the hearts and minds of a very sizable segment of the Argentine people or prevent this support from extending into a new generation. Direct military rule, government by one of the rival Radical parties, then by the other, and renewed military rule would be tried, but in 1973 Perón triumphantly returned to power. With his death, the third Señora Perón would inherit the presidency, being overthrown by the military in 1976. This coup resulted in a highly authoritarian regime and a prolonged state of virtual civil war, with the situation improving only in 1983.

The first eighteen years of this period witnessed a great chasm between what the forces that had opposed and finally overthrown Perón had hoped to accomplish in the political realm and the vastly different outcome of their efforts. At the core of this at times grotesque gap between the military's perception of reality, largely shared by the Radicals, and the objective reality of Argentina was the unprecedented continued loyalty of millions of Argentines to Perón the man, the Peronist movement, and eventually to Peronist myths. Government after government operated on the erroneous assumption that societal elements "misled" by Peronist demagoguery could be reconverted. This wildly overoptimistic thinking was closely linked to a belief that as his place of exile moved farther and farther from Argentina (Paraguay to Venezuela, then on to the Dominican Republic, and finally to Spain) and the aging process inexorably continued, Perón would cease to exercise his, to them, irrational sway over the Argentine masses. Clearly they failed to realize that charisma, like beauty, is in the eye and heart of the beholder.

The groups which so unsuccessfully strove to build a sanitized post-Perón political order failed completely to foresee the vast appeal the aging *caudillo* would have to a younger generation—who to a large extent turned him into what they wanted him to be. Hence, the military and their allies acted on the faulty premise that time was definitely and distinctly on their side. Perón and even Peronism were in their eyes—blinded, as happens so often in politics, by the distorting lenses of wishful thinking, compounded by misreading their enemy—transitory phenomena. By way of contrast, in their thinking, the armed forces, the Radical parties, and the economic elites were permanent institutions that could and would outlast what they saw as a pernicious plague.[27]

How very wrong they were is clear from the fact that since the late 1980s, Peronism has been the strongest political force in Argentina, coming under Carlos Saúl Menem to enjoy a broader and better-structured popular base than even that built by Perón, with some help from Evita, during the immediate post–World War II decade. It would seem, as students of Argentine political life have asserted, that after 1955 Argentina had two different and distinct political subcultures, one of which viewed the pre-Perón years as the country's golden age and 1943–1955 an abomination, and the other of which viewed Perón's years in power as Argentina's finest epoch, unfortunately sandwiched between two despicable eras. No wonder compromise was nearly impossible to achieve.

The "National Liberating Revolution," as the anti-Peronist forces pompously called themselves, was divided from the start. Provisional president General Eduardo Lonardi (b. 1894) was out of step with the majority of the current armed forces. He and his backers believed that it was necessary to try to work with labor leaders, who demonstrated an inclination toward some degree of cooperation with their new regime, even if they were Peronists. The liberal faction of the army strongly disagreed with any leniency toward Peronists and ousted Lonardi on November 13, 1955. General Pedro Eugenio Aramburu (b. 1903), their leader, ensconced as provisional president, cracked down hard on all aspects of Peronism, intervening in the General Labor Confederation (CGT) as well as many of its member unions. Nullifying the 1949 constitution in April 1956 and replacing it with that of 1853 had the effect of wiping out the rights workers had gained under Perón. The Peronist party was outlawed, and its party and union activists were barred from political positions. All visible Peronist symbols—pictures, plaques, statues, and buildings—were razed.

Following Lonardi's death in March 1956, Aramburu draconianly repressed an attempted Peronist countercoup in June 1956, breaking an unwritten rule of Argentine politics by having its leader, a retired general, and twenty-seven other rebel officers executed. As Aramburu consolidated his hold, most prominent nationalist generals were forced out in November, with the vice president, Admiral Isaac Rojas, shown the gate at year's end.[28] (At this point Alejandro Lanusse, to be the last military president before Perón's return to power in 1973, was a lieutenant colonel in the grenadiers regiment.)

As officers purged under Perón returned to active duty, as had occured in Brazil in the early 1930s, over a thousand army officers and large number of non-commissioned officers, as well as over a hundred naval officers, were forced out. Anti-Peronist purges extended to the labor unions. Moderate civilian allies, alienated by Aramburu's extreme measures, broke with the government and, under the leadership of future president Arturo Frondizi (b. 1908), founded a dissident Radical party. Constituent assembly elections in July 1957 saw the two Radical parties at almost even strength, as Ricardo Balbín's Radical Civic Union of the People (UCRP) edged Frondizi's Intransigent Radical Civic Union (UCRI) by 2.11 million to 1.85 million votes (24.2 percent to 21.1 percent), and blank votes, a great many cast by Peronists, reached 2.12 million—some 24.3 percent.[29] The February 23, 1958, presidential elections gave the UCRI's Frondizi a decisive 4 million to 2.4 million win over the UCRP's Balbín—on whom the military were counting to win. Frondizi's 45 percent of the vote, more than double the UCRI's proportion seven months earlier, removed any doubt that he was the beneficiary of the Peronists' support. Unhappy that a deal between Frondizi and Perón had decided the electoral outcome, the Aramburu regime acquiesced in his inauguration with obvious reluctance.[30]

Frondizi entered office on May 1—ending thirty-two months of military rule—with support of all governors and senators, as well as holding 133 out of 187 seats in the lower house. But he was soon weakened by defections over his July decision to allow foreign companies to invest in the petroleum industry. Further narrowing of his political base resulted from the resignation of Vice President Alejandro Gómez, implicated in a conspiracy centering on an army commander in chief who resisted being replaced—a development that made the Senate's presiding officer, José María Guido, next in line for the presidency. Frondizi's response was to declare a state of siege. Moreover, the military insisted on the resignation of his chief adviser, Rogélio Frigério, and, despite relegalization of the CGT, Perón broke openly with Frondizi, seriously embarrassing him by publicizing the text of their supposed secret preelection agreement.

At this point, the Argentine officer corps was deeply divided between the so-called Azules ("Blues"), believing that they should be subordinated to constitutional authority, and the Colorados ("Reds"), who held that the military should exercise power until the task of eradicating Peronism had been accomplished, "cost what it may cost." (Juan Carlos Onganía [b. 1914], who was newly promoted to brigadier general, and who would reach the presidency in 1966, was, for a time at least, more Blue than Red.) After another failed military coup in June 1959, accompanying a wave of strikes and social unrest, one of many such buffetings he would have to survive, Frondizi invited his erstwhile rival and critic Álvaro Alsogaray, a champion of private enterprise and brother of a highly placed and extremely political general, to become economics minister.[31] The ensuing austerity program ended Frondizi's honeymoon with labor. Economic growth, 5.1 percent in 1957 and a robust 6.1 percent in 1958, had tumbled precipitously to a negative 6.4 percent, accompanied by 113 percent inflation, a situation calling for this new economic doctor with a new magic elixir in his bag.[32]

As the ailing economy seemed to respond quickly to Alsogaray's prescription with GDP growth of 7.8 percent and inflation of 27 percent in 1960 and 7.1 percent economic expansion in 1961, Frondizi's fortunes appeared to be on the rise, but they would crash with a dismal economic performance in 1962—a shocking negative 1.2 percent GDP, on its way down to a negative 2.4 percent in 1963. But by 1963 Frondizi had been relieved of his office and was hence free from responsibility for a recalcitrant economy. Long before that point he had abandoned his populist grand strategy of winning the Peronist masses over to his UCRI through the benefits and lure of rapid industrialization and had settled for the calculus of survival. The first step in his disillusionment in this respect was the 1960 congressional elections, which showed that Peronist voters were still loyal to their leader; his hopes that this loyalty might fade by 1962 proved vain.[33]

The ultimate failure of the Frondizi administration, despite its often quite able and generally courageous leadership, demonstrated that intransigence and unwillingness to compromise on fundamental questions still characterized Argentina's major political actors. During his forty-seven months in office, Frondizi faced thirty-eight conspiracies and confrontations with military elements; during these, he usually backed down on some action or policy he wished to pursue in order to move the country ahead. Showing such extreme political weakness, Frondizi could not give Alsogaray the firm support required to implement effectively his policies in a difficult economic context. Moreover, electoral imperatives led to large increases in government spending prior to the 1960 midterm elections, a loosening of the purse strings that Frondizi anticipated repeating in 1962. Seeking a lightning rod, if not a sacrificial lamb for the lack of sustained economic progress, Frondizi dismissed Alsogaray in March 1961—a move certain to enrage Alsogaray's brother Julio, a seasoned conspirator.

Overall, Frondizi could not satisfy either part of his restless constituencies, neither the Peronist-labor group nor the impatient center-right-military. By late 1961, foreign policy came to be an aggravating, not just complicating, factor in his survival equation. Heading toward the second midterm elections in his scheduled tenure, Frondizi found his 1958 understanding with the Peronists that he would allow their participation in the next presidential election a two-edged sword. The military had swallowed their sworn enemy's 1960 legislative gains, since these were only partial elections, but a similarly strong performance in 1962 might give them control of the lower house, if not the senate. A gesture to mollify the Peronists, the

September 1961 award of a medal to expatriate Ernesto "Che" Guevara, now an official of Castro's Cuban regime, raised military hackles.[34]

The January 1962 meeting across the river at Punta del Este, Uruguay, of hemispheric foreign ministers to consider suspending Cuba from the OAS (Organization of American States) required a two-thirds majority vote, which the United States was hard-pressed to cobble together. The Argentine military demanded an Argentine vote against the Castro regime; Peronists, entrenched in control of the labor movement, were equally adamant that Argentina cast its vote to "save" Cuba from the underhanded blow of the "imperialists." In a futile attempt to avoid either horn of this politically explosive dilemma, Frondizi had his representative abstain. This abstention infuriated both sides, since it forced the United States to make an unsavory deal with Haitian tyrant François Duvalier in order to prevail, but did not prevent the two-thirds vote for Cuba's ouster. The Argentine military and the Peronists agreed on only one thing, that Argentina's abstention was an act of cowardice on Frondizi's part, not one of statesmanship. (In Argentine political culture, the word *intransigent* bore the positive connotation of standing firm for one's principles; compromise carried with it the negative connotation of lacking the courage of one's convictions.)

Retribution from the military would follow swiftly, with a full-blown crisis erupting on February 2. Frondizi had justified letting the Peronists run in the coming March 18 elections as providing an opportunity to destroy the myth of their invulnerability, but their Popular Union (UP) front party won the Buenos Aires gubernatorial race with 37 percent of the vote to 23 for the UCRI candidate. Nationally the two Peronist groupings, the UP and the Justicialist Front (FJ, the name replicating Perón's ideology of *Justicialsmo*, or social justice), elected 10 of 14 governors and won 32 congressional seats to the UCRI's 25 places in the lower house and the UCRP's 20. Soon, however, a coup would deprive the Peronists of the fruits of electoral victory. While frantically searching for a solution to the volcanic backlash unleashed by the Peronists' "sensational" election showing, Frondizi encountered a UCRP preferring a military coup to entering a national union-type coalition with their estranged former UCR brothers. Indeed, the situation with respect to the Radicals was, and would continue to be, reminiscent of the Protestant Reformation and the Counter-Reformation. So, unable to form a coalition, at dawn on March 29, 1962, Frondizi found himself as unceremoniously thrown out of office as Yrigoyan had been in 1930. As in that case, leaders of the rival political factions of the military agreed on the need to remove the president, although disagreeing on what should ensue.

Whereas the interventionist Colorado or *gorila* (gorilla or hard-line) faction of the armed forces, with General Julio Alsogaray (b. 1918) in the van, desired a return to military rule à la 1955–1957, influential "swingman" (pivotal figure) General Juan Carlos Onganía (b. 1914, and three years senior to Alsogaray in service) was a relative legalist, as was another president-to-be, Colonel Alejandro Augustín Lanusse (b. 1918). With a wave of induced retirements in April 1962, Onganía shot up twenty-six spots in seniority, becoming army commander in chief. Julio Alsogaray became army undersecretary; his brother Álvaro became economics minister. Thus entrenched, Onganía managed to avoid the creation of a military junta.[35] In consultation with ex-president Aramburu and other key officers, he and his backers came up with a quasi-constitutional way out. Since the vice president had resigned back in November 1958, the next in succession was the presiding officer of the upper house of the congress, José María Guido. In this confrontation of ruler versus arbiter military groupings, the latter won out on the basis of greater unity of purpose and esprit de corps.[36] By the night of September 22, the danger of a hard-line coup was over, and Guido found himself in the hands of the legalist faction.

During his less than a year and a half in office, the mild-mannered Guido was satisfied with his interim status, acting as little more than a figurehead behind whom the armed forces called the shots. The legalist elements of the army, led by Onganía and following a tradition going back to General and President Justo in the 1930s, insisted on holding presidential elections in July 1963, confident that the UCRP would win in the balloting because neither the UCRI nor the Peronists were in a position to mount a serious contest. The Colorados, behind seventy-nine-year old General Benjamin Menéndez, General Federico Toranzo Montero, and always troublesome retired admiral and one-time vice president Rojas, saw their coup plans flop in early April 1963.[37]

Following the death of a presumptive candidate, the UCRP fell back on Arturo Umberto Illia (b. 1900), a provincial leader from the interior with minimal qualifications to govern the country, particularly under difficult circumstances. Yet, overlooking the fact that the UCRP had competed with the UCRI for Peronist support in 1958, the military viewed him with favor. On July 7, 1963—with 9.7 million, some 86 percent, of the registered electorate casting their ballots—this sixty-three-year-old country doctor received a bit over 25 percent of the vote and 169 of the 476 electoral votes, which in light of 19 percent blank ballots gave him an adequate edge over the rival UCRI's Oscar Alende (with 16.4 percent of the votes) and ex-chief executive General Aramburu, who retained the support of 13.8 percent of voters.[38] As the smaller parties cast their electoral votes to Illia, he took office in October, with Guido apparently relieved to be off the hot seat. As his party held only 72 of 192 seats in the congress, the new president's alliance-building skills would be severely tested. Wisely he retained Onganía and the rest of the military high command and adopted a hands-off policy toward the military.[39]

The neo-Peronist UP had been legalized for these elections, joining the UCRI in a so-called National Popular Front. Engaged in a power struggle with dissident Peronist Augusto Vandor, entrenched in control of the "sixty-two organizations," the strongest component of the labor movement, Perón had insisted on Vicente Solano Lima of the small Popular Conservative Party as the front's presidential candidate. Two weeks before the elections Solano was removed from the ballot as being a mere stalking horse for Perón. This proscription led Perón, from exile, to order his followers to cast blank ballots. But in the partial midterm elections of March 1965, the predominantly Peronist UP won 31 percent of the vote, to the governing UCRP's 30 percent, with other neo-Peronist parties receiving 7 percent. (The Justicialist Party [PJ] had been legalized in January, but this ruling was overturned on February 26, and the PJ was forced back into the cover of a multiparty front.) This development left the government with 68 seats in the lower house, as the Peronists rose dramatically from 8 to 52 deputies. Moreover, they had carried the country's two largest cities: Buenos Aires and Córdoba.

Illia's problems began to mount with his decision to support the US intervention in the Dominican Republic, a decision resulting in bloody riots by Argentine students and workers. His inept handling of the crisis alienated both Onganía and General Lanusse, the general staff's assistant chief for operations. The former resigned over the appointment of a new army secretary and began planning Illia's ouster. In this plan the key plotter was General Alsogaray, ensconced in the strategic post of commander of the army corps in the greater Buenos Aires region.[40] Meanwhile, leaning more toward the structuralist than the monetarist side, Illia had opted for a nationalist stance and reversed Frondizi's oil concessions while initially giving favorable wage increases. Although his government's early economic results were satisfactory, with robust GDP growth of 10.3 percent in 1964 and 9.1 percent in 1965, 1966 witnessed a sharp economic slump featuring near stagnation, with a .6 percent rise in GDP (a decrease in per capita terms) and inflation back up to 32 percent. Foreign capital failed to meet the country's investment needs, even though it bought up many Argentine firms, but it served to undermine the none-too-strong entrepreneurial spirit of local capitalists. Foreign debt, which had been slightly under $380 million in 1961, rose to $526 million by 1965.[41]

As Vandor afforded an option of neo-Peronism without Perón (like Fernando Belaúnde Terry and his Popular Action Party did in Peru vis-à-vis the military's veto of APRA), the 1966–1967 round of governorship elections took on great strategic importance. In a showdown in Mendoza in April 1966, Perón's candidate defeated Vandor's by 102,000 to 62,000—giving victory to the Democratic Party with 129,000 votes. This outcome constituted an irreparable setback for the idea nourished in some military circles of negotiating "acceptable" (moderate) Peronists for the major provincial executive elections in 1967 as a prelude to a tacit alliance with Peronists independent of Perón. These members of the military had hoped that the gubernatorial elections would show that Perón's personal appeal and electoral influence had waned, but this was clearly not the case—so a very different approach would have to be found.

As Illia's shortcomings became evident, inviting invidious comparison with Frondizi, the military removed him faster than they had Frondizi. By this point many of the military had soured on civilian politicians in general and the parties in particular, holding that the Peronists, the UCRI, and the UCRP had all proved incompetent at governing. Moreover, by 1966 the armed forces had taken over many of their South American neighbors and were poised to do so in others. Mixing ideas of the Red and Blue military factions, General Onganía had garnered the support of officers who, in principle, favored civilian rule—although with the military close by as arbiter—but found it unlikely under present circumstances and were hence willing to assume a ruler role.

Finally, a coup on June 28, 1966, brought this reluctant dragon-turned-eager-beaver to power. Onganía gained public attention for his "Argentine revolution" when he promised that he would stay in power until all its goals were achieved, no matter how long it might take. To clear the way for rebuilding the country politically, all parties and legislative bodies were dissolved, and the supreme court was dismissed. Strengthening the presidential staff while reducing the number of ministries and secretariats, Onganía shifted a significant share of decisionmaking into the hands of the National Security Council (CONASE) and the National Development Council (CONADE). In the view of a perceptive scholar, the Argentine government had proven to be big, not strong or intelligent.[42]

Álvaro Alsogaray became secretary general of the presidency, a post from which he could supervise the impressive-sounding System for National Planning and Action for Development and Security. Scalded by his earlier experiences, particularly that under Frondizi, he had no problems with Onganía's strengthening of the government's repressive capabilities if it would further insulate economic planning from disruptive conflicts within the entrepreneurial class—much as was the case with Roberto Campos in Brazil at the time. This tendency had the backing of Alsogaray's brother Julio, installed as the army's commanding general. The resulting policy mix was "an intertwining of liberal orthodoxy, mercantilism, and technocratic interventionism" that reflected the debate raging in the academic and business communities.[43] This disagreement brought with it a continuing tension and rivalry between economic liberals and nationalists (by that point resolved in Brazil in favor of the former).

As his confidence increased with experience as president, Onganía increasingly sided with monetarists against structuralists and their insistence on basic reforms, installing Adalberto Krieger Vasena as a type of economic czar in December 1966. A liberal representative of industry and agro-business with close ties to transnational interests, Krieger Vasena strove to deepen Argentina's industrialization with an eye to exportation. Convinced of the need for free trade and less governmental paternalism and interference, he was neither an orthodox monetarist nor a structuralist, believing that Argentina's inflation had shifted from demand-generated to cost-pushed. In his view the answer was to hold wage increases behind the previous year's inflation through an "incomes policy" of administered wage and price controls, while providing credit to the private sector slightly ahead of the rate of these increases, but keeping expansion of the money supply behind it. This formula worked primarily to the advantage of urban industrialists and foreign investors.

In 1965, GDP growth had been a very robust 9.1 percent, plummeting to 0.6 percent in 1966 before rallying to 2.6 percent for 1967 and 4.4 percent in 1968. Concentration, centralization, and denationalization went forward, and after 1968 there was an addition to the policy mix of an increased public sector role in maintaining aggregate demand, along with an active fiscal policy. Indeed, the Onganía government's management of the economy was one of its strong points, as the period from March 1967 to May 1969 witnessed the most successful economic turnaround since that under Perón in 1952. Even with the 1969 expansion of GDP to 8.5 percent, however, not everyone was satisfied. Many entrepreneurs favored greater emphasis on privatization and dismantling of the state sector, and there was a conflict brewing in the agricultural arena between the large producers oriented to exporting cattle and grain and the smaller farmers producing for the domestic market—a cleavage found in many countries of the region.

Criticism of schemes within the administration's brain trust to create corporatist legitimacy and a "communitarian" (social cooperation) ideology also mounted. Onganía's government included a "patriarchal and traditional" group of loyalists, along with "authoritarian liberals" harboring deep reservations concerning the nationalist and corporatist leanings of "authoritarian nationalists" and technocratically inclined "professionals."[44] Both the elements that could be described as developmental nationalists and the nationalist populists had divergent ideas of what should be the aims of Onganía's heralded transformation of the nation. The former feared continued denationalization of the economy, and the latter thought that the negative effects of the present economic program could raise sociopolitical unrest to dangerous levels. The national populists went beyond opposition to orthodox economic policies, also entertaining serious misgivings about Onganía's long-range sociopolitical projects. By late May 1968, Generals Alsogaray, an avowed opponent of the nationalists, and Lanusse were questioning the corporatist project, and raising in the backrooms of the regime the question of whether Onganía was properly the interpreter of the military's "revolution" or essentially a delegate of his fellow officers, since he was president of the military junta—which had installed him—as well as of the Argentine nation.[45]

The response of this imperious, even imperial, president, who manifested pronounced Gaullist inclinations (as this dominant leader of France had triumphed over his opponents in mid-1968), was to move against both Alsogaray brothers. In August 1968, the more trustworthy Lanusse became the new army commander in chief, and Onganía began to favor the paternalists, advocates of a more active state role in the economy. With ex-president Pedro Aramburu and General Julio Alsogaray almost openly conspiring by mid-1969, the last thing Onganía needed was a social explosion. But the traumatizing *Cordobazo* broke out on June 28 with thirteen thousand workers and students riotously marching through the country's second city, Córdoba. Their ranks swollen by striking workers of foreign-owned auto plants, the next day they controlled 150 square blocks of the city's center. For several days intense media coverage treated the rest of the country to the spectacle of destructive mobs running wild. Rigorously suppressed by the army, although not without difficulty and significant bloodshed, this shocking event punctured the government's carefully cultivated image of invulnerability.[46] (At this time Médici, next door in Brazil, was in firm control of a stable and prosperous country.) To Onganía's dismay, within six months a number of guerrilla movements were active, with the growing sense of malaise fed by the leftist Peronist *"Montenero"* terrorists kidnapping and executing ex-president Aramburu for his alleged crimes against Peronism and the Argentine people.[47]

Hoping to use Krieger Vasena as a scapegoat for economic discontent, Onganía dropped his erstwhile economic pilot, who was growing unhappy with the president's turn toward the paternalists, but Onganía gained little by the move. He alienated Lanusse by naming Francisco Imaz, a retired general and Buenos Aires province governor, as interior minister without consulting the army commander in chief. As they were the protectors of the regime, the officer corps wanted a larger say in its policies, whereas Onganía acted increasingly as if he alone possessed the revealed truth, handed down to him from on high. By this point Onganía's base of support was perilously thin, and opposition to him had significantly broadened as well as deepened. In this deteriorating environment Lanusse was able to forge a consensus in early 1970 for putting an end to Onganía's corporatist designs and starting a slow transition to civilian rule. A face-to-face meeting between Onganía and Lanusse at the end of April failed to clear the air. In late May Onganía told senior commanders that his project of the "three periods" (in which the economy had to be set in order before a restructuring of society could be begun, and this restructuring needed to be completed before a new political system was constructed) might require ten to twenty years. Lanusse responded by calling for a "Great National Accord" involving closer consultation with reliable civilian forces, a proposal whose logic called for a new hand at the country's helm.[48]

Problems with labor, chronic for all Argentine military regimes, peaked in the Onganía years. Perón had left behind the best-organized and most politically sophisticated and conscious labor movement in Latin America. Subsequent governments' efforts to depoliticize it had met with very limited success; indeed, collectively these efforts added up to abject failure—beginning with Aramburu's interventions and purges of the CGT and its member unions. Labor leader Vandor made a try at Peronism without Perón, a project in which he met determined opposition from rival union boss José Alonso, toward whom the Onganía government tilted. A December 1966 general strike ended a relative honeymoon between Onganía and the trade union movement, at the same time making Vandor and his associates overconfident.

After Vandor's loss at political arm wrestling with Perón back in 1966, the government struck back hard during the second quarter of 1967 to put him on the defensive. Within a year, a dissident body, a radical populist CGT de los Argentinos led by Marxist Raimundo Ongaro had made serious inroads among the newer service sectors, particularly public sector employees and those in state enterprises. Each of the rival CGTs laid claim to about 500,000 affiliated workers. Not to be outflanked, Vandor moved to the left and sought to mend his fences with Perón. By the beginning of 1969, a substantially weakened CGT de los Argentinos was strong chiefly around Córdoba, where for better or worse it was associated with the violent events of the *Cordobazo*. Vandor's murder, perhaps at the hands of Montenero guerrillas, in the middle of 1969 left a major vacuum in the labor field and a smaller one in the political arena. Even more serious political fallout had resulted from the murder of Aramburu, who was viewed by many key figures as the man who might be used to govern the country during a transition back to civilian rule. His death required reassessment of the options.

Seeing the handwriting on the wall, in early June 1970 Onganía sought to remove Lanusse from command of the army but, after several rounds, ended up being the odd man out. In ousting Onganía from office, the armed forces acted to cut their losses before his personal discredit and snowballing public hostility could be transferred from his government to the military as an institution.[49] Despite his pledge to "deepen the revolution," the new president, General Roberto M. Levingston (b. 1920), was essentially a placeholder, one whose viability was rapidly eroded as Lanusse's influence continued to rise.

Appointment of Aldo Ferrer, a left-of-center nationalist with a reputation for being a structuralist and developmentalist, as minister of the economy enraged major business interests, who had grave reservations about his scheme for deepening vertical integration, particularly in the intermediate goods sector, while stimulating internal demand through wage increases and public works programs.[50] Suggestions by Levingston—who was beset by external sector economic difficulties related to his strategy of marginalizing the foreign sector in an attempt to build a state-domestic capital alliance—that he might want to stay on for four or five years did not sit well with major military movers and shakers, or for that matter with civilian leaders. In November a joint declaration of Perón and UCRP leader Ricardo Balbín entitled "The Hour of the People" roiled the political waters by demanding a return to democracy. It was not at all adequately offset by Levingston's issuing a "Buy Argentine" decree designed to appeal to nationalist sentiments and rally support from industrialists and businessmen.

In these circumstances Levingston's twenty-one-week government ended on March 23, 1971, when the second *Cordobazo*, of March 12–15, with the chilling spectacle of three days of rioting strikers in control of Argentina's interior industrial center, brought Lanusse to the presidency on March 24 while he retained his post as army commander. By this time "Lanusse and the more lucid sectors of the military recognized it was illusory to think that the authoritarian system could be maintained without far reaching changes."[51] Hence, the political chess game of 1971–1973 pitted a wily political strategist, General Lanusse, against an all-time true international grandmaster, Perón. After surviving an attempted coup in October 1971, Lanusse developed a strategy for engineering an impasse in which he might be drafted to enter the electoral lists and thus stay on in power. Shortly after publication of his Political Parties Law, Perón made a surprise return to Argentina in November 1972, receiving a tumultuous welcome from a half million supporters at the airport and leaving a month later—after having put his ducks in a row for the succession. Lanusse failed to mobilize sufficient military support to call off the elections at a point when at least four out of five Argentines wanted the military out of power. Moreover, Perón undermined him by making public a secret visit from a Lanusse representative in a way that forced the president to foreswear any intention to be a candidate.

Lanusse, who had legalized the *PJ* in January 1971, counted on a legal provision requiring candidates to be in the country on election day to thwart Perón, who, he was sure, would not hazard returning again against the government's express wishes. Lanusse and many other supposedly astute politicians mistakenly breathed a sigh of relief when the little-known Héctor Cámpora, the party's second vice president, received the Peronist nomination. Taking on the imposing name of the Justicialist Liberating Front (FREJULI), the Peronists added Frondizi's Independent Left Movement (MID) as an ally and nominated Vicente Solano Lima of the Popular Conservatives as Cámpora's running mate. In the March 11 balloting, the freest since Perón's original election in 1946, carried along on the slogan "Cámpora to office, Perón to power" the FREJULI candidate received 5.9 million votes, 49.6 percent of the total, to a little over 2.5 million—21.3 percent—for the UCRP's perennial hopeful, Ricardo Balbín. Francisco Manrique, a conservative of a paternalistic bent, and Oscar Alende trailed with just under 15 percent and half that, respectively. The turnout of over 11.9 million out of a registered electorate of 14.3 million—some 85 percent— was by far a new record. This electoral tidal wave gave FREJULI 45 of 69 seats in the senate, to go with 142 of 243 in the Chamber of Deputies, and all of the governorships that were up for election.[52]

The second stage of Perón's comeback was ignited when, following Perón's return to the country in late June, Cámpora and the vice president obediently resigned in early July, necessitating a new presidential election on September 23. Perón triumphed in this balloting with an impressive 62 percent of the valid vote to just over 24 percent for eternal bridesmaid Balbín. At 7.4 million votes, Perón's backing was easily an Argentine record. A persistent Manrique received almost 13 percent, a small drop from March.[53] Some 84 percent of Argentine workers voted for their champion, who enjoyed the support of three-fifths of the lower middle class, but only half that proportion of the more prosperous upper middle class. Perón, complete master of the urban regions, supplemented his sparser support in less-developed interior areas through the adhesion of regional leaders, with their control of local political structures. In addition, some conservatives who had come to fear revolution more than Peronism voted for the aging strongman in hopes that he might be able to tame the Monteneros.

Back in power after eighteen years in the political wilderness, the Peronist movement was deeply divided on a left-right cleavage overlaying a generational one. Hence, to avoid favoring one side or the other, Perón chose his third wife, María Estella Martínez de Perón (b. 1931; she used the name Isabel), a former cabaret entertainer with whom he had hooked up on his way into exile, to be vice president. Little did he dream that in just over a year this politically inexperienced young woman would be in over her head as the country's president under even more difficult conditions.

On October 12, 1973, at the age of seventy-eight, Perón returned to the presidency for what would be a short and troubled stay. Peronism was deeply divided between a new generation of youths who had grown up while Perón was in exile and looked at him as a man of the left, many accustomed to the armed struggle as Monteneros, and his old associates from before 1955, who knew his early quasi-fascistic roots and who had shifted to the right as they aged. For most of Perón's short tenure José Ben Gelbard served as economy minister, with the misfortune of having to deal with deteriorating international economic conditions. Eight and a half months after Perón's return to power, and when he was the indispensable element in holding the bifurcated party together, Perón finally did what the military had long been counting upon: He died.

Isabelita, as the widow Perón was popularly known, was poorly prepared to deal with the heavy burdens of governing a country in crisis. She was in way beyond her depth and heavily under the influence of José López Rega, a longtime right-wing associate of the late president, who soon became her lover as well as her astrologer and minister of social welfare. Argentina's first woman president ran through economic ministers at a rate that ensured there would be no coherent economic policy. Worse, if that were possible, under the sway of López Rego, the Argentine Rasputin, Isabelita gave a free hand to right-wing paramilitary groups, particularly the Argentine Anticommunist Alliance (AAA), which López Rega had founded to kidnap and kill leftist guerrillas. She also authorized the nationalization of oil exploration contracts held by Exxon and Shell, the telecommunications franchises of Siemens and IT&T, and foreign banks, a move designed to appease all the country's different varieties of nationalists.

López Rega's influence peaked in May 1975, when he was able to place a friendly general as army commander and make Italo Argentino Luder defense minister. After the first-ever general strike against a Peronist government in June 1975, the overwhelmed chief executive lost whatever small degree of control she had over the situation, a condition worsened in July by the military's depriving her of López Rega's company and advice by forcing him to flee the country to escape trial on charges embracing almost everything from corruption to sedition. In mid-October she took a five-week leave of absence, during which senate president Lüder filled in (having relinquished his cabinet post in order to return to Congress). The military's confidence that if they let her make a bigger mess of things, their eventual intervention would be warmly welcomed by the public was not misplaced. Between April 1975 and March 1976, inflation easily topped 700 percent, with the rate for March compounding into 17,000 percent a year.[54]

By early 1976, the president's credibility was gone, since almost everyone saw the coup coming, not difficult because a wide range of political, economic, and social groups were pleading with the military to take over. In meetings with top officers, these pillars of civil society were being told that they had better be sure that that was what they really wanted, because when the military did take over again, they would stay as long as they deemed necessary to get the job of restructuring and purifying the country done, using whatever measures might be necessary, no matter how extreme. Indeed, it was with a sense of relief, that the Argentine public watched the military oust Isabelita, as she was informed on March 24, 1976, that her tenure in office had been terminated by the armed forces. Five days later General Jorge Rafael Videla (b. 1925) was sworn in as the president of a military junta implementing the "Process of national reorganization." Few Argentines, most of whom had heaved a sigh of relief, had any inkling that the door was opening on the darkest days in their country's life. For the new regime unleashed a campaign of terror against all groups they considered subversive that would lead to unimaginable horrors as the "dirty war" escalated beyond any control, generating at least ten thousand "disappearances."[55]

Initially Videla chose to give economic liberalism a full chance to work under the baton of José Martinez de la Hoz, who set out to reinsert Argentina into the global economy through imposition of criteria of efficiency and comparative advantage. Protectionist import barriers were lowered, subsidies were drastically reduced, the public sector was severely cut back, and social expenditures were sharply curtailed. All this rationalization of industrial policy was accompanied by a brutal compression of real wages. In keeping with the ideas of their University of Chicago mentors, holding that hyperinflation was essentially a result of excess demand, the economic team followed an orthodox stabilization program with a mid-1977 fiscal reform and a May–November 1978 effort to "deindex" the economy while reducing costs and imposing greater market discipline.

Macroeconomic indicators at first supported the government's contention that these policies were essential for economic recovery. Between 1976 and 1978, exports exploded from $3.9 billion to $6.4 billion, whereas imports expanded modestly from $3.0 billion to $3.9 billion. The near trebling of Argentina's trade surplus to $2.6 billion and the even greater growth of foreign exchange reserves to $6 billion (from the 1976 low of $1.8 billion) were accompanied by GDP growth of 6 percent in 1977 and almost 7 percent in 1979, compared to zero growth in 1976 and a negative 4 percent in 1978. Although a quantum jump in imports in 1979 reduced the trade surplus to $1.1 billion, on record exports of $7.8 billion, foreign exchange reserves still peaked at $10.4 billion. Since GDP growth was a robust 6.8 percent and inflation dropped slightly (to 180 percent), the "new political economy" impressed more than only its architects. But this transitory picture of popular satisfaction with a temporarily booming economy would fade even faster than did national euphoria after winning the 1978 soccer World Cup—milked for all it was worth (bought and paid for as it was with bribes in money, land, and cars to the Peruvian team).[56] Indeed, the early 1980s would see the regime's bright dreams turn into the darkest of nightmares.

Colombia: Out of Step in a Positive Way

For Colombia the new period opened with delicate negotiations under way between the historically antagonistic Liberals and Conservatives on establishment of a national front as a long-term institutionalized power-sharing arrangement rather than just an ad hoc alliance to overthrow the military dictatorship of General Gustavo Rojas Pinilla—who besides being undemocratic was a threat to the traditional hegemony of those two elite-led parties. The period ended with the parties well advanced in an incrementally staged return to full political competition without reliance on the body cast provided by the National Front. The road followed required effective political leadership from a variety of individuals, rather than one or two exceptionally skilled guides.[57]

In the broad comparative picture, the Colombian National Front stands out as the clearest and most dramatic example of the political learning process in the totality of Latin American experience. Moreover, this exercise in political innovation contrasts positively in its originality and viability with the far more common practice of adopting or adapting US–western European devices and stratagems. Essentially it called for sixteen years of alternating the presidency between the two parties while evenly dividing legislative seats at all levels. In departments where one party held the governorship, the other would hold the mayoralty of its capital, switching roles every four years. To ensure "coresponsibility" for important laws, a two-thirds congressional majority was required. This involved a two-party Liberal-Conservative monopoly over the choice of candidates for the front's duration. The agreement in principle was sealed at Benidorm, Spain, in July 1956, with the final details agreed upon at Sitges, Spain, in August 1957, shortly after Rojas Pinilla's ouster.

Negotiation of this historic accord in Spain while Rojas Pinilla was still in power was a major feat of diplomacy requiring the cooperation of leaders who, until a few years earlier, had been responsible for violent partisan conflict (and who may have detested their partners-to-be). Indeed, only memories of the carnage of *La Violencia* enabled them to persist, viewing the National Front as the only sure guarantee against a return to the unthinkable. Similarly, traumatic memories of the civil war would, in the second half of the 1970s, enable all parties in post-Franco Spain to cooperate in democratization.

The National Front agreement in hand, the parties cooperated with legalist military sectors and others alienated by Rojas Pinilla's personal aggrandizement, to force the dictator out of office in May 1957. With the National Front incorporated into the constitution through a plebiscite in December 1957, early 1958 saw congressional elections giving the followers of ex-president Laureano Gómez, co-parent of the National Front, an edge over those of ex-president Mariano Ospina Pérez. Although each party would get half the seats, the Liberals held a decided edge over the Conservative Party in terms of votes, at 2.13 million to 1.56 million, as for the first time women exercised the right to vote. Alberto Lleras Camargo (b. 1906)—austere, ascetic, and intellectual—had briefly held things together as provisional president during 1943–1945, after which he enjoyed a decade as secretary general of the Organization of American States in Washington, D.C. Now, the chief architect of the National Front was not allowed to rest on his laurels; in the absence of a viable Conservative Party candidate to be the initial helmsman of the new system, he was drafted to confront the daunting task of making this experiment work in a country of some 15 million inhabitants, still more rural than urban, more agricultural than industrial, and all accustomed to an environment of political violence and repression.[58]

The Liberal Party edge over their partners fell in the 1960 congressional balloting to 1.48 million to 1.06 million: Knowing in advance that half the seats would go to each party severely dampened partisan enthusiasm. Expansion of the electorate resulted from Rojas Pinilla's having extended the franchise to women in 1954, although not giving them a chance to exercise this new right. While adopting vigorous measures to reduce banditry and rural violence, the Lleras Camargo administration also instituted a series of programs to improve the living conditions of the masses, including increased expenditures on education, expansion of the water and sewage systems, and the construction of public housing. As Lleras Camargo managed to make "cogovernment" work, engineering a substantial economic recovery accompanied by social peace, turnout for the 1962 congressional voting rose substantially, the Liberals garnering 1.7 million versus 1.3 million for the Conservatives. Within Liberal Party ranks the Revolutionary Liberal Movement (MRL) of Alfonso López Michelsen, son of ex-president Alfonso López Pumarejo, rose from 20 to 31 percent of the liberal vote, largely on the basis of López Michelsen's criticism of the front. With ex-president Ospina Pérez stronger within the Conservative Party than ex-president Laureano Gómez, the unproven Guillermo León Valencia (b. 1908) became the coalition candidate and hence the new president, as only half the 5.4 million registered voters bothered to cast their ballots in May 1962. The official nominee of the National Front was legitimized by 1.64 million voters, whereas 626,000 unhappy liberals voted for López Michelsen.[59]

Vacillating and unpredictable, León Valencia undercut much of the economic planning done by his predecessor as he struggled to govern a country whose population had risen to over seventeen million, 53 percent urban. Indeed, momentum built up under Lleras Camargo was lost, and the country came to mark time waiting for the end of León Valencia's "do-next-to-nothing" government. Deteriorating economic conditions, including rising inflation, provided conditions propitious for increasing social unrest. During León Valencia's rather ineffective government, leftist insurgents founded the National Liberation Army (ELN) in 1962 and the communist Armed Forces of the Colombian Revolution(FARC) in 1964. These negative factors contributed to a paltry 37 percent turnout in the 1964 congressional elections, with the Liberals garnering 1.14 million votes to 802,000 for the Conservatives, as ex-dictator Rojas Pinilla's vaguely Peronist National Popular Alliance (ANAPO) received 310,000 protest votes. By the second half of 1965, León Valencia was reduced to declaring a state of siege to permit harsher actions to maintain social order. He ended as one of contemporary Colombia's least-well-regarded chief executives.

In 1966, when Lleras Camargo's fifty-eight-year-old businessman cousin, Carlos Lleras Restrepo, boy wonder finance minister back in 1938, was the front's nominee, only 2.94 million voters turned out for the March congressional balloting (with the Liberal Party enjoying a slight advantage). In May 2.64 million of a registered 6.61 million voters—a mere two-fifths—participated in ratifying the two parties' choice. Some 1.9 million of these approved Lleras Restrepo as the front's new pilot.[60] As this forceful and energetic Liberal reinvigorated the economy and modernized the state, making good use of a competent cabinet and building on the foundations laid down by Lleras Camargo, López Michelsen brought his dissident Liberal Revolutionary Movement back into the mother party. To get out of the rigid body cast of the Frente, with its parity and alternation, it was agreed that the equal division of legislative seats and cabinet positions would end in 1978, to be followed by "equitable" division of offices, roughly proportional to votes received. The beginning of electoral participation by new parties was moved up to 1970 from 1974, and the two-thirds majority requirement for significant legislation was eliminated.

In the March 1968 midterm congressional balloting, with participation at 2.5 million (just 37 percent of the electorate), the Conservative Party rallied to 1.16 million votes to 989,000 for the official Liberal Party (plus a substantial showing for the MRL). In the aftermath, Lleras Restrepo lifted the state of siege imposed by his predecessor in May 1965. The Liberal Party insisted that forty-seven-year-old moderate Misael Pastrana Borrero be the Conservative Party's nominee as the front's candidate in 1970 rather than Belisario Betancur Cuartas, who probably had more support within his party. Despite low inflation and diversification of exports, this insistence on a successor who would carry on Lleras Restrepo's constructive policies almost put the National Front experiment in peril.

In April 1970, Pastrana narrowly beat out Rojas Pinilla, who managed to get on the ballot on the technical argument that ANAPO was a Conservative Party faction, not a third party. The very slim margin of 1.63 million to 1.56 million (with dissident Conservatives polling 908,000 votes) showed that the Front was running out of steam, from either voter fatigue or a public perception that it was no longer needed. Indeed, most Conservatives voted for one of the splinter candidates or even Rojas Pinilla. On the congressional side, the Liberal Party received 1.47 million votes, and ANAPO forged ahead of the profront conservatives by 1.41 million to 1.08 million.[61] As Pastrana, governing a country whose population had reached 22 million, cut back on some of Lleras Restrepo's reforms, new groups joined the political fray as well as the insurgent battlefield, the most significant being the National Liberation Army (ELN) and the 19th of April Movement (M-19), a radical offshoot of ANAPO, much as the Monteneros in Argentina were a radicalized wing of Peronism. The thorny issue of agrarian reform, which when initiated by Lleras Restrepo met with heavy opposition in the congress, was recast, with emphasis upon productivity, not redistribution. Pastrana selected the construction sector as the engine of growth for the economy because of the employment it created, which increased purchasing power and spurred demand for domestically produced consumer goods.

Since Álvaro Gómez Hurtado—Laureano's still-active son and political heir—was the official Conservative Party candidate for president in 1974, when alternation was scheduled to end, sixty-one-year-old Alfonso López Michelsen became the Liberal Party nominee, a victory behind the scenes for Julio César Turbay Ayala over grizzled veteran Lleras Restrepo. With the election truly competitive, turnout rose sharply to over 5.2 million, and López Michelsen trounced Gómez

Hurtado 2.93 million to 1.64 million, with María Eugenia Rojas de Moreno, Rojas Pinilla's very un–Evita-like daughter, trailing badly at only 500,000 votes in this contest of offspring of former presidents.[62]

The post-National Front period began in the midst of rising inflation and unemployment that led the government to implement unpopular austerity measures. During López Michelsen's turbulent term, in which economic limitations forced him to set aside his initial social reformism (embodied in his heralded To Close the Gap and Integrated Rural Development programs), the drug problem sprouted, and the military became increasingly restive. Belatedly, López Michelsen realized that drug trafficking was having seriously deleterious affects on society and politics, although it was stimulating the economy in a perverse sense. Congressional balloting in April 1976 gave the Liberal Party a 1.7 million to 1.3 million advantage over the Conservatives as almost 3.3 million Colombians participated. With labor violence stemming from rapidly rising prices triggering states of siege from 1977 on, the Conservative Party, longing to get back in power, nominated Betancur as its standard bearer for the 1978 elections. The February 1978 congressional elections saw the Liberal Party widen its margin, with 2.3 million votes to 1.65 million for their now ex-coalition partner—as only 34 percent of the electorate took part. This vote gave the Liberals 62 senate seats and 111 in the chamber to 49 and 88 for the Conservatives, as they finally regained voters from the moribund ANAPO.

Lleras Restrepo was forced to give up a comeback try by the greater Liberal support for his archrival, Julio César Turbay, who, despite being a poor campaigner who had to get campaign help from the still-revered Lleras Camargo, in June 1978 maintained the Liberal Party's hold on the presidency by only a 150,000 vote margin—at 2.5 million to 2.36 million—as only 5.1 million out of an electorate swollen to 12.6 million cast their ballots.[63] Still, Colombia had its sixth duly elected chief executive in a row, and for a second time a photo-finish election had been taken in stride. Having established democracy when most other countries were under authoritarian rule, Colombia needed no transition to democracy. It would, however, have undreamed-of problems rearing their extremely ugly heads just around the corner: intractable insurgency and the emergence of a drug industry, both of which threatened to become the base of a parallel government.

Different Paths, Varying Patterns

It is clear that semiauthoritarian Mexico was the major exception to the spread of military regimes in this period, and that Colombia escaped from military rule near its beginning. Hence, only Brazil and Argentina fit the general pattern for the 1960s and 1970s, being near the end of prolonged military domination as the period ended. It is equally clear that, having entered the period in 1956 in significantly different situations, they had followed distinct paths through it, Brazil having a much less repressive regime better managed economy, leading to its military being in a position to shape the upcoming transition. Hence, if any pattern is to emerge from the period, it must come from the experiences of the medium and smaller countries of South America.

Notes

1. This section draws heavily on Ronald M. Schneider, *"Order and Progress": A Political History of Brazil* (Boulder, CO: Westview Press, 1991), pp. 186–285, as well as the much less detailed version in Ronald M. Schneider, *Brazil: Culture and Politics in a New Industrial Powerhouse* (Boulder, CO: Westview Press, 1996), pp. 73–100. Frances Hagopian, *Traditional Politics and Regime Change in Brazil* (Cambridge, UK: Cambridge University Press, 1996), provides a systematic analysis of the factors in the "giant contribution to preserving archaic state structures and channels of mediation between state and society" made by "a set of powerful individuals."

2. Unfortunately there is no adequate biography of Kubitschek in English, although he did publish a detailed autobiography and several volumes of memoirs. In sharp contrast the most strident opposition leader is meticulously profiled in John W. F. Dulles, *Carlos Lacerda: Brazilian Crusader,* Vol. 1, *The Years 1914–1960* (Austin: University of Texas Press, 1991), and Vol. 2, *The Years 1960–1977* (Austin: University of Texas Press, 1993). Both of these books reflect a perceptive feel for the times that the author, who had spent much of his adult life in Mexico, managed to develop.

3. See Ronald M. Schneider, *Brazil Election Factbook* (Washington, DC: Institute for the Comparative Study of Political Systems, 1965), pp. 43–46, 58–61.

4. I watched US–Brazil relations closely from 1957 into 1963 as a political analyst in the State Department with a temporary field assignment to Brazil in 1962. Secretary of State John Foster Dulles, whose experience with Latin America was limited to dealing with financial claims of US investors in Central American bonds after World War I, persisted in viewing Brazil as some kind of an overgrown "banana republic." Ironically one of his sons, J.W.F. Dulles, devoted decades of his life to researching and publishing a wide variety of books that amply demonstrate the fallacy of this perspective.

5. The enigmatic Quadros died in early 1992 after a political comeback that led him once more to the São Paulo mayor's chair. Useful for the events and atmosphere of the period is J.W.F. Dulles, *Unrest in Brazil: Political Military Crises, 1955–1964* (Austin: University of Texas Press, 1970).

6. A sound history of the period is Thomas E. Skidmore, *Politics in Brazil: 1930–1964: An Experiment in Democracy* (Oxford: Oxford University Press, 1967).

7. The Chamber of Deputies had been enlarged from 326 to 409. Turnout at 14.7 million was nearly two and a half times that of 1945. I closely observed the campaigning in most regions of the country and collected results of the balloting for close study upon assuming a position at Columbia University in 1963. Consult Ollie Andrew Johnson III, *Brazilian Party Politics and the Coup of 1964* (Gainesville: University Press of Florida, 2001).

8. On Castelo, see J.W.F. Dulles, *Castello Branco: The Making of a Brazilian President* (College Station: Texas A&M University Press, 1978), and J.W.F. Dulles, *President Castello Branco: Brazilian Reformer* (College Station: Texas A&M University Press, 1980).

9. More than 2,100 individuals were punished with loss of political rights, some 4,500 (1,700 civilian and 2,800 military personnel) were forced to retire from government service. Consult María Helena Moreira Alves, *State and Opposition in Military Brazil* (Austin: University of Texas Press, 1985).

10. See the detailed treatment of these elections in Ronald M. Schneider. *The Political System of Brazil: Emergence of a "Modernizing" Authoritarian Regime, 1964–1970* (New York: Columbia University Press, 1971), pp. 178–195.

11. Useful on the aftermath of this period is María D'Alva G. Kinzo, *Legal Opposition Politics Under Authoritarian Rule in Brazil: The Case of the MDB, 1966–1979* (New York: St. Martin's Press, 1988). Also see Thomas E. Skidmore, *The Politics of Military Rule in Brazil, 1964–1985* (New York: Oxford University Press, 1988).

12. The Médici government is treated in detail in Schneider, *Political System,* pp. 297–329, and Skidmore, *Politics,* pp. 105–159.

13. On the views of Geisel and Golbery, see Alfred Stepan, *Rethinking Military Politics: Brazil and the Southern Cone* (Princeton: Princeton University Press, 1988), pp. 33–44. The administration is discussed in Skidmore, *Politics,* pp. 160–209. Golbery was an insatiable student of relevant comparative experience, who in 1969–1970 took time to read through my long manuscript (encompassing my *The Political System of Brazil*) and became intrigued by its application of Huntington's concepts to Brazilian experience from the monarchy through the 1960s. In addition to facilitating the fieldwork of Alfred Stepan, he had consultations with Huntington in 1974 as Brazil's "decompression" was being launched.

14. The best analysis of these elections was coordinated by a man who was beginning his transition from student of politics to political practitioner, and who, within sixteen years, would be Brazil's president: Fernando H. Cardoso. See Bolivar Lamounier and Fernando Henrique Cardoso, eds., *Os Partidos e as Eleições no Brasil* (Rio de Janeiro: Editôra Paz e Terra, 1975).

15. I conducted an exhausting, if not exhaustive, program of interviews and campaign observations in all major Brazilian cities from June until after election day. The results are incorporated into Schneider, *"Order and Progress,"* pp. 282–283.

16. Consult Margaret E. Keck, *The Workers Party and Democratization in Brazil* (New Haven: Yale University Press, 1992).

17. Enrique Krauze, *Mexico, Biography of Power: A History of Modern Mexico, 1810–1996* (New York: HarperCollins, 1997), pp. 625–644, covers the López Mateos years. From this point on, the most useful single book for understanding Mexican developments in a broad context is Daniel Levy and Kathleen Bruhn, with Emilio Zebadua, *Mexico, The Struggle for Democratic Development* (Berkeley: University of California Press, 2001).

18. Kenneth F. Johnson, *Mexican Democracy: A Critical Review* (New York: Praeger, 1978), p. 42.

19. López Mateos's handling of the succession process is discussed in Jorge G. Castañeda, *Perpetuating Power: How Mexican Presidents Were Chosen* (New York: New Press, 2000), pp. 4–23, 133–143. Election results are tabulated in Roderic Ai Camp, *Politics in*

Mexico: The Democratic Transformation, 4th ed. (New York: Oxford University Press, 2003), pp. 190, 193.

20. Peter H. Smith, *Labyrinths of Power: Political Recruitment in Twentieth-Century Mexico* (Princeton: Princeton University Press, 1979), p. 280.

21. Johnson, *Mexican Democracy,* p. 52. Useful up through the 1960s is Roger D. Hansen, *The Politics of Mexican Development* (Baltimore: Johns Hopkins University Press, 1974).

22. Camp, *Politics,* pp. 245–246.

23. Echeverría's management of the succession process is analyzed in Castañeda, *Perpetuating Power,* pp. 25–41, 144–153.

24. See the treatment of the 1976 election in Daniel Levy and Gabriel Szekely, *Mexico: Paradoxes of Stability and Change* (Boulder, CO: Westview Press, 1981).

25. This mismanagement is detailed in Luis Rubio and Robert Newell, *Mexico's Dilemma: The Political Origins of Economic Crisis* (Boulder, CO: Westview Press, 1984).

26. Basic sources include Luis Alberto Romero, *A History of Argentina in the Twentieth Century* (University Station: Pennsylvania State University, 2002); James Scobie, *Argentina: A City and a Nation,* 2nd ed. (New York: Oxford University Press, 1971); and David Rock, *Argentina, 1516–1982: From Spanish Colonization to the Falklands War* (Berkeley: University of California Press, 1985).

27. The thinking of the key figures of the military regime is discussed in Robert Potash, *The Army and Politics in Argentina,* Vol. 2, *1945–1962: Perón to Frondizi* (Stanford, CA: Stanford University Press, 1980), pp. 227–249. The labor-Peronist viewpoint is articulated in James W. McGuire, *Peronism Without Perón: Unions, Parties, and Democracy in Argentina* (Stanford, CA: Stanford University Press, 1997), pp. 68–83. See also Samuel J. Baily, *Labor, Nationalism, and Politics in Argentina* (New Brunswick, NJ: Rutgers University Press, 1967), and Juan E. Corradi, *The Fitful Republic: Economy, Society, and Politics in Argentina* (Boulder, CO: Westview Press, 1985).

28. The Aramburu government's repressive activities represented the harder-line faction of the military with roots in the 1951 anti-Perón conspiracy, a point at which Lonardi was already sixty-six; Aramburu was eighteen years younger. This difference of view was almost generational as the former had begun his career under the presidency of Roca in the early years of the twentieth century—just after the latter was born—and the latter finished his schooling and was commissioned during the period of Radical domination in the early 1920s. Hence, Lonardi was in his midforties at the time of the 1930 Revolution, but Aramburu was just emerging from his midtwenties. Thus Lonardi was a decade senior to Perón, and Aramburu was eight years the strongman's junior. In a hierarchical institution like the Argentine army, such seniority and age-cohort differences did matter. See Jose Luis de Imaz, *Los que Mandan (Those Who Rule)* (Albany: State University of New York Press, 1970).

29. Potash, *Army,* Vol. 2, pp. 255ff., covers the mid-1957 constituent assembly elections.

30. Ibid., Vol. 2, pp. 263–279, covers the presidential elections and their aftermath.

31. For a meticulously reconstructed account of events from mid-1959 to August 1961, see ibid., Vol. 2, pp. 308–337.

32. Useful sources on the Argentine political economy, including that at this juncture, are Gary W. Wynia, *Argentina in the Postwar Era: Politics and Economic Policy Making in a Divided Society* (Albuquerque: University of New Mexico Press, 1978), and Carlos H.

Waisman, *Reversal of Development in Argentina: Postwar Counterrevolutionary Policies and Their Structural Consequences* (Princeton: Princeton University Press, 1987).

33. As elections were for half the lower house, it was possible to let the Peronists win without their coming close to a majority. The built-in time bomb was that a repeat performance three years later would put them in control. Hence, as the balloting approached, Frondizi could not both fulfill his commitment to the Peronists and keep the military satisfied.

34. Potash, *Army*, Vol. 2, pp. 338ff., discusses the repercussions of this incident and Frondizi's consequent ouster. See also McGuire, *Peronism*, pp. 84–90.

35. Robert Potash, *The Army and Politics in Argentina*, Vol. 3, *1962–1973: From Frondizi's Fall to the Peronist Restoration* (Stanford, CA: Stanford University Press, 1996), picks up the story at this point. The aftermath of Frondizi's ouster is dealt with on pp. 4–19, and the intricate process of adhering to a legal outcome is carefully reconstructed on pp. 39–59. See also McGuire, *Peronism*, pp. 90–92, 111–153.

36. See Potash, *Army*, Vol. 3, pp. 60–62. The dance of overeager and reluctant candidates is covered on pp. 75–92.

37. On the abortive coup, see ibid., Vol. 3, pp. 93–101.

38. The elections of 1963 are dealt with in James W. Rowe, *The Argentine Elections of 1963: An Analysis* (Washington, DC: Institute for the Comparative Study of Political Systems, 1964), as well as in Potash, *Army*, Vol. 3, pp. 116–117.

39. On the Illia administration's handling of relations with the military up to mid-1965 consult ibid., Vol. 3, pp. 118–150.

40. The crucial events involving Onganía's resignation and subsequent retirement are laid out in ibid., Vol. 3, pp. 151–155. The Alsogaray-engineered conspiracy is analyzed on pp. 156–193.

41. Consult William C. Smith, *Authoritarianism and the Crisis of the Argentine Political Economy* (Stanford, CA: Stanford University Press, 1989), pp. 37–47. Also very useful, as reflecting a close understanding of the cultural context and being more eclectic in its approach, is Paul H. Lewis, *The Crisis of Argentine Capitalism* (Chapel Hill: University of North Carolina Press, 1990). On p. 256, Lewis comments on widespread tax evasion, smuggling, bribery of government officials, black marketeering, and capital flight as negative features in the late 1950s and 1960s, crying out for reform.

42. On the situation see McGuire, *Peronism*, pp. 151–159. The pithy comment is from Lewis, *Crisis*, p. 273.

43. Smith, *Authoritarianism*, pp. 48–118, discusses the Onganía regime up to mid-1968. The phrase is from p. 51.

44. See ibid., pp. 67–68.

45. See Potash, *Army*, Vol. 3, pp. 228–241, on the deterioration of Onganía's relationship with Lanusse.

46. The *Cordobazo* is discussed from different perspectives in ibid., pp. 246–255; Smith, *Authoritarianism*, pp. 127–133; and McGuire, *Peronism*, pp. 157–159.

47. Consult Richard Gillespie, *Soldiers of Perón: Argentina's Monteneros* (Oxford, UK: Clarendon Press, 1982), pp. 89–95.

48. The decline of the Onganía regime is reconstructed in Potash, *Army,* Vol. 3, pp. 255–292, and is discussed in Smith, *Authoritarianism,* pp. 120–168.

49. Potash, *Army,* Vol. 3, pp. 293–308, analyzes Onganía's ouster; pp. 309–357 cover his successor's short term. Also see McGuire, *Peronism,* pp. 150–156, and Lewis, *Crisis,* pp. 375ff.

50. On his views, see Aldo Ferrer, *The Argentine Economy,* trans. by Marjory M. Urquidi (Berkeley and Los Angeles: University of California Press, 1967).

51. Smith, *Authoritarianism,* p. 188. Lanusse's first year and a half is discussed in Potash, *Army,* Vol. 3, pp. 357–393.

52. Perón's dramatic return to power is briefly recounted in McGuire, *Peronism,* pp. 163ff., as well as in Smith, *Authoritarianism,* pp. 209–221. The military's misperceptions and ensuing miscalculations are masterfully dealt with in Potash, *Army,* Vol. 3, pp. 394–496.

53. On Perón's final stay in power, see Guido de Tella, *Argentina Under Perón, 1973–1976: The Nation's Experience with a Labour-Based Government* (New York: St. Martin's Press, 1983).

54. Great detail is available in de Tella, *Argentina,* with adequate summaries of Isabelita's short and unhappy presidency in McGuire, *Peronism,* pp. 165–170, and Smith, *Authoritarianism,* pp. 231–242.

55. Consult Paul H. Lewis, *Guerrillas and Generals: The "Dirty War" in Argentina* (Westport, CT: Praeger, 2002), and María José Moyano, *Argentina's Lost Patrol: Armed Struggle, 1969–1979* (New Haven: Yale University Press, 1995), as well as Jacobo Timmerman's moving personal account in *Prisoner Without a Name, Cell Without a Number* (New York: Random House, 1981). The Videla government is analyzed in Smith, *Authoritarianism,* pp. 231–242.

56. Not surprisingly Argentines are still very defensive about this shameful incident, which forced international soccer authorities to change the way the competition was run to eliminate advancement to the finals on the basis of goal differential rather than head-to-head knockout semifinal matches. The admiral in charge of World Cup affairs kept meticulous records that showed that the Peruvian starters, who had displayed a stingy defense in prior matches, allowed the Argentines to score goal after goal in order to overcome Brazil's five-goal advantage in total goals minus goals allowed, were paid cash, and were given a new car each and real estate. Upon the team's return to the Lima airport, the Peruvian captain faced popular outrage by crying, "Not all of us, only eight." Anyone who has the most elemental understanding of "futebol" knows that if the defense and midfield were determined to throw a game, it would be redundant to bribe the forwards, since they would be highly unlikely to receive the ball in position to score.

57. Sound histories of Colombia include David Bushnell, *The Making of Modern Colombia: A Nation in Spite of Itself* (Berkeley: University of California Press, 1993), and Frank Safford and Marco Palacios, *Colombia: Fragmented Land, Divided Society* (New York: Oxford University Press, 2002).

58. Highly useful works covering this quarter century include Harvey Kline, *Colombia: Democracy Under Assault,* rev. ed. (Boulder, CO: Westview Press, 1994); John D. Martz, *The Politics of Clientelism: Democracy and the State in Colombia* (New Brunswick, NJ: Transaction, 1997), where Lleras Camargo's administration is discussed on pp. 75–97; and Jonathan

Hartlyn, *The Politics of Coalition Rule in Colombia* (New York: Cambridge University Press, 1988).

59. On the León Valencia government, see Martz, *Politics,* pp. 99–118.

60. Ibid., pp. 119–142, treats the Lleras Restrepo administration.

61. Ibid., pp. 143–159, deals with events during Pastrana's presidency.

62. The government of the younger López is discussed in ibid., pp. 161–183.

63. Ibid., pp. 185–206, provides detail on the Turbay period. Also useful on the deteriorating situation is Richard Maullin, *Soldiers, Guerrillas, and Politics in Colombia* (Lexington, MA: Lexington Books, 1973).

9

Coups, Military Regimes, and Ends of Tunnels

Seven South American Cases, 1956–1979

Although the 1956–1979 experience of medium and small countries in South America ranged across a wide spectrum of paths, it was less diverse than in the larger countries, as only Venezuela did not go through an authoritarian military regime, having escaped from one in 1958. The opposite was true of Chile, which avoided a military takeover until 1973 but would be mired in the hold of one for another decade after the period had ended. Only Paraguay spent the entire period under a dictatorship.

Overview

Peru went through a roller-coaster period, beginning on a positive note with election of a civilian to replace General Manuel Odría in the presidency. The continuing virulent hostility of the armed forces toward the country's most significant political party caused a brief interruption of progress toward democracy in 1962–1963 and establishment of a sui generis nationalist-reformist military regime in 1968, with transition back to civilian rule barely under way at the end of the 1970s. For Venezuela this period marked a high point in establishment of a stable, highly participatory political system on the rubble of a ten-year military dictatorship. After getting through the first fifteen years reasonably well, in 1973 Chile experienced by far the most serious political crisis in its history, leading to a repressive authoritarian regime beyond Chileans' worst nightmares.

Bolivia had broken free from its negative past through its 1952 Revolution but succumbed to militarism in the mid-1960s while moving toward reestablishment of civilian rule at period's end. Ecuador continued along its disorderly semidemocratic path into the 1970s, when the demise of its many-times president José María Velasco Ibarra opened the door to military rule. Uruguay saw its democratic record besmirched by a military regime in the late 1960s, and Paraguay retained its reputation for political backwardness under the dictatorship of General Alfredo Stroessner.

Peru: Out of and Back into Military Rule

Experimentation with changing political alignments and alternative development strategies continued in Peru as industrialization gave rise to new elite sectors and middle strata not linked to APRA, massive migration to urban marginal areas, and spotty but significant social mobilization in the countryside. This experimentation was reflected in alternation of military and civilian rule as 1956–1968 would see two constitutionally elected governments separated by a yearlong interim military junta. Then 1968 would witness the beginning of a transformation-oriented military regime, which would be eased out in the mid-1970s by more traditional officers, who at the end of this period were ready to hand over power to the same civilian leader the armed forces had ousted in 1968.[1] Behind this zigzag course lay the unresolved problems of the preceding period, especially the still-intransigent military opposition to the Popular Revolutionary Alliance of the Americas (APRA).

Spurred by the economic decline that followed the Korean War boom, in late 1955 and early 1956 agro-exporters, industrialists, dissident military factions, unions, and a variety of new middle-class political organizations joined forces to oppose any plans president Manuel Odría might harbor to rig the election. In the face of spreading unrest the country's strongman relaxed censorship, but he refused to legalize APRA and threw his support to Hernando de Lavalle, a Lima businessman being put forward as a national unity candidate. Hence, in the mid-June 1956 balloting, former president Manuel Prado, a member of the urban financial elite, emerged victorious in a three-way race in which women voted for the first time, bringing participation up to around one-third of the adult population. Prado's 45 percent plurality included very substantial support from backers of the still illegal APRA. A dramatic harbinger of the future was the strong 37 percent showing of Fernando Belaúnde Terry (b. 1912), a young US-educated architect from a prominent Arequipa family who had achieved national notice as dean of the architecture school at the capital's prestigious San Marcos University. Entering the contest very late against strong opposition by the incumbent government, he emerged as the closest approximation to a charismatic leader Peru had yet produced. To a considerable extent he bottled some old *Aprista* wine in new containers, but he added a distinctive younger-generation flavor.

Despite lack of party organization, Belaúnde carried the city of Lima and most of the urban centers of the south. His support, upon which he would build for future presidential bids, came largely from newer and younger middle-class and professional elements that had emerged with the postwar surge of industrialization, from the population of southern cities, where APRA had never sunk deep roots, and from older middle-class sectors alienated by APRA's growing conservatism. On the strength of his APRA support, Prado swept the north, and he narrowly defeated Belaúnde along the central coast. Lavalle, burdened by the Odría administration's unpopularity, finished a poor third with only 18 percent, mostly coming from the more backward areas of the sierra still dominated by conservative landlords.

As no reapportionment had taken place for over three decades, the rural areas of the sierra were heavily overrepresented at the expense of the burgeoning cities of the coast. Hence, the Pradist Democratic Movement (MDP) won 75 of 180 lower-house seats and a majority of 30 out of 53 in the Senate, with *Apristas* running as independents gaining 40 and 12, respectively, while Odría-Lavalle backers moped over their mere 25 and 2. Not having fielded candidates in half the country, Belaúnde's supporters had only a token representation in the new congress. Looking ahead, Belaúnde established a new party, Popular Action (AP), spending the next six years overseeing its construction and, in the process, successfully carrying his message to all parts of the country. As put by an astute student of Peru, a contemporary of Belaúnde:

> Belaúnde does not seek to erect a "palace of ideas" as Victor Raúl [Haya de la Torre] did in the 1930s—a philosophy providing answers to all problems of public and private life. What he offers is not a doctrine but a style, or rather a style plus an eclectic principle. Some of APRA's old themes reappear, but they have been re-interpreted and brought up to date. . . . Belaúnde, however, presents a lyrical vision of Peru's destiny ranging from the socialism of the Incas to modern concepts of planning.[2]

If the future might be Belaúnde's, the present belonged to Prado. His support came from businessmen producing for the internal market, politically moderate agro-exporters, and groups in the provinces with whom he had established clientelistic ties in his earlier term as president. Although he would face stiff opposition throughout his six-year term, Prado enjoyed a much stronger political base than had Bustamante y Rivero in the country's most recent democratic experience. The military was favorably inclined toward Prado because of the successful war with Ecuador in his previous term, and the *Apristas* followed a policy of *convivéncia* (coexistence) because they were consulted on significant issues and given a leading role on labor issues, although disassociating themselves from the government's most unpopular measures.[3]

Although Prado's initial policies favored industry and other sectors producing for the internal market, and his late-term policies, particularly when Pedro Beltrán was prime minister in 1959–1961, benefited agro-exporters, the *Apristas* acted with restraint and provided him with a high degree of labor peace. For they believed that those essentially coastal interests would eventually turn against the large landowners of the sierra as inefficient and achronistic drags upon expansion of the internal market. With their core constituencies of the prewar middle class and the comfortably entrenched union leadership now among the well-situated sectors of Peruvian society, *Aprista* strategists viewed Prado's backers as an incipient bourgeoisie with whom they could form a populist alliance. The *Apristas* also looked forward to legalization as a reward for their cooperation with the administration. Ensnared in the past, they underestimated both the depth of military antagonism and the growing appeal of Belaúnde's mix of populism and nationalism. Like the Prado administration, they were all but blind to a new factor about to explode into the political equation: rural unrest in the south.

Trotskyite agronomist Hugo Blanco built a locally strong militant peasant movement in the coffee-producing La Conveníon Valley in 1958, and this would be the acorn from which revolutionary movements would grow. Peasant communities invaded wool-producing estates in the central sierra, including those of the US-owned Cerro de Pasco Corporation. Prado did not dislodge invading *comuneros* or break strikes by *colonos,* so many landowners sold plots to their tenants or even abandoned their estates. The church, changing under the influence of Vatican II, began to sell off its lands to peasants. Anticipating that agrarian reform legislation was only a matter of time, other landowners began to decapitalize their properties, transferring assets into urban investments.

In 1962 Peru faced the prospect of a fully competitive election as for the first time in thirty-one years. APRA founder and historical chief Victor Raúl Haya de la Torre (b. 1895) was allowed to run for the presidency. He faced formidable competition from both Belaúnde and ex-president Odría. The June 10 balloting gave Haya 33 percent of the vote to Belaúnde's 32.1 percent and 28.4 percent for Odría—who combined conservative rural support with that of clients from the Lima shantytowns built up under his presidency. Minor candidates divided the slim remaining slice of the electorate. While the new congress was nearing agreement on an Odría-Haya deal, the military seized power on June 18 and promptly canceled the election results on the grounds of alleged fraud—an act that received Belaúnde's support. The military junta announced that it would hold "clean" elections within a year, and to the surprise of many observers—including a large proportion of US Kennedy administration officials—it fulfilled its promise.[4] During its year in power the junta established the National Planning Institute (INP), staffing it with young civilian technocrats. In preparation for the new elections the congress was reapportioned in line with the 1961 census, membership of both houses of the congress was reduced, and a new system of proportional representation was installed.

Even with these changes, the June 1963 balloting was almost a carbon copy of that a year earlier, but the small difference was crucial. The Christian Democrats (PDC), who had received just under 3 percent of the 1962 vote, allied with Belaúnde and Popular Action, helping him near 39 percent of the vote compared to APRA's slight rise to 34 percent and Odría's dip to 26 percent. This outcome prevented a need for the decision to be made by the congress and placed Belaúnde, whom most of the military had expected to win the year before, squarely in the president's chair. However, governing would not be easy, since the AP-PDC alliance fell far short of a majority in either house of the congress, having 19 of 44 senate seats, but only 52 of 140 in the lower house. The backbone of the opposition was APRA, with 58 seats in the lower house and 18 in the upper house, generally supported by the National Odrista Union with its 24 and 7 seats.[5] This minority situation posed two special problems, since the Peruvian system contained elements of parliamentary government in that the cabinet was presided over by a prime minister requiring congressional approval and subject to a vote of censure—used to force Belaúnde to change 178 ministers during his five years in office. Moreover, there were no midterm elections: The president, senators, and deputies were elected at the same time for coterminous six-year terms. Hence, Belaúnde was to have no opportunity to improve his inadequate legislative base. Indeed, for his first four years as president, the APRA-Odría La Coalicíon held a three-fifths majority in each house. By the time this obstructionist bloc broke up, Belaúnde's Christian Democratic allies had disintegrated, with Lima mayor Luis Bedoya Reyes splitting off and founding the Popular Christian Party (PPC)—a blow, since this split negated the value of having the PDC head's daughter as his very personal and inseparable private secretary.

High hopes on the part of the Peruvian public for reforms and development by this president, fitting the profile ostensibly desired by Washington under the Alliance for Progress launched with great fanfare in February 1962, were doomed to disappointment. APRA, viewing Belaúnde as a "thief" of much of its program and an opportunist for currying military support, played an obstructionist role to the hilt. (Indeed, their attitude bore a striking similarity to the UCRP's position a short time before in Argentina, where it would rather see the military take over than cooperate with Frondizi and his UCRI branch of the Radicales.) Equally destructive were the actions of the United States, which cut off all aid to Peru and used its very considerable, often decisive, weight in international bodies such as the IMF, the World Bank (IBRD), and the Inter-American Development Bank to relegate Belaúnde's government to pariah status. As a result, Peru under Belaúnde received less foreign aid on a per capita basis than any other major Latin American country, so—unless he was willing to abandon all of his reforms and developmental projects—Belaúnde was forced to finance a growing deficit by doing increased amounts of short-term borrowing, drawing down foreign reserves, and printing money. (Again this was eerily reminiscent of the extremely shortsighted US policy toward the Kubitschek government in Brazil in 1959–1960.) Peru's foreign debt consequently rose from a modest $237 million to $695 million, and the state sector became more prominent in the economy. At the same time, domestic capital drifted out of the agro-export sector into real estate, finance, commerce, and local industrial ventures.

A dispute had been simmering for years over the US-owned International Petroleum Company (IPC), which held a concession originally issued to a British firm, then later transferred to American interests. IPC insisted that it had also acquired the original tax breaks, which under Peruvian law became void if they changed hands. Peru claimed that IPC was extremely far behind with its tax obligations, and the Belaúnde administration broke the impasse by taking over the company. Under the so-called Hickenlooper Amendment, the US government was required to cut off all aid to a country expropriating American property and investments without prompt repayment. Peru's answer was that the overdue taxes significantly exceeded the value of IPC, so in forgiving these debts Peru had paid for IPC. The Hickenlooper Amendment, unlike other similar congressional fiats designed to tie the hands of the executive branch, allowed no "wiggle room" for the executive to use its discretion, much less make an exception. Hence, Belaúnde was forced to finance his government's development projects through borrowing in European capital markets at high and rising interest rates.

His back against the wall, in August 1968 Belaúnde reached a controversial agreement by which IPC relinquished its concession to the government's petroleum company in exchange for being granted a larger role in the profitable areas of refining and marketing. To the leftists this smelled like a sellout, whereas the military used charges of a secret page missing from the version made public to justify ousting Belaúnde from office. (By the time international courts ruled in Peru's favor, Belaúnde's government was history.) For although Belaúnde certainly made mistakes, the deck was stacked against him much more than it had been against Frondizi in Argentina, much less Goulart in Brazil, and as the future would demonstrate, Peru was considerably less governable than more favored Argentina and Brazil. Hence, the harsh judgment of Belaúnde's "failures and blunders" rendered by Collier and Collier is somewhat overdrawn, although their fundamental conclusion that the blunders affected only the timing of the coup is valid, and that the armed forces' self-definition of their role gave them a determination to take the reins of government into their own hands, since

> the military increasingly believed that the democratic regime was incapable of taking needed initiatives in areas such as these, and began planning the implementation of such reforms through the militarization of the state . . . promoting fundamental economic and social reform as an indispensable

prerequisite for national security, for preempting what they perceived as the growing radicalization of Peruvian society.[6]

In the last quarter of 1967, APRA began to cooperate with the right wing of AP and in early 1968 was helping the government cope with Peru's growing economic difficulties. Bringing together the financial, industrial, and agro-export elite and encompassing private sector leaders with strong ties to foreign capital, this coalition of forces marginalized the traditional landowners of the highlands—thus earning their animosity.[7] This new coalition offered a chance for the Belaúnde government to salvage something from its term in office. Armed with a sixty-day grant of special emergency powers from the congress, a new cabinet moved swiftly and with resolve to reactivate and stabilize the economy.

Unfortunately, it was too late for Belaúnde to redeem promises of a comprehensive agrarian reform. A tidal wave of violent land seizures had taken place following Belaúnde's election in mid-1963, but late in the year he had been forced by the APRA-Odrista congressional majority to repress them guerrilla movements in the southern and central highlands and had become preoccupied with future outbreaks. This rural unrest led some military thinkers gradually to believe that agrarian reform was badly needed to head off insurgencies, if not to co-opt peasant support as Acción Democrática had done in Venezuela in 1945–1948 and again after 1958. But the military would not entrust agrarian reform to a future *Aprista* government. (Vice president Edgardo Seone, who won the AP presidential nomination for 1968 over Belaúnde's adamant misgivings, fancied himself a viable candidate, but in reality had almost no chance of being elected.)

APRA's belated cooperation with Belaúnde was motivated by its hopes not only to participate freely in the scheduled 1969 elections, but to win and be allowed to take office. In June 1968, it nominated its aging founder Haya de la Torre, and since Belaúnde was constitutionally barred from running for a second term, and the AP had no other national figure—as would be the case with the Christian Democrats in Chile in 1970—Haya de la Torre's election appeared to be a strong possibility. The military was not ready to relent in its veto of APRA in general and of bête noire Haya in particular. Since a coup close to the 1969 elections would have been too obvious a block-Haya move, incurring the risk of strong domestic reaction and international condemnation, the step had to be taken soon and appear to be directed against Belaúnde—before he could do anything to bolster his popular support.

On October 3, 1968, a coup led by armed-forces commander in chief General Juan Velasco Alvarado (b. 1910), a middle-class individual from an outlying province, brought an abrupt end to the suspense about the upcoming elections: there would be none. In the resulting "Revolutionary Government of the Armed Forces," a junta composed of the senior officer of each service branch selected Velasco Alvarado as president then assumed the post of his service's minister. The most important regional commanders were allotted what were normally civilian ministries, with key colonels lodged in a newly created cabinet secretariat, where they sought to function as the regime's brain trust.[8]

Largely unnoticed by political observers, the thinking of younger elements of the military had been undergoing critical changes since the days of the 1962–1963 junta. In a way fundamentally similar to why the global Catholic Church had drastically revised its position, these officers of generally lower middle-class provincial backgrounds had been reassessing the military's essentially conservative position in Peru's political life. The Center for Higher Military Studies (CAEM) and the intelligence schools evolved a new doctrine linking national security to development. This thinking evolved into support for agrarian reform, nationalist energy policies, and an emphasis on systematic planning. As time wore on, the progressive officers realized that the opportunity for accomplishments in these directions under Belaúnde had been lost, and since working with APRA was unthinkable, the armed forces would have to carry out changes themselves—as they perceived the case to be in Brazil (under Castelo Branco and Costa e Silva) and Argentina (under Onganía). Hence, they strongly supported Velasco's government, giving it a broad base of military support.

Initial consensus within the military began to crack as more conservative officers shied away from confrontation with the United States over the IPC dispute—which they had used to the hilt to discredit Belaúnde—and questioned stressing the social aim of redistribution over the economic goal of production, in the field of agrarian reform. During the first part of 1969, Velasco forged a coalition of military radicals and centrist developmentalists to isolate his critics. His position consolidated, and enjoying substantial popular support through government takeover of IPC, Velasco embarked on an ambitious agenda of structural reforms. Redistribution of over 8 million hectares (roughly 20 million acres) of land undercut both agro-exporting elites and *Aprista* rural unions. Major foreign firms were expropriated, and basic industry was reserved for an expanded state sector. Local capitalists were provided attractive fiscal incentives to invest in the "reformed private sector," where profit sharing and worker participation in management were instituted. As the coming to power of Allende in Chile monopolized international attention, foreign pressures were all but absent.

The alliance between the radicals and the developmentalists within the military rested upon a tripod made up of Velasco's exceptional leadership, matched only in the annals of the Peruvian armed forces by that of Odría in the 1948–1956 era; economic prosperity; and agreement of the different military currents on structural reforms. The salad days of the regime peaked in 1972 with the creation of SINAMOS, the National System of Social Mobilization, an agency designed to play a major role in a corporatist restructuring of society. In practice, there was considerable popular resistance to such top-down depoliticization, even when packaged as "popular participation." In a context of successful borrowing in the Eurodollar market, which trebled Peru's foreign debt over Velasco's tenure and certainly compared very favorably with the ultimate failure of Onganía and his successors in Argentina, the Peruvian experiment seemed to many observers to be working reasonably well.[9]

Matters began to unravel after a nearly fatal illness in February 1973 left Velasco not only debilitated, but also increasingly impulsive and impatient, a state reflected in his rejecting criticism and relying increasingly upon the more radical officers and favoring them in promotions and assignments. Velasco's problems mounted when the oil shock and the ensuing world recession led to a precipitous economic deterioration as prices for oil imports shot up, export earnings dropped, and foreign credit dried up. Moreover, a natural disaster devastated the fish meal industry, the country's second largest export. Then, too, labor and agrarian reforms and the active participation of new sectors led to increased conflict over relative shares of economic benefits and input in policy implementation. In addition, the overthrow of Allende in neighboring Chile in September 1973 removed the lightning rod of a South American government to the left of Peru's as a focus of Cold War policies of the United States and its allies. Now active participation in the Non-Aligned Movement and purchase of a large number of tanks from the Soviet Union took on a more controversial meaning. The alliance between radicals and developmentalists was coming apart. In May 1974, Admiral Vargas Caballero, the leading conservative voice in the cabinet, was forced out, and soon thereafter Velasco made public "Plan Inca," said that it had been his master plan since the beginning, and expropriated all newspapers not yet in government hands. From a comparative perspective, Peru was beginning to bear an eerie resemblance to Argentina in the final months of Onganía's government. In March 1975, Velasco suffered a stroke that accelerated his physical and mental decline. (He would die in 1977.)

In this situation ambitious General Javier Tantalean Vanini became a catalyst of division. His marital ties to a prominent *Aprista* family and the corruption in the ministry he had long occupied worried the moderates, some of whom were more attracted to what was going on under Geisel in Brazil than to the mess in Argentina or the dictatorial regime in Chile. Extraction of the armed forces from government before they became hopelessly divided and factionalized became an important goal, one requiring an exit strategy if there was to be no demoralizing retreat. So, at the end of August 1975, Velasco was eased out in favor, not of Vanini, but of war minister General Francisco Morales Bermúdez (b. 1921), who would direct the course of affairs first as prime minister, then as president.

As the radical nationalists in the military were elbowed out, Belaúnde and other leading Popular Action personalities were permitted to return to the country, and the new government courted both them and APRA as counterweights to the popular forces orphaned by its abrupt shift away from progressive social policies. By February 1977, the military government, by now fully purged of Velasquista activists, announced plans for constituent assembly elections and, in August, decreed that these would be held in June 1978. Preferring the election of a new government to this way for the military regime to buy more time, Belaúnde had the AP abstain. This action opened room, temporarily as it proved, for Luis Bedoya Reyes of the Popular Christian Party (PPC) and his version of the Chilean military government's policies to move center stage.

In this fluid political situation, Haya de la Torre and APRA attempted to seize the political initiative, while the left was highly fragmented. When the votes were in, APRA had won a plurality of 35.4 percent—close to its historical share—while the diverse elements of the left totaled 36 percent and the PPC gained second place with 24 percent. As presiding officer of the constituent assembly, the aging Haya shaped a constitution strengthening presidentialism and setting the minimum for election to the presidency at 36 percent of the vote for the 1980 balloting (up enough from the old one-third so that the 1962 election would not have ended up in the hands of the congress), subsequently rising to 40 percent. So as this period, which began in 1956 with transition to civilian rule, came to its end, Peru was again poised to trade military for civilian government through the ballot box.[10]

Venezuela: Establishment of Democracy

For Venezuela, even more than for its neighbor, Colombia, the 1956–1979 period was one of forward movement and establishment of a viable democratic system. Venezuela early found a way out of a repressive military dictatorship, one in the context of the times more retrograde than that of Gómez in the first third of the century. Then, in a demonstration that statesmanlike and pragmatic need not be antithetical and might even go hand in hand, the democratic parties would agree upon a formula reconciling power sharing with responsiveness to the electorate's wishes. Installed in office with a very broad popular mandate, a Democratic Action (AD)–led civilian government again headed by Rómulo Betancourt demonstrated to an impressive degree the absorption of lessons learned from the 1945–1948 *trienio* period.[11]

Buffeted by armed, violent opposition from both left and right, AD administrations provided ten years of responsible—at times, even creative—reformist governments under Betancourt and close associate Raúl Leoni. Then, with AD divided over the succession question, the erstwhile junior coalition partner COPEI got its chance at governing under Rafael Caldera before a reunited AD was returned to power at the end of 1973 behind Carlos Andrés Pérez. With alternation in office and loyal, responsible opposition established—no mean feat, as the far less happy experiences of many other countries amply illustrate—Venezuela would close out this period with inauguration of a second COPEI government under Luis Herrera Campíns, accompanied by the abandonment of efforts at violent revolution and the reincorporation into normal electoral-political competition of hitherto intransigently violent leftist groups.

A would-be hybrid of Trujillo and Perón and a counterpart of Rojas Pinilla next door in Colombia, dictator Marcos Pérez Jiménez, in power since 1948, faced demands for a return to democracy from a coalition of the civilian parties that had briefly flourished before the 1948 military coup. Taking the name Patriotic Junta, and clearly encouraged, if not inspired, by the National Front's contemporary success in Colombia, they spooked Pérez Jiménez in December 1957 into abruptly substituting a plebiscite for the scheduled legitimizing elections (which he had had attempted in 1952 and which had worked so well for Odría in Peru in 1950). The ploy backfired, with a national general strike backed by the church and business organizations on January 21, igniting a crisis in which the army refused to repress the protest after casualties had risen to three hundred dead and a thousand injured. Pérez Jiménez fled into exile as a military junta took over temporarily.

The parties that had overthrown the dictator agreed in midyear on a "minimum program of government," followed up by the October 1958 Pact of Punto Fijo, signed by all presidential candidates and establishing a weaker and more flexible analogue to Colombia's National Front. The leaders of the democratic parties, particularly Betancourt and Caldera, had learned well from the 1945–1948 fiasco. They, along with Jovito Villalba of the Republican Democratic Union (URD), agreed on the importance of coalitions instead of having the leading party go it alone; the need for procedural, if not substantive, consensus; avoidance of divisive extremes in party programs and concentration on common ground; encouragement of controlled and channeled growth of participation; and exclusion of the revolutionary left, including the Venezuelan Communist Party (PCV), as unsatisfiable maximalists, even though they had been allies in the struggle against the dictatorship. (In essence these thoughtful leaders were excellent Huntingtonians even before Samuel Huntington had formulated his axioms concerning reform and "reform-mongers.")

The first two governments, after an excellent brief caretaker regime under Admiral Wolfgang Larrazábal Ugeto, strove with considerable success to build legitimacy and make democracy the only game in town. Betancourt and the AD easily won the late 1958 elections, with 49 percent of the vote, and formed a broad coalition government with runner-up URD (31 percent) and COPEI, which found to its dismay that it lacked the electoral appeal it thought it had earned, garnering only 15 percent of the electoral harvest. Concerned about alleviating the fears of the groups AD had alienated in 1945–1948, Betancourt named only three AD stalwarts to his fifteen-member cabinet, along with representatives of COPEI

RÓMULO BETANCOURT

and URD as well as sympathetic independents (in recognition of the fact that the party spectrum included no entity from the right). The president negotiated an agreement on high protective tariffs, and in exchange, the business sector, represented by the Venezuelan Federation of Chambers and Associations of Commerce and Production (FEDECAMARAS), accepted a major role for the state sector in a mixed economy.[12]

When Castro as well as Trujillo tried to do Betancourt in, the armed forces decided that he must not be the communistic madman reactionaries had made him out to be. Moreover, AD's repudiation of Marxism, which led to a raucous defection in April 1960 by the great majority of its Youth Federation, who were convinced of the need for radical mobilization in support of a socialist revolution and soon became the Leftist Revolutionary Movement (MIR), was clearly genuine. For his part, Betancourt skillfully used rising oil revenues to keep the military well paid and supplied with the latest equipment. It was essential for him to do this, since the MIR, followed by the PCV, had initiated terrorist activities in the capital in late 1960, extending guerrilla movements into the countryside the following year and forming the Armed Forces of National Liberation (FALN) in 1962.

Betancourt and the AD, which had lost its lower-house majority with the 1960 defection of the radical wing and the subsequent abandonment of the coalition by the URD (which was moving left while AD was moving toward the center), suffered an even more serious defection at the beginning of 1962 by a left-wing faction, the mainstream of the party criticized for their aggressive ideological self-righteousness in line with a slogan of a public relations agency "Let us do your thinking for you." In mid-1963, a critical election year, the government ordered the arrest of all known communists and pro-Castro extremists, subsequently stripping MIR and PCV legislators of congressional immunity and imprisoning them. Meanwhile the AD and allied parties established large numbers of new unions and affiliated them with the government; they also won control of the Confederation of Venezuelan Workers (CTV) away from the PCV and other extreme left groupings. Even more important, the Betancourt government rapidly implemented an extensive agrarian reform program, coupled with aggressive organization of a rural labor movement.

Through the election in December 1963 of Betancourt's right-hand man, AD organizational secretary Raúl Leoni (b. 1906), as president, the party retained power. However, with two new, largely urban parties intensifying competition, AD's share of the vote dropped by a third to 32.8 percent, although ally COPEI increased its vote to 20.2 percent, passing the URD, which plummeted to 18 percent. Riding on a wave of urban dissatisfaction, conservative intellectual Arturo Uslar Prieti's National Democratic Front (FND) took the larger slice of the 26 percent going to the new parties, with the lesser share going to the Popular Democratic Front (FDP) of leftist elements that had defected from the MIR when that entity opted for armed struggle. Leoni's centrist administration would be troubled not only by the continued rise of virulent insurgency by Castroite extremists, but also by internal party division, since he lacked Betancourt's enormous prestige as well as his exceptional political acumen. Relying on coalition partners essential for a congressional majority, Leoni welcomed back the URD and gave business interests a role in policymaking (as had already happened with the PRI in Mexico). Opposed to abandonment of a reformist stance, progressive Luis Prieto faced off against moderate Gonzálo Barrios in a September 1967 party primary. Although very possibly having majority support among AD militants, Prieto was not the candidate Betancourt and Leoni thought was needed to hold the coalition together.

Concerned that Betancourt would seek to return to the presidency in 1973, when he would again be eligible, Prieto broke away and founded the Peoples' Electoral Movement (MEP) to run as a dissident (à la Teddy Roosevelt and his Bull Moose Party in the US presidential election of 1912). This split, just as the splits in Colombia in 1930 and 1946 did for the Liberal and Conservative Parties, allowed COPEI and Caldera to come to office in December 1968 with the narrowest of margins—28.9 percent to 28.2 percent, only 31,000 votes—from an electorate that had expanded to 4.13 million from 3.36 million just five years earlier and 2.91 million in 1958, a growth of 42 percent in a decade. The MEP polled a respectable 19.3 percent, the URD continued to fall out of favor with only 12 percent, and both the FDP and the FDN demonstrated a failure to put down roots (coming away with only 7 and 4 percent, respectively). Despite the first loss in a national election in its history, the AD still held 66 lower-house seats and 19 in the senate to 59 and 16, respectively, for COPEI.[13]

Caldera demonstrated why he had been in Betancourt's shadow since the late 1930s. His victory was a result of AD's division, not of any dramatic increase in support for him or his party. Early he legalized MIR and PCV and issued a broad amnesty that attracted most participants in the armed struggle away from guerrilla tactics, which had failed to produce results, back into "normal" political competition. Having a limited base of support in the congress, Caldera entered into an "institutional pact" with AD, providing that over the next three administrations, the party winning the presidency would name the presiding officer of the senate and the losers would get the presidency of the lower house and coparticipation in executive positions. Only after a major impasse, the parties agreed in 1970 to an informal coalition in the congress. This was facilitated by COPEI's moving toward the center when in office—as AD had done when it was the governing party—so that it overlapped multiclass parties (just as the Labor and Conservative Parties overlapped in Britain, and as Christian Democrats and Social Democrats were beginning to do in Germany.)

The presidential election of December 1973 reflected continuation of a trend toward a two-party system, as AD and COPEI combined for over 85 percent of the vote.[14] A reunited AD won behind a younger leader, Carlos Andrés Pérez (b. 1922), who received 48.8 percent of the vote to the COPEI candidate's 36.7 percent, as Betancourt wisely decided that renovation of party leadership was more important than any personal ambitions on his part. (This statesman–scholar was well aware of the irreparable harm Yrigoyen's ambitions in 1928 had done to the Radicals in Argentina.) As 1974 brought the global energy crisis and its big boom in oil revenues—with the entire Venezuelan petroleum industry by now in government hands, he could be a distribution-oriented populist. The political benefits Pérez reaped led the last of the guerrillas to give up their armed struggle and enter electoral politics.

Pérez had to concern himself more with economic policy than had his three predecessors. With growth down and inflation rising, he stepped up social welfare and investment expenditures, after 1976 giving these policies the label of "growth before redistribution." With Venezuela's rising oil revenues a cushion against increased costs of imports resulting from international inflation, he did not have to worry about depletion of foreign exchange revenues, so could concentrate on maintaining consumer purchasing power—which inevitably led to subsidized prices. As with Echeverría in Mexico, whose situation bore the greatest similarities to Venezuela's conditions, foreign borrowing appeared to be the least painful option. With AD lacking a candidate of the incumbent's stature, COPEI nominated Herrera Campíns and won back the presidency in December 1978, the margin being 46.6 percent to 43.3 percent on a record vote of 2.48 million to 2.31 million with the electorate swollen to 6.2 million—an increase of over 31 percent in ten years. On the congressional side, 38.7 percent of the vote resulted in 86 deputies and 21 senators for each of the major parties, leaving only 21 seats in the lower house for all other parties combined. Hence, when in most of the area democratic transitions were only getting under way or not yet moving forward, Venezuela's seemed fully consolidated.[15]

Chile: After a Good Start, Disaster

This was to prove a very trying roller-coaster quarter century for Chile and in many ways would be the most critical watershed in its history, its legacy becoming evident only in the ensuing period. Starting out with election of a respectable conservative, Chile would see a reformist government under Latin America's outstanding Christian Democrat, followed by election of a Marxist who would be violently overthrown halfway into his constitutional term. This traumatic event led to a military dictatorship, bringing with it a level of repression never dreamed of by essentially democratic Chileans.[16]

The period began quite favorably as, deprived of his outside mentor, Perón (ousted in September 1955), President Carlos Ibáñez del Campo decided to maintain the ship of state on an even keel by not having a candidate of his own for the 1958 succession. The January 1, 1956, general strike to protest the policy recommendations of the US-sponsored Klein-Saks economic study mission was met with a state of siege and arrest of its chief architect. In the aftermath of this fiasco the labor movement remained quiescent owing to a combination of internal recriminations and the specter of repression. Ibáñez's economic and financial officials followed orthodox policies and attempted to balance the budget. Inflation dropped in 1956 and 1957, but a surge in 1958 resulted in large part from a labor protest of wage restraints; the government was sensitive to that part of the dissatisfaction coming from white-collar workers, who were traditionally linked to the Radical Party. As would often be the case in Chile, as well as in many other countries, policy consistency was sacrificed to political conveniences, viewed around election time as necessities. This breach rekindled the debate between monetarists and structuralists, with the government moving back toward the orthodox stability measures it believed had kept 1959 inflation from rising above a disquieting 38 percent.

Following repeal in 1958 of the controversial early Cold War Law for the Defense of Democracy, Ibáñez legalized the Communist Party. As reflected by the 1957 congressional elections, the antiparty sentiment that had elevated him to office in 1952 was on the wane, but the right still benefited from quirks in the antiquated electoral law. As would be the case subsequently in Peru, reforms in 1958 greatly reduced the possibilities of the kind of voting fraud in the rural areas that had provided the conservatives with a captive electorate. By so doing, these reforms gave the parties of the center and left the incentive to seek support from the peasantry. This move toward modernizing politics also led to the incoming president's abandonment of a policy of filling key bureaucratic posts with civilian technicians and a return to staffing the executive branch with party politicians.

The 1958 presidential balloting was truly a critical election, having in its second- and third-place finishers the future victors of 1964 and 1970. Chile's constitutional reputation stood up to the test of a very close race, as Jorge Alessandri Rodríguez (b. 1896), candidate of the right-wing parties, edged out the standard bearer of the left, the Socialist Party's Salvador Allende, by less than thirty-five thousand votes. Significantly for the future, the young Christian Democratic Party (PDC), behind Eduardo Frei Montalva (b. 1911), elbowed past the over-the-hill Radicals for third place. Alessandri's winning margin was 31.6 percent of the vote to 28.9 percent for Allende, with Frei garnering an attention-getting 20.7 percent of voter preferences, while the Radical Party's near demise was sealed with its 15.6 percent—despite being favorably viewed by Washington. The very small number of votes (forty-one thousand) for a "spoiler" candidate, a defrocked Catholic priest rumored to be sponsored by the US Central-Intelligence Agency (CIA), was larger than the winner's margin. (There is little doubt that the Eisenhower administration would have mounted some covert operation to keep Allende from taking office—probably focused on thwarting his requisite selection by the congress.)[17]

Jorge Alessandri, a respected businessman with experience in both houses of congress as well as the cabinet, and son of the renowned two-time president Arturo Alessandri Palma, hero of the 1920s and 1930s (when his nemesis had been Ibáñez), steered Chile along to the major challenge of the 1964 elections. To do this, he attenuated, with tension, but not serious crises, the impact of the Cuban Revolution. His election as candidate of the Liberals and Conservatives arose out of changes that had come to maturity during the Ibáñez years. The traditional rural, clientelistic, "managed" vote the right-wing parties had depended on in the past had been undermined, so Alessandri pointed the way to a new, essentially urban coalition of the right, involving professionals, small businessmen, and, with the decline of the Radical Party, white-collar workers.[18]

Labor during the Alessandri government shifted from its antipolitics, general-strike orientation, which had proven a failure, to reentering the arena of electoral and parliamentary politics through close alignment with political parties. Opposition gains in the 1961 congressional balloting led the president to ease up on restrictive wage policies at the cost of a rise in inflation. Slippage by the right in the 1963 municipal elections caused large industrial entrepreneurs to cool toward Alessandri, who in any case was not eligible for reelection. Hence, both the Conservatives and the Liberals had to examine very closely their options for the looming presidential succession.

In 1964, Salvador Allende, a respected Socialist senator who had received less than 6 percent of the 1952 vote as a symbolic candidate and had been edged out by Alessandri in 1958, again carried the banner of the left under the Popular Action Front (FRAP) label. The right lacked a candidate with significant electoral appeal, throwing its support to the Christian Democrats' Eduardo Frei in a move to prevent a possible Allende victory. This polarized situation in an electorate that had exploded from 1.16 million in 1958 to 2.92 million led to a campaign in which funding flowed in from the United States and Western European countries on the one side and from the Soviet Union, both directly and through Cuba, on the other.[19] The result was a landslide victory for pragmatic Christian Democratic reformer Eduardo Frei, with just over 56 percent of the vote, a rare majority in a country whose multiparty politics had for over a generation led to plurality presidents needing to have their victory ratified by the congress. Yet, when one looks to the future, his not-so-easy "easy" win was misleading, since the Conservatives and Liberals had backed his election as the lesser evil and had no intention of supporting his programs.

Allende's nearly 39 percent of the vote, although far behind Frei's vote, represented a substantial gain for the left over 1958, so the runner-up was able to keep FRAP together and on the "peaceful road to socialism" as he looked ahead to 1970, when the popular centrist could not run to succeed himself. The left's strategy was to team with the right to prevent Frei from being sufficiently successful to pose the threat of a Christian Democratic victory in 1970. Hence, archenemies, although looking forward to politically, if not literally, destroying each other down the road, often worked in tandem in the congress to hamstring Frei's reform programs. Calling for "revolution in liberty" and "Chileanization" of the US-owned copper mines, Frei demonstrated awareness that a growing proportion of the population wanted more than just improved access to education and health care.

The Christian Democrats had their roots in the Conservative Party's youth wing before migrating into the Francoist-inspired Falange in the latter 1930s. Constituting themselves as a party only in 1957, they emerged in 1958 as a serious contender, a move that was as dramatic as the 1956 arrival on the Peruvian political scene of Belaúnde and Popular Action. As formulated by Frei, the party's ideals were creation of a reformist, communitarian third way between the poles of Marxism, on the one hand, and liberal capitalism, on the other. Rejecting class conflict, they wished to establish social justice by way of a humanitarian society shaped along the lines of Christian families. PDC ideologues saw the peasantry, the urban unemployed, and women as natural constituencies. In practice the party found its support within the middle class and the petty bourgeoisie and became more of a center party than one of the center-left.

With only minority support in the congress, despite garnering an unprecedented 42 percent of the vote in the 1965 congressional elections, as the rightist parties ran their own lower- and upper-house slates and adopted an oppositional stance in repudiation of his slogan of "Revolution in liberty," Frei found himself

EDUARDO FREI MONTALVA

in the classic uncomfortable position of the centrist reformer fighting a two-front war against the left and the right, while being pulled in both directions by elements within his own multiclass, catchall party. In his first two years Frei moved cautiously and thus alienated the progressive wing of his party without appeasing the right opposition, which viewed any reforms with distaste as whetting revolutionary appetites. In 1967, internal dissension came to the fore with factions seeking to improve their clout through the congressional elections. With the reformist wing headed toward alliance with Allende's forces, in 1968 the administration shifted toward the right.

If any other Chilean administration is taken as a standard, Frei's accomplishments were substantial. Despite opposition from the right, he enacted an agrarian reform program allowing expropriation of properties in excess of a certain size, with exceptions for those being efficiently managed and highly productive. By the end of his term, 3.4 million hectares, over 8 million acres of land, had been distributed to 35,000 families, and 115,000 rural workers had gained the benefits of unionization. In the mining field, Frei succeeded in getting congressional approval of majority ownership by Chileans. But with unions linked to the opposition, labor relations were generally confrontational when not conflictual. Frei's rational policy of breaking, resisting, and circumventing the labor arm of his political enemies had the effect of further radicalizing the unions. Thus, in the view of a leading observer, although aiming at depolarizing the situation, Frei's actions "aggravated polarization and worsened the deadlock."[20] As another scholar saw the situation, "In Chile, political structures that had facilitated popular participation, in a way which would not have been possible during the early stages of industrialization in Europe, proved too much of a threat to elites, and seemed too brittle to facilitate any compromise between elites and populist demands."[21]

Despite having coped reasonably well with the dilemmas inherent in this sticky situation, although after 1968 the country entered a recession, Frei was forced to sit by and see the progressive wing of his party—linked to the theology of liberation and radical agrarian reform—join Allende's alliance in 1969, a move that, along with the left wing of the crumbling Radical Party, made Allende's new, broader Popular Unity (UP) coalition more formidable than the FRAP had been. For its part, the PDC went into the campaign saddled with a candidate not only less reformist than Frei, but lacking his popularity and charisma. As in 1958, the balloting was extremely close, with Allende receiving 36.3 percent of the vote over the nominee of the National Party (a merger of the Liberals and the Conservatives), ex-president Jorge Alessandri, with 34.9 percent, as the Christian Democrats fell to 28 percent. Hence, the election went, as had all recent ones except that of 1964, into the hands of the congress, where the Christian Democrats followed the tradition of ratifying the first-place finisher—but only in return for a promise from Allende not to change the rules of the electoral game before the next presidential succession. US efforts to convince the national legislators not to vote for Allende failed, as did efforts designed to promote a military coup, the assassination of strict constitutionalist General René Schneider being the critical element.[22]

Thus, just as twelve years earlier Alessandri had narrowly edged Allende, Allende now nosed Alessandri out. Just and fair as this result may have been, its outcome proved to be tragic, as half a term of Allende, gentleman that he was, would lead to fifteen years of repressive dictatorship. For nations, as for individuals, the path to hell may be paved with good intentions, especially if these bring out very bad intentions on the part of enemies. This was certainly the case, as Allende found himself caught between the opposition and the more radical elements of his own coalition. Although this was not in itself an impossible situation, bearing some similarities to Frondizi's earlier problems in Argentina, there was one critical difference: US determination to be rid of a second Marxist regime in the hemisphere, recently demonstrated in the Dominican intervention of 1965.

Allende's Popular Unity coalition enjoyed the support of just over one-third of the congress and faced the unremitting hostility of the United States and its allies. Under these handicaps his valiant pursuit of the "peaceful road to socialism" proved unattainable. This unfortunate outcome was so even though Allende benefited from constitutional reforms in 1969–1970 that had strengthened the executive vis-à-vis the congress. As was in the cards, labor did very well under Allende's government, for which it would pay later, with the Unified Confederation of Workers (CUT) legally recognized, public employee unions legalized, and a two-thirds rise in the minimum wage in 1971, nearly twice as high a rise as the previous year's increase in the cost of living. In Allende's structuralist approach, few restraints were initially placed on wages, which generally were negotiated well in excess of government guidelines—a practice the PDC had adopted as payback for the many things the FRAP had done to make life miserable for the Frei government.[23]

The agrarian reform program was revised to greatly reduce the area of exceptions, and in a move with eventual near-fatal results, the copper mines were fully nationalized. Copper must be smelted, but refining facilities were not located in Chile, and the countries where they existed proved reluctant to buy minerals they felt had been improperly taken from their citizens. Until the ore is sold, mining creates major expenditures and no offsetting income—a lesson the Allende government learned the hardest possible way. At the same time, renewal of violent tactics in the countryside by UP's militant maximalist revolutionary wing back during Frei's administration brought strong reaction from the right, and the armed forces became increasingly divided.

Whereas socialist measures went too far for the opposition, they were only a timid beginning in the eyes of the left wing of Popular Unity. Thus, deep divisions in his government and even deeper ones within its power base increasingly hampered Allende. The Leftist Revolutionary Movement (MIR) had never embraced the *Vía Pacífica*, or the peaceful road to socialism. Dedicated to violence and having pronounced Maoist sympathies, the MIR was joined by the Movement for Unitary Popular Action (MAPU) and its followers in the labor movement in taking actions to bring about the establishment of socialism ahead of and beyond the government through land seizures and factory occupations. Extremely vociferous, these sectarian groups of the extreme left made no secret of their belief not only that existing structures and practices needed to be swept aside, but also that counterrevolutionaries and other reactionaries could expect to be sacrificed on the altar of revolution. In an unruly process of uprooting and replacing, rather than reforming and transforming, formal institutional channels of policymaking and political compromise broke down or were bypassed.[24]

Their behavior was out of line with Allende's sincere, if idealistic, belief that if nowhere else, in Chile, because of its unique characteristics and traditions, it would be possible to install socialism through democratic institutions. He was both a dedicated socialist and a convinced democrat. He felt that it was possible to unite all classes, or at least important segments of all, against monopolists, the landed oligarchy, and foreign capitalist sectors. As in the contemporary Velasco Alvarado regime in Peru, there would be three forms of economic enterprises differentiated by ownership: private; social; and mixed, with the second eventually predominating as the first was reduced in scope, often by passing into if not through the mixed model. This scenario presumed permanent tenure of the left in power, which Allende believed could be accomplished in an electoral way. Those to his left within UP felt that implantation of socialism had to be done quickly, since their confidence in maintaining power through parliamentary processes ranged from limited to nonexistent.

Popular Unity, particularly its Socialist Party component, performed well in the 1971 municipal elections, held in the midst of a short-lived boom that saw the economy grow by a robust 7.7 percent, feeding a euphoric sense of invincibility on the part of the coalition's more exalted elements. The critical test of the Via Pacífica would be the 1973 midterm congressional elections. But growing economic problems cast doubt on how the public would judge the government at that point, when short-term economic factors might blind them to the fruits the UP's actions would eventually bring. With inflation on the rise by mid-1972, and heading toward 900 percent in 1973, causing a precipitous drop in real wages, this prospect of electoral rejection became a preoccupation. The stakes of polarization were raised with the formation of a National Association of the Private Sector (FRENAP) to coordinate opposition to the government by business, finance, and industrial groups, on the one hand, and the dramatic and disruptive October 1972 truckers' strike, on the other. Along with other moves by the right, including middle-class housewives parading in the streets banging on their empty pots to protest shortages and high prices, the scenario was eerily reminiscent of Brazil in the early 1960s, leading up to Goulart's ouster at the end of the first quarter of 1964. Indeed, Brazilians were among the array of outsiders advising the anti-Allende forces.

The gains Allende had counted upon as a result of the March 1973 congressional elections did not materialize; the UP gained a scant eight seats on 34.6 percent of the vote—no real progress over 1970. Hence, the government would have to continue without adequate legislative support. The Christian Democrats had, in line with Chilean tradition, voted in 1970 for the congressional selection of Allende as the candidate with the most votes. In return they had negotiated an agreement with him that his government would not make any fundamental changes in the rules of the electoral game, an understanding that, if honored, would give the PDC a favorable prospect for returning to power in 1976, when Allende would not be eligible to stand for reelection, and Frei could run again. Frei and his associates strongly suspected that, under heavy pressure from the rebellious MIR and MAPU, which insisted on complete socialization at any cost, Allende would go along with a proposal to replace the existing congress with a Soviet-style parliament.

Having hoped to avoid this dilemma by obtaining a legislative majority in the 1973 elections, Allende was thrown into a quandary by UP's failure to get a mandate. The left's significant gains in congressional balloting since 1961—up from 22 percent to nearly 35 percent—had come chiefly at the expense of the Radical Party, which had quickly declined from over 21 percent of the vote to under 4 percent. As the Christian Democrats' share of the vote rose from 16 percent to almost 29 percent over the same span (while the right declined from 38 percent to 21 percent), there was little room for the left to keep growing unless there was an extremely sharp and "un-Chilean" shift from 1970 to 1973.

US-backed "destabilization" activities had been under way for some time, since many Republicans had not taken kindly to failure to convince the Chilean congress in 1970 to choose, as was then its legal right, Alessandri as president. (The law had subsequently been changed to provide for a runoff election instead of a congressional decision.) Earlier many of these destabilization activities had been aimed at further undermining an already poor economic situation, but newer covert operations were in the field of psychological warfare, concentrating on fears among the military that they and their families were on hit lists to be eliminated after an impending complete seizure of power by the UP. General Carlos Pratts, a liberal constitutionalist, had joined the government as a guarantor of the elections. After the congressional elections, the crisis deepened rapidly with his resignation in August at the insistence of the officer corps. The lower congressional house, where the Christian Democrats were now ready to vote with the right, on August 22 called openly for military intervention.[25]

September 11, 1973, saw General Augusto Pinochet Ugarte (b. 1915) come to power over the blood-drenched bodies of Allende and many of his supporters. Indeed, by December, fifteen hundred Allende supporters had been killed, joining the ex-president, who committed suicide rather than surrender when fighting for Chile's equivalent of the White House became hopeless. (In this gesture, he followed a precedent set by Balmaceda nine decades earlier when he was defeated in the armed struggle with the congress and the military.) Chile entered a reign of terror exceeding even what the worst days of the Argentine military regime would bring. Acutely aware of the strength of UP's organizations and the dedication of its cadres, as well as the fact that they were not thoroughly discredited in the eyes of the public (as had been the case in Brazil and soon would be in Argentina), the new holders of power set out to obliterate them.[26]

A traditional type of army officer, Pinochet had entered the military academy in 1932 at age sixteen, graduating four years later. Attending Chile's War Academy (its equivalent of the US Army Staff and Command School at Fort Leavenworth) from 1949 to 1952, and by then a major, he remained there as an instructor while also attending law school. Following a successful, but not spectacular, career as a senior officer, during which he avoided political involvement, he was selected to command the capital-area garrison at the onset of Allende's government, rising to command of the army in late August.[27] This strategic position made the reluctant conspirator the vital swingman for any coup (equivalent to Castelo Branco and Costa e Silva in Brazil in 1964).

Once dug in as head of the armed-forces junta, this throwback to the officers turned out by the German military mission in the late 1880s overcompensated for his earlier hesitancy to become involved in the plotting, exceeding any of Brazil's or even Argentina's military presidents in centralizing power and exercising it with zest—outdoing his ideological opposite, Peru's Velasco Alvarado, at his peak. Pinochet presided over a junta composed of the chiefs of the four armed services, since in Chile these included national militarized police established in the nineteenth century as a counterweight to the army. In a trajectory reminiscent of Spain's Franco in the late 1930s, Pinochet soon became Supreme Chief of the Nation and, by year's end, President of the Republic before adding the title of Chief Executive in mid-1974.

The Pinochet-led junta was extremely repressive in its opening period. With an energy and gusto not seen in Argentina until the Dirty War and never found in Brazil or Peru, it tortured and killed individuals associated with the Allende regime or active in left-wing movements. At least a thousand such "subversives" disappeared from 1973 through 1978. Despite the extreme polarization preceding the coup, most Chileans still wavered somewhere in the middle. As aptly put by a leading scholar, they were neither Marxists nor Pinochetists, but rather "dubious spectators caught in a system they had not chosen."[28] Under the force of circumstances, they became conformists.

With no political parties allowed and sectoral organizations severely restricted, the military services became avenues for a rough form of interest articulation and the junta a vehicle for a limited degree of aggregation. The most liberal, or at least the most modernization-oriented, of the services was the air force, and its General Gustavo Leigh, an often-independent, if not dissident, voice until he was purged in July 1975. The Pinochet regime did meet with considerable, even notable, success in rebuilding the country's shattered economy, a feat that eluded many military and civilian governments across the region. Initially following the path of gradualism, the government shifted to shock treatment in 1975 under the baton of Sêrgio de Castro, Chile's answer to Roberto Campos and Delfim Netto in Brazil. The country was opened up to competition by private enterprise and market forces; hence, price controls were eliminated, tariffs were reduced, the nationalization of mines was reversed, and land was returned to its former owners. From 1977 to 1981 Chile's economy expanded at annual rates of 6 to 8 percent. Continuity of what came to be called "Chicago Boys'" economic policy—for the university at which the leading lights had done their doctoral work—continued until de Castro's departure from the government in 1982.

Although restoring Chile's economic viability and fiscal solvency, Pinochet proved a much more ruthlessly dictatorial figure than Chile had ever seen. Indeed, his highly authoritarian and repressive regime, which had in mid-1977 implanted a plan for institutionalizing its permanence in power to the end of the century, was fully entrenched as the decade ended—sufficiently, as it proved, to last for another eight years.

Bolivia: Collapse of a Still-Young Democracy

During this period Bolivia would experience two elected civilian administrations that continued the work of the 1952 Revolution (essentially a cross between Peronism and Peruvian *Aprismo*) before witnessing rapid and near-complete collapse of this noble experiment in transforming this backward country. A series of military governments of differing political orientations would hold power, with only that of General Hugo Banzer Suárez (b. 1926) lasting more than a few years and providing substantial stability. As Banzer's successors were more repressive, less effective, and increasingly corrupt, this period would end with Bolivia's armed forces on the verge of being forced from office.[29]

The new period opened for Bolivia with the first MNR government drawing to a close, with a daunting agenda of "revolutionary" measures still to be enacted and implemented. Victor Paz Estenssoro had long harbored little doubt concerning who would carry on his work. Vice President Hernán Siles breezed home in the 1956 presidential race with a landslide 83 percent of the vote, five times that of the Bolivian Socialist Falange's forlorn hopeful. Not content with this large percentage of the vote, and envisioning the MNR more as an all-inclusive party along the lines of the PRI in Mexico—logical since Paz Estenssoro's original mentor, Perón, had been recently forced out of office in Argentina—Siles tried to win over the significant urban middle-class segment of the FSB's support.

Economically, the government moved increasingly in the direction of state capitalism, not the worst option in view of the weakness of private-sector entrepreneurship, but lacking feasibility in a context of falling tin prices, which undercut government revenues. Moreover, the mines faced stiff competition from both Southeast Asia and Africa. To act as a check on the army, the regime had tolerated, even encouraged, armed militias being aligned with the tinworkers' union, led by Juan Lechín—an ally in the 1952 Revolution, but now both vice president and politically ambitious leader of a restive left-wing of the MNR. The militias grew restless in the face of an economic austerity program adopted as a condition for urgently needed aid from the IMF. The results of this austerity bordered upon stagflation, with its high rates of unemployment amid punishing inflation, a bitter lesson Siles would never forget.

The 1960 presidential succession posed a difficult problem for Siles and Paz. Walter Guevara Arce led the MNR's right wing and Lechín its militant left. Both coveted the presidency; nomination of either would upset the other to the point of possible defection, if not insurrection. The solution adopted was Paz's return to office. Although the election was not as great a runaway as that of 1956, he won easily. During his new administration Paz was confronted with increasingly serious problems. State mining giant COMIBOL ran up serious operating losses, partially attributable to the fact that its heavily subsidized commissary had become a social welfare agency, with hordes of relatives and friends of miners enjoying the privilege of its use, which for many meant survival, particularly in the hard times the country was undergoing. Efforts to curb this fiscally intolerable abuse by tightening up on eligibility (not to dream of laying off excess employees) were viewed by the miners as unjustified provocations; they pointed out that they had helped protect the regime from its foes. As the miners were not only determined but also extremely well versed in the use of explosives, the government had begun to rebuild the army as a line of defense, in the meantime resorting to use of armed *campesinos* to contain the miners in times of crisis.

In a situation far from the normality of his first administration, with its dreams of harmonious democracy, Paz found himself having brought about distasteful and, in view of the future, unfortunate results. As summed up by an insightful scholar:

> He cut the government off from the few organizational anchors that previously connected it (even if negatively) to the major social sectors so that in effect it floated above society in an illusion of apolitical technocratic authority. Coercion and clientelistic manipulation were the major ways the government articulated its relationship to society. Such means of interaction were hardly likely to breed either stability, public confidence, or a sense of government legitimacy.[30]

In 1964, the dilemma facing the MNR was more serious than in 1960. Guevara Arce's defection left Lechín feeling that he was entitled to the presidency. Such an event was unthinkable in the eyes of the US government and its British and German partners in the so-called triangular plan for the modernization and reequipment of the country's highly inefficient mines. Since it exported low-value ore, with none of the more profitable smelting going on in the country, the Bolivian government was actually losing money on every ton it exported. But as tin exports provided almost all the government's foreign exchange earnings, and were needed to finance imports, much less take care of debt service, Bolivia had to keep up exports or face insolvency—which was being averted with difficulty.

International political considerations impinged heavily as the US government considered Lechín a sympathizer with Castro, if not a pawn of the Soviet Union. Thus irresistible pressure was placed on Paz to continue in power. Doing so required him to push through the congress an amendment removing the constitutional ban. With strong-arm tactics he accomplished this, along the way alienating not only the party's left wing, but also nationalistic students and both nationalist and opportunistic elements of the military. Thus, very early in his new term, attained through a close and more than somewhat questionable election, Paz was overthrown by the armed forces in the middle of serious popular demonstrations. Contrary to the overwhelming majority of unrealistically sanguine views at the time, this would prove to be a case of "out of the frying pan, into the fire," and would see slimy as well as incompetent individuals in control of the nation's destiny.

The first military president would, in retrospect, turn out to be one of the top half, certainly very far from the bottom. Air force general René Barrientos Ortuño (b. 1919), who had been serving as Paz's vice president, was a charismatic figure to the Bolivian masses. Fluent in Quechua, he was chosen for a constitutional term as president in July 1966—in a popular direct election of a military man, differing from many other cases of indirect or rigged elections. Skillfully blending repression and manipulation, Barrientos firmly implanted a model of state capitalism through which he co-opted a significant segment of the middle class. By December 1968, however, with the economy going downhill, Barrientos was governing autocratically and was in a shaky political situation in the capital, despite his popularity in the remote countryside by the time of his April 1969 death in a helicopter crash. His death opened the door to a decade of praetorianism gone wild (and was a lost opportunity for incorporation of those Indian groups neglected in the initial 1950s broadening of participation).[31]

General Alfredo Ovando Candia (b. 1917), who had been copresident immediately after the ouster of Paz and was a newly minted adept of the Peruvian nationalist reformist line, pushed aside the vice president and took power. Following his nationalization of Gulf Oil, US aid dried up. Allowing reactivation of the Bolivian Workers Confederation (COB), he adopted a populist rhetoric and mobilized young civilian politicians into political life. Ovando was unable to consolidate his hold on the presidential office, resigning under pressure in October 1970. General Juan José Torres (b. 1921) then tried to be a better imitation of Peru's Velasco Alvarado but lasted less than a year in office before being pushed out in August 1971 in favor of General Hugo Banzer Suárez (b. 1926), who, as a colonel, had served in Barrientos's first cabinet.

Banzer, the most politically astute of Bolivia's military presidents, returned to the more conservative Barrientos line while keeping a close eye on how the military was running Brazil. Attracting support from the urban middle class and business elements that had benefited from the state capitalist developmental process, Banzer built a complex center-right political coalition, transferring public resources to private hands (as the counterpart military regime in Ecuador did) through low interest rates and lax tax collection—with importers favored by an overvalued currency. Perceptions that his policies favored the eastern lowland region around Santa Cruz—where the population was lighter-skinned than in the highlands and where Bolivia's new but growing petroleum industry was centered—along with large-scale cotton, sugar, and soy cultivation did not sit well with La Paz–based and Cochabamba–based interests.

Meanwhile, Banzer fared well during a period of oil-export, foreign borrowing economic prosperity, with GDP growth averaging 5 percent a year, but he ran into heavy opposition after banning all party activity in November 1974. At that point politics reverted to a factional struggle among elites, revolving around Banzer as the lodestone of patronage (marking a significant retrogression in terms of political development). He bought substantial support by creating forty thousand new public-sector jobs, chiefly in the capital area.[32] Although the economy was growing at a rate near 5 percent a year, civilian opposition was on the rise, and military dissatisfaction was brewing. In early 1977, Banzer tried to ease pressures by promising elections for 1980, but by November, he had to move them up to 1978 and withdraw as a candidate.

The fraud-ridden July 1978 elections declared the air force's conservative general Juan Pereda Asbun to be the winner over ex-presidents Paz Estenssoro, running for the MNR and representing the center-right, and Siles, carrying the hopes of his MNR of the Left (MNRI)—with Juan Lechín and the COB continuing to occupy the left of the political spectrum. Seizing power in July in the face of mounting demands for new elections, Pereda Asbun was ousted in November by General David Padilla, who immediately promised early elections. Held in mid-1979, they saw a near tie between Paz, with 31.1 percent of the vote, and Siles, with 31.2 percent, trailed by Banzer with almost 13 percent. Failing to resolve the impasse, the congress installed Senate president Walter Guevara Arce as a caretaker. Within three months this constitutional outcome was swept aside by a bloody, nonhierarchical military coup headed by Colonel Alberto Natush Busch. He and his cronies held power for a fortnight before the female head of the lower house of the congress was chosen interim president. So the period ended with Bolivia's political future very much in doubt. However, this interrupted transition would soon resume its forward movement.

Ecuador: Velasco or the Military

Ecuador entered this period under what was for it an unusual streak of two stable civilian governments in a row. It exited the quarter century with election of a civilian government. In between it saw two more turbulent administrations by Velasco Ibarra, and both a short term and a longer term with military rule, as well as several interim political arrangements. The one permanent change would be the disappearance from the political stage of Velasco Ibarra, who had played a leading role in Ecuador's national life for much longer than anyone before or since.[33]

A contemporary of Peru's Haya de la Torre, who also wound up his long political career at the end of this period, Velasco Ibarra did not have to endure the frustration of a lifetime veto by the military as Haya did. In the presidency in 1934, he was ousted by a coup, coming back in by way of a coup in 1944 after having been defrauded of victory in 1940. Elected in 1952 and serving out a full term, he was again elected in 1960 and ousted in 1962. Velasco Ibarra's fifth and final term began with election in 1968 and ended with yet another ouster by a coup in 1972. Clearly he greatly enlivened Ecuadorian politics, but for all the decades he did this, his contributions to the country's political development were limited. For he was content to use the existing system and not try to change or significantly reform it. Intuitive and shrewd rather than a profound thinker, instinctively paternalistic and opportunistic, he had discovered at the beginning of the 1930s that the country's marginalized sectors—those ignored by the post-Eloy Alfaro political elites—were a fertile political base that allowed him to operate independently from the traditional parties. While this spellbinding demagogic populist was doing so, no modern political movements could emerge, and he was not inclined to give structure to his following, preferring to win a new host of converts each time he ran for office, appealing to whatever concerned the masses at the time while thunderously denouncing the oligarchs and praising the virtues of "his" long-suffering Ecuadorian people. In power he would build roads, schools, and hospitals—permanent works bearing his name.

In 1956, Camilo Ponce Enríquez (b. 1912), founder of the Social Christian Movement (MSC), squeaked to victory in a fraud-marred election. During his peaceful term, years in which the importance of banana production and prices continued the shift of population and power away from the sierra to the coastal region, increased attention was paid to low-level industrialization. Returned once again to the presidency in 1960, prickly populist Velasco Ibarra soon broke with his vice president and was expelled from office by a coup in November 1962. Thus Ecuador's fourteen years of constitutional order came to an end. Carlos Julio Arosamena Monroy, handicapped by a drinking problem, lasted only eight months before being ousted in favor of a military junta, itself forced from power by violent student-led riots in March 1966.

As a result Velasco Ibarra was once more elected president in June 1968, this time with only a little over one-third of the vote. Again having ruptured relations with his vice president, and confronting student protests and deteriorating economic conditions, he closed down the congress and the supreme court in June 1970. This attempt at dictatorial rule was briefly viable owing to the support afforded him by his nephew and erstwhile defense minister, General Jorge Acosta Velasco. Deprived of this prop with Acosta Velasco's forced removal by pressure from the officer corps, the aging demagogue soon fell victim to a military coup in mid–February 1972.[34]

Although Ecuador's military had ample reasons for wanting to remove Velasco Ibarra from power, they were also looking ahead to the looming presidential elections, seeing antimilitarist Guayaquil populist Assad Bucarám Elmhalim, a former street peddler turned two-time mayor, as a long-term threat—perhaps even a new Velasco Ibarra. Since Bucarám controlled the Concentration of Popular Forces (CFP) founded in the 1940s, he was a formidable front-runner. Large deposits of oil having been discovered in the trans-Andean–Amazon headwaters region of the country's remote interior, the armed forces considered themselves the best custodians of Ecuador's newfound wealth and rapidly increasing revenues. Moreover, in Brazil the military had ruled since 1964, in rival Peru the military had been in control since 1968, and the armed forces were entrenched in power in Argentina and Bolivia and soon to take over in Chile. Why should the Ecuadorian military be left out of this continental pattern, particularly as Bucarám represented coastal commercial interests whose plans for using oil revenues were likely to include populist projects for the lower classes, not the patriotic task of reequipping the country's armed forces in anticipation of renewed border conflict with Peru? After all, in their view at least, the military were Ecuador's only truly national institution.[35] So they promised a nationalist, humanist, socially responsible government but operated on the premise that what's good for the armed forces is at least not bad for the country.

General Guillermo Rodríguez Lara (b. 1923), who had moved up to army commander with the ouster of Acosta and enjoyed strong ties to Guayaquil business elites, proved to be a weak imitation of Velasco Alvarado, the military president who had been reshaping Peru since late 1968. Influential General Gustavo Jarrín Ampudia as minister of natural resources led Ecuador into the Organization of Petroleum Exporting Countries (OPEC), but many other promises were left unfulfilled under Rodríguez Lara, although agro-exporters prudently diversified into industry as a hedge. Worse than his limited political and administrative abilities, however, was the prospect that he might be looking forward to a long stay in the presidency. Having experienced most of the political plagues of the region, civilian leaders wanted at least to avoid protracted military rule—all the more since by 1974 they had had a good look at how repressive a version of it Pinochet was installing in Chile. Yet for the time being they had little leverage in the situation, for new civilian political leadership had not emerged while Velasco Ibarra was still able to cast his spell over the Ecuadorian electorate. Besides, the coast-versus-sierra cleavage was still an insurmountable obstacle to political cooperation.

Hence Rodríguez Lara and his government did not face any serious challenges, such as insurgency, urban unrest, or even a coordinated opposition. Enjoying the luxury of rising oil revenues and the fact that anticipation of Ecuador's oil finds being larger than they turned out to be made borrowing easy, he could deal favorably with labor—even the communist-controlled Ecuadorian Workers'

Confederation (CTE). An agrarian reform law decreed in 1973 had the short-run effect of quieting, if not co-opting rural workers. Business benefited the most from the military regime's policies, with taxes reduced and massive subsidies available. Yet, in the face of purchases of subsonic fighter bombers, which could only be intended for use, or threat of use, against Peru, and substantial expansion of the state's economic role, the private sector became restive, all the more as Rodríguez Lara showed signs of a populist inclination designed to build a political base—perhaps to be used for legitimizing his rule through election or plebiscite. With Quito-area business and industry well represented by the Ecuadorian Chambers of Production, their Guayaquil rival counterparts moved to establish an Ecuadorian Federation of Export Industries.

In August 1975, leaders of the Conservative, Socialist, Velasquista, and National Revolutionary Parties, with backing from a broad array of business groups, formed the Civic Junta with the announced goal of "reestablishment of constitutional order." Although Rodríguez Lara was able to put down a coup attempt in September 1975, it left his authority significantly weakened. At the beginning of 1976, he was replaced by the three service ministers agreeing on the need for austerity measures and calling themselves the Supreme Government Council. (This development resembled the replacement in Peru of Velasco Alvarado by Morales Bermúdez.) The junta's spokesman, General Poveda Burbano, opened a series of dialogues designed to assess public sentiment and possible options for an exit strategy. Three civilian commissions resulted from these discussions: one to draft a new constitution; another to revise the 1945 constitution; and a third to propose reforms of the laws governing parties and elections.

The junta agreed with the recommendations to eliminate the literacy requirement for voting and to hold a national referendum in January 1978 to choose between the two proposed constitutions. With 1.8 million, 90 percent of the registered electorate, voting, Ecuadorians opted by 43 percent to 32 percent in favor of the new national constitution rather than a revision of the 1945 one. The junta subsequently reluctantly agreed to hand power over to a duly elected government before the end of 1978. Although a decree issued by General Jarrín, now minister of government, required that a president have both parents born in the country, an ill-disguised bill of attainder against Concentration of Popular Forces (CFP) leader Assad Bucarám, the election did take place in July, with his nephew Jaime Roldós Aguilera (b. 1941) the winner, in a massive 1.03 million to 442,000 victory in late April 1979 in a long-delayed runoff with rightist Sixto Durán Ballen (b. 1921). This runner-up was a US-trained urban planner, 1970–1978 mayor of Quito, political heir of ex-president Ponce Enríquez, and a future president. The initial close electoral derby in mid-July 1978 had resulted in 28 percent for Roldós to 24 percent for Durán and 23 percent for the third-place finisher.

Rodrigo Borja of the Democratic Left (ID)—another future chief executive—finished fourth with 11 percent of the votes.[36]

Although the result was anathema to the military junta, under heavy pressure from the United States in August they handed power over to Roldós. Ecuador had emerged from military rule before the 1980s.[37] The new regime was faced with a foreign debt that had increased sevenfold in the second half of the 1970s, but it was free of Velasco Ibarra, who died in March 1979 at age eighty-six.

Uruguay: The Wilting of the Flower of Democracy

This period included toward its end the most shameful experience in Uruguay's twentieth-century life: an authoritarian military regime engaging in "Argentine-like" acts of barbarism against groups and individuals in many cases seeking to maintain or restore freedoms Uruguayans held in high esteem. Indeed, falling into the pit late, although not quite as late as Chile, Uruguay did not finish climbing back out by the end of the 1970s.[38]

The Blancos, brought to office within the plural executive system on the strength of an overwhelming majority in 1958, continued in power until 1966. Although initiating economic reforms, the Blanco government was faced with labor unrest and rising leftist agitation. In 1966, both the Blancos and the Colorados favored abandoning the collective executive in favor of a return to a presidential system, a change approved by a referendum in November, at which time the Colorados elected Oscar Daniel Gestido, a retired air force officer, to the presidency. On his death the next year, vice president Jorge Pacheco Areco took over. His austerity measures sparked widespread unrest, and the terrorist Tupamaros (National Liberation Movement), founded in 1962 by Raúl Sendic, stepped up their drive to overthrow the government and bring revolutionary change to the country. As a result Uruguay was under modified martial law from June 1968 until March of the next year.

Following violent demonstrations on the occasion of New York governor Nelson Rockefeller's fact-finding visit, Pacheco—under very heavy military pressure—imposed a modified state of siege. Elections at the end of November 1971 resulted in a virtual dead heat between the Colorado candidate, Juan María Bordaberry (b. 1928), and his Blanco rival, eventually resolved in Bordaberry's favor by the electoral court, a decision opening the way for his inauguration in March 1972. In light of the Tupamaros's audacity and successes, the congress approved Bordaberry's request to declare a state of internal war, which suspended a wide range of constitutional guarantees. Nonetheless, labor unrest escalated in the face of Bordaberry's stringent economic and social policies, despite which inflation soared and currency was devalued almost monthly. De facto became de jure in

February 1973 as Bordaberry ceded a large degree of executive authority to the armed forces, under heavy pressure from the Argentine and Brazilian military regimes to suppress the Tupamaro insurgency and stop Uruguay from being a safe haven for subversive exiles from its much larger neighbors. When the congress resisted this militarization of the government, Bordaberry dissolved the congress, installing in its place a twenty-five member appointed Council of State dominated by the military. After breaking the ensuing general strike in July, a month later the government ended union autonomy and banned labor's central organization. Acting as little more than a figurehead for the military, Bordaberry canceled the elections scheduled for 1976.

By this time significant military elements favored a gradual return to democratic rule, beginning the process in June 1976 by deposing Bordaberry. After using him as a scapegoat, they installed a National Council of twenty-five handpicked civilians and twenty-one military officers for the purpose of electing a new chief executive. Aging Aparicio Méndez Manfredini (b. 1904), a former public health minister, was given a five-year term. He promptly deprived of their political rights individuals actively involved in political affairs during the 1966–1973 period, indicating that return to a civilian president was not necessarily the same as fully reestablishing democracy.[39] But it proved to be an important first step in this direction.

Paraguay: Durable Dictatorship

This quarter century for Paraguay would be Stroessner, Stroessner, and more Stroessner. Political to his toes and confident that he was at least as able as the country's three dominant autocrats of the nineteenth century, Alfredo Stroessner (b. 1912), son of an immigrant from Bavaria who was a veteran of the Chaco War, was involved in working for and plotting against all governments since 1940. Keeping his fingers on the pulse of the Colorado Party, he came to occupy the strategic position of commanding the Asuncíon garrison, subsequently becoming commander in chief as a reward from Federico Cháves for betraying President Higínio Morínigo. After deposing Cháves in May 1954, he was elected and inaugurated in mid-August. In 1956, Stroessner consolidated his hold on power by arresting critics and advocates of democracy. Consolidating his control of the Colorado Party, he soon ran the country in a dictatorial manner reminiscent of Somoza's in Nicaragua in the 1930s and 1940s. Opponents had the choice of jail or exile, and exercising complete control over the army, he defeated exiles' efforts to invade from their refuges across the river in Argentina or Brazil. Politically adept, having exploited his rivals' penchant for underestimating him, Stroessner established a facade of constitutional rule by letting the compliant Liberal Party back into the country's extremely limited political life in 1958, followed by nonthreatening Febreristas in 1964. Indeed, he altered the electoral law to assure the runner-up party one-third of legislative seats, pure window dressing in view of the congress's rubber stamp role and the iron discipline of the two-thirds majority held by his Colorados.[40] (The 1961 extension of the franchise to women was also chiefly a public relations ploy.) Socioeconomic policy was a simple matter, since the Paraguayan economy's major revenue came from contraband. With both Brazil and Argentina having heavy protective tariffs on consumer goods to defend domestic industries, these goods were imported into Paraguay and smuggled into its much larger and vastly wealthier neighbors.

By the late 1960s and 1970s, Stroessner had another source of income for his coterie and revenue for his government. Brazil built the world's largest hydroelectric project at Itaipú on the Paraguay River. Since this was on the border between the countries, it was legally a binational project. A good share of low-tech construction work was done by Paraguay, enabling Stroessner and his favored associate, Juan Carlos Wasmosy, a pal of the dictator's son Gustavo and head of the CONEPA building consortium, to get rich off cement factories during the years of construction, as well as have a boom in jobs for unskilled workers, who were in excess supply in Paraguay. In 1974, Brazil loaned Paraguay $2 billion toward its share of costs (which reached $11 billion plus interest for a total of $21 billion). Once in operation half of Itaipú's immense production of electricity "belonged" to Paraguay, which could make use of only a very small proportion of it. The rest was sold back to Brazil, the $160 million a year providing a substantial part of Paraguay's revenues. Hence, the 1970s ended with Stroessner firmly in control and enjoying good relations with the military regimes of the only countries that really mattered to his out-of-the-way fiefdom: Brazil and Argentina.[41] Stroessner's long stranglehold on the country would finally end deep into the next period, about the same time as Chile's casting off of military tutelage at the end of the 1980s.

Similarities and Differences

The experiences of these countries were more similar in pattern than in paths followed—both in sinking into repressive military rule or striving to climb back out. Peru, Ecuador, and Bolivia shared the inception of military regimes with Brazil and Argentina—during the 1960s—whereas military regimes took over Uruguay and Chile only in 1973. Colombia and Venezuela had experienced authoritarian regimes after 1948 and reencountered democratic ways by quite similar paths in 1957–1958. Military rule was continuous in Brazil, Chile, Bolivia, Uruguay, and Paraguay, whereas it was discontinuous in Argentina, being interrupted by civilian interludes in 1958–1962 and 1973–1975. What similarities in paths and patterns existed between South America and the Central American and Caribbean subregions? The next chapter explores this key question.

Notes

1. Quite useful on Peru at this juncture are Grant Hilliker, *The Politics of Reform in Peru: The Apristas and Other Mass Parties in Latin America* (Baltimore: Johns Hopkins University Press, 1971), and Peter F. Klarén, *Peru: Society and Nationhood in the Andes* (New York: Oxford University Press, 2000).

2. François Bourricaud, *Power and Society in Contemporary Peru* (New York: Praeger, 1970), pp. 230–231. Useful for understanding this period are Peter F. Klarén, *Modernization, Dislocation, and Aprismo* (Austin: University of Texas Press, 1973), and James L. Payne, *Labor and Politics in Peru* (New Haven: Yale University Press, 1965).

3. The APRA alliance with Prado is analyzed in Ruth Berins Collier and David Collier, *Shaping the Political Arena: Critical, Junctures, the Labor Movement, and Regime Dynamics in Latin America* (Princeton: Princeton University Press, 1991), pp. 696–701.

4. The military seizure of power is studied in Arnold Payne, *The Peruvian Coup d'Etat of 1962: The Overthrow of Manuel Prado* (Washington, DC: Institute for the Comparative Study of Political Systems, 1968).

5. The extremely pragmatic, if not opportunistic, alliance of APRA with Odría is examined in Collier and Collier, *Shaping,* pp. 701–704.

6. Ibid., p. 718. The most conceptualized and sophisticated study of Peru at this juncture is Alfred Stepan, *The State and Society: Peru in Comparative Perspective* (Princeton: Princeton University Press, 1978). Other relevant works include Howard Handelman, *Struggle in the Andes: Peasant Political Mobilization in Peru* (Austin: University of Texas Press, 1975), and David Werlich, *Peru: A Short History* (Carbondale: Southern Illinois University Press, 1978). The ballyhooed IPC issue was largely a smokescreen manipulated by the military, who were determined not to let Haya de la Torre be elected as Belaúnde's successor. Belaúnde essentially had his constitutional six-year term cut to five.

7. APRA's belated cooperation with Belaúnde is covered in Collier and Collier, *Shaping,* pp. 704–706, with analysis of the party's options during this time on pp. 704–710.

8. Consult Stepan, *State,* passim., as well as Abraham F. Lowenthal, ed., *The Peruvian Experiment: Continuity and Change Under Military Rule* (Princeton: Princeton University Press, 1975).

9. A sound work on the military regime is Cynthia McClintock and Abraham F. Lowenthal, *The Peruvian Experiment Reconsidered* (Princeton: Princeton University Press, 1983). See also Cynthia McClintock, *Peasant Cooperatives and Political Change in Peru* (Princeton: Princeton University Press, 1981), and David Collier, *Squatters and Oligarchs: Authoritarian Rule and Policy Change in Peru* (Baltimore: Johns Hopkins University Press, 1976).

10. The purchase of a large number of tanks from the Soviet Union made no military sense in mountainous Peru incurred serious international liabilities, particularly since it was a credit operation that complicated subsequent foreign debt negotiations. It seems to have been part of Velasco's efforts to make Peru a significant actor within the nonaligned movement, the members of which held a "summit" in Lima on the eve of his ouster.

11. Valuable on Venezuela at this critical juncture are John D. Martz, *Acción Democrática: Evolution of a Modern Political Party in Venezuela* (Princeton: Princeton University Press,

1966); Daniel C. Hellinger, *Venezuela: Tarnished Democracy* (Boulder, CO: Westview Press, 1991); and David E. Blank, *Politics in Venezuela* (Boston: Little, Brown, 1973).

12. See Robert J. Alexander, *Rómulo Betancourt and the Transformation of Venezuela* (New Brunswick, NJ: Transaction Books, 1982).

13. Worth consulting is David E. Blank, *Venezuela: Politics in a Petroleum Republic* (New York: Praeger, 1984). Also useful is Enrique Baloyra and John D. Martz, *Political Attitudes in Venezuela: Societal Cleavages and Public Opinion* (Austin: University of Texas Press, 1979).

14. Consult John D. Martz and Enrique Baloyra, *Electoral Mobilization and Public Opinion: The Venezuelan Campaign of 1973* (Chapel Hill: University of North Carolina Press, 1976).

15. See Howard R. Penniman, ed., *Venezuela at the Polls: The National Elections of 1978* (Washington, DC: American Enterprise Institute for Public Policy Research, 1980).

16. Useful works about this period include Brian Loveman, *Chile: The Legacy of Hispanic Capitalism*, 3rd ed. (New York: Oxford University Press, 2001); Mark Falcoff, *Modern Chile 1970–1989: A Critical History* (New Brunswick, NJ: Transaction Books, 1991); and Simon Collier and William F. Slater, *A History of Chile, 1808–1994* (Cambridge, UK: Cambridge University Press, 1993).

17. Consult Arturo Valenzuela, *The Breakdown of Democratic Regimes: Chile* (Baltimore: Johns Hopkins University Press, 1978). I was working in the US State Department at this time and was able to ascertain that only four years removed from the ouster of "annoying" Guatemalan president Arbenz and with John Foster Dulles still at the helm of US foreign policy, with brother Allan heading the CIA, and with the Batista regime still entrenched in Cuba, there was no disposition on the part of the administration to "allow" Allende's coming to power in Chile.

18. The Radical Party had come to the end of its run as a political force by 1958. Despite a tendency of many scholars to be anti-Alessandri because they were pro-Allende, in light of subsequent developments evaluations of Alessandri's presidency become less unfavorable.

19. I was in Santiago shortly before the election, when, after a tragic accident involving a close relative of Frei and under the influence of convivial imbibing of excellent Chilean wine, a key member of the Allende campaign admitted that their only chance of winning would be if a Christian Democratic sound truck driven by Frei ran over Allende's mother on the steps of the cathedral—a development which he was certain would not occur.

20. Valenzuela, *Breakdown,* pp. 37–38. Quite useful is Federico G. Gil, Ricardo Lagos E. [Chile's present president], and Henry A. Landsberger, *Chile at the Turning Point: Lessons of the Socialist Years, 1970–1973*, trans. by John S. Gitlitz (Philadelphia: Institute for the Study of Human Issues, 1979).

21. Robert Pinkney, *Democracy in the Third World* (Boulder, CO: Lynne Rienner, 1994), p. 47.

22. See Peter Kornbluh, ed., *The Pinochet File: A Declassified Dossier on Atrocity and Accountability* (New York: New Press, 2003).

23. The Christian Democrats felt, quite justifiably, that the Frei government had been subjected to opportunistically partisan hamstringing by the FRAP, which frequently cooperated with the extreme right to block or eviscerate the Frei government's legislative

proposals. As Huntington points out, the far left often fears that successful reform programs will reduce the prospects of revolution and so cooperates with its mortal enemies to undermine reformers. See Samuel P. Huntington, *Political Order in Changing Societies* (New Haven:Yale University Press, 1968), Chapter Five. Because the left had obstructed the Frei government, some degree of parliamentary payback by the PDC would be both rational and justified.

24. Of interest is former US ambassador Nathaniel Davis, *The Last Two Years of Salvador Allende* (Ithaca, NY: Cornell University Press, 1985). Paul H. Lewis, *Authoritarian Regimes in Latin America: Dictators, Despots, and Tyrants* (Lanham, MD: Rowman & Littlefield, 2006), pp. 196–206, provides a very insightful analysis of the rise and fall of Allende.

25. Consult Paul E. Sigmund, *The Overthrow of Allende and the Politics of Chile, 1964–1976* (Pittsburgh: University of Pittsburgh Press, 1977), and John Dinges, *The Condor Years: How Pinochet and His Allies Brought Terrorism to Three Continents* (New York: New Press, 2003).

26. See Genaro Arriagada, *Pinochet: The Politics of Power*, trans. from Spanish (Boston: Unwin Hyman, 1988), and Mary H. Spooner, *Soldiers in a Narrow Land* (Berkeley and Los Angeles: University of California Press, 1994).

27. Very useful is J. Samuel Valenzuela and Arturo Valenzuela, *Military Rule in Chile: Dictatorship and Opposition* (Baltimore: Johns Hopkins University Press, 1986). See also Marcelo Pollack, *The New Right in Chile, 1973–97* (New York: St. Martin's Press, 1999).

28. Valenzuela, *Breakdown,* p. 163. See also Pamela Constable and Arturo Valenzuela, *Chile Under Pinochet: A Nation of Enemies* (New York: Norton, 1991).

29. Useful reading on Bolivia includes Waltrud Queiser Morales, *Bolivia: Land of Struggle* (Boulder, CO: Westview Press, 1991); Herbert S. Klein, *Bolivia: The Evolution of a Multi-Ethnic Society*, 2nd ed. (New York: Oxford University Press, 1992); and Christopher Mitchell, *The Legacy of Populism in Bolivia: From the MNR to Military Regime* (New York: Praeger, 1977). A friendly assessment of the initial postrevolution administrations is Robert J. Alexander, *The Bolivian National Revolution* (New Brunswick, NJ: Rutgers University Press, 1958).

30. James M. Malloy, *Authoritarianism and Corporatism in Latin America* (Pittsburgh: University of Pittsburgh Press, 1977), p. 475.

31. Useful are James M. Malloy, *Bolivia:The Uncompleted Revolution* (Pittsburgh: University of Pittsburgh Press, 1970), and James M. Malloy and Richard S. Thorn, eds., *Beyond the Revolution: Bolivia Since 1952* (Pittsburgh: University of Pittsburgh Press, 1971).

32. On this president, who would be back in office in the last quarter of the century, consult James S. Malloy and Eduardo Gamarra, *Revolution and Reaction: Bolivia 1964–1985* (New Brunswick, NJ: Transaction Books, 1988), and Merille S. Grindle and Pilar Domingo, eds., *Proclaiming Revolution: Bolivia in Comparative Perspective* (Cambridge: Harvard University Press, 2003). Catherine M. Conaghan and James M. Malloy, *Unsettling Statecraft: Democracy and Neoliberalism in the Central Andes* (Pittsburgh: University of Pittsburgh Press, 1994), is useful on questions of political economy.

33. See Carlos de la Torre, *Velasco Ibarra, Populist Seduction in Latin America: The Ecuadorian Experience* (Athens: Ohio University Center for International Studies, 2000).

34. For background consult David Schodt, *Ecuador: An Andean Enigma* (Boulder, CO: Westview Press, 1987), and John D. Martz, *Ecuador: Conflicting Political Culture and the Quest for Progress* (Boston: Allyn & Bacon, 1972).

35. Consult John Samuel Fitch, *The Military Coup de Etat as a Political Process: Ecuador 1948–1966* (Baltimore: Johns Hopkins University Press, 1977), and John D. Martz, *The Military in Ecuador: Policies and Politics of Authoritarian Rule* (Albuquerque: Latin American Institute of the University of New Mexico, 1988).

36. See John D. Martz, *Politics and Petroleum in Ecuador* (New Brunswick, NJ: Transaction Books, 1987).

37. Consult Allen Gerlach, *Indians, Oil, and Politics: A Recent History of Ecuador* (Wilmington, DE.: Scholarly Resources, 2002).

38. Useful for this period is Martin Weinstein, *Uruguay: Democracy at the Crossroads* (Boulder, CO: Westview Press, 1988).

39. Consult Edy Kaufman, *Uruguay in Transition: From Civilian to Military Rule* (New Brunswick, NJ: Transaction Books, 1979), as well as Charles G. Gillespie, *Negotiating Democracy: Politicians and Generals in Uruguay* (Cambridge, UK: Cambridge University Press, 1991), and Luis E. González, *Political Structures and Democracy in Uruguay* (Notre Dame, IN: University of Notre Dame Press, 1991).

40. For background, consult Riordan Roett and Richard S. Sacks, *Paraguay: The Personalist Legacy* (Boulder, CO: Westview Press, 1990). Lewis, *Authoritarian Regimes,* pp. 173–180, provides a perceptive analysis of the Stroessner regime.

41. See Paul H. Lewis, *Paraguay Under Stroessner* (Chapel Hill: University of North Carolina Press, 1980).

10

Central America
and the Caribbean, 1956–1979

Diversity Accentuated

This period witnessed greater diversity with respect to politics for this subregion than had previously existed. Not only would Cuba go through a revolution that transformed it into a communist system, but the nine states that comprised the subregion at the beginning were joined as the period progressed by a dozen newly independent nations concerned about proving their viability. Under these conditions the logical first focus of inquiry is whether any of the Central American republics established political regimes having significant similarities to those in South America. In this respect the most likely candidate is Guatemala, ethnically very much like the Andean countries, particularly Ecuador and Bolivia, and with economic and social characteristics not far different. Moreover, like Bolivia it had recently experienced revolutionary change (which, in contrast, had been ended abruptly by a 1954 counterrevolutionary coup).

Overview

Most of the Central American countries would exit the period not very far down the political development road from where they had entered it—but the trip would be turbulent for all except Costa Rica. For these six mainland countries between Mexico and Colombia the latter half of the 1950s through the 1970s saw pressures build up that would explode violently in Nicaragua and El Salvador at the very end of the period. On the other hand, Guatemala, having already experienced its revolutionary decade and the ensuing reaction, was to suffer under authoritarian military rule in the context of escalating violence and insurgency. Panama would undergo substantial transformation at the hands of a personalistic military reformer, whereas Honduras entered and exited the quarter century essentially unchanged. Indeed, the military regimes in Guatemala and Honduras bore marked resemblances to those of Bolivia and Ecuador, whereas Panama, having experienced significant positive changes under a reformist type of military figure, had greater similarity to Peru. Costa Rica continued to fine-tune and institutionalize its democratic processes, coming in the second half of the period to be Latin America's one and only full democracy, as even Chile and Uruguay succumbed to the dominant trend toward militarized authoritarianism.[1]

In the Caribbean the Trujillo Era would finally end in the Dominican Republic after the dictator's assassination in 1961, but most of the rest of the period had his chief disciple as its dominating figure. Haiti in 1957 saw the beginning of the terroristic Duvalier regime, a sultanic dictatorship that passed from father to son in 1971. By far the most dramatic development in all of Latin America was Castro's rise to power in Cuba in 1959 and his installation of a full-fledged communist system there. This event with major Cold War ramifications greatly overshadowed the emergence of a series of small nations as decolonization belated reached Jamaica, Trinidad, and a bevy of even smaller islands.

Central America: Frustration and Travail

Authoritarian rule was the norm for the Central American countries, but its pattern varied, leading them to diverging exits from the period. Only Costa Rica could feel smugly superior throughout.

Guatemala: Militarism Institutionalized

The 1954 ouster of the leftist government of Jacobo Arbenz in many ways took the country back toward the pre-1944 era. US-backed president Carlos Castillo Armas was assassinated in July 1957, an action adroitly engineered by the intelligence chief of Dominican Republic dictator Rafael Trujillo so as to seem the work of communists. This unanticipated event opened the door for election in January 1958 of aged General Miguel Ydígoras Fuentes, a one-time functionary of the 1930s–mid-1940s Ubico dictatorship.[2] By the time this rather colorful throwback conservative figure was ousted by his ambitious defense minister, Colonel Enrique Peralta Azurdia, in March 1963, a guerrilla rebellion was under way, one that would last until 1996, and a pattern of brutal repression by the armed forces and right-wing "death squads" was established. The 1966 election brought a reformist civilian to government, backed by the Revolutionary Party (PR), but only after the original candidate, his brother, had been murdered.

Well-intentioned, but prudent to a fault, ex-law-school-dean Julio César Mendes Montenegro (b. 1915) was powerless to stem the descent into a virtual civil war—having had to promise the military a free hand in counterinsurgency matters before being allowed to take office. He was hampered by being a minority president (elected with 201,000 votes to 146,000 for the government candidate and 110,000 for a dissident military aspirant). Méndez Montenegro was succeeded in 1970 through rigged elections by the officer who during his presidency had led the repressive campaign to stamp out the insurgents. Ruthless Colonel Carlos Arana Osório would reestablish the long line of military presidents, being followed in office by Colonel Kjell Eugenio Laugerud García in 1974, in a highly fraudulent election in which dissident military figure Efrian Rios Montt had the greatest popular support, and Colonel Romeo Lucas García in 1978. The presidency truly became the highest rung on the army promotion ladder, most elections featuring dissident officers running as underdogs against the outgoing president's favored successor. At the same time, the military's role expansion reached a point at which it controlled nearly fifty state institutions, including a bank exclusively devoted to making loans to officers who wished to invest in businesses or real estate. Repression under Lucas García returned to the levels of brutality reached by Arana Osório. By the late 1970s, the situation could be described as "a genuine crisis of state":

> Economically, Guatemala was in a serious tailspin, with sources of investment capital drying up, tourism declining because of the violence, and the value of export commodities declining. Politically, there was open warfare between the insurgents of the United National Guatemalan Revolution (UNRG) and the Guatemalan armed forces. Assassination, torture, kidnapping, and disappearances of social activists were routine, and Guatemala had become a pariah nation because of its atrocious human rights situation.[3]

El Salvador: Sliding into Civil War

The coup that overthrew the lackluster government of Lieutenant Colonel José María Lemos in October 1960 involved a number of collaborators of his predecessor and erstwhile mentor, 1948–1955 strongman Oscar Osório. The leftward tilt of the ensuing junta limited its tenure to a brief three months, as more conservative officers then seized power behind Colonel Julio Adalberto Rivera, who in April ran unopposed for the presidency. The material progress of Rivera's administration was closely tied to Central American economic integration and enabled him to pass power on to General Fidel Sánchez Hernández through elections in 1967.

Conditions took an adverse turn under Sánchez Hernández, the most dramatic event being the 1969 war with Honduras. Far from being a comic-opera clash over rival hopes to qualify for the 1970 soccer World Cup, this conflict high-lighted the unregulated spillover of overcrowded little El Salvador's excess popula-tion into the wide-open spaces of western Honduras. El Salvador could not face the prospect of absorbing 300,000 potential expellees from Honduras, so invaded it. Although the fighting ceased in five days, the incident spelled an end to the functioning of the Central American Common Market, which had benefited El Salvador much more than it had even less industrialized Honduras. Moreover, as many as 130,000 Salvadorans were at least temporarily driven out of Honduras.[4]

February 1972 elections saw the opposition unite to pose a formidable chal-lenge to the military-dominated National Conciliation Party (PCN). Behind for-mer San Salvador mayor José Napoleón Duarte of the Christian Democratic Party (PDC), the civilian forces finished in a dead heat with Colonel Arturo Armando Molina, who was confirmed as president by the national assembly. As his term progressed, defense minister Colonel Carlos Humberto Romero emerged as heir apparent, winning a far-from-free election in February 1977 that was met with substantial popular protests. Romero issued a Law for the Defense and Guarantee of Public Order that banned public assemblies and granted arbitrary authority to security forces.

Over the next two years, polarization marked the political scene, culminating in Romero's ouster by a junior officers' coup in mid-October 1979. This coup would be the prelude to the bloodiest and most traumatic period in El Salvador's history—perhaps the worst in the overall collective Central American experience. Revolutionary forces would find support in the countryside, where since 1961 the percentage of landless rural families had risen from 12 percent to over 40 percent.[5] As the reform option gradually disappeared and the situation of the poor deterio-rated, support for drastic and violent change grew, so when the revolutionary road succeeded next door in Nicaragua, El Salvador was ripe to follow.

Honduras: Military Supremacy

Within a year after the military seized Honduran power in 1956, ambitious Lieutenant Colonel Oswaldo López Arellano (b. 1921) overthrew the de facto president and held congressional elections in which the Liberal Party scored a sweeping victory. The national legislature soon named Ramón Villela Morales (b. 1908) to the presidency, ushering in a brief interlude of reforms and mod-ernization as well as development for this country's roughly two million inhabi-tants. But this democratic dawn was ended by a coup—only ten days before the scheduled October 1963 elections—led by the defense minister, since the Lib-eral candidate had forgotten that discretion is the better part of valor and had pledged to reduce the power of the military. With the exception of twenty months of an elected civilian government in 1971–1972, military strongmen would rule the country through 1981.

López Arellano, who had paved the way for return to civilian rule in 1957, had also ended it six years later. Working with the conservative Honduran National Party (PNH), he managed to become constitutional president in the first part of 1965, holding on until early 1971. His tenure was marred not only by his high-handed rule and tolerance of corruption, but also by the July 1969 war with El Salvador, followed by a devastating hurricane. Giving way to an elected civilian from the PNH, he waited less than two years before regaining the presidency by force in December 1972. Influenced to some degree by the Peruvian example, this time López followed a populist and developmentalist approach, but he was forced out in April 1975 as a consequence of having accepted a sizable bribe for favorable tax treatment of US tropical fruit giant United Brands. Over the next three years effective power rested with the Superior Council of the Armed Forces rather than with Colonel Juan Alberto Melgar Castro, the formal chief of state. He was pushed aside in mid-1978, and Armed Forces Chief General Policarpo Paz García took control, first as junta head, then as provisional president.[6]

Nicaragua: The Somoza Dynasty Continued

This period coincided with the rule over Nicaragua by the sons and heirs of perennial president Anastasio "Tacho" Somoza. Assassinated by an El Salvadoran political exile in 1956, Somoza left a family enterprise with its tentacles in all profitable sectors of the economy, ready, more than willing, and able to inherit power and exercise it for another twenty-three years. Luis Somoza Debayle (b. 1922), the US-educated businessman of the family, finished out the remainder of his father's term before being reelected in 1957. Under pressure from the Kennedy administration in the United States, he diplomatically stepped aside for a loyal family retainer in 1963, resuming power when the need for this window dressing no longer existed. Luis Somoza's softer form of authoritarian rule ended with a fatal heart attack in early 1967. His death allowed Anastasio Somoza Debayle (b. 1925) to take over and then be legitimized by a rigged June 1971 election in which he was credited with 71 percent of the vote. This West Point–trained namesake (down to the nickname of Tachito, or "Little Tacho") returned to old-fashioned dictatorial techniques and resumed his father's policies of maximum enrichment for the family and its loyal collaborators. He engaged in a charade of leaving office in 1972 so that under a new constitution he could be duly elected for a 1974–1981 term.

The beginning of this bon vivant autocrat's downfall came with his shameless diversion into his own pockets of international relief funds for the victims of the Christmas 1972 earthquake that devastated Managua. This scandal infused new life into the Sandinista Front for National Liberation (FSLN), whose audacious feats led to escalating, although ineffective, repression. Somoza's blatant human rights violations coincided with the coming to office in the United States of the humanistic administration of Jimmy Carter, causing a loss of the US support the dynasty had enjoyed for over four decades.[7]

A second presidential heart attack in mid-1977 caused many centrist elements to consider alternatives for the country's future. One of their leading figures, highly respected newspaper publisher Pedro Joaquín Chamorro Cardenal, was cowardly murdered in January 1978. This foul deed galvanized opposition to the corrupt and repressive dictatorship. A daring FSLN takeover of the presidential palace in August catalyzed the activities of a Broad Opposition Front (FAO), and a determined Sandinista guerrilla offensive in June 1979 led to Somoza's departure in mid-July. The old order was over, but the effort to build a new, egalitarian Nicaragua would prove exceedingly difficult and divisive.

Costa Rica: Stable Democracy (Rhode Island Scale)

This small republic shone as a lonely beacon of democracy in the 1956–1979 period, not only for Central America, but for the entire region. Narrowly defeated in 1958, the National Liberation Party (PLN) duly turned Costa Rica's presidency over to Mário Echandia Jiménez (b. 1915), a member of ex-president Otilio Ulate's National Unity Party (PUN), surging back into power again in 1962 led by Francisco José Orlich (b. 1907), a wealthy coffee grower whose fairly conservative administration was plagued by the eruption of Irazu volcano, which buried much of San José under the weight of ash that its flat tropical roofs were not designed to resist. Then the dominant party lost a tight race in 1966 to the PUN's José Joaquín Trejos Fernández. Four years later PLN founder José "Pépe" Figueres led the PLN to victory and a return to power—defeating former chief executive Echandia. This small-scale analogue of Venezuela's Democratic Action Party (led by a pint-sized near clone of Rómulo Betancourt) also triumphed in the 1974 balloting behind Daniel Oduber Quirós (b. 1921) before sustaining defeat in 1978 at the hands of Rodrigo Carazo Odio (b. 1926). In that year 860,000 voted, compared to only 137,000 in 1944, as the country's population had trebled to 2.1 million. Clearly Costa Rica had come a very long way from the 1890–1920 period, during which 22 percent of the presidencies had ended with resignation and 11 percent with coups, and an even longer way from the 1824–1889 epoch, in which civilian presidents averaged a mere 1.5 years in office, but uniformed ones averaged a robust 5.8 years.[8] Unfortunately, this consolidated, stable democracy could be only contrasted, not compared, with the other countries of Latin America (once Uruguay succumbed to military rule). In explaining Costa Rica's exceptionalism, Seligson underscores not only its relatively high levels of economic and social development and "longest and deepest tradition of democracy," but also its abolition of its armed forces almost a generation before.[9]

Panama: Only Nominally Sovereign

Historically an appendage of South America through its connection to Colombia, this small country is politically Central American in some ways and Caribbean in others. This latter characteristic dates back to the 1880s, when French concession-aires brought large numbers of blacks from the British Caribbean islands to Panama to dig the canal. The association with Central America was reinforced when at the beginning of the twentieth century the United States helped split Panama off from Colombia as part of a plan to take over the canal project. Not surprisingly, Panama has a troubled story beginning with its "protected" separation from Colombia in 1903, sponsored by a hyperactive, mission-driven, impatient Theodore Roosevelt.[10] A US railroad had opened in 1855, so Washington viewed Colombia's approval of a French canal venture in the 1890s as an infringement of the presumed "natural" rights of the United States. When Colombia's senate let the French concession expire before ratifying a new arrangement with the United States through the pending Hay-Herrán Treaty, Roosevelt decided to act.

Ignoring inconvenient congressional findings in favor of a canal in Nicaragua, Roosevelt approved of agents of the French Panama Canal Company backing a rebellion. The province of Panama had revolted on several earlier occasions, with Colombia quickly reestablishing control. The crucial difference was that this time the US navy, via the cruiser *Nashville,* prevented Colombia from doing so. Within two weeks of the November 3, 1903, rebellion, the Roosevelt administration, which had rushed to recognize the breakaway nation, signed a treaty with the new government transferring all canal rights to the United States on terms more ad-vantageous than those in the dead-letter treaty with Colombia and, on the reverse side of the coin, much more onerous for dependent, essentially protectorate-status Panama.[11]

The treaty, signed in the dead of night by French Panama Canal Company of-ficial Philippe Buena Varilla, while the new government's fully accredited repre-sentatives were en route from New York, gave the United States, in perpetuity, exclusive rights "as if it were sovereign" over a canal zone 10 miles wide running from the Atlantic to the Pacific coasts of Panama (hence cutting the country in two). The United States also retained the right to intervene in the internal affairs of the new republic for any reason related to the security and safety of the canal and its encompassing zone—governed by an official of the US War Department and garrisoned by US troops. These treaty rights, much like those the United States enjoyed in Cuba through the Platt Amendment, were exercised on five oc-casions between the opening of the canal in 1914 and 1932. But when Panama's president Domingo Obaldia died, the United States threatened annexation to prevent mixed-blood acting president Carlos A. Mendoza from completing his term. Liberal Belisario Porras (b. 1856) headed the nominally independent government in 1912–1916 and in 1918–1924, after Ramón Valdes died in office. Porras's successor, Rodolfo E. Chiari (b. 1882), a wealthy sugar planter, typified the white economic elite entrenched in power in this de facto protectorate, who were in harmony with US officials. Blocking Porras's designs to return to office, in 1928 Chiari installed Florencio H. Arosemena as his successor.

Against the backdrop of the world economic crisis, in 1931 a revolutionary group headed by upwardly mobile lower-middle-class *mestizo* Arnulfo Arias Madrid (b. 1901) seized power. The next year Arias's older brother, Harmodio (b. 1886), was elected president by a margin of 39,000 votes to 29,000. After a violent and fraud-tainted campaign, Juan Demostenes Arosemena was elected in 1936 and continued Arias's nationalist-populist policies, with Arnulfo himself winning election in 1940 (the same year that in Cuba Fulgéncio Batista would step out from behind the scenes and assume the Cuban presidency). A populist demagogue and admirer of the Axis powers, Arias was deposed the following year in a police operation partially masterminded by the United States. During the war years, with Ricardo Adolfo de la Guardia (b. 1899) as president, Panama prospered as a result of expansion of US bases and increased local procurement of foodstuffs. Extension to women of the right to vote in 1945 was in part a sign of US influence.

The closing of most of the US bases on Panamanian territory, not those located in the Canal Zone, in 1948 aggravated Panama's postwar economic ills, including unemployment, inflation, and debt, which were intensified by rapid growth of urban areas, especially Panama City. This situation facilitated the election of Arnulfo Arias once more in 1948, but his apparent victory was nullified by National Police commander José "Chichi" Remón Cantera (b. 1908), originally placed in his job by Harmodio Arias. After first installing Domingo Díaz Arosemena in office, Remón later allowed Arnulfo Arias to function as president from 1949 to 1951, only to remove him again on the pretext of abuse of power when Arias replaced the 1946 constitution with his short-lived 1941 constitution. The next year Remón had himself elected president. After negotiating modest improvements in canal arrangements through the Eisenhower-Remón Treaty of 1955, he was gunned down in a murder never fully clarified, although Panama's role in drug transshipment was involved in one way or another.[12]

Presidents Ernesto de la Guardia (b. 1904) in 1956–1960 and Roberto Francisco Chiari Ramírez in 1960–1964 were of the moneyed elite that had prospered by doing business with the Canal Zone Company, as was Marco Aurélio Robles (b. 1905), who edged out perennial candidate Arnulfo Arias in 1964. By this time national sentiment over the canal had heated up, in part inspired by Egyptian president Gamal Abdel Nasser's successful seizure of the Suez Canal in 1956. Violent student demonstrations in January 1964 showed that the limited improvements in job access brought about by revisions in the 1955 treaty had served only to increase frustration over the privileged position of "Zonians," the US citizen employees of the Canal Zone Company. Further revisions in 1967 were essentially trivial, as they reaffirmed the virtual ownership of the canal and the zone by the United States. So in May 1968 Arias again won the presidential election, but he was ousted by ambitious upstart National Guard commander Bolívar Valladares within twelve days.

Quickly pushing the rough-hewn bullyboy Valladares aside by establishing dominance over the provisional junta, able and pragmatic nationalist General Omar Torrijos (b. 1929) installed a populist, antielite regime. Dissolving the national assembly and outlawing all political parties and activities, he installed a single-party regime under the banner of his Democratic Revolutionary Party (PRD). Through carefully managed balloting in 1972, Torrijos had a National Assembly of Community Representatives elected, and it dutifully conferred upon him extraordinary powers as Chief of Government for a period of six years. He used these powers to further the work of his "dictatorship with a heart" by decreeing the first substantial land, education, health care, and labor reforms in Panama's history, along with public housing programs.[13]

Torrijos obtained a vastly improved treaty from the United States in 1977 through skillful negotiations with the Carter administration. Astutely, after negotiations had stalled with the Nixon and Ford administrations, Torrijos assumed a more democratic pose, legalizing parties and promising legislative elections in 1978. The treaty provided for continued operation and defense of the canal by the United States until the end of 1999, meanwhile granting Panama a share of the tolls. Having "forced" the United States to agree to return the canal to Panama, Torrijos enjoyed a marked increase in his already-substantial popularity. Starting the next year, and until his death in a poorly explained plane crash in 1981, this extremely intelligent politician governed through a puppet civilian president, Aristides Royo, elected by an assembly dominated by Torrijos loyalists. After that, Panamanian political development went into reverse gear, decaying to the near absurdity portrayed in John le Carré's novel *The Tailor of Panama*.

Comparative Perspective on Central America

Having had a revolution in 1944 that ushered in a decade of reform and modernization, Guatemala shared some steps, and missteps, with Bolivia on its path toward political development. In a rough sense Arévalo can be conceived of as playing a role similar to that of fellow educator Paz Estenssoro. The chief differences resided in the eight-year gap between their revolutions, the heavy US economic involvement in

Guatemala—almost complete absence in Bolivia—and Guatemala's strategic position compared to Bolivia's remoteness from any Cold War considerations. These considerations would impact on the transitions to democracy of these two countries. When the reform government of Villela Morales in Honduras is seen as a very partial and aborted parallel to the MNR revolution in Bolivia, the analogy between Honduras and Bolivia is more limited.

El Salvador's decline into protracted civil war is unparalleled elsewhere, either in Central America and the Caribbean or in the broader region. The overthrow of the Somoza dictatorship in Nicaragua at the end of this period led to a revolutionary regime far to the left of the one that had been ushered in in Guatemala in 1944, but well short of Cuba's 1959 watershed. Moreover, the United States would become actively involved in undermining the Sandinista government and reversing the country's political course. On a positive note, Costa Rica followed a sui generis path of further consolidating its democratic institutions and processes, and Panama was unique in peacefully moving forward with essentially positive political development, including a significant reduction of its dependence on the United States (which would soon be sidetracked).

The remaining task of this chapter is to examine whether there is any pattern in the political development of the Caribbean, and if so, whether there are parallels to either Central America or South America. Clearly, politics in the Caribbean, as well as in Central America, bore no significant similarity to politics in their many-times-larger neighbor, Mexico—more different from them than even from Brazil.

The Caribbean: Castro, Duvalier, and Trujillo

Dramatic events in Cuba would be the center of attention in the Caribbean during this quarter century, overshadowing even the bloody dictatorship of the Duvaliers in Haiti and the end of the Trujillo era in the Dominican Republic. Little noticed, a dozen European colonies, the vast majority of them British, would attain independence and try to find a viable niche in a region where, besides being tardy newcomers, they were in no way, shape, or form "Latin."[14]

Cuba: Revolution and Its Institutionalization

This quarter century would witness Cuba's sharp left turn down a path radically different from that of any other country in the region. The end of an extraordinarily corrupt and oppressive regime came early through a full-scale revolution, followed by the emergence of a communist political system standing in spectacular isolation at the same time as its architect, Fidel Castro Ruz (b. 1926), emerged as the first Latin American to be widely viewed as a global leader. As the 1970s came to their close, Castro was still in full flight, institutionalizing a sophisticated political system that was firmly under his control.[15] En route he defied the United States and even manipulated the Soviet Union.

Castro and a handful of other survivors of the 1953 Cuban uprising, accompanied by a few new allies, suddenly returned in late 1956 from their exile in Mexico, plunging Cuba into armed conflict. Avowing a desire to implement the 1940 democratic constitution, Castro enjoyed support of regional reformist democrats, including Venezuela's Betancourt and Costa Rica's Figueres. These notables, in turn, influenced liberal Democrats in the United States to press successfully for an end to US support for Batista. This abrupt policy change demoralized Batista supporters, who had long counted upon Washington's favor, and the tide of battle had shifted to Castro and his allies by December 1958.

On the eve of Castro's January 1, 1959, rise to power, he was far from being a communist but had begun to lean toward the more radical members of the 26th of July Movement (named after the date of the 1953 attack on the Moncada barracks), especially those influenced by young Argentine expatriate Ernesto "Che" Guevara. Acting with extraordinary political acumen and ability grounded in an astute reading of what was feasible within the international environment in terms of minimizing constraints and maximizing opportunities, Castro would, within a remarkable short time, break the hold over Cuba exercised since 1898 by the United States. In the process this thirtyish former follower of the ill-fated Eddy Chibas bested not only Washington, but also the deeply rooted tentacles of international organized crime, inflicting a dramatic defeat upon the world's most dominant power by easily repelling the US-organized invasion by exiles at the Bay of Pigs in April 1961. In so doing he elevated the Cuban Revolution to a major issue on the global scene and made himself a highly controversial, but indisputably key, world leader. One of history's great survivors, he has outlasted nine US presidents in office and may very well run his string to ten. Indeed, he came to power only three months after the late Charles de Gaulle had done so in France and at a time when current British prime minister Tony Blair was still in short pants learning which end of a cricket bat to grasp.[16]

Castro's critical choice was deciding early that breaking the chains of dependence on the United States would require finding another international patron and getting under its nuclear umbrella. In this judgment he was unquestionably correct, for Washington, still essentially oriented by the Cold War ideas of John Foster Dulles, was little disposed to abide significant independence in its backyard, much less in combination with radical structural reforms adversely impacting on US ownership and investment. The Guatemalan experience was still very fresh in Castro's mind, having occurred at the same time as his 1947 decision to follow Eddy Chibas out of the Grau San Martín camp, his determination to attempt the armed overthrow of Batista in 1953, and his option for guerrilla tactics in 1956.

FIDEL CASTRO
(CREDIT: RICARDO
STUCKERT/ABR.)

Not only had his brother Raúl been in close touch with Guatemalan exiles in Mexico as they completed their self-criticism of the Arbenz regime, but Fidel personally kibitzed this self-criticism through his increasingly intense contact with Che Guevara, who had been a participant observer in Guatemala in 1953–1954. The clear lesson Castro drew was that the United States was not yet ready to tolerate a highly nationalistic and autonomous government between it and the Panama Canal, even if it might temporize with a moderately revolutionary regime with Peronist ties in remote and economically marginal Bolivia. And Castro was determined not to let his revolution end up a victim of US intransigence, as had that of an earlier Cuban generation in 1933.[17]

Suddenly finding himself in power, Fidel shrewdly moved to make himself acceptable to Moscow as leader of a communist Cuba that had to be defended rather than as leader of a neutral Cuba that would serve as an expendable pawn in the global game of Cold War geopolitical chess. At the time seemingly unlikely, this accomplishment required both a purge of anticommunist elements in the Twenty-sixth of July Movement and marginalization of the traditional leadership of the Popular Socialist Party (PSP) along the road to Soviet sponsorship already made difficult by both the US crushing of Guatemala's revolution and Soviet aversion to national variants of communism, such as that of Tito in Yugoslavia—not to speak of Maoism—both of which were causing Moscow ulcers and sleepless nights.

Within the ranks of his close collaborators, Fidel had to sacrifice column commander Camilo Cienfuegos, who conveniently disappeared on a solo plane flight.

Agrarian reform was decreed in May 1959, and Cuban-owned businesses and real estate were socialized in October 1960, by which time large-scale nationalization of US firms was under way. Meanwhile, in July, Castro, himself prime minister, had maneuvered moderate president Manuel Urrutia out of office. A spider web of Committees for Defense of the Revolution extended controls and mobilization to the masses at the local level. The PSP, Cuba's traditional communist party, which had overwhelmingly viewed Castro as a dangerously provocative figure—categorized as a left deviationist—during the early stages of the struggle against Batista, now sought a role within Castro's regime. For his part, Castro trusted those few communists who, like Carlos Rafael Rodríguez (b. 1913), had joined him well before the overthrow of Batista.

The May 1960 restoration of full diplomatic relations between Cuba and the USSR was followed in July by US cancellation of Cuba's quota in the lucrative US sugar market. Arming a force of Cuban exiles in the United States had begun in March 1960, a CIA covert operation of which Castro was soon aware. Diplomatic ties were severed by the lame-duck Eisenhower administration in January 1961, leaving the disastrously flawed Bay of Pigs invasion to the incoming Kennedy government. With this failed April 1961 invasion and the lack of any significant Cuban opposition uprising, Castro's movement toward the Soviet Union accelerated. This approximation was reflected in Castro's May 1 declaration underscoring the coincidence of his views with communism and his December profession to be a communist. Knowing that this laying of his cards on the table would almost certainly trigger strong countermeasures from Washington, already busy at work seeking to exclude Cuba from the Inter-American System (the web of hemispheric organizations centering on the Organization of American States [OAS]), Castro strove posthaste to get under the USSR's nuclear umbrella by welcoming the secret stationing of Soviet missiles aimed at the United States.[18]

Construction of Castro's version of communism took place gradually and in stages roughly comparable to those involved in building the institutionalized single party in Mexico between 1928 and 1946. In mid-1961 a body called the Integrated Revolutionary Organizations (ORI) was created, with the PSP's Aníbal Escalante entrusted with its construction. Predictably, and almost certainly as foreseen by Castro, its hierarchy became dominated by "old communists," who subsequently sought to expand their role and influence with the administration. In March 1962, confident in the close links to the USSR provided by the stationing of its missiles, Fidel suddenly attacked the "sectarianism and privilege" shown by these orthodox PSP types. A new national directorate was installed, with Fidel as first secretary, trusted brother Raúl as second secretary, and Che Guevara, Oswaldo Dorticós, Emílio Aragones, and Blas Roca as members. Blas Roca was sidelined as editor of *Hoy,* the regime's paper, and Dorticós took over heading the Organizational Commission. (Dorticós would lose his position as Cuba's figurehead president in 1976, when a switch from a parliamentary to a presidential system gave that job to Fidel; Dorticós eventually committed suicide in 1983.) Escalante was unceremoniously bundled off to Czechoslovakia. Since this reorientation emphasized the crucial factor of Fidel's leadership, in retrospect the whole ORI experience looks like a tactical concession made by Fidel within the parameters of his strategy for convincing Moscow that Cuba was moving toward a more orthodox communism, under which Soviet influence would be strengthened.

Fidel acted quite rapidly in the aftermath of the October 1962 missile crisis to establish the United Party of the Socialist Revolution (PURS), which was ready to function on policy matters by mid-1963. At this point, facing charges of having informed the Batista regime on 26th of July Movement militants, Marcos Rodríguez implicated Joaquín Odorqui, vice minister of the Revolutionary Armed Forces and a leading PSPer, along with his wife, Edith García Buchacha. Again Castro dictated a personally advantageous and politically beneficial solution to the messy affair, protecting other PSPers from heavy negative reaction, yet teaching them a pointed lesson through Marcos Rodríguez's execution. Dissolving one's sectarian identity in the larger party seemed a sensible—indeed, for those with pre-1959 skeletons in their closets, prudent—course of action.

Finally, in October 1965, the new-model Cuban Communist Party (PCC) was unveiled with a select initial membership of only about 50,000, which would rise to 100,000 by 1970 and expand to 200,000 by late 1975. Following the 1970 failure to produce a record 10-million-ton sugar harvest, and reaching only 8.5 million tons at the cost of dislocating hundreds of thousands of workers from their regular tasks, Castro reversed his policy of economic diversification through industrialization, and *institutionalization* and *democratization* became catchwords. At the PCC's long-delayed First Congress in 1975, a new Central Committee was installed—all of its 112 members were loyal, dedicated followers of the Maximum Leader (Castro). The next year the governmental reorganization instituted a 481-member National Assembly, which elected a 31-member Council of State. Fidel, president of the Council of State and chairman of the Council of Ministers, commander in chief, and PCC first secretary, was now enshrined as a major figure of international communism. Raúl Castro was next in line as PCC second secretary, first vice president of the Council of State, and vice chairman of the Council of Ministers, as well as minister of the Revolutionary Armed Forces.[19] Fidelismo was now a fully institutionalized Marxist-Leninist system (although with a distinctive Latin flavor), a transformation facilitated by the massive emigration of the old upper and middle classes.

Dominican Republic: After Trujillo, His Lingering Legacy

The larger, eastern end of the island of Hispaniola found in this period that the end of the Trujillo era did not free them from the legacy of Trujilloism—at least not as long as his wily protégé Dr. Joaquín Balaguer y Ricardo (b. 1907) was still around, as he was into the late 1990s. Dominicans would learn the hard way that political changes did not necessarily add up to political development.

This period opened with Trujillo having completed a quarter century in power. Successfully engineering Guatemalan president Castillo Armas's assassination in 1957, he turned to a plan to put Pérez Jiménez back into power in Venezuela through Betancourt's assassination. Fortunately the plot was unsuccessful. Trujillo continued to believe that it had been a cruel trick for God to place a man of his enormous talents in such a small country. Indeed, he indulged in speculation over how much more he would have accomplished in Argentina than Perón. In an irony of fate, this rabid anticommunist outlived his usefulness and became an expendable pawn in the Cold War chess game. First, to gain the requisite Latin American support to apply economic sanctions to Cuba in mid-1959, the United States had to take the same action against Washington's longtime ally. Trujillo attempted to appease OAS members through the cosmetic act of replacing his brother Hector with his right-hand man, Dr. Joaquín Balaguer, a ploy used by the Somozas in Nicaragua about the same time. Still intending to find some way to eliminate Castro after the failure of the Bay of Pigs invasion, at the end of May, Washington appeased Latin American governments by making Trujillo the target of a US-backed assassination carried out by former Trujillo collaborators whom he had humiliated. The aim was to convince Latin American governments that the United States was against all repressive Caribbean dictators who meddled in their neighbors' affairs and was not just out to get Fidel.[20]

Trujillo had built a party to give structure and the semblance of popular support to his regime. This party proved very important in the years after his removal, since it would provide a strong foundation for Balaguer's construction of his own follow-on party. US policy was to be certain that Trujillo's sons or their uncles would not come to power. So Balaguer was soon forced to share power with a seven-member Council of State and was subsequently convinced to resign. Having presided over a liberalization bordering on a partial democratization, and having redistributed many of the Trujillo family holdings, Balaguer was well positioned for a comeback if the anti-Trujillo forces faltered—which they soon did.

The December 1962 elections gave a substantial victory to Juan Bosch, founder of the progressive Dominican Revolutionary Party (PRD). This long-term political exile found that his country of birth was far different from his adopted Costa Rica, and he tried to accomplish in months what it had taken Costa Rica many decades to build. Within seven months of taking office, Bosch fell victim to a coup led by Colonel Elias Wessín y Wessín that installed a three-man junta headed by businessman Donald Reid Cabral (who would later serve as nominal head of Balaguer's party). April 24, 1965, saw the PRD rise up in Santo Domingo to put Bosch back in office. Four days later US troops moved in to prevent a "Constitutionalist" victory. (Asserting that Bosch was still the legal president, his backers assumed the position of defenders of the constitution—which, in a strict sense, they were.) US president Lyndon B. Johnson was determined to prevent a second left-wing government from coming to power in Latin America, especially one located so close to Cuba. Frustrated by having to keep his hands off Castro—a key part of the settlement with the Soviet Union over the October 1962 Cuban missile crisis—Johnson decided to make an example of the Dominican Republic. His instrument was masked as an inter-American peace force to keep the warring parties apart, but the operation was US-directed and designed to thwart a constitutionalist victory.[21]

By September the fighting was over, and a respectable member of the elite, Hector Garcia Godoy, had been installed as provisional president. In elections held the next June, Balaguer defeated Bosch by 57 percent to 29 percent for a full constitutional term as president. Far from a demagogue, this unostentatious middle-aged bachelor was a wily politician with a paternalistic, manipulative style and a healthy respect for the power of patronage. Wiarda, a very close student of the Dominican Republic, calls him a "master of manipulative, Machiavellian Politics" and "one of the shrewdest politicians of all time in any country."[22] In a country tired of unrest, he easily won reelections in 1970 and 1974, aided by good prices for sugar that allowed economic growth of 10.6 percent a year from 1968 through 1974. He succeeded particularly well in gaining the support of women—whom he frequently appointed to administrative positions and occasionally steered through the election process into legislative positions.[23] But all winning streaks must come to an end, and Balaguer lost the 1978 election to the PRD's millionaire rancher Antonio Guzmán by a count of about 832,000 to 669,000. So the period ended with a civilian anti-Balaguer (and the Trujilloist legacy) figure in the presidency.

Haiti: The Duvalier Era

Haiti would descend into a terroristic personalist dictatorship early in the period and still be under the Duvalier dynasty when it ended. Indeed, it can justifiably be considered the most horrendous regime in Latin America's experience, certainly so if duration is taken into account. In this respect 1957 was extremely turbulent and opened the door for a generation of almost sultanic dictatorial rule. Initially five governments in six months left General Antonio Kebreu heading a junta presiding over polarized and fractionalized elections. On the right was Francophile industrialist senator Louis Dejoie, and on the left a populist leader of the urban masses, Daniel Fignolé—who boasted on his résumé of nineteen days as provisional president during the earlier turmoil. The two middle-of-the-road candidates were Magloire's finance minister and a respected middle-class black physician with a favorable reputation from his days as Estimé's health minister. The latter was viewed as the most "respectable" of the candidates, an apparent nationalist with mild reformist inclinations. Thus, François Duvalier (b. 1907), a soft-spoken advocate for the supremacy of Haiti's black heritage, was the proclaimed victor in the bitterly contested and highly controversial September 1957 elections (an outcome with enormous unforeseen impact upon the country's future).

Confounding expectations, by the time of his death in 1971 "Papa Doc" Duvalier would justifiably be viewed as a bloody dictator on the level of Uganda's reviled Idi Amin, worse by far even than the Dominican Republic's harsh, autocratic Trujillo. Unfortunately, Duvalier, himself a product of Haiti's unique and in important ways un-Latin American political culture, was a master at exploiting that culture. As caught by Fauriol, "More African and Creole than French, more illiterate than not, and historically more isolated than any other country in the Caribbean, Haitian culture has to a degree generated an enduring demoralizing attitude regarding the nation's potential."[24]

The ensuing decades provide Latin America's most dramatic illustration that not only stagnation but reversal of political development can take place. The erstwhile mild-mannered, humanistic country doctor quickly installed a regime of calculated terror so deeply rooted that his very ordinary son could take over as a teenager and carry on for a period exceeding his own despotic father's rule—easily surpassing in this respect the feat of the Somozas in Nicaragua. Moreover, the elder Duvalier, a determined despot, was able to practice his terroristic rule in defiance not only of international public opinion, but even of the Western Hemisphere's paramount power. Indeed, the limits of US hegemony are as vividly portrayed by the Haitian case as by that of Castro's Cuba, as Papa Doc (without a foreign ally, much less a sponsor) defied the West that had scorned and marginalized his country.

Dividing and weakening the armed forces; building up a loyal cross between a political police and a paramilitary arm in the form of the infamous and chillingly effective Tonton Macoutes (formally legitimized as "National Security Volunteers"); and driving the great majority of the country's professional stratum into exile as part of his campaign to undercut the mulatto elite, Duvalier succeeded at what had eluded Christophe, Dessalines, and Soulouque—absolute political power for life, not just until ouster or assassination. When threatened "unofficially" by the US government with a fate similar to that arranged for Trujillo (in whose demise in mid-1961 the CIA was deeply involved), Duvalier defied Washington and went ahead with a rigged reelection. In 1962, he skillfully exploited the US need for Haiti's vote against Castro's Cuba at the Punta del Este conference of the Organization of American States, obtaining as his reward a resumption of economic aid. He repeated this performance in 1965 with respect to OAS approval of the US intervention in the Dominican Republic.[25]

When Papa Doc died of natural causes in 1971, he left a Haiti in which all the already weak national institutions—including the church, the educational system, the media, and the armed forces—had been rendered impotent. Hence, he could die confident that his work would live on, as his nineteen-year old son, Jean-Claude, was approved as his successor in January 1971 by an announced vote of 2,391,916 to 1. Expectations of a significant liberalization were soon dashed as "Baby Doc" relied upon the bulwarks of the highly authoritarian system he inherited—much as the younger Somozas had done in Nicaragua fifteen years earlier.

The New Nations: Enriching the Laboratory

The 1956–1979 period gave birth to half a score of new countries in the region, almost all former British colonies in the Caribbean. Although initial efforts were made to prevent excessive fragmentation, a West Indies Federation died aborning, with rivalry between Jamaica and Trinidad and Tobago—the two largest entities—the major stumbling block. Hence, the region gained a plethora of mini-, micro-, and even microministates. Yet in light of the long, deliberate, and democracy-fostering decolonization process followed by the British, the early years of these countries were much more stable than the political infancy of either the Latin American countries or other post–World War II new nations. Since local self-government had already progressed, political forces learned that losing an election was not the end of the world, as other opportunities to win elections lay down the road. Moreover, with the British still in ultimate control in most cases, including the last word on patronage and subsidies, politics was not a winner-take-all proposition. A particular advantage was that because these countries remained within the British Commonwealth, they had no need to develop armed forces, so they were free of the militarism that the United States had earlier fostered in Cuba, Nicaragua, the Dominican Republic, and—to a lesser extent—Haiti. The very small military establishments of these countries, imbued with an ethos of civilian supremacy, were not involved in gaining independence, which came peacefully and gradually, often without a real change of leadership.[26]

Jamaica

In 1962, Jamaica emerged from a generation of gradually increasing self-government to status as an independent nation. Seized from the Spanish by England in 1655, it had been marked by slavery and sugar plantations, the social and economic dyad dominant down through the formal abolition of slavery in 1834, at which point 13,000 whites were far outnumbered by 200,000 blacks—soon rising to 300,000. In the 1860s, cheaper German, Scotch, and Irish labor was obtained through immigration, with Asians following. The hold of the white planter elite remained unshaken for the next century despite Marcus Garvey's establishment of the United Negro Improvement Association in 1914 and 100,000 individuals becoming Rastafarians (although they never found the savior behind whom they were to return to Africa).

In the context of the economic crisis of the 1930s, Norman Washington Manley (b. 1893) founded the People's National Party (PNP) in 1938, and in 1943 his cousin William Alexander Bustamante (b. 1884) broke away and formed the Jamaican Labour Party (JLP).[27] Elections were held in December 1944 under a constitution allowing limited domestic self-government, with the JPL winning twenty-two parliamentary seats to the PNP's five (and five others going to independents). Five years later the JLP won a much closer election, getting seventeen seats on 42.7 percent of the vote to thirteen seats on 43.5 percent for the PNP (reflecting the well-known distorting effect of single-member districts). Then in January 1955 the PNP pulled ahead, winning eighteen seats on 50.5 percent of the vote to fourteen on 39.1 percent for the JLP. In July 1959, it upped its margin to twenty-nine seats to sixteen for the JLP on 64.4 percent to 35.6 percent in an election in which the West Indies Federation was a defining issue. As internal self-government had been earned, Manley became prime minister, not just majority leader. During all this time North American companies bought up areas containing rich bauxite deposits, subsequently making infrastructural investments resulting in an urban boom.

In 1962, following a vote of 55 to 45 percent to leave the West Indies Federation, the JLP ousted the PNP by winning 26 seats to 19 (on a very close vote of 51 to 49 percent) and held power for the first decade after independence within the British Commonwealth of Nations, but the February 1967 elections were marred by widespread violence and the imposition of a state of emergency. The announced, but widely questioned, results of the election were 62.3 percent of the vote and 33 parliamentary seats for the JLP to 37.7 percent and 18 seats for the PNP. At this juncture Bustamante died and was succeeded by Donald Sangster, who also quickly passed away, making room for Hugh Shearer to become

JLP leader and prime minister. In 1972, with the economy in a deep slump, the political pendulum took a wild swing as the PNP won a landslide victory, getting 37 seats on 69.9 percent of the vote, and the JLP plummeted to 16 seats on 30.2 percent of the vote. This PNP triumph elevated to the post of prime minister the son of the PNP's founder, Michael Norman Manley (b. 1924), who had taken over from his father in 1969. Initially implementing a program of basic socioeconomic reforms, the Manley government incurred the wrath of local elites and the foreign-owned bauxite mining companies, whose vociferous complaints gained a more sympathetic hearing in Washington following Manley's development of close relations with Cuba—Jamaica's nearest neighbor.

By now a self-proclaimed "democratic socialist state," Jamaica went into its December 1976 elections under a state of emergency justified by widespread and often violent unrest. Hence, the opposition questioned the legitimacy of the governing party's overwhelming victory—47 seats on 78.3 percent of the vote to 21.7 percent and 13 seats for the JLP, continuing Manley's tenure as prime minister. He was, however, soon forced to enter into an economic stabilization agreement with the IMF that resulted in increased unemployment and a sharp decline in real wages during 1978 and 1979. Hence, the next election would see a startling reversal of fortunes.

Trinidad and Tobago

Located just off the Venezuelan coast, the second most populous of these new countries, one with an area of a bit over 5,100 square miles, was settled by the French a century after its 1492 discovery by Columbus. The French were repelled by the Spanish, who in the face of British expansionism encouraged to increase settlement in 1776. Then the British captured Trinidad in 1797, and Spain reluctantly yielded its claim in 1802. As part of the settlement of the Napoleonic Wars, Britain acquired the small adjoining isle of Tobago from the French, subsequently merging it with its larger neighbor. With slavery abolished in 1834 and blacks moving to the cities, East Indian indentured servants were brought in as plantation laborers, and their descendants made up a majority of the rural population by the time of World War I.

By good fortune Trinidad's early life as an independent nation was marked by stability and continuity under a dominant political personality operating within a framework of parliamentary democracy. For Eric E. Williams (b. 1911), an Oxford-educated historian of international note, was a practical intellectual capable of launching his small multiracial country along a more peaceful path than those followed by Jamaica or Guyana.[28] Williams encountered conservative Bhadase Sagan Maraj (b. 1919), minimally educated but charismatic (at least in the eyes of the East Indian population), and his recently formed People's Democratic Party. In 1956,

ERIC WILLIAMS
(PHOTO COURTESY OF THE
GOVERNMENT OF THE REPUBLIC
OF TRINIDAD AND TOBAGO)

Williams founded the People's National Movement (PNM), which won thirteen of twenty-four seats in elections for a parliament within the West Indies Federation. When this was dissolved, Trinidad and Tobago received full independence on August 31, 1962. Dr. Williams remained its prime minister, winning election after election until his death in late March 1981, while retaining his reputation as a social historian.

Maraj lost support when he radicalized in the 1970s, and the Democratic Labour Party (DLP) founded in 1958 by Rudranath Capildeo (b. 1920) sputtered ineffectively, as it had to oust its leader in 1969 for spending most of his time in England. In 1970, a black power movement of junior officers failed in its attempt to overthrow the popular government. In 1976, the country became a republic within the British Commonwealth. In September, in the midst of a sustained oil boom, the largely black PNM won twenty-four of thirty-six seats over the new and essentially East Indian United Labour Front (ULF), headed by Basdeo Panday—a future prime minister—and the Democratic Action Congress (DAC), a Tobago-based party. Originally dependent upon sugar, the country, possessing large deposits of petroleum and natural gas, benefited greatly from the 1970s energy crisis. This prosperity would come to a crashing end in the 1980s with the collapse of oil prices, leaving Williams's successors to cope with adversity.

Guyana

Guyana, a South American enclave bordered by Venezuela and Brazil and populated chiefly by blacks and individuals of East Indian ancestry, suffered the most traumatic late-decolonization process of any of the new countries emerging from British rule in the Western Hemisphere. The highly controversial nature of its leading political figure delayed its birth, and profound political surgery by the presiding pair of self-interested obstetricians, Britain and the United States, ensured it would be born with major political defects. As Progressive People's Party (PPP) leader Cheddi Bharrat Jagan (b. 1918), winner of the preindependence domestic self-government elections, was too radical for Washington's taste, London was convinced to hold off final independence until a way could be found to split this broad-based party. The split was accomplished by a play upon the ambitions of Jagan's erstwhile right-hand man, Linden Forbes Sampson Burnham (b. 1923). The result was a lasting rift between black and East Indian voters, the former overwhelmingly following Burnham into the People's National Congress (PNC), and the latter remaining loyal to Jagan and his US-born Marxist-Leninist wife, Janet.

The area's colonial experience had featured settlement by several European countries, consolidated under Dutch rule in 1667, with administration in the hands of the Dutch West India Company, which had to fight off other countries. The Congress of Vienna in 1815 awarded the area along the Essequibo River to Britain, which bundled the existing settlements together as British Guiana in 1831, with slavery abolished three years later—at which time the forty thousand-plus New World–born blacks slightly outnumbered those born in Africa. As many of the ex-Africans moved off the plantations to their own villages and European, chiefly Portuguese, indentured servants proved insufficient, East Indian migration picked up steam, with 240,000 East Indians brought in between 1838 and 1917. Subsequently Afro-Guyanese who served in World War I became the nucleus of a lower middle class, and the further importation of indentured servants from India were banned. Rice and bauxite overtook sugar as key exports, a result being demands to reduce the political dominance of the sugar planters— just as they were striving to gain more public investment in drainage and irrigation projects. This dissatisfaction led to the establishment by London in 1928 of a crown colony system under tight control of an appointed governor. This change reduced the ability of the electorate to influence the government, undoing reforms obtained in 1891.[29] During World War II property qualifications for voting and holding office were reduced, and elected members became a majority in the Legislative Council (in which appointed members had predominated). By 1953, all adults had the right to vote.

What would become a rather tragic political experience started on a promising note as Jagan, a dentist educated at Howard and Northwestern Universities in the

United States, who met his wife and gained his introduction to Marxism in Chicago, founded the Guyana Industrial Workers Union in 1946 and the Political Affairs Committee (PAC) the following year. Using them as a base, he and Burnham, a young black lawyer just back from school in Britain, established the Progressive People's Party (PPP) in 1950. With modified internal self-rule in effect by 1953, Jagan became Government Leader on the strength of the PPP's winning eighteen of twenty-four seats in the parliament. His leftist leanings were anathema to the US and British governments, so measures were taken to destroy the dominance of the PPP by encouraging Burnham to defect and construct a black-based party in opposition to what would then become an essentially East Indian PPP. Hence, after only 133 days of the elected PPP government, the British suspended the constitution and expelled the Jagan-headed government—imprisoning the Jagan couple for six months and appointing an interim government.

As the PPP split into Jagan and Burnham factions in 1955, the British were confident by 1957 that Burnham could win elections and were satisfied with their success in inducing him to reverse the PPP stand that independence should precede any decision on joining the West Indies Federation, a decision that would then be made after a national referendum. Hence, the British partially restored the suspended 1953 constitution and held elections in which—to Anglo-American dismay—Jagan and the PPP received nine seats on 48 percent of the vote to 26 percent and three seats for Burnham's followers. After Burnham formalized the split by founding the PNC, the next two years were marked by violent racial conflicts, as white, US-born Janet Jagan (b.1920) served as Minister of Home Affairs (in charge of police and internal security). This cleavage led to a situation in which the mid-1961 elections were fought along the divisive line "Vote for your own race." The PPP won twenty seats to eleven for the PNC and four for the United Force—a party led by Portuguese businessmen and professionals. The victors also won the right to name eight of thirteen senators and for their government to exercise internal self-government for Guyana. Jagan's subsequent trip to Washington to seek aid from the Kennedy administration was a fiasco—as Kennedy's negative opinion of Jagan was reinforced by personal contact. "Destabilization" measures by the United States and the United Kingdom, including support for strikes and CIA aid to opposition forces, characterized the next two years.[30]

At the end of 1964, Burnham and the PNC attained their Washington-London–endorsed goal of coming to power. In coalition with the United Force, which polled 12.5 percent of the vote, the PNC emerged victorious over the 45 percent plurality for the PPP. In the shadow of a long and bloody sugar industry strike, entailing 176 deaths, independence came in mid-1966, and the PNC won in 1967 elections marked by a change in proportional representation—a system that was anathema to the British, unless it suited their purposes outside Great

Britain. In 1970, Burnham declared the country a "Cooperative Republic," in which the government would own at least 51 percent of any economic enterprise, and he triumphed in the 1973 elections. Nationalizations continued, with the government lacking the managerial skills and capital needed to keep the economy operating efficiently. In an atmosphere of crisis seventy-five thousand Guyanese emigrated between 1976 and 1981. (Burnham, switching to a presidential system in 1980, would remain in power until his death in 1985.)

Bahamas

The Bahamas, a sprawling group of twenty-one small islands with a current population near 320,000, came into English hands in 1647 after earlier Dutch settlement. A British colony through World War II, when the Duke of Windsor was its governor general, in 1953 it witnessed formation of the Progressive Liberal Party (PLP) by mixed-race professionals. In reaction, Lynden Oscar Pindling (b. 1930), an ambitious black lawyer, established the United Bahamian Party (UBP), receiving a majority of legislative seats in 1962 on only 36 percent of the vote to the PLP's 45 percent (raising the question of how proportional the districts were. Known as the "black Moses," Pindling stayed in office after an 18-to-18 tie in 1967, through alliance with two independents. An extremely able although unscrupulous politician, he won 29 seats the next year and scored a clean sweep in the 1972 elections, as tourism featuring gambling provided an array of opportunities for enrichment—most on the boundary between legal and illicit—as Cuban gambling had been shut down since Castro's accession to power. Hence, Pindling was entrenched in power when independence came in 1973. The Free National Movement (FNM) constituted no more of a hindrance to him than the Republican Party did to the Daley machine in Chicago.[31]

Belize

Soon after Great Britain's first assertion of sovereignty over what it called British Honduras in 1786, until 1884, this small piece of Central America was a minor dependency of Jamaica. It came to have a complex racial makeup, including nearly half *mestizos* and over one-quarter blacks, along with a sixth Indians (chiefly of Mayan ancestry) and a small sliver of Europeans. Beginning in 1936 a minority of 5 of 13 members of the Legislative Council were chosen by a highly restricted electorate, which by 1945 comprised only 822 voters in a population of 63,000. George Cadle Price (b. 1919), from a middle-class Creole (mixed-blood) family founded the People's United Party (PUP) in 1949 and, in cooperation with the General Workers Union, and with universal adult suffrage in effect, in 1954 won 8 of the 9 elected seats in the Legislative Council on the strength of 65 percent of the votes.[32] After winning all 9 nonappointive seats in 1957, in 1961 with the legislature increased to 25 members, of whom 18 were elected, Price and the PUP scored a clean sweep. Full internal self-government came in 1964, but formal independence had to be delayed because of Guatemala's territorial claims and threat to invade if the British protective tie was severed. Meanwhile Price led his party to winning all but 2 seats in 1965 and all but 1 in 1969, slipping to 12 of 18 in 1974.

Barbados

Barbados, a small island of some 166 square miles, settled by the British in 1627, became independent in late 1966 following a relatively intense period of preparation. Sir Grantley Herbert Adams (b. 1898) studied and practiced law in England before returning to help found the Barbados Progressive League in 1938 and then organize the Barbados Workers Union—which served as the foundation for the Barbados Labour Party (BLP) in 1946. Managing to have voting requirements liberalized in 1944, the BLP gained control of the legislative council two years later, with electoral victories again in 1948, 1951 (winning 16 of 24 seats under universal suffrage), and 1956 for a parliament limited to partial domestic self-government. Its powers were expanded to full internal self-government in 1958, and Adams threw his very considerable energies into Caribbean integration, opting to be prime minister of the West Indies Federation rather than premier of Barbados—a post assumed by Hugh Cummins, under whom virtual independence was achieved in late 1961. With the federation's final collapse in mid-1962, Adams reassumed political activity in Barbados, dying in 1971.[33]

Errol W. Barrow (b. 1920), a World War II Royal Air Force pilot who returned to Barbados in 1950, split away from the BLP to establish the Democratic Labour Party (DLP) in 1954. Winning 16 seats to 5 in the December 1961 elections, Barrow presided over attainment of full independence in late 1966. In 1971 he cruised to a landslide victory as the rival BLP won only 6 of 24 legislative seats. But in 1976, after a decade and a half of DLP government, the BLP returned to power under John Michael G. M. "Tom" Adams (b. 1931)—Sir Grantley's son, who had come back from England in 1961 to rebuild the BLP (and would serve as prime minister for a decade).

Suriname

Suriname, until 1948 called Dutch Guiana, has perhaps the most diverse population out of all the post–World War II new Western Hemisphere nations. Over 35 percent are classified as "Hindustani" and another 15 percent Javanese, with just over 30 percent considered Creole (mixed African and other ancestry), along with 10 percent "bush Negro" and 3 percent each Amerindian and European. Its first major colonization was by the British in the 1650s, but in 1667 they traded it to the Dutch for New York (certainly one of the most lopsided territorial swaps in history). In the aftermath of the Napoleonic Wars, the British, French, and Dutch each took part of the larger Guiana, and Dutch Guiana saw slavery abolished in 1863. The resulting labor shortage led to importation of cheap labor from India in the 1870s and Java in the 1880s. Internal self-government with universal suffrage came by 1950. Elections for a Legislative Council brought into being the National Suriname Party (NPS) under Johan Pender and the United Hindustani Party (VHP) headed by Jaggernath Lachman, along with an array of smaller parties. In the six elections held before independence was attained in 1975, the major parties formed coalitions leading to multiethnic cabinets. During the 1960s, the leading parties allied in the name of stability but subsequently paired up with smaller ones.

In November 1973, however, Pender having died and independence being the chief issue, the NPS and three minor allies, including the Progressive Reform Party, won 22 of 39 legislative seats, dethroning the United Hindustani Party and its allies. This development led many of the losers—some 40,000, including a large proportion of the better-educated—to emigrate to the Netherlands rather than take their chances in an independent Suriname. Henck A.E. Aaron (b. 1936), leader of the NPS since 1970, became premier, taking the title of prime minister when Suriname became independent in late 1975.[34] In 1977, Aaron led the NPS to a 22-seat to 17-seat victory over a left opposition front headed by Lachman and the VHP.

Grenada

Grenada, a small island, is English-speaking, having been taken by Britain from the French in 1783. It is a predominantly black country of 133 square miles and had more than its share of political controversy during its early years as an independent country. Its first dominant figure was Eric Mathew Gairy (b. 1922), who in 1951 established the Grenada United Labour Party (GULP) and immediately won six of the eight elective seats in the Legislative Council—improving to seven of eight in 1954. Despite winning 52 percent of the vote in 1957, Gairy and the GULP came away with only two seats, so Herbert Augustus Blaize (b. 1918), who had switched to the Grenada National Party (GNP) in 1956, became the island's first chief minister in 1960. Gairy and the GULP scored a comeback in March 1961, but Blaize won six of ten seats in September 1962 after Gairy was removed from office for financial improprieties (yet GULP still received 46 percent of the vote). Associated statehood was achieved in 1967, and with seven of ten seats, Gairy was premier until early 1974, when his title changed to prime minister. Gangsterish and corrupt, relying on the so-called Mongoose Gang to intimidate critics, he was ousted by force in March 1979 and replaced by an avowedly revolutionary regime.[35] Unfortunately this regime would lead to deeper and bloodier crises.

Dominica

Dominica, a small island republic of 290 square miles, was populated in the seventeenth and early eighteenth centuries by French moving over from Martinique and Guadeloupe, but it was seized by the British in 1805. In 1955, Phyllis Shand Allfrey, a white novelist of regional note, founded the Dominica Labour Party (DLP), which won the 1971 elections. Her 1974 successor, Patrick Roland John, became the country's first prime minister with the coming of independence in November 1978, being replaced by Oliver Seraphin during mid-1979 troubles—which included an armed uprising followed shortly by Hurricanes David and Frederick. Meanwhile, Mary Eugenia Charles (b. 1919) founded the Dominica Freedom Party (DFP) in 1968, and in the 1975 elections this future dominant political figure became leader of the opposition.[36]

St. Kitts and Nevis

Robert Llewellyn Bradshaw (b. 1916), a rather authoritarian black nationalist, dominated the political life of these small islands—settled by the British in 1623 and totaling a little over 100 square miles—for almost four decades. After founding the St. Kitts-Nevis-Anguila Labour Party in 1945, he won limited self-government elections in 1946 and 1952—the latter held with universal adult suffrage. Following the 1962 collapse of the West Indies Federation, he took over as prime minister without the inclusion of Anguila. Limited independence came in early 1967, but Bradshaw died in 1978, five years before the achievement of full independence.

St. Vincent and the Grenadines

These tiny islands of St. Vincent and the Grenadines, with a combined area of 150 square miles, had been home to a unique mixture of blacks and Caribs until their deportation to Belize in the 1790s. Milton Cato of the St. Vincent's Labour Party (SVLP) was prime minister from 1967 to 1972 and 1974 to 1984, with James Mitchell (who would become the country's dominant figure) holding office briefly in 1972–1974. Independence came in late 1979, with Cato in the driver's seat.

St. Lucia

George Frederick Charles (b. 1916) came to legislative office on this small island in 1951 through his leadership of the St. Lucia Labour Party (SLP), winning reelection in 1954 and becoming SLP leader. He and the party came away in 1957 with seven of the eight elective seats on the Legislative Council. After raising this number to nine of ten in 1961, he finally lost the 1964 election to John George Melvin Compton and his United Workers Party (UWP). Compton won election after election until 1979.

Antigua and Barbuda

Antigua and Barbuda, two islands totaling 171 square miles, with almost all the population of around eighty thousand living on Antigua, were settled by the British in 1632 and used for sugar and cotton cultivation. In 1939, Vere Connell Bird, Sr. (b. 1909), founded the Antigua Trades and Labour Union (ATLU), establishing the Antigua Labour Party (ALP) in 1946. The first universal suffrage election came in 1951, with internal self-government coming in 1967. The opposition under George Walker governed from 1972 until 1976, when Bird and the ALP came back to power for an extended stay.

Latin America in 1979

By the end of the 1970s, much had changed in Latin America since 1955, although in a number of countries some of the political modifications had proved to be transitory and had begun to change back. Brazil's military government was preparing for its departure from power by taking a series of steps to turn opening of the political system into transition to democracy—with moderate elements of the administration the leading architects of decompression and liberalization. On the political plane, Mexico appeared to have changed very little, yet events would soon prove that socioeconomic changes were beginning to feed demands for change much as had been the case during the first decade of the century and the overthrow of Díaz's Porfiriato—but this time major transformations of the political system were to come peacefully rather than through revolution and civil war. Colombia had put its brief experiment with military rule behind it as early as 1957, achieving stable democracy through the innovative mechanism of the National Front (then knowing when this arrangement had outlived its usefulness). It finished the period with the grave new problems unleashed by the drug trade not yet fully evident. Argentina was enduring repressive military authoritarianism without any sign of letup—so the dramatic developments of the 1980s were hopes, not expectations. But its military leaders would soon embark on a desperate attempt to rally public support through a rash military adventure that would explode in their faces and force them to cede power back to civilian hands the next year.

The opposite was true in Venezuela, where the post-1958 democratic regime seemed to be solidly implanted, so its future decay was more a fear than a prediction. Peru had been through a great deal of turmoil, but its political development hadn't advanced significantly between the beginning and end of this period, since the government elected in 1956 was more legitimate than the hybrid government of 1979, with an elected constituent assembly but the military administration still in office. Chile, too, had experienced many developments, but its net movement was clearly back and down—from the midst of a long series of democratic governments to the most repressive of the region's authoritarian military dictatorships. Uruguay had also regressed politically but was at least showing signs of finding a road out of its nightmare, unlike Paraguay—which had spent the whole period under the Stroessner dictatorship, which would continue for another decade.

In terms of real political development little had changed in Central America. In Guatemala military rule had prevailed throughout the period, with the presidency, in effect, having become the top rung in the army's promotion ladder—a situation duplicated in Honduras. In El Salvador, where this fusion of the military with a leading political party was already the case, the country was teetering on the brink of a destructive civil war. In Nicaragua the Somoza dynasty fell from power at the very end of the period, and Costa Rica had consolidated its democracy—a very rare exception in Latin America. In some ways Panama, although still behind, had made greater progress, although this would soon come to a crashing halt.

Cuba had undergone the most comprehensive revolution ever seen in the Western Hemisphere, resulting in a communist system rooted in the personality cult of Fidelism. If Cuba had changed the most, it would be the country that changed the least from 1980 to the end of the century. Haiti under the despotic Duvaliers was essentially hell on earth, and the Dominican Republic had seen Trujillo replaced by his protégé Balaguer, essentially Trujillo Lite. The small nations gaining independence during this period ranged from being off to a remarkably good start (Trinidad and Tobago, followed by Barbados, Belize, Dominica, and St. Lucia), through showing the major shortcomings of a populist semisocialist government in Jamaica, to experiencing deep racial conflict and the evisceration of democratic processes in Guyana, and instability in Grenada. Suriname, St. Kitts and Nevis, and St. Vincent and the Grenadines were just newly embarked on independent existence.

Although the 1980s would see country after country abandoning military rule for a "transition to democracy," in some instances this change did not mean an unconditional commitment to democracy, for often this term was a politically correct catchword for a return to competitive civilian politics, which, as portrayed in Chapters 6 and 7, had in many cases been only semidemocratic. Indeed, Wiarda maintains that the military withdrew, although under pressure, "as a way of salvaging their professional, corporate, and institutional identity, unity, and respect."[37]

Notes

1. Consult Thomas W. Walker and Ariel Armony, *Repression, Resistance, and Democratic Transition in Central America* (Wilmington, DE: Scholarly Resources, 2000); Jeffrey M. Paige, *Coffee and Power: Revolution and the Rise of Democracy in Central America* (Cambridge: Harvard University Press, 1997); Ralph Lee Woodward, Jr., *Central America: A Nation Divided*, 3rd ed. (New York: Oxford University Press, 1999); and Walter LaFeber, *Inevitable Revolution: The United States in Central America* (New York: Norton, 1983).

2. See Roland H. Ebel, *Misunderstood Caudillo: Miguel Ydigoras Fuentes and the Failure of Democracy in Guatemala* (Lanham, MD: University Press of America, 1998).

3. Robert H. Trudeau, "Guatemala: Democratic Rebirth?" in Howard J. Wiarda and Harvey F. Kline, eds., *Latin American Politics and Development*, 5th ed. (Boulder, CO: Westview Press, 2000), p. 500. Also consult Susanne Jonas, *The Battle for Guatemala: Rebels, Death Squads, and U.S. Power* (Boulder, CO: Westview Press, 1991), and Piero Gleijeses, *Politics and Culture in Guatemala* (Ann Arbor: University of Michigan Center for Political Studies, Institute for Social Research, 1988).

4. See Thomas P. Anderson, *The War of the Dispossessed: Honduras and El Salvador, 1969* (Lincoln: University of Nebraska Press, 1981).

5. Tommie Sue Montgomery, *Revolution in El Salvador: Origin and Evolution* (Boulder, CO: Westview Press, 1982), and Stephen Webre, *Jose Napoleon Duarte and the Christian Democratic Party in Salvadoran Politics, 1960–1972* (Baton Rouge: Louisiana State University Press, 1979).

6. Consult James Morris, *Honduras: Caudillo Politics and Military Rulers* (Boulder, CO: Westview Press, 1984).

7. See Thomas W. Walker, *Nicaragua: The Land of Sandino*, 3rd ed. (Boulder, CO: Westview Press, 1991), as well as Donald C. Hodges, *The Intellectual Foundations of the Nicaraguan Revolution* (Austin: University of Texas Press, 1986).

8. Consult John A. Booth, *Costa Rica: Quest for Democracy* (Boulder, CO: Westview Press, 1998), pp. 40–41.

9. Mitchell A. Seligson, "Costa Rica," in Wiarda and Kline, *Latin American Politics,* p. 442.

10. Walter LaFeber, *The Panama Canal: The Crisis in Historical Perspective* (New York: Oxford University Press, 1989), and David McCullogh, *The Path Between the Seas: The Creation of the Panama Canal, 1870–1914* (New York: Simon & Schuster, 1977), and Andrew Zimbalist and John Weeks, *Panama at the Crossroads: Economic Development and Political Change in the Twentieth Century* (Berkeley and Los Angeles: University of California Press, 1991).

11. There had been frequent separatist uprisings during the second half of the nineteenth century, easily suppressed by Colombia. Panama's founding fathers knew that the United States was the only thing keeping them from being hung as traitors, so accepted a treaty that changed kilometers into miles and ninety-nine years into perpetuity. The French Panama Canal Company was the beneficiary of the modest cash payment from the United States.

12. See Larry Pippin, *The Remón Era: An Analysis of a Decade of Events in Panama 1947–1957* (Stanford, CA: Stanford University Institute of Hispanic American and Luso-Brazilian Studies, 1964), and Steve C. Ropp, *Panamanian Politics: From Guarded Nation to National Guard* (New York: Praeger, 1964).

13. Most useful is George Priestley, *Military Government and Popular Participation in Panama: The Torrijos Regime 1968–1975* (Boulder, CO: Westview Press, 1986).

14. For an overview see Franklin W. Knight, *The Caribbean: The Genesis of a Fragmented Nationalism*, 2nd ed. (New York: Oxford University Press, 1990), especially pp. 275–306.

15. Of the mountainous literature on the Cuban Revolution, standout works include Susan Eva Eckstein, *Back from the Future: Cuba Under Castro*, 2nd Ed. (New York: Routledge, 2003); Juan de Aguila, *Cuba: Dilemmas of a Revolution*, 3rd ed. (Boulder, CO: Westview Press, 1994); Louis A. Perez, Jr., *Cuba: Between Reform and Revolution*, 2nd ed. (New York: Oxford University Press, 1995), and Jorge Dominguez's monumental *Cuba: Order and Revolution* (Cambridge: Belknap Press of Harvard University Press, 1978).

16. Biographies of Castro are abundant, if often unduly favorable or excessively hostile. See Robert E. Quirk, *Fidel Castro* (New York: Norton, 1993); Tad Szulc, *Fidel: A Critical Portrait* (New York, William Morrow, 1986); and Georgie Ann Geyer, *Guerrilla Prince: The Untold Story of Fidel Castro* (Boston: Little, Brown, 1991). The newest is Brian Latell, *After Fidel: The Inside Story of Castro's Regime and Cuba's Next Leader* (New York: Palgrave Macmillan, 2005).

17. See Ronald M. Schneider, "Five Years of the Cuban Revolution," *Current History*, 46: 269 (January 1964), pp. 26–38, as well as James G. Blight and Peter Kornbluh, eds., *Politics of Illusion: The Bay of Pigs Invasion Reexamined* (Boulder, CO: Lynne Rienner, 1999), and Haynes B. Johnson, *The Bay of Pigs* (New York: Norton, 1964).

18. Consult James A. Nathan, *Anatomy of the Cuban Missile Crisis* (Westport, CT: Greenwood Press, 2001), and James G. Blight, Bruce J. Allyn, and David Welch, *Cuba on the Brink: Castro, the Missile Crisis, and the Soviet Collapse* (New York: Pantheon Books, 1993).

19. See Eckstein, *Back from the Future,* Chapter 2, as well as Aguila, *Cuba.*

20. For perspective on the country consult Howard J. Wiarda and Michael Kryzanek, *The Dominican Republic: A Caribbean Crucible* (Boulder, CO: Westview Press, 1982), and Jan Knippers Black, *The Dominican Republic: Politics and Development in an Unsovereign State* (Boston: Allen & Unwin, 1986).

21. Piero Gleijeses, *The Dominican Crisis: The 1965 Constitutionalist Revolt and American Intervention* (Baltimore: Johns Hopkins University Press, 1978), is carefully researched. Very different contemporary views are found in Dan Kurzman, *Santo Domingo: Revolt of the Damned* (New York: Putnam, 1965); John Barlow Martin, *Overtaken by Events: The Dominican Crisis from the Fall of Trujillo to the Civil War* (New York: Doubleday, 1966); and Abraham F. Lowenthal, *The Dominican Intervention* (Cambridge: Harvard University Press, 1972).

22. Howard J. Wiarda, *Dilemmas of Democracy in Latin America: Crises and Opportunities* (Lanham, MD: Rowman & Littlefield, 2005), pp. 95–99, analyzes this unusual leader.

23. Postintervention developments can be followed in Jonathan Hartlyn, *The Struggle for Democratic Politics in the Dominican Republic* (Chapel Hill: University of North Carolina Press, 1998). Balaguer is analyzed in Michael Kryzanek, *Leaders, Leadership and U.S. Policy in Latin America* (Boulder, CO: Westview Press, 1992).

24. See Bernard Diederich and Al Burt, *Papa Doc: Haiti and Its Dictator* (Maplewood, NJ: Waterfront Press, 1991); Elizabeth Abbott, *Haiti: The Duvaliers and Their Legacy* (New York: McGraw-Hill, 1988); James Ferguson, *Papa Doc, Baby Doc: Haiti and the Duvaliers* (Oxford, UK: Basil Blackwell, 1987); Patrick Bellegarde-Smith, *Haiti: The Breached Citadel* (Boulder, CO: Westview Press, 1989); Robert Fatton, Jr., *Haiti's Predatory Republic: The Unending Transition to Democracy* (Boulder, CO: Lynne Rienner, 2002); and Brian Weinstein and Aaron Segal, *Haiti: The Failure of Politics* (New York: Praeger, 1992).

25. Consult Alex Dupuy, *Haiti and the World Economy: Class, Race, and Underdevelopment Since 1700* (Boulder, CO: Westview Press, 1989), as well as Robert Rotberg, *Haiti: The Politics of Squalor* (Boston: Houghton-Mifflin, 1971).

26. The most useful comparative work is F.S.J. Ledgister, *Class Alliances and the Liberal Authoritarian State: The Roots of Post-Colonial Democracy in Jamaica, Trinidad & Tobago, and Suriname* (Trenton, N.J.: Africa World Press, 1997). See also Ralph R. Premdas, ed., *Identity, Ethnicity and Culture in the Caribbean* (St. Augustine, Trinidad & Tobago: University of the West Indies School of Continuing Studies, 1998).

27. See Michael Kaufman, *Jamaica Under Manley: Dilemmas of Socialism and Democracy* (London: Zed Books, 1985), and David Panton, *Jamaica's Michael Manley: The Great Transformation (1972–1992)* (Kingston, Jamaica: Kingston Publishers, 1993).

28. Consult Heather Cateau and S.H.H. Carrington, eds., *Capitalism and Slavery Fifty Years Later: Eric Eustace Williams—A Reassessment of the Man and His Work* (New York: Peter Lang, 2000), and Barbara L. Solow and Stanley L. Engerman, eds., *Caribbean Slavery: The Legacy of Eric Williams* (New York: Cambridge University Press, 1987), as well as Eric E. Williams, *From Columbus to Castro: A History of the Caribbean, 1492–1969* (New York: Harper & Row, 1971).

29. See Thomas J. Spinner, Jr., *A Political and Social History of Guyana, 1945–1983* (Boulder, CO: Westview Press, 1984); Alan H. Adamson, *Sugar Without Slaves: The Political Economy of British Guyana, 1838–1904* (New Haven: Yale University Press, 1972); Cheddi Jagan, *The West on Trial: My Fight for Guyana's Freedom*, rev. ed. (New York: International Publishers, 1972); Peter Simms, *Trouble in Guyana: An Account of People, Personalities, and Politics as They Were in British Guyana* (London: Allen & Unwin, 1966); and Henry B. Jeffrey and Colin Baber, *Guyana: Politics, Economics and Society: Beyond the Burnham Era* (Boulder, CO Lynne Rienner, 1986).

30. The Kennedy administration continued the hostility toward the Jagans underlying US policy since 1953. Johnson eliminated the problem by Burnham's US-UK–aided coming to power.

31. See Michael Craton, *Pindling: The Life and Times of Lynden Oscar Pindling First Prime Minister of the Bahamas 1930–2000* (Oxford, UK: Macmillan Caribbean, 2001).

32. Consult Nigel Boland, *Belize: A New Nation in Central America* (Boulder, CO: Westview Press, 1986).

33. See F. A. Hoyos, *Grantley Adams and the Social Revolution: The Story of the Movement That Changed the Pattern of West Indian Society* (London: Macmillan, 1974), which goes beyond F. A. Hoyos, *Rise of West Indian Democracy: The Life and Times of Sir Grantley Adams* (s.l: Advocate Press, 1963).

34. See Edward Dew, *The Difficult Flowering of Suriname: Ethnicity and Politics in a Plural Society* (The Hague, Netherlands: Martinus Nijhoff, 1978), and Betty Sedoc-Dulhberg, ed., *The Dutch Caribbean: Prospects for Democracy* (New York: Gordon & Breach, 1990).

35. Consult Omowale David Franklyn, *Bridging the Two Grenadas: Gairy's and Bishop's* (St. Georges, Grenada: Talented House, 1999), as well as Archie W. Singham, *The Hero and the Crowd in a Colonial Polity* (New Haven: Yale University Press, 1968).

36. See Janet Higbie, *Eugenia: The Caribbean's Iron Lady* (London: Macmillan Caribbean, 1993).

37. Wiarda, *Dilemmas,* p. 205.

11

Twilight of the Generals
and Dawn of Democracy

Political Progress, 1980–1999

As was clear by the end of the 1970s, political development in Latin America, although often painfully slow and extremely uneven, had also been significant and widespread, a fact dramatically brought home during the last two decades of the twentieth century. Movement toward developing viable, participant-representative political systems both surged ahead and demonstrated great resilience and staying power during the 1980s and 1990s. As late as the mid to late 1970s, authoritarian political regimes, some of a truly despotic nature, were entrenched in Brazil, Argentina, Peru, Chile, Bolivia, Ecuador, Uruguay, and Paraguay.

Nicaragua and Haiti were under personalist autocratic rule, and Cuba was a case apart under an autocratic, charismatic communist leader. Guatemala and Honduras had regimes much like the majority of those in South American, and El Salvador was slipping into civil war. Indeed only Colombia, Venezuela, and Costa Rica were clearly democratic. The PRI-dominated regime in Mexico showed strong authoritarian tendencies, as did the regime in Panama and, intermittently, that in the Dominican Republic. Yet by 1989 transitions to democracy were under way in the eight not-yet-democratic countries of South America, plus Guatemala, Honduras, and the Dominican Republic. Stirrings in this direction were already apparent and would soon break through in Nicaragua, El Salvador, and even Haiti.

Then mid-1993 through 1996 witnessed the most important wave of national elections in Latin America's experience—or for that matter in the experience of any region of the world. From Jamaica's parliamentary balloting of March 30, 1993, through Nicaragua's presidential election in November 1996, all but a handful of the region's countries selected chief executives through democratic constitutional processes. Indeed, as three others (Ecuador, Guyana, and the Bahamas) had experienced this positive trend during the last seven months of 1992, turnover by normal electoral means was virtually complete. During this short period only one government—that of Cuba—maintained itself in power with complete disregard for elections, although even there they were being instituted at subnational levels and for essentially consultative bodies. Not a single elected government in the region was ousted by force. This watershed time had no remote parallel in Latin American history (nor elsewhere in an area at all approaching this number of countries). Its closest approximation had been in the 1958–1961 period, but that had been a much narrower and, as it proved, shallowly rooted pendulum swing. Moreover, the scope of participation had expanded immensely since that time.

By the end of the 1990s, never had so many of the region's countries and such a high proportion of its population lived under governments of their own choosing that were fundamentally adhering to constitutional principles. At long last, viable representative political systems with substantial democratic processes predominated in this diverse and far-flung expanse. But contrary to the once-cherished belief in the United States that proximity to the "beacon of democracy" would be a powerfully positive factor, the heartland of Latin American democratic consolidation was in the most distant area: the southern portion of South America. There, where Montevideo, Buenos Aires, and Santiago are as far from New York and Washington as are the Ural Mountains or Cairo, stable democracies first took root.

Although Argentina, Chile, and Uruguay are essentially European-populated, often considered an important contributory factor to democratization, the greatest rate of progress in such positive political development was to be found in Brazil—where 81 million persons of primarily African ancestry coexist with 104 million of European extraction. And the more advanced southern part of this nation of subcontinental proportions lies further from the capital of the United States than do Moscow, or Lagos, Nigeria. Indeed, the distance from São Paulo and Rio de Janeiro to Lisbon and Madrid is roughly the same as to New York, and London or Paris is about as close to those Brazilian supercities as Los Angeles is. Equally disturbing to conventional wisdom concerning the presumptive positive political influence of the US example was the fact that a disproportionate share of Latin American laggards on the road to democratic political development were among those countries geographically closest to the United States. Thus, Cuba and Haiti had failed to find seats on the democratization bandwagon, and Mexico was late to board. Moreover, despite impressive progress in the 1990s, most of Central America had not moved decisively beyond the previous peaks from which they had slipped back.

After all the generations that had passed, slower progress toward stable democracy appeared to still be highly correlated with centers of Spanish colonial rule—

most notably the viceroyalty based in Mexico and its Central American extension; that centered on modern-day Peru, but also embracing Ecuador and Bolivia; and that subsequently headquartered in Colombia and including Venezuela and Panama. The viceroyalty set up in Buenos Aires less than a generation before independence does not enter into these calculations, as for almost all of the colonial period that area was quite peripheral and administered across the Andes from distant Lima while wide open to British influences from the South Atlantic. In this regard it is also highly suggestive that democratic laggard Cuba was exactly the place that Spanish colonial rule lasted longest, with both an early start and a very late end (the 1490s to the end of the 1890s).

Elections either increase or decrease the probability of certain policy outcomes; they do not determine that something will happen, although they can virtually eliminate certain options. In these respects the Brazilian balloting of 1994 and 1998 and the Mexican voting from 1994 through 2000 were of critical importance. In the first of these cases the elections made possible economic stability and fiscal modernization that could establish a viable base for social reforms in half of South America. The Mexican experience opened the door to determining whether Latin America's second most populous country could make an essentially peaceful transition to the kind of political democracy that Brazil had achieved between 1984 and 1994. Elsewhere in the region, elections proved a vital part of political development, although not as unambiguously as in the two major nations. In evaluating the individual cases that made up the tidal wave of return to civilian government, Wiarda injects a sober caveat. Not only had the military most often withdrawn from power rather than being forcibly ejected, but support for democracy had had a very strong pragmatic component. In his most recent interpretation, he expresses his reservations in very strong terms:

> I am not myself convinced that either the Latin military elites or the civilian elites are necessarily fully convinced of democracy's efficacy, but the Americans want it, the Europeans insist on it, world public opinion is in favor of it, and, most importantly none of the international lending agencies will provide loans or sanction investment if democracy is upset—the all-important private capital that has been so critical to Latin America's economic recovery and takeoff in the 1990s could be immediately cut off if democracy were to be overthrown.[1]

Moreover, in his opinion:

> Democracy as an ideal, as an abstract principle, still enjoys—as it has since the early nineteenth century—widespread support in Latin America. But in the often disorganized and underinstitutionalized conditions of Latin

America, people realize that democracy may not work or work very well in their context. Hence their preference for strong government, executive leadership, a nationalistic regime, top-down paternalism, and a mercantilist state that also provided abundant opportunities for employment.[2]

In this chapter the democratization process is closely examined in the two largest countries making the transition from military rule, Brazil and Argentina, as well as in long-civilianized Mexico and Colombia. Chapter 12 will consider analogous processes in the rest of the region, seeking both patterns and paths as these countries overwhelmingly made escapes from authoritarian rule.

Overview

The 1980s burgeoning of democracy saw Brazil embark upon and consolidate the longest period of stable democratic government in its history, one involving a massive expansion of participation to an electorate reaching 110 million by the end of the century. Not only did military rule come to an end after 1984, but both governmental structures and political processes also became significantly stronger and much more broadly based than during the 1946–1964 period of democracy laced with recurrent crises. Mexico underwent a wrenching process of dismantling a system of single-party hegemony and overcoming hurdles and setbacks to arrive by the end of the period on the verge of fully competitive national elections, which would result in the opposition's capturing the presidency, a feat never accomplished in the twentieth century and almost unheard of in the nation's long history. Argentina returned to democratic civilian rule in 1983, amid the trauma of a dismally unsuccessful military adventure and, with serious hiccups along the road, put together the longest-sustained democratic experience in its history, one involving far wider participation than in either its 1916–1930 halcyon years or the Perón era. In spite of very serious strains, rooted in an intractable drug and insurgency problem, Colombia had its string of popularly elected presidents serving out their full terms and turning power over to constitutionally chosen successors reach eleven by the end of the period. Along the way, the crutch initially provided by the National Front was discarded in favor of full competition.

Brazil: Transition to and Consolidation of Democracy

Political development surged ahead in the region's largest country during the 1980s and 1990s, in a near straight line and at an almost breakneck pace. Beginning with a return to direct election of governors in 1982, the transition process progressed through selection of a civilian president by an electoral college in 1984, past balloting for a congress with constituent powers in 1986 and its drafting of a new constitution in 1987–1988, and on to direct election of a younger-generation president at the end of 1989.[3] Consolidation of democracy then overcame the trying challenge of mass disillusionment and unscheduled presidential succession, for when a cloud of corruption engulfed the Fernando Collor de Mello administration in 1992, Brazil proved its political maturity through a fully constitutional process of impeachment untainted by military interference. In 1994, Brazil's rapidly expanding electorate decisively chose a very highly qualified chief executive and granted him an unprecedented second term in 1998.

As 1980 opened, João Baptista Figueiredo had settled in as president with the daunting mission of conducting Brazil's transition to elected civilian government. The economic legacy he inherited from his mentor, ex-president Ernesto Geisel, was mixed, with GDP growth for 1979 having reached a robust 7.2 percent, but inflation doubling to 77 percent. Terrorist bombings, largely the work of the extreme right although blamed on the left, escalated in May, and public refusal to swallow a whitewashing of army intelligence's provocateur role along with the president's waffling on commitment to a civilian successor led invaluable political strategist Golbery do Couto e Silva to resign in August.

The Figueiredo government reaped the debt whirlwind as it encountered the full impact of the second oil shock of 1979, with interest rates zooming to the stratosphere. Those tied to the New York prime rate rose at a dizzying pace to levels often three times that in effect when the loans had been contracted, with those linked to the LIBOR (London inter-bank offered rate) following closely behind. From a 7.7 percent average in 1977, the prime rate peaked at an unprecedented 19.4 percent in 1981, when the LIBOR was still a high 14.1 percent after a bloated 18.0 percent the preceding year. As interest payments erupted from $2.7 billion in 1978 to $7.5 billion for 1980, debt service exploded from $8 billion to $11.3 billion. Rapid export growth was eaten up by resurgent oil prices that pushed imports from $13.7 billion in 1978 to $23.0 billion in 1980. Although economic growth for 1980 was a high 9.2 percent, inflation had climbed to 110 percent—a warning of problems ahead.

The full brunt of recession was quick in arriving, with GDP in 1981 shrinking by 4.5 percent—6.6 percent in per capita terms—with minimal impact on inflation, which hovered at 95 percent as exploding debt service payments of $15.4 billion and $18.3 billion the following year depleted foreign exchange reserves. Instead of responding to the oil shock and zooming interest rates through an adjustment program that would entail economic slowdown and consequent political unpopularity, Figueiredo pushed ahead along the lines that had brought public support during the early years of his presidency, before suffering a heart attack in September 1981. In sharp contrast with the 1969 presidential incapacitation, the regime's inner circle decided to allow the civilian vice president to assume office on an interim basis, and an atmosphere of political normality was maintained.

In this context, the November 15, 1982, direct elections for the congress, the state legislatures, and the governors were a triumph of moderation and political modernization. The mixed results encouraged all major political actors to pursue their objectives through normal legal channels.[4] The progovernment PDS (Democratic Social Party) won in a majority of states, guaranteeing control of the senate, a near majority in the lower house, and a majority in the electoral college, which would choose the new president two years later. Yet return to direct elections created a situation in which the federal government would at times need to compromise. Such opposition victories as occurred were accepted by the armed forces with resignation, not the indignation that similar results had triggered in 1965. Turnout was a high 48.5 million of the registered electorate of 58.6 million. The moderate-opposition PMDB (Party of the Brazilian Democratic Movement) won in ten states with three-fifths of the country's population and nearly 75 percent of its GDP. For the first time the government party failed to get a majority of the valid votes for the lower house yet held onto its plurality, as the strongly oppositionist PDT (Democratic Workers' Party) received only 2.4 million votes—mostly in Rio de Janeiro and Rio Grande do Sul, Leonel Brizola's two strongholds—and the less strident PTB (Brazilian Labor Party) garnered 1.8 million votes, and the PT (Workers' Party), led by eternal candidate and eventual president Luis Inácio "Lula" da Silva, trailed with a disappointing 1.4 million ballots, more than three-fourths of them in São Paulo, and yielding only eight congress seats.

With the elections over, the government admitted that the country was on the verge of insolvency. Not only had 1982 been a bad year economically, but 1983 was even worse in almost every way. Inflation more than doubled, from 100 percent to 211 percent; GDP growth went from a miniscule .5 percent to a miserably negative 3.5 percent; and the current accounts deficit rose from $11.7 billion to $16.3 billion. After mid-1982, Mexico's virtual bankruptcy and foreign debt moratorium raised prospects of default and brought home to the international banking community its dangerous overexposure in Latin America. Only a hastily assembled emergency package of financing prevented Brazil's defaulting on interest payments, with amortization having been quietly suspended at midyear. By dint of a 23 percent devaluation of Brazil's currency, exports were made competitive, as Brazil embarked full steam ahead on a strategy of obtaining increased trade surpluses to offset the drying up of loans and credits so as to keep up interest payments as an inducement to banks to roll over the principal. Still, for the 1982–1988 period, the drain caused by debt service's exceeding new loans reached a staggering $39 billion, as the former totaled a monumental $140 billion.

In the short run, Brazil's success in economic damage control by drastically curbing oil imports while increasing exports was substantial, with 1983's trade surplus of $6.5 billion, eight times that of the preceding year, doubling in 1984 before slipping slightly in 1985, as, with interest rates moderating, debt service payments remained flat and exchange reserves rose from their dangerously low level. Registered foreign debt rose sharply, nearing the $100 billion level, and inflation leveled off at 224 and 235 percent, with GDP growth a satisfactory 5.3 percent in 1984 and a robust 7.9 percent the next year. Unwilling to accept a long-term recession as the price of international solvency, Figueiredo failed to implement the anti-inflation measures agreed upon with the IMF. As had been the case in 1982, the proximity of elections critical for a return to fully competitive political life made this a sound decision. Although the tiring government, limping into its sixth year, was losing control over *abertura,* it still appeared that Figueiredo's successor would come from within the governing party, if not the administration. Yet controlled political opening quickly became transition to democracy, as initiative escaped from the president's hands in the short span of June through August.[5] Figueiredo's failure to indicate a preferred successor led to sudden disaggregation of the PDS as Paulo Maluf continued his relentless drive to gain the support of convention delegates and electoral college members. This intelligent, but unscrupulous, clientelistic demagogue's success in winning the PDS nomination through lavish expenditures and promises of future favors and benefits catalyzed a backlash coalition of moderate regime elements and centrist opposition groups.

Following failure of a massive campaign in favor of direct election of the president, Minas Gerais governor Tancredo Neves emerged as the anti-Maluf contender. In the behind-the-scenes maneuvering that has historically proven key to Brazilian politics, this shrewd veteran with roots back in the Vargas era had no peer. The pragmatic moderate wing of the PMDB was joined by "Liberal Front" PDS dissidents behind vice president Aureliano Chaves in a Democratic Alliance that rapidly went from bandwagon to steamroller. Its mass rallies served as a constant reminder to the 686 electors, almost all of whom would be facing the electorate in 1986, of the political peril in going against the surging tide of public opinion—and appearing to have sold out to the blandishments of the country's consummate corrupter. Hence, on January 15, 1985, the electoral college opted for the squeaky clean, if unexciting, Neves by an overwhelming margin of 480 to 180. Yet this deserving political veteran was fated not to enjoy the fruits of victory.[6]

As had been the case in 1822, 1889, 1930, and 1946, many elements of Brazilian society expected that regime change would lead almost automatically to a substantially transformed political system. But this was a transition without rupture, one in which heavy participation by experienced politicians and powerful interests associated with the prior order would guarantee that although the bottle might be new, the contents would taste much like the old: clientelism laced with patronage and a dash of demagoguery. Transition to a viable system of competitive civilian politics after twenty-one years of military rule was by itself an arduous task, even without a transformation of long-established practices and ingrained behavior.

The first task on the new government's agenda was establishing a workable relationship between the executive and legislative branches of government while infusing responsiveness into the ponderous state machinery built up since 1964. Then came the laborious process of shaping a new constitutional framework for a complex society with enormous inequalities and developmental needs. There would be early elections for mayors of state capitals and strategic cities, appointed under the military regime, followed in 1986 by balloting for all governors, two senators per state, and a full array of federal and state legislators. Two years later would be elections in over four thousand municipalities as a prelude to 1989's first direct presidential elections in almost three decades—which required restructuring of the party system. If this political agenda were not formidable enough, there was also the task of husbanding a still fragile economic recovery and dealing with the forbidding social deficit accumulated during over nearly twenty-one years of military rule.

Ever hopeful, Brazilians had faith that Neves would find a way to pilot the country to the promised land of democracy and prosperity. Yet he would die of natural causes without even being inaugurated, leaving the task to the vice president, José Sarney (b. 1927 as José Ribamar Ferreira de Araújo Costa, but subsequently taking his father's first name as his last), an accommodationist politician from a second-line state in the northeast, viewed with reserve, if not suspicion, by most of the PMDB and virtually unknown to the Brazilian public. Liberal elements looked askance at his close ties to the military and reliance on old ARENA politicians, although recycled through brief affiliation with the Liberal Front Party (PFL). This mistrust left Sarney with no option but to follow the course that was most natural for him: governing in collaboration with the center and center-right. São Paulo congressman Ulysses Guimarães (b. 1916) assumed leadership of the center-left PMDB orphans, now junior partners in a government in which they had expected to rule the roost. The November elections of large-city mayors reinforced the PMDB's belief that it should be calling the shots, since it won in nineteen capitals and 110 of 201 other contests.

Yet much was accomplished in the early years of this accidental president's extremely challenging term. Legislation in May 1985 removed restrictions on organization of political parties, made presidential elections direct, and extended the vote to illiterates. But most of the congress had been elected in 1982 on the ticket of the military regime's governing party and were deeply suspicious of anything advocated by the PMDB's progressive wing. In the economic sphere the new government inherited an improved, and in most ways still improving, situation. Initially dependent on export expansion, economic recovery broadened into domestic commerce and agriculture. Internal consumption became the engine of economic growth as real salaries rose as part of a dramatic GDP expansion of 7.6 percent in 1986 (on the heels of 1985's 7.9 percent). Warning signs in

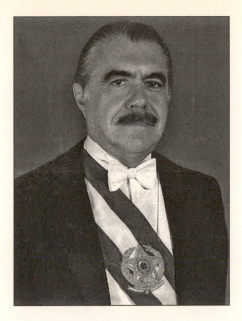

JOSÉ SARNEY

terms of falling exports and rising debt service in 1986 were overlooked in the euphoria of a spectacular drop in inflation from 235 percent in 1985 to only 65 percent for 1986.

Surging inflation at the end of 1985 and beginning of 1986 convinced Sarney to approve an economic program put together by finance minister Dílson Funaro (b. 1933) and a team of young, self-confident technocrats. Announced with great fanfare at the end of February, the Cruzado Plan fell into the category of "heterodox shock," combining a new currency (the cruzado, a cruzeiro with three zeros lopped off) with price and rent and mortgage freezes and a new wage system. Its rousing success in the short run led the government to continue it unchanged through the late-year elections. With monthly inflation rates cut to 2 percent, savings were funneled into productive investment rather than the merry-go-round of financial speculations that had become rampant. But economics, like politics, depends on collective human behavior, and an unbridled consumption boom resulted. With elections in November that would determine the nature of the governmental system and the tenure of the incumbent government, neither the president nor the PMDB could resist continuing a program that had produced massive public support for the regime. Hence, the price freeze combined with wage limitations was continued after it had begun to distort supply-demand relationships.[7]

With those adverse effects still in the future, an artificial atmosphere of prosperity guaranteed a massive electoral victory for the PMDB, with the PFL picking up the remainders. Thus, on November 15 a high proportion of the more than 69 million eligible citizens elected a congress that would also function as a constituent assembly to write a new constitution. As it would be the country's national legislature through 1990, with senators serving until early 1995, this body would play a crucial role in the consolidation of Brazil's still fledgling democratic regime. With governors and state legislatures also being chosen, the Democratic Alliance came away with all state chief executives, three-fourths of the lower house, and four-fifths of the senate. The existing opposition parties barely survived, and two dozen new parties failed to find voter responsiveness. Electing 261 federal deputies, the PMDB held a majority in the 487-member lower house, and its 45 seats gave it an even larger one in the senate. Twenty-two of twenty-three governorships went to PMDBers, although some were in coalition with the PFL. That party's 119 deputies were down only 10 from its establishment, and 16 senators were more than it had had going into the elections. The PDS paid dearly for its alignment with Maluf, as it fell from the 165 deputies and 31 senators it had had in 1985 to only 33 and 5. On the left, the PDT found little solace in 23 deputies—virtually unchanged—and the PT made much over having doubled its congressional representation, although this number was only 15 deputies on 5 percent of the vote (up from 3.3 percent in 1982).[8]

Public disillusionment came quickly as inflation began to climb toward record heights. Corrective economic policies decreed just after the elections aimed to reduce consumption and augment investment while giving the government additional revenues to decrease the public sector deficit—rather than attack it by reducing expenditures. In December the cost of living rose 7.3 percent, and in February 1987 Funaro and his PMDB economists convinced Sarney to decree a moratorium on foreign debt interest payments rather than take steps to reduce consumption—at that point the real engine of Brazil's inflation. The inevitable result was a drop in foreign investment combined with increase in remission of profits and dividends and rising capital flight. In recognition that Funaro was now a liability, Sarney replaced him in April with economist-businessman Luiz Carlos Bresser Pereira (b. 1934). Confident that, as author of books on the subject, he understood the real nature of Brazil's inflation, in June he launched a plan bearing his name. Centered on a temporary price freeze combined with a formula for keeping pay increases in check, the Bresser Plan brought inflation down, although for a very short time. In December the cost of living shot up by 14 percent as GDP growth for the year was only 3.6 percent—the lowest since the 1981–1983 recession.

In January 1988, Mailson Ferreira da Nóbrega, a career civil servant advocating a "rice and beans" alternative to his predecessors' creative heterodoxy, was named finance minister. As the changes he quickly made were already overdue, inflation for 1988 exploded from an unacceptable 416 percent in 1987 to a disconcerting 1040 percent, whereas economic growth was a depressing negative .1 percent despite a surge in exports to nearly $34 billion, producing a record $19.2 billion trade surplus, which was badly needed in light of $26.1 billion expended on debt service. On October 5 a new and in some ways contradictory constitution was promulgated, giving states and municipalities fiscal resources for which they had been accustomed to bargain with the central government and reducing the voting age to sixteen. Amendment was to be by a three-fifths majority of the congress until late 1993, at which time the congress elected in 1990 could temporarily change the constitution by a majority vote.[9]

Late 1988 elections for over 4,300 mayors and 43,600 municipal councilmen, although involving several hundred thousand candidates and mobilizing 75.8 million voters, did little to clarify the confused presidential succession picture. The two largest metropolitan centers were captured by the PT and the PDT, but neither of these parties of the left demonstrated significant strength on more than a regional level. In the midst of out-of-control inflation and disenchantment with the running of the country by the numerically dominant, but internally divided, PMDB, this party fell far short of its Cruzado Plan–inflated 1986 election triumph. Yet it remained Brazil's largest party, electing over 1,800 mayors on 25 percent of the countrywide vote compared to more than 1,400 for the PFL on just over 15 percent of the popular vote—enough to consolidate the PFL's position as the country's second-ranking party.

The party system's continuing fragmentation was reflected in the fact that the PT—despite all the hype it received in the US and European media when its Luíza Erundina (with under 38 percent of the vote) defeated the PDS's Paulo Maluf by 280,000 votes in a wide-open São Paulo electoral steeple chase—made only incremental progress toward becoming more than just a São Paulo party, coming away with only 38 mayors, winning in Porto Alegre and Vitoria, but losing in the two principal places outside of São Paulo where it had elected mayors in 1985. For its part, the PDS was a poor third nationally with close to 450 mayors, and the PDT garnered fewer than 200 mayors. The PSDB (Brazilian Social Democracy Party) proved to be still a party of many chiefs and few Indians, trailing far behind the PTB, which elected almost 400 mayors.[10]

The dreaded dragon of stagflation was a reality as 1989 opened, leading the government to announce the Spring Plan on January 15. The cruzado became the "new cruzado" by the lopping off of three zeros once again, and steps were taken to end indexation of wages, prices, and financial instruments and contracts. To prevent the 1986 fiasco, this plan was clearly of temporary duration. Hence, by February everything else took a backseat to direct election of a president for the first time since Quadros had been chosen in 1960. As on that occasion, the results would lead to extreme frustration. It was clear that the unpopularity of the Sarney government would all but eliminate its ability to influence the succession. With the stand-alone election coming near year's end, inflation at nearly 1800 percent, GDP growth at 3.3 percent, and foreign debt service exploding to $43.6 billion, Sarney's approval rating plunged—as would have happened in any other country, since management of the economy is always at or near the top of the electorate's concerns.

Only a small minority of Brazil's voters identified with the nearly two score political parties competing, if rarely competitive. Finding little appeal in ideologies and relatively uninterested in specific policies, voters were looking for a candidate, not a party and were ready to vote for a perceived savior. With many of the major party nominees in the senior citizen category, like seventy-three-year-old Ulysses Guimarães of the PMDB, who was expecting to be rewarded after three decades of electoral recess for distinguished service in restoring democracy. But a fresh new face captured the voter's fancy. Fernando Collor de Mello (b. 1948), the handsome and athletic son of an old-line northeastern politician, was the near-perfect media candidate. Indeed, before he became governor of the small north-eastern state of Alagoas, his career was in journalism, as had been his education.

Economically conservative, but socially centrist, Collor gained the nomination of a minor party, then set out with enormous energy and determination to woo the voters of the major parties. Substituting talk about modernization and blister-ing attacks upon corruption and abusive bureaucratic privileges for any profound criticism of the existing order, he made moralization and scathing denunciation of politicians the heart of his appeal. Leaving the left to Lula da Silva and Leonel Brizola and the right to Maluf, Collor went after the center, center-right, and center-left, but chiefly the great number of voters looking for someone deserving their trust.

At just over 82 million the electorate was swollen by the inclusion of sixteen and seventeen year olds. Nearly half the prospective voters were under thirty, and fewer than 15 percent above age fifty. Only a sixth had graduated from high school, 30 percent were barely able to read and write, and over a tenth were com-pletely literate. Hence, on November 15 the vast majority voted not even for the man, but for his image. When the dust settled, only Collor and Lula were left standing for the final round—a battle for the support of the majority of the elec-torate orphaned by the elimination of the also-rans upon whom they had pinned their hopes.[11] On December 17, after a final televised debate in which media pro-fessional Collor outdid the proletarian Lula, 35.1 million voters chose Collor, and 31.1 million backed Lula. Lula had picked up 19.5 million votes since the first round as opposed to 14.5 million for Collor, but Collor's 9 million-vote lead in the first round had been too much to overcome, at least with the impact of televi-sion factored in. Looking to the future, Lula and the PT had to ponder Collor's 700,000-vote margin in São Paulo, their home base.

The 1990s demonstrated that structures, practices, and attitudes built up over generations are highly resistant to change. Initial progress in political modernization was all but swept away in 1992 by corruption and influence-peddling scandals leading to impeachment of Collor, the erstwhile paladin of probity. This traumatic experience had the salutary effect of focusing the attention of the politically sophisticated minority on building stronger institutions rather than trusting all to a demagogic savior. But this was a long-term task, and in the meantime the traditional "art of not choosing between conflicting objectives" and the "proliferation of disguised mechanisms for transferring resources" persisted as the state continued to function primarily as distributor of benefits to holders of political power.[12] Moreover, the state's economic role, which had begun to expand its investments in government projects under Vargas, had grown greatly during military rule, becoming a major economic burden. From 1988 through 1993 the federal government infused $27 billion into state enterprises and received only $1.1 billion in dividends, significantly increasing its budget deficit. Even with the best of intentions, the new president could only begin to attack the most negative features of what Brazilian analysts termed O Sistema ("The System"). Events soon raised serious doubts as to his commitment to modernizing it.

Collor's initial economic program was reasonably successful. The economy's excessive liquidity was reduced by having $85 billion—most of it from the bloated "overnight" capital market that had become an inflation-feeding way of financing the government's internal debt, in 1989 an all but paralyzing 47.6 percent of GDP—frozen in blocked accounts while a new currency, the cruzeiro, was launched. Other measures, including privatization, fiscal reforms, and improved tax collection, were aimed at keeping inflation down by transforming the huge prospective public-sector operating deficit into a small surplus. In mid-1990, an industrial policy reducing protectionism and facilitating imports dealt a stiff blow to sectors of the Brazilian economy accustomed to virtually guaranteed profits at no real risk. From 80 percent in March, the rise in cost of living fell to under 15 percent in April and was halved again in May. But much more would be needed to overcome Brazil's inflationary culture, so the year's accumulation was just under 1500 percent, falling to 480 percent in 1991. Yet GDP shrank by 4.4 percent in 1990, and a minuscule 0.9 percent growth the next year was canceled out by the same slight shrinkage in 1992. Trade surpluses did remain substantial (at $10.9 billion, $10.6 billion, and $15.2 billion), and foreign debt service was cut from 1989's nearly $44 billion to a three-year average of only $17 billion.

With the initial euphoria dissipating, 84 million registered voters went to the polls on October 3, 1990, to choose which of roughly 20,000 candidates would fill 1,700 posts as governors, vice governors, senators, alternate senators, federal deputies, and state legislators. In the previous year's presidential contest the premium had been new faces, but for governors and senators Brazil's voters looked for experience and proven performance. Again the elections underscored the weakness of Brazil's political parties, and with local and regional issues playing an important role there was a strong center-right tilt to both the new the congress and the lineup of governors. The gross underrepresentation of São Paulo, combined with the grotesque overrepresentation of the smaller agrarian states, made progressive's efforts to increase their weight in the congress an uphill battle. The PMDB, weakened by the schism that had given birth to the PSDB, suffered further erosion of its erstwhile dominant position, as its erstwhile partner PFL moved up to near parity in the congress and to the lead in governorships.[13] The PSDB showed it had a long way to go, coming in sixth with only 37 deputies to the PMDB's 109 and the PFL's 86. The PDT took consolation in sixty-eight-year-old Brizola's recapturing the Rio de Janeiro governorship, and in holding even with 47 deputies, edging out the PDS at 43, for third place. Collor's National Renovation Party (PRN) finished fifth with 40 deputies. The PTB's 36 seats in the lower house pinned the PT back in eighth place with 35 (to go with a single senator and no governor, an outcome demonstrating that it was far from being a national party).

The Second Collor Plan in February 1991 featured a price and wage freeze, elimination of the overnight financial market, and abolition of monetary correction. In May, Collor fired Brazil's first female finance minister, replacing her with respected and experienced banker-diplomat Marcilio Marques Moreira (b. 1931). Drought had aggravated an agricultural disaster, and a 15 percent devaluation could not be avoided in October. But 1992's grain harvest was a near record. Also on the plus side, the 1991 census showed that population growth had been significantly less than estimated, with Brazil's 147 million inhabitants some 5 percent below projections, allowing an advantageous recalculation of per capita economic figures. Also Collor had demonstrated considerable political skill until crossing swords with Antônio Carlos Magalhães (b. 1927), back in as Bahia's governor for a third time. Assuming Collor's old pose as crusader against corruption, and backed by the media empire of Roberto Marinho, which had contributed mightily to Collor's election, Magalhães focused attention upon contradictions between the president's public statements and his unbridled behind-the-scenes wheeling and dealing.

By July congressional investigations had uncovered major campaign finance irregularities and highly organized influence peddling conducted by the president's closest collaborator. Hence, Collor saw his presidency end just after its scheduled midpoint as the impeachment process ran its course with a decisive lower-house vote on September 29 to remove him pending trial in the senate. Yet this crisis was a positive landmark, for the armed forces played no discernible role—in stark contrast to the unscheduled ends to presidential tenures in 1969, 1964, 1961, 1954–1955, 1945, and 1930. Vice President Itamar Augusto Cauteiro

Franco (b. 1930) assumed the vacated office, becoming the sixth citizen of Minas Gerais to attain Brazil's presidency (in a way, compensating for Tancredo Neves's demise in 1985).

An undistinguished politician, who after occupying the presidency would serve as his state's governor, Franco picked some able individuals to help his government escape from mediocrity, the most distinguished being his foreign minister, Fernando Henrique Cardoso, a renowned sociologist and PMDB senator from São Paulo. The October 3 municipal elections, coming on the second day of Franco's tenure, were remarkably unaffected by the national political crisis, with no party dramatically improving its position over the very mixed results of 1988. For the first time, runoffs were held in municipalities of over 200,000 registered voters, so the dust did not settle until after November 15. The top prize, São Paulo, fell to Maluf, putting an end to a streak of setbacks dating to his presidential defeat in 1984. He then merged the PDS and the Christian Democratic Party (PDC)—which had elected 211 mayors—into the Progressive Renewal Party (PPR).

In Rio de Janeiro two figures with bright political futures squared off, with César Maia (b. 1945) foiling a bid by the PT's Benedita da Silva (b. 1942) to be the first Afro-Brazilian woman to reach high elected office. (Daughter of a laundress and a construction laborer, she received 934,000 votes on the first ballot and narrowly lost the runoff with 1.36 million votes to Maia's 1.43 million.) Nationally the PMDB elected 33.7 percent of the 4,762 mayors, followed by the PFL with 20.3 percent, the PDT with 7.9 percent, and the PDS at 7.6 percent. The PSDB won 6.7 percent of mayoral races and the PTB 6.4. The PT continued its slow drive toward becoming a national party by emerging on top in only fifty-two cities. December 29 witnessed the race between the Senate's overwhelming vote to convict and Collor's vain effort to beat them to the punch by resigning.[14]

Economic performance in 1993 was mixed. Inflation shot up to a record 2670 percent, but the stagflation of recent years was broken with a lusty 4.2 percent GDP growth, back where it had been before the 1990 disaster. Exports were at a high $39 billion, producing a healthy $13-billion trade surplus and bringing foreign exchange reserves up to $32 billion. The inflow of investment, direct and portfolio, exceeded $7 billion, pushing stock market prices up 100 percent in real terms, and new foreign loans reached $10 billion. With a weather eye on the success of Argentina's anti-inflation program, Cardoso reluctantly assumed the finance ministry in May 1993, never imagining the full consequences—and benefits—of this shift of portfolios. Announced early in 1994, the Real Plan's main features went into effect at midyear, most dramatically a partial and indirect shift to a dollar-linked new currency, the real, but also including elimination of governmental deficit financing. The plan's instant success and credibility quickly transformed Cardoso into the government's stop-Lula presidential candidate, then, by August, into the leader on his way to becoming a prohibitive favorite. (In the longer run the plan would give Brazil its first eight-year president since 1946 and only the second in the history of the republic.)[15]

The October 1994 elections dwarfed even those of 1989–1990, as almost 12,000 candidates sought the favor of nearly 95 million voters to fill over 1,700 positions, a majority of them in the states. Although Lula's presidential campaign built up early momentum, since he had never really stopped running, Cardoso, who stepped down as finance minister in March, had the advantage of much stronger coalitions and candidates at the state level as he ran on an alliance of the PSDB, the PFL, and the PTB. His decisive card was the success of the Real Plan, as dramatically falling inflation rates, combined with euphoria over the July World Cup soccer triumph, left voters in an optimistic mood. Basically, Brazilian voters, having been stung the last time around, went for performance and credibility. (Whether this preference would be repeated in 2006 remained a key question.) They generally viewed Cardoso as representing the improvement in conditions during 1993 and 1994. Being author of the Real Plan was enough; added to an image for personal integrity and responsibility, as well as a more presidential demeanor than that shown by Franco, and an international reputation as a progressive scholar of development problems, to win over a large proportion of voters whose favorite party had backed its own lesser candidate.

On October 3 some 78 million voters gave Cardoso 34.4 million votes, twice Lula's 17.1 million. Cardoso carried all states except Rio Grande do Sul and the Federal District as the also-rans suffered varying degrees of single-digit electoral humiliation. Candidates associated with Cardoso won all key statehouses, with Antônio Carlos Magalhães consolidating his hold over Bahia and moving into the Senate, ex-president Sarney electing his daughter governor of their home state, to solidify his position as a power in the PMDB. All that the PT salvaged out of its overoptimistic hopes was the election of Afro-Brazilian slum-dwellers' organizer Benedita da Silva to the Senate from Rio de Janeiro—with 2.25 million votes—along with three minor figures from lesser states and two governors.

The lineup in the lower house was the PMDB 107, PFL 89, PSDB 62, PPR 53, Lula's PT 49, PP 36, Brizola's PDT 33, PTB 31, Brazilian Socialist Party (PSB) 15, Liberal Party (PL) 13, and the Communist Party of Brazil (PCdoB) 10.[16] Brazil's voters seemed to have learned well from recent experience. Overall, they demonstrated increased maturity and discrimination: Ex-governors who had done well in earlier terms were in many cases returned for a second stint; those whose terms were ending were generally rewarded with Senate seats good to 2002; capital city mayors who had performed well were often promoted to governor; and the candidates of governors who had failed to measure up to their 1990 promises paid for their sponsors' shortcomings.

So Cardoso embarked on what was expected to be a single term as president with his core coalition having 182 seats in the lower house, and parties that were clamoring to join his government having more than enough legislators to push his working majority near the three-fifths level needed for constitutional amendments—although party discipline was notoriously weak, requiring judicious use of patronage and pork. Accustomed to playing a leading role in the congress, Cardoso started auspiciously. There had been a record harvest of 75 million tons of grain in 1994, and it would rise further during Cardoso's first year in office. The new currency demonstrated great strength relative to the dollar, and foreign exchange reserves piled up to near $40 billion, while Brazil continued to run large trade surpluses despite increased imports. Inflation for 1994 was 930 percent, but for the six months the Real Plan was in effect, it was only 22 percent—well under half of the monthly rate before it went into effect—and GDP growth was a lusty 5.9 percent.

Born in 1931 in Rio de Janeiro to a family with a long tradition of army generals, Cardoso studied and made his academic career in São Paulo.[17] Fourteen at the time of Vargas's 1945 ouster and twenty-three when Vargas took his own life, Cardoso followed a long and gradual path from left toward center, particularly from the 1970s on. By the late 1950s, he had abandoned the Marxist-Leninist ideology of Florestan Fernandes, his mentor in the University of São Paulo's sociology department. Owing to close associations with individuals and movements of the far left, he found it prudent to go into exile in Chile after the military takeover in 1964. There he played a leading role in developing dependency theory (the popular political science approach of the 1960s and 1970s) before accepting a professorship at the working-class suburban branch of the University of Paris, where the spring 1968 uprisings involved many of his students and colleagues.

Following his return to Brazil later that year, Cardoso began to moderate and modify his views, founding the Brazilian Center of Analysis and Planning (CEBRAP) and conducting policy-oriented research as well as conceptual work at the same time he became involved in electoral politics. Running for the senate in 1978, he polled one-sixth the vote of the winner, but as first alternate he moved up when André Franco Montoro (b. 1916) was elected São Paulo governor in 1982. Having participated actively in discussions leading to the creation of the PT, he decided to stay with the PMDB, working as the upper-house collaborator of bellwether congressman Ulysses Guimarães. Following a narrow loss to ex-president Jânio Quadros in the 1985 race for São Paulo mayor, a valuable learning experience in political campaigning, Cardoso was comfortably returned to the senate in 1986, continuing to function as the Sarney government's leader in the congress.

In 1988, Cardoso took a major part in forming the PSDB as a split of progressive elements from the nonideological PMDB, controlled in São Paulo at that time by a practitioner of clientelistic politics, Orestes Quércia. Throughout the events of the early 1990s, Cardoso maintained credibility as a pragmatic social democrat—

**FERNANDO HENRIQUE
CARDOSO**
(CREDIT: RICARDO STUCKERT/ABR.)

staying out of Collor's cabinet because of pressure from his party before becoming foreign minister under Itamar Franco. During the 1994 campaign, assuming the appealing political persona of "FHC," he demonstrated greatly improved campaign skills, accepting advice from such electoral whizzes as Antônio Carlos Magalhães and ex-president Sarney when operating outside Brazil's developed urban center. At the same time he projected a carefully honed image of competence and reliability through the electronic media.

As president, Cardoso had ex-president Sarney and PFL leader Antônio Carlos Magalhães as major allies as they rotated in the senate presidency. (Moreover, the latter's son initially presided over the lower house.) Through many cabinet changes Pedro Sampaio Malan (b. 1943) was a fixture as finance minister. Since the Real Plan had gotten Cardoso to the presidency, he was determined to maintain its integrity against all demands from political forces for "flexibility," a euphemism for electorally popular loosening of the purse strings. Indeed, the touchstone of Cardoso's first term was continued success of his economic program.[18] In 1995, the rise in the cost of living dropped dramatically to 22 percent, followed by 9 percent in 1996 and less than half that for 1997. Although economic growth fell off to a still healthy 4.2 percent in 1995 and slipped to 2.7 percent in 1996, some 40 million new consumers had been brought into the money economy as a result of inflation's demise. In this highly favorable environment Cardoso's backers held firm in the October 1996 municipal elections.

The PSDB began its rise toward national leadership by edging out the PMDB with more than 13 million votes to just over 12.7 million, but the PMDB bested the PSDB in the election of mayors 1,295 to 921. Actually, the PFL, with almost 10.1 million votes, was second in terms of city halls won with 934. The PPR came in fourth both in votes (at 9.8 million) and in mayors elected (with 625). Still struggling to become a truly national party, the PT was fifth in electoral support with 7.9 million but, owing to its concentration in the large cities, came away with only 110 mayors, whereas the PDT's just under 7 million votes resulted in control of 436 local executives. The PTB remained a player with nearly 4.4 million votes (almost 6 percent) and 382 mayors. The PSB, PL, and PSD rounded out the top ten in Brazil's fragmented party system with 2.8 million votes and 150 *prefeitos* (mayors), 2.0 million votes and 222 mayors, and 1.2 million votes and 116 mayors, respectively. The favorable results for the progovernment parties bolstered Cardoso's prospects of reelection.

In what would be the beginning of a prolonged trend, rural areas were left out of the progress so visible in cities and towns. The predictable result was a continuing rise in violent struggles over land as the government's modest agrarian reform program whetted appetites of militant landless groups far faster than it could satisfy their desires. Still Cardoso's popularity in largely urban Brazil led to passage in 1997 of a constitutional amendment permitting presidential reelection (extended also to governors and mayors). This measure, paralleling actions taken in Argentina and Peru, greatly strengthened Cardoso's hand and removed the specter of approaching lame-duck status, as most politicians worked with the probability that he would be at the country's helm through 2002. Cracks in the global economy led to a program of fiscal constraints in late 1997 as $10 billion in foreign exchange reserves were expended fighting off a concerted attack upon the overvalued real.

Backed by an alliance of his own PSDB, the PFL, the PMDB, the PPR, and several smaller parties, and with economic growth rallying to 3.3 percent, Cardoso was able to enact major fiscal and administrative reforms in 1998 while accelerating the process of privatization of state enterprises begun under Collor and continued at a slow pace by Franco. Not even the negative impact of the Asian and Russian market collapses could derail Cardoso's reelection steamroller. In October he received 35.9 million votes to 21.5 million for Lula. Moreover, with an electorate greatly expanded to embrace two-thirds of the country's population—compared to one-sixth in 1946—the array of parties backing Cardoso rode the wave of popular support for his management of the economy to retain their decisive congressional majorities.[19] Continued political stability thus assured, an

IMF-led $42-billion financial support program was put in place in November 1998, and significant parts of the requisite fiscal, pension, and administrative reforms were duly enacted during 1999. Highly symbolic was the creation at the beginning of Cardoso's second term of a ministry of defense headed by a civilian (replacing the separate service ministries headed by military chiefs). This move was followed by devaluation of the real, which had been under attack by international speculators and now was allowed to find its market value relative to foreign currencies. By the end of 1999 international confidence in Brazil's future was again on the upswing—based on the government's demonstrated competence—although concern over social problems, particularly urban violence, rural land seizures, and ineffective police work, was on the rise. Although economic growth was a paltry 0.1 percent in 1998 and a meager 0.8 percent the next year, it was on the way to a robust 4.3 percent for 2000, as the country would enter the new century with Cardoso's experienced hand at the helm.

Mexico: From a Hegemonic System to Full Democracy

Compared to Brazil, as well as a good number of other Latin American countries, Mexico's political development for most of the 1980s and 1990s seemed limited, and in the eyes of many observers, inadequate. Yet in retrospect it appears that this once-monolithic single-party system did a better job of a controlled transition to full competitiveness than communist analogues were able to do in the former Soviet Union and Eastern Europe. Taking into account the extreme difficulty and perils of opening up a semiauthoritarian system without exposing its political processes to dangerous breakdown, Mexico handled the problem quite well. Certainly leadership passed into the hands of a younger and technically well-qualified generation, and the 1994 election was not marred by fraud as that of 1988 had been, or even the amount of fraud customary before that excess. The winner undertook to make the next elections fully free and democratic even at the risk of the PRI's loss of the power it had held since the 1920s.[20] Although corruption continued to be a major problem, Mexican's traditional high tolerance of graft and fraud was substantially diminished during the last part of this period, and the greatly increased degree of political competitiveness ushered in the beginning of higher standards and more effective controls. Comparative study of this near-universal phenomenon of politically related corruption indicates that a wave of major scandals is usually more closely related to an erosion of the tradition of impunity, hence public outcry and even outrage where resignation had reigned, than it is a reflection of increased corruption. Essentially, what was long taken for granted becomes no longer acceptable (as was the case with business practices in the United States in the early 2000s).

The great progress Mexico made toward putting an entrenched semiauthoritarian system behind and transforming it into a functioning democracy was not apparent until the end of the 1990s, when an opposition candidate won the presidential elections—unheard of since a Liberal's victory in the mid-1850s. This was a momentous event for Mexico and for Latin America, extending the benefits of competitive electoral democracy to over 100 million individuals in one fell swoop. It caught many observers by surprise, since at the beginning of this period the system of single-party hegemony established at the end of the 1920s had appeared to be firmly in place, a judgment that could still be accurately made in the mid-1980s, and many experts believed into the late 1990s that the PRI would do anything to hold onto power, not open the system up to full competition.

When the period opened, it was clear that, as had been the case for decades, it was a foregone conclusion that the next president would be whoever was the PRI standard bearer, with the incumbent president, within very loose constraints, deciding his successor's identity. Hence, by his second year as president, José López Portillo, elected at the end of 1976, knew that shaping the succession process was his top priority, along with making sure, or at least being assured, that the economy did not go completely off the tracks. Given his role as chief architect of economic policy in the preceding Echeverría administration, López Portillo was confident that he knew what had to be done. As had been the case a dozen years earlier, he, like Díaz Ordaz, would handle the succession through a process of elimination rather than starting with an heir apparent.[21] Hence, the all-important choice would eventually fall upon someone earning it as the *sexénio* progressed, not any of the early favorites. The original pair of front-runners, ensconced in the ministries of finance and planning and budget, carried on a monumental and ill-concealed struggle over the 1978 budget that exasperated the president and resulted in both of those presidential wannabes leaving the cabinet and being effectively exiled from the center of governmental and political affairs. As the central economic policy issue shifted in early 1980 to Mexico's entry into the General Agreement on Trade and Tariffs (GATT), one potential candidate after another fell by the wayside.

With economic problems mounting as 1981 wore on, López Portillo turned increasingly to the optimistic bearer of good economic tidings, planning and budget minister Miguel de la Madrid Hurtado (b. 1934). During the crucial third quarter of 1981, de la Madrid found a useful new ally in the person of young Carlos Salinas de Gortari (b. 1948), whose deficit projections were closer to de la Madrid's uncritically optimistic ones than to the finance minister's realistically pessimistic, indeed alarming, estimates. Only after de la Madrid won the battle of dueling estimates and was safely launched as the PRI candidate in late September 1981 were his and Salinas's deficit projections revised upward. In the real world, as distinguished from the insulated presidential palace, 1981 was a nearly disastrous year economically. Overproduction of oil turned into a glut resulting in sharply dropping prices for crude. This fall in oil prices, combined with stagnant exports, devalued currency, and high foreign debt, frightened investors, who pulled their money out of Mexico—turned overnight from belle of the ball to wallflower. As described by a close student of Mexican affairs:

> Instead of putting the brakes on the state's economic expansion, López Portillo actually stepped on the accelerator. In his last year in office, without warning or consultation, he announced nationalization of the domestic banking system. With a single decree, the president increased state control over the economy. . . . The move exacerbated the business community's lack of trust in the government and strongly encouraged the flight of capital from Mexico, primarily to the United States.[22]

López Portillo reacted by instituting exchange controls to protect the peso, but by 1982 inflation had soared to 100 percent, the peso had lost 40 percent of its value, and the economy was shrinking. The disillusioned president's option for finance specialist de la Madrid over PRI head Javier García Paniagua was too far along for him to reverse course when he finally came to realize that de la Madrid seemed determined to chart his own course even before the election, much less waiting until after his inauguration. In this decision, the future president may have had little choice, since his erstwhile sponsor's legacy was no longer a positive one. In the eyes of a leading Mexican statesman-scholar:

> . . . The political crisis he [de la Madrid] inherited from López Portillo in the wake of the bank nationalization and the virtual expropriation of dollar-denominated savings not only severed the fragile strands of trust between the system and the middle classes who had thrived on the former's success but also destroyed complicity and convergence of years past between the business elite and the political establishment. Nevertheless the political crisis of 1982 pales next to the country's economic collapse. De la Madrid inherited a government devoid of hard currency, without reserves, and with public finances in a shambles and the country's foreign credit practically exhausted.[23]

The 1982 election, conducted under significant reforms introduced in 1977 (the Federal Law of Political Organizations and Electoral Processes), went reasonably smoothly, with de la Madrid receiving nearly 72 percent of the vote to just over 16 percent for the sacrificial lamb candidate of the opposition National Action Party (PAN). Three-quarters of registered voters turned out on election day. This record total of 22.5 million actual voters—in a country with 73.1 million inhabitants—was three times that of 1958 and up by 5.6 million over 1976, partially disguising the fact that the PRI's winning percentage was well below the huge margins rolled up in the preceding four presidential sweepstakes. Membership requirements for parties had been lowered, and the lower house's size had been raised to 400, with 100 reserved for minority parties on the basis of proportional representation—compared to the 30–40 they had been getting since 1964. By encouraging three new splinter parties to participate through the certainty of getting at least a handful of seats, this measure had raised the non–PRI representation from 17.4 percent in 1976 to 21 percent in 1979—as the PAN actually won 4 of the 300 single-member district seats. Now the breakdown of the new chamber was 299 for the PRI to 51 for the PAN, with four minor parties awarded 17, 12, 11, and 10 seats from the proportional pool—very little change from the midterm results of 1979. Indeed, the PRI's 69.3 percent share of the vote, although down, yielded 3 more seats, and the PAN demonstrated significant, but nonspectacular progress, going from 10.8 percent of the vote to 17.5 percent.[24] Little did the president-elect imagine that this would be the last "normal"—that is, controlled—succession because of divisions taking place within his mammoth PRI as much as—or more than—because of the growth and diversification of the opposition.

With over half the government's revenues going toward debt service, prices soaring, and labor becoming unruly, de la Madrid shifted to full alignment with IMF policies, including curbing inflation, privatizing many government holdings, and lowering tariffs. To distract attention from the country's economic woes, he initiated a crusade against corruption under the banner of "moral renovation." He began to open Mexico's closed, nearly monopolistic political system by acknowledging PAN victories in a number of municipalities. In 1985, two major earthquakes in central Mexico created a heavy burden of disaster relief and reconstruction. Budgetary restraint required reduction of subsidies and cutbacks in government investments, along with a partial hiring freeze. Then, near the end of his term, a drastic devaluation of the peso triggered a staggering surge of inflation. Wage and price controls were instituted, and a $3.5-billion loan from the United States partially eased the revenue shortfall from the continuing drop in oil prices. The midterm congressional elections provided a misleading picture of normality, as the PRI's 289 seats in the lower house were 10 less than before, but the PAN also dropped 10 seats—a much more significant proportional loss from 51 to 41. The former's share of the vote slipped 4.3 percent to 65.0 percent, and the latter's 15.5 percent marked a decline of 2 percent.[25]

As the long era of PRI dominance moved toward its eventual end, Mexico's unique presidential succession process underwent significant change. López Portillo had chosen de la Madrid through a process that began with elimination of candidates with whom he had had longer and closer personal ties. From the beginning of his term, de la Madrid seriously considered only two possibilities. The first, respected finance minister Jesús Silva Herzog, born the same year as the president, was a peer of de la Madrid in almost every significant aspect. The eventual winner was Carlos Salinas, the much younger budget and planning minister, who positioned himself as a generational change who would still ensure continuity of de la Madrid's priorities. Salinas rooted his bid in a close association as a trusted collaborator of de la Madrid going back to 1979, when de la Madrid occupied the ministerial post to which he advanced in 1982 and Salinas was his closest aide. Although his personal relation with the president did not go back as far in time as that of Silva Herzog, de la Madrid and Salinas had in common that both had earned graduate degrees at Harvard.[26] Moreover, although not yet forty, Salinas was the son of an old-line PRI politico and thus not a party outsider.

Starting from behind, Salinas worked harder and with greater determination than his rival to bring about his rival's downfall. He quietly built support from within the party-government machine, while Silva Herzog, an academic rather than a political insider, was busy courting the international community, business, and the media (none of which had an impact in Mexico's peculiar process of political recruitment). Wisely, Salinas's closest alliance was forged with the presidential chief of staff, Emilio Gamboa Patrón. Battle was openly joined over the 1984 budget and reopened the next year. As revenues fell during what was known as *La Crisis* ("The Crisis," as distinct from lesser ones), Salinas refused to cut expenses, earning the gratitude of government agencies and state governors. For his part Silva Herzog fought against raising taxes to cover these expenditures, and his international and media acclaim began to irritate the extremely proud and somewhat vain de la Madrid.

When crude oil prices dropped to a devastating $8 a barrel in early 1986—a drop that cost Mexico some $6 billion in anticipated revenue—Silva Herzog increasingly appeared to the president as perhaps too concerned about his image and appearing presidential rather than about furthering the interests and objectives of the chief executive. In the escalating intramural warfare between the two economic ministries, the president sided with Salinas against further deep budget cuts. This partisanship sealed the Salinas's ascension and led to Silva Herzog's resignation. Salinas added to his prestige when the United States, the IMF, and the World Bank approved a massive $9-billion assistance program for Mexico without requiring either the spending cuts or the tax increases that his critics had insisted the international agencies would demand. All that remained was for the president to protect his chosen one by concealing his preference, publicly posing Alfredo del Mazo and Manuel Bartlett alongside Salinas as presidential possibilities so that the hard-fighting and determined Bartlett would not concentrate his fire solely on Salinas.

In March 1987, Cuauhtémoc Cárdenas Solórzano (b. 1934), son of the revered 1934–1940 president, and Porfirio Muñoz Ledo, leaders of the "democratic current" within the party, both of them feeling that they richly deserved a chance to be the official candidate, publicly split with the PRI. The interior minister's reaction seemed too conciliatory for a president hostile to PRI dissidents, costing this hopeful any slim chance that he might still have had for the coveted presidential backing. Hence, in early October 1987, the PRI ratified the president's choice of Salinas and bestowed the party's nomination on him.

The campaign saw the candidates put forth very different views of the economic situation, one in which per capita GDP was down 12.4 percent; workers had lost 40 percent of their purchasing power since de la Madrid's election; 1987 inflation stood at 160 percent; and the country's foreign debt had passed $100 billion. Although defending de la Madrid's free-market policies, of which he had been a major architect, Salinas prudently withheld endorsement of NAFTA (the North American Free Trade Agreement), in light of widespread fear that it would create a very unbalanced partnership. Cárdenas took a nationalistic line, denouncing excessive foreign influence and defending state enterprises, while calling the de la Madrid government dictatorial and depicting Salinas as representing the status quo. PAN standard bearer Manuel Clouthier, an energetic and outspoken northern businessman, advocated removing existing barriers to private investment and questioned Cárdenas's commitment to spreading democracy into all sectors of national life, depicting him as an unbridled leftist.[27]

The July 6, 1988, elections took place under changes enacted in 1986, and the momentous official results—in which participation dropped sharply to only half the registered electorate—were 50.7 percent for Salinas; 32.5 percent for Cárdenas, running on the ticket of the National Democratic Front; and 16.8 percent for PAN nominee Clouthier. This bare majority for the PRI candidate was crucial, as less than 50 percent would have required ratification by the lower house of the congress. Although passions run high, one credible analysis indicates that fraud in ballot counting was used to get Salinas's vote above 50 percent, but that it was not sufficient to rob Cárdenas of victory. Other observers are less sanguine, with Cárdenas's backers arguing that he actually received more votes than Salinas.[28] After some hesitation by the government and belligerent bluster from the opposition, Salinas was certified as having been duly elected, and public outcry died away much as it would in the United States in the aftermath of George W. Bush's disputed 2000 presidential win over Al Gore.

Cárdenas carried his home state of Michoacán by a landslide and also took Baja California del Norte, Morelos, and Mexico State, possibly also Guerrero and maybe Oaxaca. In contrast to showing a tranquil public face, the PRI was severely shaken, although not yet trembling. Its 50.4 percent of the chamber vote was sharply down from that of 1985, but the party came away with 260 seats (233 from districts and 27 from the proportional pool) in a body enlarged to 500, compared to the PAN's jump up to 101 (on a modest increase in electoral share to

17.1 percent); the Cardenista Front for National Reconstruction Party won 51 seats (with 10.5 percent of the vote), and the Party of the Democratic Revolution (PRD) 26 (putting it close on the heels of the Authentic Party of the Mexican Revolution, PARM, at 28). Thus, the divided opposition took 48 percent of the chamber seats, a quantum leap over any past performance. Cárdenas, after touring the country leading protest rallies, played a major role in organizing the PRD as a prospective national political force.

The scandals and criminal charges that surrounded Salinas after leaving office, many stemming from illicit activities by his brother and cronies, should not obscure the fact that his management of the economy was in many ways superior to that of most other Mexican presidents and a large proportion of his Latin American contemporaries. Facing an inherited mountain of foreign debt, he carried through a massive privatization of state enterprises, blocked from going further by the "untouchable" status accorded by Mexicans to Pemex. Within five years Mexico's economy went from critical to essentially sound, with GDP growth high enough, despite population growth, to chalk up sustained per capita gains. Foreign investment by the end of his term had risen from $13.5 billion to $60.6 billion (compared to an $8-billion increase under de la Madrid), and inflation had dropped from 52 percent when he took office to 8 percent in 1993. Salinas's biggest gamble, one he considered unavoidable, was negotiating, signing, and ratifying NAFTA before the end of his term. Prior to this, his heavy emphasis on privatization had augmented government revenues but had also provided opportunities for enrichment of friends and family. Some of the new revenues did go into Salinas's trademark project, the National Solidarity Program, designed to encourage grassroots organization and leadership, but also clearly useful in providing electoral support and enhancing the president's popularity.[29]

With the PRI's dominant electoral support now a thing of the past, Salinas, unlike any of his predecessors, was well aware that whomever he chose as his successor would face a stiff challenge at the polls. This meant, above other criteria, choosing a candidate who could win, perhaps even more than one who would continue his predecessor's policies and keep on some of his key associates. Salinas also realized that he would have to take into account the increased sensibilities of individuals and factions because the party was still in a state of shock over its narrow escape from disaster. As an experienced political insider, Castañeda portrays Salinas's mind-set:

> . . . The need to take excruciating pains to keep the ruling party united, not promoting pasarelas (street demonstrations and rallies) or publicly parading the candidates, to avoid encouraging feelings of defeat or open manipulation among disappointed hopefuls or their followers by refusing to place losing prospects in delicate positions, and to ensure that the real sources of

power in Mexico got to know the possible candidates and would be willing to applaud whichever of them he chose.[30]

Salinas was, however, unaware that he would have to make the choice of of a successor twice, the second time under dire circumstances and severe time constraints. Moreover, he realized that he could not afford to provoke another division of the party. As Castañeda aptly puts it, "The job description required a PRI politician with technical training and ideological, regional, personal, and age-group affinity with Salinas."[31]

Salinas attempted to manage the succession much along the lines followed by Echeverría in 1976. Early favorites quickly blotted their copybooks: in the president's view, Mexico City mayor, Manuel Camacho, was too preoccupied with keeping active in national government matters (rather than devoting himself to his present office), and finance minister Pedro Aspe, with an economics doctorate from MIT, repeated Silva Herzog's mistake of becoming the focus of too much public credit as architect of the administration's reforms and innovations. As Castañeda points out, "The idea of handing over his legacy, his place in history, and his own and his family's integrity to an individual endowed with a personality and international recognition of his own has never been a seductive one to any Mexican president."[32]

The new factor was the need for a candidate able to win against stiff competition from both Cárdenas and the PAN, indeed a stronger candidate from a political point of view than Salinas himself had been. Salinas and his sponsor, de la Madrid, were both intellectual, highly educated, technocratic types; their successor had to be someone who could go out on the campaign trail and mix it up with his challengers in a verbal slugfest if necessary, or in a personality pageant if that was what it took. The PRI had never lost. To keep this tradition going, it could not afford to back a loser, but the mood of the electorate was difficult to judge. In the 1991 midterm congressional voting—with a turnout up to 61 percent—the PRI had won a heartening 321 of 500 chamber seats, receiving 61.4 percent of the vote to the 17.7 percent that gave the PAN 90 seats (the PRD had to settle for 40, since many who had voted for Cárdenas in 1988 did not carry their enthusiasm over to little-known congressional aspirants), thus regaining the three-fifths majority lost in the midst of the torrid presidential race of 1988.[33]

In contrast to Camacho and Aspe, Luis Donaldo Colosio (b. 1950) was an expert on campaigns and elections. He had served as Salinas's campaign manager beginning in 1987. After starting the new administration as party head, and having a short experience in the senate, Colosio was named minister of social development in late 1991—an assignment that made him familiar with the country and the country with him, largely through the Solidarity Program of bringing services and benefits to the community level. The strong impingement of international

ERNESTO ZEDILLO
(CREDIT: MINISTÈRE DES AFFAIRES
ÉSTRANGÈRES—SERVICE
PHOTOGRAPHIQUE)

factors severely constrained the window for announcing the succession decision. It had to be after the November 1 Mexican State of the Union address and the US ratification of the NAFTA Treaty—a date beyond Mexican influence, much less control—and before the mid-December onset of end-of-the-year festivities. Hence, late November 1993 saw the PRI formally nominate Colosio, who compromised with Salinas on Ernesto Zedillo Ponce de León (b. 1951) as his campaign manager.

By the beginning of 1994, tension between the president and the candidate became palpable. The trigger was the peasant rebellion in Chiapas, where rebels of Mayan extraction seized several towns and, calling themselves the Zapatista Army of National Liberation (EZLN), issued a list of demands for reforms and democracy; almost 200 deaths resulted from clashes with the army.[34] This development provided Colosio's critics an opportunity to rally around the shocked president, who gave Camacho, whom Colosio had bested in the presidential succession process, the highly visible role of mediating this globally watched insurrection as the head of a team including members of the PRD and PAN. Camacho's departure from the cabinet made him legally eligible for the presidency, a fact that stirred up Colosio nightmares of a Salinas reversal. Salinas put this fear to rest only on the eve of Colosio's March 23, 1994, assassination while campaigning in Tijuana. This tragic event created a need to decide upon a new candidate in a matter of days. Once the idea of a constitutional amendment was discarded, no viable alternative to Zedillo emerged. He alone combined prospects for continuation of the president's economic policies and members of his team.

Having won the battle for the PRI's nomination, Zedillo faced real competition for election. If Salinas had been overconfident in 1988, Zedillo could not afford to be, for all eyes were peeled for electoral fraud, and he strongly desired to enjoy a greater aura of legitimacy than had the administration from which he was emerging.[35] His own party was deeply split between an open-up-to-meaningful-competition wing and a hold-the-line, clamp-down faction insisting on the need to carry PRI control into the twenty-first century at any cost. The left opposition, banded together in the PRD, was running Cárdenas for a second time and exuding a good deal of optimism. Indeed, the PRD's leadership felt that, if not the real winner in 1988, Cárdenas had come at least as tantalizingly close to victory as Mitterand had in France in 1974 before his 1981 election as president. Cárdenas, as PRI governor of his father's state of Michoacán from 1980 to 1986, had actively sought the governing party's 1988 presidential nomination, and regarded Salinas as having been too young and politically inexperienced to have earned the nomination fairly. However, in his second presidential campaign, Cárdenas had little new to say, and the collapse of the Soviet Union and the Eastern European communist regimes made his basic stump speech seem oddly dated, almost as if he were doing a rerun of 1988. The right-wing opposition PAN came up with an effective candidate in the person of Diego Fernández de Cevallos, its floor leader in the lower house, thus dividing the anti-PRI voters.

Cárdenas focused his campaign on the unfairness of existing economic, social, and political practices, promising protection of workers' rights and the environment, and calling for "true" democracy. Bluntly labeling Salinas's administration repressive and dictatorial, he cautioned that the government needed to be much more selective about foreign investment, rejecting what might infringe on national sovereignty. Fernández, having by far the best slogan in "For a Mexico without lies," pictured himself as the only true democrat in light of Cárdenas's deep roots in the PRI and association with past governments. He was by far the most skilled debater among the presidential hopefuls, and he homed in on the issue of poverty, asking Zedillo how he could praise Salinas and trumpet his administration's accomplishments when forty million Mexicans were living in poverty. Fernández appeared to be much more populist than the PAN standard bearer in 1988 had been and thus helped to soften the party's conservative reputation. Attacked from both left and right, Zedillo had little choice but to remind voters that the PRI was their best hope to meet their needs, since after all Salinas had been the engineer of the country's economic recovery.

When the dust settled after the mid-August balloting, Cárdenas had slipped badly to 16.6 percent of the vote, compared to nearly 26 percent for Fernández. The winner, with 48.8 percent, was Zedillo—as turnout had recovered sharply to nearly four-fifths of those eligible. With the law having been reformed to prevent the plurality party from allocating itself seats from the proportional pool to guarantee a majority, the new Chamber of Deputies had 300 from the PRI, 119 from PAN, 71 from the PRD, and 10 from the minor Workers' Party. In the Senate, doubled in size from 64 to 128, the breakdown was 96 for the PRI, 24 from PAN, and only 8 from the PRD. Yet the PRI's sharp drop to 50.3 percent of the congressional vote, coupled with the PAN's rise to 25.8 percent and the PRD's 16.1 percent, constituted a clear wakeup call to the lifetime ruling party.[36]

Zedillo, at forty-five, in the normal course of events would have been a contender for the 2000 elections, rather than for those of 1994, but he advanced early to the presidency, just as César Gaviria had been forced to step up ahead of time in 1990 in Colombia after the murder of Luis Carlos Galán. Graduating from the National Polytechnic Institute in 1972, between 1974 and 1978 he earned both a master's degree and a doctorate in economics at Yale, with a dissertation on the management of public debt. After almost a decade of steady career progress within the Central Bank, he moved to the number two post in the budget and planning ministry in 1987 and on to becoming its head in 1988, before assuming the secretary of education portfolio in 1992.[37] Upon his assuming the presidency on December 1, 1994—in a country whose population had swollen to 94 million—friction between Salinas and Zedillo was almost immediate, fostered by both the ex-president's brother and the finance minister, Pedro Aspe, who had been instrumental in withdrawing support from the highly overvalued peso, the results being a tailspinning exchange rate and the concomitant sharp economic contraction—with GDP shrinking by 7 percent in 1995 and bank bailouts amounting to $80 billion. As Camp sees it:

> The result of the crises caused by the devaluation of the peso is that Mexico faced negative economic growth in 1995, a loss of somewhere between 250,000 and 1 million jobs before the end of the year, a reversal of foreign investment and capital flight, a dramatic rise in inflation exceeding 50 percent yearly, an extraordinary rise in private-bank interest for mortgages and loans far above the inflation rate, and numerous business closures and bankruptcies, including the threat of important state governments declaring financial insolvency.[38]

Zedillo's administration placed the blame for the crisis, which was far more serious than that of the mid-1980s, at the door of the Salinas administration for having let the peso become excessively overvalued, whereas Salinas viewed Zedillo as having been the biggest beneficiary of his prudent avoidance of upsetting the economic picture on the eve of the elections. Salinas's brother, Raúl's arrest on a multitude of corruption charges in February 1995 and revelations that he might have misappropriated over $100 million poured gasoline on the fire. As the ex-president's own legal problems multiplied, Zedillo was freed of his legacy and able to embark on his own project for democratization. His most important decision was not, as had been the case for so long, whom to chose as his successor, but how competitive to make elections as part of the larger question of how far to go in making Mexico truly democratic—in which case, the future selection of the PRI nominee for the presidency would lose its decisive significance. Unable to count upon economic growth to bolster his administration, Zedillo had little choice but to focus upon weeding out institutionalized corruption and initiating political reforms. To this end he took the unprecedented step of selecting an attorney general from an opposition party, the PAN. Arresting the ex-president's brother on murder charges gave Zedillo's flagging popularity a boost. By 1996, the economy demonstrated signs of recovery, which Zedillo underscored by paying back two-thirds of the US emergency loan. Two years of extreme austerity paid off in GDP growth of 7.5 percent and inflation of only 15.7 percent in 1997. Yet the severely negative impact in the social sphere was reflected in a sharp rise in the proportion of those living in extreme poverty (most of whom had already been below the poverty line) from 16 percent in 1992 to 28 percent by 1999.

The July 1997 congressional elections—which also involved balloting for the Federal District governor for the first time since 1924—provided an indication of how the political winds were blowing. Cárdenas kept his presidential hopes alive by winning in the capital with a respectable 48 percent of the votes. Nationwide, the PRI came in first in the midterm congressional balloting with 39.1 percent of the votes, followed by the PAN with 26.6 percent and the PRD with 25.7 percent. The slippage from 1994, when congressional elections had coincided with presidential balloting, was significant, with the PRI falling to 239 seats (from 300), the PRD exploding from 71 to 125, and the PAN climbing very modestly to 121 (from 119). But although the PAN and PRD voted together to freeze the PRI out of top congressional offices, the PAN frequently sided with the PRI on economic and budget issues. Although the PRI lost 19 Senate seats in 1997, it retained a majority in the upper house of 77 out of 128. Importantly, the clean and fair elections significantly bolstered Zedillo's public approval.[39]

As 1999 saw attention focus on the 2000 elections—including an open battle for the PRI presidential nomination—Cárdenas began to fade because there had been unrealistic expectations of what he could do as mayor about Mexico City's manifold problems when he had to depend on the PRI-controlled federal government for financial resources. But the PAN's Vicente Fox Quesada (b. 1942), former governor of Guanajuato, towering over the other candidates at six feet six inches in his trademark cowboy boots, forged ahead of the PRI's lackluster

Francisco Labastida—winner of a hotly contested November 1999 primary. Fox's *Y* for "Ya," understood as "We've had enough; now's the time," was a catchy slogan, and as candidate of the businessman's party, his campaign did not lack for funds.[40]

Argentina: "Civil-Military Twilight" into Renovated Peronism

Although the 1980s dawned grim and unpromising for Argentina, by 1983 the sun had broken through the clouds, and by 1997 a much more broadly based regime had surpassed the duration of the middle-class democracy the country had enjoyed from 1916 to 1930. A crucial difference was that this time no global economic crash loomed on the horizon to undercut a democracy that was both significantly more mature and had substantially broader and deeper roots. Hence, it would be able to survive, although with pain and suffering, the stormy weather that would accompany the turn into the twenty-first century. A deeply ingrained pattern of military tutelage of the nation's political life was broken—since from 1930 to 1983 senior army officers occupied the presidency for all but fourteen years, with no civilian serving out his constitutional term.[41]

The distinctive feature of Argentina's escape from continued authoritarian military rule was a fundamental error in judgment on the part of the last in a series of military heads of government, which led by mid-1982 to a monumental mistake in the form of a military adventure directed against Britain. In all probability the transition to democracy would have occurred, but very likely not until the latter part of the decade and with much more suffering and bloodshed in a continuation of the "dirty war," which remains far and away the greatest trauma of Argentina's life as a nation.[42]

As the government of General Jorge Rafael Videla moved into its final stage, the rosy economic panorama of 1979 became shrouded in clouds of doubt as 1980 imports exploded to $10.5 billion, causing a $2.5 billion trade deficit and a resulting sharp drop in foreign exchange reserves to $7.6 billion. At a meager 1.2 percent, economic growth lagged behind population increase, a circumstance creating widespread dissatisfaction with a reduction of inflation that still left it at 101 percent for the year. Many banks, including the largest private one, were insolvent and had to be liquidated, with a resultant increase in pressure on the budget. Foreign debt totaled $35.6 billion at year's end, a preoccupying burden.

Deteriorating economic conditions plagued the government of General Roberto Viola (b. 1925), who took over on the basis of seniority from Videla on March 29, 1981, when the president reached the army's retirement age. Although an April 1980 bank panic had been overcome, by early 1981 grave concerns about the country's economic future led to a massive wave of capital flight. As had become customary, many of the preceding government's fiscal policies were reversed. Hence, although the trade deficit was eliminated through increasing exports and reducing imports, foreign exchange reserves were halved as GDP shrank by a staggering 6.1 percent, with industry bearing the brunt of the contraction at minus 15.2 percent. Inflation remained stable. The dreaded monster of stagflation was a highly evident fact. With the economy in shambles and violent terrorism largely subdued, at the cost of nearly thirty thousand killed, agitation for elections rose.

There was little surprise when General Leopoldo Fortunato Galtieri (b. 1926), an excellent horseman with an antiquated cavalry orientation, replaced the ailing Viola as president in November 1981, since Viola had proven to be little more than a male military equivalent of the ill-fated Isabelita Perón. The installation of Roberto Alémán as economic czar signaled a return to monetarist orthodoxy, complete with currency devaluations, a two-tiered exchange rate, and heavier use of interest rates as an instrument of fiscal policy. Retaining command of the army in his own hands, Galtieri, an Argentine General George S. Patton, Jr. (down to the britches, riding boots, and twin pistols), with something of a Douglas MacArthur complex, initiated an attack upon the Falkland—to Argentina the Malvinas—Islands in April 1982. The military hoped to rally patriotic sentiment while distracting attention from social and economic woes that had sparked a mass antigovernment labor rally in Buenos Aires. In this aim they failed abjectly, as, after sustaining a humiliating defeat, they surrendered to the British on June 14. (Galtieri's battle plan was about as brilliant as that of politically ambitious George Armstrong Custer 106 years earlier for a glorious victory over the Sioux and Cheyenne at the Little Big Horn.) At least Galtieri escaped with his life, but he was immediately replaced as army commander in chief by General Cristiano Nicolaides, and two and a half weeks later, General Reynaldo Bignone assumed the presidency with responsibility for negotiating the armed forces' withdrawal from power on the least demoralizing terms possible.[43]

With the economy in a shambles, as GDP shrank by another 5.1 percent in 1982, inflation rose to 165 percent, and foreign exchange reserves dropped to $3.2 billion, Domingo Cavallo, a young critic of the policies followed since 1976, became president of the Central Bank, hoping to do something about the ravages that financial speculation had been causing. (In the early 1990s, he would be the architect of Argentina's most successful economic plan, ironically, under a Peronist president.) In his short tenure as Argentina's central banker, he pushed through a drastic financial reform, liquidating two-fifths of the private sector's debt in only six months.

Argentina in 1983 had a very deep hole to climb out of politically. Since 1930 this once-thriving democracy had had twenty-four presidents, sixteen of them generals, and had experienced twenty-six successful coups plus at least an equal number of serious conspiratorial attempts at seizing power by force. Only two elected presidents—Generals Justo and Perón—had served out full terms during this span of over half a century. Economically the pit was equally deep, per capita GDP having shrunk by 15 percent during the last three years of military rule; a huge explosion of foreign debt, up by nearly $40 billion during the seven years of military rule; and inflation running at 400 percent a year—all of which had resulted in a massive wave of capital flight.[44]

The crucial October 3, 1983, elections brought the Radicals back to power behind Raúl Ricardo Alfonsín Foulkes (b. 1927). This military academy graduate, former congressman, and unsuccessful aspirant for his party's nomination for the 1973 presidential election received 7.66 million votes, 52 percent of the national total, carrying the more developed provinces, including the Federal Capital District (where he garnered 1.28 million votes), Buenos Aires (which gave him 2.85 million), Córdoba, and Mendoza. The Peronists, under their legal name of the Justicialist Party (PJ), ran a faltering and lackluster campaign behind a stodgy candidate, Italo Lüder, an international law professor who as Senate president had briefly occupied the presidency during Isabel Perón's 1975 forced leave of absence. The PJ polled just over 40 percent—some 5.94 million—of which 2.34 million came from Buenos Aires and 550,000 from the federal capital.[45] Yet the Peronists won control of a dozen of the country's nineteen provinces along with a 21-to-18 advantage in the senate, where 7 independents held the balance of power as a result of selection by provincial legislatures, where the Peronists were still strong, and the overrepresentation of small provinces, as in Brazil and Mexico and, for that matter, the United States. In the lower house the Radicals came away with a slim majority: 129 of 254 seats compared to 111 for the Peronists. This was the first time since the movement's founding in the mid-1940s that the Peronists had lost a major national election in which they were allowed to participate. Argentines between eighteen and twenty-seven were voting for a president for the first time and those between twenty-eight and thirty-six for just the second time. As a result of the PJ's poor electoral performance, party head Lorenzo Miguel's prestige eroded, and a struggle for party control ensued between the renewal and orthodox factions. At this nadir of leadership, labor leader Saul Ubaldini attempted to make the General Labor Confederation (CGT) the chief pole of opposition to the Alfonsín government, launching a campaign of strikes and demonstrations that had little lasting effect (but were almost inevitable, given labor's regained sense of empowerment following its ineffectiveness under the post-1976 military regime).

Alfonsín was the favored heir of the UCR's grand old man, Ricardo Balbín, who had finally passed away in late 1981. Insisting that democracy had to come before economic recovery, he forced over half the country's generals and admirals into retirement and slashed the armed forces' budget. To balance pressures from the military and human rights advocates, he started legal action against both the members of the first three post-1976 juntas and seven left-wing terrorist leaders from the dirty-war period. Although strikes were frequent, he needed to be more concerned with the sensitivities of the military, apparent when the presidential commission looking into the dirty war issued its report in July 1984. His greatest handicaps were the nearly insolvent economic situation he inherited from the military regime and the highly unrealistic public expectations that a return to democratic civilian rule would in and of itself resolve socioeconomic problems that were the result of bad policies and poor administration by evil and incompetent men—when in reality these problems had deep structural roots.[46]

Reinstalling orthodox liberal Roberto Alemán (who had served under Frondizi and Galtieri) as economics minister, Alfonsín's government ultimately proved unsuccessful in its efforts to launch the country along the road to sustained economic growth. The hole was just too deep, as Alfonsín had inherited a country in the fourth year of a deep recession, with a fiscal deficit of 15 percent of GDP and an external debt nearing $50 billion and requiring 70 percent of the country's export earnings for its servicing—with foreign exchange reserves down to a worse-than-crisis level of $102 million. Unlike in Brazil and even fiscally troubled Mexico, massive loans had not been contracted to acquire capital goods or improve productivity. Instead, huge amounts had been spent on importing unnecessary luxury goods or had left the country through capital flight. Alfonsín refused to give priority to paying off debts run up by the "illegitimate" military regime, and by 1985 the struggle to restore any substantial degree of order to the economy had failed.

Modest GDP expansion of 2.8 percent for 1983 and 2.6 percent in 1984 turned into shrinkage of 4.7 percent during 1985 before recovering in 1986 to 5.4 percent and sagging to 1.4 percent for 1987. Foreign trade stagnated; 1985 was the best year, as a trade surplus was generated on exports of $8.4 billion and imports held to $3.9 billion. This healthy surplus was halved the following year as exports shrank and imports grew, a negative trend that continued through 1987, when foreign sales of $6.2 billion and purchasing abroad of $5.6 billion cut the surplus to under $600 million. Harvard-educated Juan Sourroulle had replaced Bernardo Grinspun as economics minister in February 1985, when Argentina failed to comply with the terms of its September 1984 standby credit agreement with the IMF. Sourroulle launched the Austral Plan four months later. Based upon a heterodox shock involving and end to indexization of prices, a new currency anchored on fixed parity with the dollar, and temporary wage and price controls, its aim was to eliminate the "inertial" effects of past inflation. Government deficits were to be cut by reductions in spending and increases in taxes, and the economy was to be opened by a lowering of tariffs and the attraction of foreign investment.[47]

Although inflation for the year was 383 percent, for the six months the plan was in effect dropped to 20 percent, and down to 3 percent a month by year's end. In a move beneficial to the government budget, Alfonsín curbed the autonomy of the Fabricaciones Militares (military factories), the heart of the military-run industrial complex that had come to produce many civilian products as well as military hardware. The Peronist-controlled Senate stymied a law instituting government monitoring of union elections. The early success of the plan in dramatically curbing inflation allowed the reunited Radical Party to triumph over the Peronists by a 43 percent to 35 percent margin in the November 1985 congressional elections. (This victory may in turn have influenced President Sarney's decision to use his analogous economic plan as the horse to ride to victory in Brazil the next year.) Then, in April 1986, administered prices and a "crawling peg" system of frequent currency minidevaluations (rather than often traumatic occasional large adjustments) were phased in. As the budget deficit rose and the trade balance declined, inflation by the third quarter climbed back to 8 percent a month, totaling 87 percent for the year. On the positive side, industry expanded by 26 percent between October 1985 and September 1986, lifting GDP by 11 percent. Further midcourse corrections in the plan were made in February 1987, allowing a new agreement to be reached with the IMF. However, as had become a pernicious habit in Argentina, dramatic short-term gains from a new economic plan were mistaken for fundamental corrections, so were not followed up by needed, but politically unpopular, reforms. A December 1986 law set a deadline for filing human rights violation cases, and the June 1987 Due Obedience Law relieved military officers of responsibility if they were following orders. The regular services made little trouble, but Alfonsín never established effective control over the intelligence organizations.[48]

Congressional and governorship elections took place in September 1987 in an economic climate marked by growth slowed to a crawl, inflation rising to an annual rate of 180 percent, and foreign debt burgeoning to a staggering $57 billion—some 80 percent of GDP—up over $7 billion in a single year after holding steady during 1984–1986. These dismal economic factors impinged heavily upon the electoral outcome. In a stunning reversal from two years earlier, the Peronists elected nineteen of twenty-two governors and had a 41 percent to 37 percent edge in the congressional races. This outcome coincided with a change in control of the PJ as the orthodox wing, which had been holding on by its fingertips, gave way to the renewal faction, now led by Antonio Cafiero, who combined the party presidency with his newly won governorship of Buenos Aires.

By mid-1988, inflation was out of control at over 25 percent a month, leading to the Spring Plan in August, nonviable in the preelectoral atmosphere—since any economic plan requires governmental credibility to succeed. With the presidential campaign in full swing, inflation exploded to 80 percent in March 1989 (on its way to 200 percent in July) while its new currency, the Austral, sank like a stone from seventeen to the US dollar to over two hundred between February

CARLOS SAUL MENEM

and June. Hence, it was no surprise when the May 14, 1989, presidential elections saw Peronist Carlos Saul Menem (b. 1930) garner 47 percent of the vote to only 37 percent for the UCR's Eduardo Angeloz, Córdoba's governor. The Peronists came away with half the chamber seats, compared to a third for the Radicals. In clear recognition of the need to move forward, Alfonsín agreed to leave office six months early.[49]

Peronism, back in power because of the perceived failure of the Radical administration to manage the economy adequately, was highly rejuvenated by Menem, a demagogic maverick from the interior, who had forced the issue of Peronism adopting a primary election as a way to even the playing field with the entrenched party bosses, who would have dominated a convention. Then, in July 1988, he upset party insider Antonio Cafeiro, the Buenos Aires governor, with 53 percent of the 1.7 million ballots cast by Justicialist Party members. Now the exuberant Menem was out to prove himself a worthy successor to the charismatic *caudillo* who had inspired him in his youth. His inauguration marked a series of democratic milestones: the first time in sixty-one years that one freely elected president had handed over power to another; the first time since 1951 that there had been two constitutional presidential elections in a row; and only the second time that an election had changed the governing party.

Menem's parents had arrived in 1912 from Syria, and the future president was born nearly two decades later, after the family had prospered in the wine business. A recent law school graduate when Perón was overthrown in 1955, Menem was elected governor of La Rioja in 1973, being arrested three years later in the wake of Perón's demise, and spending five years in prison under the military regime.

With democratization he had returned to the La Rioja governorship in 1985 and established a good working relationship with president Alfonsín. Quite consciously, he decided that showmanship was a key element of electoral success in the new Argentina and developed a flamboyant style that was often viewed as over-the-top by foreign observers, but that went over very well with the Argentine populace. Much attention was given to very public attacks on him by his equally vain wife, who was upset by his dumping her soon after she became Argentina's first lady, as well as to financial scandals involving her family, but these things did Menem little political harm.

At first Menem had an economic plan drawn up by Bunge y Born, a highly successful Argentine-owned multinational commodities and feed company that had neither been in the Peronist camp nor aligned with the traditional business interests. Breaking with the practice of issuing mere stabilization plans, Menem intended to restructure as well as revitalize the economy. By the end of 1989, the congress had given him the necessary tools in the form of the Law for the Reform of the State and the Law Regarding Economic Emergency. Utilizing these special powers, Menem began a sweeping program of privatization of government-owned and mixed-capital enterprises, including utilities; suspension and elimination of direct and indirect subsidies to the private sector; and a badly needed reorganization of the financial sector. In the face of hyperinflation he stayed the course instead of abandoning his program, realizing that, in light of the grim economic and fiscal inheritance from the Alfonsín government, his policies had not had anywhere near enough time to show positive results. Indeed, when he had come to office, inflation was raging out of control at 200 percent monthly.

Privatization, downsizing of the bureaucracy, elimination of red tape through deregulation, and improvement of tax collection were pushed, as Menem's sweeping free-market reforms constituted a sharp break with the "nationalist, statist, and populist import-substitution model that had prevailed in one form or another, for most of the preceding half-century."[50] As this model had included Perón's governments, Menem demonstrated determination not to be a prisoner of the past. Much as had become prevalent in Brazil, Menem had frequent recourse to executive decrees, legally binding until repealed by the congress or declared unconstitutional by the courts. Indeed, by the end of 1993 he had issued 308 such measures—ten times as many as in Argentina's prior life as a nation.

On the labor side, like the Labour Party's Tony Blair in Britain, this Peronist did not favor the country's workers, neither strengthening the unions nor giving labor the type of influence it desired in the party and the government. Menem's reforms, although taming inflation and renewing economic growth, also led to a quantum increase in unemployment. In pursuit of the goals of state solvency and market efficiency, Menem pursued his trademark program of privatization of state enterprises, chiefly in the fields of energy and communications, netting $24 billion by 1994 by selling these businesses off outright or converting them into joint ventures. Unfortunately for the longer run, most of this financial windfall was used to cover the federal government's budget deficits rather than being invested in increasing production or used to pay down the country's mounting foreign debt.

The human costs involved the jobs of one-third of the nearly 250,000 individuals employed in public enterprises. Moreover, direct government employment was reduced from just over 2 million to 1.8 million by the laying off of 217,000 public employees, evenly divided between the federal payroll and the payrolls of the provinces and municipalities. Subsidies to the private sector were slashed from $7.9 billion in 1989 to $4.4 billion for 1992. With central government tax collections raised from $13.7 billion to $24.4 billion by 1992, small fiscal surpluses in the early 1990s replaced deficits that had averaged over 12 percent of GDP during the transition from military rule and 5 percent under Alfonsín.

In late 1990, a group of eight self-styled "renovationist" congressmen split with the PJ over Menem's decision to pardon ex-presidents Videla and Viola as well as ranking officers of their governments who had been convicted of human rights violations. At the same time, with some elements of the military restive over punishments for human rights violations during the dirty war and the closing down of a military career as a road to political advancement—as it had emphatically been when they had chosen to become officers—some sort of coup attempt was overdue in a country where even the Alfonsín government had had to deal with multiple conspiracies.[51]

As early as April 15, 1987, under Alfonsín's rather relaxed rule there had been a junior officer uprising, behind Lieutenant. Colonel Aldo Rico, protesting alleged offenses against the armed forces as an institution in the form of "unjust" trials for human rights violations. The mutineers seized control of the infantry school at the Campo de Mayo, almost bordering on the presidential palace. Riding a wave of massive support from political parties and civic organizations, Alfonsín dramatically went to the school by helicopter to demand the mutineers' surrender. Only the leader was arrested, and the 150 others received only light wrist slaps. This lack of forceful response apparently set a bad precedent, as Rico escaped in January 1988 and barricaded himself and some supporters at the Monte Caseros base. At the same time, retired air force officers seized the Buenos Aires airport. When the protest fizzled out in a few days, 282 were arrested, but only 20 brought to trial. Such kid glove treatment resulted in December in mutinous behavior by 400 at the infantry school—out of which the armed forces got a pay raise and a bonus as well as replacement of the army chief of staff. Then, under the Menem government, with 1983 presidential candidate Lüder as defense minister, on November 23, 1989, a leftist attack on the La Tablada regiment was designed to forestall a supposed coup attempt by the *Carapintadas*, face-painted elite troops, although this uprising may have been a provocation by military intelligence. On December 3,

1990, some 500 officers associated with paratrooper leader Colonel Mohammed Ali Seindelin rose up, this time only a block from the presidential palace, and were put down by forces loyal to the government after thirteen deaths and hundreds of injuries. Menem gained public approval for his vigorous response to this challenge and the subsequent life prison term given to the coup leader. The government effectively portrayed these rebels, who strove to picture themselves as fed-up patriots, as ambitious and self-serving militarists.

Relief from high inflation rates and from lack of economic growth came after the April 1991 installation of the able and innovative Domingo Cavallo as economy minister. With the president's firm backing, he implemented an economic plan bearing his name, which "dollarized" the Argentine economy by making local currency and the US dollar equal and alternative with full convertibility. Made possible by a $8-billion trade surplus in the recession year of 1990, this bold move brought inflation down sharply from an annual rate of over 1800 percent in 1990 to only 4 percent in 1994, viewed by a thankful public as a near miracle, while GDP growth averaged 8 percent a year for the first four years of the plan—the highest for any four-year period in the twentieth century. Yet, as productivity in the manufacturing sector rose one-third between 1991 and 1994, real wages dropped by 13 percent. With more serious implications for the future, the extreme exchange rate inflexibility established by the Convertibility Law of 1991 led to overvaluation of the peso, seriously compromising the ability of Argentine exports to remain competitive in international markets. Unable to use monetary policy or the exchange rate as macroeconomic instruments, Argentine governments were forced to overrely on fiscal adjustments. Events would prove that getting out of dollarization was much more difficult, especially in political terms, than entering had been.[52]

Menem's economic policies paid short- and medium-range political dividends that carried him to a tenure in office second only to that of Perón himself. The September 1991 midterm elections were a tremendous Peronist victory that could be interpreted only as a mandate for Menem. Eduardo Duhalde, his former vice president, was elected governor of Buenos Aires Province, leaving the opposition with victories only in the Federal District (the city of Buenos Aires), Córdoba, and the minor province of Neuguen. Menem and Alfonsín signed a 1993 pact for elimination of the ban on presidential reelection as part of a broader reform of the constitution, jointly gaining 211 out of 305 seats in the resulting constituent assembly (which subsequently duly approved the change).[53]

A coalition of leftist splinter parties, under the imposing name of the *Frente Grande* (Grand Front), received only 4 percent of the vote in the October 1993 congressional elections, demonstrating that it was certainly much broader than it was great. In Congress this grouping gained the adhesion of Radical Party elements alienated by what they considered Alfonsín's unprincipled reelection deal with Menem. Moreover, disgruntled UCR voters helped quadruple the Frente Grande's performance in the April 1994 constituent assembly elections to 12.7 percent, carrying the federal capital. At the same time the Peronists garnered 37.7 percent of the vote (a modest dip from 42.3 percent in the previous year's ballot-ing), and the Radical Party dropped sharply to not quite 20 percent from over 30 percent in the constituent congressional elections. Dissident Peronist senator José Octávio Bordón, leader of the 1990 defection from the PJ, folded his recently formed Open Politics for Social Integrity movement, with its acronym PAIS ("country," in the sense of fatherland), into a coalition with the Frente Grande and splinter opposition parties called FREPASO, the Fatherland Solidarity Front. This group's hopes to exploit scandals and illicit dealings by Menem family members in the upcoming presidential election proved to be wishful thinking.

In the May 1995 presidential balloting, the first for reelection of an incumbent since Perón in 1951, Menem, riding a wave of public approval for having tamed hyperinflation, received 49.5 percent of the vote, along with 137 of 257 chamber seats, in swamping FREPASO's Bordón, a former student of Brazilian president Cardoso, recipient of a respectable 29.6 percent. The UCR standard bearer was lost in the dust with 17 percent.[54] This was the first time that a Radical Party nominee finished lower than runner-up in a fair presidential election. On the congressional side, the Peronists rebounded to 43 percent, compared to the UCR's 21.8 percent and FREPASO's 21.2 percent. Yet signs that things might not go as well during Menem's second term were already evident on the economic front, as fears that the peso–dollar parity could not be maintained, combined with fallout from the Mexican crisis (colorfully called the tequilla effect), had led in early 1995 to a loss of nearly 19 percent in bank deposits, an alarming $8.5 billion. Given their long tradition of intense pressure for favors and protection from the government, Argentine economic agents were inclined to seek the quick profits of currency speculation—even if this speculation had very negative effects on the national economy.

By the 1995 elections, the positive features of the recent reform of the 1853 constitution were in effect. The right to reelection was balanced with a reduction of presidential terms to four years (as was the case in Brazil when the constitu-tional obstacle to Cardoso's reelection was removed). Popular election of senators for six-year terms (as in Brazil and Mexico) replaced the outdated practice of se-lection by provincial legislatures for nine-year terms. To eliminate the possibility of minority presidents, a plague of the Andean countries, a runoff provision was included if the front-runner did not receive 40 percent of the vote or win by 10 percent over his nearest rival. In a provision that may matter in the future, the re-quirement that presidents be Roman Catholics was dropped. Menem reshaped the party as well as its relationship to the labor movement. In his first term he "by-passed the party in filling government posts and in picking candidates for elected offices, gave party leaders little input into government policy, and increased the isolation of the national party leadership from party members and from provincial party organizations."[55] Menem continued by capturing control of the national Justicialist Party leaders he had been ignoring, taking advantage of their weak ties to the membership, unions, and provincial party leaders. In a blow to Menem's political near hegemony, in June 1997 in the first-ever election of a Federal District (Buenos Aires) mayor, Radical Party Senator Fernando de la Rúa (b. 1937) garnered 40 percent of the vote to less than 27 percent for the FREPASO candidate and not quite 18 percent for the Peronist hopeful, the appointed incumbent. For by this time lavish patronage spending and revenue sharing with the provinces needed to be cut back in the face of mounting budget deficits—an action triggering Cavallo's resignation and the subsequent airing of government dirty linen.

This reality check was confirmed shortly thereafter as the two opposition parties allied before the partial congressional elections and obtained 61 seats on nearly 46 percent of the vote to 75 on 36 percent of the ballots for Menem's PJ—down from 43 percent of the vote in 1995. This outcome dropped the Peronists to 119 seats from the 131 they had held and raised the alliance to 106 seats. Winning by a margin of over three to one in the capital and comfortably in Buenos Aires province, the opposition alliance poised for a strong run at the presidency in 1999. But first Argentina would slide into a recession in 1998, with the perplexing result that as more and more economists turned against convertibility, the Argentine public became increasingly in favor of keeping the dollar–peso peg as their only protection in a highly volatile economic situation. Desiring a third term at any price, Menem opted to go where the votes were and maintain convertibility—which allowed people the assurance that they could at any time change their holdings and accounts on a par basis into good, rock-solid US greenbacks. In making this fateful decision, the president set the stage for allowing his political ambitions to undo his very positive economic accomplishments. Menem's single-minded drive for reelection unleashed a spending race between the federal government and leading Peronist governors determined to thwart his unconstitutional gambit—with fiscal prudence tossed by the wayside. Other victims of the no-holds-barred struggle were needed tax reform, liberalization of labor markets, and revamping of the revenue-sharing system between the central government and the provinces. In the spending orgy, Argentina's already troublesome debt burden burgeoned.

Eduardo Duhalde (b. 1939), Menem's chief rival within Peronist ranks, blocked the president's efforts to gain third term, which was constitutionally highly questionable, so he received no appreciable support from the frustrated Menem when running against the Radical's de la Rúa, who had edged out Graciela Fernández to become the FREPASO-UCR alliance nominee. Thus, Argentina went to the polls on October 24, 1999, with a clear choice to make. Since over three-quarters of the record 24 million registered voters participated, they assumed in the process a share of responsibility for the subsequent performance of the winner. The UCR, eager to return to power after eleven years of Menem and Peronism, won handily with 48.5 percent of the vote for de la Rúa to 38.1 percent for Peronism's Duhalde (ex-economics czar Cavallo and his "Action for the People" trailed with a 10 percent share). In the congressional voting for half of the lower house, the UCR-FREPASO alliance came away with 63 to reach 127 chamber seats, compared to the Peronists' 50 deputies-elect (giving them only 101, including holdovers), and 17 for minor parties (who had 12 carried over).[56] Hence, the results were a continuation of a trend that saw Peronism under Menem peaking in 1995–1996—exactly when the Cavallo Plan ran out of steam. Indeed, Menem's legacy included a foreign debt that had exploded to $170 billion and an unmanageable fiscal deficit. As for the new president, his problems would start almost immediately after he took office and would overwhelm him barely halfway into his term, as Argentina sank into a grave crisis.

Colombia: Parallel Power, Rebels, and Drug Traffickers

Although Colombia's political development did not take major strides forward during the 1980s and 1990s, the country did manage to stave off the very serious threat to viable representative processes posed by the enormous wealth and power amassed by the ruthless entrepreneurs of the drug trade. Doing so without seriously violating democratic norms was no mean accomplishment; neither was success at all a foregone conclusion. Indeed, the performances of several Colombian presidents during this period compared favorably with those of both their predecessors, who allowed the country get into this predicament, and their contemporaries in other Latin American countries, especially their Andean neighbors. Moreover, political leadership at least passed into the hands of a new generation of vigorous and quite modern individuals within the country's distinctive framework of a resilient two-party system.[57]

After 1978, Colombia, a country reaching a population of 25 million, had as its president Julio César Turbay, a sixty-two-year-old middle-class descendant of Lebanese immigrants. Near the midpoint of Turbay's term, which featured a move back toward statist development and a freer hand for the military, the 19th of April Movement (M-19) insurgents held fourteen foreign ambassadors hostage for sixty-one days, a profound embarrassment to the government. Moreover, the drug trade expanded by leaps and bounds, while the authorities appeared clueless and ineffective. The resulting sense of malaise had an impact upon the country's political life, and the voter turnout for the 1980 state and municipal elections was a mere 30 percent (4.2 million out of an eligible 13.8 million), reflecting apathy as well as fear. Within this low participation the Liberal Party maintained an advantage of 2.3 million votes to 1.6 million votes in local balloting.

Still a power within the Liberal Party, Lleras Camargo favored late-1960s Bogotá mayor Virgilio Barca Vargas in 1982, and ex-president Alfonso López Michelsen, at sixty-eight, sought a comeback. This Liberal split, reminiscent of 1946, allowed the Conservative Party behind Belisario Betancur Cuarto (b. 1923) to sneak back in. The Liberals had defeated the Conservatives in the March congressional balloting by a 3.1 million to 2.2 million margin, but in May Betancur's 3.2 million votes overcame López Michelsen's 2.8 million, with dissident Luis Carlos Galán Sarmiento siphoning off 730,000 votes. Turnout rose to just above 50 percent.[58]

Betancur, a populist inclined to bypass the party and appeal directly to the middle classes, inherited a bleak economic landscape marred by recession, fiscal deficits, rising foreign debt, troublesome inflation, and high unemployment. These problems prevented him from launching new programs or redistributing income—particularly as government revenues were strained by existing patronage arrangements. Attempting to regulate the financial sectors and drifting away from the United States, Betancur encountered opposition from the military, which distrusted his efforts to negotiate an end to the insurgencies. Following the M-19's dramatic attack on the Palace of Justice in November 1985 and a devastating volcano eruption, and with the narcotics traffickers mounting a nearly parallel government in Medellín and Cali, Betancur became a virtual lame duck subject to a high degree of control by the military. Meanwhile, the March 1984 midterm elections had seen both parties splintered, with the opposition Liberals enjoying a 53 percent to 42 percent advantage over the Conservatives. Well intentioned as it was, Betancur's vaunted 1984 "National Dialogue" (of all-embracing peace talks) failed to advance the cause of domestic peace at all.

In 1986, Álvaro Gómez Hurtado tried yet again for the Conservatives as Virgilio Barco, now sixty-five, won the Liberal nod over Galán and cruised to a lopsided victory of 4.2 million to 2.6 million votes (58 percent to 36 percent of the valid ballots cast). In the congressional elections preceding the presidential balloting, the Liberals had won handily, with 49 percent for the official slate plus 7 percent for Galán's "New Liberals."[59] Coalition government ended after almost thirty years as the disappointed Conservatives refused what was, in their view, an insulting offer of three ministries. Efforts to shift to a government–loyal-opposition model failed in the face of deep divisions within each of the parties—the Liberal Party being vividly depicted by critics as a "stewpot of scorpions."

Governing a country of thirty million inhabitants, 70 percent urban, Barco, who had an engineering doctorate from MIT, sat by ineffectively as initially favorable economic conditions deteriorated after midterm. Ex-President Pastrana's son Andrés, candidate for mayor of Bogotá, was kidnapped in early 1988, as was Gómez Hurtado in May, and crime rates soared almost beyond comparison. The situation was grim as homicides passed an annual rate of 10,000 in 1980, doubled by 1988 on their way to 30,000 by 1992. (In late 1995, after yet another ill-fated presidential bid, the name of Gómez Hurtado would be added to this shameful casualty list of victims of lawlessness.) Peasant populations in guerrilla-controlled areas embraced the growing of coca, and the Armed Forces of the Colombian Revolution (FARC) instituted a tax on the production and transportation of drugs in "their" territory.

In some ways the bloodshed was equal to that of the 1948–1953 *La Violencia* period. Not only were there various competing violent guerrilla movements in combat with the military, but the drug lords had developed private armies with even better equipment and arms than the federal armed forces or the insurgents. As the campaign of military repression failed to produce results and the judicial system broke down—through a combination of bribery and intimidation—right-wing paramilitary death squads, some financed by legitimate businessmen and others by drug cartels, emerged to play a larger role. Barca's version of a peace plan left the guerrillas better off than before—in possession of "neutral zones" free from even patrol activities by the army. Meanwhile, in an effort to force the government to cancel oil exploration contracts with foreign firms, the National Liberation Army (ELN) carried out over one hundred attacks on the nation's largest oil pipeline between January 1988 and the middle of the next year.[60]

Insurgency and drug trafficking became intertwined in what was for them a symbiotic relationship. Using accumulated marijuana profits for capital, by the early 1980s Colombians became central in the global cocaine business. In 1979, Colombia had already edged past Mexico, exporting 41 tons of cocaine and nearly 16,000 tons of marijuana. A $3-billion business by that time, cocaine trafficking grew during the 1980s until the unofficial key personality of the country was drug lord Pablo Escobar Gaviria. A crusading justice minister was murdered as early as 1984, and the governor of Antioquía and the police chief of Medellín were among the summer 1989 murder harvest. As John Martz points out, many, if not most, of the insurgents were no longer ruled by ideology or a burning desire for political reform; rather, their "primary motive [is] material; they [are] flourishing with the benefits gained by robberies, kidnappings, bribery, and under-the-table deals with members of Colombia's economic elite."[61]

Liberal divisions allowed thirty-four-year-old Andrés Pastrana Arango to win the Bogotá mayoralty election, a win that launched once more a new generation of an old presidential family on the road to the country's top office. Then, in August 1989, leading Liberal Party presidential contender Galán was murdered (shades of Gaitán forty-one years earlier), and blame fell on the drug traffickers. On the positive side, the M-19 converted itself into a legal party (as Venezuelan guerrillas had done earlier, and Salvadoran insurgents would soon do). Barco had by this time decreed a state of siege.

In one month the military arrested over ten thousand persons while confiscating properties and prized possessions of drug traffickers, but not capturing any of the really big fish.

In the wake of Galán's tragic demise, his campaign manager, César Gaviria Trujillo (b. 1947), handily defeated even younger Ernesto Samper Pizano (b. 1951), the favorite of the party's left wing, for the Liberal Party's 1990 presidential nomination (an event paralleling developments in Mexico a half decade later). The late May balloting was held in a climate of terror provoked by violence unleashed by the nation's drug barons. In addition to Galán, two other presidential candidates had been slain during the campaign, and more than 300 people had been killed by a rash of bombings. In the four months immediately preceding the election, hired guns of the Medellín cartel alone gunned down 149 policemen in retaliation for the government's continued rejection of offers to pay the country's foreign debt in return for amnesty.[62] Still the March congressional elections gave the Liberals a 117- to 72-seat margin in the lower house, accompanied by a 72-to-41 advantage (including holdovers) in the Senate, as the Conservative Party's electoral support fell to 33 percent. Indeed, Conservative division was deep, with future president Andrés Pastrana's New Democratic Force faction electing 9 new senators to 5 for Gómez Hurtado's split-off. Amid a turnout of just over 40 percent of the 18 million registered voters, Gaviria won easily with 48 percent of the vote, double that received by three-time loser Gómez Hurtado, running on a dissident National Salvation Movement slate after having been denied the Conservative Party nomination. The Social Conservative Party (PSC) candidate, Rodrigo Lloreda Caicedo, was left far behind with an embarrassing 12.4 percent, which effectively ended his future political hopes. (The actual figures were 2.9 million to 1.4 million, with a movement of former guerrillas slightly more than matching the PSC's showing.) The future of the traditional Conservative Party appeared bleak after this crushing defeat, since in both 1978 and 1982 they had garnered 47 percent of the national vote. On the same ballot, 87 percent of the voters approved holding a constituent assembly to reshape the country's basic charter.

At age forty-three the country's youngest chief executive in history, Gaviria, who formed a coalition cabinet to enhance the appearance of national unity and resolve, had a good economic performance featuring shrinking the state through privatization and decentralization. Gaviria turned from the stick to the carrot, following a policy of "talking to people who were talking to the drug lords," but apparent victory with Escobar's negotiated "surrender" in June 1991 appeared ridiculously hollow in light of Escobar's July 1992 "escape" and proof that he had freely run his drug business from his private luxury prison. Failure to recapture him diminished the government in the eyes of much of the population. However, with the late 1993 death of Escobar, who had benefited from a near–Robin Hood image among the underprivileged masses of the Medellín region, Gaviria's stock soared. During his presidency a new constitution was written, followed by Liberal Party victories in the October 1991 midterm balloting that gave the party 87 of 161 chamber seats and 56 of 102 seats in the upper house, along with March 1992 state and local elections in which the Liberals won 18 of 27 governorships and elected the mayors of 18 of the country's 23 largest cities. In March 1994, Samper won the Liberal Party primary as the party scored heavily in congressional elections, but in May he was pushed hard to edge out Andrés Pastrana by 20,000 votes (2.586 million to 2.566 million or 45.1 percent to 44.8 percent) on a turnout of only 6 million out of 17 million registered, a margin rising to 133,000—on 50.6 percent to 48.5 percent—in the June runoff.[63]

Hardly was Samper settled in office when his campaign manager was arrested on charges of having accepted large contributions from Cali drug lords. The result was investigations that would hamstring the ambitious young president. Samper's campaign-financing scandal led directly to mild US destabilization efforts (stemming from his alleged financial dealings with the drug lords) and his having to stave off impeachment by wheeling and dealing with senators—many of whom had drug money skeletons in their own closets. This crisis set the stage for a Conservative Party resurgence in 1998. When the dust settled in late June, after the heated campaign, Andrés Pastrana was the winner in the runoff by 49 percent to 46 percent, becoming the first man in Colombia ever to pass the six-million-vote mark, as turnout rallied to 60 percent. But this victory came only after a neck-and-neck first-round victory, in which he trailed the Liberal candidate 34.6 percent to 34.3 percent, as half the 2.8 million votes received then by dissident Liberal Noemi Sanen, a former foreign minister, went to Pastrana rather than to his Liberal Party foe. Since the Liberals retained sizable majorities in both houses of the congress, Pastrana would be doomed to a frustrating and in most ways unproductive presidency.

Unfortunately, he (as had Betancur and Barco earlier) met with abject failure in attempts to bring about a negotiated solution to the decades of armed insurgency, the leitmotif of his administration. Pastrana's Plan Colombia left the armed insurgent groups in complete control of a very large portion of rural Colombia. Very substantial amounts of military and economic aid from the United States not only failed to bring a solution to the violence problem any nearer, but also made few appreciable inroads into the drug industry, which was flourishing at century's end.[64]

Reflections on the Four Pillars

By 1999, all four of these major countries had become consolidated democracies, at least in formal political terms. Having started the period with an unrepentant military regime entrenched in power, Argentina had come the farthest—since in

Brazil the military government had already started the transition during the last five years of the preceding period. Mexico, although not having to remove its military from power, achieved a task that had proven essentially undoable in the USSR: democratizing by loosening the hold of a hitherto hegemonic party. Moreover, this was accomplished without the trauma of a resort to arms by opponents of democracy or use of force to coerce them into acquiescence. In retrospect, the process was almost amazingly smooth and gradual. Colombia, already a democracy, succeeded in maintaining viability and competition in the face of intense threats from both revolutionary insurgents and determined and terroristic drug lords. It now remains to examine how the region's other thirty countries fared.

Notes

1. Howard J. Wiarda, *Dilemmas of Democracy in Latin America: Crises and Opportunities* (Lanham, MD: Rowman & Littlefield, 2005), p. 205.

2. Ibid., pp. 16–17.

3. Ronald M. Schneider, *"Order and Progress": A Political History of Brazil* (Boulder: CO: Westview Press, 1991), pp. 286–385, covers developments up to 1990, and Ronald M. Schneider, *Brazil: Culture and Politics in a New Industrial Power* (Boulder, CO: Westview Press, 1996), pp. 100–136, 161–168, carries the story up into early 1995. Mauricio A. Font, *Transforming Brazil: A Reform Era in Perspective* (Lanham, MD: Rowman & Littlefield, 2003), analyzes Cardoso's second term as well.

4. My detailed observations of the 1982 campaign and analyses of the results can be found in a series of twelve reports issued through the Center for Strategic and International Studies beginning in June 1982. See in particular Ronald M. Schneider, *Brazil Elections Series, Final Report: Results and Ramifications* (Washington, DC: Center for Strategic and International Studies, December 1982).

5. Analysis is contained in Ronald M. Schneider and William Perry, *Brazil Political Report* (monthly from July 1984 through February 1985 by the Center for Strategic and International Studies).

6. See Glaucio Ary Dillon Soares, "Elections and the Redemocratization of Brazil," and David V. Fleisher, "Brazil at the Crossroads: The Elections of 1982 and 1985," in Paul W. Drake and Eduardo Silva, eds., *Elections and Democratization in Latin America, 1980–1985* (San Diego: University of California at San Diego, Center for Iberian and Latin American Studies, 1986), pp.273–327. The PMDB contributed to the electoral college win for Neves with 196 deputies, 24 senators, and 51 state delegates; while the PFL produced 63, 10, and 40 of these electoral votes.

7. On the Cruzado Plan consult Werner Baer and Paul Beckerman, "The Decline and Fall of Brazil's Cruzado," *Latin American Research Review,* 34:1 (1989), pp. 35–64.

8. See Ronald M. Schneider, *Brazil's 1986 Elections*, (Washington, DC: Center for Strategic and International Studies, December 1986).

9. On the constitution consult Amaury de Souza and Bolívar Lamounier, "A feitura da nova constituição: Um resume da cultura política Brasileira," in Bolívar Lamounier, ed., *De Geisel á Collor: O balanço da Transição* (São Paulo: IDESP/Sumaré, 1990), pp. 81–134. For the political context, see Ronald M. Schneider, "Transition Without Rupture: Parties, Politicians, and the Sarney Government," in Julian Chacel, Pamela Falk, and David V. Fleischer, eds., *Brazil's Economic and Political Future* (Boulder, CO: Westview Press, 1988), pp. 188–198, and Ronald M. Schneider, "Brazil's Political Future," in Wayne A. Selcher, ed., *Political Liberalization in Brazil: Dynamics, Dilemmas, and Future Prospects* (Boulder, CO: Westview Press, 1986), pp. 217–260.

10. Lack of precise figures stems from the fact that many candidates in the hinterlands ran on coalition slates that blurred their real party identity—which they were likely to change again in bargaining with state administrations or dealing for resources and services with federal officials.

11. See the author's series of six reports, done with the collaboration of William Perry, *The 1989 Brazilian Elections*, especially No. 5, "The Final Tally" (Washington, DC: Center for Strategic and International Studies, January 1990). It appears that most of PSDB standard bearer Mario Covas's 7.8 million supporters went over to Collor, along with the lion's share of Maluf's 6 million votes and at least half of the 3.2 million electors favoring the PMDB's Ulysses Guimarães.

12. Consult Marcelo de Paiva Abreu, ed., *A Ordem de Progresso: Cem Anos de Política Econômica Republicana, 1889–1989* (Rio de Janeiro: Editora Campus, 1989), pp. 7–9.

13. See the series of studies by Ronald M. Schneider and William Perry, *The 1990 Brazilian Elections* (Washington, DC: Center for Strategic and International Studies), especially No. 1, "Pre-Election Analysis: The Setting" (September 1990); No. 2, "Pre-Election Analysis: Into the Homestretch" (September 1990); and No. 3, "Post-Election Analysis" (December 1990).

14. A thoughtful interpretation is Peter Flynn, "Collor, Corruption and Crisis: Time for Reflection," *Journal of Latin American Studies*, 25:2 (May 1993), pp. 351–371. On conditions around this time see Kurt Weyland, *Democracy Without Equity: Failures of Reform in Brazil* (Pittsburgh: University of Pittsburgh Press, 1996), and Kurt Von Mettenheim, *The Brazilian Voter: Mass Politics in Democratic Transition 1974–1986* (Pittsburgh: University of Pittsburgh Press, 1995).

15. See Fernando Henrique Cardoso (edited by Mauricio A. Font), *Charting a New Course: The Politics of Globalization and Social Transformation* (Lanham, MD: Rowman & Littlefield, 2001).

16. Results are in *Veja,* January 18, 1995, pp. 78–80, and *Istoé,* January 11, 1995, pp. 56–65.

17. See Ted G. Goertzel, *Fernando Henrique Cardoso* (New Brunswick, NJ: Transaction, 1999). Other works useful on the Cardoso period include Timothy J. Power, *Elites, Institutions, and Democratization: The Political Right in Postauthoritarian Brazil* (University Park: Pennsylvania State University Press, 1998); Peter R. Kingstone, *Crafting Coalitions for Reform: Business Preferences, Political Institutions, and Neoliberal Reform in Brazil* (University Park: Pennsylvania State University Press, 1999); Peter R. Kingstone and Timothy J. Power, eds.,

Democratic Brazil: Actors, Institutions, and Processes (Pittsburgh: University of Pittsburgh Press, 2000); and Wendy Hunter, *Eroding Military Influence in Brazil: Politicians Against Soldiers* (Chapel Hill: University of North Carolina Press, 1997). Fernando Henrique Cardoso, *The Accidental President of Brazil: a Memoir* (New York: Public Affairs Press, 2006), is also useful.

18. The plan, with careful monitoring and fine-tuning by Cardoso and his economic team remains one of the world's most successful examples of a rational and politically viable economic policy, in its essential features still being continued by his opposition—who originally denounced it as an electoral fraud—a decade later.

19. The approval for reelection is covered in Font, *Transforming Brazil,* pp. 58–61. The electorate was just under 110 million, an increase of 15 million since 1994.

20. The rich literature on this period includes Daniel Levy and Kathleen Bruhn, *Mexico, The Struggle for Democratic Development* (Berkeley: University of California Press, 2001); Kevin Middlebrook, ed., *Dilemmas of Change in Mexican Politics* (La Jolla, CA: Center for U.S.-Mexican Studies, University of California–San Diego, 2002); Wayne A. Cornelius, David Myhre, Todd Eisenstadt, and Jane Hindley, eds., *Subnational Politics and Democratization in Mexico* (La Jolla, CA: Center for U.S.-Mexican Studies, University of California–San Diego, 1999); Wayne A. Cornelius, David Myhre, Maria L. Cook, Ann L. Craig, and Jonathan Fox, eds., *Transforming State-Society Relations in Mexico: The National Solidarity Strategy* (La Jolla, CA: Center for U.S.-Mexican Studies, University of California–San Diego, 1994); Laura Randall, ed., *Changing Structure of Mexico: Political, Social, and Economic Prospects* (New York: M. E. Sharpe, 1996); and George W. Grayson, *Mexico, From Corporatism to Pluralism?* (Ft. Worth, TX: Harcourt Brace, 1998).

21. Jorge Castañeda, *Perpetuating Power: How Mexican Presidents Were Chosen* (New York: New Press, 2000), pp. 45–61, 155–175, covers López Portillo's management of succession.

22. Roderic Ai Camp, *Politics in Mexico: The Democratic Transformation*, 4th ed. (New York: Oxford University Press, 2003), p. 246.

23. Castañeda, *Perpetuating Power,* p. 63.

24. Camp, *Politics,* pp. 190 and 193, has the results of these elections.

25. Ibid., pp. 187–190 and 193, has a useful discussion of this election.

26. Castañeda, *Perpetuating Power,* pp. 63–88, 177–203, 205–211, deals with de la Madrid's term with a focus on the succession process.

27. Useful are Victoria E. Rodríguez and Peter M. Ward, eds., *Opposition Government in Mexico* (Albuquerque: University of New Mexico Press, 1995); Kathleen Bruhn, *Taking on Goliath: The Emergence of a New Left Party and the Struggle for Democracy in Mexico* (University Station: Pennsylvania State University Press, 1997); and Stephen D. Morris, *Political Reformism in Mexico: An Overview of Contemporary Mexican Politics* (Boulder, CO: Lynne Rienner, 1995).

28. Consult Camp, *Politics in Mexico,* pp. 191–193, and Castañeda, *Perpetuating Power,* pp. 230–239. See also Edgar W. Butler and Jorge A. Bustamante, eds., *Sucesion Presidencial: The 1988 Mexican Presidential Election* (Boulder, CO: Westview Press, 1991).

29. Information on Salinas is found in Castañeda, *Perpetuating Power,* especially pp. 205–206. See also Monica Serrano and Victor Bulmer-Thomas, eds., *Rebuilding the Mexican State After Salinas* (London: Institute of Latin American Studies of the University of London, 1996).

30. Castañeda, *Perpetuating Power*, p. 90, with pp. 89–129 and 212–230 treating the process by which Colosio and Zedillo were selected. On political changes preceding this crisis, see Jorge I. Dominguez and James A. McCann, *Democratizing Mexico: Public Opinion and Electoral Choices* (Baltimore: Johns Hopkins University Press, 1996).

31. Castañeda, *Perpetuating Power*, p. 94.

32. Ibid., p. 93.

33. See Camp, *Politics in Mexico*, pp. 193–194.

34. The Chiapas uprising and its ramifications are discussed in Castañeda, *Perpetuating Power*, pp. 105–109, 199–201, 222–225, 229–230. Also consult Neil Harvey, *The Chiapas Rebellion: The Struggle for Land and Democracy* (Durham, NC: Duke University Press, 1998). Background and perspective are furnished by Joe Foweraker and Ann L. Craig, eds., *Popular Movements and Political Change in Mexico* (Boulder, CO: Lynne Rienner, 1990).

35. Zedillo as candidate is discussed in Castañeda, *Perpetuating Power*, pp. 124–129; his performance is assessed in Camp, *Politics in Mexico*, pp. 3–4, 256–258.

36. Camp, *Politics in Mexico*, pp. 194–196, deals with the 1994 elections.

37. Zedillo was perhaps even more of a highly educated technocrat than Salinas or de la Madrid, although by way of Yale rather than Harvard. Roderic Ai Camp provides a wealth of material on this stratum of the Mexican governmental elite in *Mexico's Mandarins: Crafting a Power Elite for the Twenty-First Century* (Berkeley: University of California Press, 2002), and *Political Recruitment Across Two Centuries, 1884–1993* (Austin: University of Texas Press, 1995).

38. See Camp, *Politics in Mexico*, p. 250.

39. Ibid., pp. 196–197, treats this election, as does David A. Shirk, *Mexico's New Politics: The PAN and Democratic Change* (Boulder, CO: Lynne Rienner, 2004).

40. The campaign and 2000 elections are discussed in the next chapter.

41. Consult Luis Alberto Romero, *A History of Argentina in the Twentieth Century* (University Station: Pennsylvania State University Press, 2002), and David Rock, *Argentina, 1516–1982: From Spanish Colonization to the Falklands War* (Berkeley: University of California Press, 1985).

42. Useful are Paul H. Lewis, *Guerrillas and Generals: The "Dirty" War in Argentina* (Westport, CT: Praeger, 2002); María José Moyano, *Argentina's Lost Patrol: Armed Struggle, 1969–1979* (New Haven: Yale University Press, 1995); and Monica Peralta Ramos and Carlos H. Waisman, eds., *From Military Rule to Liberal Democracy in Argentina* (Boulder, CO: Westview Press, 1987).

43. On the political repercussions of the Malvinas War, see James W. McGuire, *Peronism Without Perón: Unions, Parties, and Democracy in Argentina* (Stanford, CA: Stanford University Press, 1997), pp. 176ff. On the war itself see Michael Parsons, *The Falklands War* (Stroud, UK: Sutton, 2000), and James Aulich, ed., *Framing the Falklands War: Nationhood, Culture, and Identity* (Philadelphia: Open University Press, 1992).

44. See McGuire, *Peronism*, p. 185, as well as William C. Smith, *Authoritarianism and the Crisis of the Argentine Political Economy* (Stanford, CA: Stanford University Press, 1989), pp. 241–266; the 1983 election is discussed on pp. 257–258.

45. On the Alfonsín government see Smith, *Authoritarianism*, pp. 267ff., and McGuire, *Peronism*, pp. 183–207.

46. Edward C. Epstein, ed., *The New Argentine Democracy: The Search for a Successful Formula* (Westport, CT: Praeger, 1992), is useful for the first half of this period.

47. The change of economic gurus is discussed in Smith, *Authoritarianism,* p. 287.

48. A nearly lame-duck civilian president besieged with problems managing in a few years to gain control of a renegade intelligence community accustomed to going its own way was a monumental task for even the ablest of chief executives. On civil-military relations in this period, see J. Patrice McSherry, *Incomplete Transition: Military Power and Democracy in Argentina* (New York: St. Martin's Press, 1997), and David Pion-Berlin, *Through Corridors of Power: Institutions and Civil-Military Relations in Argentina* (University Station: Pennsylvania State University Press, 1997).

49. This election reopened the question of whether some Peronist strategists had truly wished to win in 1983, when they put up a weak candidate, or had realized that popular expectations far outran possibilities for their fulfillment in the midst of economic malaise. In any case Menem was not on the radar screen as a viable contender in 1983, requiring the events of the next five years to emerge as the antiestablishment Peronist standard bearer and to take office under more favorable circumstances.

50. On Menem see McGuire, *Peronism,* pp. 216–226. Interesting ideas can be found in Javier Corrales, *Presidents Without Parties: The Politics of Economic Reform in Argentina and Venezuela in the 1990s* (University Station: Pennsylvania State University Press, 2002), and Paul H. Lewis, *Authoritarian Regimes in Latin America: Dictators, Despots, and Tyrants* (Lanham, MD: Rowman & Littlefield, 2006), pp. 234–239, perceptively analyzes Menem.

51. The military conspiracies are covered in McSherry, *Incomplete Transition,* and Pion-Berlin, ed. *Through Corridors of Power.* See also David Pion-Berlin, *Civil-Military Relations in Latin America: New Analytical Perspectives* (Chapel Hill: University of North Carolina Press, 2001), especially Pion-Berlin's essay on "Civil-Military Circumvention: How Argentine State Institutions Compensate for a Weakened Chain of Command."

52. Scandals of the Menem era are discussed in McGuire, *Peronism,* pp. 225–230.

53. A competent discussion of Argentine democratization is the chapter by Carlos H. Waisman in Larry Diamond, Jonathon Hartlyn, Juan J. Linz, and Seymour Martin Lipset, eds., *Democracy in Developing Countries: Latin America* (Boulder, CO: Lynne Rienner, 1999), pp. 71–129.

54. The formation of FREPASO and the 1995 elections are covered in McGuire, *Peronism,* pp. 249ff., as well as in Liliana de Ruz, "From Military to Menem: Elections and Political Parties in Argentina," in Joseph S. Tulchin and Allison M. Garland, eds., *Argentina: The Challenges of Modernization* (Wilmington, DE.: Scholarly Resources Books, 1998), pp. 13–152.

55. See McGuire, *Peronism,* p. 241.

56. This election was unique in that the loser would come to the presidency midway through the winner's constitutional term—in effect, splitting the presidential tenure.

57. On the first part of this period, see Harvey Kline, *Colombia: Democracy Under Assault,* rev. ed., (Boulder, CO: Westview Press, 1994), as well as Jonathan Hartlyn, *The Politics of Coalition Rule in Colombia* (New York: Cambridge University Press, 1988).

58. Betancur's term is covered in John D. Martz, *The Politics of Clientelism: Democracy and the State in Colombia* (New Brunswick, NJ: Transaction, 1997), pp. 209–241.

59. The Barca administration is treated in Martz, *Politics,* pp. 243–264, and that of Gaviria on pp. 265–289. There is a good overall treatment of the state of Colombian democracy by Jonathan Hartlyn and John Dugas in Diamond et al., eds., *Democracy,* pp. 249–397.

60. See Charles Berquist, Ricardo Peñaranda, and Gonzalo Sánchez G., eds., *Violence in Colombia 1990–2000: Waging War and Negotiating Peace* (Wilmington, DE: Scholarly Resources Books, 2001).

61. Martz, *Politics,* p. 135, as well as Harvey Kline, *State Building and Conflict Resolution in Colombia, 1986–1994* (Tuscaloosa: University of Alabama Press, 1999).

62. Gaviria is treated in Martz, *Politics,* pp. 265–289. See Russell Crandall, *Driven by Drugs: U.S. Policy Toward Colombia* (Boulder, CO: Lynne Rienner, 2002).

63. See Samper in the Hartlyn and Dugas chapter in Diamond et al., eds., *Democracy,* as well as Martz, *Politics,* pp. 297–304.

64. The younger Pastrana did not have as much to live up to as had López Michelsen, since the elder Pastrana was not in the same league as the first Alfonso López.

12

Democratization's Diverse Paths Toward Democracy, 1980–1999

During the 1956–1979 period all South American countries had experienced military dictatorships, although starting at different times. Peru had a single civilian administration at the beginning of the period, followed by a military government up to, but not through, the period's end. Venezuela, like Colombia, escaped from an oppressive military government very near the beginning, whereas Chile entered one only in 1973 and was the last to exit. Uruguay's authoritarian military episode had been mercifully short, and Paraguay left this behind for the first time in a generation after 1989. The time frame for Bolivia roughly matched that of Brazil, whereas Ecuador fluctuated between civilian and military interludes, and in Argentina the nonmilitary interruptions were shorter.

In the northern part of the region, Mexico was far from truly democratic, and Cuba was under Castro's communistic regime. Close to Cuba, Haiti was most like Paraguay: long mired in an autocracy that would persist as an anomaly in the new democratic age. The Dominican Republic, whose dictatorship had ended in the early 1960s, would continue as a semidemocracy through all but the end of the new period. Nicaragua, where a revolutionary Marxist-Leninist regime replaced the Somoza family tyranny at the very end of the 1970s, would work its way toward a Latin American "normality" it had really never experienced. In Guatemala and Honduras, military regimes had come in just before the beginning of the 1956–1979 period, and they would exit along paths similar to those of Andean South America. Costa Rica had avoided the militaristic tide of the 1960s and 1970s, whereas El Salvador certainly had not, nor did it swim with the democratic tide until the 1990s—delayed by its long civil war. Panama had not yet fully established autonomy from de facto protectorate status but would move in that direction in the late 1990s. The countries of the "New Caribbean" were still in their infant to toddler stages, all less than a generation past colonial rule. As the dynamics of political change in the four largest countries were examined in the previous chapter, the variations in the rest of the region are explored here.

Overview

Peru began the period with a return to democratic civilian rule under the same man the military had ousted in 1968. Subsequently, at long last, it elected an *Aprista* to the presidency, only to have him perform disastrously, leading the country to turn to a political outsider for a two-term administration marked by highs and lows, ending unfortunately on the latter. Venezuela resorted to reaching into the past for its presidents in a vain attempt to stave off lower-class voter disenchantment with the parties that had served the country well from the 1940s on to the beginning of the 1990s. Chile had to wait until almost the midpoint of the period to rid itself of an oppressive military regime but made up for lost time when it did return to democracy. Bolivia returned to constitutional processes at the period's inception, going back to the two men who had occupied the presidency from 1952 to 1964, before electing the general who had headed the military regime for most of the 1970s. Ecuador, with Velasco Ibarra finally gone from the scene, returned to civilian democracy under a series of far less colorful personalities, but the electorate was dissatisfied enough to regularly elect one of the incumbent's opponents as successor. Uruguay put its authoritarian interlude behind, returning to its democratic normality, and Paraguay finally got past the long era of the Stroessner dictatorship.

This was an eventful and essentially positive period for Central America, as the 1980s were a decade of violent civil war for both Nicaragua and El Salvador followed by peace and reconstruction in the 1990s. Guatemala put its bloody insurgency behind, and Honduras went on a streak of elected civilian governments more characteristic of democratic paragon Costa Rica than of a "banana republic" where the presidency had been reserved for the top-ranking military. Most of the period would be painful for Panama, but at the end the canal would finally belong to it. The Dominican Republic would spend much of the period governed, as in the preceding one, by Joaquín Balaguer but would finally have him out—although not until he was in his nineties—before the century ended. Cuba continued to have Castro for the whole period, and Haiti might get rid of the Duvaliers but find that in some ways its new military rulers were even worse.

As noted for Brazil and Argentina, outstanding political leadership was not a major factor in their climb out of the depths of the political inferno that had gotten under way in parts of the region during the late 1970s and dominated the 1980s. Political ineptitude among the military did, however, contribute significantly to erosion of support for the authoritarian option. For failure of authoritarian regimes to deliver on promises of greatly improved economic performance along with waning of the fears of possible revolutions that had led elites and panic-stricken middle sectors to turn to the military in the 1960s played much more important roles in this democratic recovery.

Peru: Disillusionment, Infatuation with Fujimori, and Illusions Destroyed

Peru had a rocky, uneven, and essentially unconsolidated transition back to civilian rule and competitive political life. Yet, despite the thorny problems posed by ingrained terrorism and an irradicable drug industry, it did move far beyond the generation-long impasse occasioned by the military's deep-seated antipathy for APRA and that party's prolonged retention of major, if not necessarily majority, popular support. By the end of the period, Peru's voters had soured on all of the existing parties and several new political movements—including that of a populist figure who would enjoy massive support for most of the 1990s.

It entered the 1980s with the *Apristas* divided and still mourning historical party leader Haya de la Torre, who had just passed away. As APRA's presidential candidate and his more conservative running mate sniped at each other, ex-president Belaúnde Terry successfully campaigned as a democratic populist, garnering 45.5 percent of the votes in the May elections compared to 27.4 percent for *Aprista* Armando Villanueva, 9.6 percent for Lima's ex-mayor Luis Bedoya of the PPC, and 13.8 percent for the several left-wing hopefuls. Villanueva gracefully stepped aside, negating the need for a runoff, and Belaúnde negotiated an alliance with his old Christian Democratic junior partners from the 1960s to obtain a majority in the congress.

One problem Belaúnde faced coming to office in July 1980 that he had not in his previous presidency was the persistent violence unleashed by the Shining Path *(Sendero Luminoso)* insurgents.[1] Advocates of a peasant-based republic through violent revolution on the principles of Mao at his most radical, the members of this group were responsible for nearly two thousand deaths in 1983 and some thirty-six hundred in 1984, along with untold acts of barbarism and destruction of property approaching the value of $1 billion. Their sensational terrorist activities cast a pall over Belaúnde's attempts to spur economic development and alleviate social problems.

When Belaúnde was unable to live up to unrealistic expectations based on a rosy retrospective view of his earlier administration, a new-look APRA came to power in 1985 behind young, handsome, and smooth-talking Alan García Pérez (b. 1949). Not only did this emulator of Spain's charismatic Prime Minister Felipe González and heartthrob Julio Iglesias draw just over 53 percent of the vote, but he also carried his party to majorities in both houses of the congress. The left made a significant comeback, with 24.7 percent of the vote for Lima mayor Alfonso Barrantes, as the incumbent governing party, Popular Action, fell into near irrelevance with only 7.3 percent. On the positive side, this was the first time in forty years that one duly elected president was succeeded by another. Yet soon the country was near chaos, as the immature president demonstrated a high-handed and autocratic style and an economic policy that wavered from one pole to the other. After promising to reverse the statist policies of the preceding governments, he abruptly turned around again. Drug traffickers and extreme-left terrorists were running amok compared to in the Belaúnde years, when the Shining Path insurgency had gotten under way, in the early 1980s, followed by the Tupac Amaro Revolutionary Movement in mid-1984.[2] Hence, by the end of the 1980s, the electorate was desperate for change, García's approval rating having plummeted from 95 percent to a dismal 15 percent. Inflation of 1722 percent in 1988 exploded to 2800 percent in 1989 as GDP fell by 9 percent, then by 12 percent. It is no surprise that an independent candidate won the late 1989 Lima mayoralty election.

Just before the national elections, the country's foreign exchange reserves were squandered, a fitting, if unfortunate, end to García's mishandling of the debt crisis. His failing performance was testimony to how APRA's inability to come to power any time in the 1930s, combined with Haya de la Torre's dominance of the party until he was a very old man, stunted development of new leadership. Indeed, García's shortcomings were magnified by the fact that as a party, the "new" APRA had a complete lack of governmental experience—although this deficiency had been against their will and should be laid at the military's doorstep. Long anticipation of what *Apristas* might do in office helped explain the unreasonably high expectations when they finally did come to power a half century or so late—more than two decades after their knocking on the door in the 1962 elections. Perversely, this lack of experience in governing also contributed to their lamentably poor performance once becoming the nation's government in the mid-1980s.

Against the ensuing background of pervasive disenchantment as well a persistent terrorist activity, a new providential man would decide to make a break with the past and rebuild the nation's political institutions. Unfortunately, Alberto Keinya Fujimori (b. 1938) was not Charles de Gaulle, and Peru was certainly not post-1958 France. For the better part of a decade Fujimori would, however, be a serviceable Peruvian version of Argentina's Menem in a country that had known no outstanding political leadership since the end of the Legúia era in 1930. (Haya de la Torre might have been such a person had the military allowed him to come to power, but he might also have been another in a series of political leaders talking the political talk much better than walking the walk.)

The 1990 race saw the old parties pushed aside by personalist campaigns of conservative author Mário Vargas Llosa (27.6 percent in the April balloting) and

Japanese-Peruvian agronomist Fujimori (24.6 percent), as APRA's standard bearer won only 19 percent and two leftist hopefuls shared 11 percent. Fujimori, head of the National Agrarian University, came from behind to win a runoff going away (56.5 percent to 34 percent) by promising an almost painless way out of the economic chaos—whereas his overconfident rival stressed the sacrifices and stern tests ahead for the nation. Peru's situation was indeed grave: GDP had fallen 30 percent in three years, out-of-control inflation was 7600 percent a year, and service on $23 billion in foreign debt was two years in arrears. Adding to public dismay was the fact that political violence had claimed close to three thousand deaths in the twelve months preceding the election.[3]

Seeking to mobilize popular support by dramatic action and to focus dissatisfaction on his opponents, in April 1992 Fujimori abruptly suspended the constitution, an act that led to a cutoff of economic aid from the United States and its allies. Bolstered by the capture of Abemael Guzmán Reynoso, supreme leader of the Shining Path insurgents, he held elections for a constituent assembly in November, and eleven months later, he gained approval of a new constitution by a narrow 52 to 48 percent margin in a national referendum. With thousands of rebels turning in their arms, Fujimori rode high on a tidal wave of popular support as inflation dropped to 15 percent and GDP grew by 13 percent in 1994, and politically related violence fell by 80 percent. This dramatic recovery, along with a brief reopening of the border war with Ecuador, paved the way for Fujimori's reelection in April 1995 with 64 percent of the vote (similar to Perón's landslide victory in 1973)—an unprecedented second consecutive term paralleling Menem's Argentine feat and preceding that of Cardoso in 1998 in Brazil.

Fujimori's centralized, executive-dominated government and free-market orientation led to massive privatization—reaching $3.5 billion by mid-1995—linked to purchasers' commitments to new investments of an equal magnitude. The year Fujimori had taken office (mid-1990), inflation had soared to over 7600 percent, falling to 139 percent in 1992, 27 percent in 1993 and 15 percent for 1994. So in October 1995 an agreement with creditors reopened access to international capital markets. With 67 of 120 seats in the congress and none of the traditional parties reaching the 5 percent vote threshold for representation, Fujimori, intimately tied to the intelligence services, was able to reduce somewhat his hitherto heavy dependence on the military, which he had redeployed away from the country's borders to concentrate on internal security. Still, his style became increasingly authoritarian, and the shady past and highly questionable dealings of his head of the National Intelligence Service (SIN) attracted adverse attention. The revamped political system remained highly personalist and poorly institutionalized. In mid-December 1996 the Tupac Amaro Revolutionary Movement proved that insurgency was still alive, dramatically grabbing the spotlight from the Shining Path by seizing over six hundred hostages at the residence of the Japanese ambassador and holding onto the most prominent politicians and diplomats until being killed by assault teams on February 22, 1997.

By that time, signs of "Fuji fatigue" were evident. Insurgency, no longer acute, remained chronic and on the upswing, having over the years cost thirty thousand lives and at least $14 billion in direct economic losses. Scandals abounded, particularly ones involving Fujimori's gray eminence, controversial intelligence chief Vladimir Montesinos. In 1999, Alejandro Toledo (b. 1963), an Indian from the interior who had begun as a shoeshine boy but later earned a Stanford doctorate in economics, led opposition to Fujimori's bid for a legally questionable third term. Fujimori and fraud would triumph in the short run, as he purged the supreme court when it ruled against him, but by the end of 2000 he would head in disgrace to exile in Japan. Sadly, better days were not necessarily ahead.

Venezuela: A Rundown Democratic System

Venezuela's political development bogged down during the 1980s and 1990s, dramatically so when compared to the great forward movement of the preceding two decades. Yet disastrous backsliding was avoided, and foundations for future progress were preserved. Leadership, one of Venezuela's strong suits in the first thirty-five years of the post–World War II era, let the country down. Concurrently, there was a failure to continue learning from the past. Political elites who had absorbed well lessons from the adversities of 1948–1958 and astutely applied them during four presidencies became overconfident and complacent. When performances of the first pair of administrations in this quarter century proved lackluster, their response, avidly seized upon by the electorate, was to go back and choose former distinguished chief executives to come back and reassume power under greatly changed circumstances. The results were acutely disappointing, but the processes of competitive civilian electoral democracy survived.[4]

As the 1980s dawned, Venezuela appeared to be in a highly favorable political situation compared to the tensions and turbulence prevailing in much of the region. Elections in December 1978 had given COPEI its second opportunity for governing, this time under Luis Herrera Campíns. The protracted insurgency had died down to sporadic flare-ups, but by 1982 economic conditions were seriously deteriorating as oil revenues, counted on for 90 percent of foreign exchange earnings and the bulk of government revenues, plunged in the final years of COPEI stewardship. With the state responsible for 65 percent of GDP and with more than 1.2 million persons on its payroll, there was great reluctance to make deep cuts in federal expenditures, which neared $23 billion in 1982.

As it entered an election year, the Herrera Campíns government faced a pressing foreign debt burden of at least $36 billion, half of it short-term, a growing trade deficit, shrinking foreign exchange reserves, surging inflation, a badly deteriorating exchange rate, and out-of-control deficit spending. In late February 1983, the Bolívar was devaluated by 40 percent, and a highly artificial exchange rate structure was imposed, followed by a temporary debt moratorium. Dissatisfaction with the government's management of the economy soared to 87 percent. Under these circumstances the AD pulled itself together to regain power at the end of 1983 behind Jaime Lusinchi (b. 1924), a veteran congressional leader. With COPEI divided between fans of ex-president Caldera and supporters of a younger aspirant, Lusinchi won by a landslide, with a margin of 3.8 million votes—a record 56.8 percent of the valid vote cast—to 2.3 million for the incumbent party. The margin of 3.3 million to 1.9 million of AD over COPEI in simultaneous congressional balloting, with less that 1.4 million for the plethora of smaller parties, gave the AD the highest proportion it had ever received in a national legislative election in Venezuela's multiparty system at 49.9 percent. This vote translated into a 29-to-13 advantage over COPEI in the senate and 112 to 61 in the 200-member Chamber of Deputies.

The 1983 election constituted the peak of two-party dominance, as Lusinchi and COPEI's Eduardo Fernández combined for 90 percent of the presidential vote, and their parties received 79 percent of the valid legislative votes. It also marked a low point for the left, as Euro-communist intellectual Teodoro Petkoff of the Movement Toward Socialism (MAS), in alliance with the Leftist Revolutionary Movement (MIR) received a dispiriting 270,000 presidential votes to go along with 5.7 percent of votes for the congress, and older Marxist warhorse José Vicente Rangel did even worse with a disheartening 220,000 votes. MIR's 1.6 percent sliver of the congressional vote matched that of the Venezuelan Communist Party (PCV), a dismal 1.7 percent. The registered electorate had grown from 1978's 6.2 million (with 5.5 million actually voting) to well over 7.5 million, of whom 6.6 million cast valid ballots.[5] Such a high degree of participation in an electorate dominated by first- and second-time voters was exceptional by any comparative standards. (In 1958, the electorate had been 2.9 million, passing 4.1 million a decade later, and exceeding 4.7 million by 1973.)

Political deterioration set in during Lusinchi's disappointingly lackluster administration. In the face of public disenchantment, AD retained power at the end of 1988 by running ex-president Carlos Andrés Pérez, associated in the public eye with the prosperity of the oil-boom-fed mid-1970s, although it had lost the control of the congress it had achieved in 1983. Disillusion set in early, as Pérez encountered a difficult economic situation that kept him from fulfilling expectations for a return to populist policies. Nonetheless, he survived rather poorly planned and organized military coup attempts in February and November 1992. Their leader, Lieutenant Colonel Hugo Chávez Frías (b. 1954), was imprisoned after the second and more serious try. (Yet it bears remembering that an even worse-planned adventure of this type had lifted Fidel Castro out of the political sideshow in Cuba in 1953, and Chávez would not have to wait long to attain Venezuela's presidency.)

Economic problems mounted, starting with a January 1993 bank crisis that cost the country $10 billion over the next year and a half, wiped out its foreign exchange reserves, helped spur inflation to an annual rate of 100 percent, and contributed mightily to a rise in unemployment to 18 percent. This time with no international oil crisis to bail him out, and evidence of corruption bursting out, the president's support eroded until the supreme court and the senate forced him to resign or be impeached in May 1993, with that year's election campaign already well under way. Not daunted by the fiasco resulting from having reached back into the past to elect a previous occupant of the presidential palace, the Venezuelan electorate decided to compound the error. In a December 1993 presidential race featuring an overcrowded field, Rafael Caldera (1969–1973) was elected as an "antiparty" candidate (like Fujimori in Peru), running against his own child, COPEI, as well as a plethora of other candidates. With a great deal of quantity, but little quality, from which to choose, only three-fifths of registered voters cast ballots. Obviously the younger generation of Venezuelans did not share the enthusiasm of their parents for the parties and system that had brought democracy after the cruel 1948–1958 authoritarian night. This experience had not been part of their lives, but being left out of the benefits was. Long preeminent, after the December 1993 elections AD dropped to only 27 percent of seats in the lower house and 32 percent of the senate. As the candidate of a catchall coalition of splinter parties calling itself Convergéncia ("Convergence"), with only 17 percent of the vote, the aging Caldera was a minority president in all senses of the word, badly needing AD support in the congress.[6] More seriously, the party system that had performed so well since the mid-1940s was clearly on its last legs.

By the mid-1990s, Venezuela's population was up 400 percent from the 1936 immediate post-Gómez era, and Caracas had grown sevenfold. The once-dominant Andean region had dropped from having nearly 20 percent of the country's population to having half that. So structural changes appear to have been needed for a system that had relied upon two major disciplined parties' keeping the congress weak in relation to the executive. This was not the type of government Caldera was inclined or able to offer. Yet, after starting very badly, once Caldera learned how much times and Venezuela had changed, he paid more attention to the views of planning minister Teodoro Petkoff, once a leader of the armed insurgency.

Having been amnestied by Caldera and calling himself an heir to Bolívar as well as a fervent admirer of Peru's Fujimori, ex-coup-maker Hugo Chávez ran successfully for the presidency at the end of 1998 as the candidate of the "patriotic pole," which included his personalistic Fifth Republic Movement (MVR), attacking the "rancid oligarchs" with devastating effect. This man of the people (son of a small-

HUGO CHÁVEZ

town schoolteacher) took office in February 1999. Independent Henrique Sallas Romer running on the Venezuelan Project (PRVZL) ticket, had eventually received the backing of both COPEI's and AD's electorally unexciting nominees but still lost to Chávez's 56.4 percent of the vote (settling for 39.5 percent). Yet Chávez came away with only a minority in the congress, where the traditional pillars AD and COPEI won fifty-five and twenty-seven seats in the chamber, with nineteen and six in the Senate (on 22 percent and 11 percent of the vote), while Sallas's PRVZL came in with twenty-four seats in the lower house and two in the Senate on 12 percent of the vote. This outcome left the opposition bulwarks well ahead of the Chávez coalition's seventy chamber and eighteen Senate seats (mainly for the MVR and its 21 percent of the vote, but also including allies Movement Toward Socialism [MAS] at 9 percent and Causa Radicál with 3 percent).

Not willing to be hampered by this congress, outdoing Fujimori Chávez gained 81.5 percent approval—if only of the 39 percent who bothered to vote—in a late April referendum on his proposal for a constituent assembly. Then, two months later, he won 117 of 128 seats for the body that wrote his kind of a strong-executive constitution.[7] This charter, ratified in mid-December 1999, also bestowed upon its architect an extended term beginning in 2000. It would prove controversial and troubled but would also mark a watershed in Venezuelan politics as well as have a broader regional impact.

Chile: The Way Back to Democracy

The period began with the Pinochet regime firmly entrenched in power and beginning to gain international acceptance, as Franco had managed to do in Spain by the late 1940s. As late as 1988, after fifteen years in power, General Augusto

Pinochet still presided over a united army, enjoyed a solid core of civilian support, and had a constitutional blueprint for remaining in power another decade—despite the demise of military regimes in all of Chile's neighbors and the rest of the region. Yet, in a very short time, he was out of power and Chile had resumed its democratic heritage.[8]

In 1980, Pinochet imposed an authoritarian new constitution, ratified through a procedurally questionable plebiscite by an announced, but widely doubted, two-thirds majority. It enshrined the duty of the armed forces to ensure the survival of the state, legalized control of the media to prevent injury to the state and the people, and outlawed both strikes and labor courts as ways of settling union-management disputes. Most significantly, the constitution provided for a plebiscite in 1988 through which the junta's candidate could receive an additional eight years as president.[9] In installing this mechanism for continuing in power, Pinochet and his advisers counted on three factors favoring legitimization of his rule: satisfaction with the country's economic situation; fear of a return to the turmoil of the early 1970s; and division of the opposition. All three of these considerations, as well as the international environment, were to undergo significant change by the time the referendum came around. To begin with the sustained economic growth, ranging from 6 to 8 percent annually from 1977 through 1981, ended abruptly in 1982 as low copper prices pulled the rug out from under loyalty-gaining social programs, modest as they were. In this context neoliberal elements organized the Independent Democratic Union (UDI) and traditional right-wingers attempted to revive the National Party (PN).[10]

Hence, by the mid-1980s, heartened by the return to civilian democracy in neighboring countries previously friendly to the Pinochet regime, Chile's political parties increasingly advocated elections and a return to competitive political processes. The strongest of these parties, the Christian Democratic Party (PDC), riding on the memory of ex-president Eduardo Frei, called openly for a no vote in the upcoming referendum. Since it was free of any involvement with the Allende government—Frei having defeated the socialist leader in 1964 and having backed his ouster in 1973—and enjoyed a close relationship with the Catholic Church, the PDC could not be attacked by the military regime as subversive or soft on communism. When a broad coalition of opposition parties, including the socialists as well as the PDC, issued a joint program on the eve of the balloting and the church carried out a massive voter registration campaign, the handwriting was on the wall for Pinochet and his supporters.

So on October 5, 1988, Chile's electorate upset Pinochet's carefully laid plans with a 54.7 percent no vote (to 34 percent favoring Pinochet's guaranteed continuance in power), as close public and international scrutiny of the balloting and vote counting stymied efforts to manipulate the electoral outcome. The question remaining was whether the regime could muster a civilian candidate capable of defeating the prodemocracy forces. Surprising the government with their unity, the opposition formed the Concertacíon dos Partidos por la Democracia (United Action of Pro-Democracy Parties) behind the PDC's Patricio Aylwin Alcozar (b. 1918) running against the regime's Hernán Buchi, the incumbent finance minister. To guarantee the military regime's acceptance of subsequent electoral outcomes, the opposition agreed to retain the 1980 constitution subject to removal of some of its most democracy-inhibiting provisions. After laborious negotiations, the modifications were approved in a May 1989 referendum. Presidential terms were reduced to six years, and the number of elected senators was raised in order to dilute the influence of the nine Pinochet-appointed senators while maintaining their existence. Still the great autonomy of the armed forces, their budget guarantees, and the exaggerated role of the national security council remained along with other authoritarian enclaves.

On December 14, 1989, Chile had its first competitive and free elections since 1970, with 55.2 percent of the valid vote, 3.5 million out of 6.8 million, going to Aylwin as he defeated the pro-Pinochet candidate by a margin of nearly 1.3 million votes and his PDC received the lion's share of the Concertacíon coalition's support (26.6 percent of the total turnout compared to 29.4 percent for Buchi's coalition of the right-wing parties). Taking office on March 11, 1990, for a four-year term, Aylwin faced the task of establishing democracy with the dictator still in control of the army and vetoing any punishment of his regime members for atrocities committed in 1973 and after. Although enjoying control of the chamber, where 51.5 percent of the vote (26 percent for the PDC) gave them sixty-nine seats, the Concertacíon lacked a majority in the senate despite winning twenty-two of its thirty-eight elected seats (thirteen for the PDC) because of a number of lifetime-appointed members, including Pinochet. On the opposition side out of a total of forty-eight the UDI had eleven seats in the chamber, and National Renovation (RN), essentially a successor to the old National Party (PN), held twenty-nine seats, second to the PDC's thirty-eight.[11]

As Pinochet was legally entrenched as both a life-term senator and army commander in chief, he enjoyed considerable bargaining power—in sharp contrast with the Argentine and Peruvian situations. Yet in some ways the residual threat posed by his presence helped maintain unity of the democratic forces beyond the point at which it otherwise might well have unraveled. For as time passed Pinochet became a sick old man preoccupied with avoiding trial and punishment abroad for his crimes against humanity. Still the government had to content itself with investigation and publicity about human rights violations, rather than prosecution and punishment. Fortunately, most of the public accepted these actions as all that was feasible under the constraining circumstances.

In 1993, Eduardo Frei Ruiz-Tagle, in his early fifties and son of Christian Democratic Party founder and 1964–1970 president Eduardo Frei Montalva,

EDUARDO FREI RUIZ-TAGLE

received 55.5 percent of the total votes for a victory of 3.7 million to 1.9 million over the right's candidate, Arturo Alessandri Besa—another bearer of a distinguished political lineage, who garnered 33.6 percent of the vote. Hence the namesake of the revered Eduardo Frei embarked upon a six-year term as consolidator of Chile's democratic transition.[12] In the lower house of the congress, seventy seats gave Concertacíon solid control, as the PDC held thirty-seven seats with each of its major allies, the Socialists and the Party for Democracy (PPD) having fifteen to the RN's twenty-nine and the UDI's fifteen. Aylwin had concentrated with some success on reducing poverty, so Frei could pay increasing attention to education and infrastructure. In 1995, GDP grew by 8.4 percent, with inflation an annual 8.2 percent and the unemployment rate down to 4.5 percent. Savings–investments equaled 31.7 percent of GDP, enabling democratic Chile to enjoy the respect for able management of the economy that had been the military regime's claim to respectability. More important, the popular support prosperity enabled the government to emerge victorious in its one major confrontation with right-wing forces.

Convicting retired general Manuel Contreras, former head of Pinochet's feared secret police, in June 1995 for the brazen 1976 murder in Washington, D.C., of Orlando Letelier, the government was faced with a four-month standoff with the military elements protecting him. In the end he was imprisoned, being given the courtesy of military, rather than civilian, guards. Then in 1997 Pinochet and the other service heads were finally retired, and judges appointed by the ex-dictator began to reach retirement age, too. At the end of the year stand-alone congressional elections gave the president's party 23 percent of the vote (compared to

27.2 percent in 1993); its allied parties fared relatively well, maintaining the government's chamber majority at 69 of 120 seats on 50.5 percent of the vote, with a turnout of 86 percent.[13] Positioning itself for the presidential succession, the PDC garnered 39 seats in the lower house (on 19 percent of the vote) to 16 for the PPD and 11 for the Socialists. On the opposition side the RN came away with 23 seats and the UDI with 17. A presidential election at the end of 1999 carried Chile forward into the second decade of reestablished democracy. In a context of rising unemployment Social Democrat Ricardo Lagos Escobar (b. 1938) of the Party for Democracy (PPD) ran against a very respectable conservative, Joaquín Lavin Infante, mayor of the wealthy suburb of Los Condes. Lagos defeated him in a tight mid-January 2000 runoff by a 51.3 percent to 48.7 percent margin—after a 48 percent to 47.5 percent squeaker on December 12, as 90 percent of registered voters cast their ballots.[14] So a former Pinochet government official narrowly lost to an Allende protégé, who to gain election pledged to continue Frei's free-market economic policies. This was a testimony to the pragmatism of Chilean politicians. With an economics doctorate from Duke University, Lagos had been education minister in Aylwin's government and public works minister under Frei, thus being highly qualified for the presidency. He would carry Chile into the twenty-first century in the best political shape of any country in the Western Hemisphere. (This conclusion was confirmed by the 2005–2006 election and is fully justified in Chapters 14 and 15.)

Bolivia: To the Future by Way of the Past

Bolivia's progress toward democracy after 1980 was generally positive and, in light of where it started, highly encouraging. Having four elected civilian presidents in a row was a major step forward in a country whose best previous experience had started with a president coming to power through a revolution and ended with the same individual (Victor Paz Estenssoro) overthrown by a military coup after having amended the constitution to enable himself to continue in office. Although the first two presidents of this 1980s democratic transition were the same two men who had held that office between 1952 and 1964, Bolivia did manage to move beyond them to chief executives of a new generation. Then, too, although a former military dictator was a perennial contender and eventually president, along the way he repeatedly accepted adverse decisions when close elections required a final decision by the congress. Indeed, the late General Hugo Banzer's participation in the country's electoral and parliamentary life may very well have served to reduce both inclination and opportunity for military intervention in the political process or armed forces' assumption of an arbiter role.[15]

The period opened with the interim president surviving two coup attempts and a narrow escape from assassination to preside over mid-1980 elections. In seeking an experienced hand to guide them through the shoals of political transition and economic crisis, Bolivians reached farther back than did their Peruvian neighbors or even the Venezuelans. Hernán Siles, who had finished his presidential term two decades earlier, came in first in the June 29, 1980, balloting, defeating veteran ex-presidents Paz and Banzer by a ratio of 34 percent, to 18 percent, to 15 percent. For the moment, at least, novices need not apply. However, politics was highly factionalized, with seventy-three parties taking part, most of them splinter groups bargaining for political crumbs from the established parties while waiting for Siles, Paz, and Banzer to vanish from the political stage—which these ambitious figures had no intention of doing. Siles's winning Democratic Popular Union (UPD) included nine other parties as well as his own National Revolutionary Movement of the Left (MNRI), and there were fourteen identifiable factions in Paz's National Revolutionary Movement (MNR).

While the congress was on the verge of ratifying Siles's election, right wing military elements behind General Luis García Mesa staged a coup leading to a yearlong regime resting on a partnership between corrupt military elements and leaders of the country's burgeoning drug traffic. Relying on the special security service of interior minister General Luis Arce Gómez, backed up by the paramilitary forces of the drug traffickers, García Meza ran an exceptionally repressive as well as thoroughly corrupt government. To curry favor with those around the capital, he signed a contract for a large sugar-refining project near La Paz. Under considerable foreign pressure and supported by the resentful Santa Cruz economic elite, the more respectable sectors of the armed forces led by Alberto Natush Busch, now a general, ousted this unholy cabal in August 1981. Two generals were unable to stabilize the situation, so in September 1982 the congress revalidated the 1980 elections, and Siles belatedly took office. A very messy transition to democracy had been accomplished.

Backed by a coalition of left and center-left parties lacking a congressional majority, Siles ran into grave problems roughly parallel to those soon encountered by Alfonsín in Argentina—an economy in shambles and unrealistically high expectations about the extent and speed of reconstruction from the negative heritage of authoritarian military rule. With parties fragmented, interest groups pressed their demands directly upon the executive, a situation different from the one that Siles had been accustomed to in his earlier presidency, when the MNR had been a nearly hegemonic party. His problems were magnified by congressional opposition not only from the right, but also from the MNR, his old party, now firmly in the hands of one-time ally Paz Estenssoro. Siles was faced with frequent military conspiracies, a hostile Santa Cruz–based business community, and an uncooperative vice president in Jaime Paz Zamora (b. 1939), an ex-guerrilla awaiting the opportunity to preside over Bolivia. Plagued by spiraling inflation, 300 percent a year into his term and rising, and growing labor unrest, Siles resisted what he considered the great mistake of his earlier presidency: entering into a stabilization program with the IMF. Instead, he declared a moratorium on debt payments that greatly weakened confidence in the economy and spurred the demand for black market dollars. With annual inflation at 2000 percent in 1984, Siles was desperate, making matters worse by entering into indirect discussions with the country's leading cocaine producer concerning payment of $2 billion in exchange for amnesty.[16] In late 1984, congressional investigations were headed off by the scheduling of new elections for mid-1985.

In looking to the past for a tried and tested chief executive, Bolivia went even farther in 1985 than it had five years before. This time Paz narrowly trailed General Banzer 26.4 percent to 28.6 percent as Siles's party garnered a pathetic 4.8 percent for its lackluster candidate. Turnout was a Bolivian record: 1.6 million. With the choice once again residing in the hands of the congress, the also-rans fell into line behind the dominant figure of the 1952–1964 period, giving Paz a 94-to-51 margin of victory. Looking ahead to 1989, a patient Banzer acquiesced—agreeing to cooperate in the congress.

Having served as president for two full terms and a sliver of a third, Paz was certain that he could do a better job than the man he had never considered in his league in ability. His New Economic Policy was designed to liberalize the economy, reduce employment in the public sector, and curb inflation by freezing public service wages while eliminating price controls. In 1984, the government's budget deficit had reached 30 percent of GDP, largely financed by issuance of government securities and expanding the money supply. With collapse of the international tin market, the militant and well-organized miners sought subsidization from the government; instead, they were met by arrest of 360 of their leaders. Paz ended the debt moratorium and renegotiated Bolivia's foreign debt, receiving $107 million in loans from the IMF after enacting tax reforms. A new electoral law, passed in 1986, recognized only parties that had received at least fifty thousand votes in the previous elections or had a membership of at least 0.5 percent of the total of the votes cast.

The May 1989 elections constituted the divide between transition and consolidation of democracy in Bolivia. The electorate was faced with clear choices uncluttered by the plethora of parties and presidential hopefuls that had characterized 1985. The governing MNR nominated ex-planning-minister Gonzalo Sánchez de Lozada (b. 1930)—raised in the United States and a University of Chicago graduate. Former vice president Jaime Paz Zamora was the Leftist Revolutionary Movement (MIR)—New Majority candidate, and Banzer, who after so long on the nation's political stage was still only sixty-two, ran a campaign reminding voters of the prosperity and order enjoyed during his previous stint in office, which had spanned most of the 1970s. In a nail-biting finish, Sánchez de Lozado garnered 23.0 percent of the nearly 1.6 million cast, edging out Banzer, who garnered 22.6 percent of the electoral harvest, and defeating Jaime Paz, recipient of a respectable 19.6 percent.

The selection process in the congress saw Banzer ally with the third-place finisher, making Paz Zamora head of a government in which—much as in the present situation in Germany—Banzer controlled a sizable share of positions and patronage, including the ministries of finance, defense, foreign relations, mines and metallurgy, and peasant and agricultural affairs. A political council presided over by Banzer monitored fulfillment of the "Government of Convergence and National Unity." Contrary to predictions of disaster, cogovernment by the "guerrilla and the gorilla" functioned reasonably well.[17] In 1993, Sánchez de Lozado's time would finally arrive—as he benefited from the rules of the game that had cost him a victory the previous time around, and with only 35.6 percent of the vote, he was ratified by the congress. In 1995, the economy was in the midst of a five-year period of 4 percent GDP growth, with foreign trade up 13 percent and inflation at 12.6 percent on its way down to 8.0 percent the following year.

In June 1997, the seventy-one-year-old Banzer, the Nationalist Democratic Action (ADN) candidate, returned to the presidency with a scant 22.3 percent of the vote, defeating, among others, ex-president Jaime Paz Zamora (with 16.3 percent) and a new MNR standard bearer (at 18 percent), in yet another election needing to be decided by the congress—which chose Banzer by a vote of 118 out of 157.[18] With 40 of 130 seats in the lower house and 13 of 27 in the senate, Banzer needed to find congressional allies among the ranks of the MIR (28 and 3) and the MNR (24 and 5) as well as the two newer significant parties: the Civic Solidarity Union (UCS) with 21 and 2 seats, and the Conscience of the Fatherland (CONDEPA) with 17 and 3. In the view of this grizzled parliamentary veteran, the more potential dance partners he had, the greater was his flexibility. Losing popularity because of his cooperation with the United States in eradicating coca production, which led to an August 1998 peasants' march on the capital, Banzer, in his long presence on Bolivia's political stage, would last until the grim reaper caught up with him in mid-2001. (Political decay for the nation would soon ensue.)

Ecuador: Catching Up with the Neighbors

Ecuador's surge of political development and democratization was substantial and sustained, although not dramatic. In a country traditionally difficult to govern, a series of civilian presidents held office after 1979. Moreover, in almost every election the winner came from the opposition to the incumbent administration, yet was allowed to take office—even in cases of very hard-fought contests resolved by paper-thin margins in runoff elections. Political progress was all the more impressive because, despite presidents usually lacking congressional majorities and often facing virulent opposition from the national legislature, constitutional normality was generally maintained.[19] Resiliency in the face of repeated and protracted crises and acute partisan rivalry is a true test of a democratic political system. This resiliency Ecuador demonstrated, for prior to this period its armed forces had found ample pretexts to intervene in analogous or even less serious circumstances.

Ecuador's transition to competitive civilian rule was launched with the January 1978 referendum on a new constitution versus a revision of the 1945 one. Over 1.8 million voted, a highly encouraging 90 percent of the electorate, and the new national charter won by a margin of 43 to 32 percent, as almost a quarter of the ballots were blank or nullified. The presidential race was thrown into an uproar the next month by the minister of government's announcement that the new president would have to be a son of native-born parents on both sides, essentially a bill of attainder directed against front-runner Assad Bucarám, a Guayaquil-based politician of Lebanese extraction. His Concentration of Popular Forces (CFP) rallied from this body blow by nominating in his stead Jaime Roldós Aguilera, Bucarám's thirty-seven-year-old nephew-in-law. In what would prove to be a move of greater-than-expected significance, history professor Oswaldo Hurtado of Popular Democracy was chosen as his running mate.

The mid-July balloting involved almost all the individuals who would govern the country during the next twenty years. The runner-up at 24 percent compared to Roldós's 31 percent, and hence a runoff contender, was fifty-seven-year-old Sixto Durán Ballen, just having finished eight years as Quito's mayor, an outcome that showed that the sierra-versus-coast antagonistic rivalry was still very much alive. In fourth place was Rodrigo Borja Cevalos (b. 1935), destined to reach the presidency two elections later.

Roldós inherited an economy struggling to meet its financial obligations, particularly an onerous foreign debt, in a context of falling oil prices. Moreover, Bucarám, bitterly disappointed that Roldós would not do his bidding, led the CPF in the congress and was frequently uncooperative with the president—who often had to veto laws sponsored by Bucarám. When politically isolated Roldós died in a plane crash in May 1981, Hurtado served out the remainder of his term. Faced by a flare-up of the long and acrimonious border dispute with Peru and hit hard by the international debt crisis, he opted for drastic austerity measures in order to achieve an accord with the IMF. The resultant currency devaluation and massive cuts in subsidies resulted in violent protests by workers.

Hurtado was followed in office in 1984 by conservative businessman León Febres Cordero Ribadeneyra (b. 1926), a wealthy US-educated Guayaquil executive, who had become congressional spokesman for the right after presiding over both the Guayaquil Chamber of Commerce and the National Chamber of Industry. A virulent antistatist, whose avid support of free-market reforms and pursuit of neoliberal policies endeared him to the Reagans, Febres Cordero's close advisers included individuals with postgraduate degrees from US universities. He did not have easy going, since his multiparty National Reconstruction Front (FRN) had run second with 27.2 percent of the vote to Rodrigo Borja's 28.7 percent before winning the May runoff by a slim 51.5 percent to 47.5 percent, and he had won the runoff only after he shifted his campaign to an insincere populist stance of "bread, housing, and development" that bolstered his coastal vote. The left, deeply divided in the presidential balloting, came away with a congressional majority, and this "progressive bloc" would deeply oppose Febres Cordero's neoliberal policies, hamstringing him whenever possible.[20] Labor unrest was pervasive even before further decline of oil prices in 1985 led to additional austerity measures and forced the president to suspend service of the mounting foreign debt. In January 1987, he was taken prisoner by paratroopers who forced him to grant amnesty to General Frank Vargas Passos for his March 1986 insubordination. The congress added to Febres Cordero's humiliation by requesting his resignation—which was not forthcoming—and Febres Cordero tried to reestablish his authority by revoking the amnesty he had granted the mutinous troops as having been extorted from him under duress.

All things may very well not come to him who waits, but patience and persistence are often necessary virtues in politics. The late François Mitterand was elected France's president in 1981 after having been in a runoff with the great Charles de Gaulle way back in 1958 and narrowly losing a second bid in 1974. Jacques Chirac would succeed Mitterand in that office in 1995, also on his third determined try. Three was also the magic number for Chile's ill-fated Salvador Allende, who had come ever so close in 1958 and been swamped in 1964 before emerging the victor in 1970. In this vein Ecuador in January 1988 saw Quito's favorite son, Rodrigo Borja of the Democratic Left (ID), finally grasp the prize that had eluded him in 1978 and had slipped out of his fingers at the last moment in 1984. Reflecting the country's continued political fragmentation, Borja received 24.8 percent of the vote on the multicandidate first ballot to 17.5 percent for runner-up Abdalá Bucarám (another of the Guayaquil Bucaráms), who would eventually win two elections later. In carrying the runoff by 47 percent to 40 percent (1.7 million votes to 1.45 million) Borja enjoyed a three-to-one margin around Quito, with Bucarám winning all along the Guayaquil-dominated coast. Although pledged to ease belt-tightening, Borja had little room to do so, as inflation was running at an annual 56 percent, and further negotiations with the IMF loomed ahead. Hence, as the basically progressive Borja enforced unpopular austerity measures, his public support slipped away.

Sixto Durán's own long wait to don Ecuador's presidential sash finally came to a happy end in 1992. Having lost in a runoff in 1978, helped engineer Febres Cordero's election in 1984, and fallen short at the finish line of the 1988 presidential sweepstakes (ending in third place), this hardy perennial of Ecuador's electoral scene saw his resolute pursuit of the country's highest office pay off twenty-two years after having become Quito's mayor. His runoff margin was 58 percent to 38 percent over the Social Christian Party (PSC)'s Jaime Nebot Saade—yet another in the string of Lebanese-extraction politicians from the coast. Problems were not long in coming. Conflict with the country's major trade union organization, the United Workers Front (FUT), was endemic, and problems rose with the Confederation of Indigenous Nations of Ecuador (CONAIE), voice of the militant sector of the country's Indian near majority. Durán's vice president and architect of his program of free-market reforms, Alberto Dahik Garzozi, fled the country in November 1995 when faced with corruption charges. He was followed soon by a stream of other government officials. A referendum that would have strengthened presidential authority (largely inspired by Fujimori's recent success in neighboring Peru) having been defeated, Durán, lacking a viable base of support in the congress, could only hang tough and hope to elect his successor.[21]

In the 1996 balloting, Durán's ex-foreign minister, Jaime Nebot Saade, ran slightly ahead of the tenacious Abdalá Bucarám Ortiz (b. 1952; nephew of Assad Bucarám and brother-in-law of deceased president Roldós) in a rare contest between two Guayaquil-based candidates. They got 27 percent and 25 percent of the vote, respectively, over two other serious contenders, one a popular TV figure who tried, as did Bucarám and Nebot, to appeal to the politically marginalized Indians. There was a July runoff, which Bucarám won by 54 percent to 46 percent. Despite this narrow margin between two very different candidates, a polarized electorate accepted the results, which constituted a frustrating loss for those whose high hopes of victory had been dashed by the final hours of vote counting. On the congressional side, the Durán–Nebot–led Social Christians came away with 28 of 82 seats, a slim lead over the Ecuadorian Roldosist Party (PRE) of the new president.

As the century neared its end, problems morphed into crises, and the more-than-flamboyant Bucarám, who egoistically considered himself an apt pupil of the late Velasco Ibarra, and who adopted some of Argentine counterpart Menem's demagogic style without any of the substance of his performance, was declared "mentally impaired" by the congress and removed. The congress refused to let the vice president, a woman, take office, turning instead to its own presiding officer. His maneuvering for a full term as well as the army commander's overt ambitions were thwarted by a widespread and deeply rooted demand for new and free elections.

In response to clear popular desires, a constituent assembly was elected in November 1997. Opening for business in December, it promptly provided for new presidential voting. This was duly held in May 1998, with Quito mayor Jamil Mahuad Witt (b. 1950) of the Popular Democracy Party edging out Álvaro Noboa of the PRE 51 to 49 percent in an all-Lebanese-descent runoff in July. The original multicandidate race had seen Mahuad with 35.2 percent to Noboa's 26.5 percent, trailed by ex-president Borja, who retained the support of 15 percent of the electorate. Although 1996 runner-up Jaime Nebot decided not to run for the presidency, his PSC came in first in the congressional balloting. After his August 1998 inauguration, Mahaud managed to cobble together a legislative majority and end a war with Peru in just six weeks. But the economy was his downfall, as El Niño winds devastated coastal agriculture in 1998, and service on a $16-billion foreign debt—eating up 40 percent of government revenues—put the nation's finances out of kilter. Replacing easily avoided taxes with a 1 percent tax on financial transactions led to massive capital flight, reaching $400 million in January 1999 alone.[22] With the economy shrinking by 7.3 percent in 1999, inflation rising by 60 percent, and poverty doubling since his inauguration, Mahaud would resort to desperate measures that would be exploited by his enemies to bring him down. (His downfall would usher in a protracted period of sociopolitical turbulence.)

Uruguay: Regaining Its Democratic Reputation

A new era opened in Uruguay in 1980 with relegalization of the Blanco and Colorado Parties and restoration of political rights to most of those who had lost them under the military regime. When submitted to a popular referendum in November, a proposed new constitution was decisively rejected (57 to 43 percent), so noncompetitive election of a candidate agreed to by the two parties and approved by the military was canceled. Uruguayans wanted a full return to competitive political life. Stung by this setback, the military could still veto the most popular candidate of the 1971 balloting, Wilson Ferreira of the Blanco Party. On the other hand, the military agreed that all their special prerogatives with respect to the country's political life would expire after one year of constitutional rule. On September 1, 1981, General Gregorio Álvarez (b. 1925), who had headed the Armed Forces Commission of Political Affairs from 1974 to 1978, was installed as president for a presidential term ending in March 1985.

In November 1984, a new election took place, with the military exercising a veto power over the nominees—especially retired general Liber Seregni of the Broad Front, but including the Blancos' Wilson Ferreira. The winner was the Colorado Party's Julio María Sanguinetti (b. 1936), polling only 28.3 percent of the vote, but benefiting from the long-entrenched practice of summing of votes of all candidates of a particular party. Sanguinetti's landmark accomplishment was an amnesty at the end of 1986 for members of the military accused of committing human rights violations since 1973.[23] This controversial measure was eventually finally ratified by the Uruguayan voters in an April 1989 referendum. The electorate would also remember him for the 17 percent GDP growth achieved in 1986–1987. In November 1989, Luis Alberto Lacalle (b. 1941) from the National Party was elected president with only 22.5 percent of the vote, devoting himself to implementing a full return to the country's democratic traditions, beginning with an all-embracing political amnesty. Economic stagnation and rising inflation forced this first Blanco president in the twentieth century to implement an austerity program of wage restraints, spending cuts, and privatization of state-run enterprises.

Opposition to Lacalle's economic policies paved the way for Sanguinetti's return to office in November 1994, as, with 32 percent of the vote, he edged out the Blanco candidate by less than 23,000 votes; Tabaré Vásquez, who had been elected mayor of Montevideo by the Broad Front in 1989, and who was running as the Progressive Encounter (EP) standard bearer, was just another 13,000 votes behind. This close call convinced the Colorados and Blancos to cooperate in 1996 in enacting a measure that would head off an EP win in 1999. The newly mandated primaries were held in April, with presidential balloting accompanying the congressional elections in October, a runoff vote in November, and municipal elections in May of the next year. (Prior to this time, parties could run several candidates for president, with all their votes being transferred to the party's front-runner.)

Running for the fifth time at the end of October 1999, Colorado Party leader Jorge Batlle Ibáñez (b. 1927) trailed the left's candidate, once again Tabaré Vásquez, by 40.1 percent to 32.8 percent, the National Party (Blancos) disastrously far behind with 22.3 percent. But in a runoff on November 28 Batlle defeated the left's leader by 54 percent to 46 percent, promising "no new taxes." Supporters of the third candidate in the regular election, ex-president Lacalle, who had been weakened by a nasty primary battle, threw most of their votes to Batlle in the runoff.[24] This centrist descendant of the nation's most famous historical political figure took office on May 1, 2000, with a divided congress in which his party needed to ally with the Blancos to have a majority. Significant change on the political scene was under way.

Paraguay: Better Late Than Never

Paraguay, a laggard country, would belatedly make its uneasy transition to democracy in the context of all of its neighbors having done so. Having completed a quarter century in power by the time the 1980s opened, dictator Alfredo Stroessner had been grooming his playboy son Gustavo to take over—eventually. As the durable autocrat began to feel his age, he took steps beyond his usual practice of sharing the profits of international narcotics traffic, money laundering, and contraband to ensure that the succession would be a family matter. This turn of events, manifested in the compulsory retirement of senior generals at the end of 1988 and their replacement by allies of the heir apparent, abruptly turned Stroessner's right-hand man, General Andrés Rodríguez, into a reborn democrat. Ousting the ailing seventy-six-year-old Stroessner in February 1989 and hustling him into exile, Rodríguez called for early elections. Although many observers misguidedly praised him for this "democratic" move, it was really designed to guarantee his election, since there was no time for exiles to return and reorganize their parties.[25] Not surprisingly under the circumstances, on May 1 Rodríguez received 72.4 percent of the votes to 20.3 percent for Domingo Laíno, leader of the Authentic Radical Liberal Party (PLRA), which had been belatedly legalized in March. The fact that 1.2 million voters made up only 53.4 percent of the officially registered electorate testified to how padded were the electoral rolls inherited from the dictatorship. Post-Stroessner Paraguay was significantly different from the sparsely inhabited backwater country he had come to rule in 1954.

In May 1991, municipal elections, in which the turnout was a significant proportion of an electorate pared to 1.7 million, the Colorados, running up a margin of 43.4 percent to 33.3 percent for the PLRA, won everywhere except in the capital. Constituent assembly elections in December broke the same way, with the Colorados gaining 122 of 198 seats on 55.1 percent of the vote to 55 seats on 27 percent electoral support for the PLRA. Under the 1992 constitution Rodríguez picked as his successor the country's richest man, fifty-four-year-old Juan Carlos Wasmosy, who had amassed much of his fortune in partnership with the deposed dictator. Although he lost the primary to ex-chief justice Luis Maria Argaña, Rodríguez pressured the electoral tribunal to reverse its results. Winning in September 1993 by a margin of 39.9 percent to 32.1 over the PLRA's Laíno, with the left's Encuentro National (EN) polling 23.1 percent, Wasmosy presided over an orderly term. The Colorados' 42 percent share of congressional voting gave it 38 seats in the chamber along with 29 in the senate, well ahead of the PLRA (with 35 percent of the votes cast in the legislative race), but short of a majority. With Argaña's Colorado Conciliation Movement controlling 22 seats in the lower house and 10 in the upper, and opposing him, the president moved toward alliance with the Liberal Party.

General Lino Oviedo, entrenched as army head, wanted to become the new Stroessner. He provoked a crisis at the end of 1994 when Wasmosy was visiting Brazil and was removed from his post in April 1996 when he threatened to kill the president. Nominated for the presidency by the Colorado Party, he was arrested for plotting in December 1997. Oviedo was freed the following August only after the inauguration of fifty-four-year-old Raúl Cubas Grau, victor over the sixty-two-year-old Laíno in the May 1998 presidential balloting by 54 percent to 42.5 percent. Cubas had been Oviedo's erstwhile vice-presidential running mate until the former was sentenced to prison, so was widely considered a stand-in elected on the slogan "Cubas in office; Oviedo in power."[26] In March 1999, Vice President Argaña, distinctly not an Oviedo ally, was assassinated, the blame falling on President Cubas, who was forced to resign, making senate leader Luis Angel González Macchi (b. 1947) the new chief executive. From exile in Argentina and Brazil

Oviedo strove to mount coups. To put this inveterate plotter on the defensive, the government sought his extradition. Clearly the country's strongman tradition hung on doggedly, but the infant democracy showed determination.

Central America: Different Roads to Democracy

This period began with massive bloodshed in El Salvador, a revolution turning into bitter civil war in Nicaragua, continued violent repression of a largely indigenous insurgency in Guatemala, a thoroughly corrupt military regime in Panama, and a seemingly entrenched military power in Honduras. Only Costa Rica was a functioning democracy. By the period's end twenty years later, all insurgencies had been replaced by peace, and each of the six countries enjoyed civilian democratic government. Overall, this subregion underwent greater political development during the 1980s and 1990s than in the first eight decades of the century—a remarkable accomplishment.[27]

Guatemala: Getting Past the Generals

The 1980s opened inauspiciously under a third military president in a row (the seventh out of eight since 1951). In 1978, this melancholy string had continued with General Fernando Romeo Lucas García, who presided over the slaughter of forty indigenous leaders who had seized the Spanish Embassy. Following a coup in March 1982, reborn Evangelical Christian general Efraín Ríos Montt (b. 1924), a victim of fraud in 1974, proclaimed himself president. While talking of transition to an elected civilian government, he took a totally forceful approach to the country's debilitating civil strife, continuing efforts to crush the insurgents with renewed intensity. His reward was being forced out in August 1983 by disgruntled fellow officers. General Oscar Mejía Victores then presided over the election of Christian Democratic mayor of Guatemala City Marco Vinicio Cerezo Arévalo (b. 1942) at the end of 1985, with turnout a respectable 61 percent. At last Guatemala's transition to democracy was under way, although with baby steps.

Although not drastically improving the country's situation, this well-meaning civilian showed more initiative in this direction than had Guatemala's most recent civilian president, survival-oriented Julio César Mendes Montenegro in 1967–1970. Yet his rather lackluster administration cost the Christian Democrats a significant share of their popularity. The November 1990 elections were thrown into disarray when ex-president Ríos Montt and his slate were ruled off the ballot at the eleventh hour. In the ensuing highly competitive first round, Jorge Carpio Nicolle, 1985 runner-up, edged out conservative Evangelical businessman Jorge Serrano Elias (b. 1945) of the Solidarity Action Movement (MAS) by 25.7 percent to 24.3 percent, with the Christian Democratic standard bearer and Guatemala City mayor Álvaro Arzú Yrigoyen (b. 1946) each garnering 17.5 percent. The January 1991 runoff saw Serrano surge to victory with over 60 percent of the limited number of votes (a 43 percent turnout) and immediately take office.

Inspired by Fujimori's success with a "self-coup" in Peru, Serrano tried ineptly to gain extraordinary powers the same way in March 1993. This attempt was a complete fiasco, for the Guatemalan situation differed markedly from that of Peru, and this backfiring power grab allowed human rights ombudsman Ramiro de León Carpio to become interim chief executive. Subsequently confirmed by a plebiscite, he provided an environment of peace and moderate economic growth, combined with manageable inflation conducive to free and highly competitive elections at the end of 1995. After falling just short of a majority in the multicandidate November 1995 balloting, Álvaro Arzú of the conservative Party of National Advancement (PAN) edged out Alfonso Portillo Cabrera, a civilian surrogate for one-time authoritarian strongman Rios Montt and his right-wing Guatemalan Republican Front (FRG), by a razor-thin margin of 31,000 votes in a January 1996 runoff. The August 1994 legislative elections had seen the FRG surge from 10 percent of the vote to 40 percent and the PAN rise from 10 percent to 30 percent as the Christian Democrats fell to 16 percent and the National Center Union to 10 percent—changes marking a very decided shift to the right. Arzú's inauguration ushered in a touchy period of maneuvering to put an end to the violent civil strife that had claimed at least 140,000 lives since 1961. Yet, for all the remaining difficulties, this first decade of civilian rule marked a significant advance over a past in which popularly elected civilians had held the presidency only from 1945 through 1950 and 1967–1970. Still, 70 percent of Guatemala's Indians were not effectively integrated into national life.[28]

On November 30, 1999, Portillo Cabrera of the FRG won a landslide victory, garnering 43.6 percent of the vote to 27.8 percent for his nearest competitor, Oscar Berger Perdomo—upped to 68.3 percent to 31.7 percent in the runoff—and giving the FRG 63 of 115 congressional seats to 37 for the erstwhile ruling PAN, as the New National Alliance (ANN) came away with 11 to go with the 11.3 percent of the vote its Álvaro Colom had garnered in his initial presidential bid. Thus the far right replaced the center-right in power. Forty-eight years old and a leftist rebel in his youth, Portillo had been a Christian Democratic stalwart from 1990 to 1995, when he ran for the presidency as the FRG's stand-in for Ríos Montt, losing in the runoff. Distancing himself from the old general, he now won a runoff with the candidate backed by the incumbent Arzú (PAN) administration. At seventy-five, Ríos Montt became the head of the congress in which the FRG held a majority. He would not, however, long influence the course of affairs.

El Salvador: Ending Civil War

The young officers who overthrew increasingly repressive General Romero in October 1979 were unable to establish control over a deteriorating political situation in El Salvador. Three civilians—a moderate, a liberal, and a progressive—were included in the junta along with two army officers. Criticized by senior military for moving too far too fast with reforms, they resigned in early January 1980, being replaced by Christian Democratic figures. An agrarian reform program was announced and banks, as well as the marketing of coffee and sugar, were taken over by the government. Still, death squad activity increased and the resumption of military assistance by the Carter administration in the United States was matched by a rise of guerrillas to around ten thousand.

With insurgency on the upswing, inspired by the Sandinistas' success in neighboring Nicaragua, newly elevated Archbishop Oscar Arnulfo Romero y Galdanyez (b. 1917) became the focal point of efforts at mediation. Following his murder in March, the country rapidly slid into a protracted civil war. As the new US Reagan administration increased support for the government, the various rebel groups, unified since October 1980 in the Farabundo Martí Front for National Liberation (FMLN), demonstrated resilience and staying power.[29]

With José Napoléon Duarte (b. 1926), defrauded of the presidency in 1972, now heading the junta, elections were held in March 1982 for a constituent assembly. Duarte's Christian Democrats garnered 35.5 percent of the vote to 25.8 percent for the far-right ARENA (Nationalist Republican Alliance) and 16.8 percent for the once-hegemonic National Conciliation Party (PCN). By this time 30,000 lives had already been sacrificed, and over 400,000 Salvadorans had fled the country. As the conflict raged on, presidential elections in 1984 placed the moderately reformist Duarte in the presidency. In 1986, a massive earthquake devastated the country as Duarte was dying of cancer. The United States continued to back the Salvadoran military's dream of crushing the "rebellion." Bolstered by the Sandinistas' continuing success in Nicaragua, the FMLN also strove for victory by force of arms, but its November 1989 "final push" failed to spark an urban uprising. Meanwhile the toll in deaths and destruction mounted. Hence, the 1988 elections saw ARENA return to power behind Alfredo Cristiano (b. 1948), a wealthy coffee grower and moderate conservative who called for a direct dialogue to end the decade-long civil war. ARENA's 54 percent of the vote to 36 percent for the Christian Democrats reflected disenchantment with the course of affairs. As stalemate continued on the battlefield and the Soviet bloc disintegrated, peace talks in Mexico reached a tentative accord in April 1991, followed by a formal signing in mid-January 1992 and a cease-fire effective on February 1. With intermittent violence continuing, the army was cut in half—from 63,000 to 31,500—and many of he most hard-line officers compulsorily retired at midyear.

Following two years of 5 percent economic growth, 1994 saw the election of ARENA's Armando Calderón Sol (b. 1948) with only half the registered electorate participating despite favorable economic growth in 1992 and 1993. In the April runoff, he improved to 68 percent from his 49 percent plurality in March, and an opposition coalition could rise to only 32 percent from its 25 percent in the first round. Yet this outcome offered some hope to the former armed opposition, as the left's vote in 1989 had been under 4 percent, rising in 1991's congressional balloting to 12.5 percent, a good result in relative terms, although less so in absolute figures. Although the economy stagnated in 1996, Calderón Sol moved toward consolidating peace and approximating democracy by implementing agreements on a new national police with 20 percent carried over from the old force, 20 percent ex-guerrillas, and 60 percent individuals not involved in the twelve-year civil war.[30]

In March 1997, midterm balloting in the context of economic stagnation, the left coalition received 32.1 percent of the vote to 33.3 percent for the governing ARENA party. This outcome translated into 27 seats to 28 in the 84-member congress, a significant gain over the 21 to 39 outcome in 1993. At the municipal level, the left rose from control of 13 towns to control of 54, including the capital, as ARENA fell from 210 to 145. In the March 1999 presidential election, Francisco Flores Pérez (b. 1959) of Calderón Sol's ARENA party won handily with 52 percent of the vote to 29 percent for the FMLN standard bearer, as only two-fifths of eligible voters turned out. An ex-president of the national legislature and a 1981 political science graduate of Amherst, the winner represented the rise of a younger generation to national political leadership—in a country sorely needing forward-looking leaders.

Honduras: Civilian Rule at Last

This was a red-letter period for Honduras, which for the first time in its history firmly established not only civilian government, but also democratic civilian government, although, this political development did not come easily. In November 1981, four years before a similar move in Guatemala and while El Salvador was racked by civil war, the first direct presidential elections in over a quarter century closed the book on military rule in Honduras. The presidency would no longer be the top rung on the army promotion ladder, as General Policarpo Paz García left office and the Liberal Party won a substantial electoral victory by 637,000 to 491,000 behind Dr. Roberto Suazo Córdova (b. 1927), a physician from a small interior city. Although subject to a significant degree of military tutelage as long as the conflict in Nicaragua was continuing, particularly until General Gustavo

Álvarez Martínez was replaced as armed forces chief in 1984, Suazo Córdova was a reasonably effective chief executive—more so than other initial civilian presidents such as Cerezo in Guatemala or Violeta Chamorro in Nicaragua.

Liberal José Azcona del Hoyo (b. 1927), victor in 1985 by 787,000 to 701,000 and an enemy of Suazo Cordova, presided over a disappointing administration, leaving his party rather discredited as corruption, rife under his predecessor, continued. Hence, November 1989 saw election of the National Party's Rafael Leonardo Callejas Romero (b. 1943)—an also-ran the last time out—with a record 917,000 votes (to 777,000 for the Liberal Party candidate—future president Carlos Flores Facusse). This marked the first time in fifty-seven years that an opposition candidate had been freely elected and allowed to take office. Callejas's term coincided with greatly diminished US presence and interest as the Cold War ended and the Nicaraguan civil war came to a close, but this term, too, was marred by corruption. In late 1993, Honduras experienced a fourth consecutive competitive election, the victor being the Liberal Party's Carlos Roberto Reina, a somewhat stodgy seventy-year-old, who polled 823,000 votes to 661,000 for his PNH rival. So alternation of parties in power had established a solid beachhead, not just a toehold, in Honduras.[31] Reina met with a modest degree of success in curbing the worst excesses of corruption and increased spending on social programs.

A fifth straight essentially free and competitive election on November 30, 1997, pitted Flores Facusse, a forty-seven-year-old Liberal newspaper publisher and congressional leader, against the Nationalists' Nora Gunera de Melgar, a former Tegucigalpa mayor. Flores won by a substantial 53 percent to 42.5 percent, running up big margins in the two major cities, Tegucigalpa and San Pedro Sula, as three-quarters of registered voters turned out, a sign of increased interest in politics as part of a generalized realization that the succession of liberal presidents had managed to limit the military's political influence. With Flores's inauguration in late January 1998, the civilian electoral road to the presidency appeared to be quite firmly consolidated. The new congress saw the Liberal Party with a 67 to 55 edge. In the autumn of 1998, Hurricane Mitch had a devastating impact upon the country, with thousands killed and 75 percent of banana plantings and a quarter of coffee fields destroyed—along with vital transportation infrastructure. So Flores had to concentrate on relief and reconstruction but did place the armed forces under a civilian minister for the first time since 1957.

Nicaragua: Peaceful Abandonment of Marxism

During the 1980s and 1990s, Nicaragua worked its way out of civil war to a series of three essentially democratic elections, the middle one of which transferred power from an entrenched Marxist-Leninist regime to a coalition of its opponents. In many ways this was the most dramatic course of events in any country in the Western Hemisphere during the period, and it had a significant psychological impact throughout the region.[32] The overthrow of the entrenched Somoza dictatorship took place only a few scant months before the 1980s dawned. As allies from the antiauthoritarian struggle were cast aside or fell by the wayside, the government became coherently and cohesively Sandinista, with major decisions made by the FSLN's nine-man national directorate. With President Carter and the Democrats still in office in the United States, the revolutionary regime's early months transpired in a nonthreatening international environment. The leitmotif of 1980 was the massive and essentially successful literacy campaign that attracted favorable international attention.

This relative honeymoon changed rapidly in 1981 as the Reagan administration terminated economic assistance, threw its decisive weight against aid from international bodies, and furnished increasing support to counterrevolutionary forces. US governmental determination to "destabilize" the Sandinistas rose in 1982–1983, accompanied by a policy of economic strangulation that helped push annual inflation to 1800 percent. In response to the increasingly aggressive US policy, polarization within Nicaragua mounted. Moreover, the government became increasingly dependent upon the Soviet Union. Despite the continuing armed struggle by the Contras, with a backbone of former Somoza National Guard cadres, the Sandinista government, confident of its popular support, moved ahead with elections during 1984. Riding a 75 percent turnout on November 4, despite concerted US efforts to have the opposition boycott the election, the FSLN was an easy winner, garnering 67 percent of the votes for its Daniel Ortega Saavedra (b. 1945) to be president, at the same time gaining 61 of 96 seats in the National Assembly on 63 percent of the vote. Armed with constituent powers, this body then drafted a new radical constitution.

The electoral victory had little impact upon the conflict tearing the country apart and contributing to 6 percent negative economic growth year after year. The United States devoted at least another $100 million in aid to the Contras, leading to the proclamation of a new state of emergency in Nicaragua in October 1985, suspending press freedom, the right to assemble, and the right to strike. Signature, along with four other Central American presidents in August 1987, of a peace accord involved a commitment by Ortega to respect democratic pluralism, hold free elections, and resolve the country's internal conflicts. The National Reconciliation Committee set up to work toward the peace accord's implementation may have been partly window dressing, but it eventually resulted in the lifting of the state of emergency and a cease-fire. Opposition groups formed the National Opposition Union (UNO) in mid-1989, uneasily holding together during the intense and divisive campaign.

Still confident of its support among the electorate, and too internationally committed to back down now that the Soviet Union was in the process of collapse, on February 25, 1990, the communist government once again held elections, counting on opposition division to keep them in office. To their surprise and dismay, Violeta Barrios de Chamorro (b. 1929), widow of the martyred anti-Somoza symbol, defeated Ortega by 54.7 percent to 40.8 percent—with voter participation rising to a high 86 percent. Essentially these were the country's first broad-based, fully competitive elections and the only case of peaceful handing over of power from government to opposition since at least 1928—a transfer of power that had taken place under US military occupation. The Sandinista Revolution was at an end. With 51 seats in the national assembly to 39 for the FSLN, the Chamorro government could begin dismantling the revolution and rebuilding the devastated economy—which had shrunk by an additional 18.6 percent in 1988–1990.[33] As a pragmatic gesture of reconciliation, Chamorro retained Ortega as commander of the armed forces in return for the FSLN's agreement to a drastic reduction in the military and a disbanding of the internal security forces attached to the interior ministry. Antonio Lacayo, the president's son-in-law and holder of a master's degree in management from the Massachusetts Institute of Technology, coordinated the day-to-day administration of the government. By paying off $360 million in arrears to international financial institutions, Nicaragua was reinstated as a member of the international financial community. Although hyperinflation was curbed within a year, no major influx of foreign investment followed, and the Nicaraguan economy remained in the doldrums.[34]

A presidential election on November 22, 1996, with a full array of choices from one extreme of the political spectrum to the other was a major stride along the road to democratic political development. Sandinista hopes for a return to power were dashed by Ortega's defeat at the hands of the Liberal Alliance's Arnaldo Alemán Laczyo (b. 1946), who polled 905,000 votes—just under half those cast—to 670,000 for the Sandinista ex-president, with nine minor candidates splitting the rest. The Liberal Alliance won 42 legislative seats to 36 for the FSLN, leaving the balance of power in the hands of 15 congress members from minor parties. Most of these allied with the Liberals to annul all acts passed by the lame-duck congress (between election and inauguration). The Chamorro government had sharply reduced foreign debt from $12.7 billion to $3.9 billion, with economic growth resumed in 1995 and 1996, but with a severe trade deficit of $390 million on exports of only $710 million. Still, it was no mean feat to have cut inflation from 1989's 14,000 percent to only 12 percent.

Alemán, a specialist in corporate and banking law and mayor of Managua during the Chamorro government, met with limited success during his five years as president, although GDP grew by 4.1 percent in 1998, 7.4 percent the next year, and 5.5 percent in 2000. Many of his close associates had been linked to the Somoza regime, and the administration's penchant for privatization provided opportunities for illicit, or at least unethical, enrichment. Nicaragua, already the area's poorest country, was devastated like Honduras by Hurricane Mitch in the fall of 1998, with many thousands killed and a large number of houses destroyed. By 2000, Alemán was being investigated for illegal acts by the country's comptroller general, who alleged that the president and his relatives had increased their assets ninefold since taking office.[35]

Costa Rica: Basking in Democracy

Democracy continued on an even keel in Costa Rica, the garden spot of Central America, during the 1980s and 1990s. Returning to power in 1982 behind Luis Alberto Monge Álvarez (b. 1926) within a context of economic woes bordering on collapse, the National Liberation Party (PLN), historically the country's leading political party, overcame the challenge of moving beyond its original leadership generation with great success in 1986, through the election of Oscar Arias Sánchez (b. 1941), a 52-to-46 percent winner who went on to win a Nobel Peace Prize for his determined efforts to ease the US–Nicaragua conflict. In 1990, the opposition United Christian Socialist Party (PUSC) regained the presidency with Rafael Angel Calderón Fournier (b. 1949), son of pre-1948 president Calderón Guardia, by a 51-to-47 percent edge. Four years later the PLN came back behind thirty-nine-year-old José María Figueres Olsen, son of its founder.

Thus offspring of the antagonists of the 1948 crisis peacefully took part in the country's eleventh consecutive democratic transfer of power from one popularly elected president to another—even though the margin of victory was only twenty-nine thousand votes, less that 2 percent of the total, as turnout was, for this model little democracy, a normal 81 percent. The younger Figueres, who had a slim 28–24 congressional majority, pursued free-market economic policies that contributed to division within the party. The country's enviable democratic record continued in February 1998 as conservative Miguel Angel Rodríguez (b. 1944) of the PUSC was elected over the PLN's José Miguel Corrales by 46.9 percent to 44.4 percent, only a marginal shift from the previous election, although with a lower turnout of 72 percent, but yielding an opposite result, as the small community of independent voters seemed to be able to determine the outcome of Costa Rica's elections.[36] Corrales's party had 27 of the 57 legislative seats to 23 for the PLN but accomplished few significant changes. Indeed, bright as this period had been, Costa Rica, like Nicaragua, would soon be tainted by scandal.

Panama: Breaking the Military's Hold

General Omar Torrijos turned the presidency over to Aristides Royo in 1978 and perished in a plane crash in 1981. In mid-1982, the new leader of the Panamanian Defense Forces (FDP), General Ruben Paredes, replaced Royo with Ricardo de la

Espriella, and a new constitution was approved by popular referendum the following April—by which time General Manuel Noriega (b. 1936), FDP chief of intelligence, had elbowed Paredes out of his way and then ousted the president in favor
of his vice president, Jorge Illueca. This game of political musical chairs continued
with a fraud-ridden election in which the victim was the ever-persistent Arnulfo
Arias. Elected in May 1984, puppet president Nicolás Ardito Barletta resigned in
September 1985 after the murder of Noriega critic Dr. Hugo Spadafora, being replaced by marionette Eric Delvalle, as Noriega continued to call the shots.[37]

Noriega came under sharp criticism in the United States for acts of political
repression and involvement in drug-running activities. In mid-1987 the United
States cut off economic and military aid and early the next year indicted Noriega
on drug-trafficking charges. When the president, Delvalle, attempted to dismiss
him, Noriega mobilized enough political and military support to force him into
hiding. Panama headed toward chaos as the United States imposed a freeze on assets held in US banks, and a general strike organized by business interests brought
the economy to a standstill. Neither the United States nor the OAS would accept
the results of the rigged 1989 presidential elections, in which the Civil Opposition
Democratic Alliance (ADOC) ran Guillermo Endara Gallimany (b. 1936), a representative of the white elite, against Noriega's man. Both sides claimed victory, but
a Catholic Church–sponsored survey credited Endara with three-fourths of the
votes, and former US president Jimmy Carter denounced massive electoral fraud.
With the country's electoral tribunal declaring the results null and void, the Panamanian strongman ousted President Delvalle and in November bullied the national assembly into granting him full powers as head of state and "leader of the
struggle for national liberation." Shortly thereafter Noriega declared a state of war
against the United States. The US response was swift and decisive.

On December 20 "Operation Just Cause" began with the landing of 26,000
US troops. Noriega was captured and taken to the United States for trial. Arias associate Endara was promptly installed as president on the strength of his presumed
recent electoral victory. In April 1992, Noriega was found guilty on eight drug-
related counts and sentenced to forty years' imprisonment. As the Panamanian
economy—devastated by the $2 billion in destruction and related costs from the
US intervention—remained in the doldrums with a crushing debt burden and extremely high unemployment, and the unpopular Endara appeared to be spending
excessive time and energy on his new young bride, all of the rather poor lot of
candidates in the May 1994 presidential sweepstakes looked better than the discredited incumbent, whose approval rating fell to a pathetic 9 percent.

With much of the population alienated by what they saw as a return to the
pre-Torrijos pattern of elitist, light-skinned, US-backed governments, the seemingly best-qualified contender, wealthy businessman Ernesto Pérez Balladares
(b. 1947), an economics graduate from Notre Dame with an MBA from the Uni-

versity of Pennsylvania's Wharton School, supported by what remained of the Torrijos-Noriega machine, beat out Arnulfo Arias's widow, California-based salsa singer Ruben Blades, and the incumbent government's candidate by 33 percent to 30 percent to 17 percent to 16 percent, respectively. The new government brought inflation down to 2 percent by 1996, and unemployment was more than halved to 14 percent.

In May 1999, Mireya Moscoso de Gruber, fifty-one-year-old widow of Arnulfo Arias, won the big prize—key because the next year would see the canal and the Canal Zone finally revert to Panamanian control.[38] Her election occurred only after the electorate had rejected a constitutional amendment that would have allowed Pérez Balladares to stand for reelection. For to say the least, he was not in a league with those South American chief executives who had recently been successful in legalizing reelection: Cardoso, Menem, and Fujimori. The widow Arias defeated thirty-five-year-old Martín Torrijos, son of the late populist national leader, by 45 percent to 38 percent, gaining 34 seats in the 72-member national legislature to 18 for Torrijos's PRD—but his day would soon come.

The Caribbean: Falling Behind the Others

Compared even to its Central American neighbors, the "Old" Caribbean shared only marginally in Latin America's democratic surge. The Dominican Republic broke a log jam, which enabled it to begin to move forward in terms of political development. Cuba largely marked time as it coped with the demise of the Soviet Union. Unfortunate Haiti endured several forms of trauma that would plague it into the next century.

Dominican Republic: Getting Past Balaguer

Most of the 1980s and 1990s were a reinstallation and continuation of Joaquín Balaguer's rule over the Dominican Republic. The period opened with Antonio Guzmán of the Dominican Revolutionary Party (PRD) in office and becoming so mired in scandals that he committed suicide in July 1982. Although retaining a strong base in the country's interior, Balaguer lost in that year to the PRD's Salvador Jorge Blanco (b. 1926). Recession stemming from an economic adjustment program and leading to large-scale popular protests in 1984 created nostalgia for the "good old days" that allowed Balaguer to return to power in 1986 on the strength of 41 percent of the vote, with reelection in 1990 by a very narrow margin of 35 percent to 34 percent over old rival Juan Bosch—who at eighty was three years younger than Balaguer. The closeness of the May 1994 election in which he barely edged out the PRD's José Francisco Peña Gómez, by 43.6 percent to 42.9 percent, combined with his extremely advanced age, led Balaguer to

JOAQUÍN BALAGUER

agree under US pressure to a shortened term with new elections in 1996—when he would complete a remarkable twenty-two of thirty years in the presidency (in addition to his brief tenure at the end of Trujillo's reign).[39]

In mid-1996, the electoral process, which Balaguer had exploited for three decades, finally brought an end to his excessively protracted domination of the country. Peña Gómez, who had taken over leadership of the PRD when Bosch split away in 1973, led substantially on the first ballot over young US-born Leonel Fernández Reyna of the Dominican Liberation Party (PLD). But Peña Gómez, a veteran dark-skinned intellectual making his third bid for the presidency at age fifty-nine, fell afoul of Balaguer's intense animosity, as in the June 30 runoff he could only add marginally to the 46 percent of the vote he had secured on May 16. In sharp contrast, forty-two-year-old Fernández benefited from the elimination of Balaguer's candidate, who had received 15 percent of the vote in the first balloting. Hence, Fernández glided into office by a scant seventy-two thousand votes, 51 percent of the votes compared to his earlier 39 percent share. With just a single senator (of 30) and only 10 percent of the 120-member lower house, he was forced to grant Balaguer an initial major voice in governmental decisions. For the old fox's Christian Social Reform Party (PRSC) held 11 seats in the upper house and had 44 in the chamber, compared to the opposition PRD's 15 and 57. But economic recovery resulting in GDP growth of 7.3 percent in 1996 and 8.2 percent for 1997 would prove to be political money in the bank when Fernández subsequently sought a return to the presidency.

The political scene was further shaken in May 1998, when Peña Gómez died eleven days before congressional elections. The wave of sympathy gave the PRD control of the congress with 83 of 149 seats in the chamber and 24 of 30 in the senate, as well as control of nine-tenths of the country's municipalities. Fernández's PLD rose from 13 to 49 places in the chamber and from 2 to 4 in the Senate, whereas Balaguer's PRSC dropped from 50 to 17 in the lower house and 14 to 2 in the upper house. Despite the ninety-one-year-old Balaguer's protestations of further electoral plans, which he did pursue into the next century, his era was effectively finished.[40]

The significance of this changing of the political guard in the Dominican Republic should not be underestimated. Successfully navigating the treacherous shoals and perilous rapids of an extremely heated and down-to-the-wire succession race generally contributes more to consolidation and institutionalization of democracy than does a less intense process. Given Balaguer's roots as a pillar of the Trujillo regime dating back to the 1930s, it was both essential and difficult for the Dominican Republic to get past his old-style, highly personalist politics if it was to be able to develop the kinds of programmatic parties and ancillary political vehicles needed to confront the new century. This remained a daunting challenge, since participants in Dominican politics had undergone her or his political socialization under the Trujillo legacy as continued by Balaguer, which provided stability and continuity at the cost of retarding political development.

Haiti: Out with the Duvaliers, In with the Military

By the beginning of the 1980s, the second Duvalier dynasty dictator had settled into power as the country became accustomed to the absence of its greatest tyrant. "Baby Doc," as Jean-Claude Duvalier was generally known, married in 1980 into an elite mulatto family, with his mother and wife subsequently fighting for influence over him. As the international environment became more hostile, and economic performance continued to be insufficient for any purpose other than enrichment of the regime's inner circle, repression again escalated. By the early 1980s foreign influences the father had so effectively curbed had regained leverage, and Pope John Paul II's visit in 1983 encouraged opposition to the unjust and repressive order. Riots broke out in November 1985, and the armed forces refrained from using force against antigovernment demonstrators. So at the beginning of February 1986 the United States took satisfaction in Duvalier's abrupt departure from power and the region.[41] Yet this was later than the sweeping wave of transitions to democracy that characterized Latin America in the 1979–1984 period as well as after the fall of entrenched authoritarian regimes outside the region in places like South Korea and the Philippines.

Most importantly and tragically, the end of rule by the Duvaliers did not bring an end to dictatorial government, much less lead to representative government or democracy. The March 1987 democratic constitution was rendered inoperative by the 1988 seizure of power by Lieutenant General Henri Namphy. Prior to this coup, the November 1987 elections had been violently aborted—leading to US suspension of all except humanitarian aid—then rescheduled for January 1988, at which time an extremely small and generally unenthusiastic turnout elected Professor Leslie F. Manigat, a supposedly "reformed" ex-Duvalierist, to a five-year term, which in fact lasted only five months. In turn General Namphy would serve less than three months as president before being ousted in September by General Prosper Avril—a former financial adviser of the Duvaliers who was no improvement. Ousting Avril in March 1990, General Herval Abraham became the power behind figurehead president Ertha Pascal Trouillot. Along side these power-oriented and highly corrupt military figures, increasingly involved in Haiti's becoming a major conduit of drugs from South America to the United States, only one new political leader had emerged by the end of the 1980s, popular radical Catholic priest Jean-Bertrand Aristide (b. 1953). This future two-time president gained national prominence as leader of protests against the July 1987 massacre of peasants in the drought-stricken northeast, and he continued to condemn the bloody activities of Duvalierist death squads acting with government-provided impunity. In December 1990, Aristide won election to the presidency and took office in early February 1991. The program of his Lavalas ("Cleansing Flood") movement featured decentralization of political institutions, agrarian reform, and a literacy campaign, but before even preliminary steps could be taken, Aristide was overthrown on September 30, 1991, by a coup led by General Raoul Cédras.[42]

Under military rule the situation in Haiti went from bad to worse, with high government officials increasingly involved in the international drug trade as well as brutally repressing any manifestations of opposition. After long delay, while Aristide pled his case and waited for action in the United States, the Clinton administration—spurred by the influx of Haitian "boat people"—moved in September 1994 to oust the Cédras regime and, in mid-October, reinstalled Aristide in office, leaving significant international public order forces to stabilize the situation—beginning with the thankless task of creating a minimally effective police force. The poverty-stricken country remained dependent upon outside economic aid and financial support. Frustrated by Aristide's high-handed "papal" style and the absence of a functioning legislature, Smarck Michel resigned as prime minister before finishing a year in office. Local and parliamentary elections were scheduled for late June of the following year, with eighteen-year-olds and up eligible to vote for 27 senators and an 83-member lower house. After makeup elections and runoffs, Aristide's Lavalas party held decisive congressional majorities, with 17 seats in the upper house and 65 in the chamber of deputies. Yet the mid-December presidential election was marked a by very low turnout of 28 percent of the registered electorate, with 88 percent of these voting for the candidate of the Lavalas Political Organization (OPL).[43]

The inauguration of colorless René Préval on February 7, 1996, was a landmark of sorts, the first transfer of power from one constitutionally elected president to another in the 192 years of Haiti's independence. The tasks facing this shy fifty-one-year-old agronomist were intimidating, and prospects for progress were limited. Much, if not most, of the public appeared to be looking past him to the next election, with the certain candidacy and highly probable election of Aristide once more, since he had reorganized the OPL into the Fanmi Lavalas (FL, Cleansing Flood) and acted more like a chief executive taking a sabbatical than an ex-president. Indeed, Haiti's road to the end-of-century elections was very rough. On January 11, 1999, President Préval established a new government by decree—for no cabinet had functioned since Prime Minister Rosney Smarth had resigned in June 1997. Parliament passed a law extending its own term, an act Préval declared unconstitutional. After rejecting three nominations for prime minister made by the president, in December 1998 the national legislature approved Jacques Edouard Alexis, while demanding the right to reject his cabinet. The supreme court refused to get involved in this controversy, so the impasse continued. But once again belief that things were so bad that they couldn't get much worse proved to be wishful thinking.

Cuba: From Ahead of the Times to Against the Tide

Cuba provided the major exception to the adoption and consolidation of competitive democratic systems in the 1980s and 1990s. To a remarkable degree Castro continued in the first of these decades to further institutionalize a single-party Marxist-Leninist system just as the Soviet-led communist world entered into decay, crisis, and collapse. Yet this should not have been a highly surprising development, for Cuba was still a much younger nation than any other Hispanic American country, Brazil, or Haiti. Moreover, in sharp contrast to European communist nations or the rest of Latin America, save the former British Caribbean states, Cuba was in the full sense of the word insular—with no territorially contiguous neighbor.

Castro had always considered his Cuba sui generis, and having originally adopted communism pragmatically within the Cold War context, he subsequently found its highly centralized, extremely hierarchical structures ideally suited to maintaining himself firmly entrenched in power. For his purposes it wasn't broken, so he saw no need to fix it—or even dream of abandoning it. This is not to say that political changes were completely absent from Cuba during the last decades of the twentieth century, but rather that they were aimed at preserving stability, not fostering democratization. Indeed, the Revolutionary Armed Forces (FAR) had been expanded to over 200,000, with nearly 100,000 reservists and a larger number in the militia and territorial troops (a kind of national guard). The

Second PCC Congress in December 1980 had seen little personnel movement other than retirement from the Secretariat of its two oldest members, Blas Roca and Carlos Rafael Rodríguez, and addition of eleven new alternates to the Political Bureau. The Central Committee was expanded from 112 to 148, with the number of alternates increased from 12 to 77 (in keeping with the PCC's substantial growth in size). Eighty percent of the Central Committee's full members were reelected, and half the alternates promoted to fill the vacancies. Remaining at 36, the military's proportion of the Central Committee fell, but the armed forces were well represented among the new alternates. Municipal Assemblies of People's Power were elected in October 1981 with a total of 10,755 members, 8 percent women. Still, all 499 members of the 1981–1986 National Assembly were PCC members, and this makeup changed little in the 1986 balloting.[44] But with Gorbachev's glasnost and perestroika in the Soviet Union, Fidel began to implant his own policy moving in the opposite direction.

The end of the Cold War and collapse of the Soviet Union was a devastating blow to the Cuban economy and posed a critical challenge to Castro's extraordinary leadership abilities. By 1992, the substantial aid, subsidies, and trade preferences, valued at at least $5–6 billion annually, to which Cuba was accustomed had been abruptly ended. Acknowledging that this "special period" would be a time of great difficulties, Castro rallied the Cuban people behind the "humanist revolution" and opposition to the machinations of US imperialism. Tirelessly touring the country, he exhorted the people to make the necessary sacrifices to preserve the revolution and Cuba's independence. At the same time he took steps to ensure the unity and loyalty of the party and government. The campaign to "rectify errors and negative tendencies" involved show trials in 1989 aimed at putting an end to high-level corruption. General Arnaldo Ochoa and three others were sentenced to death, and the head of Fidel's personal security detail and the transportation minister received twenty-year prison terms.[45]

In contrast to the limited cosmetic change at the Third Party Congress in 1986, significant adjustments in the PCC's top organs were adopted by the Fourth Party Congress in 1991. The Political Bureau was expanded from fourteen to twenty-five members, with Fidel reconfirmed as first secretary and Raúl as second secretary. Subsequently the National Assembly of People's Power elections in 1993 were for the first time direct—rather than by the provincial assemblies—and many of these part-time national legislators were nonmembers of the party. With only one nominee permitted for each seat, the announced turnout was 99 percent—of which 89 percent were said to have voted a straight party ticket, with 7.2 percent of the ballots ruled invalid.

For the 1993–1998 period Fidel remained at the apex of Cuba's interlocking power pyramid, seconded in all of these offices by Raúl Castro, who, in addition to being PCC second secretary, remained first vice president of both the Council of State and Council of Ministers as well as armed-forces minister. (The national assembly meets twice a year, delegating its authority to the Council of State the rest of the time. The Council of State body includes its president, who is chief of state and chief of government, the six vice presidents, a secretary, and twenty-three other members. The Council of Ministers is presided over by the president of the Council of State and includes most of that body's hierarchy plus other high executives.) Below the Castro brothers, by a considerable distance, the regime's inner circle included General Abelardo Colomé Ibarra as vice president of the Council of State and interior minister as well as Political Bureau member; Osmany Cienfuegos Gorriara, a member of all three of these key bodies; and Juan Almeida Bosque and Carlos Lage Dávila, Political Bureau members and Council of State vice presidents, the latter also serving as vice director of the presidential staff. The members of the National Assembly of Peoples' Power elected in July 1995 for a five-year term were 70 percent party members or cadres of the mass organizations. The announced turnout was just over 97 percent, with 11.3 percent of ballots ruled invalid. The early 1998 election by the assembly reaffirmed the leadership structure for another term running to March 2003.

Fidel had amply demonstrated his intention to keep a tight rein on both party and government. The 1989 purge and execution of senior army officers on corruption and drug-trafficking charges and the subsequent expulsion of Political Bureau member Carlos Aldana Escalante in 1992 underscore this determination to prevent slacking off even though the leader had moved into his seventies. Indeed, despite years of predictions concerning the imminence of a regime crisis, Castro entered the twenty-first century in a position fundamentally more analogous to that of fabled Venezuelan strongman Juan Vicente Gómez in the mid-1930s, who died in full control of the country, than to that of Mexico's Díaz a century before (when he still had a decade ahead of him before being forced from office). Like Gómez or China's late Mao Tse-tung, Fidel looked as if he might remain fully in power until a natural death. Meanwhile, the black market became an essential recourse for millions of Cubans, and success in extending life expectancy combined with a sharp drop in fertility rates led to an increasingly "graying" population. Yet economic disaster was avoided, courtesy of resurgence in tourism. With Fidel noticeably aging, what would come after him became a question of increasing concern.[46]

The "New Caribbean": Rough Going for Many but Not All

The countries that had become independent in the preceding period continued to cope with problems rooted in small size and limited economic viability, aggravated in the cases of Trinidad and Tobago and Guyana by racial cleavages. The greatest unrest was the violent turn of events in Grenada, resulting in US armed intervention.[47] Yet most of these young states developed new leadership, and only a few remained under the control of their original leaders or direct family descendents. (The ranks of the latter included Suriname, Dominica, St. Vincent and the Grenadines, and Antigua and Barbuda.)

Jamaica

The period from 1980 to the end of the century saw Jamaica weather stormy political seas before arriving at a viable and essentially democratic calm. In the face of major shortfalls in fulfilling goals of the 1978 extended-facilities agreement, the IMF suspended disbursements at the end of 1979. Michael Manley's People's National Party (PNP) government, citing rising oil costs, soaring interest rates, and unforeseen expenditures for repairing severe flood damage as justifications for a waiver, bristled when this request was rejected—suspecting that US opposition had been decisive. Manley reacted by calling new elections for late 1980 with the IMF's role as the central issue in a campaign in which a thousand were killed.[48] With real GDP down over 16 percent since 1974 and unemployment up to 31 percent, the economy was certainly the main focus of political debate. Opposition leader Edward Seaga (b. 1930), leader of the Jamaican Labor Party (JLP) since 1974, lambasted Manley's handling of the economy, while the prime minister attempted to shift the blame to international factors and actors. As imports rose to over $1 billion, the trade deficit for 1979 nearly doubled to $242 million, reflected in the current accounts' deficit jumping to $228 million. In 1978, inflation had trebled to nearly 50 percent, coming down to 31 percent for 1979, but real wages were in a tailspin under restrictive wage policies. Most dramatic of the manifold signs of growing social unrest was the explosive upsurge of violence in Kingston.

Following an alleged coup attempt in late June, considered by some the invention of a desperate Manley, the October election resulted in a resounding victory for Seaga and the JLP, which came away with fifty-one of sixty parliamentary seats (on a landslide 85 percent of the vote) and stayed in power through an election boycotted by the PNP in 1983. Relations with the new US government of Ronald Reagan improved dramatically through the early and mid-1980s as Seaga's probusiness policies dispelled the clouds. The 1989 elections, however, saw Manley return to power with a new moderate and pragmatic image, garnering 45 seats on 75 percent of the vote. Upon his health-impelled retirement in March 1992, new PNP leader Percival J. Patterson (b. 1935), who in early 1993 led the party to a 52 to 8-seat triumph on 60 percent of the vote (as the JLP fell to only 26.3 percent of the vote), accelerated Jamaica's transition to a free-market economy. In December 1997, Patterson won a new term as prime minister with 50 seats on 56 percent of the vote to only 10 on 39 percent for the JLP in a modest turnout of 60 percent of registered voters. Patterson was on his way to a record-challenging tenure in office, but one in which material achievements would be few.

Trinidad and Tobago

With the 1981 death of founding father Eric Williams, George Michael Chambers (b. 1930) became the country's second prime minister, keeping the People's National Movement (PNM) in power with 26 seats won in November's parliamentary elections. Both price and production of oil were dropping as the 1980s went on, catching the government overextended in construction of infrastructure works—for in 1980 oil constituted 94 percent of export earnings and 65 percent of government revenues. In an adverse economic climate in which the GDP registered a negative growth of 6.1 percent a year from 1982 through 1987, the four opposition parties formed the National Alliance for Reconstruction (NAR) in 1984, and a 33 percent currency devaluation at the end of 1985 was very unpopular. Hence, it was no great surprise when, in an environment of corruption and drug-trafficking charges, Chambers and the PNM lost the late-1986 election, getting only 3 of 36 seats on 31 percent of the vote to the NAR's 33 seats on two-thirds of the vote. This turnabout opened up an era of competitive politics as the Democratic Action Congress (DAC), a Tobago-based party never seriously contesting more than that small island's pair of seats, came to hold a balance-of-power position. As the PNM reorganized in 1987 behind ex-energy minister Patrick A.M. Manning (b. 1946), the NAR governed with Tobago's Arthur N.R. Robinson, a deputy prime minister under Eric Williams for six years and finance minister for a decade, as prime minister. Accusing Robinson and the NAR leadership of racism, Basdeo Panday (b. 1933) broke away in 1989, founding the United National Congress (UNC).[49]

In a context of economic austerity, Jamrat al Muslimeen—a movement of Afro-Trinidadian Muslim converts—staged a mid-1990 uprising under the leadership of former policeman Yasin Abu Bakr, taking the prime minister and most of the government hostages, blowing up police headquarters, and seizing the television station to broadcast their demands for immediate new elections. In five days of looting 23 persons were killed and 500 (mostly looters) wounded. Having gained freedom by promising an amnesty, the government refused to honor the promise as being extorted from them under duress. But the 114 individuals charged with murder and treason mounted appeals that eventually resulted in their being ordered to pay for damages. The end-of-1991 elections saw the NAR drop dramatically to only 24 percent of the vote and two seats as the PNM won 21 seats on 45 percent of the vote and Panday's UNC won 13 seats with a healthy 29 percent of the ballots cast. Manning became prime minister until the late 1995 voting ended in an impasse. The PNM led with 49 percent—heavily concentrated in its urban strongholds. The UNC was close behind with 45.8 percent of the voter preferences, and seats were tied at 17-to-17.

With the support of the two Tobago legislators, this electoral impasse brought Trinidad its first Indian prime minister in Panday, with former prime minister Arthur N.R. Robinson, key in the Tobago alliance with Panday, moving to the largely ceremonial post of president by a 46 to 18 vote a few months later. Over the next six years prosperity reigned as GDP growth averaged 5.6 percent annually and the country enjoyed a natural-gas boom that compensated for the drop in crude oil exports, which at 225,000 barrels a day had constituted 80 percent of exports in the 1970s.[50] Fortunately the petrochemical industry continued its growth, and the country became the world's second largest exporter of ammonia. In this favorable atmosphere, GDP growth for 1997 was 4 percent and inflation only 3.8 percent. Still, crime was on the rise, and tensions between ethnic groups were simmering. Moreover, dissension was threatening the tenuous hold on power of a prime minister who acted more as if he possessed a solid parliamentary majority than as if every vote was critical.

Guyana

In 1980, a new constitution instituted a presidential system, with Forbes Burnham continuing as the country's chief executive. At the same time Walter Rodney—prominent Marxist intellectual, spokesman for the Working People's Alliance, and virulent critic of Burnham—was victim of a car bomb. Subsequently press censorship was tightened and the PPP (Progressive People's Party) increasingly harassed. With Burnham's death in August 1985, his vice president, Hugh Desmond Hoyte (b. 1929), became president as well as leader of the People's National Congress (PNC). He moved slowly away from Burnham's authoritarian and statist stance, inviting foreign aid and investment. Hoyte won the fraud-ridden December 1985 elections in a landslide, with 79 percent of the vote yielding 42 of 53 legislative seats. As export earnings continued to fall, the government resorted to increased borrowing, which by 1988 had raised foreign debt to $1.7 billion—six times the country's official GDP—with arrears passing $1 billion. Hoyte had little choice but to adopt a pro-US stance and seek IMF assistance.[51]

Considerable social unrest accompanied the austerity policies adopted as a result, and leading to 1992 elections that returned Cheddi Jagan and the PPP to power after twenty-eight years—although the PNC left office grudgingly, accompanied by a good deal of rioting. With the Cold War only a historical memory along with Jagan's radicalism, mining and agriculture led an economic recovery. Jagan died in March 1997. His seventy-seven-year-old widow Janet took his job, and Samuel Hines stayed on as prime minister. Then, in the mid-December 1997 elections, the PPP trounced Hoyte's PNC by 53.3 percent to

40.6 percent, gaining 29 of the 53 parliamentary seats, and the widow Jagan was confirmed in the presidency. Resigning in August 1999 due to ill health, she was replaced by the PPP's Bharrat Jagdeo (b. 1964). (The country's original generation of leadership would come to its end in late 2002 with Hoyte's death.)

Belize

One new country came onto the Central America–Caribbean stage after 1980, as Belize, originally settled by English woodcutters, finally became independent from Britain in 1981. Self-government had been attained in 1964, but this tiny country of 200,000 inhabitants had remained a nominal British colony because of Guatemala's territorial claims and its belligerent threat of backing bluster with invasion. With a narrow victory in 1979 by a margin of 52 percent for his Peoples United Party (PUP) to 47 percent for the United Democratic Party (UDP), George Price, the country's dominant political figure since 1950, became prime minister and could still boast of never having lost an election.[52] The prime minister was finally upset at the end of 1984 by the UDP under Manuel Esquivel (b. 1940), but Price and the UDP rebounded in 1989. A period of spirited political competition marked the 1990s, as in mid-1993 the PUP won 51 percent of the vote, but the UDP ousted it from office courtesy of having won 16 of 29 seats in Parliament. In a dramatic turnaround, the PUP gained 26 of 29 seats in August 1998 balloting, making new leader Said Musa (b. 1944) prime minister and leaving the erstwhile governing UDP with only three members in parliament. The influx of refugees from Central America's armed conflicts had come to be a major problem.

Barbados

The period opened with J.M.G.M. "Tom" Adams in office and his Barbados Labour Party (BLP) going on to win 17 of 27 parliamentary seats in 1981. With Adams's sudden death at age fifty-one in early 1985, H. Bernard St. John (b. 1930) took over until the mid-1986 elections, held in an environment of high unemployment, returned the center-left Democratic Labour Party (DLP) to power with 24 of 27 seats on 59.4 percent of the vote. This dramatic reversal of fortune made Errol Barrow once again the prime minister until his death the next year. His succession by L. Erskine Sandiford caused Richard "Richie" Haynes to lead a schism that resulted in establishment of the National Democratic Party (NDP). Still, Sandiford and the DLP emerged victorious in the early 1991 elections, with 18 seats to 10 for the BLP, but lost power in September 1994 to the BLP and its new leader, economist Owen Arthur (b. 1949), who led it to a 19-of-28-seat landslide (as the hitherto governing party retained only 8 seats). In the January 1999 elections the BLP won 26 seats on 65 percent of the vote, compared to only a pair on 35 percent of the vote for the opposition. This election gave Arthur a second five-year term as prime minister and left the DLP to ponder what it needed to do to mount a comeback.[53] Meanwhile, offshore banking came to be a pivotal economic factor.

Suriname

The constitutional, but corrupt, government was violently overthrown in early 1980 by a movement led by Sergeant Major Desire "Desi" Bouterse with support from the left-leaning Nationalist Republican Party (PNR)—whose Henk Chin-A-Sen was installed as prime minister, tutored by an eight-member National Military Council composed of young officers. In August the legislature was dissolved and a state of emergency decreed. Following a March 1981 attempted coup by Hindustani officers, a Revolutionary People's Front was set up at year's end, and the president and cabinet were dismissed in February 1982. In December Bouterse, now a lieutenant colonel, arrested and killed most of his leading opponents in what would be known as the December Murders. This barbarous act led to the Dutch withdrawing their substantial economic support.[54]

After purging the officer corps, the ruthless strongman established a mixed military-civilian cabinet with Errol Alibux as a pliable facade prime minister. With bauxite prices falling, opposition to the regime, including the Surinamese Liberation Army led by Ronnie Brunswyk, emerged and took to the streets. By mid-1986 plotting was under way that led Bouterse to issue a new constitution suitable to his interests, and then to hold elections in December 1987. Despite his organization of a National Democratic Party (NDB) under his new puppet prime minister Jules Wijdenbosch, the multiethnic National Front for Democracy and Development (FDO) won 41 of 51 seats and, from the ranks of the United Hindustani Party (VHP), elected a pro-Western businessman, Ramsewak Shankar, as president for a five-year term beginning in January 1988, with former prime minister Henck Aaron as vice president and prime minister.

By the end of 1990, the army was running amok and was involved in growing drug trafficking. It ousted the Shankar government and reinstalled Wijdenbosch. In mid-1991, the New Front (NF), the old FDO, won 30 of 51 seats to 12 for Bouterse's party and 9 for the new Democratic Alternative. Runaldo Ronald Venetiaan (b. 1936) became president and Jules Adjodhia prime minister. Suriname experienced yet another political reversal in mid-1996 when the governing NF fell to 24 seats on 45 percent of the vote and the NDP rose to 36 percent and

16 seats but found enough parliamentary allies to take over. Having Wijdenbosch rather than the much more controversial Bouterse as its candidate, the NDP triumphed in the electoral college-like United People's Assembly by 438 to 407 votes, with Wijdenbosch assuming the presidential office in September. By early 1999, corruption was rampant and the economy in a tailspin as bauxite prices collapsed. In an effort to save his political skin, Wijdenbosch purged Bouterse after a vote of no confidence had received 27 votes to only 10 in support of the president. Because another ten members of Parliament abstained the vote was short of the thirty-four needed to force Wijdenbosch out.[55] But he expelled Bouterse in the interest of political survival. The period ended with a beleaguered president holding on by his political fingertips and agreeing to move the elections up a year to May 2000.

Bahamas

The politics of the Bahamas, a small tourism and gambling-enriched country, continued to be dominated by Lynden Pindling, who as head of the Progressive Liberal Party (PLP) was opposition leader from 1964 to January 1967, when an 18-to-18 tie in parliamentary seats allowed him to become premier courtesy of an alliance with an independent legislator. When independence came in 1973, he became prime minister, winning reelection in mid-1982 and again in early 1987, this time with an advantage of 31-to-16 seat despite allegations that drugs passing through the islands had reached astronomical values, with handsome profits accruing to government luminaries. In 1997 the opposition Free National Movement (FNM) pulled off a stunning upset, winning 34 of 40 seats on the strength of 58 percent of the vote. As a result, Pindling retired from political life, and Perry Christie became the PLP leader. Hubert Ingraham of the FNM became prime minister as Christie strove to rejuvenate the historically dominant PLP. Contributing to rising social tensions was the fact that a fifth of the population were illegal Haitian immigrants.

Grenada

Maurice Rupert Bishop (b. 1944) had a short and troubled period of dominance. Jailed when Grenada gained its independence in early 1974, he led his New Jewel Movement (NJM) in seizing power in March 1979. Bishop's "workers' and farmers' government" initially enjoyed the support of a large proportion of the little island's 100,000 inhabitants as it facilitated grassroots participation and concentrated on reducing the high illiteracy rate and establishing basic social welfare programs—with technical and limited financial support from Cuba, other communist countries, and several unaligned nations. An internal power struggle developed as followers of Bernard Coard became a party within the party that gained control of the NJM's central committee by fall 1983. While Bishop and his closest associates were in Czechoslovakia seeking power generators, Coard—who accused Bishop of having drawn away from Leninist principles—began to disarm the worker and farmer militia units.

On Bishop's October 8 return by way of Cuba, Coard accused him of trying to make Castro the arbiter of NJM internal affairs, and Bishop was arrested four days later. Freed by rioting masses on October 19, Bishop was recaptured by troops loyal to Coard and immediately executed along with other government officials. In response, the Reagan administration promptly launched "Operation Urgent Fury," a complete military success within hours—quickly overcoming the small number of Cuban soldiers and militia working to enlarge Grenada's airport.[56] In the aftermath of the traumatic revolution-intervention, aging former premier Herbert Augustus Blaize merged his Grenada National Party into the New National Party (NNP), which then emerged victorious in the December 1984 balloting—winning 14 of 17 seats in Parliament. Still Eric Gairy's Grenada United Labour Party (GULP) retained the support of 38 percent of the electorate. Upon Blaize's death at the end of 1989, Ben Jones led the party to defeat at the hands of the New Democratic Party (NDP) headed by Nicholas Brathwaite, who had served as interim prime minister in 1983–1984. The NNP was resurgent in mid-1995 under Keith Mitchell (b. 1946) with 8 seats on 32.7 percent of the vote before winning all 15 seats in the January 1999 election, keeping Mitchell in office—the first time since the US intervention that the incumbent party had won an election.

St. Kitts and Nevis

In 1980, the long-dominant St. Kitts-Nevis Labour Party (SKNLP) lost to an alliance of the People's Action Movement (PAM) and the Nevis Reformation Party (NRP), ushering in a decade and a half of PAM rule that saw Kennedy A. Simmons holding the finance, foreign affairs, and home office portfolios along with the prime ministership. At the end of 1993, the SKNLP staged a comeback with Denzil Llewellyn Douglas (b. 1953) leading it to 54 percent of the vote and 4 of the 8 St. Kitts parliamentary seats, but the PAM's Simmons stayed in office with a minority government. Badly hurt by scandals concerning drugs and money laundering, the PAM won only a single seat in mid-1995 allowing the SKNLP to come to power with 58 percent of the vote and Douglas to become prime minister. He consolidated his leadership and by the end of the period was on his way to extending his tenure via new elections.

Dominica

The mid-1980 elections inaugurated a new era for this newly independent little country as the Dominican Freedom Party (DFP) won 17 of 21 parliamentary seats and made Mary Eugenia Charles (b. 1918) prime minister. Surviving two attempted coups in 1981, this spunky lady guided her party to another victory in 1985, winning 15 seats to 6 for the party whose twenty-year domination it had broken in 1980. Meanwhile, ex-prime minister Patrick John was convicted of trying to overthrow her government, and the Dominica Labour Party (DLP) and three smaller political entities merged into the Labour Party of Dominica (LPD). In mid-1990 the DFP held onto office by a single seat, and five years later Dame Mary Charles was succeeded as its leader by Brian Alleyne, who promptly lost the mid-1995 election. Eleven of the twenty-one seats went to the new United Workers Party (UWP) of Edison Jones.[57] Unfortunately for him, a sharp drop in banana exports ensued.

St. Vincent and the Grenadines

Robert Milton Cato (b. 1915), founder of the St. Vincent Labour Party (SVLP) in 1954, had headed these very small islands' government in 1967–1972, returning to office in 1974. With independence in 1979, he became prime minister until mid-1984. Then James F. "Son" Mitchell and the National Democratic Party (NDP) started a long stay in power by winning 12 of 15 parliamentary seats—and occasioning Cato's retirement from politics—before scoring a clean sweep in 1989 and 12 of 15 again in 1994. In 1998 the opposition, merged in the Unity Labour Party (ULP), received 54.6 percent of the vote, but the NDP held onto a one-seat majority, and Mitchell embarked on his fourth five-year term in office.

St. Lucia

Centrist John George Melvin Compton (b. 1926) of the United Workers Party (UWP) headed this little island's government from 1964 through independence in 1979 before losing the July election by a decisive 12-seat to 5-seat margin in Parliament to the St. Lucia Labour Party (SLP). The SLP promptly split between followers of Prime Minister Allan Louisy and populist George Odlum, this split leading to the former's resignation in 1982. Staging a comeback, Compton became prime minister for a second time, lasting until his resignation in March 1996—by which time he had accumulated twenty-nine years in office. Vaughn Lewis served as prime minister until the landslide May 1997 victory of the SLP behind its new leader, Kennedy "Kenny" Anthony (b. 1951), with 16 of 17 seats on 60 percent of the vote. This tiny republic took pride in poet Derek Walcott's 1983 Nobel Prize in Literature to go along with W. Arthur Lewis's economic laureate from 1973.

Antigua and Barbuda

After Antigua separated from St. Kitts and Nevis, Vere Connell Bird, Sr., dominated political life. Full internal self-government came in early 1967, making him premier. After losing to the Progressive Labour Movement (PLM) in 1971, his Antigua Labour Party (ALP) staged a comeback in 1976, winning again in 1980. Becoming prime minister when independence came in late 1981, Bird won election after election, including 16 of 17 parliamentary seats over a fragmented opposition in 1984, before stepping down at age eighty-four in favor of his son Lester Bryant Bird in September 1993. The ALP won with greater difficulty in early 1994 as its share of the vote dropped from 63.8 to 54.4 percent. Vere C. Bird, Jr., emerged as a guiding force behind his brother, since a skeleton in his political closet kept him from the top office: As defense minister in 1990 he was the central figure in an arms-dealing scandal in which Israeli weapons ended up with Colombian guerrillas. The March 1999 elections gave the ALP another victory as it gained a seat, although slipping slightly to 52.6 percent of the vote—in that tiny country 17,000 votes to 14,800.[58] Hence, Lester Bird remained prime minister as opponents searched for a viable alternative.

Latin America at Century's End

As the twentieth century closed, Latin America had certainly progressed a significant distance down the road to political development, compared to where it had been in 1979, much less in the mid-1950s. A long roll of countries had undergone transitions to democracy during the period, and many of them were consolidated into freely elected and competitive political systems—although operating within a political culture much closer to that of the southern European nations than to that of Anglo-American pluralism. Moreover, Mexico was well advanced in the direction of democratization—just a year away from having the opposition attain power in a peaceful and orderly manner, something never before achieved, not just absent for the seven decades of PRI dominance. If anything, the temptation was to look back at the progress made instead of looking to the challenges still ahead. But attention would soon shift, for just as throughout the course of political development elsewhere, gains in the realm of formal democracy gave rise to demands for its extension into the social sphere, and dramatic headway with respect to participation unleashed pressures for the translation of a newly achieved voice in electoral politics into greater economic equality. In Latin America this "deepening" of democracy would be the initial political challenge in the new century, which is the subject of the next chapter.

Notes

1. There is a competent treatment of Peru's troubled situation by Cynthia McClintock in Diamond, Hartlyn, Linz, and Lipset, eds., *Democracy in Developing Countries: Latin America,* (Boulder, CO: Lynne Reinner, 1999), pp. 309–365. Useful for the first part of the period is Catherine M. Conaghan and James M. Malloy, *Unsettling Statecraft: Democracy and Neoliberalism in the Central Andes* (Pittsburgh: University of Pittsburgh Press, 1994)—also covering Bolivia. Jo-Marie Burt and Philip Mauceri, eds., *Politics in the Andes: Industry, Conflict, Reform* (Pittsburgh: University of Pittsburgh Press, 2004), studies four other countries along with Peru.

2. The rich literature on the Peruvian insurgencies includes Steve J. Stern, ed., *Shining and Other Paths: War and Society in Peru, 1980–1995* (Durham, NC: Duke University Press, 1998); David Scott Palmer, ed., *The Shining Path of Peru* (New York: St. Martin's Press, 1992); and Cynthia McClintock, ed., *Revolutionary Movements in Latin America: El Salvador's FMLN and Peru's Shining Path* (Washington, DC: United States Institute of Peace Press, 1998).

3. Fujimori's reelection is discussed by McClintock in Diamond et al., eds., *Democracy.* As in the contemporary cases of Menem in Argentina and Cardoso in Brazil, the decisive battle was in getting the constitution amended, the election being almost anticlimactic. Paul H. Lewis, *Authoritarian Regimes in Latin America: Dictators, Despots, and Tyrants* (Lanham, MD: Rowman & Littlefield, 2006), pp. 239–242, discusses Peru in this period.

4. Useful through the 1980s is Daniel C. Hellinger, *Venezuela: A Tarnished Democracy* (Boulder, CO: Westview Press, 1991). His coverage is extended in Steve Ellner and Daniel Hellinger, eds., *Venezuelan Politics in the Chávez Era: Class, Polarization, and Conflict,* paperback ed. (Boulder, CO: Lynne Rienner, 2004). For a perceptive analysis of the decline of Venezuela's democracy see the chapter by Daniel H. Levine and Brian F. Crisp in Diamond et al., eds., *Democracy,* pp. 367–426. See also the vivid portrayal of Chávez in Lewis, *Authoritarian Regimes,* pp. 242–246.

5. On the 1983 elections see my series of four studies, especially No. 4, *Venezuelan Election Project: Results and Future Prospects* (Washington, DC: Center for Strategic and International Studies, January 1984). Those of 1988 are discussed in Hellinger, *Venezuela.*

6. The fact that Caldera was elected with a minimal plurality by a coalition of splinter and ad hoc parties running against not only AD but even his old party COPEI was a strong indication of voter disillusionment with the parties that had dominated the political scene since 1958. Essentially, those parties, like APRA and AP in Peru, had failed to adjust to an electorate swollen by the entrance of both young "first-timers" and the urban underclass. Interesting ideas are expressed in Javier Corrales, *Presidents Without Parties: The Politics of Economic Reform in Argentina and Venezuela in the 1990s* (University Station: Pennsylvania State University Press, 2002).

7. Consult Ellner and Hellinger, eds., *Venezuelan Politics.*

8. On the Pinochet period see J. Samuel Valenzuela and Arturo Valenzuela, eds., *Military Rule in Chile: Dictatorship and Repression* (Baltimore: Johns Hopkins University Press, 1986); Pamela Constable and Arturo Valenzuela, *A Nation of Enemies: Chile Under Pinochet* (New York: Norton, 1991); and Mary Helen Spooner, *Soldiers in a Narrow Land: The Pinochet Regime in Chile* (Berkeley and Los Angeles: University of California Press, 1994).

9. The chapter by Arturo Valenzuela in Diamond et al., eds., *Democracy,* pp. 191–247, provides a coherent analysis of the reestablishment of democratic political life in Chile.

10. See Marcelo Pollock, *The New Right in Chile, 1973–97* (New York: St. Martin's Press, 1999), pp. 73–81, as well as Paul E. Sigmund, ed., *Chile 1973–1998: The Coup and Its Consequences* (Princeton: Princeton University Program in Latin American Studies, 1999).

11. Pollock, *New Right,* pp. 83ff.

12. On the elections see ibid., pp. 164–193, 184–195, with the nature of National Renovation (RN) discussed on pp. 115–116, and the congressional lineup on pp. 149ff.

13. On the election, see ibid., pp. 164, 174–180. Frei's victory repeated the 1958 success of another presidential son, which in turn had multiple precedents in Chile's nineteenth century. Of course, this phenomenon is not unheard-of in the United States, just not as frequent. On balance Frei performed better than had the younger Alfonso López in Colombia or his contemporary, the junior Figueres in Costa Rica.

14. Consult ibid., pp. 153, 180–184. The closeness of the election combined with the decline in the Concertacíon's share of the vote, in part reflecting Christian Democrat's reluctance to cast their ballots for a socialist, gave the opposition reason to look forward to the new century.

15. Of value on the 1980s is Waltrud Queiser Morales, *Bolivia: Land of Struggle* (Boulder, CO: Westview Press, 1991).

16. Useful on the early years of this period is James M. Malloy and Eduardo Gamara, *Revolution and Reaction: Bolivia 1964–1985* (New Brunswick, NJ: Transaction Books, 1988).

17. Consult Waltrud Queiser Morales, *A Brief History of Bolivia* (New York: Facts on File, 2003).

18. Banzer demonstrated considerably greater political acumen in returning to the presidency than had Ibáñez in Chile in 1952. He did it his way, not piggybacking on the success of a powerful sponsor and an influential movement such as Perón provided to Ibáñez.

19. Essential on Ecuador is John D. Martz, *Politics and Petroleum in Ecuador* (New Brunswick, NJ: Transaction Books, 1987). Useful on the early years of this period is David Schodt, *Ecuador: An Andean Enigma* (Boulder, CO: Westview Press, 1987).

20. Consult Allen Gerlach, *Indians, Oil, and Politics: A Recent History of Ecuador* (Wilmington, DE: Scholarly Resources Books, 2002).

21. To understand the emergence of the Indians as a political factor, see Melina Selverson-Scher, *Ethnopolitics in Ecuador: Indigenous Rights and the Strengthening of Democracy* (Boulder, CO: Lynne Rienner, 2001), as well as Erick D. Langer, ed., *Contemporary Indigenous Movements in Latin America* (Wilmington, DE: Scholarly Resources Books, 1998). The Confederation of Indigenous Nations of Ecuador (CONAIE) was established in 1986 but only gradually acquired skill in the political realm.

22. The Ecuadorian leadership problem differed from those of Peru, Venezuela, and Bolivia, where well-institutionalized parties were running out of steam. In a country where

personalities had counted for so much and parties for so little, the military's vetoing of Assad Bucarám, the one man who might have filled the vacuum left by Velasco Ibarra's death, entailed grave consequences by opening the door to a succession of individuals able to gain election by mobilizing support of a fifth to a fourth of the voters, but—given the shortness of the presidential term—unable to construct the alliances necessary to govern effectively.

23. On Uruguay consult Martin Weinstein, *Uruguay: Democracy at the Crossroads* (Boulder, CO: Westview Press, 1988).

24. For details of the restoration of democracy consult Luis E. González, *Political Structures and Democracy in Uruguay* (South Bend, IN: Notre Dame University Press, 1991), and Charles G. Gillespie, *Negotiating Democracy: Politicians and Generals in Uruguay* (Cambridge, UK: Cambridge University Press, 1991).

25. Riordan Roett and Richard S. Sacks, *Paraguay: The Personalist Legacy* (Boulder, CO: Westview Press, 1990), is quite useful on the 1980s.

26. Essential is Peter Lambert and Andrew Nickson, *The Transition to Democracy in Paraguay* (New York: St. Martin's Press, 1997).

27. John A. Booth, Christine J. Wade, and Thomas W. Walker, *Understanding Central America,* 4th ed. (Boulder, CO: Westview Press, 2006), provides an excellent overview of the subregion. See also Thomas W. Walker and Ariel Armony, *Repression, Resistance, and Democratic Transition in Central America* (Wilmington, DE: Scholarly Resources Books, 2000), supplemented by Ralph Lee Woodward, Jr., *Central America: A Nation Divided*, 3rd ed. (New York: Oxford University Press, 1999).

28. The period is covered in Christopher Chase-Dunn, Susanne Jonas, and Nelson Amaro, eds., *Globalization on the Ground: Post-Bellum Guatemalan Democracy and Development* (Lanham. MD: Roman & Littlefield, 2001); Susanne Jonas, *The Battle for Guatemala: Rebels, Death Squads, and U.S. Power* (Boulder, CO: Westview Press, 1991); and Susanne Jonas, *Of Centaurs and Doves: Guatemala's Peace Process* (Boulder, CO: Westview Press, 2000).

29. See Tommie Sue Mongomery, *Revolution in El Salvador: Origins and Evolution* (Boulder, CO: Westview Press, 1982), and Philip J. Williams and Knut Walter, *Militarization and Demilitarization in El Salvador's Transition to Democracy* (Pittsburgh: University of Pittsburgh Press, 1997).

30. Consult Tommie Sue Mongomery, *Revolution in El Salvador: From Civil Strife to Civil Peace* (Boulder, CO: Westview Press, 1995) as well as Joseph S. Tulchin and Gary Bland, eds., *Is There a Transition to Democracy in El Salvador* (Boulder, CO. Lynne Rienner Publishers, 1992).

31. See James Morris, *Honduras: Caudillo Politics and Military Rulers* (Boulder, CO: Westview Press, 1984), for the opening years of this period. The story can be picked up in Walker and Armony, *Repression, Reaction, and Democratic Transition*. See also Eva Loser, *The 1989 Honduran Elections: Pre-Election Report* (Washington, DC: Center for Strategic and International Studies, November 1989), as well as Mark B. Rosenberg and Philip L. Shepherd, eds., *Honduras Confronts Its Future: Contending Perspectives on Critical Issues* (Boulder, CO: Lynne Rienner, 1986).

32. See Thomas W. Walker, ed., *Nicaragua Without Illusions: Regime Transition and Structural Adjustment in the 1990s* (Wilmington, DE: Scholarly Resources Books, 1999).

33. The election was extremely closely monitored. See the treatment in Jorge I. Dominguez and Marc Lindenberg, eds., *Democratic Transitions in Central America* (Gainesville: University Press of Florida, 1997), and, for perspective, William M. LeoGrande, *Our Own Backyard: The United States in Central America, 1977–1992* (Chapel Hill: University of North Carolina Press, 1998), as well as Louis W. Goodman, William M. LeoGrande, and Johanna Mendelson Forman, eds., *Political Parties and Democracy in Central America* (Boulder, CO: Westview Press, 1992).

34. See David Close, *Nicaragua: The Chamorro Years* (Boulder, CO: Lynne Rienner, 1999).

35. David Close and Kalowatie Deonandan, eds., *Undoing Democracy: The Politics of Electoral Caudillismo* (Lanham, MD: Lexington Books, 2004), is highly critical of the Alemán government.

36. John A. Booth, *Costa Rica: Quest for Democracy* (Boulder, CO: Westview Press, 1998), includes even the 1998 elections, and Fabricio Edouard Lehoucq, "Costa Rica: Paradise in Doubt," *Journal of Democracy*, 16:3 (July 2005), pp. 140–154, is quite up to date. Additional analysis is contained in the chapter by John A. Booth in Diamond et al., eds., *Democracy*, pp. 429–468, and Jeffery M. Paige, *Coffee and Power: Revolution and the Rise of Democracy in Central America* (Cambridge: Harvard University Press, 1997), provides a comparative perspective including Nicaragua and El Salvador.

37. Consult Margaret E. Scranton, *The Noriega Years: U.S.–Panamanian Relations, 1981–1990* (Boulder, CO: Lynne Rienner, 1991); R. M. Koster and Guillermo Sanchez, *In the Time of Tyrants: Panama, 1968–1990* (New York: Norton, 1990); and John Dinges, *Our Man in Panama: How General Noriega Used the United States—and Made Millions in Drugs and Arms* (New York: Random House, 1990).

38. For perspective see Walter LaFeber, *The Panama Canal: The Crisis in Historical Perspective* (New York: Oxford University Press, 1989).

39. Consult Howard J. Wiarda and Michael Kryzanek, *The Dominican Republic: A Caribbean Crucible*, rev. ed. (Boulder, CO: Westview Press, 1992).

40. Jonathan Hartlyn, *The Struggle for Democratic Politics in the Dominican Republic* (Chapel Hill: University of North Carolina Press, 1998), analyzes events past the mid-1990s, as does the chapter by Rosario Espinal and Jonathan Hartlyn in Diamond et al., eds., *Democracy*, pp. 469–518. Very useful is Ramonina Brea, Rosario Espinal, and Fernando Valerio-Holguin, eds., *La Republica Dominicana en el Umbral del Siglo XXI: Cultura, Politica y Cambio Social* (Santo Domingo, Dominican Republic: Pontifica Universidad Catolica Madre y Maestra, 1999).

41. Consult Robert Fatton, Jr., *Haiti's Predatory Republic: The Unending Transition to Democracy* (Boulder, CO: Lynne Rienner, 2002); Alex Dupuy, *Haiti in the New World Order: The Limits of the Democratic Revolution* (Boulder, CO: Westview Press, 1997); and Chetan Kumar, *Building Peace in Haiti* (Boulder, CO: Westview Press, 1999).

42. See Elizabeth Abbot, *Haiti: The Duvaliers and Their Legacy* (New York: McGraw-Hill, 1988), and Fatton, *Haiti's Predatory Republic*.

43. The extremely fragmented opposition, expectation that a Lavalas victory was inevitable, and lack of enthusiasm for the uninspiring candidate were among the factors contributing to the low turnout. Useful for perspective are Georges A. Fauriol, ed., *Haitian*

Frustrations, Dilemmas for U.S. Policy (Washington, DC: Center for Strategic and International Studies, 1995), and Robert I. Rotberg, ed., *Haiti Renewed, Political and Economic Prospects* (Washington, DC: Brookings Institution–World Peace Foundation, 1997).

44. On this period consult Juan M. de Aguila, *Cuba: Dilemmas of a Revolution*, 3rd ed. (Boulder, CO: Westview Press, 1994); Louis A. Perez, Jr., *Cuba: Between Reform and Revolution*, 2nd ed. (New York: Oxford University Press, 1995); Hugh Thomas, *Cuba: Or the Pursuit of Freedom*, updated ed. (New York: Da Capo Press, 1998); and Susan E. Eckstein, *Back from the Future: Cuba Under Castro* (New York: Routledge, 2003), particularly Chapters 3 and 4.

45. See Eckstein, *Back from the Future,* pp. 84–85. This meticulous scholar places the value of free military arms and aid at $10 billion, with Soviet loans and credits running at a rate of $1.463 billion plus $162 million from Eastern European countries.

46. Peter Roman, *People's Power: Cuba's Experience with Representative Government* (Lanham, MD: Rowman & Littlefield, 2003), stresses the democratic features of the Cuban regime. Many of the "whither Cuba" symposia have little lasting value, an exception being Susan Kaufman Purcell and David Rothkopf, eds., *Cuba: The Contours of Change* (Boulder, CO: Lynne Rienner, 2000). On societal changes see Eckstein, *Back from the Future,* Chapter 5, especially pp. 140ff., as well as Juan M. de Aguila, "Development, Revolution, and Decay in Cuba" in Howard J. Wiarda and Harvey F. Kline, eds., *Latin American Politics and Development*, 5th ed. (Boulder, CO: Westview Press, 2000), pp. 400–446.

47. For the old and new Caribbeans see Jorge I. Dominguez, Robert A. Pastor, and R. Delise Worrell, eds., *Democracy in the Caribbean: Political, Economic, and Social Perspectives* (Baltimore: Johns Hopkins University Press, 1993).

48. See David Panton, *Jamaica's Michael Manley: The Great Transformation (1972–1992)* (Kingston, Jamaica: Kingston Publishers, 1993).

49. In the absence of significant scholarly monographs, one of the few adequate sources for accompanying events in this small country is the annual (originally biennial) volumes on *South America, Central America, and the Caribbean* (London: Europa Publications, 1986–2004).

50. Trinidad, as the region's one significant producer of petroleum products—hence the basis of a more viable economy—as well as a location much more proximate to South America's northern coast than to the rest of the Caribbean (particularly Cuba, Haiti, and the Dominican Republic), enjoys relative freedom from undesirable foreign pressures compared to other countries of the region.

51. With the end of the Cold War and the aging of the Jagans, and in light of security threats in the Middle East, official US interest in and involvement with Guyana's politics waned to the point of virtual disappearance. As in the case of Suriname, Washington came to accept the fact that Brazil had a much more immediate concern about its small neighbors and very probably possessed superior assets for dealing with them.

52. See Nigel Boland, *Belize: A New Nation in Central America* (Boulder, CO: Westview Press, 1986).

53. Consult the country entries in the fifth through ninth editions of *South America, Central America, and the Caribbean,* cited in note 49 above.

54. See Henk E. Chin and Hans Buddingh, *Surinam: Politics, Economics, and Society* (London and New York: F. P. Pinter, 1987), and Edward Dew, *The Trouble in Surinam, 1975–1993* (Westport, CT: Praeger, 1994).

55. Consult Europa Publications' *South America, Central America, and the Caribbean*, especially the sixth edition (1997), the seventh edition (1999), and the eighth edition (2000); see note 49 above.

56. See the sixth, seventh, and eighth editions of *South America, Central America, and the Caribbean*; see note 49 above.

57. Consult the country entries in *South America, Central America, and the Caribbean* volumes published in 1995, 1997, 1999, and 2000; see note 49 above.

58. See the country entries in *South America, Central America, and the Caribbean*, particularly the sixth edition (1997), the seventh edition (1999), and the eighth edition (2000); see note 49 above.

13

Entering the New Century

Tides and Currents, 2000–2005

The 1990s for Latin America had been a decade characterized by generally middle-of-the-road neocapitalist governments relying heavily upon participating in globalization by opening up their economies and privatizing investment-starved state enterprises in keeping with the so-called Washington Consensus among most of the region's leaders (which assumed that free-market economies and freer trade were congruent with increased democracy). The results of this strategy were often disappointing to downright disillusioning for the majority of the population—especially the underprivileged lower classes. As a consequence, the twenty-first century began with a wave of efforts to find ways of combining newly established democratic politics with populist, if not necessarily clearly progressive, social policies. In the ongoing tension between badly needed economic growth and fear of reawakening the dreadful dragon of inflation, 1990s progress in taming the latter subsequently tempted policymakers to embrace the former as public opinion increasingly shifted in favor of priority for development over price stability, sometimes very vocally. This attitude provided a very serious challenge to several Latin American countries, since the less fortunate sectors of society, although sometimes expressing a theoretical preference for democracy, are more concerned with development and security. They, unlike their better-off compatriots, often prefer strong, even authoritarian, government—if it delivers in the economic realm—to democracies that fail to do so and do not firmly maintain order.[1]

Hence, a very important question for Latin America as a whole is whether or not democratic governments in the first decade of the twenty-first century will prove increasingly responsive to social sectors that heretofore have either received empty promises or merely token benefits. These broad elements at the bottom of the social pyramid fall into two major groupings: the urban underprivileged and the neglected rural masses—each in absolute, if not relative, terms more numerous in Brazil than in any other country, followed by Mexico. Authoritarian regimes of the 1960s and 1970s throughout Latin America had very little motivation to concern themselves with either segment; the initial wave of democratic administrations first gave priority to economic reconstruction before turning to the concerns of the urban middle classes and organized skilled workers. Even administrations four or five times removed from their country's initial democratic transformation have found that a priority for economic stability severely circumscribed the growth required for more distributive policies.

In Brazil not only did Cardoso leave social justice and income redistribution on the back burner, but Lula da Silva, his historically much more leftist successor, continued this strategy. The conservative victory behind Fox in 1999 guaranteed there would be no shift toward distributive policies in Mexico until at least after the 2006 elections, and Colombia opted for a middle-of-the-road chief executive in 2002, with his reelection likely in 2006, pushing any priority for social issues up past 2010. Moreover, Argentina's turn-of-the-decade economic and social collapse condemned the administration of Kirchner to a situation where, in 2003–2005, economic recovery of necessity dominated the policy agenda. Hence, for the 382 million of the region's 565 million inhabitants dwelling in the four largest countries, social justice continues to be limited chiefly to the levels of political rhetoric and campaign debate, not of current policy. And in most of the medium-sized countries similar imperatives prevail, and important social groups become increasingly restless. Moreover, governments embracing neoliberal programs have run into roadblocks to their implementation by presumed allies and even from within their own ranks. For as Wiarda poses the problem in extreme terms:

> To the extent state size is reduced or state-owned companies privatized, so are the opportunities forfeited for patronage, government jobs, contracts, corruption, special access, insider knowledge, and opportunities for self-enrichment. No politician in Latin America or elsewhere can favor policies that undermine the jobs and/or patronage base of his political support.[2]

Given significant structural differences in the economies of the various Latin American countries, there was a sharpened awareness among politically relevant groups that what is needed, or what may be politically feasible, in one country is not the same as in another—even if they might be neighbors geographically. Hence, a growing division emerged between those nations in which democracy and development appear to go hand in hand and those where formally democratic governments fall short in the sphere of economic performance, particularly where this shortcoming is compounded by dramatic rises in crime and public disorder.[3] Management of the economy had become the number one priority for governments, especially in the more urban and developed countries, but less favored sectors of society expected to see positive results reflected in their levels of living, not just in macroeconomic indicators. In this respect the challenges in the opening years of the twenty-first century were daunting and show few signs of easing. For the region as a whole, the performances of giants Brazil and Mexico are increasingly important, but the electorate in each country is little interested in overall Latin American figures, even positive ones, if their nation lags behind and their sector of society is still being shortchanged. Indeed, only the privileged upper strata have any concept of Latin America, much less a sense of Latin Americanness.

Overview

Hence, it should not have been surprising that the early 2000s marked the inception of a new period of increasing political volatility for much of South America. Given Brazil's great bulk, the most important single development in that part of the region was Lula da Silva's election to Brazil's presidency in late 2002. His limited formal education, lack of administrative experience, radical left background, with its potential for an unsettling effect upon foreign investment, and his party's extremely weak position in the congress combined to raise questions as to whether he would or could build on the foundations for sustained development established in this largest of Latin American nations during Fernando Henrique Cardoso's double term in office. Following an initially promising start, in which action was taken on reforms stalled in the preelection phase of the preceding government, financial scandals and economic stagnation forged to the front in the first part of 2004, although the economy rallied in the second half of the year, before municipal elections in early October showed how fragmented political preferences remained. Then in mid-2005, campaign finance and bribery scandals hit the government with hurricane force.

The most significant development for the North American part of the region was the coming to power of a freely elected opposition president in Mexico at the end of 2000. Vicente Fox's subsequent performance in office was critical in maintaining competitive political life in the region's second most important country, and like his counterpart in Brazil, he lacked a congressional majority. With a six-year nonrenewable term, he had to strive to build a record on which his party could run in a heated three-way race in which the left opposition enjoyed the early advantage of a candidate with high name recognition in Andrés Manuel López Obredor, entrenched as Mexico City's mayor. Unfortunately for Fox, global events and developments in the United States continued to impinge negatively on his performance, leading to a resurgence of support for the middle-of-the-road party ousted from power in 2000. Hence, his influence on the mid-2006 elections waned, and he appeared destined to be a political one-hit wonder.

The most dramatic development in the opening years of the new period for the region as a whole was the chaos in Argentina, which led to a revolving-door presidency and the holding of new elections in early 2003, followed by a concerted effort at recovery. This attention-attracting panorama at the southern tip of Latin America was combined with the elevation to power in Colombia, through its 2002 elections, of a hard-hitting law-and-order politician committed to reversing the tolerance shown to the guerrillas by his predecessor. Next door in Venezuela, the cause for concern was mounting unrest bordering on rebellion directed against the left-leaning personalist Hugo Chávez, culminating in an unsuccessful recall campaign in mid-2004 and a strengthening of Chávez's prestige in the region. Peru's slumbering political volcano showed signs of renewed activity as a new president in 2001 demonstrated very little ability to deal with the basic problems of a country still mired in hundreds of corruption trials dating back to the decade-long Fujimori regime. Bright spots of democratic stability in Chile and Uruguay were balanced by instability in Ecuador and a mounting crisis in Bolivia—two countries where neglected Indian masses were insisting on a voice in national affairs and ready to follow whoever would take their demands seriously. Hence, the beginning of the second decade of elected government in Paraguay drew little attention.

In Central America the main question was whether, in an adverse international environment of terrorist tensions, economic malaise, and generally fumbling leadership, the democratic gains of the 1990s could be preserved. Yet to a significant degree these six nations managed to continue progress toward stable representative political processes. The same was not true of the older countries of the Caribbean, with near chaos in Haiti, some backsliding in the Dominican Republic, and the aging of a regime becoming increasingly personalist in Cuba. The newer Caribbean countries, some of marginal economic viability, had gains in most offset by reversals in a few while leadership was waiting to see what implications faltering efforts toward regional economic integration might have for them.

Since 2006 will see critical elections in almost all the major and intermediate countries of the region, their recent electoral developments require close examination. This is most essential for Brazil with its great expanse, massive electorate, and extremely fluid multiparty system as well as its current political crisis. Everywhere voter concerns, issues, and responses from contenders take on increasing relevance as attention turns to electoral campaigns.

Brazil: From Cardoso to Lula to 2006

The 2000s opened with Brazil entering year two of Fernando Henrique Cardoso's second administration. As congressional consideration of social security, pension, and tax reforms essential to sound governmental finances and controllable fiscal deficits stalled, the country's thousand top politicians, along with hordes of lesser politicos, turned their attention to positioning themselves, engaging in slate making, arranging finances, and beginning to campaign for the October 2000 nationwide municipal elections—which marked the onset of maneuvering for late 2002 elections not only for the presidency, but for all governorships and national and state legislative positions (as had occurred in 1998).[4] This time, however, with the incumbent ineligible to run for another term, the municipal elections might significantly impact the presidential succession.

Trends observable in the late 1990s were confirmed by the nationwide balloting in all 5,559 municipalities at the beginning of October 2000, following intense campaigning varying from very modern techniques in the great urban centers to tried-and-true patronal and rural machine methods in the vast hinterlands. With a record 84.5 million turnout, up sharply from 1996's 74.1 million, change was incremental, not dramatic, hence providing only limited clues to what might be expected two years later in the presidential sweepstakes. Just under 40 percent of the voters came from the country's one hundred largest cities, showing that, contrary to the media attention lavished on metropolitan areas, a majority of the electorate was still to be found in medium and small cities and rural towns. The leftist Workers' Party (PT)'s increase to 14.1 percent of electoral support (over 11.9 million votes), although far below its leaders' optimistic predictions, finally established it as one of Brazil's big four, although still the least of them. On the other side of the political spectrum, the conservative Liberal Front Party (PFL) essentially held its ground with 15.4 percent (13.0 million votes). The Brazilian Social Democracy Party (PSDB), Cardoso's own party, retained the lead in the electoral derby by a nose over the more clientelistic—hence less cohesive—Party of the Brazilian Democratic Movement (PMDB) at 16.0 to 15.7 percent (over 13.5 million to nearly 13.3 million voters). A number of the medium-sized parties demonstrated electoral viability, but not to a degree that would justify dreams of going it alone on a national scale in 2002.[5]

In the second-division race, significant in such a fragmented party system, in which the four leading parties together had the support of just over three-fifths of the electorate, the Brazilian Popular Party (PPB) led with 8.1 percent of the national vote (6.8 million supporters) over the Brazilian Labor Party (PTB) at 6.9 percent (5.8 million backers), with the declining Democratic Workers' Party (PDT) at 6.6 percent (with the preference of 5.6 million voters). The Brazilian Socialist Party (PSB), the Popular Socialist Party (PPS), and the Liberal Party (PL) avoided being relegated to insignificance by holding on to 4.6, 4.2, and 3.0 percent of voter preferences, respectively. The same was not true of the fast-sliding Social Democratic Party (PSD), the Green Party (PV), the Social Christian Party (PSC), and the Communist Party of Brazil (PCdoB). Thus it was clear that the political preferences of the huge Brazilian electorate remained extremely divided.

(It was apparent that a threshold, such as Germany's 5 percent rule, although probably forcing the merger of splinter parties, would not in itself lead to a transformation of Brazil's political fragmentation, as seven parties received between 6 and 16 percent of the vote, and two others near 5 percent, still leaving more votes in total to the small splinters than any of the leading parties garnered.)

In terms of offices won, the PMDB led with 1,257 mayors and 11,373 city council members, compared to 1,028 and 9,649 for the PFL, with 990 and 8,515 for the PSDB (totaling 3,275 and 29,537, respectively, some three-fifths of the total). These results demonstrated that although these three were national parties enjoying support from large numbers of elected officials in addition to the many times larger number of functionaries these dignitaries employed, they were far from dominant. At 618 mayors and a healthy 7,064 local legislators, the PPB, strongest in São Paulo, showed residual strength well ahead of the PTB's 398 mayors and 4,989 municipal council members or the decaying PDT's scant harvest of 288 *prefeitos* and 3,765 aldermen. Seventh place went to the PL with 234 mayors and 2,890 municipal councilors, with the PT's lack of strength outside the major cities reflected in an eighth-place harvest of only 187 mayors and 2,485 *vereadores* (city councilmen). Despite their weakness in rural areas and medium-sized cities, opposition parties, led by the PT, combined to capture twelve state capitals (up from eight) and twenty-seven of the largest sixty-two cities, compared to ten cities four years earlier. The proportion of women winning mayoral posts remained static at 5.7 percent. Although the requirement for the share of women on party slates rose from 20 to 30 percent, the number elected to city councils rose only marginally to 11.6 percent.

International attention was—as is so often the case—heavily focused on São Paulo, the vast metropolis where the PT's vivacious Marta Suplicy, a psychologist famed as the country's leading guru on sexual and marital problems as well as estranged wife of a senator who had been the PT's candidate for governor, emerged victorious in the October 29 runoff by a 59 percent to 41 percent margin over multiterm former governor and ex-mayor Paulo Maluf, poster boy for old-style corruption (and perennial presidential hopeful). Her victory did not reflect great strength for the PT, as her increase from only 38 percent in the first round came via endorsement as a lesser evil by the PSDB (including the president), whose candidate had missed getting into the runoff in place of Maluf by a mere 6,000 votes. (Maluf, who refuses to disappear from Brazil's political stage, subsequently improved much more sharply from his 17 percent core support.)

In Rio de Janeiro, Brazil's other urban conglomerate of over ten million, the front-runner in the first round, the PFL candidate, lost in a close runoff to the PTB's César Maia (as the PT's Benedita da Silva fell by the wayside with only 20 percent of the vote). In four weeks Maia dramatically increased his share of the vote from 23 to 51 percent, whereas his opponent could only improve from 35 to

49 percent, but this highly competent administrator remained a regional, rather than a national, leader. In the country's third city, Belo Horizonte, the PSB's candidate coasted to a 55 percent to 45 percent runoff victory after having led the PSDB standard bearer on national election day with 44 percent to only 31. But his ill health in April 2001 elevated his PT vice mayor, Fernando Pimentel, to this prominent post. In other urban centers with populations of over two million the results were very mixed. Salvador went easily to the PFL without a runoff, a result narrowly avoided in Porto Alegre, where the PT's Tarso Genro garnered 49 percent of voter preferences on his way to a 64 percent to 36 percent cakewalk on October 29. In Recife the PFL incumbent came tantalizingly close to victory in the initial balloting with 49 percent, only to see the tables turned in the runoff as the PT's João Paulo Lima e Silva nosed him out with 51 percent of the vote as he stood still at 49 percent. In Curitiba the PFL's standard bearer hung on for a 51 percent to 49 percent runoff victory over his PT challenger. In Fortaleza presidential hopeful Ciro Gomes failed to propel his ex-wife into the second round of balloting, as the PMDB candidate upped his vote from 33 percent to 54 percent for that party's most prominent electoral trophy. The country's biggest winner was not even on the ballot, as in Bahia PFL strongman Antônio Carlos Magalhães demonstrated his continued political clout, coming away with control of 94 percent of the state's 417 city halls, including the metropolis of Salvador. Ex-president José Sarney nearly kept up with him, emerging from the elections with 200 of 217 Maranhão municipalities controlled by his allies, 73 of them from the PFL and a large number of others affiliated with the PMDB—in which he kept his membership while having his daughter, the state's governor, enrolled in the PFL. Although the presidency remained beyond the reach of these senior citizens, their position as major determiners of who will be the contenders were solidified.

In the aftermath of the elections, President Cardoso sought in vain to find a strategy to enact priority legislation during 2001 before national and state electoral considerations came to the fore once more. His success in this direction was very limited, and he gradually became a limping rooster, two steps short of a classic lame duck (a president whose successor has already been chosen rather than one just hobbled or crippled by his erstwhile supporters climbing on the bandwagons of possible successors—a major consideration in multiparty systems). One of Cardoso's problems, fatal if he wished to manage the succession process, was his inability to bring about sustained economic growth sufficient to generate an increase in per capita income. His reelection had been greatly facilitated by GDP growth of 2.7 percent in 1996, rising to 3.2 percent for 1997. Then in 1999 economic growth was an anemic 1.4 percent, and memories of recovery to 4.1 percent in 2000 could not make up for a pronounced slump in 2001. Brazilian voters are skeptical about final economic data released early the next year; they are extremely wary of preliminary figures issued in the course of an election campaign—particularly if their personal experience tells them that prices they deal with in everyday life are on the rise. Hence, the fact that 2002 turned out to be a fairly good year in economic terms did not really help the administration's candidate.

In sharp contrast with Argentina's contemporary unprecedented woes, the Brazilian economy performed at least marginally well in Cardoso's eighth and final year in office. The public debt to GDP ratio in 2002 was a worrisome 58 percent, but the federal government's primary fiscal surplus was over 3 percent of GDP and the trade surplus was a robust $13 billion—breaking the old 1994 record of $10.5 billion only three years after enduring a $6-billion trade deficit in 1999 (on the heels of an $8.6-billion imbalance in 1998). Despite troublesome trade barriers, commerce with the United States and its NAFTA partners came to exceed that with the European Union, which came to 23 percent of Brazil's diversified total, with the rest of Latin America just behind as a trading partner, and Asia coming on strong. Moreover, Brazil began to carry the day within the mechanisms of the World Trade Organization (WTO) in its challenging of unfair subsidies and restrictions on the part of the industrialized powers.

Lula's presidential campaign had, in effect, been going on nearly continuously since his first bid in 1989—embracing his determined, if unsuccessful, runs in 1994 and 1998. Now despite a flurry of wild predictions of a huge surge in PT voters, this mature campaigner knew after three losses in a row that to win he needed to build a broad coalition of parties, including some that were still part of Cardoso's legislative base. In this enterprise Lula had three things going for him. First, his electoral allies knew that he would have to keep his promises to them, for there was no way that he could come close to building a majority in either house of the congress without having them as valued partners. Lula's second reinforcing asset was the fact that these parties had a long record of adhering to whatever government was in power, being accustomed to the patronage and perks of being part of the government and unsuited to, as well as unfamiliar with, the role of opposition. His third advantage was the appreciation on the part of important PFL, PMDB, PTB, and even some PPB leaders of his popularity with the masses—a part of which they would like to have rub off on their anointed candidates during what promised to be very difficult races at the state level.

Lula was soon relieved of his worry that Cardoso would find a way to unify much of his 1998 backing behind a coalition candidate. Once the PSDB was adamant that the administration's standard bearer had to come from its ranks, only wings of the factionalized PMDB and divided PFL could possibly join behind him. Major figures of these large parties who would not do so included ex-president Sarney in the former and the longtime political boss of Bahia, Antônio Carlos Magalhães, in the latter, each of whom had recently presided over the congress as entrenched members of the innermost senatorial circle. Since their sup-

**LUIZ INÁCIO
LULA DA SILVA**
(CREDIT: RICARDO STUCKERT/ABR.)

port would not be available until they had explored other opportunities, Lula demonstrated his availability for alliances by selecting seventy-one-year-old José Alencar of the small centrist Liberal Party (PL), a successful Minas Gerais business-man, to serve as his running mate. Along with Lula, Governors Roseana Sarney of Maranhão and Anthony Garotinho in Rio de Janeiro emerged as the early fron-trunners, but their candidacies wilted under government-aided attacks by its can-didate, health minister José Serra. Ms. Sarney was laid low by exploitation of financial scandals involving her husband and ran for the senate instead. Garotinho, despite division of the Evangelical movement upon whom his hopes rested, con-tinued in the race.

In the first round of balloting on October 6, Lula garnered 39.2 million votes (46.4 percent) to Serra's 19.6 million (23.2 percent). Garotinho made a respectable showing with 15.1 million votes (17.9 percent), and Ciro Gomes slipped from his 1998 third-place performance with 10.1 million ballots cast in his favor (12.0 per-cent). An impressive 94.3 million, some 82 percent of a registered electorate of 115.3 million, went to the polls.[6] The October 27 runoff was anticlimactic as Lula trounced Serra 52.8 million to 33.4 million—57.6 percent to 36.4 percent (62.5 percent to 37.5 percent in terms of valid votes). On the congressional side, the PT elected 91 to the 513-member lower house compared to 84 for the PFL, the

PMDB's 74, and 71 for the PSDB. Fifth place went to the PPB at 49, followed at a distance by the PTB and PL with 26 each and the PSB and PDT at 22 and 21 seats. Counting holdovers, the PFL and PMDB led in the Senate with 19 each, trailed by the PT with 14 and the PSDB with 11. The PDT held 5 seats, and the PTB, PSB, and PL each held 4 of the 81 seats. The PT's just under 18 percent of the Chamber of Deputies and slightly less in the Senate left Lula with a major challenge in mounting a congressional majority, reflecting his party's continued fragility in many parts of the country—worrisome in light of his determination to seek reelection in 2006. (In the midst of Cardoso's 1998 win, the PT had elected 59 deputies.)

This weakness of the PT compared to the popularity of its candidate was confirmed in the governorship elections, where the PT won only 3 of 27 races, no improvement over 1998. The PSDB, despite its presidential candidate's defeat, led with 7 states (containing 52 million voters) and the PMDB with 5 (embracing an electorate of 24 million), as the PFL and PSB with 4 each also outperformed Lula's party. Thirteen of these races were determined on October 6, with the other fourteen resolved through runoffs. The PT was victorious only in the relatively unimportant state of Matto Grosso do Sul and extremely small Piauí and Acre, whereas the PSDB, Serra's party, carried off the major prizes, São Paulo and Minas Gerais, the country's two most populous states, along with medium-sized Ceará. Presidential show horse Garotinho's PSB triumphed in his home state of Rio de Janeiro, where his wife was elected governor (by 4.1 million votes to less than 2.0 million for the PT's acting governor Benedita da Silva, thus all but putting an end to this dynamic black woman's hopes to play a role on the national scene). The PMDB swept the South—Rio Grande do Sul, Paraná, and Santa Catarina, as well as winning control of the Federal District and retaining the governorship of Pernambuco, all in all a formidable power base. Bahia and Maranhão were the PFL's major electoral spoils. The state of São Paulo has a population equaling that of California (near that of Argentina or Colombia), and Minas Gerais is on a par with Texas or New York. Rio de Janeiro has some 14 million inhabitants, and Bahia is nearing that mark, with Rio Grande do Sul reaching 11 million, Paraná closing in on 10 million, and Pernambuco exceeding 8 million— so they are the electoral plums. Still, Ceará, at well over 7 million, and Maranhão, approaching that mark, are far from insignificant electoral bases.

A very important consideration for the future was the inescapable fact that in very large part Lula's election was a result of support by dissident leaders of the Cardoso-era governing coalition, eager to even scores and strengthen their position within their own parties. Ex-president Sarney blamed Serra for unfairly derailing his daughter's once-flourishing presidential campaign, whereas Antônio Carlos Magalhães resented having been forced to resign not only the senate presidency but even his senate seat over what he considered a minor technical violation of rules. With a Serra victory, the rivals of these two lords of Brazilian politics would consolidate control over the PMDB and the PFL, respectively; by helping elect Lula this pair of hardy political perennials could look forward to being crucial power brokers in the fragmented 2003–2006 congress and influence the presidential succession. Neither of these grizzled veteran wizards of Brazilian politics had any reason to remain allied with the new president except in terms of a satisfactory arrangement with respect to cabinet posts and patronage in politically strategic agencies. Both sage veterans of political wars kept a wary weather eye out for opportunities to increase their influence—a development more likely the greater the difficulties encountered by the administration's PT nucleus. Indeed, by mid-2004, with the administration bogged down in scandals, an insider saying was that Sarney exercised greater influence in the presidential palace than he had during the last years of his own presidency. (By late 2005 this would be all the more so.) Hence, while stockpiling financial resources for future campaigns, Lula focused on the task at hand: how to obtain a working majority in the congress.

Lula handled the potentially treacherous task of organizing his government with skill and a solid perception of political realities. He and his closest associates knew that translating his landslide electoral victory into effective support for his administration would be as difficult as it was essential. Starting with well under one-fifth of the seats in each house of the congress for his own party, the president-elect needed to turn his erstwhile electoral allies into reliable coalition partners. As this task included the essentially conservative PFL as well as a PMDB with a strong conservative wing, Lula and his closest advisers realized that, in accommodating the other parties' demands in the areas of both patronage and policy, they ran a serious risk of alienating the more radical ideological elements of their own party—its so-called Shiite wing. Pragmatically, they decided that this was a price they were willing to pay and moved toward the center, while taking steps to isolate and marginalize party extremists.[7] Hence, the heterogeneous administration cobbled together in the two months between the end of victory celebrations and inauguration day at the beginning of 2003 met the situation's political requirements. In addition, despite its political diversity, this administration held together well compared to previous initial cabinets, with most of its key figures surviving the shakedown cruise and staying around at least into the administration's second year in office.

Lula also demonstrated considerable skill in establishing reasonable working relationships with governors of the most important states and, where this was not possible, with mayors of major metropolitan centers—particularly when, as in the case of São Paulo, they came from the PT's ranks. For behind the rhetoric of electoral politics all major political actors shared a realization that Brazil had essentially found the road toward economic viability during the Cardoso years and had no desire to jeopardize the foundations that were finally in place. As a leading newsmagazine pointed out just after the election, government funds and employment, "the historical canals through which political power exercised its will," had changed fundamentally in terms of the reduction in the size of the state, leaving much less in the way of patronage to be passed on to regional bosses in return for votes. Moreover, expenditures at the state and local level were now disciplined by the 2001 Law of Fiscal Responsibility, and federal budgetary outlays no longer passed through the hands of governors, congressmen, and mayors before reaching their intended objective.[8]

The central figures in Lula's administration were longtime close associate, PT head, and campaign manager José Dirceu Oliveira da Silva (b. 1946), originally from Minas Gerais, as chief presidential assistant (essentially combining the duties of the White House chief of staff Andrew Card and those of Karl Rove) and Antonio Palocci (b. 1960), a medical doctor from São Paulo and advocate of stimulating exports, as finance minister. A two-term mayor of the sizable city of Ribeirão Preto, he had played a major role in 2002 campaign fund-raising. Important supporting roles were filled by economics professor Guido Mantenga (b. 1949) with the planning portfolio; personal intimate José Genoino (b. 1946), yet another *Paulista*, who had been the PT's losing candidate for governor of São Paulo, installed as the PT's president; Luiz Dulci (b. 1956), labor activist and PT general secretary from Minas Gerais, as secretary general of the presidency; and close personal friend, Luiz Gushiken (b. 1950), a São Paulo bank workers' leader, ensconced in the newly created position of minister of government communications. Dirceu came to function as a quasi prime minister before being laid low along with many of the others in the monumental campaign finance scandal of 2005.

In acknowledgement of the PT's strength in Rio Grande do Sul, that state received four cabinet posts, including ex-governors Olivio Dutra as minister of urban affairs and Tarso Genro in charge of the Economic and Social Development Council. Former Federal District governor Cristovam Buarque was initially given the education portfolio (later passed to Genro), and Aldo Rebelo of the PPS, like Genoino once a guerrilla, became minister of political articulation. Cabinet positions were also allocated to representatives of those allied parties not ideologically aligned with the PT. Thus Ciro Gomes, fourth-place finisher in the presidential sweepstakes, became minister of regional integration, Rio de Janeiro congressman Miro Teixeira was named minister of communications, and Pernambucan Eduardo Campos became minister of science and technology.

Contrary to expectations of those remembering Lula's historical militant socialism and the PT's ideology, but in keeping with his newly found belief that without sustained development distributionist policies would lack viability, there was a striking continuity with the policies of the outgoing administration. This was also highly conditioned by the new chief executive's need to rely heavily on the same parties as had his predecessor within a presidential system with many semiparliamentary features, and with ex-president Sarney presiding over the senate (as he had done for portions of Cardoso' administration). Priority was given to enactment of the very social security, pension, and tax reforms that Lula and the PT had vehemently opposed when they were the backbone of the opposition to Cardoso's government—and which were well advanced in the legislative process until sidelined by electoral politics in 2002.[9] In addition there were the imperatives of an IMF requirement for a primary budget surplus of 3.75 percent of GDP in 2003 and the perceived need for $14 to $16 billion in new foreign investments and financing to supplement the hoped-for record billion trade surplus in order to keep Brazil's balance of payments in order.

Party switching is commonplace in Brazil, and the government soon managed to expand and consolidate its legislative base by attracting congress members seeking the ample advantages of executive favor. By 2004, the PSDB had lost 23 seats and the PFL 21, while the major gainer was the PTB, doubling its chamber representation from its original 26, followed by the PL, which (with a splinter junior partner) went up from 27 to 47. This notable success came with a heavy delayed price as the government would be shaken to its foundations starting in mid-May 2005 over damning evidence that many of these party jumpers had been paid to jump with illegal funds used by the PT. (Many times in politics those perceived as shrewd operators assume that they have gotten away with a covert masterstroke, only to have the lid blown off down the road.) The PMDB picked up three senate seats as alternates replaced elected senators who took executive positions at the national or state levels.

The president's most notable success was in adding parties to his coalition through a combination of patronage and policy moderation. First, the PMDB came aboard in mid-2003, followed soon after by the PPB, recast as the Popular Party (PP). This broadening of its congressional base allowed the administration to win the crucial votes on pension reform in August with 358 votes, of which 80 came from the PT and 61 from authentically left parties. Not only did a greater number, 152, come from the government's center and center-right allies, but 62 yes votes came from the opposition. In following months this phenomenon was repeated even more dramatically with respect to fiscal and tax reforms, as the PT furnished 87 votes, other left parties 62, and the relative center a whopping 186, as opposition dissidents shrank to 39.[10]

The administration hoped for a groundswell of support to propel the PT along the road to becoming a truly national party. Campaigning for the most important local elections not only in Brazil's experience, but by a large margin for the entire Latin American region, took place in a mixed political environment. On the negative side, by April 2004 Lula found himself mired in a corruption scandal that had erupted in mid-February when a videotape surfaced showing his congressional liaison soliciting hundreds of thousands of dollars in campaign contributions from the boss of an illegal numbers game (*jogo de bicho,* or "animal game," in local parlance). Impunity and political favors were promised in return for this contribution, and in late March the government was forced to admit publicly that this kind of "administrative improprieties" had continued after Lula and the PT took office. With his government described by political analysts as paralyzed and the party as divided and perplexed, Lula's approval rating sank below 50 percent for the first time. Presidential chief of staff José Dirceu came under heavy attack for allegedly covering up a series of incidents of party-related corruption, a development that led the government to increased dependence on Sarney to keep the congress from open rebellion. Little did anyone dream that a year later a related scandal would hit the administration like a tsunami. As the economy grew in 2003 by a meager 0.5 percent, revelation that during his first year in office the left-leaning president had invested in development projects only a tenth of the amount Cardoso had in his final year in office further undercut the administration and, by putting it on the defensive, discombobulated its original electoral strategy of seeking to turn the local balloting into a referendum on the national administration.[11]

Significant economic recovery from midyear was a badly needed boon for the government. Economic growth for the year reached 5.2 percent, and burgeoning exports—at $94 billion, up sharply from $73 billion for the preceding year, which in turn constituted a 21 percent rise over 2002—provided a trade surplus of a record $33.6 billion (compared to the old mark of $24.8 billion in 2003). Thus, per capita GDP was again on the rise. For after reaching 5.7 percent in the decade beginning in 1971, this crucial index of economic health was marginally negative for the next ten years (down 0.37 percent), before rising a very modest 1.1 percent from 1991 through 2000—all on the strength of that year's 4.3 percent economic expansion, nearly 3 percent over population growth. Belief that resumption of economic growth was sustainable helped alleviate the problem of public sector debt, which had risen above half of GDP. The profile of the government's domestic indebtedness had already improved with a sharp drop in its dollar-indexed proportion—to an all-time low of one-seventh. By the third quarter the beneficial effects were being felt in the international area with improved debt ratings and a drop in the sovereign debt spread (the premium over the prime rate paid for international perceptions of repayment risk). Industrial production began to rise in August 2003, and a year later output was running nearly 10 percent over the corresponding month of the previous year and up nearly 8 percent since the beginning of 2004. Auto manufacturing and exports were growing at an encouraging rate, with domestic sales also picking up. The big question was whether economic recovery would balance out the bad news on the sociopolitical front sufficiently to permit the PT to expand its electoral base beyond the large cities, thus improving Lula's chances of reelection, or whether a rival party would emerge as a heavyweight foe capable of mounting a formidable challenge.

What happened electorally in nearly 5,500 medium and small municipalities in Brazil in October 2004 turned out to be substantially more important than the results in the major cities that monopolized media attention. Two things were certain from the results: first, this municipal balloting accurately reflected what the total national electorate of 121.4 million individuals—twice the number of Latin America's next largest country, Mexico—wanted from local authorities and politicians; second, given the nature of Brazil's fragmented multiparty system as well as its particular brand of federalism, the very mixed character of the results kept them from casting much light on presidential succession.[12] The most dramatic immediate impact was the runoff defeat of São Paulo mayor Marta Suplicy by the runner-up from the 2002 presidential sweepstakes. José Serra's election in this city of nearly 7.8 million voters both resurrected his presidential hopes and, to the extent coattails were perceived to be involved, transformed the PSDB's able, young, and personable two-term governor of that electorally huge state, Geraldo Alckmin, into an alternative presidential candidate for his party. Indeed, he would be viewed as one around whom other moderate parties might coalesce as had been the case with Cardoso in 1994 and 1998. (São Paulo state has over 27 million registered voters, twice as many as runner-up Minas Gerais.) In contrast to the 2000 mayoral election, this time it was the PSDB's candidate who benefited in the runoff from the support of a majority of third-place finisher Maluf's "orphans." Thus, after leading 43.6 percent to 35.8 percent in the initial balloting, four weeks later Serra garnered 54.9 percent of the runoff vote compared to the devastated incumbent's 45.1 percent for a massive victory margin of 590,000 votes. "Marta's" defeat, along with the PT's loss of important interior cities such as Campinas and Ribeirao Preto, cost the party many thousands of patronage positions, which in most cases fell into PSDB hands. (Statewide the PSDB elected over 200 mayors compared to 56 for the PT.) This slippage was the first of a series of events negatively impacting Lula's reelection hopes.

In Rio de Janeiro, with over 4.4 million voters, the PFL's César Maia, an incumbent who had also held the post in 1992–1996 and enjoyed the backing of the PSDB, was easily reelected mayor with 50.1 percent of the vote on October 1 over a fragmented opposition (as the PT candidate languished in fifth place with a dismal 6.3 percent share of the votes, continuing the party's chronic failure to establish a base in the country's second largest city). The PFL also carried the most populous suburb, and the PMDB won in three of the state's major cities.[13] PT incumbent Fernando Pimentel won reelection in Belo Horizonte (with an electorate of 1.7 million) on the strength of an impressive 68.5 percent of the vote, and the PT also carried the largest of its industrial suburbs, whereas center and right parties did well in the rest of this large state. Salvador's 1.6 million voters handed Antônio Carlos Magalhães—dominant in the state since the late 1960s—

a major setback as his candidate lost to the PDT's young João Henrique Carneiro, who received 43.7 percent of the vote in the first round before garnering three-fourths of the ballots in the runaway runoff as the PT's candidate failed to make the second round. (Yet Magalhães still controlled 345 of the 417 municipalities in the country's fourth most populous state—some of them of significant size.)

In Fortaleza, with an electorate of nearly 1.4 million, a PT maverick triumphed over the PFL candidate with 56 percent of the runoff vote. Curitiba's 1.2 million voters gave the PSDB's Carlos Alberto Richa, a 52.8 percent runoff victory over the PT standard bearer. PT incumbent João Paulo Lima e Silva in Recife, with its electorate of over a million, was an easy winner with 56.1 percent of the vote, but his counterpart in Porto Alegre (also with a million voters), Raúl Pont, went down to a stunning 53.3 percent to 46.7 percent runoff defeat. Although the PT came away with two more state capital than they had previously held, as a result of losing São Paulo and Porto Alegre the population of these cities was only half what the party had controlled going into the elections. (In places of 10,000 to 50,000 the PT won 124 to the PSDB's 294, while in smaller cities the ratio was 219 to 516.)

Nationally the relative shares of voter support and offices won reflected a moderate acceleration of trends visible over the past dozen years rather than any sharp shift. For while attention focused on the major metropolitan centers, some 96 cities with electorates of over 150,000 contained a total of 46.4 million voters, nearly 38 percent of the country's total, and an even larger proportion of the electorate, some 46 percent, resided in communities of under 50,000 inhabitants. With its victory in São Paulo city as well as other major centers in that extremely populous state (nearly equal to Argentina or Colombia), the PSDB, while closely trailing the PT in total national first-round votes 15.7 million to 16.3 million (16.5 percent to 17.1 percent), came away with a marked advantage in terms of offices, with 874 mayors to 411 (sixth place) as well as a healthy lead in population governed. Given the clientelistic nature of Brazilian politics, this gave the leading opposition party a leg up on the crucial 2006 balloting.

Since the number of Brazilians casting ballots was up to 95.2 million from 84.5 million in 2000, the PSDB managed to gain 2.2 million votes compared to the PT's 4.4 million. Indeed, while slipping to third place with 14.2 million votes (15.0 percent), the PMDB garnered almost a million more than it had the previous time around and still retained the lead with 1,056 mayors (a drop from 1,257). The PFL sagged from 13.0 million votes to 11.3 million (15.4 percent to 11.8 percent) and came in third with 794 mayors, increasing the likelihood that it would seek to join a coalition in 2006.[14] But although the PSDB and PT—the parties of the leading presidential contenders—forged to the fore, two-thirds of Brazilian voters continued to prefer other parties (the PMDB, PFL, and PP almost equaling the two leaders, leaving another third for the lesser parties).

Following the also mixed outcome of the runoffs, Lula encountered difficulty in reformulating the congressional base of his government. Elected as the man, he governed with great reliance upon a small group of intimates he felt, given his total lack of previous executive experience, knew more than he did about running the government, but his faith would soon prove misplaced. Meanwhile, election results that weakened opportunistic ally Antônio Carlos Magalhães's influence within the PFL while strengthening the position of César Maia, combined with the growth of the PSDB relative to the PMDB and PP, created a need to satisfy these parties' voracious patronage appetites, along with those of the PTB and PPS, at the expense of vote-poor but militant left-wing allies such as the PCdoB. Cabinet shuffling became both more frequent and more difficult as the congressional strength of parties continued to change down to the end-of-September deadline after which party switchers would be ineligible to run for reelection. Since the beginning of the administration, 163 of 513 deputies had changed their party affiliations, many more than once.

If the 2004 elections had brought a major disappointment, 2005 was a nightmare for Lula and his party. First, the administration failed to elect the presiding officer of the lower house, thus losing the ability to determine its agenda. Hence, by May vital reform legislation was stalled, and although congressional allies remained as part of the government bloc, their support became less reliable as the question of presidential succession loomed. Then politics was thrown into confusion and the government into disarray in midyear by a series of financial scandals dwarfing those of a year earlier, but involving some of the same pivotal figures. Revelations concerning substantial bribes for lucrative contracts in the post office, where the PTB was ensconced as a reward for congressional support, merged with disclosure of a scheme of payments to congress members for switching to parties allied with the PT. Under the relentless glare of the press and the start of new congressional investigations, all roads eventually led to the powerful and arrogant José Dirceu.

Soon the administration's strongman was forced to resign and was expelled from Congress. Other presidential intimates, including the PT's secretary general and treasurer, were deeply implicated in a scheme with its roots back in the murky dealings of campaign financing for Lula's 2002 presidential run. Indeed, these illegal activities were clearly larger and more systematic than those resulting in Collor's 1992 impeachment. Hence, both the leading contenders for the presidency in 1989, for all their pious denunciations of corrupt political practices, could not resist milking the same cash cows to fatten their campaign war chests. The PPS broke with the government over the scandal.

Concerned about maintaining foreign confidence in the economy—Brazil's strongest trump with 3.5 percent growth, exports up 25 percent for a record $40-billion trade surplus, and foreign debt down to 50 percent of GDP from 65 percent in 2000—the opposition at first refrained from attacking the president, while maximizing the damage done to his party, its allies, and Lula's reelection prospects. The PSDB was determined to run a candidate—Serra, with São Paulo governor Alckmin and Minas Gerais's Acéio Neves in reserve—and considered that a greatly weakened president, one perhaps having to answer impeachment charges, was a favorable scenario. After all, the government was all but paralyzed. Moreover, to insulate Lula from culpability, his defenders were forced to depict him as unaware of what was going on within the presidential office and the intertwined PT national leadership—involving his closest associates. Although keeping Lula from looking like a knave, this approach to damage control ran the risk of having him appear instead to be a fool. Indeed, by mid-November polls showed Serra would defeat him in a runoff, as 46.7 percent of respondents said they wouldn't vote for Lula under any conditions, whereas only 27.3 percent said he was the one candidate for whom they would vote. (At the same time his favorable and unfavorable performance ratings were about even, whereas those of his government were decidedly negative.) To make things worse, the mysterious death back in 2002 of the PT mayor of Santo André (a large São Paulo industrial suburb) was disinterred—with strong indications of complicity by chief presidential aide Celso Carvalho, as well as evidence that finance minister Palocci had been the architect of the graft scheme in place at that time in cities controlled by the PT, and then transplanted into financing the national campaign.

Another bothersome problem for Lula arose over the control of his own party. In 2001, his moderates received 51 percent of convention votes against 36 percent for the radicals and 13 percent for a less extreme group. Now many PT militants were criticizing the government's economic policies and insisting that the president should follow party ideology, not heed the wishes of his allies.[15] Lula needed a decisive vote of confidence from the party faithful in order to allay growing doubts concerning the strength of his core support, but in September the government managed to put in former labor minister Ricardo Berzoino as PT president with great difficulty and only after important elements including a number of congressmen, ex-education minister Buarque, and other party founders had jumped ship. The vice president also broke with the government, leading a group of PL congress members into the Renovating Municipalist Party established by the Universal Church of the Kingdom of God and its extremely entrepreneurial founder, Bishop Edir Maceo. Furthermore, the finance minister was increasingly implicated in the scandals as well as being attacked by the new presidential chief of staff and others in the government who felt that massive spending on popular programs was the only road left for Lula's retaining power through another term. No wonder the beleaguered government looked to the end-of-the-year summer holidays for a chance to lick its wounds—despite the consolation of having narrowly elected Aldo Rebelo as teh Chamber president.

Mexico: Democracy Established, Progress Stalemated

The significance of recent developments in Mexico should not in any way be underestimated. They constitute the greatest step in that country's political development since the halcyon days of the Cárdenas administration in the late 1930s. With the opposition victory in the July 2000 presidential elections, federalism and separation of powers, long vitiated by the hegemonic position of the PRI, finally had an opportunity to emerge as vital aspects of a broadly participant, highly competitive political system. The greater responsiveness to "outsider" elements of society provided by this transformation greatly reduced the prospect of widespread, protracted political unrest.[16] Camp eloquently captures the watershed nature of this development:

> The victory of a party other than PRI essentially stood the Mexican political model on its head, destroying permanently the incestuous, monopolistic relationship between state and party. Such a relationship no longer exists. The future of the Mexican electoral process from 2000 forward relies heavily on the behavior and organizational strength of the three leading political parties, the PAN, PRI, and PRD, and on citizen perceptions of their candidates. It also relies on citizen views of the performance of the parties' candidates in office, particularly in executive posts.[17]

The once stodgy and Catholic Church–linked National Action Party (PAN) had been reinvigorated during the 1980s as ranchers and industrialists alienated from the governing PRI by the 1982 bank nationalizations entered its right-of-center opposition. PAN's respectable showing in 1994 coupled with the country's financial competitiveness crisis of that year and the next led to continued growth of the PAN, further stimulated by indications of Institutional Revolutionary Party (PRI) vulnerability as well as increasing signs of government intentions to conduct free elections in 2000.[18] Hence, the tall, quasi-charismatic Fox's dynamic campaign resulted in a plurality of 42.5 percent of the national vote, to 36.1 percent for the PRI's unexciting Francisco Labastida Ochoa and only 16.6 percent for the PRD's Cárdenas. The PAN along with its small ally, the Green Party, came away with 38.2 percent of the chamber vote and 208 seats, while the PRI retained 209 seats on 36.9 percent of the vote. The PRD ran a poor third, winning only 51 seats on 18.7 percent of the vote. The PRI lost control of the senate, with only 60 seats (including holdovers), but the PAN still trailed at 51 senators, three times the PRD's 17 seats.[19]

In contrast to the alliances crucial to Lula's election in Brazil, the outcome of Mexico's presidential succession was the product of long-term trends of levels of economic and social development, regionalism, and urbanization. For some time the opposition had been strong in the relatively high-income Federal District and Baja California; now they fared even better. (This situation paralleled developments in Brazil with respect to the São Paulo and Rio de Janeiro areas beginning in 1978.) As with the government party in Brazil in the final stages of the authoritarian regime, essentially the first half of the 1980s, the PRI's base of electoral support increasingly narrowed to the less-developed and less-urban areas of the country—which were also the educational laggards. As Camp points out, Fox was backed by 60 percent of university-educated voters and 53 percent of those who had made it through high school, whereas for Labastida these figures were 22 percent and 28 percent—insufficient to compensate for the fact that he racked up votes among those whose formal education was limited to six years or less—since in Mexico these numbered only two-fifths of the voters.[20] Mexico, perhaps even more than Brazil, has become an urban country, and Fox obtained the lion's share of urban votes, whereas the rural bastion of the PRI contained only a fifth of the electorate. (This voter behavior confirms an observation I made many years ago that in most cases little can be done to change the political behavior of rural populations unless they cease to be rural via the mechanism of internal migration to towns and cities.) Like Lula in Brazil, Fox was viewed as the candidate of change. He transcended the limits of his party's popularity through a personal organization known as the Friends of Fox.[21]

The first opposition president in the memory of any living Mexican came to office with only minority support in the congress and amid expectations that were unreasonably high, since it was such an unprecedented event. Fox soon found that, no matter how arduous campaigning might have been, governing was much more frustrating and stressful. The euphoria of breaking the PRI's seven decades of hegemonic rule dissipated quickly in the face of a public expecting rapid changes and immediate results. Fox's task of organizing his government was much easier than that Lula was to encounter in Brazil two years later, since he drew only on his party and respected independents, but in the end these would not result in a congressional base of support. He would have to negotiate with the PRI and PRD on a case-by-case basis as his predecessor had learned to do, particularly after 1997. In contrast to Lula, he did not have to abandon his historical ideological positions, nor did he have to worry about dissipating the suspicions and overcoming the reservations of foreign investors—as did both Lula and Argentina's Kirchner. On the negative side, he faced opposition from two highly organized parties, one with a broader national base than his PAN and positioned to occupy the center of the political spectrum, while the other was firmly entrenched on the left.

Fox organized his administration, criticized for lack of cabinet coherence, and operated the resulting government showing little regard for the PAN machinery still controlled by 1994 standard bearer Diego Fernández de Cevallos and party traditionalists. He had to deal early with the conflict between foreign minister Jorge Castañeda, an expert on presidential succession with roots well left of the party, and interior minister Santiago Creel—who strongly desired to be the 2006 nominee. Castañeda, whose presidential aspirations were increasingly apparent, was subsequently eased out of the government. Meanwhile, Lázaro Cárdenas Batel of the PRD was elected governor of Michoacán, following in the footsteps of his father and revered grandfather. To further complicate Fox's task, the ingrained inefficiency of huge petroleum entity Pemex was a burdensome carryover from the statist traditions of the long PRI era. In 2002, major oil producer Mexico ran up a trade deficit just under $8 billion while spending $10 billion on petrochemical imports. Even Venezuela's oil company produced 195 barrels a day of crude oil per worker, more than double Pemex's meager 87 barrels (with a private giant like Royal Dutch Shell reaching 300 barrels per employee). To aggravate matters, Mexico's foreign debt had by this time ballooned to $76 billion, as foreign direct investment fell from $16 billion in 2000 to $11 billion for 2002.

Many of the benefits of NAFTA predated Fox's assumption of power, and after September 11, 2001, his vaunted rancher-to-rancher relationship with US president George W. Bush was buried in the debris of the World Trade Center, with any special relationship between the two countries forgotten amid the hubbub of the war on terrorism. Fox had counted upon making progress on bothersome bilateral issues to distract Mexican attention from limited movement on domestic issues, and his ace in the hole was the prospect of special treatment for the millions of Mexican migrants concentrated in those parts of the United States that had been forcibly taken from Mexico in the mid-nineteenth century. Economically the four million Mexicans illegally in the United States were a vital part of the Mexican economy through at least $14 billion a year in remittances (a third higher by some estimates). Adding to Fox's woes, the midterm congressional balloting of July 2003 did not bring the relief for which he was hoping. Instead, the PRI rebounded to 223 chamber seats on 35 percent of the vote (plus 17 seats for their Green Party allies), whereas with the support of 30.5 percent of voters the PAN dropped to 155 seats—only 30 percent of the total. The PRD recovered from its poor 2000 showing by electing 96 to the lower house compared to the 53 it had held. With a low 42 percent turnout, the balloting was no real indication of what 2006 might bring. In the eyes of a seasoned observer, Mexico had "a constitutionally mandated majority presidential system operating like a parliamentary system."[22]

In an effort to divert attention from legislative stalemate, in mid-2004 a special prosecutor appointed by Fox sought to indict aging ex-president Luis Echeverría and several members of his government for the killings of student protesters back in 1971. This was another step in a flawed strategy of launching investigations "aggressive enough to undermine the chance of legislative cooperation, but not decisive enough to satisfy the appetite for vengeance."[23] At the end of August, on the eve of his state of the nation address, and facing protest marches by dissatisfied workers and farmers, Fox threatened to establish a truth commission to investigate abuses committed by the PRI during its long dominance if the supreme court refused to hear the case against Echeverría. But despite such public muscle flexing, he was reaching the point where he would have to struggle against continued erosion of his authority as he entered the stage of his term analogous to that of Cardoso in Brazil following the 2000 municipal elections—a semilame duck. Like Belaúnde Terry in Peru in the early 1980s as well as Cardoso in 2002, this freewheeling personalist appeared to have no viable successor at hand—and precious little time to come up with one. (Negative public reaction to a trial balloon concerning his politically ambitious wife, Marta Sahagun, had forced her to issue a disclaimer of interest or intent.) Fox remained personally popular, but this did not extend to his party or government.

Hence, following the few, if strategic, gubernatorial elections of 2004, Mexico's electoral outlook was as uncertain as that of Brazil, with the mid-2006 election at least as likely to bring the PRI back to power as to continue the PAN's brief hold on the presidency, and the PRD's fortunes appearing to be on the rise in urban centers. The PRI, winner of four of six recent governorship elections (including Oaxaca, Veracruz, and Baja California del Norte) underwent reorganization at the hands of party president Roberto Madrazo Pintado (b. 1952), who became the party's nominee in November 2005. He paid lip service to modernization but resorted to all the old win-at-any-cost tactics of the pre-Zedillo PRI.[24] The PRD's early front-runner was Mexico City's progressive mayor Andrés Manuel López Obredor (b. 1954), a very popular figure whom the government was trying to ensnare in a web of corruption charges. Conservative ex-energy minister Felipe Calderón Hinojosa (b. 1962) exploited serious miscues by Creel to wrest the PAN nomination from the erstwhile favorite. Although the next chief executive will be one of these three, he will be a minority president faced like Fox with limited prospects of enacting a significant portion of his program.

Argentina: Climbing Back from Crisis

The new century started disastrously for Argentina. Indeed, Fernando de la Rúa soon had ample reason to rue his apparent good fortune in having won the 1999 presidential election, as the April 2000 congressional revision of the employment law—removing safeguards and benefits the workers had enjoyed since Perón's time—led to strikes and disturbances. This social unrest was aggravated in October when the vice president drawn from the ranks of FREPASO (Fatherland Solidarity Front) resigned in protest over the president's refusal to break with unsavory Radical politicians—accused of having bribed senators to make the labor law more flexible. The result was a situation the president publicly recognized as "a veritable catastrophe."

The Argentine economic crisis, which began as a reasonably mild recession in 1998, had deepened by 2002 into the worst crisis in the country's history (comparable only to that of 1930, which combined the full impact of the world depression with the overthrow of the Yrigoyen government), one that was tearing the social fabric apart and producing political chaos. The nation's per capita GDP, highest of major countries in the region at roughly $11,000 in terms of purchasing price parity, declined precipitously, as GDP dropped to near its 1993 level and unemployment soared well above 20 percent. Admitting defeat in dealing with the situation, the outwardly highly qualified government defaulted on the country's massive foreign debt of about $155 billion before it devastated savings and investment by making a hollow mockery out of currency convertibility as local money lost three-quarters of its value relative to the dollar. As one informed observer portrayed the political impact of what was generally considered "collapse" of the Argentine economy:

> The toll on politics has been no less dramatic: between October 2000 and August 2002, there were five cabinet crises, two presidential resignations, one Senate crisis, and five ministers of the economy. The streets in downtown Buenos Aires are now full of abandoned retail stores and angry protesters. Que se vayan todos! (Kick everyone out!) reads the omni-present graffiti.[25]

Argentines wondered how it could be that a mere decade since their country had supposedly saved itself from hyperinflation and despair by pegging its currency to the dollar, and despite tens and tens of billions of dollars in loans from the IMF—accompanied by fulsome praise of the country's economic management from the international financial community—they had wound up in an unimaginable disaster. The public was understandably perplexed, since for the first time in many of their lifetimes Argentina had seemingly gotten its politics and economy in order during the decade-long administration of Carlos Saúl Menem (1989–1999). Some of the most extensive market reforms in the world had been initiated, civilian control over the military had been consolidated, and stronger instruments of governmental accountability instituted. The historically bitterly hostile major parties had even negotiated an unprecedented pact to reform the constitution in 1994, and the stable democracy previewed in the halcyon days of 1916–1930 appeared to have arrived. Indeed, in early 2000 a Harvard political scientist heralded "The Normalization of Argentine Politics."[26]

The era of twenty-four presidents in twenty-eight years (1930–1958) that had followed the collapse of the early twentieth century democratic experience were almost universally held to be part of the country's past—alongside the repressive military rule preceding 1983's reestablishment of democracy. Moreover, important macroeconomic indicators were positive in 2001, including a trade surplus of $7.5 billion (compared to a deficit of $3.1 billion in 1998) that cut the current accounts deficit from $11.9 billion to under $4.6 billion. What most Argentine's had overlooked was that by the end of 2000 a foreign debt nearing $150 billion equaled 51.4 percent of GDP, and the $25.5 billion required for debt service used up 71.3 percent of export earnings. As Argentina started down the slippery slope to insolvency, the IMF increased its support, supplying a loan of $13.7 billion at the end of 2000 and arranging $26 billion in financing from other sources—asking in return for pension reform and curbs on fiscal transfers to the provincial governments—paralleling steps recently taken in Brazil. The IMF's largesse was tied to the Argentine government's maintaining a stringent monetary policy and further tightening fiscal policies.

Bringing Carvallo back as economics minister, the de la Rúa administration pursued deficit reduction, considered by the IMF crucial for macroeconomic stability. Cuts of $1.6 billion (about 3 percent of the federal budget) were announced in early July, on the eve of a major government bond offering, and with the presidency undergoing angioplasty. Instead of reassuring investors, shaken by his proposal to replace the dollar as currency peg by a mixed basket of stable currencies, this further austerity move was interpreted as a sign that the crisis was deepening. Hence, bonds could be sold only at 14 percent interest, 50 percent higher than the preceding month. After the IMF came up with an additional $8 billion in August, the government announced near year's end additional drastic budget cuts totaling $9.2 billion, nearly 18 percent of approved expenditures.[27]

Not surprisingly the electorate was upset, cutting the pro-government vote nearly in half from late 1999 as congressional elections in mid-October (for 130 of 251 chamber seats and 72 in the Senate) gave the Peronists 65 lower-house seats and 40 in the upper Senate to 35 and 25 for the governing UCR and its allies—resulting in a strong plurality in the chamber and a majority in the upper house, with FREPASO and a small party each having 17 seats—mostly carryovers. Spoiled and blank ballots reached historic highs, especially in Buenos Aires, which contained two-fifths of the country's electorate. The election did not change the fact that to maintain its highly overvalued currency, Argentina required large dollar reserves, since in theory anyone at any time was entitled to exchange each peso for a dollar. Only the huge IMF loans made a continuation of this policy possible—at the cost of increasing foreign debt to an unpayable level—at least in political terms, if technically possible in strictly economic ones. Public and private foreign debt reached $146 billion in 2001, with reserves halved (from $35 billion to only $18 billion). The extremely high ratio of debt to export earnings came at a time GDP shrank by an additional 11 percent. At the end of the year Argentina defaulted on debt service, seeking to force creditors to settle for as little as 25 cents on the dollar—something the creditors stubbornly resisted (later insisting that the economically recovering country, having escaped disaster, could afford a far less deep discount on renegotiated debt). Massive bank runs resulted in a breakdown of convertibility only partially contained by Cavallo's imposition of strict limits on withdrawals and currency movements, leading the IMF to withhold a scheduled $1.26-billion disbursement.

With the middle class badly hurt and the informal (off-the-books) economy starved almost out of existence, rampant unrest featuring widespread looting and twenty-seven deaths forced de la Rúa to resign on December 20, an action leading to the temporary elevation to the presidency of the Senate's Adolfo Rodríguez Saá, a modestly charismatic Peronist, as word that Argentina's rich had spirited $20 billion out of the country led to renewed rioting. Following Rodríguez Saá's resignation after only ten days in office, the presidency passed to chamber presiding officer Eduardo Camano. As soon as the New Year's holiday was over, the nation found itself in the paradoxical situation of the man who had lost the election only two years earlier being invited to assume the presidency. Duhalde soon found that he had made a bad deal in return for not much more than a footnote in history, as he was unable to mobilize congressional or public support for his emergency measures. Yet this grave political crisis, like Collor's removal from office in Brazil a decade earlier, was handled constitutionally, with the congress playing the central role and the military remaining a highly interested, but sideline, observer. Three days later currency parity was ended—and the value of the peso dropped precipitously by over 70 percent. Unemployment soon exceeded 25 percent, and half of all Argentines found themselves below the poverty line—compared to 22 percent in 1994.

The supreme court threw a monkey wrench into the executive's plans by declaring the freezing of bank accounts unconstitutional and trying to overturn the government's enactment of a six-month ban on legal challenges to limits on bank withdrawals. In late April Cavallo resigned in the face of IMF intransigence and lack of support for plans to exchange frozen accounts for government bonds. Roberto Lavagne became Argentina's sixth economic minister in a year (a dramatic contrast with Pedro Malan's eight-year stint in Brazil). Buffeted by political ill winds from all directions, Duhalde called presidential elections for late March 2003—following the precedent of Alfonsín in 1988 by cutting six months off his already-truncated term. In November, fed up with IMF insistence on policy changes before providing further help, the government failed to make a payment due to that international body, holding that it had failed to support Argentina's efforts to renegotiate $55 billion owed to private foreign investors. At the same time, the year's inflation was held to 40 percent, confounding critics and observers who had predicted runaway hyperinflation. Indeed, the country's economic recovery was already under way.[28]

Presidential succession split Duhalde's Peronists three ways. Ex-president Menem led the April 27, 2003, balloting with 24.3 percent, followed closely by Néstor Carlos Kirchner (b. 1950), who had just finished twelve years as governor of a Patagonian province. Former economics minister Roberto López Murphy finished in the money with 16.4 percent to 14.1 percent for both anticorruption crusader Eliza Carrío and the third Peronist, Rodríguez Saá—who had briefly held down the presidency in December 2001. With public opinion polls showing 60 percent support for Kirchner—Peronism's new face—Menem avoided an embarrassing defeat by conceding the runoff, allowing Kirchner to take office in late May 2003. On the positive side, turnout was nearly 80 percent, and blank and spoiled ballots dropped to 2.5 percent—a clear indication that individuals alienated from the political process in 2001 had opted to play a constructive role in avoiding further political decay.

After six consecutive years of decline, the battered Argentine economy grew by 8.7 percent in 2003. This growth further increased the popularity of the new president as he exploited the fact that Peronism was a "loose and heterogeneous confederation of provincial party bosses" to reestablish presidential leadership to where it had been in Menem's salad days.[29] With a term running well into 2007, Kirchner was aware that he could become the dean of Latin American presidents should Lula fail to gain reelection. Meanwhile, he burnished a nationalist reputation and began to reverse Menem's sweeping privatizations. But Argentina's recovery faced a setback in March 2004 in the form of a severe energy shortage. Although drought was a contributing factor, the main culprit was lack of investment in production and distribution following the utility privatizations of the Menem era—despite contractual obligations by the purchasers to do so. Owners of the large utility companies blamed their inaction on a court-imposed freeze on rates and the sharp devaluation of the peso, combining with inflation to yield low rates and leading to revenues falling behind costs.

Bolstered by over 8 percent economic growth again in 2004, Kirchner's government took a firm stand on sharply reducing foreign debt through a program of exchanging existing bonds for new ones with a deep reduction in face value. This move paid off with a March 2005 agreement on $103 billion in bonds held by private investors at a 70 percent discount. Foreign exchange reserves were up to nearly $20 billion as a current-accounts surplus was achieved. By playing hardball with creditors and refusing to let debt renegotiation take priority over social needs, Kirchner sought to stem Brazil's bid to be recognized as the region's spokesman. Indeed, his increasingly protectionist trade policies took the blush off hitherto close relations with Brazil.[30] Kirchner's lack of a congressional majority, since rival Peronists had done well in 2003, was remedied by the partial congressional elections of late October. His wife, fifty-three-year-old Cristina Fernández de Kirchner, gave up her Senate seat from her small hometown province to run in the crucial Buenos Aires constituency, decisively winning by 46 percent to 20 percent. In the process she defeated the wife of ex-president Duhalde and helped bring in 69 congress members on her well-tailored coattails compared to only 11 for Duhalde's bloc (as the UCR won 19 seats), thus giving the president a very strong plurality in the chamber to go along with his majority in the upper house—where his candidates won 17 of the 24 seats being contested (to only 4 for Duhalde's Peronist faction and 3 for the Radicals). Hence, Kirchner's prospects for reelection in early 2007 seemed as strong as Cardoso's had been in Brazil at the analogous stage of fifteen months to post time back in mid-1997.

Colombia: Getting Serious with Insurgency

The troubled country of Colombia entered the new century mired in the Andrés Pastrana administration's futile efforts at negotiating peace with the entrenched insurgents, a policy belatedly abandoned in February 2002. A month later the Liberal Party won 54 of the 161 seats in the chamber and 29 of 102 in the senate to the Conservative Party's 21 and 13 seats. But the largest representation was the host of minor parties backing Alvaro Uribe Vélez (b. 1952) for the presidency. In late May this dissident Liberal running as an independent, received 53 percent of the vote to 31.7 percent for Horacio Serpa, as many former Conservatives flocked to his side.[31] A one-time mayor of Bogotá and unsuccessful presidential aspirant, Uribe was inaugurated in August. Despite protracted peace talks, no results were reached with respect to the major guerrilla groups, and at the beginning of 2004 the government launched a major offensive in the vast region stretching from just south of the capital to the Ecuadorean border. This shift in policy was spurred by sharply falling oil production—which customarily produced a third of government revenues—and the consequent need to attract new investment by demonstrating that the government was in control. The 2001 decision to reduce the mandatory share of state enterprise *Ecopetrol* in joint ventures from 50 to 30 percent and the subsequent institution of a sliding scale of royalties proved inadequate, in the face of the risks to lives and property posed by the rebels, to spur a significant upturn in investment by foreign petroleum companies.

By early 2004, Plan Colombia, a bilateral program with the United States initiated in 1999 and aimed against drug trafficking and insurgency, was beginning to show limited results in terms of strengthening the Colombian army.[32] Despite sharp increases in US assistance, which had risen from $67 million in 1996 to $1 billion by 2001, accompanied by and increase in military advisers and civilian security consultants, only very modest progress was made in the direction of disarming the fifteen-thousand-man antirebel United Self-Defense Forces of Colombia, author of mass killings and protector of drug trafficking. Indeed, in many ways these paramilitary groups, which enjoy powerful military and political

ÁLVARO URIBE

backing, even within the congress, constitute a greater obstacle to political normality than do the entrenched rebel groups they use as their justification for existence. Like the rebels, they enjoy a sizable safe haven ceded to them by the
government on the flawed reasoning that safety from attacks and interference
would increase their willingness to disarm.[33] On the political front, local and de-
partmental elections in early October brought in Luis Garzón, a 2002 presidential
contender and head of the new leftist Independent Democratic Pole Party, as
mayor of Bogotá. At the end of November 2004, as GDP growth reached 4 percent, the constitution was amended to allow Uribe to run for a second term in
2006, and a year later the supreme court up held the amendment's legality, with a
very positive public reception.

Peru: After Fujimori, Political Disenchantment

Running for a coalition called Peru Posible ("Possible Peru"), Indian-ancestry
Alejandro Toledo Manrique (b. 1946) encountered blatant electoral fraud in the
April 2000 presidential balloting, which credited incumbent third-term-seeker
Alberto Fujimori with 49.8 percent of the votes to his 40.3 percent. Convinced
that the end-of-May runoff was rigged, Toledo dropped out at the last minute,
permitting Fujimori to claim 57 percent of the vote and to be reinaugurated in
late July. Three weeks later the lid blew off a scandal involving intelligence chief
and presidential crony Vladimiro Montesinos's illegal sale of weapons to Colom-

bia's FARC guerrillas. The surfacing of a videotape showing Montesinos making a large cash payoff to a congressman quickly followed this grave misdeed, a revelation that in turn led to a nearly unanimous congressional vote to disband the National Intelligence Service. (In mid-2001, Montesinos was arrested in Venezuela, and a year later he was convicted of abuse of authority and sentenced to nine years in prison, with five more added on another charge in March 2003 and more than fifty additional indictments pending.) When proof of a secret $48-million account emerged in October, and with the opposition taking control of the congress, the jig was finally up. Fujimori was voted out of power in mid-November as having a "moral incapacity" to fill the office and rushed unceremoniously into exile in Japan.

As both vice presidents resigned, a caretaker government under congressional head Valentin Paniagua held elections in April 2001, in which Toledo, holder of a Stanford University doctorate in economics despite his beginnings as a poor shoeshine boy, defeated ex-president Alan García by 36.5 percent to 25.8 percent, with Lourdes Flores of the National Unity Party (PUN) coming in a strong third. In the early June runoff, García picked up the lion's share of Flores's votes, receiving 47.8 percent of the vote to Toledo's 52.2 percent, falling just short of a comeback victory. (Once again, this was a warning not to count a supposedly discredited Latin American ex-president out, particularly if—like García—he had the chutzpah to say that he had made every mistake possible in his first term, so that now the nation deserved the benefit of the lessons he had learned from this dismal performance.) Toledo's Possible Peru party came away with 41 congressional seats. The Popular Revolutionary Alliance of the Americas (APRA) won 27, and PUN won 15. The parties of the Fujimori regime collapsed from 52 to a lonely 4 congressmen.

Off to a bumbling start, Toledo sought to salvage his political reputation and regain some degree of popular support by pursuing a far-reaching anticorruption investigation that by 2004 had led to charges against over fourteen hundred politicians and government officials. Yet this effort, already tarnished by Toledo's decision to ignore the serious study of the problem conducted by his interim predecessor, backfired when at the beginning of the year a former close adviser of Toledo's was accused of conspiring with an army general to bribe judges.[34] As scandals mounted, the president replaced the crusading prosecutor in charge of the investigations, paying a significant price for this desperate move in the form of further erosion of his already minimal public support. In mid-August 2005, Toledo tried to rally his stumbling government by elevating internationally respected finance minister Pedro Pablo Kuczynski to the post of prime minister, a move vainly designed to put the spotlight on him as a possible presidential contender (Toledo was harboring hopes of duplicating Cardoso's 1994 success in Brazil). But Toledo's approval ratings fell into single digits. In this context, even though he was legally ineligible to run for office and faced multiple indictments, in November Fujimori dramatically flew from his safe haven in Japan to Chile, where protracted extradition proceedings could keep his name on Peruvian front pages. In the chaotic situation of Peruvian politics, where he still was the favorite of a significant minority, Fujimori hoped public opinion would pressure the courts to allow his candidacy.

Venezuela: Chávez, *Caudillo,* or Would-Be Castro?

Under the brand-new constitution, which had given him an extended term, President Hugo Chávez handpicked a 21-member "mini-congress" at the beginning of February 2000, subsequently postponing elections for an additional six-year term and a single-chamber national legislature from late May to the end of July.[35] At that time a low turnout yielded a 57 percent endorsement of Chávez, an avowed admirer of Bolívar, Castro, Fujimori, and Panama's late Omar Torrijos. His Fifth Republic Movement (MVR) won 80 of 165 congressional seats on 44.4 percent of the vote, as its ally, the Movement Toward Socialism (MAS) came away with 21 posts. Once nearly hegemonic, Democratic Action (AD) led the opposition with 30 seats on 26.1 percent of the vote, with its traditional rival Christian Socialist Party COPEI, settling for a mere 8 congress members and an anemic 5.1 percent electoral support. Only 6.6 million of 11.7 million registered voters bothered to vote—as a large proportion of Chávez's foes did not support the opposition candidate.[36] Local elections in December evoked a meager turnout of just 23 percent of eligible voters. On the economic front a new hydrocarbons law enacted in 2001 raised royalties from 16.7 percent to 30 percent and limited foreign participation in new oil projects to 49 percent. These provisions gave Chávez both increased government revenues and nationalist support in a rapidly polarizing political environment.

A protracted oil workers' strike at the end of 2001 and the beginning of 2002 led to widespread violence once the Venezuelan Labor Confederation (CTV) and the Federation of Chambers and Associations of Commerce and Production (FEDECAMARAS) threw their support behind the strike. After seventeen individuals were killed near the presidential palace on April 11, dissident army units arrested Chávez and installed a junta under FEDECAMARAS president Pedro Carmona. A pro-Chávez uprising by the presidential guard restored him to power within two days, as much because of as despite clear signs of US backing for the provisional regime. A general strike from November 2002 to February 2003 ended only after international mediation resulting in a shaky agreement for a recall election the next year. As Chávez loyalists replaced striking workers, PDVSA's (the cumbersome acronym for what had been known as Petroven) revenues declined by over 12 percent in the third quarter of 2003 as oil exports fell by 27 percent. When the recall was finally held on August 15, Chávez emerged relegitimized as his supporters prevailed by a 59 percent to 41 percent margin with a 70 percent turnout of an electorate reaching 14 million.

Buoyed by soaring petroleum prices, which, rising 47 percent in 2004, spurred dramatic GDP growth of 17 percent, more than making up for 2002's 9 percent drop, Chávez prepared for a bid to remain in power beyond the late 2006 elections. Having packed the supreme court with an additional twelve justices and won every plebiscite held, Chávez was riding high.[37] October 2003 regional elections that left the government with control of all but two states had strengthened his hand, particularly as nine new governors were ex-military allies, and his popularity ratings in 2004–2005 consistently ran above 70 percent. Congressional balloting in December 2005 reflected Chávez's continued support, as all significant opposition parties boycotted the elections. Meanwhile, this populist *caudillo* raised eyebrows abroad by his anti–US rhetoric and gestures and the purchase in the first part of 2005 of $7 billion in armaments, including 100,000 Russian AK-47 rifles. Moreover, he has used subsidized oil exports to create dependency on Venezuela in some of the small Caribbean islands as well as to support leftist movements in South American countries.

Chile: Consolidating Democracy's Poster Boy

In mid-December 1999, there had been a near tie in Chile's third consecutive free and competitive presidential election, settled in favor of social democrat Ricardo Lagos Escobar (b. 1938) of the Party for Democracy (PPD) over his conservative opponent by a mere 2.6 percent of the runoff vote—after a minuscule 0.5 percent margin on election day attributed by many observers to Joaquín Lavin's effective use of television. A year later municipal elections demonstrated the governing alliance Concertacíon's continued dominance as it elected 169 mayors and 1,039 municipal council members, and the Christian Democratic Party (PDC) remained its senior partner with 85 mayors and 424 local legislators. The conservative opposition's Alliance for Chile won 165 city halls, chiefly in smaller communities, accompanied by only 684 local legislators, led by National Renewal (RN) with control of 72 city halls and 292 municipal lawmakers. The left was all but shut out, electing a single mayor and only 23 council members.[38] In November 2001, the governing alliance received 62 of 120 chamber seats on the strength of 48 percent of the vote. Again the PDC was the strongest leg of the Concertacíon, with 23 seats to 20 for the PPD and 10 for the Socialist Party (PS). The opposition Alliance for Chile earned 57 seats on 44 percent of the vote, with the Independent Democratic Union (UDI) getting the lion's share of 31, to 18 for the RN. With one-half of the senate's 38 elected seats at stake, that body came away almost evenly divided as the *Concertacíon* edged the Alliance 20 to 16.[39]

By early 2005, maneuvering for the presidential balloting at year's end was under way. With the economy continuing its strong performance and the county enjoying social peace, especially compared to its Andean neighbors, the center-left coalition remained in a strong position to continue in office. Michelle Bachelet (b. 1951), former defense minister and the preferred candidate of the incumbent chief executive, obtained the Concertacíon nomination and finished first in the December 11 balloting, but she was forced into a mid-January 2006 runoff with one of the country's richest men running for the RN (and edging out the UDI's Lavin).

Ecuador: Trouble Incorporating the Indian Masses

Ecuador began the new century coping with the instability resulting from the political awakening of the indigenous population excluded from the progress of the 1980s and most of the 1990s. The period opened with president Jamil Mahuad in desperate straits. His announcement in January 2000 of plans to exchange the sucre for the US dollar at a rate of 25,000 to 1 and make the dollar the country's currency proved to be his swan song. On January 21 he was overthrown following rioting by Indians brought into the capital and egged on by politically ambitious midgrade army officers led by Colonel Lúcio Edwin Gutiérrez Borbua (b. 1957). The congress fled to Guayaquil, where it quickly named sixty-two-year-old vice president Gustavo Naboa to the presidency. International pressure caused the military to go along with this constitutional outcome to make this former head of Guayaquil's Catholic University, who was to govern until January 2003 elections, its sixth president in four years. As oil prices continued to recover strongly from the 1998 low of eleven dollars a barrel, in April 2000 the new government entered into a $2-billion agreement with the IMF, and Naboa followed market-oriented economic policies.

In late November 2002, dark-skinned and Indian-featured Gutiérrez, the architect of Mahuad's overthrow, who promised a war against corruption and to listen to the poor, including the Indians, defeated banana tycoon Álvaro Naboa (b. 1950) by 54 percent of the votes to 46 percent in a runoff election following the fragmented results of the previous month's multicandidate electoral sweepstakes, as well as the October 2002 congressional balloting. As was the case in Venezuela with the rise of Chávez, lower-class voters were seeking a voice, and disaffected middle sectors were searching for a new face. With only a fifth of the seats, Gutiérrez's January 21 Patriotic Movement lacked the congressional support mustered by three-time loser Naboa, often viewed as an opportunistic populist demagogue seeking to distract attention from his position as the country's wealthiest individual. Once again, as in Venezuela and Bolivia, traditional parties, corruption, and globalization were the targets of effective negative campaigning by a would-be Andean facsimile of Perón—this time overcoming his opponent's lavish campaign spending on the electronic media.

Governing did not become any easier when in August 2003 the president dropped from the cabinet the three ministers of the indigenous Pachakutik Plurinational Unity Movement (MUPP), which had given him 8 of the 121 seats in the congress. In a desperate attempt to stave off impeachment by a hostile congress, the president struck a deal with discredited ex-president Abdalá Bucarám to push through amnesty for his corruption charges in return for the Roldosist Party's support for his replacing the members of the supreme court. Despite 6.6 percent GDP growth for 2004, this blatant manipulation of government processes backfired on Gutiérrez in late April 2005 when a rising wave of demonstrations involving chiefly increasingly militant Indians forced him out of office. His replacement until the upcoming elections was sixty-six-year-old vice president Alfredo Palacios.

Bolivia: Pressure for a Second Revolution

The new century witnessed continuation of the Bolivian people's quest for new leadership that would do for the base of the socioeconomic pyramid what the 1952 Revolution had done for the middle sectors and the highland Indian communities. Evo Morales, a representative of the lowlands Indians, heavily dependent on growing coca leaves and hence staunchly opposed to any government cooperating with the United States in coca eradication projects, gained stature when expelled from the congress at the beginning of 2001 under US pressure. In August cancer caught up with seventy-five-year-old President Hugo Banzer, who resigned (dying the next May) and was succeeded by his vice president, José F. Quiroga Ramírez (b. 1961). An industrial engineer from Texas A&M, Quiroga had served as finance minister under Paz Zamora in 1992.

Elected for a second time in June 2002, with only 22.5 percent of the vote, Gonzalo Sánchez de Lozado of the National Revolutionary Movement (MNR) edged out two candidates with nearly 21 percent each (including coca producers' champion Evo Morales) as well as ex-president Jaime Paz Zamora, who fell to 16.3 percent of voter preferences. The congress, in which the MNR had 36 deputies and 11 senators to the Movement Toward Socialism (MAS)'s 27 and 8, selected Sánchez de Lozado by a vote of 84 to 43 over Morales.[40] The result left much unrest and dissatisfaction, especially in the Cochabamba and Santa Cruz areas. For although the economy had grown at an annual average of 3.5 percent from 1990 through 2001, this number had dropped to 2.4 percent in 2000 and to only 1.2 percent in 2001—negative in per capita terms. Although management of the economy was the strong point on the president's résumé, he was unable to pull Bolivia out of the recession he had inherited.

Indigenous groups violently protested a foreign-backed project to build a $5-billion pipeline to facilitate exports of natural gas (whose eventual consumers would be the United States and Mexico). Spreading unrest that entailed eighty deaths forced Sánchez de Lozada, by now seventy-three years old, to resign in mid-October 2003 and flee the country. He was replaced by fifty-year-old independent corruption fighter Carlos Mesa Gisbert, a historian by profession. In mid-April 2004, mass demonstrations narrowly failed to topple Mesa's government after it signed a natural gas export agreement with Argentina. In the October 2004 municipal elections, voters, especially those outside major urban centers, abandoned traditional parties in favor of a bevy of new movements. As tensions continued to rise, Mesa resigned in early June 2005, being replaced by Eduardo Rodríguez, head of the supreme court—as the presiding officers of the congress stepped aside. Unable to stabilize the deteriorating situation, in November the acting president called for new elections for December 18, in which the forty-six-year-old Morales won decisively over former short-term chief executive Jorge Quiroga, averting the need for the newly elected congress to become involved.

Uruguay: Rise of the Left

The small democracy of Uruguay began the new century with a close election in which the left made a strong bid to come to power, obtaining 38.5 percent of the vote for its longtime standard bearer, Tabaré Vásquez, to 31.3 percent for the Colorados' Jorge Batlle, as former president Alberto Lacalle of the National Party (Blancos) trailed with 21.3 percent. In the resulting runoff Batlle prevailed by 51.6 percent to 44.1 percent. Taking office at the beginning of March 2000, Batlle found his former opponent to have the largest representation in each house of the congress, 40 of 99 seats in the chamber and 12 of 30 in the senate, to his party's 32 and 10, necessitating a continuation of cooperation between the Colorados and their historic rivals, the Blancos, who retained 23 seats in the lower house and 7 in the upper Senate, to prevail over Vásquez's "Progressive Encounter in the Broad Front." The main task facing Batlle was economic recovery from the 1999–2000 recession, which had ended three years of 5 percent annual GDP growth, a formidable task in the face of dominant neighbor Argentina's crisis (although economic expansion in 2004 reached 10 percent).

On October 31, 2004, Uruguayans went to the polls once again, with sixty-four-year-old hardy perennial Tabaré Vásquez and the ponderously named Progressive Encounter–Broad Front–New Majority finally coming to power on the strength of 52 percent of voter preferences and 53 of 99 seats in the lower house along with 17 of 30 in the senate.[41] The Blanco candidate trailed with 35 percent, but the governing Colorados absorbed a crushing defeat, retaining support of only 11 percent of the electorate. A heterogeneous alliance of small parties ranging from communists to Christian Democrats, the Broad Front's core is composed of one-time Tupamaro guerrillas. Given Uruguay's weak and delicate position between Brazil (nearly fifty times more populous) and Argentina (with twelve times Uruguay's population), policy limits for the Vásquez government, upon taking office in March 2005, were largely set by those of Lula and Kirchner.

Paraguay: Still Well Behind, but Moving

By the middle of 2002, President Luis A. González Macchi was fending off impeachment, trying to reach the scheduled April 2003 elections. At that time the Colorados kept their fifty-six-year streak going, electing Oscar Nicanor Duarte Freitas (b. 1956) on 37.1 percent of the vote to 24 percent for former vice president Julio César Franco and 21.3 percent for businessman Pedro Nicolás Fadul. A radical populist stand-in for exiled conspirator General Lino Oviedo was held to 13.5 percent of voter preferences. The long-dominant Colorados won 37 of 80 seats in the lower house, but only 16 of 45 in the Senate. The new chief executive in this country with a very limited tradition of competitive politics (beginning only after the 1954–1989 Stroessner dictatorship) was an advocate of free-market economics who denounced corruption during the campaign but was unlikely to do much about it—since the Colorados had long been deeply enmeshed in it and contraband, money laundering, and narcotics trafficking are still mainstays of the country's economic life.

In the early months of 2005, Duarte Freitas pushed through legislation barring foreign ownership of land within 50 kilometers of the border. This law threatened some 200,000 Brazilians, who have long provided a major proportion of Paraguay's commercial agricultural production. (The political crisis in Brazil that erupted shortly thereafter may have been a boon to the Paraguayan government.)

Central America: Consolidating Democratic Gains

In the six countries of Central America, the political progress achieved during the 1980s and 1990s continued to weather the challenges that arose along the road to sustained political development. Costa Rica misfired a bit over corruption; Guatemala and Honduras continued their strings of competitive elections into a third decade; El Salvador and Nicaragua strove to further heal the wounds of their recent civil wars; and Panama moved on to a younger political generation.

Guatemala: Staying on the Road to Democracy

Only two-fifths of the 4.5 million registered voters turned out at Christmastime 1999 to give Alfonso Portillo (b. 1951) a crushing runoff victory. At the end of 2003, conservative businessman Oscar Berger (b. 1946), former Guatemala City mayor and the runner-up the last time around, defeated Álvaro Colom Cabelleros, who had finished in third place, by a margin of 54 percent to 46 percent.[42] The voters had shifted back from right toward center-right with almost half the electorate preferring a moderately progressive candidate—lending him four times the electoral support they had in 1999. Moreover, although human rights issues remained from the long era of civil strife, their frequency and intensity were diminished.[43] The left, which held eight seats in the congress on the strength of fewer than 8 percent of the vote, sought to regroup behind the leadership of Nineth Montenegro and the New National Alliance (ANN) in time to contest the 2007 elections. Meanwhile, controversy centered on the environmental impact of large-scale gold mining by a Canadian company.

El Salvador: Ongoing Political Reconciliation

Progress toward a truly competitive political system continued in March 2000 as the left opposition continued the gains it had made since the end of El Salvador's devastating civil war. The Faribundo Martí Front for National Liberation (FMLN) reelected the mayor of San Salvador and pulled ahead of the right-wing Nationalist Republican Alliance (ARENA) with 31 seats to 29 in the 84-member national legislature, as the National Conciliation Party (PCN) came away with 14—although only a third of the eligible voters took part in the balloting. Moreover, the FMLN went up to control of 77 municipalities as the governing party dropped from 161 to 127. In March 2003, with turnout remaining low, the FMLN maintained their legislative edge at 31 to 27 (with 16 for the PCN); privatization of health services was a major campaign issue.

As 2.1 million citizens cast their ballots, the March 2004 presidential elections gave a new-generation ARENA leader, thirty-nine-year-old Antonio "Tony" Soca, a decisive victory with 58 percent of the vote (five more percentage points than incumbent Francisco Flores had garnered in 1999) over an old-guard left-wing former guerrilla, Schaflek Handel (b. 1930), who polled 36 percent.[44] Soca's election meant that by the end of his term ARENA would have been in power for two full decades. Despite modest economic gains, poverty had declined sharply from the over 60 percent level prevailing in the early 1990s. This improvement was largely a result of remittances by the roughly two million Salvadorans living abroad, particularly those in the United States. Indeed, the US dollar was adopted in 2001 as the country's monetary standard. Hence, possible changes in US immigration policy are a subject of great concern to hundreds of thousands dependent upon remittances in a country that had a very limited domestic economy. With congressional and municipal elections looming in March 2006, critics of the aging Handel's leadership of the left, including the popular mayor of the capital city, formed the Revolutionary Democratic Front (FDR).

Honduras: Alternation Established

In November 2001, Ricardo Maduro (b. 1946) of the National Party was elected president and came away with 61 of the 128 legislative seats as the Liberal Party lost its previous majority, falling to 55 seats. Taking office at the beginning of 2002, this former businessman and banker, who had turned to politics only after his son had been killed by kidnappers, followed a law-and-order agenda featuring controversial antigang legislation and harsh prison conditions. Elections on November 27, 2005, pitted Porfirio "Pépe" Lobo Sosa, a traditionalist ally of the president, against the Liberal's Manuel Mel Zelaya Rosales, supported by the 1998–2002 chief executive. With economic growth a satisfactory 5 percent in 2004 and 4 percent for 2005, the major issue was crime, particularly the gangs fed by youths expelled from the United States as undesirable criminals. Voters preferred Zelaya's promise to attack social problems to his rival's "crush-crime" approach.

Nicaragua: Overcoming Ingrained Corruption

In November 2001, Daniel Ortega and the FSLN failed again to get back into power as aging Enrique Bolaños Geyer (b. 1928) of the Constitutional Liberal Party (PLC) won the presidency by a 56.3 percent to 42.3 percent margin and came away with a 47 to 43 edge in the national legislature. Vice president in the outgoing administration, Bolaños had taken Sandinista gains in the November 2000 local elections as a wakeup call. Shaking off tutelage by outgoing President Arnaldo Alemán, Bolaños took on the corruption issue, and Alemán, more discredited than Salinas had been in Mexico a few years earlier, was accused of illegal dealings involving over $100 million and was arrested at the end of 2002. With elections scheduled for late 2006, but likely to be moved forward, Ortega (still only fifty-nine) strove energetically to take advantage of widespread disenchantment with corruption and poor economic performance. Sandinista ranks were, however, divided as ex-Managua mayor Herty Lewites, the country's most popular public figure, denounced Ortega's past of opportunistic ties with Alemán and founded the Sandinista Renovation Movement (MRS).

Costa Rica: Lowered Tolerance of Wrongdoing

In April 2000, the national legislature rejected President Miguel Angel Ro-dríguez's proposed privatization legislation and his popularity continued to sink. For its part the generally dominant National Liberation Party (PLN) was deeply split over ex-president Arias Sánchez's desire to run again and the issue of free trade. Hence, dissidents formed the Citizen's Action Party (PAC). Abel Pacheco de la Espriella (b. 1933) of the president's United Christian Socialist Party (PUSC) received 38.5 percent of the vote in a three-way race, leading Rolando Monge Araya of the PLN and Otton Solis of the PAC, who polled 30.9 percent and 26 percent, respectively—before disposing of Monge in an April 2002 runoff by a comfortable margin of 58 percent to 42 percent, as voter participation was 69 percent, low for this little democracy. (This was the first runoff since 1936, as the two leading parties usually averaged over 95 percent of the total.) With these three parties having 19, 17, and 14 seats in the 57-member legislative assembly, the 6 votes of a minor party took on unusual importance. GDP growth of 5.6 percent for 2003 helped keep this small democracy on an even keel.

There was a change in early October 2004 when Miguel Angel Rodríguez was forced to resign as secretary general of the Organization of American States after being accused of serious fiscal crimes when president of Costa Rica in 1998–2002. Shortly thereafter, ex-president Rafael A. Calderón (1990–1994) was arrested for involvement in a major scandal of overbilling and kickbacks centering on purchase of medical equipment for a leading hospital (which allegedly netted him $450,000 on a $40-million transaction). Then former president José María Figueres Olsen was accused of influence peddling. President Pacheco strove energetically to stay free of the suspicions engendered by the activities of these predecessors and the recent ex-president of neighboring Nicaragua.[45]

There are twenty women in the fifty-seven-member congress. As the gender gap in Costa Rican politics is the smallest in the region, it was not surprising that women were among the early front-runners for the 2006 elections. But in the campaign, which formally opened in October 2005, the PLN banked on former president Oscar Arias Sánchez to defeat former runner-up Otton Solis, this time candidate of the Union for Change faction of the PUSC in the presidential sweepstakes scheduled for February 2006.

Panama: Accent on Youth

At the beginning of May 2004, Panama elected forty-year-old Martín Torrijos to replace Mireya Moscoso. Martín Torrijos is the son of the 1968–1981 neo-Peronist strongman who built the strongest political party ever seen in this country of narrow interest groups masquerading as parties. In the peculiar context of

Panamanian politics this constituted a decision to look forward, rather than back, since the loser in a 46 percent to 29 percent drubbing was less than mediocre ex-president Guillermo Endara. Enjoying a bare legislative majority, Torrijos resurrected plans for widening the canal and reconstructing its locks so that supertankers, as well as large ore and grain carriers, could once again make use of it. To this end he needed to attract very large amounts of foreign financing, but the short-term economic benefits of massive construction and longer-range increase in canal tolls would be of great use in bolstering social projects.

The Caribbean: Little Reason for Optimism

The Caribbean continued to fall farther behind the rest of Latin America, with Haiti becoming more of a basket case, the Dominican Republic slipping back from its post-Balaguer gains, and Cuba stagnating in the fifth decade of the Castro era.

Cuba: Stability and Stagnation

In comparison to the significant adjustments of the 1990s elsewhere, Cuba changed little in the first years of the new century. In his mid-seventies and in power for over forty years, Castro was not inclined to innovate, but policies already in place were having unintended as well as intended effects. Despite effective damage control measures during the closing years of the old century, economic problems were catching up with Cuba. Its sugar yield was down to half that of the 1980s peak years, and the world price was extremely low, so earnings of $450 million were the lowest in three decades.[46] Informal dollarization had proven a double-edged sword for the regime. It helped erode state-sector productivity along with socialist values and the bases of egalitarian stratification of society upon which legitimacy rested. Although efforts to attract tourism met with substantial success, direct foreign investment was only one-seventh that received by the Dominican Republic.[47] Indeed, 70 percent of dollars in Cuba were the result of remittances from relatives in the United States, a flow that reached $700 million annually, going predominantly to white Cubans in the Havana area, thus greatly increasing income inequality.[48] As Eckstein perceptively points out, on the political side:

> The government and Party managed to keep domestic opposition weak, divided, and isolated. They did so through selective use of repression, including periodic arrest and imprisonment of dissidents and continued denial of dissident access to the state-controlled media.[49]

Yet by late 2004, Castro appeared to be aware of the seeds of economic transformation planted by the country's informal dollarization and sought to maintain the stream of regime-bolstering revenue while containing its erosive effects on the system.[50] Thus in November he ended the policy in effect since 1993 of allowing the circulation of dollars as parallel legal tender. Henceforth "convertible" pesos had to be purchased even by recipients of remittances from the United States, with the government charging a 10 percent tax. Portrayed as a patriotic response to the George W. Bush administration's new restrictions on remittances and visits, the measure was designed to channel dollars into the national treasury and, by enforcing a one-to-one rate of exchange, curtail the great advantages enjoyed by recipients of remittances compared to the rest of the population.

Castro's dramatic 2005 pratfall, in which he fractured several bones, focused attention upon the fact that he was seventy-eight, with his designated successor, Raúl Castro, not far behind at seventy-three. The post-1993 economic reforms had disproportionately benefited the military, who were allowed to expand their range of business activities and investments. Speculation on the *caudillo*'s heir expanded to include his son, Fidel Castro Díaz-Balart, as well as economic czar Carlos Lage and Ricardo Alarcón, president of the National Assembly of People's Power (Cuba's legislature).[51] This body had last been elected at the beginning of 2003, when an announced 8 million votes (a turnout over 97 percent) elected 609 unopposed progovernment candidates.

Dominican Republic: Decay and Hopes for Resurrection

In mid-May 2000, with incumbent president Lionel Fernández ineligible for a second consecutive term and longtime dominant political leader Joaquín Balaguer an ailing ninety-two, Rafael Hipólito Mejía Domínguez (b. 1941), candidate of the Dominican Revolutionary Party (PRD), garnered 49.9 percent of the vote to 24.9 percent for the standard bearer of the Dominican Liberal Party (PLD) and only 24.6 percent for Balaguer seeking yet another term as leader of the Christian Social Reform Party (PRSC). Although having 24 of 32 Senate posts, with only 73 of 149 seats in the lower house, the PRD needed Balaguer's cooperation. This situation remained essentially unchanged after the mid-2002 congressional elections, although the PRD improved its already dominant position in the upper house, since, while the PLD fell from 49 to 41 seats in the chamber, the PRSC gained from 17 to 36. Encouraging for its future, however, the PLD carried the capital city, and an era was finally put to rest in midyear with Balaguer's death.

The Mejía government was hit with a major bank failure in May 2003 that occasioned a bailout equivalent to nearly a fifth of the country's annual economic output. Moreover, the spendthrift populist followed policies resulting in trade deficits of $3.5 to $3.7 billion each year. GDP growth, which had reached 7.5 percent in 1998 before peaking at 8.8 percent in 1999, weakened in the transition year of 2000 before falling to 3.2 percent in 2001 and 4.4 percent in 2002 and turning negative for 2003 as the peso lost half its value. Foreign debt soared from 20 percent of GDP to 40 percent, some $6 billion, and the country's extreme dependence on petroleum imports constituted a major obstacle to economic recovery—leading to discussion of dollarization with consequent loss of control over fiscal policy. Thus it was not surprising that many Dominicans looked back fondly on Fernández's previous administration and swept him back into office in May 2004 by 54 percent to 36 percent over the incumbent president. Whether they did him much of a favor remained to be seen, as he assumed office in August with the country perilously near the brink of insolvency, with inflation near 50 percent and unemployment over 17 percent, prices for some basic foods having doubled over the preceding twelve months, electricity falling far short of demand, and gasoline and propane scarce. Moreover, residual nostalgia for the Balaguer era persisted.

Haiti: The Hemisphere's Basket Case

With progress occurring in traditionally laggard countries, such as Honduras and Paraguay, Haiti entered the new century as Latin America's most backward country. As time went on it became increasingly apparent that the explanation of Haiti's political underdevelopment is rooted in the country's outdated social structures, which in turn heavily reflect its primitive economy. Sadly, it is not yet in any crucial respect a modern country, being more analogous to the second-tier countries of Africa than to the least-developed of Latin America's other countries. The great majority of the Haitian population still reside in rural areas, where agriculture is largely subsistence and production woefully outdated by today's international standards. Its current political travails dramatically underscore the retrograde nature of its social structures. Organization is an extremely scarce commodity, with politics highly fragmented as well as personalized—if not quasi-tribalized.

Aristide's Lavalas Party swept the May–June 2000 parliamentary and local elections, leading the opposition to boycott the November presidential balloting, thus making Aristide the winner in a walkover (being credited with 91.6 percent of the vote). Manipulation of the preliminary balloting led the United States and its allies to interrupt aid disbursements. When René Préval transferred the presidency back to Aristide in February 2001, it was the first time an elected Haitian president had ever served his full term, then given way to an elected successor. This modest streak was not to continue. The November 2000 conviction of ex-strongman Raoul Cédras and a number of his associates for the murder of fifteen slum dwellers back in 1995 and the sentencing to life at hard labor was little more than an empty gesture, since it was in absentia. Social and economic conditions entered into decline from their already precarious levels.

By the beginning of 2004, opposition to Aristide had grown to encompass much of the country and was hard at work to oust the high-handed populist.

Matters came to a head in early February in the aftermath of a badly managed celebrations of the bicentennial of independence and a wave of violence against former boat people by strong-arm squads connected to the president. By February 27 the situation had deteriorated to the point where the United States sent in marines and international bodies sought to engineer a solution to the increasingly chaotic violence. On February 29 Aristide departed for exile in South Africa, claiming that the resignation document he had signed had been coerced. Supreme court head Boniface Alexandre was sworn in as president with aging Gerard Latortue, a United Nations functionary, selected by a panel to be prime minister. Since the army had been disbanded in 1995 and the police were notoriously ineffective, an international peace force assumed responsibility for order, with Brazil eventually contributing a significant contingent (much as it had in the Dominican Republic in 1965), thus allowing the United States to reduce its presence. The so-called National Resistance Front for the Liberation of Haiti, including forces closely associated with the exceedingly corrupt and repressive military governments as well as elements of the former army seeking its reconstitution, controlled large portions of the country but were prevented from seizing power in the capital.[52] In 2005, violence and unrest remained at such high levels that the scheduled national elections were repeatedly postponed until at least January 2006.

The New Caribbean: Maturation and Growing Pains

By the early years of the twenty-first century, many of the countries that had gained their independence after World War II had had a longer and richer experience with self-government than had others that had not attained independence until the late 1970s or early 1980s. This circumstance was reflected in uneven political performance that saw stability in Trinidad and Tobago, rising opposition to the entrenched administration in Jamaica, campaigning for the 2006 elections in Guyana, and important national voting in Suriname.[53] As three of the four countries that had not gotten past their originally dominant leaders and their direct heirs by 1999 did so in these years, Suriname remained the only one still to find new leadership.

Jamaica

In mid–October 2002, the People's National Party (PNP) of Prime Minister P. J. Patterson, the incumbent since 1992, won 34 seats in parliament to 26 for the Jamaica Labour Party (JLP). Its fourth victory in a row came on a low turnout of 57 percent of registered voters. Subsequently the opposition came back strongly in the mid-2003 local elections. With the constitutional issue of becoming a republic catalyzing concern among political elites, Patterson assumed a strongly pro-

Aristide position in 2004, going so far as giving the ousted Haitian leader tempo-rary asylum. Within government party ranks speculation rose over his eventual successor as 2006 elections loomed on the horizon.

Trinidad and Tobago

The new century opened with increasing conflict between the head of govern-ment and the president, leading to friction between both of them and the judici-ary. Crime was on the rise, and the minister of local government was implicated in the murder of a prominent opposition businessman. In elections at the end of 2000 Prime Minister Badseo Panday and his essentially East Indian United Na-tional Congress (UNC) prevailed 52 percent to 46 percent—19 seats to 16—over former prime minister Patrick Manning and his predominantly black People's National Movement (PNM), as the National Alliance for Reconstruction (NAR), holder of a single seat, denounced both of the major parties for exploiting racism. Panday encountered major problems with his health and corruption charges—re-sulting in the defection of attorney general Ramesh Maharaj. In the early elec-tions at the end of 2001, the UNC at 49.7 percent retained a slight popular edge over the PNM and its 46.3 percent of the vote—as the break-off dissidents earned only 2.5 percent and the NAR continued its collapse, garnering a paltry 1.5 per-cent of voter preferences. With the seats evenly divided (at 18-to-18), President Arthur N. R. Robinson used his prerogative to name the PNM's Patrick A.M. Manning prime minister.

Challenging this action as illegal and unconstitutional, Panday managed to keep parliament from meeting for six months, a period in which the new govern-ment conducted many corruption investigations into the affairs of the Panday ad-ministration. President Robinson, whose term had been extended for an additional year, took steps to sue the former prime minister for asserting that his choice of Manning was racially motivated. Manning called the third general elec-tion in less than two years, and in late 2002 his PNM won 20 seats to the UNC's 16, remaining in power. George Maxwell Richards (b. 1931) was chosen as the new president, and the governing party emerged victorious in 83 of 126 districts in the mid-2003 municipal elections. Meanwhile, murders and kidnappings multi-plied, many involving rival drug gangs. With the population of 1.3 million bal-anced at 40 percent black and 40 percent East Indian, with 18.5 percent mixed and less than 1 percent white, Trinidad appeared in danger of becoming trapped in the type of vicious racially divisive politics that has plagued Guyana.

On the positive side, Trinidad has emerged in recent years as the hemisphere's leading supplier of liquefied natural gas, providing 80 percent of the US imports of this energy source—up from 31 percent in 1999. This sudden boom led to 13 percent GDP growth in 2003 and nearly as high a rate of economic expansion in

2004. An iron and steel complex and two of the world's largest methanol plants have sprung up south of Port of Spain at Point Lisas alongside the established array of ammonia plants. At nearly $5 billion annually, Liquid Natural Gas (LNG) has eclipsed the former chief export, oil, still the source of $1.4 billion a year. The government not only is a partner in building an LNG terminal off the coast of Louisiana but is also investing $700 million in building a pipeline to Barbados and other eastern Caribbean islands. With unemployment at 10 percent and roughly a fifth of the population living in poverty, demands were rising for channeling the expanding government income into social as well as economic development. So far the government's response seems to be showy public works such as a new central market for Port of Spain, as well as a rapid transit system.

Guyana

In March 2001, the Progressive Peoples Party (PPP) received 53.1 percent of the vote to 41.7 percent for the Desmond Hoyte–led Peoples National Party (PNC), gaining a 34-to-27 advantage in the 65-seat legislature and giving Bharrat Jagdeo (in since August 1999) a new five-year term as president. Unfortunately, stability did not translate into progress, as the country's socioeconomic problems in some ways worsened. Moreover, the opposition, now led by Robert Corbin, called for major revisions of the electoral system before the election scheduled for mid-2006.

Belize

In early 2003, elections the incumbent People's United Party (PUP) received 53.2 percent of the vote and 22 of 29 parliamentary seats compared to the 46 percent of votes, but only 7 seats, of the United Democratic Party (UDP), maintaining Said Musa in office as rising crime, blamed by some politicians on recent immigrants, became a focus of controversy.

Barbados

The new century opened with the Barbados Labour Party (BLP) entrenched in office on the strength of its early 1999 electoral near clean sweep with 26 of 28 seats in parliament on 65 percent of the vote. In May 2003 it retained power behind Owen S. Arthur with 23 of 30 seats, although the opposition Democratic Labour Party (DLP) raised its vote share of from 35 to 44 percent. Under this economist, offshore banking became a more critical element in a very unevenly spread prosperity, and the country became embroiled in a dispute over fishing rights with Trinidad and Tobago.

Suriname

In late May 2000, ex-president Ronald Venetiaan's New Front (NF) stormed back into power with 33 of 51 seats in the national legislature on 47 percent of the vote as incumbent President Jules Widjenbosch and the National Democratic Party (NDP) suffered a stunning collapse, receiving only 9 percent of the vote. In August, Venetiaan became president on the strength of 37 of 51 legislative votes, with Jules Ajodhia back in as prime minister, while former dictator "Desi" Bouterse remained occupied fighting Dutch drug-trafficking convictions. As the government pressed ahead with badly needed measures to end economic stagnation, ex-prime minister Errol Alibux was indicted on charges of having defrauded the government, and investigations were opened into the infamous December Murders.

Hence, the late May 2005 elections, in which 60 percent of the 330,000 registered voters took part, resulted in a plurality of 23 seats (a drop of ten) for the NF, as Bouterse's NDP rose sharply to 15. The A-Combination (AC), led by Ronny Brunswijk—head of the 1980s insurrectionary Jungle Commando Group—representing the neglected Maroon (sometimes called bushnegro) minority, received 5 seats, one less than ex-president Widjenbosch's Alliance for Prosperity (Volksallia Voor Vooruitgang, VVV). Selection of the president dragged on until August as the incumbent and the ex-dictator competed for votes from the lesser parties. When in July neither could marshal the required two-thirds (34) of the United People's Assembly, the election went to a much larger and more broadly based body, where Venetiaan retained the presidency by a healthy margin of 560 to 315.

Bahamas

The May 2002 elections saw the Free National Movement (FNM) fall from electoral grace, retaining only seven of its 34 seats (on 41 percent of the vote) as the Progressive Liberal Party (PLP) jumped from 5 seats to 29 of 40 parliamentary seats on the strength of 52 percent of the vote, making Perry Christie the new prime minister (in place of one-time law partner Hubert Ingraham).

Grenada

At the end of 2003, incumbent prime minister Keith Mitchell's New National Party (NNP) survived a narrow escape, falling to 8 seats as the National Democratic Congress (NDC) behind Tillman Thomas won the other seven. Offshore banking has become a major prop of the economy, and sale of passports to foreigners of questionable business dealings roils the political waters.

Dominica

At the beginning of 2000, the Dominica Labour Party (DLP) behind Roosevelt "Rosie" Douglas won 10 seats in the 21-member parliament on 42.9 percent of the vote, allying with the Dominican Freedom Party (DFP), whose once-dominant electoral fortunes had declined to 2 seats, to make Douglas prime minister. His sudden death in October elevated Pierre Charles (b. 1954) to the head of government as Vernon Lorden Shaw continued as the tiny island republic's president, and the United Worker's Party (UWP) of former prime minister Edison Jones reaccustomed itself to the role of opposition it had held until mid-1995. Charles's abrupt demise in January 2004 brought thirty-one-year-old Roosevelt Skerritt to the chief executive position. National balloting on May 5, 2005, in an atmosphere of economic growth, saw Skerritt and the DLP retain power with a 12 to 8 legislative majority.

St. Kitts and Nevis

In March 2000, the St. Kitts–Nevis Labour Party (SKNLP) received 53.9 percent of the St. Kitts vote and all eight of the dominant island's seats to keep Denzil Llewellyn Douglas, the incumbent since mid-1995, in office. In late 2004, he renewed his lease as prime minister courtesy of carrying 7 of the 8 St. Kitts seats, while the opposition leader lost his constituency in Nevis (which has 3 seats for its eleven thousand inhabitants).

St. Vincent and the Grenadines

After Prime Minister James Mitchell of the National Democratic Party (NDP) retired at age sixty-nine from political life in late 2000, Ralph Goncalves (b. 1946) led the opposition Unity Labour Party (ULP) to victory in the March 2001 balloting, garnering 57 percent of the vote and 12 of the 15 seats in parliament. Violent crime became a major political issue along with he extensive cultivation of marijuana as the country headed for its next elections.

St. Lucia

At the end of 2001, Prime Minister Kenny D. Anthony (b. 1950), in office since mid-1997, led the St. Lucia Labour Party (SLP) to victory with 14 of 17 parliamentary seats on 54.2 percent of the vote. Dr. Anthony—an administrative one-man band—held the finance, economic planning, financial services, economic affairs, and information portfolios along with his prime ministerial responsibilities, perhaps prudent in light of the country's heavy debt burden. In a surprising move

in early 2005 George Melvin Compton, a long-term prime minister who had retired from political life in 1996, regained control of the United Workers Party
(UWP) and declared himself once again a candidate for the country's top elective
post at the age of seventy-nine.

Antigua and Barbuda

The Bird dynasty, winners once again in 1999, continued their hold on this tiny
country through the mid-2003 balloting, in which Lester B. Bird of the Antigua
Labour Party (ALP) retained the prime minister's post along with the ministries of
defense, foreign affairs, justice, public works, and four other portfolios. With sugar
essentially out of business and tourism down, offshore financial services and tele-
marketing partially took up the economic slack. Still, in March 2004 Baldwin
Spencer of the United Progressive Party (UPP), taking advantage of the first voter
reregistration in three decades, ended the Bird family's long hold on power, one
that had resulted in foreign debt of $1.1 billion—an alarming 135 percent of the
country's small GDP, which was growing at only 2 percent a year. Both Lester
Bird and Vere Bird, Jr., lost their seats as the UPP came away with a majority of 12
to 15. Since two-fifths of the labor force (mostly hired by the Birds) are on the
government payroll, the new administration's talk of retrenchment raised the
hackles of the ALP-tied labor unions.

As tourism has lagged, the country has come to depend heavily upon overseas
online gambling. Since the United States raised legal obstacles, Spencer cut a deal
with a recently naturalized millionaire from Texas to sell him two small islets for
construction of a luxury resort complex. Naturally speculation runs rampant
about how much money may have passed into whose hands.

Bermuda

Bermuda, a popular tourist destination, remains a British colony, although it has
enjoyed full internal self-government since 1968. The United Bermudan Party
(UBP) is multiracial, and the proindependence Progress Labour Party (PLP) is almost exclusively black. In 1976, the PLP garnered 46 percent of the vote and 14
of 40 legislative seats, leaving the UBP entrenched in power. Premier in 1982,
John W. Swan saw his party win decisively in 1985 before slipping a few seats in
1989. After a 22-to-18 escape from electoral defeat in the October 1993 balloting,
in early 1997 Swan resigned, being replaced by Pamela Gordon. This leadership
shuffle did not help the party, and the November 1998 elections saw the PLP
surge into office for the first time behind Jennifer Smith on the strength of 54.2
percent of the vote and 26 seats to the UBP's 44.1 percent of electoral preferences
and 14 places in the legislature.

After European criticism of Bermuda as an out-of-control tax haven, in mid-2003 Smith led the PLP to a narrowed victory, holding on to 22 of 36 seats on 51.6 percent of the vote to the UBP's 48 percent of the ballots. Having carried her own constituency by only 8 votes, she was forced to resign, being replaced by W. Alexander Scott.

Where Latin America Stands

At the end of Chapter 7 the unifying themes of this work were assessed as they stood in the mid-1950s (which happens to be when I finished my course work and began research for my first book, thus devoting myself full time to study and observation of the area). Significant change has occurred with respect to all the basic concerns during the ensuing half century, but those with deep cultural roots continue to prove resistant, even resilient. For most of the region the authoritarian corporatist political culture, although in remission, demonstrates disturbing signs of resurgence among some sectors of society. The views of Wiarda quoted in Chapter 1 may require some qualification and softening, but they are a reminder that centuries of tradition are not easily swept away in a world where they have demonstrated a strong capacity to adapt and survive. Certainly these views are less universally held, particularly among groups that have embraced Pentecostal brands of Protestantism in place of Catholicism, most apparent in Brazil, Chile, and perhaps Guatemala.

With the burgeoning of civil society and voluntary organizations in recent decades, as well as more ample and better-administered social welfare programs, patron-client relationships are not the norm they still were in the 1950s and 1960s. Nevertheless, they are still fundamental in the hinterlands. As with traditional political culture, their national impact has been diminished by the very high degree of urbanization that Latin America has experienced, with a reversal of the urban-rural proportions since the 1950s. As recent elections have dramatically demonstrated, along with this urbanization participation has greatly expanded, with the registered electorate exceeding 60 percent of the total population in many countries and passing two-thirds in cases such as Brazil. At the same time, there is often deep frustration with the disconnection between voting and seeing congruent results in terms of desired policies. There as much as elsewhere those whom a person votes for leave much to be desired when it comes to implementing their campaign promises. With the generalized trend toward national legislatures playing a larger role in shaping public policy than has usually been the case in Latin America, not all voter focus is on the executive. Moreover, in truly federal systems such as Brazil and Argentina and as is slowly developing with respect to Mexico and Colombia, many citizens encounter more satisfactory results from electing governors, mayors, and municipal council members than from electing remote presidents and distant national legislators.

Related to these salutary trends, leadership and leadership styles have undergone very considerable evolution away from the *caudillo* phenomenon that still exerted substantial influence in some of the less politically developed countries through World War II and into the 1950s. This complex subject receives major attention in the concluding chapter, as does violence, which has diversified in form, having come to be increasingly related to protests by minorities excluded from an effective voice in national affairs—also discussed in the next chapter. The current era is free of either a predominant ideology, as positivism was dominant in the 1871–1899 period, or contending world ideologies like communism and fascism in the 1920s to the mid-1940s and Marxism-Leninism versus the American capitalist-democratic doctrine through the Cold War. As a result personalities, images, and—in some cases—performance have come to the fore.

Just because corruption has become more of a political issue in very recent years does not necessarily mean that it is more pervasive. Indeed, the attention it receives is both healthy and a sign of political development. What was long taken for granted as inevitable or a necessary evil is now being viewed as an eradicable evil to be combated. When it interacts with drug trafficking, it is a more serious problem, one that receives attention in the final chapter. One more of our continuing issues remains to be addressed: the political role of the military and whether patterns of civil-military relations have been established that guarantee that the armed forces will no longer intervene as arbiters or moderators as they did so massively in the 1960s. This topic, too, is analyzed in the concluding chapter.

It is clear that for almost all Latin Americans, from the largest countries to the smallest, 2006 will be a critical year. Most of them are scheduled to participate in selecting new governments. Some nations may provide continuity, whereas many others are likely to opt for significant change. In all cases, this account of Latin America's political experiences has explained the contexts in which these contests will take place and has identified the key actors. Now it is time to pull together the findings of this account of Latin America's political development.

Notes

1. This is thoughtfully analyzed by Howard J. Wiarda in *Dilemmas of Democracy in Latin America: Crises and Opportunity* (Lanham, MD: Rowman & Littlefield, 2005). A thought-stimulating volume is Douglas A. Chalmers, María do Carmo Campello de Souza, and Atilio A. Boron, eds., *The Right and Democracy in Latin America* (New York: Praeger, 1992). Peter H. Smith, *Democracy in Latin America: Political Change in Comparative Perspective* (New York: Oxford University Press, 2005), is an excellent, topically organized, analytical

treatment that is current just beyond 2000 and contains very little discussion of particular countries.

2. Wiarda, *Dilemmas,* p. 204.

3. Consult Manuel Antonio Garreton and Edward Newman, eds., *Democracy in Latin America: (Re)Constructing Political Society* (New York: United Nations University Press, 2001), and Manuel Antonio Garreton, Marcelo Cavarozzi, Peter S. Cleaves, Gary Gereffi, and Jonathan Hartlyn, *Latin America in the Twenty-First Century: Toward a New Sociopolitical Matrix* (Boulder, CO: Lynne Rienner, 2003).

4. Mauricio A. Font, *Transforming Brazil* (Lanham, MD: Rowman & Littlefield, 2003), covers many political topics up to the 2002 elections, but on other topics ends by 2001. The story is carried a bit further in some of the essays in Mauricio Font and Anthony P. Spanakos, eds., *Reforming Brazil* (Lanham, MD: Lexington Books, 2004).

5. Changes from 1996 were very limited for the three largest parties as well as the PPB and many of the midsized parties. The PT demonstrated the greatest growth, a gain from 10.6 percent of the vote to 14.1 percent, hardly spectacular and coming essentially at the expense of the PDT, reflecting the declining appeal of its aging leader, Brizola, contrasted with Lula's moderating and maturing stature. The PDT fell from 13.4 percent to 6.6 percent as its loss of nearly 4.4 million votes corresponded closely to the PT's gain of almost 4.1 million. Very useful work on this and other elections has been done by Professor David Fleischer of the Universidade Federal de Brasília.

6. See Andrei Meirelles and Gerson Camarotti, "Xadrez no Congresso," *Época* (October 28, 2002), pp. 80–81, as well as the Brazilian daily press of the period.

7. Consult Thomas Traumann, "Lula en Novo Tom," *Época* (October 28, 2002), pp. 59–62.

8. Delmo Moreira, "O Brasil que Fica de Herança," *Época* (October 28, 2002), pp. 54–58.

9. For perspective see Eliana Cardoso, "Monetary and Fiscal Reform," and Sonia Diaibe, "Social Policy Reform," in Font and Spanakos, eds., *Reforming Brazil,* pp. 29–51, 71–91.

10. Consult Solano Nascimento, "Deputados Cangurus," *Veja* (February 11, 2004), pp. 54–55.

11. See Barry Bearak, "Poor Man's Burden," *New York Times Magazine* (June 17, 2004), pp. 30–35, 50, 56, 59.

12. Consult especially the three major weekly news magazines, beginning with *Época* (August 30, 2004), *Veja* (September 15, 2004), and *ISTOÉ* (September 15, 2004), and continuing to mid-November. Polling, particularly by IBOPE, Datafolha, and Vox Populi, is generally more accurate than that done in the United States, largely because of the much higher turnout in Brazil, since in US polls a very large proportion of those responding will not actually vote on election day, whereas 85 percent do in Brazil.

13. A good treatment of the political wars in Rio de Janeiro is contained in *Época* (September 15, 2003), pp. 54–66. All major Brazilian daily papers gave comprehensive coverage to the elections, that of the *Folha de S. Paulo* being the most detailed.

14. Strictly applying the criteria for the number of municipal legislators, the courts reduced the total from 60,276 to 51,748. Election results can be found in *Época,* October 11,

October 18, and November 8, 2004, as well as *Veja* and *ISTOÉ* of October 6, October 13, and November 10, 2004.

15. Emir Sader, "Taking Lula's Measure," *New Left Review,* 33 (May–June 2005), pp. 58–80, is an articulate leftist critique of the PT government by a disaffected party founder. More balanced is Wendy Hunter and Timothy J. Power, "Lula's Brazil at Midterm," *Journal of Democracy,* 16:3 (July 2005), pp. 127–139.

16. Useful works getting into this period include Luis Rubio and Susan Kaufman Purcell, eds., *Mexico Under Fox* (Boulder, CO: Lynne Rienner, 2004); David A. Shirk, *Mexico's New Politics: The PAN and Democratic Change* (Boulder, CO: Lynne Rienner, 2004); and Joseph S. Tulchin and Andrew D. Selee, eds., *Mexico's Politics and Society in Transition* (Boulder, CO: Lynne Rienner, 2003). To see how far the PAN had come since its early days consult Donald Mabry, *Mexico's Acción Nacional: A Catholic Alternative to Revolution* (Syracuse, NY: Syracuse University Press, 1973).

17. Roderic Ai Camp, *Politics in Mexico: The Democratic Transformation*, 4th ed. (New York: Oxford University Press, 2003), p. 197. See also Roderic Ai Camp, *Mexico's Military on the Democratic Stage* (Northport, CT: Praeger, 2005).

18. The election is discussed in Camp, *Politics*, pp. 174–176, 199–205, and in greater detail in Chappell Lawson and Jorge Dominguez, eds., *Mexico's 2000 Elections* (Cambridge, UK: Cambridge University Press, 2000), and Joseph Klesner, *The 2000 Mexican Presidential and Congressional Elections: Pre-Election Report* (Washington, DC: Center for Strategic and International Studies, 2000).

19. See Camp, *Politics,* pp. 190–193.

20. Camp, *Politics in Mexico. . . ,* p. 202.

21. Ibid., p. 204.

22. M. Delal Baer, "Mexico at an Impasse, *Foreign Affairs*, 83:1 (January–February 2004), p. 106. See also Chappell H. Lawson, "Fox's Mexico at Mid-Term," *Journal of Democracy*, 15:1 (January 2004), pp. 139–152.

23. Baer, "Mexico," p. 102.

24. See Denise Dresser, "Fox's Mexico: Democracy Paralyzed," *Current History*, No. 679 (February 2005), pp. 64–68, where she calls Madrazo "the old system at its worst," as well as Joseph L. Klesner, "Electoral Competition and the New Party Hope in Mexico," *Latin American Politics and Society*, 47:2 (Summer 2005), pp. 103–142.

25. See Javier Corrales, "The Politics of Argentina's Meltdown," *World Policy Journal*, 19:3 (Fall 2000), pp. 29–36.

26. Steven Levitsky, "The 'Normalization' of Argentine Politics," *Journal of Democracy*, 11:2 (April 2000), pp. 56–69.

27. Also very useful is Hector E. Shamis, "Argentina: Crisis and Democratic Consolidation," *Journal of Democracy*, 13:2 (April, 2002), pp. 81–94.

28. Steven Levitsky and Maria Victoria Murillo, "Argentina Weathers the Storm," *Journal of Democracy*, 14:4 (October 2003), pp. 152–166.

29. Ibid., p. 164.

30. See José Eduardo Barella, "Ninguem Paga a Ninguem na Argentina," *Veja* (September 17, 2003), pp. 102–103, and Chrystiane Silva and Carlos Rydlewski, "Diplomacia do Faz-de-Conta," *Veja* (September 15, 2004), pp. 112–114.

31. Consult Eduardo Posada-Carbo, "Colombia's Resilient Democracy," *Current History*, No. 670 (February 2004), pp. 68–73.

32. Consult Arlene B. Tickner, "Colombia and the United States: From Counternarcotics to Counterterror," *Current History*, No. 661 (February 2003), pp. 77–85, as well as Russell Crandall, *Driven by Drugs: U.S. Policy Toward Colombia* (Boulder, CO: Lynne Rienner, 2002).

33. See Juan Forero, "Safeguarding Colombia's Oil," *New York Times* (October 22, 2004), p. W.1.

34. See Juan Forero, "Peruvians Fight Graft One Case at a Time," *New York Times*, (April 5, 2004), p. A.2; and Juan Forero, "Peruvians Tired of Toledo, but Worry About Ousting Him," *New York Times* (August 5, 2004), p. A.8.

35. Useful on Venezuela is Jennifer McCoy and David Meyers, *The Unraveling of Representative Democracy in Venezuela* (Baltimore: Johns Hopkins University Press, 2004), and Steve Ellner and Daniel Hellinger, eds., *Venezuelan Politics in the Chávez Era: Class, Polarization, and Conflict* (Boulder, CO: Lynne Rienner, 2004). See also Jennifer McCoy, "One Act in an Unfinished Drama," *Journal of Democracy*, 16:1 (January 2005), pp. 109–123.

36. See José E. Molina V. and Carmen Pérez B., "Radical Change at the Ballot Box: Venezuela's 2000 Elections," *Latin American Politics and Society*, 46:1 (Spring 2004), pp. 103–134.

37. Consult "O clone do Totalitarismo," *Veja* (May 4, 2005), pp. 152–162.

38. See Paul W. Posner, "Local Democracy and the Transformation of Popular Participation in Chile," *Latin American Politics and Society*, 46:3 (Fall 2004), pp. 55–58, and John M. Carey and Peter M. Scavelis, "Insurance for Good Losers and the Survival of Chile's Concertacíon," *Latin American Politics and Society*, 47:2 (Summer 2005), pp. 1–22.

39. Peter Siavelis, "Electoral System Coalitional Disintegration and the Future of Chile's Concertacíon," *Latin American Research Review*, 40:1 (2005), pp. 56–82.

40. Many observers believed that US insistence on Morales's expulsion from the congress is what lifted him from relative obscurity and made him a political force.

41. See Larry Rohter, "Aided by Uruguay's Problems, Left is Expected to Gain Power," *New York Times*, (October 31, 2004), p. I.18; and Larry Rohter, "Uruguay's Left Makes History by Winning Presidential Ballot," *New York Times*, (November 1, 2004), p. A.11.

42. Consult John A. Booth, Christine J. Wade, and Thomas W. Walker, *Understanding Central America: Global Forces, Rebellion, and Regime Change*, 4th ed. (Boulder, CO: Westview Press, 2006).

43. See J. Mark Ruhl, "The Guatemalan Military Since the Peace Accords: The Failure of Reforms Under Arzú and Portillo," *Latin American Politics and Society*, 47:1 (Spring 2005), pp. 55–85.

44. See David Holiday, "El Salvador's 'Model' Democracy," *Current History*, No. 679 (February 2005), pp. 69–76.

45. See Fabrice Edouard Lehoucq, "Costa Rica: Paradise in Doubt," *Journal of Democracy*, 16:3 (July 2005), pp. 140–154.

46. Susan Eva Eckstein, *Back from the Future: Cuba Under Castro* (New York: Routledge, 2003), pp. 222–224.

47. Ibid., pp. 219–221.

48. Ibid., pp. 233–234.

49. Ibid., p. 241.

50. Ibid., p. 243.

51. See Javier Coralles, "Cuba After Fidel," *Current History*, No. 679 (February 2005), pp. 69–76.

52. The Haitian crisis received heavy, if episodic and essentially descriptive, coverage in the major newspapers from late January well into February 2004. A sound treatment is Daniel P. Erikson, "Haiti After Aristide: Still at the Brink," *Current History*, No. 679 (February 2005), pp. 83–90.

53. Consult the country entries in Europa Publications' *South America, Central America, and the Caribbean*, 10th edition (2002), 11th edition (2003), 12th edition (2004), and 13th edition (2005).

14

Comparative Perspectives on Latin America's Political Development

As has been amply documented throughout the just completed trip through the region, Latin America's political experience has been marked on the dark side by corruption, egoism, injustice, inertia, inequality, violence, exclusion, and short-sightedness. But these negative factors have often been balanced by courage, determination, persistence, resilience, imagination, responsiveness, and occasionally innovation. Although the picture is still very mixed, as is the case on most of the earth, these positive elements are becoming more widespread and pervasive, gradually displacing their dysfunctional opposites from center stage and pushing them toward the wings—although not entirely eliminating them from the drama of national life, much less from its setting. Although politically motivated violence persists, it has been eliminated in many countries, brought under control in others, contained in a few more, and remains rampant in only a handful. At the same time consolidation of democratic political processes based on broad popular participation, linked to increasingly effective governmental structures, and rooted in a congruently modernizing political culture is well advanced in a majority of Latin American countries, which contain the overwhelming bulk of the region's population. This current state stands in sharp, even stark, contrast to the situation as recently as the late 1970s and carrying over into the 1980s, when authoritarian military regimes were still entrenched in such leading countries as Brazil, Argentina, and Chile.

This progress is all the more notable since, as has been shown in the preceding chapters, many Latin American countries have undergone divisive experiences that left long-lasting traumatic aftermaths impeding rational political development. Some of these conflicts unfortunately persisted for a full generation or, in a few cases, even beyond. Although a good number of these have been overcome in recent years and others have had their negative impact attenuated, several still persist, retarding progress toward viable competitive political processes in certain countries. But in contrast to cases in the past where animosities prevented civil cooperation even well beyond the generation in which they were rooted, more recent experience is marked with examples of pragmatic outcomes. Since democratic politics necessarily often involves difficult compromises and uneasy alliances between yesterday's—and very possibly tomorrow's—rivals, if not opponents or even enemies, this is a salutary trend.[1]

A major measure of democratic stability is the handing over of power from one freely elected chief executive to another. An even more significant landmark, and a much rarer one, is replacement of a democratically elected president by a popularly selected one of a different political persuasion. Both these highly favorable occurrences have been markedly more frequent since the 1990s than ever before in the region's experience. Indeed, they have become commonplace and expected. With the exclusion of Cuba, where Castro has been in power for over four and a half decades, and with the caveat of Haiti, where Aristide was ousted from power before finishing his encore term, having been elected to succeed his duly elected successor. All other countries have fundamentally met this important political development criterion—most of them repeatedly. Such alternation or even rotation of parties in power is still extremely rare in most parts of the world.

Latin America's experience dramatically underscores the fact that there is no quick and easy path to political development. Indeed, except for a pair of city-state–sized, rather insulated, and somewhat artificial "hothouse" cases analogous to Denmark and Switzerland—Costa Rica and Uruguay—political development in Latin America has followed a very tortuous and painful zigzag course, with generations often prone to repeat mistakes of preceding ones. In large part this laborious progress is rooted in the major authoritarian corporatist components of Latin America's political culture. As captured by Wiarda:

> Most Latin American countries have the *formal institutions* of democracy—elections, legislatures, political parties, and so on—but are not very democratic underneath. They are *electoral democracies* but not *liberal democracies*. They have the *institutions* of democracy (relatively easy to change) but not its underlying *practices* or *political culture*. [Italics in the original.][2]

But the region also demonstrates that over a span of generations political culture can change sufficiently to support and even nourish democratic processes despite a country's extremely authoritarian starting point and subsequent highly antidemocratic experiences along the way. Overall, change in political culture is most strongly correlated with the scale and timing of postindependence immigration, but it can eventually occur without a significant influx of new and different people. Only in the case of Mexico, however, is proximity to the United States a major factor modifying political culture; otherwise it is the result of processes far more broadly based and profound than the US example, or "Yankee" influence.

As Latin America moves past the opening years of this new century, it has become one of the more politically developed regions of the world. In good part this headway was to be expected, given the substantial length of experience as "independent" nations of most of its components—ranging from a century and three-quarters to two centuries. The region's rise on the political development scene also reflects the emergence, almost always near the bottom of the pile, of a host of new nations in the aftermath of World War II and, more recently, the breakup of the Soviet Union and Yugoslavia, which has provided a relative, but not absolute, boost. Yet much of this distinct improvement in the region's political status is the result of hard work and lessons learned—although often belatedly. Although a number of first- and second-try democracies show signs of stress and strain, there are solid reasons to doubt that most of this progress is merely another "false dawn" like the one in Argentina in 1912–1930 or Brazil between 1946 and 1964.

In this respect, it must be asked to what degree establishment of democracy in Latin America required countries to become essentially urbanized? For it is a strikingly evident fact that the region's consolidating democracies at the beginning of the twenty-first century are overwhelmingly urban, in contrast to the situation prevailing when the wave of democratic regimes that emerged in the late 1950s and early 1960s collapsed. Latin American societies have undergone vast changes in the past generation, ones that have transformed the societal foundations of political life. A decided majority of Latin America's population is now urban; soon urbanites will become the overwhelming population bulk. Hence, the patrimonialism of the past, although still an important drag upon political development, is definitely on the wane—though more modern forms of clientelism survive and in some countries even flourish.

Spurts of Political Development

The question of under what circumstances surges in political development have taken place in Latin America—and why they have eventually run out of momentum—has even more relevance to comparative study than it does to a current understanding of this region. Looking back, one finds that such leaps forward have resulted from an accumulation of fundamental socioeconomic changes that have rendered the existing political regime obsolete and created a gap between those privileged by the political status quo, but no longer creating the nation's wealth, and those individuals and groups that, having been elevated by the ongoing socioeconomic transformations, seek a commensurate voice in political affairs.

When political participation was much more restricted, leadership was the fundamental catalyst of whether a political development surge would be accomplished sooner or later. Very often the key to prompt fulfillment was realization by individuals already on the political stage, but blocked in the quest for the nation's highest office, that the support of these emergent elements was key to their own aspirations. Hence, measures had to be taken to empower them. Usually coming from the "modernizing" wing of a dominant political party, as in turn-of-the-century Argentina, once in power these leaders adopted policies that shifted public resources into the hands of the new elites to enhance their productivity. In most cases these newly dominant elements would eventually use their political influence for profitability instead of productivity. If their heyday was prolonged, they would become the old oligarchs in a repeat of the dialectic that had opened their way to power. In other cases the elite they had displaced might have found new allies—often in the military—to dislodge them from power and provide for a temporary comeback, as in Argentina between 1930 and 1943.

Surges of political development are likely to occur sooner if catalyzing, or at least facilitating, leadership has emerged, and to be delayed to the extent that entrenched elites resort effectively to control and cooptation. The record is clear on this point. In Brazil a constitutional monarchy that served the country well from the 1820s through the 1860s survived the 1870s with minimal modification. Then the shift of the country's economic center of gravity from the tropical plantation agriculture of the northeast to coffee production in the center-south led to vigorous and persistent demands from the new economic elite for a major increase in their voice within the parliamentary regime. In the absence of a drastic reapportionment of representation within this federal imperial system, totally infeasible in light of the determination of the declining elites to hold onto their governmental clout, the rising coffee-related economic elite had to await the establishment of a republic as a necessary, but not sufficient, condition for attaining political domination. In fact, their progress in this direction was severely limited during the initial presidencies of military figures with roots deep in the old order and socialized well before midcentury. Hence, adoption of a republic did not bring with it any immediate political development.

Aside from replacing the monarch with an elected president, the 1891 constitution left the foundations of the old political order virtually intact. When São Paulo coffee interests finally reached the presidency after 1894, the first civilian chief executive was forced to concentrate on repressing insurrection, and the second coped with a crippling financial crisis stemming from sharply dropping coffee revenues. Since the very restricted electorate had no real choice within a party system of severely limited competition (based on preemptive elite agreement on an official candidate), little political development took place. At the same time, however, economic growth had exceeded 80 percent during the first two decades after the founding of the republic, causing consequent changes in society, particularly in the area of internal migration and urbanization. The resulting dissatisfaction led to the election in 1910 of an anti–São Paulo military figure. Although Hermes da Fonseca failed to overcome the engrained patronal-patrimonial heritage of Brazil's political life, his administration did set in motion a wave of discontent that eventuated in the 1930 Revolution and the rise of the middle class toward a decisive role in political affairs.

With the most politically advanced urban elements polarized between the ideological mobilization of violence-oriented communists and local fascists, Vargas skillfully guided Brazil along a centrist path. Although refraining from organization of a party (a far more daunting task in this sprawling subcontinent than anywhere else in the region), the paternalistic Vargas greatly expanded executive structures within a corporatist framework, especially between 1937 and 1944. Self-representation of interests within proliferating agencies and councils did more toward establishing a base of eventual pluralistic politics than a manipulated party system might have. Vargas masterfully accommodated emerging interests while easing the decline of traditional elites.

As the Great Depression morphed into wartime prosperity, an economic and social transformation had take place since Vargas first came to power in 1930—largely as a result of his policies. Industrial growth spurred urbanization, and internal economic activity overtook external demand as Brazil's economic engine. Meanwhile, a labor movement had been built from the top down, and preparing for a return to competitive politics, Vargas formed a party based largely upon labor to supplement a party that was essentially a holding company of regional notables and their machines.

Following an interim term presided over by one of his close military associates, Vargas returned triumphantly to office in 1950 on an unprecedented wave of popular support, nearly four million votes. In his tragically shortened final term as president, Vargas was unable to carry political development forward except in the realm of respect for legislative and judicial autonomy. He did, however, give further impetus to industrialization despite realizing that it would undercut the traditional leg of his support. Although his foes managed to destabilize the aging leader's government, even after his suicide in 1954 Vargas had the last laugh as a disciple elected the next year pushed ahead with Vargas-type policies in a democratic context of highly competitive politics through the single term allowed him by the 1946 constitution. Unfortunately, the opposition candidate who dazzled the electorate in 1960 lacked the requisite patience for the job, and his vice-presidential successor fell short in competence. Hence, the military seized power in 1964. Political development would be resumed only in a much more complex economy and society in 1985, this time without outstanding leadership.

For Mexico, significant political development took place even later than in Brazil. Promising beginnings made in the middle of the nineteenth century by Juárez and the Liberals were swept aside by the French intervention, whose aftermath was the developmentally oriented Díaz dictatorship. Over its thirty-five-year span administrative structures began to flourish, but the political system remained authoritarian even as the economy grew and diversified. In the absence of unifying leadership, the 1910 Revolution led not to a reformed political system, but to the chaos of protracted civil war and warlord politics, leaving any significant construction of political institutions until the 1930s and also setting back economic and social development.

Building upon Calles's steps to channel presidential succession away from the battlefield and into the political arena, Cárdenas developed the party, rather than himself, as the backbone of an expansionist and inclusive corporatist political system. Hence, at the end of his extremely fruitful presidency in 1940, he was able to turn political and governmental affairs over to a series of competent, rather than illustrious successors who had to strive to measure up to the high standards he had set. The PRI worked admirably to bring stability in the place of violence as well as to restrain the political role of the military, but the party would have far less success—in the short run, at least—in adapting to societal changes resulting from the economic development that gained speed during and after World War II. Indeed, Mexico moved steadily toward becoming an urban, industrialized nation within a somewhat suffocating straitjacket of widening political participation, without a viable competitor for the omnipresent government party. (This path stood in sharp contrast to that of Brazil, where the leader stayed at center stage until the mid-1950s, and the armed forces, rather than any of the poorly structured and weakly supported political parties, were the chief national institution.)

By the late 1980s, Mexico had become urban, increasingly industrial, and societally complex. As a result, the PRI was steadily less capable of aggregating the widening range of interests and broadened scope of demands. Co-optative concessions to the opposition tended to encourage the National Action Party (PAN) in the industrial cities of the north, and incompatible ambitions led to a schism in PRI ranks giving rise to a rival party of its left, one with Cárdenas's son as its standard bearer. As a result, the president elected in the mid-1990s opted for a course of democratization, turning the 2000 elections fully competitive and opening the way for an opposition victory. In this respect, the Zedillo administration contributed, in its low-keyed manner, almost as critical an element to Mexican political development as Cárdenas had done with far greater flourish and drama sixty years earlier.

Argentina was a global leader in political development in the period when Brazil was mired in a fraud-ridden elite system and Mexico was knee-deep in fraternal bloodshed. Argentina reached the 1870s having only recently united its swollen urban head with its somewhat stunted interior body. Under these conditions, Roca's centralizing and power-concentrating political system after 1880 did see significant political development, although focused on growth of the federal executive. Young and vigorous, Roca worked with the National Autonomist Party (PAN), essentially a collection of notables who negotiated government policy while ensuring the manipulated—and if need be, fraudulent—election of their candidate. Although four individuals occupied the presidency between the end of Roca's first tem in 1886 and the beginning of his second a dozen years later, he remained the guarantor of this republic by and for the elites in a country awash in a flood of immigrants.

Following the Roca Era, Argentina exploded into its political golden age, one in which it shone on the global scene as a stable and democratic nation when these qualities were scarce even in Europe. Sustained economic development and heavy immigration resulted in a vast increase in urbanizations and growth of industry as well as emergence of politically ambitious middle-class elements. Tory reformer Sáenz Peña followed up the disintegration of the old PAN by pushing through the congress both the secret ballot and nearly universal manhood suffrage. As a result, the long-oppressed radicals came peacefully to power in 1916 and remained there until 1930. Hence, effective incorporation of the middle class into competitive political life was complete at an early date. Unfortunately, the onset of the Great Depression would also spell the demise of this "false dawn" of democracy, just as Brazil and Mexico would begin to move forward with their derailed political development.

Argentina's political development would decay over the next fifteen years before resuming in a limited mode during the decade-long presidency of Perón beginning in 1945. Peronism had as its backbone the urban labor movement, which had gained significance in Argentina before elsewhere in Latin America. A mobilizational type of populist nationalist movement, Peronism survived its leader's ouster in 1955, celebrating his return to power eighteen years later. The corporatist facets of Peronism had withered away in the interim, as the intervening military regime had dismantled its structures. Since the military came back in with a vengeance in 1976, political development was essentially on hiatus from 1955 through 1983. Yet the cumulative effect of stuttering economic development was increased societal complexity.

After their return to power in 1989, Peronist presidents first had to deal with repairing the institutional damage done by the authoritarian regime, then cope with the social changes brought on by Argentina's transformation into an increasingly urban industrial country. Indeed, the successful pursuit of economic development through most of Menem's decade in power increased the institutional gap as it led to the near demise of the Radical Party without anything coming close to replacing it as Peronism's competitor. The result in the political sphere has been a fragmentation of Peronism into rival currents that Kirchner is currently striving to overcome, combined with the absence of a significant rival party.

Colombia's quest for political development has been hindered by absence of any dynamic, transforming leader analogous to Vargas, Cárdenas, or Perón. Rafael Nuñez established the basis of a narrowly based elite republican system during the 1880s. But at the end of the century a bloody civil war turned this into an essentially one-party regime—that of the Conservative Party victors. The 1920s saw significant economic development as oil and bananas came to supplement coffee as major export crops. With opposition to Conservative domination mounting, Liberals took advantage of the ruling party's disarray in 1930 to regain the presidency. Four years later López strove, without adequate congressional support, to deal with social problems in the hostile context of economic distress. Replaced by a very centrist party rival, he came back in 1942 but was hamstrung in trying to reform the political system by an alliance of Conservative foes and Liberal rivals, resigning in 1945 and leaving politics in disarray.

With the charismatic Gaitán's assassination three years later, the way was opened for the worst the Conservative Party could produce to come to power in the aftermath of the most intensive politically motivated slaughter in the region's experience. Only in 1958, under the National Front agreement between the major parties, initially guided by Lleras Camargo, was political development resumed, both aided and hindered by this institutional body cast. The phasing out of the National Front in the late 1970s and early 1980s returned the country to full competition within a democratic framework severely strained by protracted insurgency and insidious drug trafficking. Uribe has broken the sway of the two historically dominant parties.

For its part Peru underwent an authoritarian brand of political development beginning in the final years of the 1800s. Piérola, after an initial term cut short in 1881 by Peru's defeat in the Second War of the Pacific, returned to power in 1895 as a conservative, yet populist, semi-*caudillo*. Although the economy diversified, Lima grew by leaps and bounds, and new economic elites emerged—each tied to a major export and the region from which it came. The first impact on lagging political development was the return to power in 1919 of one-time president Legúia, using a broad reformist coalition of new social sectors to oust the hitherto dominant elite coalition. Resorting to force in the face of electoral fraud, he seized power and held it to 1930, relying on corruption, nepotism, and cronyism rather than building political structures. Under his development-oriented rule, Lima grew an additional two-thirds, and public works were concentrated there— increasing tension between the capital and the interior.

Any minimal foundations for nationalizing the scope of politics laid down by Legúia were squandered by the senseless conflict between the military and the *Apristas* that severely warped political life for a generation, a good part of it spent under military rule. Between 1963 and 1968 Belaúnde Terry was stymied in efforts at substantial reform by lack of legislative support. Ousting him at the tail end of his term to prevent election of their *Aprista* nemesis, the military tried with much drama and little lasting result to carry on modernization with a leftist flavor that included going back to preconquest communitarian roots. Unable to maintain unity, they gave way to civilian rule in 1980, but one after another, some sooner, one later, the military rulers failed to fulfill promises and left office with their parties discredited. Political development found itself stuck in reverse gear, as the Fujimori decade of the 1990s was barren of institution buildings.

Political development for Venezuela would begin belatedly on the foundations of a *caudillo* system installed by Guzmán Blanco in the 1870s and 1880s and perfected by Gómez during his long 1908–1935 reign. During this time the oil boom brought immigration and shifted power away from the Andean ranching region. The dictator's death removed the chief barrier to political development, which, after a hesitant start, gained momentum during the 1945–1948 AD interlude. The following decade of military dictatorship failed to fully uproot the organizations established under Betancourt's leadership. So after a decade of military rule ended in 1958, he and his party returned and were able to incorporate the labor movement and much of the peasantry through effective institutions, despite rapid expansion of the electorate. Substantial as was this surge of political development, it ran out of steam within twenty-five years. Unfortunately, the quality of leadership provided by the "Generation of '28" was not matched in the 1980s and 1990s. Still, the electoral processes survived intact, but millions of new voters left out of the benefits from the development of the 1960s and 1970s turned to Chávez, a much more demagogic and inflammatory as well as less-educated leader.

Dramatically different from Venezuela, Chile began its political development early, essentially having no problem of national unification and consolidation. Portales laid foundations for a viable representative system in the early independence years, and by 1870 modern (for the times even when compared to Britain and the United States) political parties competed for the electorate's favor. With the franchise expanded in the late 1870s, Chile shrugged off the trauma of a brief civil war in 1891 over a presidential attempt to overpower the congress. Its "parliamentary republic," in marked contrast with Peru's "aristocratic republic" at the same time, saw refinement of its political institutions continue until the precipitous drop in earnings from nitrates in the 1920s coincided with heavy urbanization. With the Radical Party's Alessandri elected over conservative opposition in 1920, a new, more presidential constitution was of little help in stemming political decay. The military regime installed in 1927 proved mercifully short-lived, and Alessandri was swept back into office by a 1932 landslide. The heavily middle-class Radicals retained power in 1938 with considerable support from the left, extending their sway in 1942 with a developmentally oriented administration and in 1946 with a coalition extending over to the Socialist and Communist Parties. Certainly Chile merited being viewed as a politically highly developed democracy.

Yet the Cold War's intrusion led to a cynical dumping of the left, which contributed to an antiparty reaction in 1952, bringing the 1927–1930 military president back in as a pseudo-Peronist. Chilean democracy would appear to flourish for two more decades, running up an enviable record of electoral honesty and parliamentary representativeness peaking with the 1964 election of Christian Democrat Frei. Six years later the rules of the democratic game led to an impending disaster as socialist Allende was elevated to the presidency with a thin 1.4 percent margin over the conservative 1958–1964 chief executive in a three-way race. The "Peaceful Road to Socialism" had succeeded in its first step, but Allende would find it impossible to socialize the nation without tampering with the basic rules of the electoral game. When the 1973 congressional elections failed to give his government more than a respectable plurality (on less than 35 percent of the vote), Allende was in a position analogous to that of Balmaceda in 1891, with the aggravating factor of a determined US-backed campaign to destabilize his government. Within five months the congress called for the military to step in, and Chile's vaunted democracy hurtled off the tracks, replaced by the armored streamliner of a repressive military regime. This dramatic and tragic reversal did not spell an end to political development in Chile. As economic growth continued under Pinochet, democratic groups, even long bitter rivals, came together for Pinochet's replacement as they had in 1958 in Colombia and Venezuela, in 1979 in Peru, in 1983 in Argentina, and in Brazil the next year. With Christian Democrats and socialists joining in a National Front type of alliance, the democratic elections forced upon Pinochet at the end of 1989 brought in the first of a new series of reformist civilian presidents who would rebuild Chile's political system into a model for the region. The restored democracy has already outlasted the span of the Pinochet regime and is going strong.

These seven major countries of Latin America, comprising 80 percent of its population, have followed quite distinct paths toward political development. Collectively, despite Peru's continuing problems, they have made very substantial progress in coping with daunting obstacles along the way. Several have had the benefit of outstanding leadership at critical junctures. With few exceptions, the smaller countries have been less fortunate and are less well advanced along the road.

Ecuador, between 1895 and 1911, established elite-dominated republican institutions under Alfaro, a trend cut short by his violent death. Collapse of the cocoa boom in 1925 eroded toleration of the corruption of political processes by his greedy successors, the result being a coup by young officers. The extreme presidential instability of the 1930s ushered in a generation dominated by the antithesis of political development in the person of Velasco Ibarra, a populist demagogue expert at wooing the voters, but incapable of staying the course when in office (after 1934, again beginning in 1944, a 1952–1956 term, a return in 1960, and a final performance from 1969 to 1972). A tough act to follow, at least as a political campaigner, he left a heritage of popular response to demagogic promises and the irrelevance of political parties that persists to the present day, along with a damaging tradition of unceremoniously ousting presidents who fail to satisfy the expectations they had raised in winning election (with no end in sight).

Bolivia has arrived at the same unsatisfactory point as Ecuador, but by a path including a revolution and reformist party analogous to Venezuela's and free of a colorful, dominating figure like Ecuador's. Instead of the lessening regional conflict between the sierra and coastal regions, Bolivia (which has no seacoast) is plagued by increasing tensions between its western highlands and the eastern lowlands, the restless source of most of its limited wealth. Lacking significant political development until its 1952 Revolution, Bolivia briefly attained a degree of democracy embracing the small middle class and the erstwhile labor elite (tin miners) plus indigenous majority, who benefited from the mid-1950s agrarian reform. Paz Estenssoro built the MNR into a cross between Peronism and the PRI, only to see it splinter over the issue of his irreplaceability, which led to a long succession of military governments from the mid-1960s to the early 1980s. Subsequently, encore performances by three aging ex-presidents underscored the failure of new leadership to emerge. With oil and natural gas reserves and production of coca leaf as the country's dynamic economic factors, narrowly based societal modernization took place, chiefly around Santa Cruz in the lowland east, rather than in the densely populated highlands, the highlanders demanding nationalization of the petroleum riches and diversion of the income to their benefit, and lowland business interests preferring secession to loss of control of the wealth of "their" area. No political development can occur under these conditions, and an Indian representative of the coca growers will now try his hand at finding a formula for viability in what some observers have viewed as a "nonviable" country.

Guatemala, the Central American country most similar to Ecuador and Bolivia, followed a course like that of Venezuela—*caudillo* dictators—up through World War II. It then had a revolutionary decade from 1944 to 1954 analogous in important ways to Bolivia's a bit later. The great geopolitical differences and contrasting foreign investment situations of Bolivia and Guatemala led to a US-supported counterrevolution in Guatemala that ushered in three decades of military rule, which all but wiped out the post-1944 foundations for political development. Still wracked by undeclared civil war that victimized chiefly the indigenous population, Guatemala slowly and hesitatingly undertook political development at the end of 1985. A series of competitive elections, a novelty for this largest of the Central American and Caribbean countries, have kept power in the hands of business-oriented interests without effective incorporation of the masses.

Honduras and El Salvador, together almost as populous as their common neighbor, have both experienced limited political development, with much greater trauma for the latter. After World War II, changes were essentially from neo-*caudillo* dictators to rule by the professional military. Honduras made the transition to freely elected civilian presidents in 1981, but El Salvador had to go through a protracted civil war to arrive at that point by 1994. Nicaragua followed a different path, with a family dynasty type of dictatorial regime ending in revolution in 1979. A Marxist-Leninist government held power amid a state of civil war until voted out in early 1990. Unfortunately, the three ensuing civilian governments have proven corrupt and ineffective, and the country remains mired as the subregion's poorest.

Costa Rica, only half as populous as Honduras or El Salvador, has made the greatest headway in political development. After the emergence of quite stable electoral politics, although on a very small scale, by the 1880s Costa Rica continued on this exemplary road until an effort by an unusually ambitious president to perpetuate himself in power through electoral fraud led to a brief civil war in the late 1940s, from which democratic processes emerged strengthened. Figueres's moderately progressive National Liberation Party has won a majority of the long series of highly competitive elections held since that time but has repeatedly accepted defeat at the polls, resolving to try harder the next time. A contrast is Costa Rica's slightly less populous neighbor, Panama, which languished as a US protectorate until General Torrijos established a significant degree of autonomy between 1969 and his sudden death in 1981. Even then, as dramatically shown by the 1989 armed intervention to depose General Noriega, the United States exercised undue influence until after the return of the canal's control to Panama in 2000. Finally some degree of political development may be resumed under the presidency of Torrijos's son now that the US presence has been greatly reduced.

The Dominican Republic's political development experience at first approximated that of Nicaragua. With US sponsorship, the Trujillo family was well on its way to becoming a dynasty when its patriarch was assassinated in 1961. The United States went to great trouble both to prevent a within-the-family succession or continuation of his right-hand man in office. But Balaguer proved a shrewd politician, building a strong party on the foundations of that used by his late mentor, and repeatedly winning election to the presidency, which he held from 1966 to 1978 and from 1986 through 1996. The election of a young, US-educated president that year and his return to office through the 2004 balloting finally opened the way for political development to make belated and hesitant headway, but this is a necessary, not a sufficient, condition.

Unfortunately, the same cannot be said for Haiti. From 1957 through 1986 the Duvaliers, father and son, ran a terroristic sultanic regime in the hemisphere's poorest country, one in which the mass of the population lived in subsistence agriculture or swelled the squalid slums of its two main cities. Ouster of the younger Duvalier led to a short period of brutal, corrupt, and drug-influenced military governments before election of Aristide in late 1990. Overthrown after only eight months, he gave way to renewed military misrule, ended in late 1994 by a US-armed intervention restoring Aristide to office. His 1996–2001 successor never really achieved full control of the government, and Aristide was returned to office. Conditions went from bad to worse, culminating in his ouster in early 2004, with chaos slightly mitigated by foreign peace-keeping forces.

Although one would be hard-pressed to uncover any trace of political development in Haiti, nearby in Cuba a high degree of organization and stability prevails. A US protectorate, first by law, then de facto, until the 1930s, Cuba then came under the control of a Trujillo–Somoza type of military dictator. Batista ceded office to a civilian successor in 1944, but after rampant corruption discredited this stab at formal democracy, he returned to power in 1952. By the end of 1958, armed insurrection led by Castro had caused him to flee the country. Castro ably constructed an effective Marxist-Leninist system with himself firmly ensconced as its unquestioned leader, fine-tuning it after the fall of the Soviet Union (during his thirty-third year in power). The question is whether his hegemonic single-party system will eventually prove amenable to increased competition, like the PRI in Mexico.

Among the smallest countries of South America, one, Uruguay, experienced a path to political development resembling in part that of both Chile and Costa Rica, whereas Paraguay was one of the last to get moving in this regard. José Batlle y Ordóñez constructed a stable welfare state in Uruguay during the first two decades of the twentieth century, but like Chile's democracy, it succumbed to military authoritarianism between 1973 and 1984. As in Chile, this proved to be a painful interlude, which has since overcome by a return to competitive civilian politics. Paraguay's military dictatorship, culmination of a tradition going back to independence, came to its end only in 1989, so political development is still at an early stage, but at least a return to military rule has been avoided, and parties have established roots among the electorate—which is no longer inexperienced.

As to countries, chiefly in the Caribbean, that have attained independence since the 1960s, political development varies from the established parliamentary republic of Trinidad and Tobago down to the extreme tentativeness and fragility of representative processes in Suriname.

Conceptualization

Since the historical examples of the process outlined above took place before the great expansion of political participation and the establishment of elections rather that the use of the armed forces as the ultimate arbiter, their application to contemporary Latin America and its future may be subject to qualification. Yet they may be highly instructive for later-developing regions. In this regard Latin American experience strongly confirms the view that it is the social conditions resulting from economic development, not the latter's level in and of itself, that influence electoral outcomes—with leadership playing a major role in determining how long the apparently inevitable time lag will be.[3] Hence, it is useful to compare the time line of political development with that of political leaders provided in the next chapter.

In answering the question of to what extent does Latin America's political development mesh with experience elsewhere, it is highly informative to view the region in the perspective of the most widely influential effort to build comparative propositions concerning the relationship between societal changes and the course of national political life. Samuel Huntington's ideas on political development as formulated in his 1968 classic *Political Order in Changing Societies* have proven essentially sound in the light of Latin American experience.[4] In Brazil social mobilization—changes in the social order that undercut existing political culture—in the early twentieth century outpaced political institutionalization (which strengthens political structures and processes by giving them complexity, coherence, autonomy, and adaptability). By the late 1920s, this left the country in a clearly praetorian position of inadequate interest-mediating organizations and channels relative to increased pressures for participation. The outcome was regime change through the 1930 Revolution, leading to a system in which Vargas' leadership made the new mix of structures and processes sufficient for a time in terms of adaptability, complexity, and coherence, basic components of political institutionalization, although lacking in the dimension of autonomy.

As the economic development and social change unleashed by Vargas's policies spurred further social mobilization, particularly during World War II and his final term in the early 1950s, the political system was again praetorian by 1964, the result being the establishment of an authoritarian military regime.

Cumulative economic development and modernization under governments pursuing growth gave rise to further social mobilization (through the impact of industrialization, urbanization, increased education, and the spread of mass media). Since political institutionalization lagged badly, the military itself adopted a decision to expand adaptability, autonomy, and coherence to go along with the increased complexity through reestablishing competitive political processes capable of channeling the vastly expanded demands for participation. Thus, despite its continuing social mobilization in the 1980s, Brazil's political system became and has remained civic—indeed, increasingly so. By the 1990s, Brazil came to possess a political infrastructure of mediating structures and participatory processes adequate to the advanced level of mobilization that had been reached in its urban industrial society, although in need of further strengthening. (As president from 1995 through 2002, social scientist Cardoso paid heed to political development needs.)

In Mexico the developmental thrust of the Díaz era led to a surging tide of social mobilization while political institutionalization stood still. Hence, an extremely praetorian situation at the beginning of the twentieth century resulted in a revolution that failed to institutionalize itself politically, bringing on a protracted period of instability whose destructive effects retarded social mobilization. This instability ended in the late 1920s and 1930s through establishment of a hegemonic party that provided a great deal of complexity and sufficient coherence, along with a modicum of adaptability, for several decades before facing the challenges posed by further social mobilization through a growing degree of autonomy in the 1990s. Thus Mexico avoided the praetorianism that plagued most of the region in the 1960s and 1970s and subsequently became an increasingly civic political system before it became democratic, supporting the proposition that political development should move ahead in advance of democratization (as economic growth usually precedes redistribution).

Argentina, although for decades ahead of the game in terms of its absolute level of political institutionalization, had slipped by 1930 into a praetorian situation through the surge of social mobilization unleashed by sustained early-twentieth-century economic growth and societal modernization. Rescued by semidemocratic and mobilizational Peronism in the mid to late 1940s, Argentina slipped back into praetorianism when faltering institutionalization stalled relative to accentuated social mobilization by the mid 1950s. As authoritarian military regimes failed to foster significant political institutionalization, Argentina remained mired in praetorian conditions until the early 1980s, when, much as in Brazil, reestablishment of competitive political life brought with it a flourishing of political institutionalization that caught up with social mobilization—which in the Argentine case slowed sharply as a result of having already reached a very high level.

Huntington's global-universal scheme also helps clarify the course of Colombia's political life. There, political institutionalization closed the gap with relatively slow social mobilization during the 1930s, only to see a marginally civic system derailed in the late 1940s by charismatic populist Gaitán's assassination and the consequent precipitous decline in adaptability and coherence. The resulting descent into a blood-drenched praetorian period was ended by reestablishment of a balance between social mobilization and political institutionalization by means of the innovative National Front system of power sharing established in 1958. Despite the emergence of grave insurgency and drug-trafficking problems, the resurrected civic system has survived in the face of continuing social mobilization, with elections serving as much-needed escape valves for societal tensions. The balance could be described as bare solvency, with little reserve institutionalization against a stormy day. (Uribe is in a position to build on this.)

Peru, Venezuela, and Chile have all followed political development paths congruent with basic elements of Huntington's inductive and empirical theorizing. In particular they bear out his conceptualization of the relationship between reform and revolution, including the former's role in the achievement of "containment" rather than revolution as the outcome of praetorian situations. In Venezuela the loyalty-gaining reforms of post-1958 AD administrations (building on agrarian reform initiatives of the AD's earlier brief stay in power) led to mobilization of the rural masses within a civic political system rather than against it. Hence, even though alienated urban groups attempted to launch armed revolution, they were never able to forge an alliance with significant elements of the rural population. Thus Venezuela remained a civic system for nearly a generation despite continuing social mobilization. Only in the last half of the 1990s did its political institutionalization lose adaptability and decline in coherence. Even then, the country did not move into the praetorian realm, continuing to decide who would hold power through the ballot box even in a highly polarized atmosphere. Indeed, Chávez became president through electoral processes and emerged victorious in a series of frequent tests at the polls, including those in both August and October 2004, and continues to enjoy widespread mass support.

In the case of Chile, reform proved to be more a catalyst of revolution than an alternative to it, for reasons compatible with Huntington's appraisal of this equation, yet even the establishment of a Marxist government came through constitutional processes. There social mobilization was matched by political institutionalization until the economic crisis of the mid to late 1920s, which accelerated the erosion of established political beliefs and values to the point of their breakdown. Still a full-blown praetorian situation was avoided as the Ibáñez regime proved to be transitory, with the country back on the civic path within five years and staying there for another four decades. The systematically reformist Frei government in the last half of the 1960s attempted the strategy, which was working in Venezuela, of undercutting revolutionary tendencies through loyalty-gaining reforms.

Under the different circumstances of Chile—where the miners were the most important segment of the labor movement—there were well-established parties to the left of the Christian Democrats, and a praetorian regime had not recently been ousted as in Venezuela in 1958. Thus, reforms had at least as much a catalytic effect (whetting appetites for more) as an ameliorative one. The civic political order survived in the 1970 elections through elevation of the radical left to power, but as the Allende government's policies accelerated social mobilization that undermined fragile and in some ways brittle institutionalization, upsetting the attenuated civic balance, the country slid rapidly into praetorianism. Instead of having a revolutionary outcome this crisis resulted in a counterrevolutionary military coup. Subsequently, the Pinochet regime failed to keep its restrictive version of political institutionalization ahead of the substantial social mobilization resulting from the societal effects of sustained economic development through which the military hoped to gain legitimacy. The late 1980s return to competitive politics resurrected the institutional pillars of the previous civic system, strengthening them through the broad-based inclusionary Concertacíon and reestablishing a decidedly civic balance.

Peru provides a stiffer test of the limits of Huntington's scheme for conceptualizing the course of political development. Since his propositions are probabilistic, never intended to be determinist, this caveat need not be perplexing or disconcerting—two adjectives that unfortunately too frequently do apply to Peru's troubled political life. To a significantly greater degree than in Colombia, the crux of the problem is that Peruvian nation building is still incomplete owing to both geographic and ethnic factors. In important respects Lima is just the effective capital of the country's heartland, not of the outlying areas. Moreover, the army's generation-long veto of the *Apristas*—extending from the early 1930s into the mid-1980s—by excluding the most broad-based political movement from a central and continuous role in the country's political institutionalization prevented the system from being truly civic. Hence, it was susceptible to military intervention.

Beyond these seven major countries, containing almost four-fifths of Latin Americans, the applicability of Huntington's analytical framework—or any other, for that matter—is limited in many cases by the degree to which political life has been profoundly affected by external factors and actors, particularly the United States. This is certainly true of Cuba, the Dominican Republic, Panama, Nicaragua, and Guatemala, as well as Haiti, in terms of US occupation, direct armed intervention, or organization and orchestration of seizures of power. But Uruguay, Paraguay, and Costa Rica are fundamentally congruent with Huntington's propositions, and Ecuador and Bolivia are partially subject to the same incomplete nation-building restriction as Peru.

Huntington's original analytical scheme was concerned with political development in terms of stability and viability, not with whether political development leads to democracy. But Latin America's experience also underscores the essential validity of views propounded at the end of the 1960s by Dankwart A. Rustow concerning the fact that democratization is a lengthy and generally discontinuous process. He saw its genesis in a "preparatory phase," during which "well-entrenched social forces" engage in a prolonged and inconclusive struggle over fundamental class, ethnic, and religious conflicts.[5] This struggle is likely to be the result of emergence of a new elite "that arouses a depressed and previously leaderless social group into concerted action." The forces and issues involved can vary widely from case to case and even over the course of the transition in a single country. Hence, it is highly desirable that a country face up to its particular conflicts and devise or adopt "effective procedures for their accommodation." Since polarization and intensity are hallmarks of the struggle, progress toward democracy is far from ensured, much less inevitable. Moreover, the minimum period for bringing about democracy is likely to be at least a generation, of which a major proportion is taken up by the preparatory phase.

The shift to the "decision phase" comes when these exhausting and often violent struggles end in stalemate. Then angry and frustrated elites may decide that their interests could be better served by a basic compromise on procedures rather than continuing the conflict. They calculate that it is feasible to employ their bargaining skills to get the better of their rivals in "some crucial aspect" of democratic processes that has been mutually accepted. There are different types of sponsors, content, and motives from case to case, but for all parties the compromise tends to be a second-best outcome, if not a lesser evil. Once agreed to by the contending elites, this generally "distasteful" (or at least reluctant) option for democracy gains acceptance first from professional politicians, then from the politically active citizens, in what Rustow calls the "habituation phase."

Over time this "novel prescription for taking joint chances on the unknown" works to the benefit of the more democratically inclined political actors and their followers. But failure to resolve some urgent early political question may well lead to erosion of this acceptance and even lead to a demise of democracy. Although compromise can usually be found on economic issues and social policy, religious, national, and racial divisions prove more intractable. Rustow sagely points out that each of the major tasks along the slow road toward democracy has its own logic and natural protagonists. Hence, democratization is apt to be a stop-and-go process, at times requiring societal changes to catch up with those in the political realm, or even the emergence of political leaders whose socialization, and thus political culture, differs from that of the preceding phase. What Rustow did not take into account when writing over thirty-five years ago was the possibility that a military seizure of power might derail democracies—an adverse development that became a tidal wave in much of the world, but that fortunately, in a wide array of Latin American countries, only interrupted the habituation phase, necessitating a renewed decision in favor of democracy.

How does Latin America's experience fit with this scheme? Reasonably well at a basic level. In Brazil a very restricted elite-dominated formal democracy existed from 1894 through 1930 on the foundation of the earlier constitutional monarchy. It foundered on the question of full incorporation of the middle class. Following the paternalistically authoritarian Vargas era—a response to sharp political polarization that had led to armed conflict—a reborn electoral democracy survived from 1946 into 1964. Its failure to resolve issues concerning greater participation for the working class triggered two decades of authoritarian military rule. A much more broadly based democratic regime emerged in 1985 and became both institutionalized and stabilized in a renewed process of habituation. Hence, successful democratization was eventually accomplished on the fourth try within a century of a republican framework of government.

For Mexico the road to democratization has also been highly discontinuous, but much more violent. The battle for power that lasted from 1910 to the late 1920s led to formation of a hegemonic governing party rather than real political competition. With significant democratic features implanted under Cárdenas (1934–1940), the party's long string of electoral successes pushed the final decision phase into the late 1990s, with habituation still at an early stage. Mexico stands in marked contrast with Argentina, where in 1912–1914 the basic decision was undertaken to go beyond the constrained elite democracy of the preceding four decades. Sadly, the military's seizure of power in 1930 renewed a prolonged struggle that ended with a decision to reinstall full democracy in 1983. Colombia saw its habituation to democratic processes interrupted in the late 1940s with Laureano Gómez's violent crusade against the Liberals, but within a decade most Conservatives had opted for a return to democratic processes within the conciliating framework of the National Front. Despite elements wedded to violence, habituation to democracy has progressed for the great majority.

Peru poses a phenomenon Rustow failed to foresee: the decision of the armed forces to veto a major political movement for over a half century. Although a decision phase that included the military opened in the late 1970s, habituation has proven difficult, in large part owing to an absence of national unity (Rustow's single precondition) rooted in the limited political incorporation of the very sizable indigenous element of its population. For Venezuela, the preparatory phase lasted until 1958, the ensuing decision phase being relatively short, as habituation began within a decade. Much earlier than any other country in the region, Chile made the decision to adopt some significant democratic procedure back in the 1830s, and habituation ran nearly its full course in another generation. A century later the Pinochet dictatorship constituted a temporary, although traumatic, aberration. Among the smaller countries, the democratization process outlined by Rustow worked with success in Costa Rica and Uruguay and has belatedly gotten under way in Guatemala, El Salvador, Honduras, Panama, the Dominican Republic, and even Nicaragua and Paraguay. For their part, Ecuador and Bolivia suffer from a lack of national unity, and Cuba and Haiti have never progressed out of the preparation phase.

Latin America's recent experience has been, on balance, decidedly positive with respect to formal democracy and its emphasis upon free elections, universal suffrage, and a reasonable degree of administrative accountability to elected authorities as well as freedom of expression and association. The region has also made outstanding progress in broadening participation, along with substantial, if still quite uneven, headway in eliminating systematic differences in participation across class and ethnic lines. With respect to gender, the gap in the more developed of its countries is comparable to that in English-speaking North America and western Europe—with the rate of improvement probably higher. But "deepening" of democracy in terms of reducing social and economic inequalities presents a less rosy picture. A significant school of thought holds that "the structure of the state and state-society relations are critically important to the chances of democracy."[6] The state needs enough strength and autonomy to avoid being an instrument for advancing interests of dominant groups. Instead, it should be responsive to pressures from civil society. This responsiveness, the authors argue, is often lacking as mobilization of subordinate classes declined with the disappearance of obvious threats to the democratic system, and parties generally failed to forcefully and effectively articulate the demands of these social strata. High voter turnout by the masses, although a good thing, often does not result in the translation of their interests into government policies:

> The political space left empty by weak popular organizations and the failure of political parties to establish organizational ties to subordinate classes have been filled by clientelistic networks. These networks link lower class individuals and informed social groups to individual politicians; they serve at best as transmitters of temporary particularistic favors, not as channels to mobilize citizens into influencing policy formation.[7]

These authors single out countries with weak parties: Brazil, Peru, Bolivia, and Ecuador. Clearly the current situations in these countries, as discussed in the preceding chapter, support this contention.

There is also considerable validity to their concerns about presidents coming to power through loose electoral coalitions, rather than being elevated to office by a strong party whose legislative support they require, and often viewing legislatures and courts as obstacles to their exercise of power. This position on the part of chief executives undermines the congress and the judiciary as levers for affecting policy and renders the public pressuring the party they voted for generally ineffective. Yet, as has been shown, there are many countries in which the legislative branch is a meaningful part of the policymaking process and parties are as effective as they are in a number of Europe's older democracies. Indeed, in Brazil, Mexico, Argentina, and Colombia the present chief executives do need to treat their national legislatures as "legitimate partners in Government" (as these authors entreat), whereas in Ecuador the congress has demonstrated a penchant for removing highhanded presidents from office.

Moving to the question of just how the past affects the present, I would argue that all cases bear out the contention of Scott Mainwaring and Arturo Valenzuela, two leading figures in the contemporary study of Latin American politics, that an approach stressing "path dependency" helps bridge the gap between structural dependency because of its emphasis upon the past as determining the future and its antithesis of "replacement," which holds that the present essentially negates or at least neutralizes the past. In this view, structural, institutional, and cultural constraints impose broad limits or shape the general nature of outcomes that are then determined by contingent choices that impact upon political, economic, and social trajectories.[8] I would add that legacies of the past not only linger, but sometimes even resurge.

Conditioning Factors

With respect to Latin America of the early twenty-first century, as social scientists we must concentrate on what explains the great differences in degree of ability to obtain and maintain democratic processes among the region's countries. As individuals deeply concerned with Latin America's future, we must ask whether there is anything about the recent decades of sustained headway toward democratic political development that justifies optimism that this time the pendulum might not swing back as was the case in the early 1960s as well as in the late 1940s. The chief factor linking societal transformations to political change appears to be the great expansion of political participation, which engenders and spreads a sense of political efficacy, a feeling of some small share of responsibility in the results obtained by popularly elected governments, and a stake in their survival. Although during the post–World War II populist era in many countries governments were chosen by electorates greatly expanded over any previous democratic interlude, voters were still a distinct minority of the population.

The vast expansion of the electorate in recent decades in the great majority of Latin American countries is of the greatest significance with respect to democratic political development. The challenge of broadened participation has been both critical and difficult in all countries that have eventually succeeded in developing into stable democracies—witness the travails of even Britain, the United States, France, and Germany. In this realm, compared to earlier global experience Latin America has done very well in greatly increasing the number and proportion of voters without seriously destabilizing the fundamental institutions of its political systems. Brazil and Mexico provide dramatic cases. Brazil's registered electorate of over 125 million now includes two-thirds of its population, an elevenfold increase compared to only 11.5 million eligible voters in 1950, when Vargas was swept back into power, and more than double the 58.6 million registered as late as 1982. Mexicans with a voice in choosing their governmental officeholders have increased exponentially since 1952, the last balloting before women could vote, and now exceed 70 million.

Numbers and proportions do not tell the whole story. Racial and ethnic factors also play a significant role in the integration of societal sectors into national political life. For first the middle sectors and then the urban working class incorporation into politics was most easily—hence, in most cases, first—accomplished in those few countries, like Argentina, where no significant racial or ethnic factor was involved. There, as in neighboring Uruguay and, to a more limited extent, Chile, those knocking on the door for admittance into the political arena were essentially European, as were the elites that were being asked to accommodate to their inclusion in what had hitherto been a quite restricted club. This adjustment was eased by the fact that the broadened membership would as a practical matter remain stratified on the basis of social status, since the elites possessed formidable political assets beyond their mere individual votes.

In the case of Brazil, broadening of political access to include recent immigrants moved ahead much faster and farther than it did with respect to Afro-Brazilians, color proving to be a far greater deterrent than just socioeconomic factors. Hence, the factory workers who benefited under Vargas in the 1930s and 1940s were overwhelmingly white, as, for that matter, were the workers appealed to by Goulart in the early 1960s or even the cadres of the contemporary Workers' Party (which, as one of its recently disaffected founders laments, remains more a party of unions than of workers).[9] In Mexico the relative continued political marginalization of the rural proletariat is far from unrelated to its high proportion of Indians, and meaningful participation of many rural sectors is facilitated by their identification as essentially *mestizo*. Elements feeling left out have found a home in the Party of the Democratic Revolution (PRD), which has the support of at least a third of the Mexican electorate—twice the proportion of Workers' Party (PT) votes in Brazil. In Argentina all significant elements of society have been incorporated into national life through Peronism. In Colombia such groupings long ago channeled their frustrations and alienation into insurgency, and in Venezuela they have become the backbone of Chávez's support.

The Andean countries have begun to incorporate their indigenous populations into national political life—generally with at least short-term destabilizing effects. In Bolivia this matter is complicated by the issue of coca cultivation, but it is also limited by the post-1952 political inclusion of many of the highland Indians.[10] In Ecuador the politicization of the Indians merges with ecological movements directed against the oil companies. As a practical political matter in the majority of countries, the growing numbers of individuals with minority racial or ethnic heritages residing in urban centers are significantly less excluded from the political process than those living in distant rural areas, and there is a continuing flow of the latter toward the cities. Some governments have attempted to make life in small cities less unbearable, but in the absence of greater responsiveness to concerns on the periphery, as well as needs as viewed from the center, the stream of people to urban centers will continue.

It is in the happy combination of increasingly urban and modern societies, vastly broadened political participation, a more favorable international environment, and a growing capacity to learn from past experience that optimism concerning Latin America's political future is rooted. This situation is fairly general throughout this far-flung and diverse region, but its core is the South American continent, particularly giant Brazil and its Southern Cone neighbors of Argentina, Chile, and Uruguay. Yet only two decades ago these same countries constituted the backbone of authoritarian militarism in the hemisphere. Hence, it appears that the foundations for a democratic order are cumulative, perhaps even sedimentary. At least, this is a proposition meriting examination in the years ahead.

From the perspective of the end of 2005, the long-term political future of South America appears quite promising, especially in the southern and eastern areas. Anchored by Brazil, Argentina, Chile, and Uruguay, a substantial degree of essentially democratic stability has a good chance of extending itself over time into the Andean region, with large and troubled Peru constituting the most critical element. (In many ways it, along with its smaller Andean neighbors, Ecuador and Bolivia, seems to have the greatest similarities to the conditions of Iraq and Afghanistan.) Venezuela needs its talented middle classes to recapture some of the determination shown by an earlier generation in the 1958–1983 period, an enterprise requiring, as does Peru's challenge, effective leadership. Colombia's next administrations must confront the dual challenge of curbing the insidious influence of narcopolitics and bringing an end to the endemic problem of violence and insurgency—or at least containing it in enclaves away from population centers. Hemmed in by these larger countries, and in some ways subject to their influence, Ecuador, Bolivia, and Paraguay will either cope with their problems or present limited and containable threats to the political health of the continent.

A sound and stable South America, which contains two-thirds of the region's population, would be little affected by problems that might exist in Central America and the Caribbean—subregions of small and geographically remote to isolated countries. Fortunately, Central America is in by far the best political shape in its often quite troubled history. Moreover, from a South American perspective both Central America and the island republics are essentially the concern and responsibility of Mexico and, ultimately, the United States. As Mexico—which vastly outweighs all of Central America and the Caribbean taken together—has recently added democracy to its vaunted stability, the picture in this regard is more positive than at any previous juncture.

Incorporating major new groups into national political life is almost always a confrontational and conflict-generating process that places great strains upon a political system, often destabilizing it. This has certainly been the pervasive experience of Latin American countries. But although much remains to be done, as previously discussed, the crucial uphill portion of this Herculean task has been accomplished in much of the region and is moving forward in most of the rest. Experience shows that once this bringing of an excluded element of the population into effective political participation has been substantially completed, not only is a major source of tensions and dissension removed, but the broadened popular base also helps further stabilize the political system. Emergence of greater procedural consensus—agreement on the rules of the governmental game—allows intense competition of distributive issues without placing the underlying stability of structures and processes in serious jeopardy. Once the executive branch's attention can focus upon effectively brokering rival claims to policy benefits rather than be diverted to, if not preoccupied by, the calculus of survival, its prospects for satisfactory performance are greatly enhanced.

If Latin American countries on the whole have made impressive progress with regard to the challenges of participation and incorporation, has this progress been matched in the area of distribution and social justice? Although the answer is a qualified no, the historical sequence in older democratic parts of the world generally involved a significant time lag, for it is largely only through effective political participation that underdog groups gain a more equitable share of socioeconomic goods and benefits. Hence, the most relevant question is whether there is strong evidence of this scenario at least beginning to occur in Latin America. Since Brazil is the region's economic engine and largest society, with one of the world's most skewed income distributions, significant movement there would have a heavy impact upon the regional equation. Although Mexico could—and should—do more than it has in this regard (and would likely do so under a PRD government), the region's number two country is not such an extreme case and has more of a foundation to build upon. Whether either of the giants will give priority to reducing inequalities depends heavily upon how emphatically their electorates call for this remedy in their critical 2006 elections.

Analogous to incorporation of new groups already discussed, there are certain socioeconomic problems profoundly impacting on politics that must be dealt with along the course of political development. Painful as it may be to bite the bullet on some of those that are never easy and universally involve confrontation if not open conflict, once successfully disposed of, these challenges are removed from the agenda of tests still to be encountered and met. For countries that have avoided the issue or bought time with palliative measures, agrarian reform is the most pressing. In the long run its emergence into the active political arena is not only necessary, but also salutary, even if temporarily destabilizing. Agrarian reform in its broadest sense of alterations in land tenure patterns sufficient to provide land and employment to a sizable portion of the marginalized rural masses is often the most difficult, intractable, and violence-generating of the distributive-participatory tasks faced on the road to construction of a socially just and inclusive polity. Since the interests adversely affected are most often well entrenched in the country's existing power structure—much as slaveholders were in the past—decisive action is often postponed until tensions in some area have escalated into widespread violence. Understandable as such procrastination may be, its continuation in the face of clear symptoms of growing unrest is politically shortsighted. Once again, at present it is hulking Brazil that faces the greatest need to move farther and faster in this field, one in which Mexico took decisive action beginning in 1934, though it needs to create a new generation of beneficiaries.

Where the Region Stands

As Latin America moves to the end of the first decade of the new millennium, many of the democratic gains from the 1980s and 1990s have been consolidated. Brazil has been free from military tutelage for over two decades, and Mexico has escaped from the constraints of the long PRI power monopoly and become a highly competitive electoral democracy. These positive trends have opened opportunity for further democratic political development but do not guarantee that it will occur. Argentines, having come out of one of their most troubled political crossings, may finally be liberated from the unrealistic belief that they will triumph over any adversity, if not be immune to many of the region's woes, because, after all, they were a displaced corner of Europe, not really Latin American (which to many Argentines means having a mixed population). Colombia has developed a significant, although not entirely laudable, capability for coexisting with intractable insurgency and at the same time being unable to do more than contain, not necessarily curb, much less eliminate, it. At best this country has become a political diabetic, able to reduce the most threatening symptoms and avert a fatal outcome at the expense of a highly constrained political lifestyle. Perhaps some Colombians take too much consolation from the fact that continuing violence, which pervades most aspects of urban life, is far below the levels of the Thousand Days' War (over a century ago) or *La Violencia* of 1948–1953. As elsewhere, in Latin American countries' complacency may be psychologically comforting, but impatience is more likely to spur reforms and progress.

So, although the panorama is essentially favorable, especially if compared to any previous time, there are still dark clouds on the horizon. In a few cases old crises have remerged or new challenges come to the fore to undermine democratic stability, if not to place it in serious jeopardy. The geographic area of greatest weakness extends around South America's upper and central Andean regions from Venezuela down to Peru, although the most troubling single case in recent years has been that of urban European Argentina, where the 2002 replacement of its democratically elected president by the man he had defeated in 1999 only temporarily eased the acuteness of a political crisis rooted in what was perhaps the deepest and most rapid economic deterioration any Latin American country has experienced—exceeding even those set off by the onset of the Great Depression. But showing praiseworthy resilience, Argentina began to climb out of the crisis by carrying off the election of a new president in 2003 smoothly and in accordance with constitutional rules—and has stabilized since. Andean unease has distracted attention from substantial progress in Central America—the area of greatest instability and violence in the 1980s—in narrowing its political development gap with respect to its southern neighbors, as well as a general steadiness in the Caribbean—both the old and the new states—marred by the contemporary Haitian crisis. In that subregion stability has allowed observers the luxury of focusing on Fidel Castro's eventual demise, not because of any acute crisis in Cuba, but because of actuarial odds—as was the case with Franco in Spain three decades ago—since Castro has moved well into his late seventies.

In a global situation dominated by the US-led "war on terrorism," with its focus on the Middle East and Asia, the centrality of the Brazilian third of the region to other Latin American countries continues to grow. There, the eight years of unaccustomed stability under distinguished social scientist Fernando Henrique Cardoso was pushed back into history by the election in 2002 of his, on paper at least, polar opposite, Lula da Silva. Continued progress in Brazil would not guarantee forward movement for the South American continent, of which it is nearly half, much less for the rest of Latin America. But backsliding or decay there would hamstring advances and negate even significant gains in countries of lesser weight, as well as have a heavy negative impact on regional averages. Other than the situation of the United States in North America, no country on earth is as dominant in its region as is Brazil in South America. Both Europe and Asia have multiple leading countries, while Africa, in the same sense of the word, has none. Similarly, in the northern portion of Latin America Mexico dwarfs all other countries combined.

Democracy: The Only Game in Town?

Political development in Latin America has unquestionably taken enormous strides over the past century; it has leapt forward during the past fifty years, and has made very significant, even dramatic, progress during the most recent quarter century. Even over the short span of the last decade, headway toward stable representative political systems with a substantial degree of institutionalization and a broad base of participation has been made, often against adverse headwinds. In progressing toward consolidation of democratic processes the most important threshold to be crossed is that of recognition by all significant power contenders that democracy has become the "only game in town" with elections—not military coups or revolutions—deciding who will control the machinery of government. Such a near-universal commitment to the ballot box as the fundamental arbiter of who will hold government office is difficult to attain. Once reached and consolidated, this kind of electoral democracy generally remains viable unless resulting governments fail woefully in their responsibility to manage the economy with some degree of competence.

The realization that the electoral process has become definitive—rendering other, sometimes deeply rooted, ways of gaining power obsolete—is arrived at only through a protracted process and is both painful and only reluctantly accepted by elements on both the right and the left. These polarized and intransigent actors cling tenaciously to their favored practice of winning through force rather than persuasion.[11] At long last, democratic electoral politics has become the only game in town in the vast majority of the region's countries, where only twenty-five years ago competitive elections were rarely held, and if they did take place, their results were often brushed aside by authoritarian military regimes. This favorable development, in almost all cases following on the heels of authoritarian military regimes, has come about through a variety of paths.

Munck and Leff stress that modes of transition shape the ensuing regime and course of politics by affecting "the pattern of elite competition, institutional rules crafted during the period of transition, and disposition of key actors to accept or reject the new rules of the game."[12] These authors' scheme of transition modes is based on the identity of the actors impelling change and the strategies they employ. The former ranges from the incumbent elite through a combination of incumbent and counterelites, to counterelites alone. Strategies run from accommodation through its combination with confrontation, to essentially confrontational. In the resulting matrix, reform from below, transaction, extrication, and rupture are possible modes for transition (as are conservative reform, social revolution, and revolution from above).

Chile, where the impetus came from the opposition following an accommodationist strategy, illustrates reform from below, resulting in fairly balanced elite competition. In contrast, Argentina, with moderate elements of both the regime and the opposition as agents of change, using a strategy involving more confrontation than accommodation, but having the opponents of military rule playing the major role, illustrates reform through rupture. There the lack of opposition to democratization led to an early breakup of the antiauthoritarian alliance, as both the Radicals and the Peronists strove to become hegemonic, unlike the Christian Democrats and Socialists, who remained allied in Chile. In this scheme, Brazil, with a similar mix of actors, who used much more accommodation than confrontation, exemplifies reform through transaction. This reform resulted in a very complex transition process, in which a plethora of political parties competed, with lines blurred between ex-regime and former opposition elements—and the eventual alignments still being worked out.

As Colombia and Venezuela had their transitions from authoritarian military regimes in the late 1950s, they do not easily fit a conceptualization based essentially on 1980s developments. Both would seem to come fairly close to reform from below, followed by competition between two parties operating within a framework of cooperation roughly analogous to Chile's Concertacíon. This scheme is not fully appropriate for Mexico, which did not have an authoritarian military regime, but it could be said that the impetus for change came chiefly from the opposition, abetted by reformist elements within the governing party. However, this transition was a process of infusing formally democratic institutions, already in place, with truly competitive content. For its part, Peru falls somewhere between the reform through transaction and extrication modes, being somewhat more confrontational in the strategy of opposition elements, but still more accommodationist than not, and with regime moderates being the most significant actors.

The region's essentially democratic conditions can and should, in both the empirical and normative senses of that word, be maintained if the social and economic benefits of political participation, through effective leverage on distribution, are extended to the previously excluded sectors of society. The grave difficulties democracy has encountered in Venezuela, for example, stem from distribution of public goods remaining skewed toward the social elements brought into meaningful political participation by Democratic Action or COPEI in the late 1950s and 1960s. The same opportunities for a better level of living were not effectively extended to an expanding urban underclass that remained essentially invisible to the middle class and organized skilled workers who, after getting theirs were not anxious to share the wealth. As a result they ended up with Chávez as president and running the risk of a more adverse redistribution. Since it is not clear what Venezuelans have learned from this experience, the expectation that it will be a wakeup call to middle sectors and skilled workers in other countries is unjustified. Hopefully, socially responsible leadership in countries with emerging social groups are in most cases sufficiently intelligent to realize the danger of letting groups achieve a degree of political power without being willing to see them use it for their economic improvement.

None of these considerations diminishes the importance of the fact that far greater numbers of Latin Americans than ever before believe that elections are the normal and proper way to decide who will exercise governmental authority. This belief greatly reinforces the complementary view that constitutional governmental processes are a meaningful and effective way to decide public policies. If at the root this is still perceived as involving a large element of who gets what at the expense of whom, there is a lessening tendency to view this as a rigid zero-sum game in which anyone's gains translate almost mechanically into someone else's losses.

Violence and Militarism

Although violence is still far from absent in Latin American politics, it has greatly decreased over time. As clearly shown in this study, the early decades of national existence were marked by violence and conflict, with force usually deciding who would hold power. However, the longest and bloodiest periods of resort to force came one, two, or even three generations after independence. Starting with the Thousand Days' War in Colombia at the very end of the nineteenth century, massive and protracted civil strife moved to Mexico in the second and third decades of the twentieth century before exploding in Colombia in 1948 and continuing in a chronic rather than acute stage down to the present.[13] At the beginning of the 1990s, civil war still devastated Nicaragua and El Salvador, and Guatemala had witnessed equally intense violence and counterviolence raging for two decades, away from the world's attention because it occurred in peripheral rural areas, victimized chiefly indigenous populations, and lacked Cold War or drug-trafficking implications. Terrorism still ran rampant in Peru, and violence was at times volcanic in Colombia.

In the late 1990s, violence increased in the region's two largest countries as armed struggles over land in the vast interior of Brazil accelerated, and the Zapatista rebels in southern Mexico, involving more theatrical posturing than actual violence, compensated for peace achieved in the Central American and Peruvian cases, temporarily satisfying the media's appetite for blood (until this was sated by gorier developments in other parts of the world). Lost from sight was the calming influence of the refusal of the Cardoso and Zedillo administrations to overreact, and their use of these two countries' federalism to decentralize the issue. In all the region, Mexico deserves high marks for overcoming a heritage of intense conflict beginning with its conquest and extending through a bloody independence struggle, war against a foreign-imposed monarch in the 1860s, and two decades of revolution and civil war after 1910.

In the opening years of the twenty-first century, large-scale organized insurgencies have become relatively rare. Moreover, compared to southeast Europe, much less Africa and Asia, organized armed violence is isolated and sporadic. Indeed, although all loss of life is to be deplored, that attributable to politics in Latin America has become minimal compared to the bloodbaths in central Africa, the countries of its eastern "Horn," along the southern fringe of the former USSR, and into Southeast Asia by way of Sri Lanka and outlying parts of Indonesia. Indeed, for Latin America crime-related urban violence has become a much more serious problem, one calling for attention to social problems, not military repression.

The dramatic shift from the "normality" of military rule as late as the 1970s and early 1980s to its complete disappearance in little more than a decade does not guarantee that this historical and deep-seated phenomenon has been effectively banished, never to rear its ugly head again. Military intervention in politics has always been a function of inclination and opportunity, conditioned by tradition. The adequate performance of civilian governments in the 1990s and early 2000s has greatly diminished opportunities, and relatively long periods of civilian governments help weaken a "savior of the nation" tradition important for legitimizing coups. Much less can be said with certainty concerning inclinations, for armed forces are hierarchical institutions in which there is a substantial time lag between initial socialization and arrival at a level giving an officer some weight in decisionmaking.

Permanent and adequately institutionalized civilian supremacy over the military is still far from established in a number of Latin American countries. Mexico in the 1930s and early 1940s shows that the less individuals select a military career with political ambitions in mind, the lower is the collective inclination to seek opportunity or pretext to intervene. Yet Mexico's success in taming militarism was greatly facilitated by the fact that the professionalized officer corps was decimated, if not destroyed, in the 1911–1928 fighting. Moreover, the elimination of intraparty competition through establishment of the hegemonic PRI all but eliminated the opportunity factor. Indeed, Mexico's uniqueness for a long generation was a hegemonic party dominated for six years at a time by an extremely powerful president, who then ceded leadership to a successor essentially of his choice. In this manner order and stability prevailed under civilian rule from the 1930s through the 1990s.[14] As this time span included at least two protracted periods of military interventions and authoritarian regimes for most of the rest of Latin America, it was no mean accomplishment, although in some ways a cross between a political body cast and a societal straightjacket. For ingrained negative behavior combined with facilitating institutional arrangements often proves impervious to mild political medication.

It is still to be seen whether changes in recruitment and socialization are sufficient to engender and maintain a sea change in such a deeply rooted tradition. Most critical in this respect is the fact that the choice to follow a military career is most often made by an individual's midteen years. Hence, if this option is influenced by a belief that becoming an officer is a promising road to high political office, or at least major influence as an arbiter of politics, the effect may be felt as much as four decades to a half century down the road—the point where top military rank is finally attained. Thus, the virus of militarism may lay dormant for many years, or even decades, after civilians come to occupy the presidency. After all that time, the military may still harbor ambitious men whose eyes have long been fixed on political power. A quarter century of civilian rule went down the drain in Argentina in 1930, and prior to 1973, Chile had experienced over four decades of civilian rule broken only by the fully constitutional election of a long-retired former military executive in 1952.

Despite this caution, the prospects for rampant military interventionism in the region as a whole are at an all-time low.[15] Mexico has enjoyed civilian supremacy for a generation and a half; Colombia since 1957. Brazil's armed forces have adjusted well to near abandonment of the once-treasured "moderating-power" role. In Argentina the military as an institution still bears deep scars from its dismal performance as the nation's self-appointed savior in 1976–1983. This sobering experience is reinforced by the officer corps' perception that none of the military governments of 1955–1973 came close to performing well. In the special case of Chile, statesmanlike behavior on the part of the democratic politicians carried the country through the potentially dangerous period when ex-authoritarian strongman Pinochet still held command of the army. This was roughly paralleled in Nicaragua, where former Sandinista president Ortega's brother controlled the armed forces under the government whose election had ousted his party from office. These exceptional results took place in the aftermath of protracted political trauma and were greatly facilitated by a strong desire to avoid any situation that might provide an opportunity for resurgent militarism.

A few places, including Peru and, under worsening conditions, Bolivia and Ecuador, are going through political crises that, if prolonged, could lead to military preoccupation outweighing negative memories of experience as rulers of their country. However, for Latin America as a whole, including even these danger spots, the point has finally been reached at which teenagers selecting a career have not witnessed recent examples of military officers achieving national political power.

Where do external factors come in? Although many of the military coups in the 1960s and 1970s deeply rooted in the Cold War era enjoyed the backing of foreign powers, especially the United States, the situation has changed drastically. Indeed, in light of the leading role of external forces in fostering democratization in recent years, it is imperative to review what role they have played in the political development of Latin America. Although differing significantly in distinct time periods, in no instance has democratization been accomplished through foreign occupation (as in the cases of Japan and Germany after World War II). In the nineteenth century both US armed intervention and the more sustained French occupation in Mexico were clearly detrimental to political development, and they had a distinctly antidemocratic impact. The US military government of Cuba at the turn of the century and the direct, armed interventions of the Wilsonian era in Haiti, the Dominican Republic, and Nicaragua also resulted in militarized dictatorships. Moreover, the intense tutelage exercised over Panama by the United States led in the post–World War II period to military domination of its governments. To be sure, the understanding of the processes of political development prevailing at those times provided no useful guidance as to how democracy might be encouraged.

At the present time, interference in the internal affairs of other countries has to be justified as being aimed at supporting democracy and can remove only antidemocratic governments with highly negative records on human rights. Thus the present intervention in Haiti by the United States and its allies claims an entirely different rationale than the 1965 "anticommunist" intervention in the Dominican Republic. Ambitious military figures cannot expect support for efforts to seize power. Indeed, they are aware that collective sanctions are a very likely consequence for their resulting "illegitimate" governments.

Notes

1. Recent scholarship on the region as a whole includes a number of books providing insight and provoking thought. Among them are Peter H. Smith, *Democracy in Latin America: Political Change in Comparative Perspective* (New York: Oxford University Press, 2005); Manuel Antonio Garreton, Peter Cleaves, Marcelo Cavarozzi, Jonathan Hartlyn, and Gary Gereffi, *Latin America in the Twenty-first Century: Toward a New Sociopolitical Matrix* (Boulder, CO: Lynne Rienner, 2002); Mark Falcoff, *A Culture of Its Own: Taking Latin America Seriously* (New Brunswick, NJ: Transaction Books, 1998); Forrest D. Colburn, *Latin America at the End of Politics* (Princeton: Princeton University Press, 2002); Jose Nun, *Democracy: Government of the People or Government of the Politicians?* (Lanham, MD: Rowman & Littlefield, 2003); Manuel Antonio Garreton M. and Edward Newman, eds., *(Re)Constructing Democracy in Latin America* (New York: United Nations University Press, 2001); and Ronaldo Munck, *Contemporary Latin America* (New York: Palgrave/Macmillan, 2003).

2. Howard J. Wiarda, *Dilemmas of Democracy in Latin America: Crises and Opportunity* (Lanham, MD: Rowman & Littlefield, 2005), p. 230. For background consult Howard J. Wiarda and Margaret MacLeish Mott, eds., *Politics and Social Change in Latin America: Still a Distinct Tradition?*, 4th ed. (Westport, CT: Praeger, 2003). A thought-provoking analysis by a Latin American thinker is Alvaro Vargas Llosa, *Liberty for Latin America: How to Undo Five Hundred Years of Oppression* (New York: Farrar, Straus, & Giroux, 2005).

3. A contradictory literature has finally shaken down to a generalized agreement that rather than a relationship between high levels of economic development or rates of economic growth and democratization, economic factors impact upon the political realm largely through their societal effects. Stimulating works enriching this debate include Patrice Franko, *The Puzzle of Latin American Economic Development*, 2nd ed. (Lanham, MD: Rowman & Littlefield, 2003), and Charles H. Wood and Bryan R. Roberts, eds., *Rethinking Development in Latin America* (University Station: Pennsylvania State University Press, 2005), as well as Evelyne Huber, ed., *Models of Capitalism: Lessons for Latin America* (University Station: Pennsylvania State University Press, 2002). On further conceptualization see Peter H.

Smith, ed., *Latin America in Comparative Perspective: New Approaches to Methods and Analysis* (Boulder, CO: Westview Press, 1995).

4. Samuel P. Huntington, *Political Order in Changing Societies* (New Haven: Yale University Press, 1968).

5. See Dankwart A. Rustow, "Transitions to Democracy: Toward a Dynamic Model," *Comparative Politics*, 2:2 (April 1970), pp. 337–363, reprinted in Lisa Anderson, ed., *Transitions to Democracy* (New York: Columbia University Press, 1999), pp. 14–41.

6. Evelyne Huber, Dietrich Rueschemeyer, and John D. Stephens, "The Paradoxes of Contemporary Democracy: Formal, Participatory, and Social Dimensions" in Anderson, ed., *Transitions, p.* 171. For a perceptive view of possible tensions between democracy and liberty, see Fareed Zakaria, *The Future of Freedom: Illiberal Democracy at Home and Abroad* (New York: Norton, 2003).

7. Huber, Rueschemeyer, and Stephens, "Paradoxes," p. 181.

8. Scott Mainwaring and Arturo Valenzuela, eds., *Politics, Society, and Democracy: Latin America* (Boulder, CO: Westview Press, 1998), p. 105.

9. Cristovam Buarque speaking at the Bildner Center for Hemispheric Affairs of the City University of New York Graduate Center, November 2005.

10. On the political incorporation of native populations consult Kay B. Warren and Jean Jackson, eds., *Indigenous Movements, Self-Representation, and the State in Latin America* (Austin: University of Texas Press, 2002), and Donna Lee Van Cott, ed., *Indigenous Peoples and Democracy in Latin America* (New York: St. Martin's Press, 1994).

11. See Juan J. Linz and Alfred Stepan, *Problems of Democratic Transition and Consolidation: Southern Europe, South America, and Post-Communist Europe* (Baltimore: Johns Hopkins University Press, 1996), particularly pp. 5–6.

12. Gerardo L. Munck and Carol Skolnik Leff, "Modes of Transition to Democratization: South America and Eastern Europe in Comparative Perspective" in Anderson, ed., *Transitions,* pp. 193–194.

13. Consult Miguel Angel Centeno, *Blood and Debt: War and the Nation-State in Latin America* (University Station: Pennsylvania State University Press, 2002), and David R. Mares, *Violent Peace: Militarized Interstate Bargaining in Latin America* (New York: Columbia University Press, 2001).

14. Roderic A. Camp, *Mexico's Military on the Democratic Stage* (Northport, CT: Praeger, 2005).

15. See J. Samuel Fitch, *The Armed Forces and Democracy in Latin America* (Baltimore: Johns Hopkins University Press, 1998); Richard L. Millett and Michael Gold-Biss, eds., *Beyond Praetorianism: The Latin American Military in Transition* (Boulder, CO: Lynne Rienner, 1996); Kirk S. Bowman, *Militarization, Democracy, and Development: The Perils of Praetorianism in Latin America* (University Station: Pennsylvania State University Press, 2002); Brian Loveman, *Por la Patria: Politics and the Armed Forces in Latin America* (Wilmington, DE: Scholarly Resources Books, 1999); and Craig L. Arceneaux, *Bounded Missions: Military Regimes and Democratization in the Southern Cone and Brazil* (University Station: Pennsylvania State University Press, 2001).

15

Conclusions and a Look into the Future

Political development is a long-term and almost never a straight-line process. It was only in the mid-1960s that Latin America was entering a period when authoritarian military regimes would be all but universal, a situation that prevailed for nearly two decades. Only forty years farther back, shortly before Castro's birth, governments were almost without exception the result of elite-dominated successions resulting from fraudulent elections if not naked seizures of power. The few exceptions were destined to succumb to the political fallout of the world economic crisis unleashed in 1929–1930. Indeed, at that time, when World War I had given way to the optimistic 1920s in the developed world epitomized by western Europe and the United States, Brazil was caught up in a series of military uprisings that would culminate in its 1930 Revolution. Mexico was still immersed in the long bloody civil war that its 1910 Revolution had substituted for a repressive dictatorship. Colombia was a one-party oligarchic regime resulting from the fratricidal slaughter of its Thousand Days' War at the turn into the twentieth century. Although Argentina was enjoying a heady dose of democracy, this house of cards would come tumbling down with the dawn of a new decade in 1930. Chile was on the brink of trading constitutional civilian rule for a military dictator, and Venezuela had long been under an autocrat who had an equally long tenure still before him. Cuba suffered under dictatorship slightly mitigated by US power and propensity to intervene. Only Uruguay and Costa Rica among the region's many smaller countries had any substantial degree of democracy and respect for the rights of their citizens.

As already shown, change in the region since that time has been more profound and substantial than it was in Europe during any equivalent time span. Yet, documenting how much more politically developed and broadly participant Latin

America is today compared to forty, eighty, or a hundred years ago is, in and of itself, only part of the story. What is truly important is an understanding of why and how this progress came about as well as an appreciation of the challenges and obstacles to its continuation.

Beyond the changes in political structures and processes already examined, the past most pervasively influences the present through the political socialization all persons undergo, particularly in their early years. Everyone is subject to particularly intense impact from traumatic events such as wars or protracted economic crises. Fortunately, in this respect most of Latin America's countries are to one degree or another distancing themselves from past national traumas. Only those few persons well into their seventies have even fading childhood memories of the Great Depression of the 1930s, and World War II is still a vivid memory only for the limited segment of the population turning the corner from their sixties into the seventies. With democratization dating back to the late 1970s or early 1980s for most of the region, traumatic memories of the military regimes prevalent in the 1960s and 1970s are essentially the province of individuals at least in their midforties, and in some countries already in their fifties. The middle-aged individuals holding a high proportion of the region's political offices had their prime socializing experiences during the late 1940s and the more populist 1950s.

Until 2010, this fading of the fairly recent past (in terms of processes, personalities, and events) will be accentuated, with tens of millions of individuals born after 1980 already politically active and those born after 1990 entering the political arena in significant numbers. Electoral democracy is fast being taken for granted by an increasing proportion of the population, remaining a novelty perhaps only in Mexico, and still largely unknown in Haiti and experienced in a restricted manner in Cuba. Indeed, in recent years Cuba's exceptionalism has become more of a curiosity in the region than a concern, much less the preoccupation it once was. The Cuban Revolution as a feasible model for emulation remains in the hearts of some, but the minds of far fewer. There is reason to be interested in what may transpire after Castro but little cause to believe it will have a significant impact on other countries. Indeed, its ripple effect will be felt more in Florida than even in other parts of the Caribbean, much less mainland Latin America.

Leadership: Essential Element or Desirable Catalyst?

One of the most serious lacks in contemporary Latin America is leadership. A critical factor in mobilizing developmental advances in any part of the world, leadership has been in serious decline globally for most of the past generation. In the world as a whole the high point with respect to political leadership was the middle of the twentieth century. The vast majority of the great leaders of that generation had been born in the latter part of the nineteenth century, most of them in the

1890s. In Europe this flowering of outstanding leaders included Britain's Winston Churchill as its forerunner followed by Charles de Gaulle across the channel in France, Francisco Franco in Spain, Benito Mussolini in Italy, Adolf Hitler in southern Germany, Josip Broz—later rechristened politically as Tito—in the Balkans, and, a touch earlier, a sterner counterpart emerging from the lower extremes of the USSR, who would become a world shaker as Stalin. Across the Atlantic in the Western Hemisphere, precursors Theodore Roosevelt and Woodrow Wilson were followed by Franklin D. Roosevelt.

Latin America was not left out of this global phenomenon (which included Turkey's Kemal Ataturk, India's Mohandas Gandhi and Jawaharlal Nehru, and Indonesia's Sukarno), with Cárdenas in Mexico, Vargas in Brazil, and Perón in Argentina—this youngest of these three nation shapers being born in 1895. But just as the rest of the world, including the United States, has subsequently failed to produce individuals comparable to this generation, Latin America has furnished only Fidel Castro. Since scholars have not yet come up with adequate explanations for this global occurrence, clues from Latin American experience have significant value.

In Latin America the contemporary era has seen very little quality political leadership in Argentina, a country that from the late nineteenth through much of the twentieth century gave rise to Roca, Yrigoyen, and the Peróns, with even Menem a standout on a number of criteria. Brazil, favored with Vargas, Kubitschek, and Cardoso during the post–World War I era, sees Lula possibly just avoiding serious missteps, as Sarney did, as much as being a real prospect to fill the shoes of any of his distinguished predecessors. Colombians, unable to point to an outstanding leader since Rafael Reyes early in the twentieth century, lament the premature death of Gaitán and are forced to reassess past presidents such as Alfonso López less unfavorably, as each of the more recent ones has been lackluster at best. In Mexico, Fox is notable for having gained office rather than for any accomplishments as president, and to find a figure worthy of admiration the public must hark back to Cárdenas—now sixty-five years out of office—and jump back all the way to Juárez in the third quarter of the nineteenth century. (Although Díaz was great in terms of impact, he was certainly not highly admirable.) In Peru's late 1980s disaster Alan García has been reevaluated upward in light of Fujimori's ultimate disgrace and Toledos's extremely pedestrian performance, and Hugo Chávez's controversial role in Venezuela follows a series of at-best marginally adequate presidential performances in a country that just a generation ago produced both a Rómulo Betancourt and a Rafael Caldera. Nor are there any shining stars in the smaller countries, where hopes rather than reasonable expectations underlie the optimism surrounding the newest occupants of presidential palaces.

It is highly sobering to reflect that the contemporary ho-hum crop of chief executives has resulted from broad-based and often highly competitive electoral

LEADERSHIP TIMELINE 1870–2000

	1870	1880	1890	1900	1910	1920	1930	1940	1950	1960	1970	1980	1990	2000
Brazil	1111111111111111			44442222	3333		111111111111		1111 1111	222		22222444442222	111111	
Mexico	11111	333333333333333333333333333333		44444		33333333311111			22222				22222	
Argentina		11111		11111		22222	22 444444		11111111		4444 11 4444		3333322222222	
Colombia		333333333333					3333	33311	111				3333	
Peru		55	555	333	333333333		55555	55555555555553333333333333				3333	555555555	
Venezuela	2222222222222222222222222222				44444444444444444444444444			111		11111	4444		4444	
Chile						11111 444 111111			44444		22222555555555555555555522222222222222			
Ecuador			4444	44444			33	333	3333	33 3333				
Bolivia									222255552222	5555555	555222		5555	
Uruguay				1111	1111							3333	3333	
Paraguay									5555555555555555555555555555555555					
Guatemala	222222222		5555555555555555555					2222555						
Costa Rica	3333333			444444444		44444444			1 1111		1111			
Nicaragua			555555555555555					555555555555555				444444444		
Honduras							5555555555555		4 444					
El Salvador														
Panama											22222222			
Cuba								55555555	5555511111111111111111111111111111111111111111					
Dominican Republic											33333333333		3333333333	
Haiti														
Jamaica														
Trinidad											1111111111111111			
Guyana										333333			33333	

NOTE: Tenures of the highest rated leaders are signified by a line of 1's; the next most able with 2's; followed by 3's, 4's, and 5's down through the 75 distinguished individuals featured in Appendix A. Hence, it is the empty space that illustrates run-of-the-mill to inadequate leadership.

politics. This fact leads to the uncomfortable question of whether these leadership doldrums are despite democracy or in some significant ways because of it. Hence, it becomes imperative to scrutinize critically the present processes of political recruitment in these countries (to which significant attention has been given in the preceding chapter). Why have federal systems with governorships as executive training grounds not provide more qualified candidates? As in the United States, why is this potential advantage only partially realized in practice? How important are political party systems in advancing or blocking the rise of able executives? Given the need to mobilize massive electoral support, has it become more important to be a skilled campaigner than to possess attributes of political leadership that would create a more effective president once in office? With the elevated cost of campaigns, has wealth or the ability to raise enormous sums of money come to overshadow executive abilities and political acumen? Since a veil of incompleteness clouds the present, answers must be sought in the recent past, with antecedent experience useful for discerning trends or at least directions of change. From this perspective, on balance the picture is not very hopeful.

The Second-Chance Phenomenon

Latin America has a very deep and widespread tradition, far more pronounced than in any other part of the world, of seemingly discredited leaders making surprising—often stunning—political comebacks. Beginning in Mexico soon after independence with Antonio López de Santa Ana—in his case time after time after time—this Lazarus phenomenon included Augustín Gamarra, Ramón Castilla, Nicolás de Piérola, and later Augusto Legúia in Peru as well as Tomás Cipriano de Mosquera and Rafael Nuñez in Colombia; the trio of José Antonio Paéz, José Tadeo Monagas, and Carlos Soublette in Venezuela; José Miguel Velasco in Bolivia; Manuel Gondra in Paraguay; and Fructuroso Rivera and Venáncio Flores in Uruguay. The Caribbean had the duo of Pedro Santana and Buenaventura Baéz, and subsequently that of Juan Isidro Jiménez and Horácio Vásquez in the Dominican Republic. These returns to power can be explained largely by their frequently involving forceful usurpation of power, the indirect election process in many of these countries, and by the very small populations of a large proportion of them— and particularly limited urbanization.

However, this trend continued unabated around the bend into the twentieth century with Julio Roca and Hipólito Yrigoyen in Argentina; Brazil's Rodrigues Alves; Leonidas Plaza Gutiérrez, José Pardo, and Oscar Benevides in Peru; Bolivia's Ismael Montes; Eloy Alfaro in Ecuador; José Batlle y Ordóñez and Alfredo Baldomir in Uruguay; Belisario Porras in Panama; Francisco Dueñas three times in El Salvador; and finally both Ricardo Jiménez and Cleto González in Costa Rica.

Many of these cases can be explained by the very restricted electorates involved and the even more limited pool of electable candidates, but the encore performance phenomenon persisted into periods of great demographic growth accompanied by even greater expansion of the region's electorates. Indeed, such cases peaked during the second half of the twentieth century, being particularly pronounced and dramatic in South America. In Argentina Juan Perón returned triumphantly to power in 1973, some eighteen years after having been sent packing into exile. In Chile Carlos Ibáñez accomplished a similar feat in 1952, after being pushed out in disgrace in 1930. His earlier rule had been sandwiched between a first administration by Arturo Alessandri, marked by his resignation, and a reprise through electoral victory in 1932. (Alessandri's son Jorge would be president for the 1958–1964 period.)

Back from the ashes was an even more frequently repeated scenario in Bolivia, where Victor Paz Estenssoro, ousted by coup after a manipulated reelection in 1964 following successfully completed terms in 1952–1956 and 1960–1964, was brought back in 1985, succeeding Hernán Siles, who had been his successor in 1956 and reinstalled as president in 1982. Subsequently Hugo Banzer, in power as a military strongman from 1971 to 1978, returned to the presidency through the 1997 elections, reincarnated as a populist. Gonzalo Sánchez de Lozado, elected to that office in 1994, won election again in 2002 but did not manage to serve out his term, being ousted by civil unrest. Farther up in the Andes, Ecuador witnessed an even more extreme case of this phenomenon as José María Velasco Ibarra was repeatedly restored to office by the electorate from the 1940s to the 1970s even though only one of his five administrations lasted its full term.

These cases are only part of Latin America's political return-from-the-grave phenomenon. Brazil's dramatic experience was that of Getúlio Vargas, whose first stay in power (1930–1945) ended with a forced resignation, followed by a sensational electoral triumph in 1950 and then suicide four years later. Colombia's version saw Alfonso López serving an elected term from 1934 to 1938; returned to office in 1942, he was forced out before the next scheduled elections. The provisional president at that juncture, Alberto Lleras Camargo, was the elected chief executive in 1958–1962, and in 1974 López's son and namesake won the presidency. Peru saw Manuel Prado as its president in 1939–1945 and again for 1956–1962, and Fernando Belaúnde Terry occupied the presidency from 1963 to 1968 before being elected again for the 1980–1985 term. This development was less dramatic than Venezuela's selection of 1968–1973 president Rafael Caldera to be its chief executive again in 1993 over the opposition of the party he had founded decades before—even though the electorate's decision in 1988 to bring back 1974–1978 president Carlos Andrés Pérez had led to Pérez's forced retirement a year before the end of his elected term. In the Dominican Republic, Rafael Trujillo's absences from the presidency during his long rule over the country were essentially in the form of sabbaticals, but his protégé Joaquín Balaguer not once, but twice, won back the presidency after he had been forced to relinquish it (1966 and 1986). The man who finally replaced the aged Balaguer in 1996, Leonel Fernández, staged a comeback of his own in 2004. Jean-Bertrand Aristide was elected Haiti's president at the end of 1990, and after ouster by a coup nine months later, reassumed office in October 1994, serving until the end of the next year. Following a term by a political ally, this controversial individual was again elected in November 2000, being forced out once more in February 2004—swearing that he would be back. Not only did Costa Rica's highly popular José Figueres serve constitutionally from 1953–1958 and 1970–1974, but his son was elected president for the 1994–1998 term. In a rather parallel situation, Julio María Sanguinetti was elected Uruguay's president for the 1985–1989 period, following the end of the military regime, and returned through the ballot box for 1994–1999.

Panama was not to be left out in this respect as Arnulfo Arias succeeded his brother in 1940 and, after being ousted in 1941, won reelection again in 1948— this time surviving in office until 1951. Older, but apparently not wiser, he was elected a third time in 1968, lasting in office only a matter of days. (In 1999, his much younger widow won the presidential sweepstakes largely on the residual magic of his name). In Guyana, Chedi Jagan spent four and a half months in power in 1953, returned to office in the elections of 1957, and once again returned at the end of the century—this third time made final by his death. During the 1950s Paul Magloire had two stints at Haiti's helm, and in Jamaica, Michael Manley, son of a previous chief of government, was in and out of power and back in again within the framework of that country's parliamentary system. Also parliamentary, Trinidad and Tobago in its equally short life has seen repeat performances by Patrick Manning, despite having had a single head of government from before independence until 1981. In Cuba from the 1930s through the 1950s, both Ramón Grau San Martín and Fulgéncio Batista occupied the presidency two separate times, the latter elected for the 1940–1944 term and returned to power in 1952. This back-for-another-try practice was subsequently broken only by Castro's remaining in power without interruption for more than a generation since Batista's ouster at the end of 1958. This extreme continuism is certainly no improvement over an in-and-out-and-in pattern, which allows a significant element of choice.

As shown in preceding chapters, as late as the 1980s and 1990s the pool of serious contenders for the presidency in a majority of Latin American nations included former holders of that high office, providing voters a choice between proven performance and promise and potential. Subsequently this situation has changed drastically, with recruitment of presidents now centering on unproven aspirants. If Lula da Silva is not reelected in Brazil in late 2006, the winner will not be one of his predecessors. Mexico has a strict one-term-only limit, as did

Colombia until 2006. In Argentina Carlos Saúl Menem seems finally effectively out of the picture, and both Fernando de la Rúa aand Eduardo Duhalde are discredited as having been unable to last more than half a term and "leading" the country into near ruin. Fujimori in Peru is in exile, talking tough about returning to the presidency although not currently eligible, but there is a good chance for Alan García to rebound. Whatever happens in Venezuela, there will be no return to the pre-Chávez chief executives—since his last two predecessors were themselves throwbacks to an earlier era. Chile has not looked backward for a presidential contender in over a half century, and Ecuador did this only for the late Velasco Ibarra. Bolivia has all but run out of available ex-presidents, although one short-termer ran at the end of 2005. Given these considerations, determining why Latin American countries have been so prone to reevaluate presidents and give them a second chance—along with comparative analysis of encore versus initial performances—may finally be left to historians.

Lasting Legacies: Parties and Movements Versus Myths and Traditions

Which leaders catalyzed the most profound transformations in their countries? The roster in order of enduring political development includes Brazil's Vargas (1930–1945 and 1951–1954), Cárdenas in Mexico (1934–1940), Perón of Argentina (1945–1955 and 1973–1974), Cuba's Castro (1959–?), Betancourt in Venezuela (1946–1947 and 1958–1963), and Lleras Camargo of Colombia (1945–1946 and 1958–1962). From the smaller countries the most notable architects of political development are Batlle y Ordóñez in Uruguay and Figueres of Costa Rica, along with Bolivia's Paz Estenssoro and perhaps Torrijos in Panama. (They and many others are ranked in Appendix A.)

When it comes to depth instead of stars, Brazil, aside from Vargas, has enjoyed quality political leadership only from 1956 through 1960 with Kubitschek, a Vargas heir, and Cardoso (1995–2002). Surviving mediocre leadership much of the time, it was launched into political decay by Bernardes and Washington Luís in the 1920s as well as through the manifold shortcomings of Quadros and Goulart in 1961 to early 1964. From the downfall of the Díaz regime in 1911, Mexico's political leadership, with the lonely exception of Cárdenas, rarely rose above merely competent, a deficit offset by the staying power and occasional episodes of adaptability demonstrated by the PRI. On balance, Argentina's process of political recruitment functioned best as it entered the twentieth century, with Roca, Sáenz Peña, and Yrigoyen all effective before the fifteen-year interregnum of Perón, whose institutional legacy provided both Menem for a decade and the country's present chief executive. Even Justo in the 1930s would have been above the norm for most of the region's countries.

By way of contrast, Colombia's leadership rarely rose above adequacy and more often fell below a passing mark than above it (with Alfonso López and César Gaviria the only ones to even stand comparison with Lleras Camargo). Other than Betancourt, in pre-Chávez Venezuela only Caldera in his first term was more than an average chief executive, and in Peru, Legúia and Fujimori, the best of a poor lot of performers, ended poorly, with Belaúnde nearer their level than down with the rest. Chile has had its ups and downs, not out of place for its relatively small population, with the first Alessandri closest to a star, followed a third of a century later by the elder Frei. It has, however, had a series of quite competent chief executives since the reestablishment of democracy in 1990. The best jobs of finding decent leadership from a small pool have been done by Costa Rica and Uruguay.

The proof of the pudding with regard to leadership lies in the extent and duration of legacy, broadly defined. Perón and Peronism in Argentina rank first in this respect, since more than thirty years after the great man's death Peronists remain the country's leading political force. Vargas, although the parties he founded did not survive the military regime as major factors, influenced a very wide range of today's political leaders and forces. More important, he initiated fundamental social and economic changes in Brazil that are the foundation of recent progress. Less positive, but very profound and persistent, is the ongoing heritage of Trujillo and Balaguer in the Dominican Republic—where the latter occupied the presidency until 1996. Castro is likely to rate with these transforming leaders, but the legacy of a regime still in power is subject to only tentative assessment, and the durability of Castroism without Castro is yet to be proven.

As a coherent effort at comprehensive implementation of the Mexican Revolution, delayed by civil war and warlordism, Cárdenas's epoch in Mexico stands out and remains a point of reference for contemporary politicians. Although strong vestiges of the Somoza Era persist in Nicaragua, more were negated by the Sandinista Revolution, so on balance, Paz Estenssoro and Hernán Siles and the 1952 Bolivian Revolution have a more durable as well as a more positive legacy. On the down side, without the deeply embedded *caudillo* tradition in Venezuela, embodied in the twentieth century by Juan Vicente Gómez, who channeled it toward militarism, there would be no Hugo Chávez today. Velasco Ibarra established no political party to carry on his idiosyncratic politics in Ecuador but can be considered the inspiration for the Concentration of Popular Forces, overall the country's most successful political party, as well as serving as a human textbook for a series of populist leaders there.

"What might have been" has little place in serious political science work, but in the case of one of Latin America's major countries, a particular counterfactual scenario is informative. Gaitán represented a rare type of leadership, with a transformational project and a mobilizational ability otherwise absent from the

Colombian scene. The country's worst years, those of *La Violencia*'s bloodbath, were those immediately after his assassination in 1948. Had this radical populist liberal reached the presidency in 1950, as was a very strong possibility if not a foregone conclusion, this trauma might have been avoided, along with its troublesome aftermath—including the Rojas Pinilla military regime. Gaitán's track record up to his death in the prime of his life and at the apex of his popularity strongly indicates that such success was a real possibility, for in several important respects he had the potential to be a transformational leader on the level of Vargas or Perón. A somewhat analogous case is that of Peru, where Haya de la Torre and the *Apristas* were barred from power for a generation by that country's military, at a great cost not only to democracy, but to any form of basic political development. Both Colombia and Peru, and their combined inhabitants numbering well over 70 million, have paid dearly for these lost opportunities.

Leadership and the Future

Aside from the merits of individual leaders, there has been progress in the broader picture of who holds and exercises power. A century ago entrenched economic elites dominated Latin American politics, often almost unchallenged; seventy years ago the impact of the world economic crisis was the determinant factor; then forty years ago the military became the arbiter of national destiny throughout the region. At least now, in all but a few cases of relatively small countries, the decision as to who will govern is in the hands of the people, and complex social orders have led to increasingly pluralistic politics. Indeed, the past two decades have involved a sometimes-difficult learning process about how to exercise this newly won power wisely as well as more effectively. In this regard greater independence and concentration on the country's current situation are more common than in the past. Now more than before, neighbors may have governments of the determined right, or of the hopeful left, or of the uncertain center, but these are at least governments chosen by the people in response to their own perceived needs and recent experience. Although some bad choices have been made and more are likely in the future, this thoughtful voting constitutes a major step forward along the boulder-strewn road to political development.

It is readily apparent that leadership has been and continues to be a vital variable, although a frustratingly idiosyncratic one, conditioned by contextual factors and cultural values. Often in the past, it has been and now generally is in short supply around the rest of the world; it is also in short supply in Latin America. Brazil seems to be in reasonably good shape for having had political recruitment interrupted by two decades of military rule. José Sarney, who was chosen in 1984 to balance a ticket, not to govern the country through its transition into a fully competitive democracy, must be judged to have been at least adequate. (Indeed, his performance with respect to guiding a first postauthoritarian government was far better than that of Alfonsín, Belaúnde, or Silas; Aylwin's task in Chile was a much easier one.) Then came substandard presidents Collor de Mello and Itamar Franco, the first of whom conned an inexperienced electorate, and the second of whom, Collor's vice president, had never been chosen to preside over the nation's destinies. By contrast Cardoso was superbly prepared for the position, and Lula da Silva initially performed better than many observers expected, until floundering in a sea of scandal, and still could win a second term in the late 2006 election. If he does not win, his good qualities, added to those of his predecessor, not only raise the bar, at least back to where it was in the late 1950s, but almost guarantee that whoever replaces him will have to possess the strong presidential credentials that already characterize the early front-runners.

Mexico provides cause for concern because Vicente Fox turned out to have been a much better campaigner than chief executive and because no matter what his performance, he cannot be reelected. On the positive side, Mexico's system is now truly competitive, and having lost last time around for the first time in history, the PRI has worked diligently to field a qualified candidate in an effort to regain power, as has the PAN in its desire to stay in office, and the PRD in its hope to finally get into power. Offering longer-term hope, Mexico's congress, long a rubber stamp, finally seems to be emerging as a leadership proving ground, and since Mexico is operating more like a true federal system than during the centralization imposed by PRI hegemony, it is approaching in this respect Argentina, if not Brazil. Its governors can now gain valuable political as well as administrative experience.

By contrast, Argentina's recent track record raises warning signs. Both Fernando de la Rúa and Eduardo Duhalde, effective campaigners as well as experienced administrators at the state and metropolitan levels, abysmally failed as presidents. Clearly more effective than either of them, Kirchner has not yet risen to the level reached by Menem during his first eight years in office, but off a strong start, he may do so. Moreover, having a truly federal system, Argentina has governorships as well as cabinet positions and congressional leadership posts as training grounds and structures for political recruitment. Colombia's profound problems have eluded solution under a series of unremarkable presidents, in part at least because of the confining constraints of a single four-year term, which prematurely shifted political attention to the succession question. With the late 2004 constitutional amendment Uribe has escaped this fate but must still take advantage of his strong chance of reelection. Over time governorships and metropolitan mayoral offices may come to play roles more similar to those in Brazil and Argentina.

Peru and Venezuela afford cause for serious preoccupation, not just concern. Alejandro Toledo has been only adequate on his best days, which have been alarmingly few. Positive for much of his extended presidency, Fujimori's final legacy casts a pall over the Peruvian political scene—where the mixed performance of Belaúnde (1963–1968 and 1980–1985) and the subsequent fiasco of Alan García set a fairly low standard. Political recruitment remains excessively unstructured there, but even more so in the case of Venezuela. Hugo Chávez rose from being a military plotter with no normal political or governmental experience, and he is too concerned about his personal continuation in office à la Castro to groom any successor. But anti-Chávez groups are characterized by the absence of any dynamic leadership, and his reelection in 2006 is a strong possibility. Indeed, his intention is to rival Guzmán Blanco and even Gómez in length of tenure. Moreover, the vaunted democratic era of the 1960s and 1970s was spectacularly unable to handle leadership renovation, repeatedly reaching far into the past to bring former presidents back to office, in a clear admission of failure to produce new leaders.

Chile has put together a string of competent chief executives since its return to democracy, but Bolivia has not gotten on the track since running out of historical figures to reinstall (Siles, Paz Estenssoro, and Banzer before the fiasco of Sánchez de Lozado). Now it has turned to election of Morales, a radical charismatic representative of the restless masses, particularly coca growers. Ecuador, since the era of Velasco Ibarra, has produced far more seriously flawed and ultimately unsuccessful presidents than it has ones who have even been adequate, and it is still plagued by the sierra versus coast cleavage. Uruguay continues a tradition of doing quite well for a country with such a small pool from which to draw, but Paraguay has not yet found a way to tap the best-qualified elements of its very limited recruitment base. Guatemala encountered difficulty in freeing itself from continuing influence, although not rule, by a controversial former military strongman (Ríos Montt), a problem that passage of time has resolved. El Salvador, Honduras, and Costa Rica (like Uruguay) have done reasonably well in political recruitment, given their small pools of possibilities. Nicaragua and Panama have found the road rougher—the former because of the discontinuity imposed by the period of Sandinista rule, the latter owing to the recentness of direct US interference. Panama's 2004 choice combines youth with direct descent from the one truly able political leader that small country has yet produced (Omar Torrijos).

Out in the Caribbean, Castro remains the region's only globally renowned leader, but nearing eighty, he is in the winter of his years. Furthermore, there are of necessity grave reservations as to the future, since no mechanisms for ensuring a competent successor are in place. Haiti's leadership situation is worse than dire, since Aristide looked passable only against the very low bar of that troubled country's background of incompetency, despotism, or a combination of these two negative qualities in the occupants of its presidential palace. The runaway winner in early 2006 was an individual dwarfed by Aristide when he previously held office—and in many ways he was the best of the lot. The Dominican Republic is less leadership-bereft, largely by comparison, not by positive quality. The Trujillo-Balaguer era is only a few years past and still has a distorting influence upon the present generation of leading politicians, most of whom are just that—not true political leaders, but leading politicians in a context lacking quality competition. The immediate question is whether in a return to the presidency, this time free of Balaguer's influence, Leonel Fernández can improve upon his earlier term. From Jamaica to Guyana, the English-speaking small and even smaller countries have markedly undistinguished to near inadequate leadership, leaving Trinidadians nostalgic for Eric Williams, Jamaicans fondly remembering the Manleys (father and son), and Guyanans longing for Cheddi Jagan, or in some cases even for Forbes Burnham. Extremely severe size limitations and deep racial cleavages in the even smaller Caribbean states make any overall change for the better unlikely in the short term, although one or two out of a dozen might be lucky and beat the odds.

The greatly increased participation through elections in selecting national rulers has not, in most of Latin America, improved their quality. Indeed, the democratic imperative of gaining congressional approval of their policies and actions has diminished the effectiveness of many presidents. Most dramatically, for three-quarters of a century Mexican chief executives benefited from automatic legislative approval of their initiatives. The current president is the first to face a congress that is not only independent, but also essentially hostile. Brazil's incumbent finds his own party a distinct minority within a multiparty congressional coalition to which he must make major policy concessions—to a much higher degree than was the case for his 1995–2002 predecessor. Of the region's four major countries, only in Colombia does the president possess a clear legislative majority, and this by way of support by a variety of parties. Until the October 2005 legislative elections, Argentina's Kirchner had to deal with divisions in Peronist ranks. Minority presidents lacking congressional majorities are common among the midsized and smaller countries, impasse and stalemate being frequent results.

Over the longer haul the quality of political leadership in Latin America could well improve for two reasons. First, the restoration of democratic processes, including filling offices through competitive elections, dates back in most countries to the early and mid-1980s. This amount of time allows for emergence and maturation of a new generation of leaders not decimated or stunted by the authoritarian experiences of the 1960s and 1970s. Second, although women still have the decidedly short end of the officeholding stick, the gender disparity is slowly narrowing. More women as mayors, governors, national legislators, and department heads broadens and deepens the pool of potential candidates and has already increased the possibilities for them to become chief executive. Isabelita Perón in Argentina in the mid-1970s, Violetta Chamorro in Nicaragua in the early 1990s, and Miryea Moscoso in

Panama reflect an encouraging trend in this regard, since the first was her husband's constitutional heir and the second a symbol of her martyred husband. But the third is the widow long-deceased former president who was in distant exile, and she was all but unknown to a large proportion of voters. Then Bachelet in Chile over the end of 2005 and beginning of 2006 was elected entirely on her own merits. Progress is uneven, but it is encouraging that substantial change in reducing the political handicap of being a woman has occurred in Brazil, and that Peru has already seen a woman leading in the late stages of a presidential campaign. Mexico, unfortunately, lags behind—with the slow and faltering progress in this regard in its giant northern neighbor not setting a particularly good example. (Cuba, Costa Rica, and Argentina rank seventh, eighth, and eleventh in the world in terms of women serving in the national legislature, well ahead of the United States in 69th place, France in 82nd place, and Japan trailing at number 134.)

The mid-1990s trend toward elimination of the no-reelection rules in a number of Latin American countries was, on balance, a step forward. As has been amply demonstrated, the talent pool is often limited, so ruling out an exceptionally able chief executive—as was the case with Juscelino Kubitschek in Brazil in 1960—could lead to a decidedly inferior successor. Moreover, if Jânio Quadros, who did replace Kubitschek, could have contemplated the possibility of two terms to complete his comprehensive agenda for putting Brazil's administrative house in order, he might well not have thrown the country's political life into disarray through an ill-conceived bid to gain exceptional decree powers. Forcing a president to sit out two terms in Venezuela—in this case, a full decade—meant they might return when times and tasks have changed considerably, or when they are well past their prime, or even both, as with Caldera. But elimination of this provision has allowed Chávez to perpetuate himself in office. A single four-year term, as in Colombia until 2006, has been a more serious limitation than Mexico's single six-year term, which, however, is only marginally more restrictive than the eight-year limit in Brazil and the United States.

If competence is increasingly likely among Latin American leaders (except perhaps those few emerging without administrative experience as was the case with Lula), "visionary" leadership is less likely to achieve power—if managing at all to emerge to contender status. "Transforming" leaders have been rare, except for the happy coincidence of Vargas, Perón, and Cárdenas at the same time, since in the past a large proportion of them have been erstwhile visionaries, their visions tempered by the heavy responsibilities of office.[1] "Radical" leaders are apt to be elevated to power only in countries where—as in Venezuela in the 1990s—a large proportion of the politically participant population (often newly enfranchised) feel that they have been denied a fair share of governmental benefits.

Is There a Latin American Family of Nations?

As elsewhere in the world, Latin American countries do influence each other by actions upon, or even within, the country being influenced. There is, however, very little evidence that developments in one Latin American country significantly affect events in another, either by individual example or by demonstration effect. The major exception seems to have involved South America in the early 1950s. In this instance the Peronist experience in Argentina extended its influence into a majority of the continent's nations. Although a portion of this extension was a result of the Argentine regime's conscious efforts to exert influence, a substantial proportion resulted because governments or opposition forces in these countries perceived the Peronist model as suitable for, or at least adaptable to, their circumstances.

The Peróns were unquestionably charismatic leaders as well as skillful political operators, and Peronism was a political phenomenon with aspects of style, program, and political philosophy appropriate for other sections of the continent. In the Cold War setting, at that time at least, the communist path was not viable in the Western Hemisphere—for Guatemala was very distant from South American countries and at an early stage of selecting a few elements of that road, and Cuba was still virtually a US puppet under Batista's yoke. Hence, Perón's talk of a third way between the excesses of either communism or right-wing capitalism held considerable appeal to Bolivia, Chile, Venezuela, and Colombia, and even to some Vargista elements in Brazil. By the first part of 1953, governments in all these countries were looking closely at Peronism, and in Chile and Bolivia presidents openly proclaimed their affinity. Evita's mid-1953 death not only forced Perón to focus on domestic matters but caused him to shift toward the defensive and underscored the potential weaknesses of his model, one that never did show brightly in the strictly economic field. By late August 1954, Vargas was dead and the interim Brazilian government was friendly to the United States and hostile to Perón for his past ties to Vargas. Hence, Brazil's interest in emulating Peronism turned into a fleeting infatuation instead of a lasting attraction. With Perón's removal from office in September 1955, the affinities of political strategies that had briefly prevailed quickly dissipated and disappeared.

From 1959 into the 1960s much was made of the appeal of Castro and his Cuban Revolution, many observers predicting sweeping and profound changes throughout the region as a result—many because that was what they ardently wanted; others because it was their worst nightmare. Yet Cuba failed to become a model for any other country to follow. The Allende regime in Chile was both strikingly different and deeply rooted in Chilean idiosyncrasies. And instead of fulfilling his boast to turn the Andes into the Sierra Maestra of South America (a reference to the Cuban Revolution), Che Guevara met his death in Bolivia without even having made a serious impact on that one isolated country.

With rare exceptions of "intimate" or "penetrated" neighbors, Latin American publics have paid very little attention to what was happening in other countries of the region. Until recently, this lack of interest was perhaps reasonable, as events in other countries had no significant impact upon their lives or even the course of their national affairs. Now greater attention is becoming not only rational, but also highly desirable, particularly in economic interchanges. Argentina, not only Uruguay and Paraguay, is heavily affected by Brazilian economic performance through that country's great specific weight within Mercosur, or the Southern Cone Common Market. Politically concerned Chileans are increasingly aware that close ties to Mercosur are an important option, hence some knowledge of what is going on in Brazil should supplement preoccupation with neighboring Argentina and Peru. Bolivia's traditional concern with looking westward at Peru and Chile is turning toward Brazil as involvement in Mercosur becomes an important issue. Since Spanish and Portuguese are more similar on the printed page than in their spoken forms, spread of print media across national borders has facilitated "knowing thy neighbor" even if she or he lives down the block. However, the most significant influence on some Latin Americans being less misinformed about other countries is television. Pictures not only speak as eloquently as thousands of words but also do not require familiarity with the language of their subjects.

It remains an open question whether this pervasive lack of influence of one country's experiences on another—or others—may be changed by the effects of continued economic integration, as clearly has been the case in Europe. For a long period such economic cooperation was limited to relatively minor subregional groupings such as Central America, the New Caribbean, or the west coast South American countries of the ineffective Andean Pact. Beginning near the end of the authoritarian period, but picking up momentum through the late 1980s and 1990s, a solid edifice of a dynamic free trade area began to take shape with previously hostile rivals Brazil and Argentina at its core. Under their leadership and encompassing other newly industrialized countries of South America, the Southern Cone Common Market came into existence. Its name is misleading, for the heart of Mercosur is massive Brazil, not its more southern Argentine, Uruguyan, and Paraguayan full partners or associate member Chile. Candidates Venezuela, Bolivia, and Peru, like Brazil, are hardly part of a geographic Southern Cone, but the entity's name could very easily be changed since the *sur* could stand for "south"—as in South American.[2]

The vast expansion of intraregional commerce that followed Mercosur's inception helped underwrite sustained economic growth facilitating political stability and democratization. Desire to qualify for admission to Mercosur has had some influence upon policies of governments in Peru and Bolivia. Mercosur's success has been unwelcome to US administrations, which have a conflicting plan for Western Hemisphere economic integration. May 2003 witnessed a less than enthusiastically integration-disposed president becoming Argentina's sixth chief executive in two years; he provided a beginning for sorely needed policy continuity. As a populist in the Peronist lineage, Kirchner is inclined—like his Brazilian counterpart Lula—to find an independent road in international matters, one featuring reduced dependence on the United States. It is clear that these countries have no intention of facilitating the kind of hemispheric economic integration sought by the United States. Instead of piecemeal adhesions, they envision an economically unified South America dealing with Washington from a position of strength.

Convergence, or Each in Its Own Way?

Although there is no "typical" Latin American country, the range of variation in the political sphere has been reduced compared to that of any time in the past. The prior peak of convergence was in the late 1960s and early 1970s, when authoritarian military governments prevailed alongside a semiauthoritarian civilian regime in Mexico. Indeed, the case might well be made that the similarities of those repressive regimes helped erase some of the preceding country-to-country differences, and that the ensuing processes of transition to democracy reinforced similarities. For all its problems, Haiti is less exceptional than it was during the long Duvalier era—ended less than two decades ago, so that Cuba is now the most distant from the region's norms. There is now some real sense of discussing central tendencies in terms of a basic Latin American mode—which fits the greatest number of countries—instead of an essentially meaningless mean (homogenizing average) or misleading median (merely the midpoint along a continuum of differences). The following questions remain: How many must fit in how narrowly defined a model? What degree and manner of weighting or distribution should be used if the regional mode isn't going to be decided by the English-speaking mini-countries of the Antilles?

Brazil differs from any synthetic model in scale even more than degree, and certainly more than kind. Mexico has finally emerged from not-so-splendid isolation as a hegemonic single-party regime to having a competitive multiparty system. Colombia no longer has the rigid, elite-dominated, vertical two-party system it had for generations. Argentina is becoming more Latin American. Long accustomed to viewing their country as a displaced, if not misplaced, corner of Europe, Argentines increasingly realize that, like it or not, they are South Americans. Indeed, most of them are aware that what happens in the Brazilian economy has a more direct, greater, and more immediate impact upon their lives than do European developments. Not only have their recent troubles imparted an unaccustomed degree of

humility, but passage of time has blunted the still politically significant ethnic differences. Their Italian forebears are by now history; they themselves are not first- or
second-generation descendants of immigrants, but fourth- or even fifth-generation
Argentines who have an attenuated immigrant heritage—like many of the Brazilian businessmen with whom they often come in contact, although not the dark-
skinned masses found in less proximate areas north of those they visit (and not
represented among Brazilian business travelers).

Clearly Brazil and Mexico have had no impact upon each other's political development. They view themselves as being very different, and in fact, they are in
almost all visible aspects. The distinguishing features of their political life have
been very distinct: settlement in the second quarter of the sixteenth century versus significant colonization a generation later; a native civilization as the backbone
of a traditional agricultural order versus massive importation of African slave labor
for the same purpose; heart of the Spanish Empire in the New World versus the
New World's seat of the Portuguese Empire; a violent independence struggle involving repression of efforts to turn it in the direction of social revolution versus
remaining a monarchy under the Portuguese royal family; violence-laced *caudillo*
rule through the middle of the nineteenth century versus peaceful stability under
an emperor; and loss of nearly half its territory at midcentury to an aggressive
neighbor versus defeat of all separatist movements.

Following the 1850s the two countries continued to follow very divergent
paths: imposition by a European power of a foreign monarch versus national consolidation under a beloved Brazilian-born monarch; emergence of an authoritarian militarist holding onto power for thirty-five years versus establishment of a
republic and entrenchment in its control of a civilian agro-exporting elite; a violent revolution leading into nearly two decades of extremely bloody civil war versus orderly presidential succession through negotiated prearrangement of electoral
outcomes; creation of a hegemonic party system in the 1930s and 1940s versus a
paternalistic authoritarian strongman ruling without parties; marginalization of
the military through the dominant ruling party versus increased military intervention in the country's political life, followed by two decades of authoritarian military rule; all this bringing the two countries up to the mid-1980s.

Since that time the differences have been significantly reduced. Mexico moved
toward multiparty electoral competition as Brazil resumed a highly competitive
political life. Mexico had a string of highly educated technocrats in its presidency,
and Brazil entrusted its to an outstanding academic social scientist for two terms.
Finally, both turned at almost the same moment to longtime opposition leaders
strikingly different from their predecessors in background, outlook, and style. This
development constituted a significant functional convergence from opposite directions but occurred with very little attention to, and no real thought about,

what the other country was doing. Rather it was rooted in the requisites of large, urban, modernizing industrial systems. Yet, at the level of political behavior, Brazil and Mexico have long enjoyed a fundamental similarity going beyond just the persistence of clientelistic politics—a near universal factor throughout the region as well as in much of the rest of the world. Parallels between the *panelinha* in the former and its Mexican counterpart, the *camarilla,* are striking.

> The brokering, clientelistic nature of the Brazilian political-governmental system reflects the pervasive role of the *panelinha*, an informal group of a closed nature bound together by common interests and personal ties. Its essence lies in having members in a variety of complementary positions in the sociopolitical-economic structure, and in its negative manifestations it may give rise to a kind of amoral cronyism. One of the most important of the types of personal links that maintain connections among interests, organizations, and agencies, *panelinha* is difficult to identify and trace, since there is no formal record of its existence.[3]

Many of the features of Mexican political culture predispose the political system to rely on camarillas. A camarilla is a group of people who have political interests in common and rely upon one another to improve their chances within the political leadership.[4]

The largest and most important *camarillas*—those reaching the presidential cabinet—typically have been assembled over a long period of time, through an elaborate process of personal alliance building.[5]

Similarly, Mexico's pervasive nepotism and its counterpart in Brazil are more than kissing cousins: "Involving relatives plus a full array of in-laws, the *parentela* (extended web of relatives and family associates) has on its fringes an assortment of informally adopted individuals and even family retainers."[6]

If Brazil and Mexico have had almost no direct or even indirect impact on one another's political lives, the same is true of Mexico and Argentina and of Mexico and Colombia. Admittedly, the differences along the road were not as dramatic as in the case of the two largest countries. Points of similarity can be found between their *caudillo* periods, those of Rosas and Santa Ana, both barely lasting into the 1850s. Far less dictatorial and repressive, the Roca era in Argentina shares with Díaz's Porfiriato a rise through military prowess and emphasis on development through centralization and concentration of power, as well as a basic coincidence in time. But their legacies were almost polar opposites: the coming of middle-class democracy in Argentina by the early twentieth century; abject failure to manage this political feat and an ensuing protracted bloodbath for Mexico. At a very fundamental level there were similarities between Cárdenas's installation of a corporatist-populist regime in

Mexico and Peronism in Argentina—as well as between both and the Vargas era in Brazil. After again following divergent paths in the 1960s and 1970s, since Mexico avoided military rule and Argentina endured a worse form of it than Brazil did, in broad terms Argentina since 1983 has followed a course similar to that sketched in the preceding paragraph for both Mexico and Brazil.

If three of the four largest countries have ended up since the mid-1980s on parallel if far from identical paths, what has happened with the fourth country? The answer is that although Colombia may not now be quite as different from the other three as it was during most of their journeys along the path (since it is not as well defined as any road) of political development, Colombia clearly had no leader bearing more than the remotest similarity to the other countries' charismatic corporatist-populist reformers. To try to fit Alfonso López into this mold would be an exercise in sophism as much as futility. The best that can be done in this direction is to say that Gaitán might have been the fourth musketeer if this political D'Artagnan had not been killed before the rendezvous.

Did events in one country ever have a demonstrated impact on others? Only rarely and in limited ways. Perón's success in exporting his model in the early 1950s has already been discussed. The Velasco Alvarado regime in Peru had some effect upon military politics in Bolivia in the brief 1968–1973 period, as well as a very limited impact in Ecuador. Once Perón was out of power, the erstwhile Peronist franchise holders in Colombia and Venezuela at least exchanged laments over being politically orphaned, and it is likely that Betancourt compared notes with Lleras Camargo, if not on how to bring about the political demises of the dictators, at least on how to fill the ensuing vacuum. At an earlier point in time in the Caribbean, it is probable—given their common parentage—that Trujillo, Somoza, and Batista kibitzed on the strategies of one another's 1930s–1950s post-US intervention dictatorships. Central America provides a slightly different case, given its relative compactness and common experiences into the 1930s. But even there, one country's familiarity is chiefly with its immediate neighbors (Guatemala with El Salvador and Honduras; Costa Rica with Nicaragua and Panama).

Learning from Experience, or Plunging Blindly Ahead?

What can we conclude with respect to learning experiences? Evaluating the political learning experiences of peoples and countries clearly contains a highly subjective component. Yet, since it is an essential underpinning of both conclusions about the past and predictions concerning future political development, this evaluation must be undertaken.[7] Few Latin American countries demonstrated much in this respect as long as their political systems were elite-dominated and had restricted effective electoral participation. At earlier points, each country had a very limited past to draw upon for lessons, and governing groups had not broken the habit of looking more at the United States or, in a few cases, western Europe for lessons rather than focusing nearer to home. For their part, marginalized and excluded groups understandably considered contemporary macropolitical developments irrelevant to a future in which they might gain a voice in shaping the course of their country's politics. Moreover, only when elections rather than coups became the decisive factor in determining who would hold office and exercise power could lessons of the past be applied to more effective pursuit of developmental goals.

If there has not been a cumulative and at least partially cross-national political learning process in Latin America—somewhat analogous to that emerging in southern Europe, as manifested since the 1970s—then hopes for democratic political development in African and Asian regions must be tempered and scaled back. Should such a salutary drawing of lessons from past trauma take hold in Latin America in the early twenty-first century, as may be starting to happen, it would not necessarily mean that the same will happen in the countries of Africa and Asia. However, there is a possibility that it might. Hence, the challenge for comparative studies is to ascertain what can be done to enhance this prospect and foster such learning from experience.

A compelling lesson from Latin America's experience is that successful democratization requires a significant degree of political development. Much of this development may take place during "false dawns," early and ultimately impermanent efforts at establishing democracy. As Huntington points out on a global basis, the first two waves of democratization were followed by demoralizing reverse waves. Worldwide that reverse wave beginning in 1922 swept away democracy in thirteen of the seventeen countries that had embraced it between 1910 and 1931, and the second, starting in the early 1960s, reduced democratic regimes from a peak of fifty-two to only thirty. Twenty-three of the twenty-nine countries democratizing between 1974 and 1990 (the third wave) had had prior democratic experience.[8]

These "cyclical," "second-try," and "interrupted" democracies included Brazil, Argentina, Colombia, Peru, Venezuela, Chile, Ecuador, Bolivia, Uruguay, Guatemala, El Salvador, Honduras, Costa Rica, and Panama—both a majority of the Latin American countries and half of all the reestablishments of democracy in the world. In South America only Paraguay was on its initial try at democracy (beginning in 1984), joined by Nicaragua in Central America and, going back farther in time, by Cuba and Haiti. (The recently independent nations emerging from colonialism fall into Huntington's decolonization pattern, with Guyana by now lying between "second try," and "interrupted.")

Most important, all instances of democratization in Latin America have been protracted processes involving disheartening setbacks followed—often after the passage of considerable time—by resolute efforts to regain lost ground before shifting to making new headway. Indeed, as shown in Chapter 4, the exception often made for Costa Rica does not stand up to close scrutiny when we push the time horizon back into the latter part of the nineteenth century rather than using 1900 as the starting point. Hence, those countries elsewhere in the world stalled along the road, or even sidetracked, have no reason to become disheartened and every reason to seek answers from the Latin American nations to questions about how they might get moving again.

For Brazil, drawing meaningful lessons from its own past experience and applying them in the political arena has been both slow and partial but shows signs of accelerating. Moreover, given Brazil's many facets of uniqueness—size and population, Portuguese and monarchical heritage, and the near equal mix of European- and African-origin peoples (the latter exceeding in number that component throughout the rest of the region)—the experience of other countries has been considered essentially irrelevant. Many of the same considerations apply in Mexico's case. Here the Cárdenas period in the 1930s and, in more limited ways, the Zedillo administration (1995–2000), with its conscious effort to adapt to changed conditions, offer rays of hope, but the jury must remain out until Mexico at least gets past Fox into the next administration. Largely in light of their particular bilateral relationship with the United States, Mexicans essentially feel that the rest of Latin America holds no lessons for them. Hence, over half the region's inhabitants are insular in their view of the possible sources of any relevant lessons.

Argentina appears finally to have developed a capacity for learning from previous setbacks and failures on the road to political development, and although both Colombia and Venezuela have demonstrated a good deal in this respect in the past, their record since the 1990s reflects at least partial amnesia. Moreover, given differing patterns and paths for almost all their national lives, neither views the other as significantly similar. In the former, the National Front was an outstanding example of recrafting institutions and procedures to prevent a recurrence of past problems, and in the latter, after 1958 Acción Democrática, systematically applied lessons from 1945–1948 failures. Chile has been a quite good learner, as has Uruguay, but Peru is near the opposite pole, generally failing to see lessons from its own history Bolivia, Ecuador, and Paraguay are indifferent learners. As for Central America and the Caribbean, the results of a cumulative political learning experience are mixed, spotty, and questionable—with Costa Rica, El Salvador, and Panama showing the most promise. Some elements in each country look at their neighbors' experiences, but few find them relevant to their own concerns.

Whither Latin America?

As the late Roger Hilsman reminds us, the future crouches in the present, while the present is itself still emerging from the past.[9] How this process has and is occurring affords no certainty for understanding what lies ahead, but it does provide significant clues. In a changing world straight-line projections are extremely hazardous, but not to try to peer through the dusk of uncertainty and the fog of impermanence—at least down to the next corner and reflect on what may lie around the corner—it would be to shirk a scholar's responsibility to put knowledge and understanding to work on behalf of more reasonably informed public policy. As shown above, all political participants, leaders and followers alike, are very much products of the political socialization they underwent as much as a half century earlier. Combining this salient fact with the persistence of many practices and the inertia of structures and procedures confirms the lesson of Latin America's history that substantial change for the region as a whole is very likely to be slow and gradual.

Estimating where Latin America may be in 2010 requires just peering down the road rather than even looking around the corner. At the end of 2005, the dawn of the next decade is only as far ahead as 2000 is behind. For many countries this time span encompasses only the completion of the present administration and a single presidential succession. In Brazil, Mexico, Colombia, Peru, Venezuela, and Chile (among others), presidential elections come in 2006, and in Argentina, early the following year. The calendar for 2005 contained a minimum of scheduled changes of government for the region, and 2004 was marked by only scattered presidential successions. This continuity provides a favorable context for further consolidation of democratic gains made in recent years. Although there may well be isolated ups and downs, no reverse swing of the pendulum looms on the horizon. If, as seems highly possible and even probable (although far from certain), the region can reach the end of the decade without recourse to coups and a resurgence of militarism, its historical cycle of political booms and busts may well have been broken. With most transitions to democracy dating back at least to the first half of the 1980s, democracy would by 2010 have endured for twenty-five to thirty years.

Does this mean that the future of democracy in Latin America is guaranteed? Clearly not, for a serious and prolonged economic downturn could destabilize what are generally still immature democracies. But in terms of political development, many of these countries are strapping and healthy adolescents, and some are vigorous young adults. This condition contrasts very favorably with the infirm and infant statuses that characterized the democratically inclined Latin American polities leveled to the ground by the bulldozers of Cold War militarism during 1962–1973.

To venture beyond 2010 becomes an exercise in futurology, a quite different and much more speculative matter, since contingencies, both internal and international, multiply and uncertainties proliferate. Any such predictions must rest upon the accuracy of those already made for the shorter run, so it is upon these that the final considerations in this book are focused. As the twenty-first century moves forward, the fundamental question hanging over Latin America is whether the dramatic trend toward democratization since 1980 can be consolidated—both by being extended to the laggards and by being deepened in the other countries. Having begun at the end of the 1970s, this predominance of positive political development has already outlasted typical swings of the pendulum in Latin American political life. If there are no international crises, which in the past have impinged upon, often shortening, previous democratic surges—like the world depression at the beginning of the 1930s or the Cold War beginning in the late 1940s—this time the answer is largely in the hands of the region's own inhabitants: elites, masses, and the often amorphous sectors in between.

Will the countries of Latin America find their political bearings in the years ahead and manage to combine democracy with social progress and economic development?[10] This is the 565-million-person question over which the first years of the new millennium cast some gray clouds of gloom, although not necessarily of doom. The hope of dedicated radicals of the left that there was a quick, if violent, road to the Promised Land is all but dead, lingering only as a treasured illusion of the past. The belief of the right that neoliberal policies anchored in privatization and relative price stability would usher in an era of prosperity as well as stability has also proved illusionary, as the downside of globalization has made itself felt. As so often in the past, world developments—this time the war on terrorism—have pushed the region to the familiar ground of being a low priority for the United States and the other industrial powers. To change this status, Latin American nations will first have to deal more effectively with their own sociopolitical problems and then—having demonstrated their competence—act on the international scene with much greater unity of purpose.

Each country of Latin America faces a salient priority problem for the near future. For most of the countries, the immediate challenge is to recognize what this problem is and to find the necessary resolve to at least begin its amelioration—even if a lasting solution may be a long-term task. For some countries the problems are more pressing and more intractable than for others. Standing in the way of solutions are not only lack of resources, both material and human, serious as this is in many cases, but also failure to create widespread awareness of the need for action. Denial, so prevalent in individual human behavior, too often proves to be a collective phenomenon—especially when recognition of the critical shortcoming brings with it difficult and unpleasant choices. Protracted denial and the inaction it entails only aggravate the problem and increase the costs of dealing with it. Indeed, they may do so beyond the capability of the political system to cope effectively.

In terms of political maladies, Colombia remains the most critical case among the major Latin American nations, followed by Peru and Venezuela. Colombia's problems might be likened to serious cardiovascular problems, Peru's problems viewed as an instance of advanced cancer, and Venezuela's problems being seen more as psychological ills. Colombia continues deeply divided, and its resolve is still questionable. Peru appears to run from one kind of a doctor to another seeking a more favorable diagnosis, rather than contemplating a serious treatment plan, and Venezuela's dual political personalities require integration into a single one—a task aided by the vast financial resources at its government's disposal, should they be employed wisely as in the Betancourt era (after 1958).

Although, as has been shown, it is hazardous to speak of the "learning process" of a body politic, educationally advanced Argentina appeared for a long time and in important respects to be a slow learner, with many Argentines accustomed to a European-type lifestyle and clinging hard to hope for a miracle cure rather than fully accepting the need for bitter medicine and possibly painful surgery. Fortunately, at the beginning of 2003 that key country belatedly showed some awareness of the life-threatening nature of its infirmities and elected a government pledged to pursue painful treatment if necessary to restore the country to the robust health it enjoyed before 1930 and largely recaptured under Perón. Argentina needs to remember that, lacking the natural resources essential for heavy industry, its highly educated population is its greatest asset in a high-tech and increasingly service-oriented world. Its political structures and processes are adequate to the country's needs as long as its political culture continues to evolve away from that existing in the yesterdays of the agro-exporting elites. Fortunately, Argentina has no significant sector of its society that is not yet participating meaningfully in its political life.

Unfortunately, for many students of the region, Argentina's past condemns it to be considered culpable until it proves that it has undergone a thorough rehabilitation. Perceptively, but unforgivingly, Wiarda characterizes it as "its own worst enemy" and, in a play on the title of the famous song from the musical *Evita,* urges, "Don't cry for Argentina." In support of his contention that in this case "development leads not to peaceful democracy, but to sclerosis, fragmentation politics, strife, and national unraveling," he marshals formidable prosecutorial arguments. Even putting aside Argentina's past political sins, dealing with the 2001 crisis he finds:

> The country and its citizens continued to spend wildly and way beyond their means, forcing the country into near-bankruptcy. The party system was divisive and both it and the leadership failed to respond to the pending crisis. In addition, and again like Venezuela, the country remained as much corporatist as it was democratic, with all the different groups interested only in their own interests, hiving off whole sectors of public policy for themselves, and so ripping the system off that by 2001–2002 Argentina was nearing economic and political collapse.[11]

The malaise had deep-rooted social, cultural, and political as well as economic causes:

The origin lies in Argentina's chronic inability to live within its means, the pretensions of its elites and middle classes to live an affluent, First World lifestyle that they cannot afford, and their inability to come to grips realistically with the fact that Argentina is a Third World country and not a wealthy, European-style welfare state.

In Wiarda's view, "Corruption, special favoritism, patronage, and clientelism are the paths to political advancement there." Holding that Argentines wallow in denial and scapegoating, this seasoned observer contends that Argentina has become the country par excellence of entitlements, including being on the public payroll and receiving "special favors" from the government. No element of society is excluded from Wiarda's indictment. Moreover, he considers Kirchner's policies superficial reforms that "do not get at Argentina's serious underlying problems." Indeed, they may actually serve to deepen them.

Despite these caveats rooted in the country's past life, Argentina has moved forward, although very recently, in dealing with its most pressing challenges. The worst crisis in its history bottomed out early in the new century, and the country encountered a viable electoral outcome in 2003. The Kirchner government's management of a still-fragile economic recovery is crucial to its stability and authority. In this respect it initially benefited from relatively low expectations rather than the unreasonably high hopes that have complicated previous crises. But staving off disaster is an acceptable outcome only in the short run, so success by one administration will not be enough to fully reestablish faith in the system and its leadership. Much will depend on the performance of the successor, in whose selection the experienced and comparatively sophisticated Argentine electorate will hopefully exercise great care and discrimination—which would include the option of rewarding Kirchner with a second term. Argentina's well-structured party system is a significant asset in this quest for sustained political development.[12]

Brazil has laboriously achieved a relatively high degree of political development without benefit of effectively integrative political parties. In light of its great size—over four times that of Mexico, three times that of Argentina, and seven and half times that of Colombia—and great diversity, the creation of truly national parties with coherent programmatic content continues to be an intimidating task. Yet it remains the most important structural one, as substantial progress in this direction is required for full consolidation of recent political gains. In the policy arena Brazil must continue with agrarian reform, the massive problem on which the Cardoso administration made a significant beginning, and to which the present government has pledged to give a higher priority. In light of the problem's vast scale, very little was done until Cardoso's eight-year administration. Then a good deal was accomplished just before and after the turn of the century in absolute terms, but no great dent was made in the accumulated backlog, as health, educa-tion, and urban food programs received higher priority. After a slow start, the pres-ent administration began to build up some momentum on this front, yet, for electoral reasons if for no other, it still favors the squeaky wheels of urban groups over the protest actions of the landless. Such unrest most often occurs on large landholdings, far from the cities, that are home to most officials of this administra-tion, like all previous ones. In terms of long-range enlightened self-interest, agrar-ian reform should be given a much higher priority by the next administration, no matter who heads it.[13] However, if we take into account the short-range political imperatives, one or two steps up the ladder are all that can realistically be expected during the rest of this decade. For the peculiarities of Brazil's electoral system mil-itate against responsiveness to the agrarian reform constituency, and it rewards not offending powerful advocates of the status quo.

Hence, in the political realm, Brazil urgently needs to enact and put into effect reforms long discussed, but not acted upon. At the heart of the problem is Brazil's highly defective electoral system, nominally a form of proportional representation, but one that in effect has candidates most directly in competition with members of their own party and spreading their campaign efforts across an excessively wide constituency—the entire state. Here Brazil needs to innovate as creatively as the German Federal Republic did after World War II, not continue debating whether to copy the system the Germans crafted for their specific problems and needs. Again, as in so many Latin American cases, as well as in Afro-Asian countries, the need is to adapt, not adopt. The present system has the most damaging effects in the major states, beginning with the absurdity of having seventy members of Con-gress, as well as the whole state legislature, elected at large from a state with a pop-ulation greater than that of California—precisely the tragicomic situation in São Paulo. Hence, Brazil should consider the following proposal, put forth to the Castelo Branco government in the mid-1960s.[14]

Since most of Brazil's large and middle-sized states are naturally divided into quite generally recognized regions with fairly distinct political as well as socioeco-nomic characteristics, why not make these regions the constituencies? As each would be entitled to from 7 to 10 congressional seats (about what the smallest states have now), the basic outlines of Brazil's enshrined method of proportional representation could be retained. The greatest advantage of moving in this direc-tion is that it might stand a chance of being enacted, and even implemented, for members of the congress have proved extremely reluctant to make changes that might endanger their personal chances of reelection, which a shift to single-member districts or even the German hybrid system would do. At the same time, rich and well-known candidates running statewide would not, as they do at pres-ent, be able to bring in a half dozen or more obscure members of their party through their excess votes, and the obscenely elevated cost of campaigning could be brought back under control. This plan might also allow for finally managing to reduce the extreme underrepresentation of modern urban areas, stemming from outdated constitutional limits on the number of seats for each of the largest states, which cause serious malapportionment for the lower house in a system in which equal representation for each state in the senate has already given the small, often backward, states undue power.

From the 1930s on, Mexico created the political equivalent of a full body cast to escape the chronic civil strife unleashed by its 1910 Revolution. Its daunting challenge from the 1990s forward has been, and continues to be, how to fully dismantle the hegemonic PRI structure without losing the valuable benefits of stability that it brought for over a generation. This process cannot be hurried, since there are potential political development advantages to the victory of any one of the three significant parties in the 2006 presidential contest—as long as the elections are free and fully competitive, and the results are respected. There are no party or electoral system problems as in Brazil. Rather, the priority need is continuing change in Mexico's political culture, particularly as it bears upon the behavior of interest groups still caught midstream in transition from attitudes shaped in a corporatist system to ways of thinking congruent with increasing pluralism. As is always the case, thinking has to change before behavior can.

In the policy arena, Mexico has three urgent needs. The first is to improve levels of living for the rural and small-town masses. A situation in which a very large proportion of the populace believes that its hopes for a better life lie in the breadwinners' leaving home and finding work among the vast US underclass of illegal unskilled workers is politically unhealthy. There is something very wrong in a Mexican president's staking his political future on convincing the United States to make the lives of these millions of expatriate Mexicans, and the lot of tens of millions of their family members left behind, less insufferable. The underlying imperative is to create better employment opportunities and more adequate social programs within Mexico. In light of the low rate of population increase, these goals are not unattainable in a context of sustained economic growth.

Relations with the United States are not important to Mexico—they are absolutely paramount. The relationship is so asymmetrical as to render the term *lopsided* a gross understatement. As has often been noted, when the United States sneezes, a number of Latin American countries catch cold, but only Mexico comes down with pneumonia. Ironically, it is this extreme degree of dependence that gives Mexico some degree of leverage in its dealings with its behemoth of a neighbor. For the threat of an unstoppable torrent of illegal immigration unleashed by socioeconomic deterioration in Mexico is, along with the heavy financial stake of US banks and investors, the prime factor in giving Mexico a meaningful priority in US foreign policy.

At the present, the bilateral relationship, which in many ways can be summed up as "too close for comfort," is essentially going nowhere. President Fox, originally lacking a congressional majority, failed to improve his situation in the midterm elections. Given Mexico's rigid one-term-and-never-again constitutional provision, he rapidly moved toward near-lame-duck status. His potential trump card of migration concessions from his great "amigo" in the White House has been devalued by both the passage of time and the disinclination of President George W. Bush to give priority to such a politically divisive issue at a time when the war on terrorism holds center stage in the foreign policy realm. The best hope lies in upgrading current legislative proposals for a guest worker program.

The second pressing policy need if Mexico is to consolidate its newly established democracy, is to curb the cancerous growth of drug trafficking and its pervasive corruption of the law enforcement and judicial systems. The huge amounts of money mobilized by the Mexican producers of marijuana and the transshippers of South American cocaine have enabled them in the past to corrupt even the highest levels of Mexico's antidrug forces, something now evident as well in Guatemala. Outward indications of progress by the Fox administration cannot be relied upon because, by definition, successful criminal penetration of law enforcement, like properly executed covert intelligence operations, remains unknown to the public. This rooting out of police corruption by the drug traffickers needs to become a priority for all three major parties and a crusade for the administration taking office at the end of 2006.

Colombia's salient challenge is very different from those of Argentina, Brazil, and Mexico. The pervasively corrupting influence of the entrenched illegal drugs industry has undermined the country's formal electoral democracy, characterized by well-rooted and highly competitive national parties. Hence, the priority need is to find a way to accomplish what administration after administration has failed to do: reestablish control over areas long dominated by well-armed and experienced insurgent movements. Failing that, efforts to curb the drug trade are doomed to failure, further undermining public faith in government. This is a long-term task that has been inhibited by Colombia's democratic political system, in which presidents have had a single four-year term. In effect this limit meant that noticeable progress had to be made in, at most, three years, before attention turned to the selection of the next governmental gladiator. (It remains to be seen whether the recent removal of this restriction will enable two-term presidents to accomplish more.) Brazil, Argentina, and Peru all removed their one-term restrictions in the mid-1990s, doing so after being convinced that the incumbent chief executive had proven so exceptionally effective that not to give him a chance to continue his good work would have been the height of foolishness. The prospects for Colombia's coming up with its equivalent of Cardoso, Menem, or even Fujimori in the near future are not strong, but perceptions rule in politics, and it appears that a very substantial proportion of the Colombian population view another four years of Uribe as preferable to the alternatives. (See the Epilogue.)

Admittedly, drug and insurgency problems, even separately, present a formidable political challenge; when combined, their containment may well strain a political system's capabilities to their limit, and a solution may be unattainable. Drug production and export vastly enhance the resources available for corruption. Beleaguered revolutionaries turn to providing protection to the drug traffickers in return for financing of arms purchases. The relationship is symbiotic, as the more serious the drug problem, the more the government must divert resources to combating it, reducing the ability to concentrate on anti-insurgency measures. Firmly established in Colombia, this unholy alliance is still a pressing problem for Peru and an increasingly troublesome prospect for Bolivia.

It is here in the Andes that the question of whether geography still exercises a significant impact upon politics arises. Improvements in transportation and communications have greatly reduced the salience of geographic considerations in most of the region. Yet in Colombia the mountainous terrain still affects political life. Trifurcation of the Andes isolates Bogotá from other major population centers, with Medellín and Cali lying on the other side of the major cordillera and Cartagena and Baranquilla located on the Caribbean coast (with Bucaramanga sitting well inland near Venezuela). Topography has greatly complicated the battle against insurgency and drug trafficking, and in Bolivia and Ecuador it continues to aggravate intense regionalism.

Peru's most pressing challenge is to devise and implement a program to eliminate the roots of violent insurrection, rather than just "manage" and contain the threat provided by the Sendero Luminoso and Tupac Amaru revolutionary movements. A lasting solution must go beyond Fujimori's formula, for a very large proportion of the Peruvian public realizes that its success was impermanent, if not fleeting. Moreover, the resources available to any Peruvian president are very limited in comparison to resources of the four larger and much richer countries. Unfortunately, the current administration is barely keeping its head above water and no significantly better alternative is on the horizon.

For Venezuela the priority problem has been moving on to new leadership after having spent most of the 1990s under presidents who had reached their political prime during the 1960s and 1970s. The result of the established parties' failure to renovate their leadership cadres was the explosion to power of Chávez, who in important ways has aggravated the problem through adoption of an updated version of paternalistic caudillism rather than modernization of governmental structures and political processes. Wiarda sees Venezuela as another example of the noxious legacy of authoritarian corporatism. In his considered judgment:

Venezuela had a harder time than earlier thought in transitioning from an organic to inorganic (or individualistic) and democratic society. It had a well-developed party system, but the parties were corrupt; they governed under a gentlemen's agreement (the Punto Fijo) that provided for a rotation in office among the elites but kept other, newer claimants out of public office and the spoils it afforded.[15]

Development in Venezuela, in other words, did not lead to a more liberal, pluralist, or socially just society. Instead it led to ever greater corruption and patronage-dominated politics as the parties "bought off" entire corporatized sectors of society.

Wiarda views the rise of Chávez as a natural, not necessarily desirable, outcome of this political degeneration, and him as an advocate of Jean Jacques Rousseau's concept of "great, charismatic leaders" embodying the country's "general will" and governing through "plebiscitary" democracy. In this perspective, Chávez articulates Latin American opposition to neoliberal policies, and his profile is likely to rise as those of Castro and Lula decline. With oil revenues swollen by the upward surge of crude prices, he need not fear the economic consequences of lambasting the United States.

Bolivia has not yet found any adequate source of income as an alternative to coca leaf and paste for its large population of Indian subsistence farmers. In extreme frustration over eradication efforts adversely impacting their already extremely low level of living, many of these farmers have given their support to movements and candidates promising to free them from such restrictions. Indeed, one of these, Evo Morales, who is committed to strongly nationalistic policies, assumed the presidency in early 2006. Ecuador, although free from the drug problem, shares the challenge of incorporating its indigenous masses into national political life. Paraguay's major issue is, in the face of ambitious military figures, to stay on the constitutional road it has followed for only part of a generation, and with very limited resources, Uruguay faces the demand for greater social benefits.

Central American countries need to consolidate the gains made in recent years and continue to improve the quality of their democratic regimes. In this regard the prosecution of past chief executives in Nicaragua and Costa Rica is a positive sign, and in Panama the young president faces the challenge of reinvigorating the social policies instituted by his late father more than a quarter century ago. El Salvador is ripe for a reformist turn, a development that would not be out of place for Honduras, and Guatemala needs to accelerate the integration of its indigenous masses.

In the Caribbean, Cuba's challenge in the years ahead is the dual task of engineering a viable succession to Castro, who has been in power since 1959, and finding a road to reincorporation within the Latin American community of nations. Although the latter task could conceivably precede the former, it is most likely that new leadership will prove a precondition to completion, if not necessarily to initiation, of effective inclusion in emerging regional schemes of economic integration. The key challenge to the Dominican Republic is to leave behind the negative aspects of the protracted Trujillo–Balaguer era and demonstrate that the country can be governed effectively by leaders and institutions distinct from the personalist rule of that political dynasty, which covered all but ten years of the 1930–1996 period. The encore administration of Leonel Fernández inaugurated in mid-2004 needs to rise to this intimidating challenge against the background of four disastrous years of misgovernment intervening since Fernández's initial 1996–2000 term.

Haiti remains the "sick man" of Latin America. The case can readily be made that very little political development has taken place there during the past half century. Indeed, in some respects Haiti appeared more stable, if not advanced, during the Estimé administration a generation ago than it does now. Certainly, it did not then lag as far behind the other least-developed countries of the region as it does at present. (Paraguay was the penultimate in the mid-1950s, followed by Honduras, and both have since moved forward.) Indeed, during the early 1960s, when the John F. Kennedy administration in the United States was engaged in a series of basic political development studies on a variety of developing countries, especially in Latin America, it was unable to identify individuals or organizations within Haiti having a significant potential for contributing to the country's political advancement. Although much of the responsibility for this sad state of affairs rested then with the Duvalier dictatorship, the situation has since improved only marginally. Unfortunately, there is not even a significant and respectable organized-labor movement in Haiti to serve as a foundation for a modern reformist political party—as underscored by the chaotic electoral process at the end of 2005 and carrying over into the next year.

Thus only in Haiti is the central question one of fundamental political viability. Dictatorship there is still very recent, and faith in electoral processes is tentative where not extremely limited. Shaky internal order requires a continuing foreign police presence, and governmental structures are generally ineffective. For powerful historical reasons rooted in deep animosity, even progress next door in the Dominican Republic carries negligible weight in terms of demonstrable effect or positive "contagion." Developments in the rest of Latin America are considered by all but a handful of Haiti's political actors to be of no real relevance. Since the country has been independent for two centuries, it provides a sad reminder that political development is not automatic, much less inevitable. Fortunately, the much more favorable circumstances in the small countries of the "new" Caribbean, just winding up their first generation of independence, demonstrate that absence of a white European population component is not a barrier to political development—an extremely important fact in light of the racial composition of countries seeking democratic political development at present.

Latin America and the World

What is happening politically in Latin America today is still not viewed in most of the world as of any great concern. Gradually, however, Brazil is stirring up greater curiosity, if not serious interest, in larger portions of the world than was the case even in the 1994–2002 period. Few of the globe's less-developed countries could identify with the accomplishments of a government headed by one of the world's leading social scientists. For many of these countries, Brazil's current experience under an authentic representative of its disadvantaged masses is far more relevant and, for a few at least, hope-inspiring. Indeed, this once-strident socialist's acceptance of free-market capitalism and the need to put development ahead of redistribution, resulting in the pursuit of social justice through the distribution of the fruits of growth stemming from sustained investment, may well be the West's most attractive billboard and convincing showcase in gaining the hearts and minds of Africa—nearly a quarter of the world's nations. The more that people of that continent can see life improving for the eighty-one million Afro-Brazilians, the greater may be their interest in Brazil's formula for democracy and development (although the level of Africa's awareness of Latin America is still dismayingly low).

Argentina's dramatic decline in the early 2000s decade and its being overshadowed by its huge northern neighbor, as well as Mexico's ensnarement in an unavoidable junior partnership with the United States, has served to enhance European interest in Brazil, and even more as it manifests its independence from the United States on global trade issues and demonstrates an increasing ability to be a leader of like-minded countries outside Latin America. (This European interest is reflected in substantial support for Brazil's bid for selection as a permanent member of an enlarged UN Security Council.) Chile may be handling its affairs with competence bordering upon distinction, but it remains a small country that is geographically remote to most of the region as well as to Europe, whereas Brazil's heterogeneity as well as its great size and central location makes it a much more broadly relevant example. As Brazil's exports have greatly expanded and should show continued growth, its deepening as well as extending network of trade relations both enhances ties and underscores mutuality of interests. Trade relations is an asset skillfully capitalized upon by Brazil's highly professional diplomatic service, which Lula has wisely left under the direction of a cosmopolitan career professional, risen through the ranks like most of his predecessors, and well known globally from his previous postings.

The current international situation presents opportunities as well as challenges to Latin America. It is not a distinct culture or civilization in Huntington's sense (as are the Islamic and Asiatic religion areas). For, like North America, South America is very clearly an offshoot of western Europe, as is most of the Caribbean and Central America. Mexico still fits this categorization but is slowly sliding toward becoming a variant of the predominant English-speaking portion of North America, particularly the United States. Overwhelmingly Christian and speaking the tongues of the Iberian Peninsula, the region also has its economic ties essentially with Europe and the United States. Indeed, this Latin American affinity to the North Atlantic community of nations may turn out to be that civilization's saving grace in the more pessimistic of Huntington's scenarios. Combined with the increased incorporation of the eastern European countries as the West's buffer against the Muslim world, Latin America's continuing population growth helps offset the global demographic shift away from the still-dominant western European civilization and culture.[16]

In a world in which the Islamic countries enjoy a much higher rate of demographic expansion than the Christian West (with half the world being neither), Latin America's relative weight within the West is on the rise. Including Latin America, the West is a solid four-continent bloc (including Australia and New Zealand "down under"), with Islam confined to a third of Asia and less than half of Africa. Within the Western Hemisphere, Latin America's population already outweighs that of the United States and Canada by a margin approaching two to one, as Brazil and Mexico together essentially match the United States. Not only has this region's population growth greatly outstripped that of Europe or the United States, but immigration from Latin America accounts for a very significant part of the latter's slowing climb toward the 300 million mark.

Increasingly, it seems that differences between the North American portion of sprawling Latin America and its larger southern continent are no longer diminishing but instead may be growing. If former cultural outsider Brazil has become significantly more Latin American, Mexico seems to be becoming less so as a result of increasingly intimate interaction with the United States. As a part of this unequal, but far from one-way, process, the southwestern region of the United States—from second most populous Texas across to a California close to rivaling Colombia or Argentina in its number of inhabitants—is increasingly Mexicanized. This process is only in a secondary sense a process of Latin Americanization or being Hispanicized in a broader sense, but it does have such an effect when combined with the large and diverse "Latino" population in New York and the heavy concentration of Cubans and Haitians in southern Florida (soon to overtake New York as the country's third most populous state). At the same time, however, Mexico, by losing its uniqueness with the end of PRI hegemony and the narrow presidential succession process the PRI entailed, has become more like the rest of the region politically. Since it greatly outweighs all of Central America and the Caribbean, Mexico exerts a very heavy influence in the respect of similarity versus difference involving the North American and South American portions of Latin America. (It is useful to remember that Europe, which is geographically much more compact, is still a far from homogeneous region, including as it does the British Isles in the west and parts of Russia in the east and ranging from Scandinavia in the north to Greece and part of Turkey in its south.)

In sum, electoral democracy is well rooted in Latin America, and participation has become very broad, although its quality in a number of countries still leaves much to be desired. The social dimension of democracy remains a matter of concern, especially with regard to income inequality. Progress in this and other facets of justice is the region's greatest challenge. In this regard Chile leads the way, but will the larger countries follow? In any case, Latin America has come to be an important part of the global scene and a very significant component of the community of democratic nations. Moreover, its best days still lie ahead, as many of its countries are just achieving maturity and are on the brink of fulfilling their potential. Its successes in these realms make Latin America worthy of examination and possible emulation by nations less well advanced along the road to political development. Past failures and setbacks also provide lessons about overcoming obstacles to the development of viable political systems that are responsive to the will of their citizens. The impact of the wave of 2006 presidential successions in terms of advancing or retarding this trend is discussed in the Epilogue.

Notes

1. These types are discussed in Arnold M. Ludwig, *King of the Mountain: The Nature of Political Leadership* (Lexington: The University Press of Kentucky, 2002), pp. 31–41.

2. Consult Francisco Dominguez and Marcos Guedes de Oliveira, eds., *Mercosur: Between Integration and Democracy* (Pieterlen, Switzerland: Peter Lang AG, 2004), as well as Laura Gomez-Mera, "Explaining MERCOSUR's Survival: Strategic Sources of Argentine-Brazilian Convergence," *Journal of Latin American Studies*, 37:1 (February 2005), pp. 109ff.

3. Ronald M. Schneider, *Brazil: Culture and Politics in a New Industrial Powerhouse* (Boulder, CO: Westview Press, 1996), p. 194.

4. Roderic Ai Camp, *Politics in Mexico: The Democratic Transition*, 4th ed. (New York: Oxford University Press, 2003), p. 117.

5. Wayne A. Cornelius, "Politics in Mexico," in Gabriel A. Almond, G. Bingham Powell, Jr., Kaare Strom, and Russell J. Dalton, *Comparative Politics Today: A World View*, updated 7th ed. (New York: Longman, 2003), p. 492.

6. Schneider, *Brazil*, p. 193.

7. See Jenifer L. McCoy, ed., *Do Politicians Learn from Political Crises?* (Boulder, CO: Lynne Rienner, 1999).

8. See Samuel P. Huntington, *The Third Wave: Democratization in the Late Twentieth Century* (Norman: University of Oklahoma Press, 1991), pp. 41–44.

9. Roger Hilsman, *The Crouching Future: International Politics and U.S. Foreign Policy, a Forecast* (Garden City, NY: Doubleday, 1975).

10. Present shortcomings are discussed in Susan Eva Eckstein and Timothy P. Wickham-Crowley, eds., *What Justice? Whose Justice? Fighting for Fairness in Latin America* (Berkeley: University of California Press, 2003).

11. Howard J. Wiarda, *Dilemmas of Democracy in Latin America: Crises and Opportunities* (Lanham, MD: Rowman & Littlefield, 2005), pp. 110–115, with quotes from pp. 110, 111, 112, 115.

12. Smith regards Argentina as having one of the more institutionalized party systems, with long-lived parties and high voter identity (low electoral volatility). See Peter H. Smith, *Democracy in Latin America: Political Change in Comparative Perspective* (New York: Oxford University Press, 2005), pp. 176–182. By sharp contrast, Brazil has very low institutionalization of its party system; it is also next to the bottom (trailed only by Peru) in electoral volatility and popular affinity for its political parties.

13. On the agrarian situation, see Bjorn Maybury-Lewis, *The Politics of the Possible: The Brazilian Rural Workers' Trades Union Movement, 1964–1985* (Philadelphia: Temple University Press, 1994), and Anthony W. Pereira, *The End of the Peasantry* (Pittsburgh: University of Pittsburgh Press, 1997).

14. I conceived of this proposal and discussed it with the late Luiz Navarro de Brito, a doctor in political science from the Sorbonne, and noted intellectual Luiz Vianna Filho when they headed Brazil's presidential staff in 1966. Unfortunately, the former passed away prematurely, and the latter became involved in governing the state of Bahia while the national government became authoritarian and antireform.

15. Wiarda, *Dilemmas,* pp. 104–109, with quotes from pp. 104–105, 106–107.

16. Samuel P. Huntington, *The Clash of Civilizations and the Remaking of World Order* (New York: Simon & Schuster, 1996).

Epilogue

Latin America's Critical 2006 Elections

The year 2005 ended for Latin America with a momentous question hanging in the air: Was the political tide turning toward radical champions of the newly participant masses? Put in personal terms, did Hugo Chávez represent a significant trend or will he prove to be—as was the case with Castro four decades ago or the Sandinistas half as far back—only a spectacular exception to the prevailing predominance of middle-of-the road, middle-class governments? Given the relative dearth of presidential successions during 2004–2005, the conflicting answers put forth by informed observers have been rooted in the shifting sands of speculation, heavily influenced by personal political preferences. By the end of 2006, however, it would be clear if indeed there were such a trend, a swing in a different direction, or a mixed bag of voter preferences and electoral outcomes.

Twelve countries including all but one of the seven most populous (Argentina, which would come along in early 2007) were choosing their governments for the next four to six years. In most cases the electorate and prospective turnout were setting new records. Indeed, over 250 million voters took part in this thunderous wave of voting, providing the most broadly based indicator of policy preferences and priorities across the region that has ever been available. Since the presidential term in Mexico will extend for six years and in a few others for five, while four is increasingly the norm, this heavy concentration of elections will not be repeated in the near future.

Although the two most significant elections would not occur until after the midpoint of this crucial year, with Mexico at the beginning of July and Brazil coming along on October 1, the campaigns in these giant countries nearing a joint population of 300 million, two-thirds of whom are eligible to vote, were already well advanced by early May, and quite reliable polling data was available. To this point the eight countries that had held elections within the past twelve months (including four in 2005) provided indications that the political winds were blowing nearly as diversely as are their geographic locales and varied climates. Kicking off the succession procession, as discussed in Chapter 13, Suriname and Dominica reelected their incumbents in May 2005, while at the end of November Honduras—where alternation of power between two historical parties is well established—chose a Liberal Party (PLH) leader over a staunch advocate of law-and-order measures to curb its alarmingly rising crime. Yet in Congress the Liberals held 62 of 128 seats to 55 for the National Party (PNH), requiring alliances with minor parties to enact legislation.

On December 18 poverty-stricken and chronically unstable Bolivia opted to entrust its political fortunes to the champion of its neglected Indian masses. Evo Morales, Cochabamba-based spokesman for the country's numerous coca growers (one of the very few economically viable sectors of its troubled economy) pledged to squeeze far greater revenues out of the country's extensive natural gas reserves—presently being developed by foreign enterprises. This raised questions about the future role of Brazil's mixed-capital state corporation, *Petrobrás,* Bolivia's largest economic entity, as well as massive Spanish investments and Argentina's position as a customer second only to Brazil. Two-fifths of Bolivia's fast growing production of soy, centered in the autonomy-minded eastern lowlands around Santa Cruz, is in Brazilian hands, and the highway to the east designed to make this crop more competitive is being built and financed by Brazil. Needless to say, the Bolivian government was hoping for Lula da Silva to be reelected in their large and powerful neighbor, meanwhile counting upon its political campaign to divert attention from Bolivian matters.

While Castro and Chávez may be very active cheerleaders for an ideological approach by the new government, they can do little for it in the material realm. Already Brazil and Argentina were trying hard to pull Morales into their orbit through membership in Mercosur. There was no track record upon which to predict this populist's actions, but his legislative base is far less broad than that of Chávez, and Bolivia's only access to the sea is down the Paraná-La Plata river system through Brazil and Argentina. Demands that Chile relinquish part of the territory won in the Second War of the Pacific have fallen upon deaf ears.

By way of sharp contrast, a week before Bolivia's elections Veronica Michelle Bachelet Jeria (b. 1951) had opened a lead in the first round of the presidential sweepstakes in prosperous and stable democratic Chile. In early January 2006, Bachelet, an avowed agnostic and proudly independent single mother, improved from 45.9 percent of the vote in the first round to 53.5 percent. The 500,000-vote margin for the *Concertacíon* standard bearer was an improvement over incumbent Ricardo Lagos's narrow win five years earlier. A spunky daughter of an air force general who paid with his life for his loyalty to Allende, she turned back multimillionaire businessman Sebastian Piñero in a campaign by stressing competence and experience while being free of demagogic promises or pledges of drastic sea changes.

A medical doctor who lived in the United States both as a preteen and thirty-five years later as a student at the Inter-American Defense College, the new president studied in East Germany after her 1975 exile from Chile. For as a Socialist student leader, she had undergone imprisonment and torture in the wake of Allende's ouster. Following the end of the Pinochet regime, she acted as an adviser to the health ministry and graduated from the Chilean War College. When Lagos became president, she served first as health minister, then made her unique mark in the sensitive and strategic position of a female defense minister before winning the triple crown of Socialist Party nomination, having been selected over a Christian Democratic rival as the coalition's candidate, and election to the presidency. Her triumph reflected voters' choice to continue the string of enlightened centrist governments Chile had had since the 1989 return to democracy. She enjoyed a strong position in Congress with 65 of 120 seats in the Chamber and 20 of 38 in the upper house. Her cabinet, comprised equally of men and women, contained a plurality of Christian Democrats including Alejandro Foxley, Aylwin's finance minister, as foreign minister, as well as the outgoing president's son.

The next three months did little to clarify these early mixed signals as on February 5 Central America's political gem, Costa Rica, in a cliffhanger of an election chose 1986–1990 chief executive (and Nobel Peace Prize winner) Oscar Arias Sánchez of the traditionally leading National Liberation Party (PLN) over challenger Otton Solis of the Citizens' Action Party (PAC) by a paper-thin margin of 40.9 to 39.8 percent (665,000 to 646,000), as nearly two-thirds of the more than 2.5 million eligible voters turned out. Since both candidates came out strongly against corruption, the conditions for participation in the Central American Free Trade Agreement was the major issue in this most economically advanced of the subregion's countries. In legislative balloting the PLN came away with 28 seats on 36.5 percent of the vote to the PAC's 20 seats with 25.7 percent as the incumbent PUSC sagged badly to only 7.7 percent of voter preferences and a mere 4 seats. This left minor parties having 5 seats in the 57-member Congress.

On February 7 laggard and deeply troubled Haiti[1] staged its oft-postponed presidential balloting among over thirty generally undistinguished hopefuls, with the hands-down winner being ex-president Réne Préval (sixty-three), widely viewed as a stand-in for exiled chief executive Jean-Bertrand Aristide. Despite the presence of a large contingent of international peacekeepers, the balloting entailed some violence and a significant element of fraud (albeit only when compared to other Latin American elections, not to those in Africa and the Mid-East). After a decision to exclude controversial blank votes from the count, Préval was credited with 51 percent of the vote compared to under 12 percent for his nearest rival, eliminating need for a runoff. In the April 21 runoff legislative elections (in which turnout was only 30 percent) the president-elect's *Espwa* (Hope) electoral vehicle on 11 of the 27 Senate seats along with 20 of 85 in the lower house, but needed help from Aristide's *Lavalas* and even the Peoples' Struggle Organization (OPL) for a parliamentary majority.

The major question in observers' minds is how long armed international forces, currently numbering close to ten thousand, will remain and what degree of stability can they provide in this deeply divided country of extremely weak institutions? Once they relinquish a decisive voice, will Préval act with a meaningful degree of independence, or will popular pressure cause him to allow Aristide's return? In contrast to Aristide, Préval has strong links to elements of the country's elite and professes to be on a quest to unite the deeply divided country.

Although the presidency was not at stake, congressional and municipal elections in El Salvador on March 12, involving 3.8 million voters, confirmed the governing Nationalist Republican Alliance (ARENA) party's leading position with 34 of 84 congressional seats, along with 10 for its ally the National Reconciliation Party (PCN), compared to 32 for the leftist Faribundo Marti National Liberation Front (FMLN).

As elections moved to larger venues, April 9 saw Peru, the region's fifth most populous country, stagger through hotly contested balloting in which the runner-up and the third place finisher from 2001, ex-president Alan García of the Peruvian Aprista Party (PAP) edged out 2001 near-winner Lourdes Flores from the conservative National Unity (UN) to get into an early June runoff with pro-Chávez former military officer Ollanta Humala of the Union for Peru (UPP). The resulting alliance with Flores gave García an initial advantage (as they had totaled 49 percent of the April vote to Humala's 30.6 percent). The deciding factor would be the behavior of the supporters of the fourth and fifth place finishers, ex-president Valentín Paniagua and a stand-in for ex-president Fujimori. As usual in light of Peru's political fragmentation, the new chief executive would lack a legislative majority as the April balloting left the PAP with 45 seats, the UN 40, and the PNP with only 30 of the 120 places in the unicameral Congress, while 14 seats went to the Fujimori alliance for the Future (AF) led by his daughter.[2]

These results through April, which spanned the region geographically, left its political panorama showing no clearly defined trend. This significantly lessened the probability that Latin America's 2006 presidential successions would mark a pronounced turn, much less a watershed. But the rest of the year would define at least the short-term political future for a distinct majority of Latin Americans— for the three most populous countries were still to go to the polls.

Looking down this road, Colombia appeared certain to give an unprecedented second consecutive term to center-rightist Álvaro Uribe, whose multiparty coalition led by Radical Change (CR), *Colombia Democrática* (CD), the National Unity Party (P de la U), and the remnants of the discredited Conservative Party (PC) was victorious in the March 12 congressional balloting, coming away with 61 of the 102 Senate seats to go along with a88 in the 166-member lower house—as the opposition Liberal Party (PL) lost one-third of the seats it had held. Despite efforts of the leftist guerrillas to intimidate voters in the country side, 40 percent of the 26 million eligible voters cast their ballots.

Reliable opinion polls gave Uribe a 25 percent lead over his nearest competitor, Liberal Horacio Serpa (a two-time loser in presidential elections), just a few weeks before the May 28 balloting, indicating that he was likely to avoid a runoff, which he would almost certainly win. A major cloud was the stuttering process of disarming the right-wing United Self-Defense Forces (AUC) and the issue of the extent of their leaders' influence in Congress—estimated at 20 to 35 percent in the outgoing congress.

July 2's Mexican voting involves the future of nearly one-fifth of the region's population with Andrés Manuel López Obredor of the Party of theDemocratic Revolution (PRD), running as candidate of the Alliance for the Well Being of All (ABT), running neck and neck with Felipe Calderón of the governing National Action Party (PAN) as Roberto Madrazo of the Institutional Revolutionary Party (PRI) trailed in the polls with only 25 percent as the hotly contested campaign entered its final stage. Balloting on March 12 in populous Mexico State, which coils around the Federal District and contains 9 million voters, indicated that the PRD had gained ground there since the last election, with the PAN in slight decline, and the PRI losing its once dominant position. (Mexico has no runoff provision.)

López Obredor focused his campaign on the issues of poverty and the need for state control of the critical energy sector, while Calderón, well financed and with an appealing personality, stressed the generally sound economic situation and the need to attract foreign investment to keep development on track. This left the PRI to stake out an intermediate position and seek to arouse nostalgia for the Zedillo years (1995–2000)—a strategy hampered by its candidate's lack of personal appeal.

In any case, Congress is likely to be divided fairly equally among the three major parties. This means that a return to pre–2000 essentially center-right policies is a possibility as is a continuation of a PAN administration more linked to the party than Fox's has been. Even if López Obredor emerges the victor, he will face similar constraints to those Lula encountered when he came to office in Brazil four years earlier, especially the need for congressional support from the center and center-right. Indeed, López Obredor took great care during the campaign to distance himself from Chávez and to project respected Cambridge-trained economist Rogelio de la O as his chief economic advisor; prestigious National Autonomous University of Mexico (UNAM) rector Juan Ramón de la Fuente as his domestic policy guru, and career diplomat José María Pérez Gay as future foreign minister.[3] He has pledged that half of his cabinet would be women.

Poverty-stricken and racially divided Guyana's almost certain reelection of Bharrat Jagdeo of the Progressive People's Party (PPP) in September would maintain the status quo, as would the electoral confirmation as prime minister in Jamaica of Portia Simpson-Miller, who replaced P. J. Patterson as leader of the dominant Peoples' National Party (PNP) in March. On October 15 unruly Ecuador will choose among an array of veteran aspirants led be congressional leader Cynthia Viteri of the conservative Social Christian Party (PSC)—a compromise between its Jaime Nebot and Leon Febres Cordero wings—and two-time runner up banana magnate Álvaro Naboa for the Renovating Institutional National Action Party (PRIAN), and former vice president Leon Roldós campaigning under the banner of the Patriotic Society Party (PSP). Ex-president Lucio Gutiérrez is seeking to be declared eligible, and the Ecuadorian Roldosist Party (PRE) of equally controversial Abdalá Bucarám has not yet entered the fray. With the issues closely tied to domestic Ecuadorian topics, including incorporation of the politically frustrated indigenous masses, who still lack a mobilizing leader, the likelihood of a clear-cut winner seems slim.

The left's best hope for a gain is in Nicaragua, where former *Sandinista* president Daniel Ortega's bid to return to office is threatened by the strong campaign of much younger dissident "Henry" Lewites, who is running fairly close behind Eduardo Montealegre of the Nicaraguan Liberal Alliance (ALN)-Constitutional Liberal Party (PLC) coalition in the election coming in November. For the expected landslide reelection of Chávez the same month would not be a net gain for the left, since he has been in power since 1998.[4]

Thus, whether the region's political pendulum swings one way or the other is reduced essentially to the electoral outcome in Brazil, with its one-third of the region's population. On October 1 a possible 126 million voters will either determine its 2007–2010 president or set up a late-year final showdown involving the two frontrunners. As incumbent Luis Inácio Lula da Silva and his Workers' Party (PT) struggle to overcome the heavy burden of his administration's accumulation of misdeeds and missteps, and counting on economic performance to pull him through to a second term, the Brazilian Social Democracy Party (PSDB)'s Geraldo Alckmin, also supported by the Party of the Liberal Front (PFL), has consolidated an electoral base of about 35 percent—equal to that of Lula. As most supporters of the Party of the Brazilian Democratic Movement (PMDB)'s Anthony Garotinho, who is out to match his third place finish from 2002, are likely to back Alckmin in a runoff, the consensus of the country's usually quite accurate public opinion polls indicate high prospects for a very close second-round outcome between Alckmin and Lula.

Yet with five months of intense campaigning still ahead, the electoral panorama could undergo significant change. As shown in Chapter 13, in Brazil the presidential outcome is linked to state races that are heavily influenced by alliances that—

given its fragmented and far-from-disciplined party system—may differ from alignments at the national level. (This stands in sharp contrast with the far-less-fluid situation in Mexico, where 60 to 70 percent of voters demonstrate strong party loyalty.) In late March the supreme court upheld "verticalization," of coalitions, barring the prevailing practice of formal alliances at the state levels at odds with those in the presidential race. In any event, since the country's huge electorate is concentrated in a few large states, the campaigns in these states will once again greatly influence the national outcome.

In São Paulo, with a whopping 28 million voters, the PSDB–PFL alliance enjoys the advantage of controlling both the statehouse and São Paulo city hall, along with having a very strong gubernatorial candidate in Serra. (The PSDB was the leading party there in both the 2002 state and 2004 municipal balloting, so the question is by how much the PSDB–PFL will win.) In number two Minas Gerais, whose electorate has reached 14 million, the PSDB–PFL forces are counting on the coattails of popular governor Aécio Neves, who is running for reelection, to pull their presidential candidate to victory—particularly if Alckmin pledges not to seek a second term (thus opening the way for their favorite son). In Rio de Janeiro, whose electorate has reached nearing 10 million, the PT has traditionally been very weak and the PSDB far from robust. Garotinho, with his wife entrenched in the governorship and running as the PMDB nominee, should garner a good proportion of these votes, while pro-Serra forces count on the popularity of Rio de Janeiro mayor César Maia to pile up a significant margin over Lula—with Garotinho's votes falling to them in the expected runoff.

The fourth largest electorate—Bahia's at well over 9 million—provides a test of the strength of Antônio Carlos Magalhães's PFL, with the PSDB its junior partner there in this transitional state from the developed south to the less modernized northeast. In contrast, Rio Grande do Sul, with 8 million votes, sees the PT with strong roots, but the PMDB holding the governorship. The outcome will depend to a significant degree upon whether its governor, defeated by Garotinho for the presidential nomination, puts his shoulder to the wheel, as well as the depth of the PT dissidence supporting Heloisa Helena of the radical Party of Socialism and Liberty (PSOL).

Although these five largest states contain 55 percent of the country's voters, the next group of vote-rich states, totaling another 28 percent of the electorate, have the potential to tip the scales in a close election. Paraná and its more than 6 million voters has proven to be a good state for the PSDB and PMDB, while Pernambuco's electorate of 6 million figures large in Lula's reelection hopes. In Ceará, with 5.5 million potential ballots, the chief question is if the leadership of PSDB national president Tasso Jereisatti will outshine homegrown presidential wannabe Ciro Gomes, who served in Lula's cabinet. Santa Catarina's more than 4 million voters are likely to aid Alckmin, while a large proportion of Maranhao's nearly 4 million voters still follow the lead of ex-president José Sarney, whose daughter is a recent former governor now representing the state in the Senate. She is affiliated with the PFL, while her father plays a leading role in the PMDB.

To the uncertain degree that performance of congressional slates influences presidential voting, the opposition enjoys a distinct advantage because of incumbents and regional power brokers. The big unknown is the impact of campaign finance reforms that did away with such staples of Brazilian campaigning as musical shows combined with election rallies and certain types of showy and expensive advertising. Then, too, how much will the scandals stemming from 2002 and the increased vigilance of the electoral courts inhibit parties from the massive flows of illegal financing that have characterized Brazilian elections? But even if Lula should rebound and earn a second term, this would not indicate a voter swing to the left, since his margin would be a small fraction of what it was when he was first elected in 2002.

Notes

1. Sara DeGraff provided valuable assistance in overcoming the slowness of election results in Haiti.

2. Very useful for understanding Peru's confused and volatile political situation are Catherine Conaghan, *Fujimori's Peru: Deception in the Public Sphere* (Pittsburgh, PA: University of Pittsburgh Press, 2005) and Paul Drake and Eric Hershberg, eds., *State and Society in Conflict: Comparative Perspectives on the Andrean Crises* (Pittsburgh, PA: University of Pittsburgh Press, 2006).

3. See Allyson Lucinda Benton, "Mexico's (Temporary) Turn to the Left—Campaign Rhetoric Only!" *Current History*, No. 688 (February 2006), pp. 69–73 as well as Alejandro Alvarez Bejar, "Mexico's 2006 Elections: The Rise of Populism and the End of Neoliberalism?" *Latin American Perspectives*, Vol. 33, No. 2 (March 2006), pp. 17–32.

4. Consult Phil Gruson, "Chavez's Venezuela," *Current History*, No. 688 (February 20, 2006), pp. 58–63.

Appendix A

Ranking of Latin American Political Leaders, 1870–2005

Leader	Country	Constituency	Tenure	Political Development	Social Modernization	Economic Management	Statesmanship	Moral Example	Program	Legacy	Total
Getulio Vargas	Brazil	5	5	5	4	5	5	5	4	4	42
Lazaro Cardenas	Mexico	5	3	5	4	4	5	5	5	5	41
Juan D. Peron	Argentina	4	5	5	4	4	5	3	5	5	39
Pedro II	Brazil	5	5+2	3	5	4	5	5	4	3	39
Fidel Castro	Cuba	2	5+2	5	5	2	5	5	5	2	37
Juscelino Kubitschek	Brazil	5	2	4	3	5	5	5	5	3	37
Jose Batlle y Ordonez	Uruguay	1	3	5	5	4	3	5	5	5	36
Alberto Lleras C.	Colombia	4	2	5	3	3	5	5	4	4	36
Arturo Alessandri	Chile	2	4	5	4	3	4	5	5	5	36
Benito Juarez	Mexico	5	5	3	3	2	4	5	5	3	35
Fernando H. Cardoso	Brazil	3	3	4	3	4	4	4	4	2	34
Romulo Betancourt	Venezuela	3	3	5	4	4	4	5	4	4	34
Jose Figueres	Costa Rica	1	4	5	3	4	3	4	4	4	34
Eric Williams	Trinidad	1	5	4	3	4	4	3	4	4	33
Ernesto Zedillo	Mexico	5	3	5	2	3	3	4	4	4	33
Julio Roca	Argentina	4	4	5	3	4	2	4	3	4	33
Eduardo Frei	Chile	2	3	4	3	3	4	5	4	3	32
Victor Paz E.	Bolivia	2	2	4	4	3	3	5	4	3	32
Patricio Aylwin	Chile	2	2	5	4	3	3	4	4	4	31
Antonio Guzman Blanco	Venezuela	3	5	3	3	4	3	4	2	2	31
Adolfo Lopez Mateos	Mexico	5	3	3	3	3	4	4	3	3	31
Humberto Castello Branco	Brazil	5	2	3	2	3	3	5	4	3	31
Ricardo Lagos E.	Chile	2	3	4	3	3	4	4	4	4	31
Juan Jose Arevalo	Guatemala	2	2	4	3	4	3	4	3	3	30
Eduardo Frei Ruiz-Tagle	Chile	2	3	3	3	3	4	4	4	4	30
Ernesto Geisel	Brazil	5	2	4	2	3	3	4	3	4	30
Hipolito Yrigoyen	Argentina	4	3	5	4	3	2	3	3	2	29
Omar Torrijos	Panama	1	4	3	3	3	4	3	3	3	29
Carlos Saul Menem	Argentina	4	4	3	3	3	2	2	2	3	29
Augusto Leguia	Peru	3	5	4	3	4	3	3	3	1	29
Plutarco Elias Calles	Mexico	5	4	4	2	3	2	3	3	4	29
Justo Rufino Barrios	Guatemala	2	4	3	3	4	3	5	3	3	29
Jose Sarney	Brazil	5	2	4	3	4	3	3	3	2	29
Manuel F. Campos Salles	Brazil	5	2	4	3	4	2	3	3	3	29
Tomas Guardia G.	Costa Rica	1	4	4	3	4	2	3	3	4	28
Alfonso Lopez	Colombia	4	3	3	3	3	2	3	3	3	27
Fernando Belaunde T.	Peru	3	4	3	3	3	2	3	3	3	27
Julio M. Sanguinetti	Uruguay	1	4	3	2	3	3	4	3	3	27
Porfirio Diaz	Mexico	5	5+2	2	2	4	3	2	3	0	26
Rafael Nunez	Colombia	4	3	3	2	3	2	3	3	2	26
Cesar Gavaria	Colombia	4	2	3	2	3	3	3	3	3	26
Hermes da Fonseca	Brazil	5	2	3	2	3	3	2	3	2	25

Leader	Country	Constituency	Tenure	Political Development	Social Modernization	Economic Management	Statesmanship	Moral Example	Program	Legacy	Total
Juan Velasco Alvarado	Peru	3	3	3	3	3	2	3	3	2	25
Raul Alfonsin	Argentina	4	3	4	2	3	2	3	2	2	25
Joao Baptista Figueiredo	Brazil	5	3	4	2	2	2	2	2	3	25
Ricardo Jimenez	Costa Rica	1	4	3	2	3	2	4	2	4	25
Cleto Gonzalez	Costa Rica	1	4	3	2	3	2	4	2	4	25
Eloy Alfaro	Ecuador	2	5	3	2	3	2	2	3	2	24
Cheddi Jagan	Guyana	1	4	4	2	2	2	3	3	3	24
Joaquin Balaguer	Dominican Republic	1	5	2	3	3	2	3	2	3	24
Jose Maria Velasco Ibarra	Ecuador	2	5	3	3	3	2	3	1	2	24
Ramon Villela Morales	Honduras	1	3	3	3	2	3	4	2	3	24
Agustin Justo	Argentina	4	3	3	3	4	3	3	2	2	24
Juan Carlos Ongania	Argentina	4	2	3	2	4	2	2	3	2	24
Rafael Caldera	Venezuela	3	4	2	3	2	2	3	3	1	23
Prudente de Moraes	Brazil	5	2	3	3	2	2	2	2	2	23
Rafael L. Trujillo	Dominican Republic	1	5+1	3	2	3	2	1	2	2	22
Juan Vicente Gomez	Venezuela	3	5+1	2	2	3	2	1	2	1	22
Carlos Ibanez	Chile	2	4	2	2	3	2	2	3	2	22
Venustiano Carranza	Mexico	5	3	1	2	2	2	3	3	2	22
Rafael Videla	Argentina	4	3	2	4	1	2	3	2	1	22
Daniel Ortega	Nicaragua	1	4	2	2	3	2	2	4	2	22
Alberto Fujimori	Peru	3	4	3	2	3	2	1	2	1	21
Salvador Allende	Chile	2	2	2	3	1	2	4	4	1	21
Manuel Odria	Peru	3	3	2	3	3	2	2	2	2	21
Nicolas Pierola	Peru	3	3	2	3	3	2	2	2	1	21
Manuel Prado	Peru	3	4	2	2	3	2	2	2	1	21
Fulgencio Batista	Cuba	2	5+1	2	1	4	2	2	1	0	21
Anastacio Somoza	Nicaragua	1	5	2	1	3	2	1	2	3	20
Jacobo Arbenz	Guatemala	2	2	2	3	2	2	3	3	1	20
Manuel Santos Zelaya	Nicaragua	1	5	2	2	3	1	3	2	1	20
Augusto Pinochet	Chile	2	5	1	2	4	2	1	2	1	19
Hernan Siles	Bolivia	1	3	3	2	2	2	3	2	1	18
Hugo Banzer	Bolivia	1	4	3	1	2	2	2	1	2	18
Manuel EstradaCabrera	Guatemala	2	5	1	1	2	2	1	1	2	17

The clock is still running on Brazil's Lula da Silva, Nestor Kirchner of Argentina, Colombia's Alvaro Uribe and Hugo Chavez of Venezuela, while it has run out on Mexico's Vicente Fox. (The next two in the ratings, Alfredo Stroessner and Tiburcio Carias Andino, were in a virtual tie with fellow dictator Estrada Cabrera.

This ranking is based on my adaptation of "The Political Greatness Scale" developed by Arnold M. Ludwig in *King of the Mountain: The Nature of Political Leadership* (Lexington: The University Press of Kentucky, 2002), pp. 274–315 and 403–408. This psychiatrist's eleven-factor scale overemphasized creation of a new nation, territorial aggrandizement, and participation in wars. I have replaced these three dimensions with political development as well as substantially modifying his categories of ideology, economic prosperity, size of constituency, and staying power to better fit Latin America—as well as most of the rest of the ex-colonial world. All nine components have been calculated on a 0 to 5 scale (whereas Ludwig gave higher weight to population and tenure in office than to other achievements) for in my opinion leadership involves success in attaining, retaining, and exercising power.

Only the top 75 leaders are included as lower scores reflect undistinguished performance. Emperor Pedro II of Brazil is included because his long rule extended eighteen years beyond the 1870 starting point, while Fidel Castro is the only active leader included since he has already been in power well beyond the time required for the maximum longevity score. These individuals are listed in order of aggregate scores, with quintiles including 1–15 (great by any standards); 16–30 (clearly outstanding); 31–45 (decidedly memorable); 46–60 (distinguished); and 61–75 (a cut above the rest). These are used to code periods on the "Political Leadership Timeline" in Chapter 14. Well-known names not included (such as Duvalier) may have stood out in some respect, usually longevity, but their overall performance was lackluster, averaging less than 2 out of a possible 5.

CRITERIA

Size of Constituency: 5 points for current populations of over 100 million; 4 points for above 30 million; 3 points for more than 20 million; 2 points above 10 million; 1 point for 9 million or less. This reflects the higher degree of competition to rise to the top in more populous countries.

Years in Power: 5 points for 16 or more years in effective control of a nation's government, with additional points for surpassing 25 and 35 years; 4 points for 10 to 15 years; 3 for 6 to 9 years; 2 points for 3 to 5 years; and 1 point for under three years.

Political Development: The major consideration is the degree to which the leader strengthened the capabilities of the political system and dealt effectively with threats to its viability. Hence success in guiding the country through the Great Depression or establishing democratic rule after authoritarian regimes or periods of civil strife carry heavy weight.

Social Modernization: Did the leader help catalyze societal changes, channel those transformations already underway, or merely facilitate them through eliminating or minimizing obstacles? Did the leader give major impetus to ending stagnation or accelerating growth? Particular credit is given for dealing effectively with major inherited or externally caused crises. (Given the lead-lag factors involved, comparison is made with the immediately preceding and ensuing goverrments' performances.)

Statesmanship: Performance with respect to conduct of foreign policy and coping with international problems and pressures as well as leadership in regional or sub-regional affairs. No credit is given for grandstanding and self-promotion that does not lead to real accomplishments.

Moral Example: Beginning with avoidance of corruption and scandals, this criteria moves through evidence of placing the good of the country and welfare of its people before personal gain or accentuated partisanship. Breaking with well-established negative practices in these respects carries parti- cular weight.

Programatic Foundation: To what extent does the leader possess a coherent intellectual/philosophical basis for his policies, and does he stick with it under pressure or yield to expediency? Does the leader have a roadmap for or a vision of his country's future? This is admittedly treacherous ground as in real world situations the line between pragmatism and opportunism is often poorly defined, especially when the calculus of political sur- vival kicks in. Hence consideration of the leader's base of congressional support needs to be taken into account. Coherence of policies carries more weight than lofty public pronouncements that are often belied in practice.

Legacy: The low end is leaving the country in worse shape politically than it was before the leader's tenure. Overthrow and repudiation of his poli- cies is a dramatic measure, while low popularity is common and may prove transitory. At the high end, establishment of a political movement that can successfully compete for office years and even decades later is a major and rare accomplishment, as is adoption of important portions of the leader's policies by his erstwhile critics and opponents.

As is shown by the total scores, only 26 Latin American political leaders have scored 30 points or higher, with just 12 more reaching an average score of 3 (and aggregate of 27). While 19 countries are represented on this honor roll, many others have no one in the top 75.

Glossary

abertura	Political "opening," an early stage in transition from an authoritarian regime toward democracy.
acuerdos	"Accords" or "agreements" usually in the nature of backroom deals among political brokers.
affranchis	A "freedman" class of former slaves in the late eighteenth and early nineteenth century Haiti.
alcabala	Spanish colonial sales tax.
alcaldes mayors	Town or district executives in Spanish colonies.
Apristas	Followers of the APRA party in Peru.
argolla	Used with *la* (the), a label for the early twentieth century Ecuadorian economic elite closely tied to the Agricultural Bank. Freely translated, it means those "stuffed to the gills" (overfed) in the sense of being "fat cats."
audiencias	The second level of Spanish colonial administration, subordinate to viceroyalties. Literally a chief judicial tribunal headed by *oidores*.
ayuntamientos	Urban governing councils introduced to parts of Spanish America on the eve of independence.
bandeirantes	Individuals taking part in *bandeiras* in colonial Brazil, essentially explorers rather than settlers.
bandeiras	Adventurous exploration expeditions into the interior of colonial Brazil.
bandido	"Bandit," a term applied to both criminals and political opponents.
braceros	Mexican harvest workers in the United States in the 1940s into the 1960s.
caboclos	Originally a term for mixed blood individuals in Brazil that later became a colloquial expression for "hillbillies," "yokels," or "hicks."
cacique	A native Indian chief, in recent times used to mean a type of local political boss.
callampas	Urban slums of Lima, Peru, so named for their tendency to spring up like "mushrooms."
camarilla	In Mexico a group of persons who rely on one another to advance their shared political interests and individual leadership bids.
campesinos	Rural laborers and subsistence farmers, often imprecisely rendered into English as the narrower category of peasants.
capitanias	"Captaincies," the original Portuguese colonies in the New World, which later became provinces within a viceroyalty of Brazil.
cartorial	Used in Brazil in reference to the nature of a political system in which appointments to governmental office were exchanged for electoral support and public employment used to satisfy the clientelistic needs of the elite.
castas	The several types of mixed blood populations in seventeenth century Spanish America, particularly in Mexico.

caudillos	Spanish American personalist political leaders first arising in the aftermath of the wars for independence who utilized private armies to control a region of the country and then to seize control of the capital city.
científicos	Usually used with los as a name for the positivist technocratic elite of the Diaz regime in Mexico.
colegiado	The unique plural executive governmental system employed by Uruguay for much of the twentieth century.
colonos	Peruvian rural workers.
compromiso	A generally bilateral agreement or commitment in the political realm.
comuneros	Populations of essentially indigenous communities who in the late colonial period sometimes rose up in opposition to the so-called Bourbon reforms and demanded a voice in political decisions. In twentieth century Peru it means rural dwellers living in communities rather than on the landed estates.
concertación	Literally "working in concert" to denote a type of formal political alliance with a defined purpose (rather than only transitory convenience.)
conquistadores	"The name given to the original generation of "conquerors" of Latin America, especially the followers of Hernan Cortez and Francisco Pizzaro.
continuismo	The pronounced tendency up through World War II for Latin American chief executives to remain in power beyond and despite constitutional limitations.
convergencia	"Convergence."
convivencia	"Coexistence," the term for political collaboration between strange bedfellows. Particularly applied to the alliance of conservatives and *Apristas* in Peru during the late1950s and early 1960s.
coronel, pl. coroneis	The name given to political bosses in the interior of Brazil, especially in the northeastern region, derived from their holding commissioned ranks in the National Guard during the monarchy.
coronelismo	The type of patron-client political processes shaped by the *coroneis*.
corregidores	Formally *corregidores de Indios*. Local level Spanish colonial officials roughly equivalent to Indian agents in nineteenth century US terms.
corregimentos	Interior areas subject to rule by *corregidores*.
cortes	The Spanish national legislature.
criollos	Europeans born in the New World; in English "Creoles."
derrubadas	Political efforts by the Brazilian government of Floriano Pexioto in 1890–1891 to oust provincial governors who had sided with his predecessor.
descamisados	Literally "shirtless ones," the term for the Buenos Aires lower class followers of the Perons.
dispositivo militar	The structure of military support arranged by Brazilian presidents to assure their survival in office.
distensão	In English "decompression," a stage of dismantling the most authoritarian features of the Brazilian military regime followed by the government of Ernesto Geisel in the mid-1970s.
dizimo	A highly unpopular tithe tax (10 percent) levied by the Portuguese government in colonial Brazil.
donátario	The "donatary" or recipient of a major land grant (*capitania*) in the New World from the Portuguese monarch.
ejido	A collective holding of agricultural lands by Mexican Indian communities.
encomenderos	Individuals granted an *encomienda* by the Spanish crown.

encomienda	A Spanish colonial grant of the services of a community of Indians in return for converting them to Christianity and providing protection.
engenhos	Sugar plantations in colonial Brazil.
estancias	The name in southern South America, especially Argentina, for large agricultural land holdings.
estanciero	The owner of an *estancia*.
fazenda	The Portuguese equivalent of a *hacienda* or *estancia*, that is a large rural land holding.
fazendeiro	The owner of a *fazenda*; collectively *fazendeiros* are the dominant elite of large landowners in the colonial and early independence periods of Brazil.
Frente Nacional	The National Front, a formal co-governing arrangement between the two dominant political parties in Colombia in order to reestablish democracy in the late 1950s.
fueros	Special legal rights including that of their own courts enjoyed by the military and the church in colonial and early independence New Spain.
Gaucho	Literally "cowboy," a resident of the Brazilian state of Rio Grande do Sul.
gobernacion	"Government," often the name for the ministry in charge of governmental affairs and internal security.
gorila	Colloquial term for hard-line right-wing advocates of continued military rule, especially in Argentina.
hacendados	Large land holders (owners of *haciendas*) in most of Spanish America.
haciendas	The name in most of Spanish America for large rural land holdings.
Inconfidência Mineira	An unsuccessful 1789 conspiracy against royal authority inBrazil.
jogo de bicho	Brazil's version of the numbers game, with animals instead of numbers.
linha dura	Literally "hard line," that is militantly intransigent. Usually applied to the faction of a military establishment advocating control of the government by the armed forces.
llanero	A cowboy of the Venezuelan *llanos* or plains.
logias	"Lodges," a name used for politically active, often conspiratorial, military cliques, especially in Argentina.
mamelucos	The offspring of Indian mothers and European fathers in colonial Brazil.
Mapuches	A fierce Indian tribe in central Chile whose defeat opened the way for settlement and development of what became the country's heartland.
mestizo	An individual of mixed European and Indian ancestry.
Mineiros	The inhabitants of the key Brazilian state of Minas Gerais.
mita	The name in colonial Peru for the *encomienda/repartimento* with respect to forced labor of Indians on roads and other public works.
oidores	The chief judges of *audiencias*.
pampean	Referring to inhabitants of the fertile *pampas* (grassland plains) covering much of northern Argentina.
panelinha	A Brazilian form of political networking that revolves around mutual support through having a member well placed in every key area of society and government.
parentela	A form of social network in Brazil involving close cooperation among members of a broadly extended family and their influential contacts.
pau Brasil	A redish dyewood from which Brazil got its name.
Paulistas	The residents of São Paulo.
pelucones	The conservative "big wigs" in Chilean politics of the 1820s and 1830s.
peninsulares	Individuals born in Spain who migrated to the New World in the colonial period.

pipolos	The liberal "newcomers" or "pipsqueaks" in Chilean politics of the 1820s and 1830s.
poder moderador	"Moderating Power," meaning the authority of the Brazilian emperor to function as the fourth branch of government, particularly as the manipulating balance wheel of the parliamentary system.
Porfiriato	The thirty-five year rule of Porfirio Diaz in Mexico beginning in the mid-1870s.
Porteños	The residents of Buenos Aires.
prefeitos	Brazilian mayors.
puta	Spanish for whore, used pejoratively in political life for enemies.
quilombo	Communities formed by run away slaves in seventeenth century Brazil.
ranchero	"Rancher," a Mexican term for a rural landholder who did work on his ranch as distinct from an aristocratic *hacendado*.
Reconquista	The long and violent struggle to recover control of Spain from Muslim rule by Catholic forces (reconquest) completed in 1492.
reducciones	Self-sustaining settlements into which Guarani Indians were gathered by the Jesuits and colonial administrators in the region of today's Paraguay and adjoining parts of Brazil, Argentina, and Uruguay.
reerguimento	Brazil's financial "resurrection" under President Rodrigues Alves in 1903–1905.
repartimento	A grant to Spanish colonial landowners of labor on roads and public works of those Indians not subject to the *encomienda*. (In Peru it was called the *mita*.)
rurales	The brutal rural police of the Diaz regime in Mexico.
salvações	Political efforts by the Brazilian government of Hermes da Fonseca on the eve of World War I to oust entrenched oligarchical political machines in the hinterland.
seismarias	Subsidiary land grants in colonial Brazil to entrepreneurs who would organize their settlement.
sexenio	Mexico's single six-year presidential term.
tenentes	Literally "lieutenants," a name for reform-minded activist young officers in Brazil during the 1920s and 1930s.
tenentismo	The political movement catalyzed and led by the *tenentes*.
unitarios	Advocates of a unitary government in Argentina in the first half of the nineteenth century.
vereadores	Municipal councilmen in Brazil.
viceroy	A very high royal governor of a vast portion of the New World literally functioning in the stead of the king (rey or rei).
visitador	A type of inspector general sent to the colonies by the Spanish crown to conduct an administrative audit, most frequently at the end of a viceroy's tenure.

Index